MW01480649

1993 EDITION

THE SMART CONSUMER'S DIRECTORY

1993 EDITION

THE SMART CONSUMER'S DIRECTORY

publishers since 1798

THOMAS NELSON PUBLISHERS
Nashville

Published in Nashville, Tennessee by Thomas Nelson, Publishers and distributed in Canada by Lawson Falle, Ltd., Cambridge, Ontario.

Library of Congress Cataloging-in-Publication Data

Smart consumer's directory.
p. cm.
ISBN 0-8407-4503-6
1. Consumer protection—United States—Directories. 2. Consumer education—United States—Directories. 3. Toll-free telephone calls—United States—Directories. I. Thomas Nelson Publishers.
HC110.C63S55 1992
381'.33'02573—dc20 92-9380
CIP

1 2 3 4 5 6 7 8 — 98 97 96 95 94 93 92

Acknowledgments

Consumers Resource Handbook, U.S. Office of Consumer Affairs. Washington, D.C.: U.S. Government Printing Office, 1992; *How To Complain* based on *How To Write A Wrong,* Federal Trade Commission, U.S. Government Printing Office; *Lost or Stolen Credit and ATM Cards; Credit Billing Errors,* Federal Trade Commission, Washington, D.C.: U.S. Government Printing Office, 1987, 1988; *Franchise and Business Opportunities; New Car Buying Guide,* Federal Trade Commission; *Agencies on Aging* based on *Resource Directory for Older People,* U.S. Department of Health and Human Services, Washington, D.C.: U.S. Government Printing Office, 1989; *International Travel Tips,* based on *Travel Tips for Older Americans,* Department of State, Bureau of Consular Affairs, Washington, D.C.: U.S. Government Printing Office, 1989; *Where To Write for Vital Records,* U.S. Department of Human Services. *Consumer Credit,* based on *Consumer Handbook To Credit Protection Laws,* Board of Governors of the Federal Reserve System, 1989; *Obtaining Student Loans,* based on *The Student Guide,* U.S. Department of Education, 1991–92; *Home Mortgage Guidelines,* based on *Wise Home Buying,* U.S. Department of Housing and Urban Development, Washington, D.C.: U.S. Government Printing Office, 1987; *Second Mortgage Financing,* Federal Trade Commission, 1986; *Mortgage Refinancing,* Board of Governors of the Federal Reserve System.

Contents

Introduction

Our society has become so complex that even the most knowledgeable and careful consumer has difficulty conducting day-to-day business. Getting the most for your money, making a complaint if something goes wrong, and who to turn to for help, are problems that we all face.

Today, we conduct most of our business with strangers—whether with mail order businesses in distant states, or banks where we are only an account number.

The Smart Consumer's Directory can help. Included in Part I are consumer tips on airline travel, selecting child care, lost or stolen credit and ATM cards, how to correct billing errors, investigating franchise and business opportunities, shopping by mail, and choosing a long distance telephone service.

Part II is a consumer assistance directory. Many companies have consumer affairs or customer relations departments to answer questions or complaints. The addresses and telephone numbers of more than 800 companies are listed in the "Corporate Consumer Contacts" section. Popular magazines, a new car buying guide, a list of names and addresses of car manufacturers, consumer and public information hotlines, a list of Better Business Bureaus by state, plus state and federal agencies, some with toll-free 800 numbers, are only a few of the many listings in this section.

Getting ready to go on vacation? Whether it's a trip around the world, or a picnic at the nearest state park, check Part III, "Recreation, Travel and Leisure," for important tips about foreign travel, toll-free numbers for airline and hotel reservations, information about cruises, TV show tickets, a list of the 10 most popular theme parks in the U.S., and much more. National parks are listed by state along with popular attractions from all 50 states. Major league sports teams are listed by state with addresses and phone numbers.

In our mobile society, people often reside far from their place of birth. Vital statistics and where and how to get them is the subject of Part IV, "Where to Write for Vital Records," a listing by state of offices from which you may obtain birth, death, marriage, and divorce records.

The Federal Information Center (FIC), administered by the General Services Administration, can help you find information about Federal government services, programs, and regulations. A list of metropolitan area and state toll-free numbers which can be called only within that state are given in Part II. If your area is not listed, call **1-(301)-722-9098.**

Every effort has been made to ensure the accuracy of the information listed here, but if a toll-free number has changed, the correct information can usually be obtained by calling the toll-free operator at **1-(800)-555-1212.**

SOURCES OF HELP

Libraries

Local libraries can be a good source of help. Many of the publications mentioned in this book can be found in public libraries. Some university and other private libraries also allow individuals to use their reference materials. Check your local telephone directory for the location of nearby libraries.

Media Programs

Local newspapers and radio and television stations often have "Action Line" or "Hot Line" services. These programs might be able to help consumers with their problems. Sometimes these programs, because of their influence in the community, are successful in helping to resolve consumer complaints. Some action lines select only the most severe problems or those that occur most frequently. They might not be able to handle every complaint. To find these services, check with your local newspapers, radio and television stations, or local library.

Occupational and Professional Licensing Boards

Many state agencies license or register members of various professions, including doctors, lawyers, nurses, accountants, pharmacists, funeral directors, plumbers, electricians, car repair shops, employment agencies, collection agencies, beauticians, and television and radio repair shops.

In addition to setting licensing standards, these boards also issue rules and regulations, prepare and give examinations, issue, deny or revoke licenses, bring disciplinary actions and handle consumer complaints.

Many boards have referral services or consumer education materials to help you select a professional. If you have a complaint and contact a licensing agency, the agency will contact the professional on your behalf. If necessary, they might conduct an investigation and take disciplinary action against the professional. This action can include probation or license suspension or revocation.

To find the local office of an occupational or professional licensing board, check your local telephone directory under the headings of "Licensing Boards" or "Professional Associations" or look for the name of the individual agency. If there is no local office, contact the state consumer office.

Legal Help

Please note that some of the sources of help listed have a policy of declining complaints from consumers who have sought prior legal counsel.

Small Claims Courts

Small claims courts were established to resolve disputes involving claims for small debts and accounts. While the maximum amounts that can be claimed or awarded differ from state to state, court procedures generally are simple, inexpensive, quick and informal. Court fees are minimal, and you often get your filing fee back if you win your case. Generally, you will not need a lawyer. In fact, in some states, lawyers are not permitted. If you live in a state that allows lawyers and the party you are suing brings one, do not be intimidated. The court is informal, and most judges make allowances for consumers who appear without lawyers.

Remember, even though the court is informal, the ruling must be followed, just like the ruling of any other court. If the party bringing the suit wins the case, the party who lost often will follow the court's decision without additional legal action. Sometimes, however, losing parties will not obey the decision. In these cases, the winning party can go back to court and ask for the order to be "enforced." Depending on local laws, the court might, for example, order property to be taken by law enforcement officials and sold. The winning party will get the money from the sale up to the amount owed. Alternatively, if the person who owes the money receives a salary, the court might order the employer to garnishee or deduct money from each paycheck and give it to the winner of the lawsuit.

Check your local telephone book under the municipal, county or state government headings for small claims court offices. When you contact the court, ask the court clerk how to use the small claims court. To better understand the process, sit in on a small claims court session before taking your case to court. Many small claims courts have created dispute resolution programs to help citizens resolve their disputes. These dispute resolution processes (e.g., mediation and conciliation) often simplify the process. For example, in mediation, both people involved in the small claims dispute meet, sometimes in the evenings or weekends, and with the assistance of a neutral, third-party mediator, discuss the situation and create their own agreement.

Research indicates that if both people show up for the mediation, 85–90% of the time an agreement is reached. Just as importantly, researchers learned in follow-up, six months after the session, that 85% of the agreements were "substantially fulfilled." Considering this, when you contact your small claims court, ask first about their mediation or conciliation process.

For additional information about dispute resolution, contact:

American Bar Association
Standing Committee on Dispute Resolution
1800 M Street, N.W.
Washington, D.C. 20036
(202) 331-2258

Legal Aid Offices

Legal Aid offices help individuals who cannot afford to hire private lawyers. There are more than 1,000 of these offices around the country staffed by lawyers, paralegals and law students. All offer free legal services to those who qualify. Funding is provided by a variety of sources, including Federal, state and local governments and private donations. Many law schools nationwide conduct clinics in which law students, as part of their training, assist practicing lawyers with these cases.

Legal Aid offices generally offer legal assistance with such problems as landlord-tenant relations, credit, utilities, family issues (e.g., divorce and adoption), social security, welfare, unemployment and workmen's compensation. Each Legal Aid office has its own board of directors which determines the priorities of the office and the kinds of cases handled. If the Legal Aid office in your area does not handle your type of case, it should be able to refer you to other local, state or national organizations that can provide advice or help. Check the telephone directory or call your local consumer protection office to find the address and telephone number of the Legal Aid or Legal Services office near you. If you would like a directory of Legal Aid offices around the country, contact the National Legal Aid and Defender Association, 1625 K Street, N.W., 8th Floor, Washington, D.C. 20006, (202) 452-0620.

Legal Services Corporation

The Legal Services Corporation (LSC) was created by Congress in 1974. There are LSC offices in all 50 states, Puerto Rico, the Virgin Islands, Guam and Micronesia. To find the LSC office nearest you, check the telephone directory, call the Federal Information Center (FIC) (301) 722-9098, or call the LSC Public Affairs Office at (202) 336-8800. If you wish to buy a full directory of all LSC programs, write or call:

Public Affairs
Legal Services Corporation
400 Virginia Avenue, S.W.
Washington, D.C. 20024-2751
(202) 336-8800

Finding a Lawyer

If you need help finding a lawyer, check with the Lawyer Referral Service of your state, city or county bar association listed in local telephone directories.

Complaints about a lawyer should be referred to your state, county or city bar association.

OTHER CONSUMER INFORMATION

Consumer Credit Counseling Services

Counseling services provide assistance to individuals having difficulty budgeting their money and/or meeting necessary monthly expenses. Many organizations, including credit unions, family service centers and religious organizations, offer some type of free or low-cost credit counseling.

The Consumer Credit Counseling Service (CCCS) is one non-profit organization that provides money management techniques, debt payment plans and educational programs. Counselors take into consideration the needs of the client, as well as the needs of the creditor, when working out a debt repayment plan. You can find the CCCS office nearest you by contacting the National Foundation for Consumer Credit, Inc., 8611 Second Avenue, Suite 100, Silver Spring, MD 20910-3372, 1 (800) 388-CCCS (toll free).

Consumer Groups

Private and voluntary consumer organizations usually are created to advocate specific consumer interests. In some communities, they will help individual consumers with complaints. However, in most cases, they have no enforcement authority. To find out if such a group is in your community, contact your state or local government consumer protection office.

Consumer Information Catalog

The *Consumer Information Catalog* lists approximately 200 free or low-cost Federal booklets with helpful information for consumers. Topics include careers and education, cars, child care, the environment, Federal benefits, financial planning, food and nutrition, health, housing, small business and more. This free *Catalog* is published quarterly by the Consumer Information Center of the U.S. General Services Administration. Single copies of the *Catalog* only may be ordered by sending your name and address to *Catalog,* Consumer Information Center, Pueblo, CO 81009 or by calling (719) 948-4000.

Non-profit groups that can distribute 25 copies or more each quarter can automatically receive copies by writing for a bulk mail card.

Part I

The Smart Consumer

GETTING THE MOST FOR YOUR MONEY AND AVOIDING CONSUMER PROBLEMS

Today's marketplace offers a variety of products and services. In order to be a smart consumer, here are some things to think about before and after you make a purchase.

Before you buy

- Think about what you really need and what product or service features are most important to you.
- Compare brands. Ask for word-of-mouth recommendations and look for expert product comparison reports. Check your local library for magazines and other publications that compare products and services.
- Compare stores. Look for a store with a good reputation and plan ahead to take advantage of sales.
- Check with your local Better Business Bureau (BBB) or consumer protection office to find out about the company's complaint record.
- Check for any extra charges, for example, delivery fees, installation charges and service costs.
- Read warranties to understand what you must do and what the manufacturer must do if you have a problem.
- Read contract terms carefully. Make sure all blank spaces are filled in before you sign a contract.
- Ask the salesperson to explain the store's return or exchange policy.
- Do not assume an item is a bargain just because it is advertised as one.

After you buy

- Read and follow the instructions on how to use the product or service.
- For safety and to protect your warranties, use the product only for the purposes outlined by the manufacturer's instructions.
- Read and understand the warranty. Keep in mind that you might have additional warranty rights in your state. Check with your state or local consumer office for more information.
- Keep all sales receipts, warranties, service contracts and instructions.
- If trouble develops, report the problem to the company as soon as possible. Trying to fix the product yourself might cancel your rights to service under the warranty.
- Keep a file of your efforts to resolve the problem, including the names of the individuals you speak with and the date, time and outcome of the conversation. Keep copies of the letters you send to the company and any replies it sends to you.

HANDLING YOUR OWN COMPLAINT

How to Complain

Before you complain, be sure that you have something to complain about. If that fancy set of box kites you ordered two months ago for your grandson's birthday still hasn't been delivered and the birthday party is tomorrow, you should check with your post office to be certain the kites aren't being held there for you to pick up—before you fire off a complaint.

If the expensive cleaning products you bought from a salesperson at your door do not do the job as promised, you might want to save your complaint until you carefully read the instructions.

But once you are as certain as you can be that you have a problem you can't solve alone, complain—and do it quickly!

The faster you complain, the better your chances for a satisfactory settlement. Some companies may not be liable if you fail to complain within a certain period of time. In dealings with door-to-door sellers, remember, you have three business days to change your mind and cancel your purchase.

Some companies may be unable to make the adjustment you want if you don't complain soon enough. As soon as you have determined that you have something to complain about, that is the time to sit down and prepare your letter.

Why are you complaining? Identify your specific problem with the product or service. The more precisely you understand what you don't like about your purchase, the easier it will be to convey your complaint to the seller or manufacturer.

- Does the product or service fail to do what the ads or salesperson promised? In what ways does it fail to perform?
- Are you complaining about the terms of payment? Did you get a bill for more than you agreed to pay?
- Have you been waiting longer than you should under the law, usually 30 days, for something to come from a mail order firm?
- Is the product simply in need of repair? Was it damaged when you got it?

These are the kinds of questions you should answer for yourself in preparing a letter of complaint.

What do you want done about your complaint? Do you want:

- A refund? A *cash* refund? Or will you settle for a credit slip or gift certificate?
- A replacement? A different size, color, or model?
- Repairs? How soon do you want them completed?
- Removal of the charge from your credit account? Do you also want the interest that has accumulated removed from your account? (You may have to write a letter to your credit card company to inform them.)

Sometimes you need more than your complaint to get what you want. To make an effective complaint, you should consider what papers you have to support your story and make your case with the seller.

Here are some of the things that you should assemble and make copies of when writing a complaint letter:

- Cancelled checks
- Bills
- Sales receipts
- Warranties
- Contracts

For quick reference, you should also write down the following information, much of which you can find on sales receipts, warranties, or other brochures or papers the seller gives you:

- The date and location of your purchase. This information is of particular importance if your purchase was covered by the "Cooling Off Rule."
- The model number or serial number or any identifying codes that will help you describe exactly what you bought.
- Your account number if you used a credit card or other charge account to pay for your purchase.
- Any written or verbal promises that the seller made to you. For example, if a section of an ad you answered in buying by mail claimed the product was "Guaranteed for One Full Year or Your Money Back, No Questions Asked!", keep the ad. To be safe, keep a copy of all ads you answer for reference later. If the promise or claim was made over the phone or in a conversation with the seller, try to remember just what was said and write it down before you forget.
- The name, address, and telephone number of the seller and if possible, the manufacturer. You may be able to find this information on papers that came with your purchase. If it's not there, you can still get your complaint through to someone who can help you.

You should know that the law says that any misrepresentation of fact that is used to induce you to buy something is a deceptive business practice. That means that if a magazine seller tells you the cost will be twice as high tomorrow if you don't buy today, but it will really be the same, the salesperson is probably using illegal tactics.

If we could chisel in marble just one rule about complaining it would be this:

DO IT IN WRITING!

More than any other reason, people are denied their consumer rights because they fail to write a record of the problem.

Too often, your first response may be to call or visit the seller and demand action. If that first visit or call works, that's fine. But if it doesn't, you need a written account of the problem. For example, if the seller promises to take care of the matter but then *doesn't,* you have no proof that you made that verbal complaint.

Always write a letter. You also may want to phone or visit the merchant to explain your problem in person, but be sure to document the conversation. Complaining personally can be a good way to let the seller know that you are dissatisfied. But when you complain in person, keep these points in mind:

- Complain first to the person who took your money.

- Go to someone who can do something about your complaint. Ask to speak to the manager, owner, or person in charge.
- Be prepared. Carry copies with you, never originals, of all the information you have gathered to support your complaint, such as receipts, bills, and cancelled checks. Make photocopies of your originals at a library or copy store.
- Don't be put off. You may not only have to be persistent, you may also have to be unflappable in the face of the seller's efforts to diminish or dismiss your complaint.
- Keep cool. You can't be made to feel foolish when you know it would be foolish *not* to complain. Besides, you should have an insurance policy to back you up—your complaint letter.

The First Complaint Letter

This letter is important for many reasons:

- It puts your complaint on record with the company.
- It preserves your rights under the law.
- It ensures that the company knows your side of the story.

A SAMPLE COMPLAINT LETTER

Your Address
City, State, Zip Code
Date

Complaint Department
Name of Company or Organization
Address
City, State, Zip Code

Dear Sir or Madam:

I am writing about (describe the product, including serial and model number, service, issue, law, or event).

I have had trouble with it because (describe problem briefly. Also include the date and place of purchase). Enclosed please find (copies of bills, contracts, cancelled checks, sales receipts, etc.).

I thought you would like to know of my dissatisfaction and (state previous efforts. Identify the consumer protection agency to which you are sending a carbon copy of the letter).

I look forward to your reply within the next 30 days explaining what you intend to do about my problem.

Sincerely,

Your Name

Enclosures
cc: Names of organizations receiving copies of your letter.

- It can help get government agencies involved in your case, if necessary. Or, it can alert the agencies to the company's questionable business practices.
- It can lay the foundation for any future legal case and help you in drafting later letters, if you need to write more than once.
- It lets the company know you are serious about pursuing your complaint. A business may ignore your complaint until it sees something in writing.

Style

Be calm, but not apologetic; be firm, but not hostile. If you include everything you should in your letter (see the sample letter in this section), the company will get your message. Tell the company who else is getting a copy of your letter to let it know you are serious.

If at all possible, type your letter. If you can't type, print so that the reader won't miss a word.

Make your sentences short and to-the-point. Keep the letter as brief as possible yet include everything the company needs to know about your complaint.

Use this checklist to be sure you have included everything you need to make your letter effective and complete:

- Provide your name, your address, and phone numbers where you can be reached during the day and evening.
- Describe what you bought and say when you bought it. Include model, make numbers, and names if possible.
- State where you made your purchase—in your home, at a friend's home, from a catalog, through an ad in a newspaper or magazine, on television or radio, or at a store.
- State the problem. Give a history of what is wrong with the product or services you bought. Tell the company why you are dissatisfied.
- Enclose copies, NOT ORIGINALS, of everything relevant to the sale: warranties, contracts, cancelled checks, sales receipts, bills, etc.
- State what you want the company to do about your complaint. Demand satisfaction but tell the company what will satisfy you—a refund, a replacement, or repairs.
- Tell the company when you want it to respond. Be reasonable. Allow two or three weeks.
- Give the name or names of offices, agencies, or associations you intend to go to for help if your problem isn't solved.
- Tell the company to whom you are sending a copy of your letter.

Now do all of the things your letter says you are going to do:

- Keep track on your calendar of the number of days you have given the company to respond. Circle the deadline date. And if you haven't heard from them by then, take additional action.
- Send copies of your letter to one or more of these organizations, offices or agencies:

* Local or county consumer office;
* State consumer office;
* State Attorney General;
* Trade associations, such as the Direct Marketing Association or the Direct Selling Association;
* The Better Business Bureau, or the Chamber of Commerce, if you cannot locate a BBB near you;
* Your state senator or legislator or U.S. Representative or Senator;
* The American Association of Retired Persons' National Consumer Assistance Center;
* Local, state, or federal offices or agencies like the Federal Trade Commission, the Office on Aging, or the U.S. Postal Service.

You can find the addresses for the agencies and associations and other sources of information throughout this book. Some groups also will be listed in your telephone book.

Keep copies of every letter you write, and also keep any correspondence you receive from the company.

Photocopies from machines in most libraries and some do-it-yourself copying shops usually cost about 10¢ per page. Look under "copy" in your telephone book.

When you have any telephone conversations with a company representative, write down the date of the conversation, the name and position of the person with whom you spoke, and his or her telephone number.

Send your letter by certified mail if you think you may need proof later that the company received your letter. You will receive a notice telling you when and where the letter was delivered.

Send your first letter to the company that sold you the product or service. If you cannot find the address of that company on any of the materials that came with your purchase or contract, you can probably find the address in the phone book. You can also ask your local library for help.

Direct your letter to the person or department you believe can do something about your complaint. Most companies have consumer complaint departments, so direct your letter to them.

If you think only the president or another person in the company can solve your problem, write to him or her. The library has many directories that list the highest officers of most companies.

Depending on the nature of your complaint, you may want to write directly to the manufacturer and bypass, or only send a copy to, the seller.

You may want to contact the manufacturer directly if:

- Your complaint concerns a defect in the product;
- Your problem involves getting repairs; or
- You have a dispute regarding the terms of the warranty.

The Second Complaint Letter

The second letter should repeat the first letter's message with some additions. The second letter should:

- Restate the problem;
- Tell the company when you last wrote and point out that your letter of a certain date has not been answered; and
- Notify the company that you are now going to ask for help from one or more of the agencies who received copies of your first letter.

When asking an outside, or third, party for help, you need to write a letter (and phone if you wish) giving them information to help you:

- Ask the party to assist you, and list what you already have done for yourself and when you did it;
- Provide copies, not originals, of whatever correspondence you have had with the company;
- Note what the company's response has been to your letters, calls or visits, and why it was not satisfactory; and
- Give the helping agency your name, address, and phone number. Be sure to keep a copy of this letter as well.

When the third party enters the dispute, the company gets three messages:

1. You are determined to pursue the case and will not give up easily.

2. The confrontation may now be made public. This could mean bad publicity or lost business for the company.

3. You may have on your side people with the experience, sophistication, and resources to correct the problem and obtain a fair settlement.

How the business reacts to the widening of your case to include a third party depends on many things, including how sensitive the business is to publicity, how much faith it has in the fairness and legality of its actions, how experienced the company is in such matters, and how much money the company has.

When a third party is involved, some companies take action on the complaint. Some companies may solve the problem for the sake of goodwill. Other companies may do nothing, fearing action could give their products or services a bad image.

But at this point, when you've already done everything you can on your own behalf, it may do a lot of good to ask a third party for help.

Here are some of the organizations and agencies you may want to contact:

Consumer Offices

There are consumer offices in most counties, cities, and states. Local offices can be especially helpful because they are nearby, which makes contacting them easier, and because they are familiar with local businesses and laws.

You can find the consumer office nearest you in your phone book. Look under the name of the city and then under municipal listings for "Consumer." These are government agencies and do not charge for their help.

If you cannot find a phone number or address right away, try dialing your information operator—411. If the operator cannot help you, contact your local library and ask for help in getting in touch with your local consumer office.

If there is no consumer office near where you live, contact your county or state consumer office. Some states have separate departments of consumer affairs. Others have divisions within the office of the governor or some other high official, like the state Attorney General.

If the business you are complaining about is located in another state, try to contact that state's consumer office or ask your own state office to help you contact the right office in the other state.

Better Business Bureaus

These are non-profit organizations sponsored by private businesses. Most offer these basic services:

- Provide general information on products and services;
- Take written complaints and will contact the company on your behalf; and
- Record how well the companies handled complaints filed against them in the past. Don't always expect the bureau to tell you much about other complaints, but all offices will tell you if complaints have been registered.

BBB's do offer complaint mediation between consumers and merchants as well as legally binding arbitration in some cases. Local offices are listed in your phone book. If you call one of them, be prepared to explain the problem and don't forget to ask for a complaint form.

If your complaint is not resolved through informal mediation, you and the merchant involved may agree to submit your dispute to a panel of disinterested third persons who will be chosen by the two of you. The BBB has a pool of volunteer arbitrators and can provide the panel free of charge. Hearings are informal so you can present evidence and ask questions.

The award, or settlement, made at the conclusion of the hearing is legally binding on both parties and can be enforced in court.

Dispute Resolution Panels

These panels can be an effective forum for resolving disputes between a customer and a company without resorting to court action. The rules for these panels vary, but all are available at no cost to the consumer and can provide prompt action, as well as public accountability for the business.

This way of settling a complaint uses the services of a neutral panel or arbitrator to decide disputes. The panels sometimes are composed of a majority of consumer representatives. Industry trade associations, like the Better Business Bureau, the Home Appliance Manufacturers' Association, and the National Automobile Dealer's Association, sponsor such panels. And so do some private companies like Ford and Chrysler.

The panel or arbitrator listens to both sides of the dispute and then makes a decision about what should be done. In most cases, both sides must agree to abide by that decision. In some instances, the decision is binding only on the business.

The business you are complaining to may suggest this way of settling your dispute or you may ask for it. You can get information about the panels from your local consumer protection office or the Council of Better Business Bureaus, 1515 Wilson Boulevard, Arlington, VA 22209.

Media

Hundreds of newspapers, television and radio stations operate "action lines" and other programs designed to help their readers and listeners settle complaints and help motivate businesses to solve customer's problems.

While these operations can be very successful in cutting red tape and finding answers to complicated problems, it is important to remember that their purpose also is to maintain an audience. They may not be able to help all who ask them, and they may choose particularly unusual or colorful complaints to keep their audiences interested. Even if you decide not to rely solely on an action line, sending the reporters a copy of your complaint letter indicates the seriousness of your pursuit.

Small Claims Court

These are "people's courts" where you can tell your problem to the judge in your own words. Although this is an informal action, and is used for the resolution of minor disputes over small sums of money (usually less than $500), you must appear in court when your case is scheduled. Generally, you can sue only for money. Most states and localities have such courts within their district, municipal or superior court system, but they usually cannot help you resolve problems with companies located outside their jurisdiction.

If you cannot find a listing in the phone book for small claims court, ask your local consumer office for help.

Forming Your Own Consumer Complaint Group

Groups of this kind have been formed in communities throughout the country to help consumers help themselves. The group is *not* an organization of paid consumer counselors or lawyers, but a group of consumers organized to accomplish a goal. The group sends complaint letters to merchants and may organize a delegation to visit the merchant and negotiate a settlement. More information on these groups is available from the Consumer Federation of America in Washington, D.C.

As a consumer, you have the right to expect quality products and services at fair prices. If something goes wrong, there are things you can do to resolve the problem. Here are some suggestions for handling your own complaint.

1. First, contact the seller if you have a complaint.
2. If that does not resolve your problem, contact the company headquarters.
3. If your problem is still unresolved get in touch with the consumer organization or local, state and Federal offices that provide help in cases like yours.
4. Taking legal action should be the last resort. However, if you decide to exercise this right, be aware that you might have to act within a certain time period. Check with your lawyer about any statutes that apply to your case.

Save records

Start a file about your complaint. Include copies of sales receipts, repair orders, warranties, canceled checks and contracts which will back up your complaint and help resolve your problem.

Describe the problem

When you complain, be sure to describe the problem, what (if anything) you have done already to try to resolve it and what you think is a fair solution. Do you want your money back? Would you like the product repaired? Do you want the product exchanged?

Go back to where you made the purchase

Contact the business that sold you the item or performed the service. Calmly and accurately explain the problem and what action you would like taken. Avoid displays of anger; they usually don't help. If a salesperson is not helpful, ask for the supervisor or manager and restate your case. Most consumer problems are resolved at this level.

Allow each person you contact time to resolve your problem before contacting someone else for help.

Keep a record of your efforts and include notes about whom you spoke with and what was done about the problem. Save copies of any letters you send to the company as well as letters sent to you.

Don't give up

If you are not satisfied with the response at the local level, don't give up. Call or write a letter to the person responsible for consumer complaints at the company's headquarters. Many companies have toll free telephone numbers. Often these toll free "800" numbers are printed on product packaging. Check your local library for a directory of toll free telephone numbers or call 1 (800) 555-1212 to learn whether a company has a toll free number. If you're writing a letter, send your letter to the consumer office or the president of the company.

HOW TO WRITE A COMPLAINT LETTER

Where to write

If talking with a salesperson or higher-level company representative does not solve the problem, you will need to write a letter to the company to resolve your complaint.

Check the reference section of your local library. The following books might help you locate useful company and brand name information:

- *Standard & Poor's Register of Corporations, Directors and Executives;*
- *Standard Directory of Advertisers;*
- *Thomas Register of American Manufacturers;*
- *Trade Names Dictionary;* and
- *Dun & Bradstreet Directory.*

What to write

- The letter should include your name, address, home or work telephone numbers, and account number, if appropriate.

The Letter of Complaint

(Your Address)
(Your City, State, Zip Code)
(Date)

(Name of Contact Person)
(Title)
(Company Name)
(Street Address)
(City, State, Zip Code)

(Dear Contact Person):

On (date), I purchased (or had repaired) a (name of the product with serial or model number or service performed). I made this purchase at (location, date and other important details of the transaction).

Unfortunately, your product (or service) has not performed well (or the service was inadequate) because (state the problem).

Therefore, to resolve the problem, I would appreciate your (state the specific action you want). Enclosed are copies (copies, NOT originals) of my records (receipts, guarantees, warranties, canceled checks, contracts, model and serial numbers, and any other documents).

I look forward to your reply and a resolution to my problem, and will wait (set a time limit) before seeking third-party assistance. Please contact me at the above address or by phone at (home or office numbers with area codes).

Sincerely,

(your name)
(your account number)

- Make your letter brief and to the point. List all the important facts about your purchase, including the date and place you made the purchase and any information you can give about the product, for example, the serial or model number.
- If you are writing to complain about a service you received, describe the service and who performed it.
- State exactly what you want done about the problem and how long you are willing to wait to resolve it. Be reasonable.
- Include copies of all documents regarding your problem; be sure to send COPIES, NOT ORIGINALS.
- Don't write an angry, sarcastic or threatening letter. The person reading your letter probably was not responsible for your problem, but might be very helpful in resolving it. Type your letter if possible. If it is handwritten, make sure it is neat and easy to read.
- Keep a copy of all letters to and from the company and all related documents.
- The sample letter following is a guide to help you write a complaint letter. Remember, if you write a letter to a Better Business Bureau, government agency, trade association or other source of help, give information about what you have done so far to try to get your complaint resolved.

How to mail your letter

The complaint letter should be sent by certified mail, with a return receipt requested. This will cost more, but the receipt will provide evidence that the letter was received and who signed for it. However, to protect against the letter being misplaced or lost en route, you might want to send it by registered mail. This will cost more than certified mail, but it guarantees that all post office personnel handling the letter will sign off on it.

CONSUMER TIPS

This section contains several suggestions to help you become a smarter consumer. It includes tips on how to choose child care, find the best school for you or your child, and protect your privacy. Remember to check with your local consumer protection office and Better Business Bureau for other consumer information on a variety of topics.

Airline Travel

Almost every day, newspapers and radio and television stations advertise discount and special offer airline tickets. To find the offer that best meets your needs, use the following guidelines:

1. Travel agents are sources of information about fares, schedules and baggage limits, as well as local businesses that can issue airline tickets and boarding passes. In addition, travel agencies sometimes purchase discount seats to popular destinations. So check with travel agents, even if the airlines are sold out. Remember, by being an informed consumer, you can help with your agent's search for bargain fares by sharing information your agent might not have seen yet.
2. When making your airline reservation, always ask about fees or penalties for changing or canceling a reservation or a paid ticket. There might be a variety of ticket prices, with varying penalties and conditions. Choose the one that best fits your needs. In general, the less expensive the fare, the more restrictions it is likely to include. So, if price is important to you, book early and make sure your plans will not change!
3. Read the disclosure statement on the back of your ticket. It explains your rights and responsibilities as a passenger, as well as the airline's liability for overbooking seats or for losing or damaging luggage. However, not all passenger rights are included on the back of an airline ticket; some are incorporated by reference. Travelers wanting more information should ask the airline for a copy of its "Conditions of Carriage." In addition, the U.S. Department of Transportation publishes a booklet called "Fly Rights," which is available from the Consumer Information Center.
4. When flights are overbooked, airlines must ask for volunteers to give up their reservations in exchange for compensation of the airline's choosing. If you volunteer, be sure to get any compensation arrangements in writing.
5. If you are "bumped" or involuntarily reassigned to a later flight, the airline must provide a written statement of your rights and entitled compensation. The complete rules for compensation are available at all airport ticket counters and boarding locations.

Selecting Child Care

Choosing child care is an important issue for many parents. Some alternatives are day care centers, family child care homes, pre-schools, in-house caregivers (nannies) and co-op child care programs. Parents should look at the available child care alternatives and pick one that best meets their needs. Here are some questions parents should ask when looking for child care:

1. What are the licensing laws for day care providers in your city, county or state? Your local consumer protection office is a good place to start checking for this information.

2. Do caregivers have references? What about special training in child development and education? How many children does each adult watch?

3. Is the home or center clean? Are such potential poisons as cleaning supplies out of reach and locked up? Are meals and snacks nutritious, adequate, and safely prepared and served? Is there enough space inside and outside in which the children can play? Is the playground fenced?

4. If the center is large, do visitors and children sign in and out? What are the safety precautions in case of fire or other emergencies?

5. What about sick children? Do they stay home? What if a child needs medical help? Is someone on staff trained in first aid, including cardiopulmonary resuscitation (CPR) and the Heimlich Maneuver?

6. What are the fees for half-days, overtime or sick children? Are you required to pay for days a child does not attend, for example, during a family vacation?

7. How does the staff discipline children? How much of each day is filled with planned activities? Are activities geared to the child's age and development?

8. Are the children's drawings or projects displayed and changed often? Is there a designated space for your child's belongings?

9. Do caregivers tell you what your child did that day? Do they discuss how your child is doing overall?

After your child is in a program, you should ask:

1. Does your child talk happily about the program?

2. Do you meet new employees? Do they talk to your child?

For employers, the Department of Labor Women's Bureau Work and Family Clearinghouse provides information about child and elder care. For more information, call 1 (800) 827-5335 (toll free).

Credit Cards

The following suggestions can help you when selecting a credit card company or using your credit cards.

1. Keep in a safe place a list of your credit card numbers, expiration dates and the phone number of each card issuer.

2. Credit card issuers offer a wide variety of terms (annual percentage rate, methods of calculating the balance subject to the finance charge, minimum monthly payments and actual membership fees). When selecting a card, compare the terms offered by several card issuers to find the card that best suits your needs.

3. When you use your credit card, watch your card after giving it to a clerk. Promptly take back the card after the clerk is finished with it and make sure it's yours.

4. Tear up the carbons when you take your credit card receipt.

5. Never sign a blank receipt; draw a line through any blank spaces above the total when you sign receipts.

6. Save your purchase receipts until the credit card bill arrives. Then, open the bill

promptly and compare it with your receipts to check for possible unauthorized charges and billing errors.

7. Write the card issuer promptly to report any questionable charges. Telephoning the card issuer to discuss the billing problem *does not* preserve your rights. Do not include written inquiries with your payment. Instead, check the billing statement for the correct address for billing questions. The inquiry must be in writing and must be sent within 60 days to guarantee your rights under the Fair Credit Billing Act.

8. Never give your credit card number over the telephone unless you made the call or have an account with the company calling you. Never put your card number on a post card or on the outside of an envelope.

9. Sign new cards as soon as they arrive. Cut up and throw away expired cards.

10. When writing checks for retail purchases and to protect yourself against fraud, you may refuse to allow a merchant to write your credit card number on your check. However, if you refuse, the merchant might legally refuse to sell you the product. There is probably no harm in allowing a merchant to verify that you hold a major credit card and to note the issuer and the expiration date on the check.

11. If a merchant indicates he or she is using credit cards as back-ups for bounced checks, or refuses your sale because you refuse to provide personal information (including your phone number) on the bankcard sales slip, report the store to the credit card company. The merchant might be violating his or her arrangement with the credit card companies. In your letter to the credit card company, provide the name and location of the merchant.

Lost or Stolen Credit and ATM Cards

Credit Billing Errors

Increasingly, people find it convenient to shop with credit cards or to bank at automated teller machines (ATMs) with ATM cards. But the ease with which these cards can be used also makes them very attractive to thieves.

Loss or theft of credit and ATM cards is a serious consumer problem. However, the Fair Credit Billing Act (FCBA) and the Electronic Fund Transfer Act (EFTA) establish procedures for you and your creditors to follow to resolve problems with credit card and electronic fund transfer accounts. Here are some suggestions on what to do if any of your credit cards are missing or stolen, how to protect your cards, and what you can expect from a credit card registration or protection service.

Reducing Your Financial Loss

There are at least two good financial reasons for you to report the loss or theft of your credit and ATM cards quickly. First, the sooner you report the loss, the more likely you will limit your liability if someone uses your card without your permission. Most card fraud occurs within the first 48 hours after a card is stolen.

Second, the sooner you report any loss, the more card costs can be kept down. You pay higher interest rates and annual fees because card fraud costs issuers hundreds of millions of dollars each year.

If any of your cards are missing or stolen, report the loss as soon as possible to your card issuers. Some companies have toll-free or WATS numbers printed on their statements and 24-hour service to accept such emergency information. For your own protection, you should follow up your phone calls with a letter to each card issuer. The letter should give your card number, say when your card was missing, and mention the date you called in the loss.

These are toll-free numbers of some of the major credit cards to report lost or stolen cards:

American Express	800-528-2121
Carte Blanche	800-525-9135
Diner's Club	(except Colorado) 800-525-9135
	(within Colorado) 800-332-9340
Discover Card	800-858-5588
Master Card	800-556-5678
	(TDD)800-225-1208
Mobil Oil Credit Corp.	800-225-9547
Visa	
Classic Card	800-336-8472
Gold Card	800-847-2911

You may wish to check your homeowner's insurance policy to see if it covers your liability for card thefts. If not, some insurance companies will allow you to change your current policy to include protection for card losses.

- **Credit Card Loss.** If you report the loss *before* these cards are used, the FCBA says the card issuer cannot hold you responsible for any unauthorized charges. If a thief uses your cards before you report them missing, the most you will owe for unauthorized charges on each card is $50. This is true even if a thief is able to use your credit card at an ATM machine to access your credit account.

However, it is not enough simply to report your credit card loss. After the card loss, review your billing statements carefully. If your statements show any charges not made by you, send a letter to the card issuer describing each questionable charge on your account. Again, tell the card issuer the date your card was lost or stolen and when you reported it to them. Be sure to send the letter to the address provided for billing errors. Do *not* send it with a payment or to the address where you send your payments unless you are directed to do so.

- **ATM Card Loss.** If you report an ATM card missing *before* it is used without your permission, the EFTA says the card issuer cannot hold you responsible for any unauthorized withdrawals. If unauthorized use occurs before you report it, the amount you can be held responsible for depends upon how quickly you report the loss to the card issuer. For example, if you report the loss within two business days after you realize your card is missing, you will not be responsible for more than $50 for unauthorized use.

You could lose as much as $500 because of an unauthorized withdrawal from your bank account if you do not tell the card issuer within the two business days after you discover the loss. And, you risk *unlimited* loss if, within 60 days after your bank statement is mailed to you, you do not report an unauthorized transfer or withdrawal. That means you could lose all the money in your bank account and the unused portion of your maximum line of credit established for overdrafts.

If any unauthorized transactions appear on your bank statement, report them to the card issuer as soon as you can. As with a credit card, once you have reported the loss of your ATM card you cannot be held liable for additional amounts, even if more unauthorized transactions are made.

Protecting Your Cards

The best protections against card fraud are to know where your cards are at all times and to keep them secure. For ATM card protection, it is important to keep your Personal Identification Number (PIN) a secret. Memorize this number. Statistics show that in one-third of ATM card frauds, cardholders wrote their PINS on their ATM cards or on slips of paper they kept with their cards.

The following suggestions may help you protect your credit and ATM card accounts.

For credit cards:

- Never give your account number to persons who contact you by phone unless you make the call;
- Never put your account number on the outside of an envelope or on a postcard;
- Draw a line through blank spaces on charge slips above the total so the amount cannot be changed;
- Do not sign a blank charge slip unless absolutely necessary;
- Rip up carbons from the charge slip and save your receipts to check against your monthly billing statements.
- Open billing statements promptly and compare them with your receipts. If there are any mistakes or differences, report them as soon as possible to the special address listed on the billing statement for "billing inquiries." Under the FCBA, the card issuer must investigate billing errors if you report them within 60 days of the date your card issuer mailed you the statement.
- Keep in a safe place (away from where you keep your cards) a record of your card numbers, expiration dates, and the telephone numbers of each credit-card company for the emergency reporting of losses;
- Carry only those cards that you regularly need, especially when traveling.

For ATM cards:

- Select a PIN (personal identification number) that is different from other numbers noted in your wallet, such as your address, birthdate, phone, or social security number;
- Memorize your PIN;
- Do not write your PIN on your ATM card or carry your PIN in your wallet or purse;
- Never put your PIN on the outside of a deposit slip, an envelope, or on a postcard;
- Examine all ATM receipts and bank statements as soon as possible.

Card Registration Service

Many companies offer card registration and protection services that will notify all companies where you have credit and ATM card accounts in case your card is lost or stolen. With this service, you need make only one phone call to report all card losses instead of calling each card issuer individually. Also, most services will request replacement cards on your behalf. Registration services usually cost $10 to $35 yearly.

Purchasing a card registration service may be a convenience to you, but it is not required by card issuers. The Fair Credit Billing Act and Electronic Fund Transfer Act give you the right to contact credit companies and ATM card issuers directly in the event of loss or suspected unauthorized card use.

If you do decide to buy a registration service, compare offers and look for one that will best suit your needs. Read the service contract carefully to check the company's obligations and your liability. For example, will the company reimburse you if it fails to notify charge card loss promptly after you report the loss? If not, you could be liable for unauthorized charges.

Getting More Information

For additional information about credit or ATM card fraud or credit card billing problems, send for: Credit and Charge Card Fraud; Fair Credit Billing; or Credit Billing Blues. These fact sheets are available free from the Federal Trade Commission, Public Reference, Washington, D.C. 20580.

The FTC cannot solve individual credit-dispute problems for consumers. It can act, however, when it sees a pattern of possible law violations. If you have a complaint or question about credit cards issued by department stores, oil companies, or other non-bank creditors, write to: Credit Cards, Correspondence Branch, FTC, Washington, D.C. 20580.

If your credit or ATM card is issued by a national bank, send any correspondence to the Office of the Comptroller of the Currency, Consumer Activities Division, Washington, D.C. 20219. If your card is issued by a savings and loan institution or a federal savings bank, contact the Federal Home Loan Bank Board, Office of Community Investments, Washington, D.C. 20552. For all other banks, write to the Federal Reserve Board, Division of Consumer and Community Affairs, Washington, D.C. 20551.

Credit Billing Errors? Use FCBA

At certain times of the year, you may find yourself facing particularly large credit card bills. At those times especially, the Federal Trade Commission (FTC) advises you to review your billing statements with care.

Credit card billing errors *do* occur, but they are simple to resolve if you know how to use the Fair Credit Billing Act. Under this law, you must send the creditor a written notice about the problem to avoid paying for any charges you dispute. Many consumers forfeit their rights under this Act because they rely on calling the company to correct a billing problem. You can call if you wish, but phoning does not trigger the legal safeguards provided under the Fair Credit Billing Act.

To take full advantage of your rights under the law, this is what you need to do:

1. Write the bank, other financial institutions, or retailer who issued the card. Your notice must be received within 60 days after the issuer mailed the first bill containing the error. In your letter include: your name and account number; the date, type, and dollar amount of the charge you are disputing; and why you think there was a mistake.

2. Be sure to send the letter to the special address for billing inquiries, as designated by the card issuer. You frequently can find the proper address on your bill under a heading such as "send inquiries to."

3. Do not put your letter in the same envelope as your payment. To be sure the card issuer receives your letter, you also may wish to send it by certified mail.

If you follow the above requirements, here is what the creditor is required to do:

1. Acknowledge your letter in writing within 30 days after it is received, unless the problem has been resolved within that time.

2. Conduct a reasonable investigation and, within no more than 90 days, either explain why the bill is correct or correct the error.

3. Include documents showing that the charge was correct, if the creditor states the bill is correct and if you asked for "proof" in your letter.

Under the FCBA, the card issuer cannot close your account just because you disputed a bill under the law.

If you continue to have problems with the card issuer, you might wish to seek legal advice or contact your local consumer protection agency. For more information about this law, contact the FTC for a free brochure. Write: "Fair Credit Billing," Public Reference, Federal Trade Commission, Washington, D.C. 20580.

For more information on establishing and protecting your credit see the chapter "Consumer Credit," p. 237.

Environmental Tips

How to dispose of everyday trash or garbage (often called solid waste) is an issue of interest to many consumers, businesses, environmentalists and government officials. Here are some tips designed to help you understand the garbage, or solid waste, disposal issue. These tips also might help you evaluate the environmental claims some companies are making about their products and packages.

1. The Environmental Protection Agency (EPA) has outlined a three-part solid waste management plan. It includes source reduction or reducing the amount of waste created in the first place, recycling and composting, waste-to-energy incineration and landfilling.

2. The EPA also has issued its suggestions on how individual consumers can help solve the solid waste problem. They are:

REDUCE the amount of waste that you throw away,

REUSE products whenever possible, and

RECYCLE as many products and packages as you possibly can.

3. If you wish to use environmental claims to compare products, specific claims are usually more meaningful. Two examples of specific claims could be "50% less packaging than an earlier container" or "contains 25–30% recycled content." Claims about a product or package like "environmentally friendly" or "safe

for the environment" can be misleading because they are so broad and vague. Environmental issues are very complex. If you have questions about a company's environmental claims, call or write the company.

4. The environmental benefits of a "degradable" product depend on how it is handled after disposal. A degradable product will break down if exposed to air, water, light and/or micro-organisms over time. Therefore, a degradable product might be appropriate for a composting system, if there is a composting system nearby that can safely and effectively compost the discarded product into a usable product. However, if the degradable product will end up in a landfill, and that is where more than 70% of waste ends up now, it might not degrade in any meaningful way because landfills are designed to keep out air, water and light. Additionally, if the product will be incinerated or recycled, the degradability of the product is not important. Check with your local solid waste management office to find out what waste disposal system is used in your community. If there is a composting facility in your area, be sure to ask what kinds of compostable materials it will accept. For example, some composting programs are limited to yard waste, leaves, etc.

5. It is technically possible to recycle many materials, for example, paper, metal, glass and plastic. The key question is whether these materials can be recycled in your community. Does your community ask you to separate one or more types of materials from the rest of your trash for curbside pick-up? Or, is there a drop-off recycling center that accepts that type of material? If a product labeled "recyclable" is not separated from the rest of your trash, it is not likely to be recycled. Check with your local solid waste management office to find out which products and packages are recyclable in your community.

6. Many products are being made from recycled materials. This helps "complete the loop" of recycling by using recycled materials to make new products. If you wish to buy a product made primarily from recycled material, check to see if the percentage of recycled material is listed on the product or package.

For additional information about environmental claims or the garbage disposal programs in your community, contact your state or local consumer protection office. This office will be able to refer you to the local solid waste management authority.

Franchise and Business Opportunities

Buying a franchise or a business opportunity may be appealing if you want to be your own boss, but have limited capital and business experience. However, without carefully investigating a business before you purchase, you may make a serious mistake. It is important to find out if a particular business is right for you and if it has the potential to yield the financial return you expect. A Federal Trade Commission rule requires that franchise and business opportunity sellers provide certain information to help you in your decision.

Under the FTC rule, a franchise or business opportunity seller must give you a detailed disclosure document at least ten business days before you pay any money or legally commit yourself to a purchase. This document gives 20 important items of information about the business, including:

- the names, addresses, and telephone numbers of other purchasers;

- a fully-audited financial statement of the seller;
- the background and experience of the business's key executives;
- the cost required to start and maintain the business; and
- the responsibilities you and the seller will have to each other once you buy.

The Disclosure Statement

The disclosure document is a valuable tool that not only helps you obtain information about a proposed business, but assists you in comparing it with other businesses. If you are not given a disclosure document, ask why you did not receive one. Some franchise or business opportunity sellers may not be required to give you a disclosure document. If any franchise or business opportunity says it is not covered by the rule, you may want to verify it with the FTC, an attorney, or a business advisor. Even if the business is not legally required to give the document, you still may want to ask for the data to help you make an informed investment decision.

Here are some important things to do before buying a business:

- *Study the disclosure document* and proposed contracts carefully.
- *Talk to current owners*. The disclosure document must list the names and addresses of other people who currently own and operate the franchise or business opportunity. These people are likely to be important sources of information. Try to call a number of owners to find out about the company. Ask them how the information in the disclosure document matches their experiences with the company. Remember, a list of company-selected references cannot be substituted for the list of franchises or business opportunity owners required under the FTC rule.
- *Investigate earnings claims*. Earnings claims are only estimates. The FTC rule requires companies to have in writing the facts on which they base their earnings claims. Make sure you understand the basis for a seller's earnings claims.

  Sellers also must tell you in writing the number and percentage of other owners who have done as well as they claim you will do. Remember, broad sales claims about a successful area of business—such as, "Be a part of our four billion dollar industry"—may have no bearing on the likelihood of your own success. Keep in mind that once you buy the business, you may be competing with other franchise owners or independent business people with more experience.
- *Shop around: compare franchises with other available business opportunities*. You may discover that other companies offer benefits not available from the first company you considered. *The Franchise Opportunities Handbook,* published annually by the U.S. Department of Commerce, describes more than 1,400 companies that offer franchises. Contact other companies and ask for their disclosure documents. Then you can compare offerings.
- *Listen carefully to the sales presentation*. Some sales tactics should signal caution. For example, if you are pressured to sign immediately "because prices will go up tomorrow," or "another buyer wants this deal," you should slow down, not accelerate, your purchase decision. A seller with a good offer does not have to use this sort of pressure. Remember, under the FTC rule, the seller must wait at

least ten business days after giving you the required documents before you may pay any money or sign any agreement. Be on guard if the salesperson makes the job sound too easy. The thought of "easy money" may be appealing, but, as we all know, success usually requires hard work.

- *Get the seller's promises in writing.* Any important promises you get from a salesperson should be written into the contract you sign. If the salesperson says one thing but the contract says nothing about it or says something different, your contract is what counts. Whatever the reasons, if a seller balks at putting verbal promises in writing, you should be alert to potential problems. You might want to look for another business.
- *Consider getting professional advice.* Unless you have had considerable business experience, you may want to get a lawyer, an accountant, or a business advisor to read the disclosure document and proposed contract to counsel you and help you get the best deal. Remember, the initial money and time you spend on getting professional assistance and verifying facts, such as making phone calls to owners, could save you from a major loss on a bad investment.

Health Hoaxes, Food Fads and Dangerous Diets

Consumers spend millions of dollars each year on phony medicines and treatments, food fads, and weight loss products and diets that simply do not work and might be dangerous. The information below will help you avoid buying unproven health and diet products or programs.

1. If a health claim sounds too good to be true, there's a good chance it is. Be skeptical about claims offering "miracle or secret cures" or "scientific breakthroughs." True cures or breakthroughs are always publicized widely in the media; there are no secret cures.

2. Check with a licensed health professional or credible health organization (for example, the American Cancer Society or the American Dietetics Association) before buying "cures" or "miracle diets." Science has not yet found a cure for arthritis, as the Arthritis Foundation could tell you, so products that promise to cure you of the disease are phony.

3. Be aware that health frauds, food fads and fake diet products might rob you of more than your money. They might ruin your health or even take your life.

Home Improvements

Hiring a contractor to renovate your home, add a room or make some other improvement can be a confusing maze of contracts, licenses, permits and payment schedules. The suggestions listed below can help guide you through that maze.

1. Compare costs by getting more than one estimate or bid. Each estimate should be based on the same building specifications, materials and time frame.

2. Before choosing a contractor, check with state, county or local consumer protection agencies to see if any complaints have been filed against the contractor. Ask about information on unresolved cases and how long a contracting company has been in business under its current name.

3. Ask a potential contractor for a list of previous customers whom you could call

to find out about work quality and if they would hire that contractor for future work.

4. Check with your local building inspections department to see if licensing and/or bonding are required of contractors in your area. If so, ask to see the contractor's license and bonding papers.

5. Before signing a written contract, be sure it includes the contractor's full name, address, phone number and professional license number (where required), a thorough description of the work to be done, grade and quality of materials to be used, agreed upon starting and completion dates, total cost, payment schedule, warranty, how debris will be removed and any other agreement information. Never sign a partially blank contract. Fill in or draw a line through any blank spaces.

6. Most contractors have liability and compensation insurance to protect the customer from a lawsuit in the event of an accident. Ask to see a copy of the insurance certificate.

7. If the work requires a building permit, let the contractor apply for it in his name. That way, if the work does not pass inspection, you are not financially responsible for any corrections that must be made.

8. When you sign a non-emergency home improvement contract in your home and in the presence of a contractor (or contractor's representative), you usually have three business days in which to cancel the contract. You must be told about your cancellation rights and be provided with cancellation forms. If you decide to cancel, it is recommended that you send a notice of cancellation by telegram or certified mail, return receipt requested.

9. For a remodeling job involving many subcontractors and a substantial amount of money, it is wise to protect yourself from liens against your home in case the contractor does not pay subcontractors or suppliers. If state law permits, add a release-of-lien clause to the contract or place your payments in an escrow account until the work is completed.

10. If you cannot pay for a project without a loan, add a clause to your contract stating it is valid only if financing is obtained.

11. When signing a contract, limit your first payment to not more than 30% of the contract price. The remaining payments should depend on the progress of the work. Ten percent of the contract amount should be held back until the job is complete, and all problems, if any, are corrected. Some states have home improvement laws that specify the amount of deposit and payment schedule. Check with your state and local consumer protection offices to see if there is such a law in your community.

12. Thoroughly inspect the contractor's work before making final payment or signing a completion certificate.

Door-To-Door Sales

All of us have bought something from a door-to-door salesperson at some time in our lives. It can be handy to do our shopping at home. We often can see the full selection of goods without counter shopping in a crowded department store. And we get the luxury of personalized service that can be hard to come by in big stores. But there may be times when buying from a door-to-door salesperson leaves us disappointed. We may be unhappy later with what we bought or confused and dissatisfied by how much we end up paying.

It used to be that a peddler could get your name on the dotted line and with a handshake be off quicker than you could count your change. Not any more. Thanks to industry standards and a Federal Trade Commission rule, we can change our minds about door-to-door purchases.

The Federal Trade Commission rule is called the "Cooling Off Rule." It gives every buyer three days to change his or her mind about many purchases made on doorsteps, or anywhere away from the seller's place of business. For the rule to apply, the purchase must cost $25 or more. There are exceptions to this rule, however.

But before you get into a position where you need to use the "Cooling Off Rule," take precautions to keep from getting into hot water in the first place.

- Find out just who is knocking at your door. Some door-to-door salespeople may use gimmicks to get your attention and get you to sign for something before you know who they represent. Ask to see the seller's identification. Posing as a door-to-door salesperson can be a good cover for burglars and other criminals.
- Don't buy on the spot. Even if the item or service is something you really need or want, you probably can live without it long enough to find out if you are getting a good deal.
- Shop around. You can price products or services by phone if you can't do it in person. Most of the things peddled door-to-door are available from other sellers. Contact a few of them to compare what they offer to what the door-to-door salesperson is touting.
- Do not sign anything until you get satisfactory answers to these questions:

  * What are you getting and exactly how much are you going to pay—including tax, interest, or other charges? If someone says you are going to get something free, make sure it really is *free*. If you have to sign a paper to receive the free item, don't do it!
  * What will the product or service do and not do? If you are getting a new vacuum cleaner, for instance, find out if it will remove dog hair as well as it picks up kitty litter.
  * Exactly what does the warranty cover on the product or service you're buying? If you know for certain that your roof needs fixing, and you are going to pay someone to fix it, ask the seller to state in writing what happens if the repair doesn't do the job.
  * How long does the guarantee or warranty last? For example, if your new roof isn't warranteed for more than a couple of months, then you may not be getting a very good deal.
  * What are the company's policies on refunds and exchanges? Can you get a refund, or must you take another product in its place?
  * What happens if you need to reach the seller or someone in the company? You should have the name, address, and telephone number of either the salesperson or a company contact, and preferably both.
  * Does the sales contract match the claims made by the seller? Are the terms of

the sale the same? If there is a finance charge, is its annual rate of interest clearly stated?

Two things to remember when you want to sign a contract:

1. Make sure all the blank spaces in your contract are filled in before you sign it.
2. Get a copy of any contract or any other document you sign and keep it handy for future use.

In all sales transactions, get as much as possible in writing. If the salesperson promises you that your vacuum cleaner will last 15 years, get it in writing from the seller. If the seller insists that the roof repair you're buying will last 10 years, get it in writing.

How to Cancel

The Federal Trade Commission requires door-to-door sellers of goods or services valued at $25 or more to tell you your cancellation rights. And your contract *must* include information about your right to cancel.

You should be given two copies of a cancellation form or receipt. These should be dated and should show the name and address of the seller and the date by which the buyer may cancel.

To cancel your purchase:

NOTICE OF CANCELLATION

Date of Transaction:

You may cancel this transaction, without any penalty or obligation, within three business days from the above date.

If you cancel, any property traded in, any payments made by you under the contract or sale, and any negotiable instrument executed by you will be returned within 10 business days following receipt by the seller of your cancellation notice, and any security interest arising out of the transaction will be cancelled.

If you cancel, you must make available to the seller at your residence, in substantially as good condition as when received, any goods delivered to you under this contract or sale; or you may, if you wish, comply with the instructions of the seller regarding the return shipment of the goods at the seller's expense and risk.

If you do make the goods available to the seller and the seller does not pick them up within 20 days of the date of your notice of cancellation, you may retain or dispose of the goods without any further obligation. If you fail to make the goods available to the seller or if you agree to return the goods to the seller and fail to do so, then you remain liable for performance of all obligations under the contract.

To cancel this transaction, mail or deliver a signed and dated copy of this cancellation notice, or send a telegram, to (name of seller) at (address of seller's place of business) not later than midnight of (date), saying,

I hereby cancel this transaction.

Your Signature Date

- *Act fast*. The law gives you three days. Any time before midnight of the third business day *after* the date on the contract, you can cancel by mailing or delivering a cancellation notice to the address given for cancellation. Count three *business* days. Do not count Sundays or holidays. For example: If you signed the contract on a Friday, you would have until midnight the following Tuesday to cancel (assuming that neither Saturday, Monday nor Tuesday was a holiday).
- *Sign and date the cancellation form*. The seller should include the form with your contract. If the seller does not do this, then write one of your own and keep a copy. On page 27 is the FTC's model "notice of cancellation" that sellers must provide, as required by the FTC rule.
- Keep copies for yourself of everything you send to the seller, including your dated cancellation form. Never send originals of anything you cannot replace, such as cancelled checks, receipts, guarantees, promises the seller made in writing, or your contract and warranties, if any.

  Once you have notified the seller you choose to cancel the sale, the seller *must* do these things within 10 days:

  1. Refund any money you paid for the merchandise.

  2. Return any goods or property that you used as a trade-in.

  3. Cancel and return any promissory note you may have signed.

  4. Tell you whether you can keep any merchandise that was left with you—any "free" gifts, for example.

  5. Pick up within 20 days any merchandise left with you or pay you for any return mail shipping costs to send back the merchandise.

If the seller does not do what the law requires, the seller may be penalized under the law.

But remember: if the salesperson has complied with the law, you *can* be held responsible for all agreements in the contract you signed if you fail to do what is required of you (like cancelling within the allotted three days).

When Don't You Get to "Cool Off"?

There are situations in which you do not have the right to cancel a contract. The Federal Trade Commission's "Cooling Off Rule" does *not* apply to all sales of products and services. You do not have three days to cancel any contract you wish you hadn't made. Specifically, it does not cover sales that are:

- under $25;
- for real estate, insurance, or securities;
- for emergency home repairs when you waive the right to cancel;
- made entirely by mail or by phone;
- made at the seller's normal place of business, such as a store outlet; or
- initiated by you for repair or maintenance on your personal property.

What Else Should You Know About the Rule?

Whether the salesperson is invited or uninvited to your home, the rule still applies, and you have your right to cancel. The rule applies to any place you buy something—

at other people's homes, on street corners, anywhere—except for the seller's normal place of business.

As an older person, you can be at a real disadvantage when dealing with unknown sellers. The stories of elderly people who were talked into thousands of dollars worth of unnecessary home repairs are legendary and heartbreaking.

Refusing to buy on the spot is one good way to avoid future disappointments and unnecessary expense. Buying later, instead of now, is not likely to cost you a once-in-a-lifetime bargain. If you wait to buy until you are sure you are getting what you really want, and at the best possible price, an honest salesperson will wait, too.

When Should You Complain?

When you have done all you can do to exercise your right to cancel in three days, but the seller fails to live up to his legal responsibilities, complain.

Some organizations that may be of some help are:

- Your state, county or local consumer protection office or your state Attorney General's office;
- The Federal Trade Commission, which enforces the "Cooling Off Rule," 6th and Pennsylvania Avenue, N.W., Washington, D.C. 20580; and
- The Direct Selling Association, which can assist you with your complaint if the seller belongs to the organization, 1730 M Street, N.W., Washington, D.C. 20036.

Home Shopping

Today, there are many ways to buy products or services. Some consumers buy items through mail order, telephone, or even television shopping programs. Keep the following tips in mind:

1. Be suspicious of exaggerated product claims or very low prices and read product descriptions carefully. Sometimes, pictures of products are misleading.

2. If you have any doubts about the company, check with the U.S. Postal Service, your state or local consumer protection agency, or Better Business Bureau before ordering.

3. Ask about the firm's return policy. If it is not stated, ask before you order. For example, does the company pay charges for shipping and return? Is a warranty or guarantee available? Does the company sometimes substitute comparable goods for the product you want to order?

4. If you buy by telephone, make clear exactly what you are ordering and how much it costs before you give your credit card number; watch out for incidental charges.

5. Keep a complete record of your order, including the company's name, address and telephone number, price of the items ordered, any handling or other charges, date of your order, and your method of payment. Keep copies of canceled checks and/or statements. If you're ordering by telephone, get the names of any company representatives with whom you speak.

6. If you order by mail, your order should be shipped within 30 days after the company receives your completed order, unless another period is agreed upon when

placing the order or is stated in an advertisement. If your order is delayed, a notice of delay should be sent to you within the promised shipping period, along with an option to cancel the order.

7. If you want to buy a product based on a telephone call *from* an unfamiliar company, ask for the name, address and phone number where you can reach the caller after considering the offer. It is best to request and read written information before deciding to buy.

8. Never give your credit card, bank account or Social Security number over the telephone as proof of your identity, unless you placed the call or have an account with the company you are calling.

9. Postal regulations allow you to write a check payable to the sender, rather than the delivery company, for cash on delivery (C.O.D.) orders. If, after examining the merchandise, you feel there has been misrepresentation or fraud, you can stop payment on the check and file a complaint with the U.S. Postal Inspector's Office.

10. You can have a charge removed from your credit card bill if you did not receive the goods or services or if your order was obtained through misrepresentation or fraud. You must notify the credit card company *in writing*, at the billing inquiries/disputes address, within 60 days after the charge first appeared on your bill.

Mail Order Sales

It has been said that if you shop by mail, the whole world is your department store. You can buy hams from Virginia, handicrafts from New Hampshire, woolens from Maine, apple-peelers from Alabama, or oranges from Florida.

Shopping by mail is a way to buy specialty items without leaving your house. It's a way to find products that are hard to find in stores without wearing yourself out in the search.

Buying from catalogs, magazines, and other publications gives you all the time you need to make up your mind. The "store" opens and closes when you want it to. If you want to shop at 3 A.M. when you can't sleep, or browse through the merchandise over a cup of coffee, you can when you shop by mail.

Shopping by mail also can be thrifty when there is a discount for buying directly from the source.

But the leisure and convenience you get with mail order sometimes can be offset by a long wait for your merchandise or by your disappointment when the item isn't what you wanted.

And when your mail order arrives late or not at all, you may not know what to do.

The Federal Trade Commission has a rule that gives you certain rights when you shop by mail. The U.S. Postal Service enforces various fraud laws under its authority which can apply to mail order purchases.

It is easy to be fooled when you order by mail. You can help protect yourself if you first:

- Deal with reliable companies. If you don't know the company, you might want to check with a consumer protection office near you, which in turn may check with offices near the company. Or check with the Direct Marketing Association.
- Read the ads for the product very carefully. Don't rely on pictures alone since

they may be misleading. And if there are some claims in the ads that sound "too good to be true," then maybe they are. Write the company for more details.

- Never send cash for a mail order purchase. A cancelled check, money order receipt, or credit card bill may be the only way to prove your money was received and cashed by the seller if a dispute occurs about payment.
- Keep a copy of your order blank and write down or copy the name of the company, its address, and when you sent your order.

Know your rights under the law:

1. You must receive the merchandise when the seller says you will.

2. The seller must ship the goods to you *no later* than 30 days after your properly completed order arrives, unless the advertising specifies otherwise.

3. The seller, if unable to meet the required shipping date, must send you an option notice giving you the right to cancel and receive a prompt refund, or to agree to the delay.

4. You can cancel your order and get your money back if you don't get what you ordered shortly after 30 days of the date specified in the advertising.

But beware. If you don't answer the seller's first notice of a delay, where the revised shipping date is 30 days or less, you are agreeing to a later shipping date and will have to live with it.

It is up to the seller to provide you with a stamped envelope, a pre-paid post card, or some way to send back your answer at no cost to you.

Remember, the seller must:

- Notify you there will be a delay;
- Tell you if the delay is going to be less than or more than 30 days;
- Mail you your refund within seven business days; and
- Take no more than one billing cycle to adjust your account if you paid by charge card. If adjustment takes longer, the Fair Credit Billing Act says you can stop payment on the disputed charge by notifying the credit card company in writing.

The Mail Order Rule does *not* apply to orders for:

- Film development;
- Seeds or growing plants;
- "C.O.D." payments; or
- Magazine subscriptions after the first issue.

The rule also does not apply if you use an "800" number to place your order and charge it directly to a credit card, or if your credit account is charged *after* the merchandise has been shipped.

Whose Stuff Is This Anyway?

Most of us have received things in the mail at some time or other that we never ordered. The law says, quite simply, unordered merchandise is yours to keep. You may legally consider it a gift, and you cannot be forced to pay for it or return it.

. . . A woman who had a long-running dispute with a cosmetics company over a jar of face cream was surprised and confused when, after months of letters protesting that she had not received the cream although she paid for it, found *two* jars of the expensive preparation in her mail box.

"What should I do with the second jar?" she asked the consumer office. "I only paid for one jar. Do I have to return the other?"

The answer? *No.*

There are only two kinds of merchandise that legally can be sent to you through the mail without your consent. They are:

- Free samples clearly labeled as such; and
- Goods mailed by charities seeking contributions, such as key rings or other small items.

You can keep these items, and it is illegal for any seller to try to force you to return anything you did not order. If the seller tries to bill you for something you didn't order, ask the seller for proof that you placed the order.

What the Postman Didn't Bring

There are many ways to send things these days besides the U.S. Postal Service. United Parcel Service (UPS) is one of them. If you get something that is delivered by a private delivery service that you did not order, you must do two things before you can keep the item:

1. You must tell the sender that you received merchandise you did not order, preferably in writing so you can prove it later if you are billed.

2. You must give the sender a reasonable amount of time, such as 30 days, to pick up the merchandise at the *sender's* expense. Tell the sender what you will do with the merchandise if it is not picked up—keep it, toss it out, whatever.

If you decide to return the merchandise, you should be able to find the address and phone number for most delivery services, such as United Parcel Service (UPS), in your telephone book.

If You Have a Complaint

If you have a problem with a mail order company, make your complaint known. If you think the product doesn't live up to its sales claims, or if your purchase doesn't arrive when it should, or the item simply isn't what you ordered, complain.

First make the problem known to the seller. Also, send a copy of your letter to the U.S. Postal Service, Washington, D.C. 20260, and to the Federal Trade Commission, Washington, D.C. 20580. A list of FTC regional offices follows this article. It may help if you let the seller know you've contacted various agencies. Although the FTC does not intervene in private disputes between you and a mail order seller, it does investigate problems in which a pattern of violations is clear.

If you wish to receive catalogs by mail or place an order, following is a list of catalog names and telephone catalog order numbers.

Catalog Names and Numbers

CATALOG COMPANY	CATALOG ORDERS
American Express	800-528-8000
Arizona Mail Order	602-747-5000
Austad's	605-336-3135
Avon Fashions	800-322-1119
Bass Pro Shop	800-227-7776
	(TDD No., 800-442-5788)
Bedford Fair	919-763-5600
Blair Fashions	800-458-6057
Bradford Exchange	800-323-5577
Brookstone	603-924-9541
Brownstone Studio	800-221-2468
Cabela's	800-237-4444
Campmor	800-526-4784
Carol Wright Gifts	402-474-4465
CBN Publishing	800-446-7323 (ex VA)
Chadwick's of Boston	508-583-6600
Clifford & Wills	800-922-0114
Collin Street Bakery	903-872-8111
Colonial Garden Kitchens	800-752-5552
Colonial Williamsburg Mail Order Dept.	800-446-9240 (ex VA)
C.O.M.B.	800-328-0609
The Company Store	800-323-8000
Crutchfield	800-446-1640
Damark	800-729-9000
Eddie Bauer	800-426-8020
	(TDD No., 800-462-6757)
Figi's	715-387-6311
Fingerhut	800-233-3588
Franklin Mint	800-843-6468
Fuller Brush	800-522-0024
Gander Mountain	800-558-9410
	(TDD No., 800-558-3554)
Haband	201-942-1010
Hamilton Collection	800-228-2945
Hammacher Schlemmer	800-543-3366
Harry & David	800-547-3033
International Male	800-854-2795
Jackson and Perkins	800-292-4769
James River Traders	800-445-2405
J.C. Penney	800-222-6161
	(TDD No., 800-527-7889)

CATALOG COMPANY	CATALOG ORDERS
J. Crew	800-562-0258
Johnny Appleseed's	800-767-6666
Jos. A. Bank Clothiers	800-285-2265
King-Size	800-343-9678
K-Paul's Louisiana Mailorder	800-457-2857
Land's End	800-356-4444
	(TDD No., 800-541-3459)
Lane Bryant	800-477-7070
	(TDD No., 800-456-7161)
Laura Ashley	800-367-2000
L'Eggs	919-744-1170
	(TDD No., 919-744-5300)
Leichtung Workshops	800-321-6840
Lillian Vernon	914-633-6300
L.L. Bean	800-221-4221
	(TDD No., 800-545-0090)
Mark Cross	800-223-1678
Metropolitan Museum of Art	800-468-7386
Miles Kimball	414-231-4886
Mind's Eye	800-227-2020
Neiman-Marcus	800-825-8000
	(TDD No., 800-533-1312)
Old Pueblo Traders	602-747-5000
Omaha Steaks	800-228-9055
Orvis	800-541-3541
REI	800-426-4840
Roaman's	800-274-7130
Sears	800-366-3000
	(TDD No., 800-729-2828)
Service Merchandise	800-251-1212
The Sharper Image	800-344-4444
Smithsonian Institution	703-455-1700
Spiegel	800-345-4500
Spiegel Ultimate Outlet	800-332-6000
Swiss Colony	608-324-6000
The Talbots	800-882-5268
	(TDD No., 800-624-9179)
The Tog Shop	912-924-9371
Victoria's Secret	800-888-8200
Walter Drake	800-525-9291
Williams-Sonoma	800-541-2233
Wisconsin Cheeseman	608-258-3000

TDD: Telecommunications Device for the Deaf

Federal Trade Commission Headquarters

6th & Pennsylvania Avenue, N.W.
Washington, D.C. 20580
(202) 326-2222

Federal Trade Commission Regional Offices

1718 Peachtree Street, N.W.
Atlanta, Georgia 30367
(404) 347-4836

10 Causeway Street
Boston, Massachusetts 02222
(617) 565-7240

55 East Monroe Street
Chicago, Illinois 60603
(312) 353-4423

118 St. Clair Avenue
Cleveland, Ohio 44114
(216) 522-4210

100 N. Central Expressway
Dallas, Texas 75201
(214) 767-5503

1405 Curtis Street
Denver, Colorado 80202
(303) 844-2271

11000 Wilshire Boulevard
Los Angeles, California 90024
(310) 209-7890

26 Federal Plaza
New York, New York 10278
(212) 264-1207

901 Market Street
San Francisco, California 94103
(415) 995-5220

915 Second Avenue
Seattle, Washington 98174
(206) 442-4655

Unwanted Catalogs and Telephone Sales Calls

The Direct Marketing Association (DMA) operates the Mail Preference Service and Telephone Preference Service. If you wish to have your name removed from the lists maintained by companies subscribing to these DMA services write to: Mail Preference Service or Telephone Preference Service, Direct Marketing Association, 11 West 42nd St., P.O. Box 3861, New York, N.Y. 10163-3861.

Include your complete name and address, including apartment number and zip code.

Long Distance Telephone Service

Calling family and friends long distance is no longer a simple matter of picking up the telephone and dialing. Consumers now have choices that can save money and improve service. Here are some tips that will help you pick a long distance telephone company.

1. To compare long distance telephone carriers, think about the types of calls you make. When, how often, and where do you call? This information helps you select the carrier offering the best value for your long distance dollar. Be sure to look for the company that provides the best overall value in terms of price, service, features and quality.

2. Check prices by asking the company to describe or provide written information on charges for different distances during its daytime, evening, night and weekend hours. Ask about one-time only and regular charges. Is there a subscription fee, monthly service fee or monthly minimum charge? Ask about the availability of calling plans. There are several types of calling plans. Which plan works best for you depends on where and when you call and how long you talk. Major long distance companies can analyze your bills and help you choose the best plan for you.

3. Consider services. Decide which services are important to you: 24-hour operator services and customer service for billing and other inquiries; immediate credit for misdialed and unanswered numbers; domestic and international services; calling cards; third-number billed directory assistance; and/or domestic and international directory assistance and person-to-person calling. Not all carriers provide service to

all areas. Make sure the one you choose provides service to the areas you call most often.

4. Judge the quality of the carrier's performance. Are the calls clear? Do the calls connect quickly and on the first try? Are the bills accurate and easy to understand? A trial period might help you decide whether the quality of phone service is adequate. Before signing up, be sure you understand the terms of the carrier's cancellation policy and the costs involved in switching to another carrier.

5. Review the facts before making a decision. When you contact long distance carriers to gather information, make it clear that you are just asking for information and not signing up for service.

6. If you have a complaint about long distance services, first try to resolve your complaint with the company providing the service. If you are unsuccessful in your efforts to resolve the complaint yourself, then file a complaint with the appropriate regulatory commission. If the calls were placed within your state, the complaint should be filed with your state public utilities commission. If the calls were placed to another state or another country, the complaint should be filed with the Federal Communications Commission.

7. If you are making long distance calls away from home, know your long distance company's access code and dial that code. Listen for the name of your long distance company. If you are not sure you have reached your long distance company, call the operator that serves the phone you are using and ask what company you have reached. If it is not the one you want, hang up and try the access code or use a different phone.

Remember, it is not safe to assume that because you are using a particular company's calling card, you will be served by that company. Some companies take your card information and bill you for the call at their rates without telling you who is handling your call.

There might be times you cannot reach your preferred long distance company, and it is not convenient to look for another phone. In this case, you might wish to ask the operator of the company that serves the phone you are using to give you the charge for making a call of "X" minutes to the city you are calling.

8. When making calls from a hotel, ask what long distance company serves the hotel. If it is not your company, ask if you can reach your long distance company from the hotel's phones. It is also a good idea to ask what surcharges the hotel places on local and long distance calls, regardless of which telephone company handles the calls.

Mail Fraud

More and more consumers are receiving misleading or downright fraudulent mail promotions. These promotions take several forms. Some examples are:

- sweepstakes that require you to pay an entry fee or order a product;
- notices of prizes that require you to call a 900 number or buy a product;
- mailings that look like they are from government agencies, but they are not;
- classified "employment" or "business opportunity" advertisements promising easy money for little work; and
- prize awards that ask for your credit card or bank account number.

Consumers should be particularly suspicious of one of the most prevalent forms of mail fraud, notices that you have received a prize, in some cases, a very expensive prize like a car or vacation. Usually, you have to purchase a product, for example, a lifetime supply of cosmetics or large amounts of vitamins, to be eligible to receive the prize. In fact, few of the prizes are awarded, and of those received, many are worthless.

The Alliance Against Fraud in Telemarketing, administered by the National Consumers League, has information about the dangers of these types of mail solicitations.

Contact your state or local consumer office or Better Business Bureau if you have any doubts about promotions you have received through the mail.

Remember, if it sounds too good to be true, it almost certainly is.

900 Numbers

Consumers can take advantage of a variety of helpful information services by using 900 numbers. Generally, four different types of companies work together to provide 900 number services. They are:

- information providers—the business or person who created the 900 number program and is responsible for its content;
- service bureaus—a business providing a message storage system to help the information provider answer the calls to the 900 number (not all information providers hire outside service bureaus; some have their own message storage equipment);
- long distance carriers—the long distance company hired by the information provider to carry the 900 number programs (this is not necessarily the long distance company which provides your regular long distance service); and
- local phone companies—the business responsible for billing the 900 number services.

The tips listed below will help you use these numbers wisely and cost effectively.

1. There is a fee for every 900 number call, and the cost varies from call to call, so be sure you know what the fee is before you dial. Usually, there are two charges: 1) a connection fee to make the call; and 2) an additional fee based on the length of your call.

2. If you have a billing problem and cannot resolve it through your local phone company, complain directly to the long distance carrier involved. The following long distance companies have toll free numbers to handle 900 number complaints:

AT&T 1 (800) 222-0300*
MCI 1 (800) 444-3333
US Sprint 1 (800) 366-0707

*Note: If AT&T gives you a different 800 number on the long distance page of your phone bill that lists the 900 number charges, call that 800 number instead.

3. If you have a billing or other problem, you should also complain to the information provider and service bureau. The long distance carrier can provide you with the name and address of the information provider and service bureau.

4. If your problem is not resolved by contacting your local phone company, long distance carrier, service bureau or information provider, you should contact the Federal Trade Commission, 6th and Pennsylvania Avenue, N.W., Washington, D.C. 20580, or the Federal Communications Commission, 1919 M Street, N.W., Washington, D.C. 20554. If you received the solicitation for the 900 number in the mail, contact the Chief Postal Inspector, U.S. Postal Service, Washington, D.C. 20260-2100, (202) 268-4267. You also can contact your state attorney general's office, local Better Business Bureau or Consumer Credit Counseling Services.

5. Arrangements can be made with the local phone company so that 900 numbers cannot be dialed from your phone. There might be a fee for this service. Call your local phone company for more information.

Protecting Your Credit Rating and Personal Privacy

Here are some suggestions about how you can protect the privacy of your credit, medical and insurance records, as well as other personal information:

Personal Information

When you are filling out an application for credit, insurance or a job, ask how the information you give about yourself will be used. Who has access to it? Will the information be exchanged with other companies? How long is the information kept? How often is it updated?

Medical and insurance records

The Medical Information Bureau (MIB) is a data bank used by insurance companies. Medical and some non-medical information about you is collected from insurers and, with your authorization, shared when you apply for individual life, health or disability insurance. You can obtain a copy of your MIB file by writing to Medical Information Bureau, P.O. Box 105, Essex Station, Boston, MA 02112.

Periodically discuss your MIB file and other medical records with your doctor to verify the accuracy of your file.

Credit records

Credit bureaus keep records about how you pay your bills and how much credit you have, among other things. For a small fee, you can find out what's in your credit record and the names of the companies that have asked for information about you. If you are denied credit based on information in your credit bureau file, there is no cost to learn what's in your credit report. The creditor will tell you which credit bureau to write or call.

Get a copy of your credit report at least once a year, or before major credit purchases, and check for inaccuracies.

If you find a mistake in your credit report, the credit bureau must check it and correct it for you. Any negative information that cannot be proven must be removed. However, correct information about late payments can stay on your record for seven years. More severe credit problems, bankruptcy, for example, can stay on your record for up to 10 years. You also can add to your file a 100-word statement of explanation for a credit problem. Remember, when you make a correction in your credit file, make sure the correction is made at all three credit bureaus.

All three major credit bureau companies (TRW, Equifax and Trans Union) will agree to not release your name for marketing purposes. Their addresses are listed in the "Corporate Consumer Contacts" section.

As of April 30, 1992, TRW Inc. has announced that consumers will be able to receive one free copy of their credit report each year.

To request a free report, send your name, spouse's name if married, home address with zip code for last five years, Social Security number and year of birth to:

TRW Inc.
National Consumer Relations Center
12606 Greenville Ave.
P.O. Box 749029
Dallas, TX 75374-9029

or call 214 235-1200, ext. 251.

Product Safety Warnings and Recalls

Every year, in order to prevent injury to consumers, Federal agencies recall or issue warnings about hundreds of products, including food, drugs, cars and other vehicles, home and garden products, appliances, recreational boats and toys. Hazards might occur because of design flaws, production defects, new scientific information about dangers from materials previously thought safe, accidental contamination, tampering, unforeseen misuse of products or failure to meet safety standards.

Consumers are critically important in these product safety efforts because they *identify* product safety problems and because they *respond* to the warnings and recalls. In fact, product recalls and warnings can protect consumers only if consumers react to them. Yet, only two percent to 50% of consumers respond to recall notices.

The U.S. Office of Consumer Affairs has prepared a leaflet that explains which Federal agencies issue consumer product safety warnings and recalls, the kinds of products each of them covers, and how to let them know about product safety problems, or find out about warnings or recalls they have announced. For a free copy, write to:

Recalls
Item 634X
Pueblo, Colorado 81009

Choosing A School

Whether you're looking for a school for your child or seeking to improve your own skills, education is a decision that should be made carefully. The guidelines below are designed to help you with that decision.

Choosing a school for a child

There are many types of schools, public schools, magnet schools and private schools.

Public schools are grouped into city, county or regional school districts. Check with your local consumer protection office or look in the telephone book to find the address of your local school district office. Ask about school options for your area.

Then, exercise your options to choose the school that best matches your child's unique learning style.

Become involved in your child's education and other needs both at home and at school.

The U.S. Department of Education has published a booklet, "Choosing a School for Your Child." Free copies of the booklet can be ordered by writing to Choosing a School, Consumer Information Center, Pueblo, Colorado 81009.

Choosing a job training program

If you are looking for a job training program, avoid scams by checking with your local consumer protection office or Better Business Bureau before you enroll.

Before going back to school, check to see if local employers or others, for example, your local community college or high school extension, offer the type of training you want. These programs are generally less expensive and you do not have to sign a contract for extended payments.

Be sure the skills the school teaches will be useful to you and are being used in the workplace.

When selecting a job training program, you should ask the following questions:

- If you must learn how to use equipment, does the school have enough equipment so every student can practice using it? Is the equipment up-to-date?
- How many recent students graduated? How many found jobs in their fields? Did the school help them find jobs, and how long did it take? How do current and past students feel about the school's program? Ask to talk with former students.
- Does the program include on-the-job training? Do teachers work with industry and update their skills regularly?
- Do you have to take out a loan to pay for the program in advance? How are refunds handled in case the school doesn't deliver on its promises, or if you have to drop out for other reasons?
- Find out what the student loan default rate is for the school you are considering. Call 1 (800) 4-FED-AID.
- Report cases of fraud to the U.S. Department of Education at 1 (800) MIS-USED.

Paying for job training or college

There are several sources of financial aid, including scholarships, grants and loans. Scholarships and grants *do not* have to be repaid, but loans *do*.

Check with your local library for information about financial aid and check with the school about its financial aid programs.

The Department of Education, which oversees Federal financial aid programs for job training or college, can answer your questions about how to apply for Federal financial aid, how to solve loan problems or how to report possible fraud.

Remember, loans must be repaid. Because of the large number of students who do not pay back their loans, the Department of Education and other financial aid providers have stiff penalties for those who do not repay the loans.

Service Contracts

If you are buying a car or major appliance, you may be offered a service contract. To many consumers, buying a service contract is like buying "peace of mind" from repair hassles. An estimated 50% of all new car buyers, and many used-car and major appliance buyers, purchase service contracts. The cost can range from $50 to $500, depending on the length and amount of coverage provided. Some consumers, however, may be paying for *more* protection than they need.

Before you buy a service contract, consider the following:

- *What does a service contract offer?* A service contract, like a warranty, provides repair and/or maintenance for a specific time period. Warranties, however, are included in the price of the product, while service contracts cost extra and are sold separately.
- *What is covered by the service contract?* A service contract may cover only certain parts of the product or specific repairs. Read the contract carefully and, if it does not list something as specifically covered, assume that it is not. Service contracts do not cover repairs resulting from misuse or failure to maintain the product properly. Also, you may be obligated to take certain action, such as notifying the company of problems, to insure that the service contract is not voided.
- *What will the service contract give you that the warranty will not?* Before considering a service contract, make sure you know what your warranty coverage is. Carefully compare the coverage of your warranty to the coverage offered by the service contract to decide if the service contract is worth the additional expense. For more information about warranties, write for "Warranties," a free brochure from the Federal Trade Commission, Washington, D.C. 20580.
- *What other costs will you have?* You may have other expenses after you buy a service contract. Service contracts, like insurance policies, often have deductible amounts. Or, you may be charged each time the item is serviced. Some expenses are limited or excluded. For example, auto service contracts may not completely cover towing or rental car expenses. In addition, you also may have to pay cancellation or transfer fees if you sell the covered product or wish to end the contract.
- *Where can you get service?* If the service contract is offered by a local retailer or dealer, you may only be able to get local service. Consider the possibility that problems may develop while you are traveling or after you move away from the area.
- *Who is responsible for the contract?* The Federal Trade Commission often gets letters from consumers who ask what they can do about a service contract company that has gone out of business and cannot repay claims. Unfortunately, there is little recourse available to these consumers. The best way to avoid this situation is to make sure, before you sign a contract, that the company is reputable and has insurance.

- *Can you purchase a service contract later?* You may be better able to decide if you need a service contract after you have owned the product for some time. Consider waiting until your warranty period expires to buy a service contract.

Smoke Detectors

When fire occurs in your home, your chances for survival are twice as good when smoke detectors are present. Smoke detectors, when properly installed and maintained, provide early warning when fires occur. Early warning increases your chances for survival and allows the fire department to save more of your property. For this reason, many cities and states have laws requiring smoke detectors in homes. Check with your local fire department or state fire marshal for additional information about what might be required in your community.

Following the tips below will help you use your smoke detectors to the best advantage.

For minimum protection, install a smoke detector outside of each bedroom or sleeping area in your home and keep your bedroom doors closed while you are asleep. For greater protection, install smoke detectors on every floor of your home. Be sure to install the detectors away from air vents.

Keep your smoke detectors properly maintained. Test them at least once a month to ensure that the detectors are working properly. At least once a year, clean the detectors by dusting them with a vacuum cleaner. Batteries in battery-operated detectors should be changed annually. Use only the type of batteries recommended on the detector.

If your smoke detector sounds an alarm when no smoke is present, consult with the manufacturer or with your local fire department. If smoke from cooking causes the detector to sound an alarm, *do not remove* the batteries or disconnect the power source. Simply fan the smoke away from the detector until the alarm stops. If this happens frequently, it might be necessary to relocate the detector or install a different type.

Develop a fire escape plan and review the plan often with all members of the household. The plan should include:

- helping children and elderly people who might need special assistance;
- getting out of the house when fire occurs and using a neighbor's telephone, rather than your own, to notify the fire department; and
- picking a place outside the house where all members of the family will meet to ensure that everyone got out safely.

For additional information on smoke detectors, contact the U.S. Fire Administration, 16825 South Seton Avenue, Emmitsburg, MD 21727.

Used Cars and Car Repair

The following guidelines will help you buy a used car or get your car repaired.

Used Cars

1. Decide what kind of car you need and how much you can afford to spend. Talk to owners of similar cars.

2. Decide whether you want to buy from a dealer or private owner. A car bought from a private owner usually has no warranty.

3. In a private sale, check to be sure the seller is the registered owner of the car. Make sure you get the car's title and registration, bill of sale and copies of all other financial transaction papers necessary to register the car in your name.

4. If you're buying from a dealer, read the contract carefully before you sign, take the time to ask questions about unclear terms and keep a copy of the contract.

5. Look for and read the *Buyer's Guide* which must be displayed in the window of all used cars sold by dealers. The *Buyer's Guide* explains who must pay for repairs after purchase. It will tell you if there is a warranty on the car, what the warranty covers and whether a service contract is available.

6. Comparison shop for price, condition, warranty and mileage for the model(s) you are interested in buying. Compare available interest rates and other terms of financial agreements.

7. To estimate the total cost of the car, add the cost of interest for financing, the cost of a service contract (if any), and service or repair expenses you are likely to pay.

8. Before buying the car, have a mechanic inspect it.

9. Check the reliability of the dealer with your state or local consumer protection agency. Check the local Better Business Bureau to see if there are complaints against the dealer.

Car Repair

1. Check the terms of your car's warranty. The warranty might require the dealer to perform routine maintenance and any needed repairs.

2. Before having your car repaired, check the repair shop's complaint record with your state or local consumer protection office or local Better Business Bureau.

3. Some repair shops have mechanics certified by the National Institute for Automotive Service Excellence (ASE) to perform one or more types of services. Be aware, however, that repair shops can display the ASE sign even if they have just one mechanic certified in one tested specialty.

4. Don't tell the mechanic what you think needs to be fixed or replaced, unless it's obvious. Instead, describe the problem and its symptoms. Let the mechanic determine what needs fixing.

5. For major repairs, think about getting a second opinion, even if the car must be towed to another shop.

6. Before you leave the car, make sure you have a written estimate and that the work order reflects what you want done. Ask the mechanic to contact you before making repairs not covered in the work order.

7. If additional work is done without your permission, you don't have to pay for the unapproved work and you have the right to have your bill adjusted.

8. Ask to inspect and/or keep all replaced parts.

9. Keep copies of all work orders and receipts and get all warranties in writing.

10. Many states have "lemon" laws for new cars with recurring problems. Contact your local or state consumer office for more details.

Warranties and Guarantees

An important feature to consider before buying a product or service is the warranty that comes with it. When reviewing warranties, use the guidelines below.

1. Do not wait until the product fails or needs repair to find out what is covered in the warranty.

2. If the product costs $15 or more, the law says that the seller must let you examine any warranty before you buy, if you ask to see it. So use your rights to compare the terms and conditions of warranties (or guarantees) on products or services before you buy. Look for the warranty that best meets your needs.

3. When purchasing a product or service, ask these questions:

- How long is the warranty, and when does it start and end?
- What is covered? Which parts? What kinds of problems?
- Will the warranty pay for 100% of repair costs, or will it pay for parts, but not the labor to do the repairs? Will it pay for testing the product before it is repaired? Will it pay for shipping and/or a loaner?
- What do you have to do and when? Are regular inspections or maintenance required? Do you have to ship the product out of state for repairs?
- Who offers the warranty, manufacturer or retailer? How reliable are they?

4. Keep sales receipts and warranties in a safe place.

5. Some states have additional warranty rights for consumers. Check with your state or local consumer protection office to find the laws in your state.

Part II

Consumer Assistance Directory

CORPORATE CONSUMER CONTACTS

This section lists the names and addresses of more than 750 corporate headquarters, and in many cases, the name of the person to contact. Most listings also include toll-free "800" numbers.

Unless otherwise noted, all "800" numbers are toll free and can be used from anywhere in the continental United States. Many companies have Telecommunications Devices for the Deaf (TDDs). All TDD and "800" numbers are in bold type.

In some cases, you will see a company name or brand name listed with the instructions to see another company listed elsewhere in this section. For example: **Admiral, see Maycor.** This means questions about Admiral products should be directed to the consumer contact at Maycor because Maycor handles the complaints for the Admiral brand.

If you do not find the product name in this section, check the product label or warranty for the name and address of the manufacturer. Public libraries also have information that might be helpful. The *Standard & Poor's Register of Corporations, Directors and Executives, Trade Names Dictionary, Standard Directory of Advertisers,* and *Dun & Bradstreet Directory* are four sources that list information about most firms. If you cannot find the name of the manufacturer, the *Thomas Register of American Manufacturers* lists the manufacturers of thousands of products.

Remember, to save time, first take your complaint back to where you bought the product. If you contact the company's headquarters first, the consumer contact probably will direct you back to the local store where you made the purchase.

A

Ms. Anna Wright
Agency Complaint Coordinator
AAMCO Transmissions, Inc.
One Presidential Boulevard
Bala Cynwyd, PA 19004-9990
(215) 668-2900
1 (800) 523-0401 (toll free)

Audience Information
ABC Inc./Capitol Cities
New York, NY 10023
(212) 456-7777

Mrs. Susan Shaw
Consumer Affairs Assistant
AETNA Life and Casualty
151 Farmington Avenue
Hartford, CT 06156
(203) 273-2645
1 (800) 243-0185
(toll free outside CT)

AJAY Leisure Products
1501 East Wisconsin Street
Delavan, WI 53115
(414) 728-5521
1 (800) 558-3276 (toll free)

Ms. Susan Mach
Director of Consumer Affairs
AT&T
295 North Maple Avenue
Room 2334F2
Basking Ridge, NJ 07920
(201) 221-4003

Customer Service
Ace Hardware
2200 Kensington Court
Oak Brook, IL 60521
(708) 990-6600

Admiral
see Maycor

Airwick Industries, Inc.
see Reckitt & Colman Household Products

Ms. Patricia E. Arnold
Director, Consumer Affairs
Alaska Airlines
P.O. Box 68900
Seattle, WA 98168
(206) 431-7286
(consumer affairs)
(206) 431-7197
(customer relations/baggage, air cargo and freight claims)
(206) 431-3753
(existing refunds and lost ticket
applications file information)

Ms. Michelle Evans
Manager, Consumer Relations Department
Alberto Culver Company
2525 Armitage Avenue
Melrose Park, IL 60160
(708) 450-3000

Mrs. Leah Reed
Supervisor, Customer Service Department

Allied Van Lines
P.O. Box 4403
Chicago, IL 60680
(708) 717-3590

Mr. Michael Foort
Customer Relations Manager
Allstate Insurance Company
Allstate Plaza—F4
Northbrook, IL 60062
(708) 402-6005

Ms. Lydia Morikawa
Manager, Customer Relations
Aloha Airlines
P.O. Box 30028
Honolulu, HI 96820
(808) 836-4293

Mr. Tom Onushco and Ms. Gail Donnelly
Consumer Representatives
Consumer Services
Alpo Pet Foods
P.O. Box 2187
Allentown, PA 18001
(215) 395-3301
1 (800) 366-6033 (toll free)

Mrs. Kathy Ford
Manager, Customer Relations
Amana Refrigeration, Inc.
Amana, IA 52204
1 (800) 843-0304
(toll free—product questions)

Ms. Susan M. Sampsell
Manager, Consumer Affairs
America West Airlines
4000 East Skyharbor Boulevard
Phoenix, AZ 85034
(602) 894-0800

Ms. J. L. Ferguson
Manager, Consumer Relations
American Airlines, Inc.
P.O. Box 619612 MD 2400
DFW International Airport, TX 75261-9612
(817) 967-2000

Approved Auto Repair
American Automobile Association
Mailspace 15
1000 AAA Drive
Heathrow, FL 32746-5063
(written complaints only)

American Cyanamid Company
see Lederle Consumer Health Products Division

Mr. Martin J. Hummel, Vice President
Corporate Customer Relations
American Express Company
American Express Tower
World Financial Center
New York, NY 10285
(212) 640-5619
1 (800) 528-4800
(toll free—green card inquiries)
1 (800) 327-2177
(toll free—gold card inquiries)
1 (800) 525-3355
(toll free—platinum card inquiries)

Customer Service
American Family Publishers
P.O. Box 62000
Tampa, FL 33662
1 (800) AFP-2400 (toll free)

Ms. Sue Holiday
Consumer Correspondent
American Greetings Corporation
10500 American Road
Cleveland, OH 44144
(216) 252-7300
1 (800) 321-3040 (toll free outside OH)

Ms. Linda Mulrenan
Director, Consumer Affairs
American Home Food Products, Inc.
685 Third Avenue
New York, NY 10017
(212) 878-6323

American Learning Corporation
see Encyclopaedia Britannica

Mr. Ronald J. Fojtlin, Manager
Customer and Product Services
American Standard, Inc.
P.O. Box 6820
Piscataway, NJ 08855-6820
1 (800) 223-0651 (toll free in NJ)
1 (800) 223-0068 (toll free outside NJ)
(608) 787-2000 (Trane/CAC, Inc.)

Mr. Troy D'Ambrosio
Vice President, Corporate Communications
American Stores Company
P.O. Box 27447
Salt Lake City, UT 84127
(801) 539-0112
1 (800) 541-2863 (toll free)

Mr. Anthony L. Fera
Manager, Consumer Relations
American Tourister, Inc.
91 Main Street
Warren, RI 02885
(401) 247-2100
1 (800) 635-5505 (toll free outside RI)

Mr. Peter Lincoln
Director of Corporate Communications
Ameritech
1050 Connecticut Avenue, N.W., Suite 730
Washington, D.C. 20036
(202) 955-3058

Amerongen, Inc.
see Budget Rent-A-Car Corporation

Mrs. Joanne Stevens, Manager
Customer Relations and Consumer Affairs

Amoco Oil Company
200 East Randolph Drive
Chicago, IL 60601
(312) 856-4074

Mr. Alex T. Langston, Jr.
Director, Customer Relations
Amtrak
Washington Union Station
60 Massachusetts Avenue, N.E.
Washington, D.C. 20002
(202) 906-2121
1 (800) USA-RAIL
(toll free reservations and information)
1 (800) 356-5393
(toll free—credit card inquiries only)

Mr. John Brown, Manager and Senior Corporate Counsel
Corporate Government Affairs
Amway Corporation
7575 East Fulton Road
Ada, MI 49355
(616) 676-6733
1 (800) 548-3878 (toll free TDD)

Mr. Jeff Solsbig, Supervisor
Product Service and Repair
Andersen Corporation
100 4th Avenue, North
Bayport, MN 55003
(612) 439-5150

Mr. Craig Hetterscheidt
Manager, Consumer Relations
Anheuser-Busch, Inc.
One Busch Place
St. Louis, MO 63118-1852
(314) 577-3093

Corporate Relations
Aon Corporation
123 North Wacker Drive
Chicago, IL 60606
(312) 701-3000
1 (800) 621-2108 (toll free)

Customer Relations Department
Apple Computer, Inc.
20525 Mariani Avenue
Cupertino, CA 95014
1 (800) 776-2333
(toll free—complaints and questions)
1 (800) 538-9696
(toll free—dealer information)

Aramis, Inc.
see Estee Lauder, Inc.

Customer Service
Arizona Mail Order
3740 East 34th Street
Tucson, AZ 85713
(602) 748-8600

Arm & Hammer
see Church & Dwight Co., Inc.

Mr. Harry Robinson
Consumer Relations Adminstrator
Armorall Products Corporation
6 Liberty
Aliso Vijo, CA 92656
(714) 362-0600
1 (800) 747-4104 (toll free outside CA)

Consumer Services
Armour Food Company
9 Conagra Drive
Omaha, NE 68102-1679
(402) 595-7000

Mr. Fred Fuest
Manager, Consumer Affairs
Armstrong Tire Division
Pirelli/Armstrong Tire Corporation
500 Sargent Drive
New Haven, CT 06536
1 (800) 243-0167 (toll free)

Ms. Jane W. Deibler
Manager, Consumer Affairs
Armstrong World Industries
P.O. Box 3001
Lancaster, PA 17604
(717) 396-4401
1 (800) 233-3823 (toll free)

Mr. Lawrence Seigel
Atari Video Game Systems
330 North Eisenhower Lane
Lombard, IL 60148
(708) 629-6500

Ms. Alice Benzing
Consumer Compliance Officer
Atlantic Financial
2401 Walnut Street
Philadelphia, PA 19103
(215) 972-4530
1 (800) 233-1198 (toll free)

Mr. Thomas C. Butler
Manager, Customer Relations
Atlantic Richfield Company
ARCO Products Company
1055 W. 7th Street
Los Angeles, CA 90051-0570
1 (800) 322-ARCO (toll free)

Mr. J. R. Patterson, Vice President
Customer Service and Insurance
Atlas Van Lines
1212 St. George Road
P.O. Box 509
Evansville, IN 47703-0509
1 (800) 457-3705 (toll free)

Ms. Lynne Lappin
Supervisor, Customer Service
Avis Rent-A-Car System
900 Old Country Road
Garden City, NY 11530
(516) 222-4200

Customer Service
Avon Fashions, Inc.
5000 City Line Road
Hampton, VA 23661
(804) 827-9000

Ms. Lynn Baron, Manager
Consumer Information Center
Avon Products, Inc.
9 West 57th Street
New York, NY 10019
(212) 546-7777

B

Mr. Frederick J. Wilson
Assistant General Counsel
Bacardi Imports, Inc.
2100 Biscayne Boulevard
Miami, FL 33137
(305) 573-8511

Baldwin Piano & Organ Company
422 Wards Corner Rd.
Loveland, OH 45140-8390
(614) 693-2982

Bali
Sara Lee Corporation
3330 Healy Drive
P.O. Box 5100
Winston-Salem, NC 27103
(919) 768-8611
1 (800) 654-6122 (toll free)

Corporate Communications
Bally Manufacturing Corporation
8700 West Bryn Mawr
Chicago, IL 60631
(312) 399-1300

Quality of Services
Bank of America, NT & SA
Bank of America Center
555 California Street, 19th Floor
Department 3538
San Francisco, CA 94104
(415) 622-3590

Mr. Michael Pascale, Vice President
Public and Investor Relations
The Bank of New York Company
48 Wall Street, 16th Floor
New York, NY 10286
(212) 495-2066

Barnett Banks, Inc.
P.O. Box 40789
Jacksonville, FL 32231
(904) 791-7720

Mr. John Clapp
Quality Assurance Manager
R. G. Barry Corporation
13405 Yarmouth Road, N.W.
Pickerington, OH 43147
(614) 864-6400
1 (800) 848-7560 (toll free outside OH)

Bass Pro Shop
1935 South Campbell
Springfield, MO 65898
1 (800) BASS-PRO (toll free)

Customer Service
Eddie Bauer
1330 5th Avenue & Union Street
Seattle, WA 98101
(206) 622-2766

Ms. Karen Haase
Manager, Consumer Affairs
Contact Lens & General Eye Care Products
Bausch and Lomb
Personal Products Division
1400 North Goodman Street
Rochester, NY 14692
1 (800) 553-5340 (toll free)

Ms. Janice Glerum
Director, Customer Service
Contact Lenses
Bausch and Lomb
Professional Products Division
1400 North Goodman Street
Rochester, NY 14609
1 (800) 552-7388 (toll free)

Ms. Ethel Killenbeck
Manager, Consumer Affairs
Sunglasses Division
Bausch and Lomb
P.O. Box 478
Rochester, NY 14692-0478
1 (800) 343-5594 (toll free)

Bayer USA
500 Grant St., One Mellon Ctr.
Pittsburgh, PA 15219
(412) 394-5578

Customer Service
L. L. Bean, Inc.
Casco Street
Freeport, ME 04033-0001
(207) 865-9407 (TDD)
1 (800) 341-4341 (toll free)

Customer Service Department
Bear Creek Corporation
2518 South Pacific Highway
P.O. Box 299
Medford, OR 97501
(503) 776-2400

Beatrice Cheese, Inc.
Cheese Division
770 North Springdale Road
Waukesha, WI 53186
(414) 782-2750

Mr. Charles F. Baer, President
Consumer Products Division
Becton Dickinson and Company
One Becton Drive
Franklin Lakes, NJ 07417
(201) 848-6800
1 (800) 627-1579 (toll free)

Beiersdorf, Inc.
P.O. Box 5529
Norwalk, CT 06856-5529
(203) 853-8008
1 (800) 233-2340 (toll free outside CT)

Mr. Fred Cooke
Assistant to the President
Bell Atlantic Corporation
1133 20th Street, N.W.
Washington, D.C. 20036
(202) 392-1358

BellSouth Telephone Operations
(Southern Bell and South Central Bell)
Consumer Affairs Manager
600 North 19th Street, 12th Floor
Birmingham, AL 35203
(205) 321-2892
1 (800) 251-5325 (toll free TDD)
1 (800) 544-5000 (toll free voice line for disabled customers)

Mr. Keith Kard, Director
Marketing and Public Relations
Benihana of Tokyo
8685 Northwest 53rd Terrace
Miami, FL 33166
(305) 593-0770
1 (800) 327-3369 (toll free)

Ms. Sue B. Huffman
Director, Consumer Affairs
Best Foods
CPC International, Inc.
P.O. Box 8000 International Plaza
Englewood Cliffs, NJ 07632
(201) 894-2324

Mr. John Morgan
Manager, Customer Service
Best Western International
P.O. Box 10203
Phoenix, AZ 85064-0203
(602) 780-6181

Consumer Relations Department
BIC Corporation
500 Bic Drive
Milford, CT 06460
(203) 783-2000

Birds Eye
see General Foods

Mr. Floyd Coonce
Manager, Consumer Assistance
Black and Decker Home Appliances
6 Armstrong Road
Shelton, CT 06484
(203) 926-3218

Consumer Services
Black and Decker Power Tools
626 Hanover Pike
Hampstead, MD 21074
(301) 527-7100
1 (800) 762-6672 (toll free)

Mr. Jerry Weber
Senior Vice President of Operations
Blockbuster Entertainment Corporation
901 East Las Olas Boulevard
Ft. Lauderdale, FL 33301
(305) 524-8200

Ms. Lori Hunt
Customer Services Representative
Block Drug Company, Inc.
257 Cornelison Avenue
Jersey City, NJ 07302
(201) 434-3000, ext. 308
1 (800) 365-6500 (toll free outside NJ)

Customer Service Department
Bloomingdale's by Mail, Ltd.
475 Knotter Drive
P.O. Box 593
Cheshire, CT 06410-9933
(203) 271-1313 (mail order inquiries only)

Ms. Allison Rader
Consumer Relations
Blue Bell, Inc.
P.O. Box 21488
Greensboro, NC 27420
(919) 373-3564, 4036

Consumer Affairs
Blue Cross and Blue Shield Association
655 15th Street, N.W., Suite 350
Washington, DC 20005
(202) 626-4780

Ms. Karen Braswell
Marketing Manager
Bojangles
P.O. Box 240239
Charlotte, NC 28224
(704) 527-2675, ext. 226

Consumer Response Department
Borden, Inc.
180 East Broad Street
Columbus, OH 43215
(614) 225-4511

Boyle-Midway Household Products, Inc.
see Reckitt & Colman Household Products

Ms. Stephanie Smith
Manager, Consumer Affairs
Bradlees Discount Department Stores
One Bradlees Circle
P.O. Box 9015
Braintree, MA 02184-9015
(617) 380-5468

Breck Hair Care Products
see Lederle Consumer Health Products Division

Customer Service
Brights Creek
5000 City Lane Road
Hampton, VA 23661
(804) 827-1850

Mr. Raymond Heimbuch
Manager, Consumer Affairs
Bristol-Myers Products
685 Routes 202/206 North
Somerville, NJ 08876-1279
1 (800) 468-7746 (toll free)

Mr. John L. Skule, III
Vice President, Industry and Public Affairs
Bristol-Myers Squibb Pharmaceutical Group
P.O. Box 4000
Princeton, NJ 08543-4000
(609) 921-4000
1 (800) 332-2056 (toll free)

Brita, USA
see Clorox Company

Customer Relations
British Airways
75-20 Astoria Blvd.
Jackson Heights, NY 11370
(718) 397-4000

Ms. Deborah A. Volz
Consumer Relations Manager
Brown-Forman Beverage Company
P.O. Box 1080
Louisville, KY 40201
1 (800) 753-1177 (toll free)

Consumer Care Information
Brown Group, Inc.

P.O. Box 354
St. Louis, MO 63166
1 (800) 766-6465 (toll free)

Customer Relations
Budget Rent-A-Car Corporation
P.O. Box 111580
Carrollton, TX 75011-1589
1 (800) 621-2844 (toll free)

Investor Service Center
Bull & Bear Group, Inc.
11 Hanover Square
New York, NY 10005
(212) 363-1100
1 (800) 847-4200 (toll free)

Manager, Customer Relations
Bulova Watch Company
26-15 Brooklyn Queens Expressway East
Woodside, NY 11377
(718) 204-3300 (consumer relations)
(718) 204-3222 (repairs)

Burger King Corporation
17777 Old Cutler Rd.
Miami, FL 33151-6341
(305) 378-7011

Mr. Monroe Milstein, President
Burlington Coat Factory Warehouse Corporation
1830 Route 130 North
Burlington, NJ 08016
(609) 387-7800

Public Relations
Burlington Industries
3330 West Friendly Avenue
Greensboro, NC 27420
(919) 379-3376

Burpee Seed Company
300 Park Avenue
Warminster, PA 18974

Mrs. Dorie Monroe
Professional Services Manager
Burroughs Wellcome Company
3030 Cornwallis Road
Research Triangle Park, NC 27709
(919) 248-3000

C

Caterpillar, Inc.
100 NE Adams St.
Peoria, IL 61629-0001
(309) 675-1000

Mr. Ray Faiola, Director
CBS Broadcast Group
Audience Services
Program Information Office
524 West 57th Street
New York, NY 10019
(212) 975-3166

CIBA-GEIGY Corporation Agricultural Division
410 Swing Road
Greensboro, NC 27409
(919) 632-6000
1 (800) 334-9481 (toll free)

CIBA-GEIGY Corporation Pharmaceuticals Division
556 Morris Avenue
Summit, NJ 07901-1398
(908) 277-5000

CIBA Vision Corporation
2910 Amwiler Court
Atlanta, GA 30360
1 (800) 241-5999 (toll free)
1 (800) 227-1524, ext. 4828 (toll free—consumer relations)

Customer Service
CIE America
2515 McCave Way
P.O. Box 19663
Irvine, CA 92713-9663
1 (800) 877-1421 (toll free)

CIE Terminals
see CIE America

Mr. Mark A. Whiter
Director, Customer Relations
CIGNA Property and Casualty Companies
1600 Arch Street
Philadelphia, PA 19103
(215) 523-2729

Claus, Santa
(also Mrs. Claus, Elves & Reindeer)
North Pole, 30351
(official Postal Service address)

Consumer Affairs Department
CPC International Inc.
International Plaza
Box 8000
Englewood Cliffs, NJ 07632
(201) 894-4000

Mr. Paul Reisbord
President and Chairman of the Board
C&R Clothiers
8660 Hayden Place
Culver City, CA 90232
(310) 559-8200

CVN
see QVC Network

Customer Relations Department
CVS
One CVS Drive
Woonsocket, RI 02895-0988
(401) 765-1500
1 (800) 444-1140 (toll free)

Cabela's, Inc.
812 13th Avenue
Sidney, NE 69160-8888
1 (800) 237-8888 (toll free)

Ms. Darlene Stovall
Consumer Affairs Analyst
Cadbury Schweppes
Beverages Division
High Ridge Park
P.O. Box 3800
Stamford, CT 06905
(203) 968-7673
(203) 968-5895 (consumer affairs)
1 (800) 426-4891 (toll free)

Cadbury Schweppes Confections
see Hershey

Ms. Kathleen Ellwood
Manager, Consumer Relations
Caloric Modern Maid Corporation
403 North Main Street
Topton, PA 19562-1499
(215) 682-4211

Mr. Drew Fox
Director, Consumer Relations
Campbell Soup Company
Campbell Place
Camden, NJ 08103-1799
(609) 342-3714

Mr. Lloyd Rockwell
Vice President, Winery Operations
Canandaigua Wine Company
116 Buffalo Street
Canandaigua, NY 14424
(716) 394-3630

Corporate Consumer Affairs
Canon U.S.A., Inc.
One Canon Plaza
Lake Success, NY 11042-9960
(516) 488-6700

Ms. Pat Biederman
Passenger Service Manager
Carnival Cruise Lines
3655 Northwest 87th Avenue
Miami, FL 33178-2428
1 (800) 327-7373 (toll free)

Mr. James Witz
Consumer Relations Manager
Carrier Air Conditioning Company
P.O. Box 4808
Syracuse, NY 13221
1 (800) 227-7437 (toll free)
Bryant Heating and Air Conditioning
1 (800) 428-4326 (toll free)
Day & Night Heating and Air Conditioning
1 (800) 428-4326 (toll free)
Payne Heating and Air Conditioning
1 (800) 428-4326 (toll free)

Carte Blanche
see Diners Club

Ms. Mary Mumolo
Senior Manager, Consumer Relations
Carter Hawley Hale Stores
388 North Mission Road
Los Angeles, CA 90031
(213) 227-2423

Consumer Affairs Department
Carter-Wallace Inc.
1345 Avenue of the Americas
New York, NY 10105
(212) 339-5000

Retail Operations
Carvel Corporation
201 Saw Mill River Road
Yonkers, NY 10701
(written inquiries only)

Customer Service Department
Casio, Inc.
570 Mount Pleasant Avenue
Dover, NJ 07801
(201) 361-5400

Mr. Bruce Wagner
Customer Service Supervisor
Champion Spark Plug Company
P.O. Box 910
Toledo, OH 43661
(419) 535-2458
1 (800) 537-8984 (toll free outside OH)
1 (800) 537-9996 (toll free in OH)

Ms. Stacey French
Customer Relations Coordinator
Chanel, Inc.
9 West 57th Street, 44th Floor
New York, NY 10019
(212) 688-5055

Ms. Lila A. Lesley, Consumer Affairs
Consumer Products Division
Chattem, Inc.
1715 West 38th Street
Chattanooga, TN 37409
(615) 821-4571, ext. 211
1 (800) 366-6833 (toll free outside TN)

Mr. Walter Dabek
Director, Consumer Information
Chesebrough-Pond's, USA.
33 Benedict Place
Greenwich, CT 06830-6000
1 (800) 852-8558 (toll free in CT)
1 (800) 242-0203 (toll free outside CT)

Ms. Kathy Yeu
Director, Consumer Affairs
Chemical Bank
277 Park Avenue
New York, NY 10172
(212) 310-5800

ChemLawn Services Corporation
8275 North High Street
Columbus, OH 43235
(614) 888-3572
1 (800) 888-3572 (toll free)

Mr. W. P. Howell, Supervisor
Dealer and Consumer Affairs
Chevron U.S.A. Inc.
P.O. Box H
Concord, CA 94524
(415) 827-6412
1 (800) CHEVRON (toll free)

Complaint Department
Chi-Chi's, Inc.
10200 Linn Station Road
Louisville, KY 40223
(502) 426-3900

Chuck E. Cheese
see Integra

Mrs. Cathy R. Marino, Manager
Consumer Relations
Church & Dwight Company, Inc.
469 North Harrison Street
Princeton, NJ 08540-7648
(609) 683-5900
1 (800) 624-2889 (toll free in NJ)
1 (800) 524-1328 (toll free outside NJ)

Church's Fried Chicken, Inc.
see Popeye's

Cincinnati Microwave
One Microwave Plaza
Cincinnati, OH 45249-9502
(513) 489-5400
1 (800) 543-1608 (toll free)

Circuit City Stores, Inc.
2040 Thalbro Street
Richmond, VA 23230
(804) 257-4292
1 (800) 251-2665 (toll free)

Ms. Dinah Nemeroff, Vice President
Corporate Director of Customer Affairs
Citicorp/Citibank
399 Park Avenue
New York, NY 10043
(212) 559-0043

Ms. Ellen Peressini, Executive Secretary
Citizen Watch Company of America, Inc.
8506 Osage Avenue
Los Angeles, CA 90045
(310) 215-9660
1 (800) 321-1023 (toll free)

Ms. Carol Leet, Director
Consumer Affairs Dept.
Clairol, Inc.
345 Park Avenue
New York, NY 10154
1 (800) 223-5800 (toll free voice/TDD)
1 (800) HISPANA (toll free Spanish voice/TDD)

Clinique Laboratories, Inc.
see Estee Lauder, Inc.

Ms. C. Kay Whitehurst
Consumer Services Manager
Clorox Company
1221 Broadway
Oakland, CA 94612-1888
(415) 271-7283
1 (800) 292-2200
(toll free—laundry brands)
1 (800) 537-2823
(toll free—charcoal and food brands)
1 (800) 227-1860
(toll free—household surface cleaners)
1 (800) 426-6228
(toll free—insecticides)
1 (800) 242-7482
(toll free—water purification systems)

Consumer Affairs Department
Club Med Sales, Inc.
40 West 57th Street
New York, NY 10019
(212) 977-2100

Mr. Roger Nunley, Director
Industry and Consumer Affairs
Coca-Cola Company
P.O. Drawer 1734
Atlanta, GA 30301
1 (800) 438-2653 (toll free)

Coldwell Banker
see Sears, Roebuck and Co.

Ms. Grace Richardson
Vice President, Consumer Affairs
Colgate-Palmolive Company
300 Park Avenue
New York, NY 10022-7499
1 (800) 221-4607
(toll free—oral care products)
1 (800) 338-8388
(toll free—household products)

Mr. Tom Kelly
Senior Vice President, Operations
Colonial Penn Group, Inc.
11 Penn Center Plaza
1818 Market Street, 26th Floor
Philadelphia, PA 19181
(215) 988-8531
1 (800) 523-1700 (toll free-auto and homeowner customer service)
1 (800) 523-4000 (toll free-health customer service)
1 (800) 523-9100 (toll free-life customer service)

Columbia House
A Division of SONY Music Entertainment, Inc.
P.O. Box 4450
New York, NY 10101-4450
1 (800) 457-0500
(toll free—records and tapes)
1 (800) 457-0866
(toll free—videos)

Ms. Teresa C. Infantino
Executive Vice President
Combe Incorporated
1101 Westchester Avenue
White Plains, NY 10604-3597
(914) 694-5454
1 (800) 431-2610 (toll free)

Combined Insurance Company of America
see Aon Corporation

Commerce Drug Division
see Del Laboratories, Inc.

Ms. M. Teresa Abreu
Manager, Customer Relations
Commodore Business Machines, Inc.
1200 Wilson Drive
West Chester, PA 19380
(215) 431-9100

Customer Relations Department
Compaq Computer Corporation
P.O. Box 692000
Houston, TX 77269-2000
1 (800) 345-1518 (toll free)

Comprehensive Care Corporation
1795 Clarkson Road
Chesterfield, MO 63017
(314) 537-1288
1 (800) 678-2273 (toll free)

Ms. Janet M. Venditti
Manager, Consumer Affairs
Congoleum Corporation
Technical Operations Center
861 Sloan Avenue
Trenton, NJ 08619
(609) 584-3000
1 (800) 274-3266 (toll free)

Consumers Products Group
see Commodore Business Machines, Inc.

Supervisors Department
Contempo Casuals
5433 West Jefferson Boulevard
Los Angeles, CA 90016
(213) 936-2131
1 (800) 368-5923 (toll free)

Ms. Ann R. Yanulavich
Director, Customer Relations
Continental Airlines, Inc.
3663 North Belt East, Suite 500
Houston, TX 77032
(713) 987-6500

Ms. Barbi Rose 2CR
Manager, Consumer Affairs
Continental Baking Company
Checkerboard Square
St. Louis, MO 63164
(314) 982-4953

Control Data Contact Center
Control Data Corporation
8100 34th Avenue South
P.O. Box 0
Minneapolis, MN 55440-4700
(612) 853-3400
1 (800) 232-1985 (toll free)

Customer Service
Converse, Inc.
One Fordham Road
North Reading, MA 01864-2680
1 (800) 343-2667 (toll free)
1 (800) 428-2667 (toll free)

Conwood Company, L.P.
813 Ridge Lake Boulevard
Memphis, TN 38120
(901) 761-2050

Ms. Margie Hausburg
Quality Assurance Analyst
Coors Brewing Company
Consumer Hotline
Golden, CO 80401
1 (800) 642-6116 (toll free)

Coppertone
see Schering-Plough HealthCare Products, Inc.

Ms. Suzanne Scannelli, Supervisor
Corning/Revere Consumer Information Center
Corning Incorporated
1300 Hopeman Parkway
Waynesboro, VA 22980
(703) 949-9143

Ms. Connie J. Shelby
Director, Consumer Affairs
Cosmair, Inc.
P.O. Box 98
Westfield, NJ 07091-9987
1 (800) 631-7358 (toll free)

Ms. Aggie Merkel, Supervisor
Member and Consumer Relations
Cotter & Company
2740 North Clybourn Avenue
Chicago, IL 60614-1088
(312) 975-2700

Service Department
Craftmatic/Contour Organization, Inc.
2500 Interplex Drive
Trevose, PA 19053-6998
(215) 639-1310
1 (800) 677-8200 (toll free)

Consumer Affairs Division
Jenny Craig International
445 Marineview Avenue
Del Mar, CA 92014
(619) 259-7000

Mr. George Turner
Assistant Vice President, Operations
Crown Books
3300 75th Avenue
Landover, MD 20785
(301) 731-1200

Cruise America Motor Home Rental and Sales
5959 Blue Lagoon Drive
Miami, FL 33126-2066
(305) 262-9611
1 (800) 327-7778 (toll free)

Mr. Peter Cammarata
Director, Sales and Marketing Operations
Cuisinarts Corporation
P.O. Box 120067
Stamford, CT 06913-0741
(203) 975-4600
1 (800) 726-0190 (toll free outside NJ)
(609) 426-1300 (in NJ)

Ms. Kathleen Bayer
Special Assistant to the President for Consumer Affairs
Culligan International Company
One Culligan Parkway
Northbrook, IL 60062
(708) 205-5757

Mr. Marvin E. Eisenstadt, President
Cumberland Packing Corporation
Two Cumberland Street
Brooklyn, NY 11205
(718) 858-4200
1 (800) 336-0363 (toll free in NY)
1 (800) 231-1123 (toll free outside NY)

Mr. Tony Saulino
Department Head, Customer Service
Current, Inc.
P.O. Box 2559
Colorado Springs, CO 80901
1 (800) 525-7170 (toll free)

Customer Care Department
Curtis Mathes Corporation
1450 Flatcreek Road
Athens, TX 75751
(214) 675-6886

Curtis-Young Corporation
2550 Haddonfield Rd.
Pennsauken, NJ 08110-1194
(609) 665-6650

D

d-Con
see L&F Products

Ms. Joan Calkins
Manager, Customer Service
DHL Corporation
1820 Gateway Drive, Suite 300
San Mateo, CA 94404
1 (800) CALL-DHL (toll free)

Dairy Queen
see International Dairy Queen

Ms. Becky Ryan
Director, Consumer Relations
Dannon Company, Inc.
P.O. Box 44235
Jacksonville, FL 32256
1 (800) 321-2174 (toll free)

Ms. Stephanie McDermott, Manager
Customer Service Department
Danskin
P.O. Box 15016
York, PA 17405-7016
1 (800) 87-DANSKIN (toll free)

Data General Corporation
4400 Computer Dr.
Westborough, MA 01580
(508) 366-8911

Ms. Avis Carlson, Manager
Central Consumer Relations
The Department Stores of the Dayton Hudson Corporation
Box 875
700 Nicollet Mall
Minneapolis, MN 55402
(612) 375-3382

Dean Witter Financial Services Group
see Sears, Roebuck and Co.

Dearfoam
see R. G. Barry Corporation

Deere & Company
John Deere Road
Moline, IL 61265-8098
(309) 765-8000

Ms. Margaret Sanders
Consumer Relations Department
Del Laboratories, Inc.
565 Broad Hollow Road
Farmingdale, NY 11735
(516) 293-7070

Ms. Janet M. Acklam
Manager, Consumer Affairs
Del Monte Corporation
P.O. Box 193575
San Francisco, CA 94119
1 (800) 543-3090 (toll free)

Public Relations
Delco Remy Division
General Motors Corporation
2401 Columbus Avenue
Mail Code 1-310
Anderson, IN 46018-9986
(317) 646-2000

Mr. Fred Elsberry
Director, Consumer Affairs
Delta Air Lines
Hartsfield Atlanta International Airport
Atlanta, GA 30320
(404) 715-1402

Ms. Barbara Smith
Product Service Manager
Delta Faucets
P.O. Box 40980
Indianapolis, IN 46280
(317) 848-1812

Operations
Denny's, Inc.
P.O. Box 3800
Spartanburg, SC 29304-3800
(803) 596-8000

Mr. George Andrassy, Vice President
Research and Development
Dep Corporation
2101 East Via Arado
Rancho Dominguez, CA 90220-6189
(310) 604-0777
1 (800) 367-2855 (toll free)

Ms. Julie Jason
Manager, Customer Service
DeVry, Inc.
2201 West Howard Street
Evanston, IL 60202
(708) 328-8100
1 (800) 225-8000 (toll free)

Ms. Lisa L. Ridle, Director
Consumer Information Center
The Dial Corporation
Dial Tower
Phoenix, AZ 85077-1606
(602) 207-5518
1 (800) 528-0849 (toll free—foods division)
1 (800) 45-PUREX (toll free—household and laundry division)
1 (800) 258-DIAL (toll free—personal care division)

Customer Relations
Diet Center, Inc.
921 Penn Avenue
Pittsburgh, PA 15222-3814
(412) 338-8700
1 (800) 333-2581 (toll free)

Customer Assistance Department
Digital Equipment Corporation
40 Old Bolton Road
Stow, MA 01777-1215
(508) 493-7161
1 (800) 332-4636 (toll free)

Customer Relations
Dillard Department Stores, Inc.
1600 Cantrell Road
Little Rock, AR 72201
(501) 376-5200

Ms. Betsy Seeley
Vice President, Customer Service
Diners Club International
183 Inverness Drive West
Englewood, CO 80112
(303) 799-9000
1 (800) 525-9135 (toll free)
(303) 649-2824 (TDD)

Discover Credit Card
see Sears, Roebuck and Co.

Ms. Helen Robinson
Manager, Consumer Response
Dole Packaged Foods
ATTN: Consumer Response Department
50 California Street, 19th Floor
San Francisco, CA 94111
1 (800) 232-8888 (toll free)

Mr. David Black, President
Operations
Domino's Pizza, Inc.
P.O. Box 997
Ann Arbor, MI 48106-0997
(313) 930-3030

Mr. Robert J. Posch, Jr.
Vice President, Legal Affairs
Doubleday Book & Music Clubs, Inc.
501 Franklin Avenue
Garden City, NY 11530-5806
(516) 873-4628

Ms. Sharon Clark
Manager, Consumer Affairs
DowBrands
P.O. Box 68511
Indianapolis, IN 46268-0511
1 (800) 428-4795 (toll free)

Mr. Jim Ball, Vice President
Corporate Communications
Ms. Wynema Hamilton, Coordinator
Consumer Affairs
Dr Pepper Co./The Seven-Up Co./Premier Beverages
P.O. Box 655086
Dallas, TX 75265-5086
(214) 360-7000

Customer Service Department
Walter Drake & Sons
Drake Building
Colorado Springs, CO 80940-0001
(719) 596-3140

Ms. Jane Lagusch
Corporate Secretary to the President
Drug Emporium, Inc.
155 Hidden Ravines Drive
Powell, OH 43065
(614) 548-7080

Dulcolax
Boehringer Ingelheim
90 East Ridge
P.O. Box 368
Ridgefield, CT 06877-0368
(203) 798-9988

Mr. Robert M. Rosenberg
Chairman of the Board
Dunkin Donuts of America
P.O. Box 317
Randolph, MA 02368
(617) 961-4000

Mr. Thomas M. Johnson
Manager, Consumer Affairs
Dunlop Tire Corporation
P.O. Box 1109
Buffalo, NY 14240-1109
(716) 879-8258
1 (800) 548-4714 (toll free)

Product Information Center
E.I. duPont de Nemours & Co.
1007 Market Street
Wilmington, DE 19880-0010
1 (800) 441-7515 (toll free)

Consumer Affairs Department
Duracell USA
Division of Duracell, Inc.
Berkshire Industrial Park
Bethel, CT 06801
(203) 796-4000
1 (800) 551-2355
(toll free—8:30 a.m.-5 p.m. EST)

Consumer Affairs Department
Durkee-French Foods
A Division of Rickett & Colman Inc.
1655 Valley Road
P.O. Box 939
Wayne, NJ 07474-0939
(201) 633-6800

E

Mr. John Vaeth
Eastman Kodak Company
343 State Street
Rochester, NY 14650-0811
1 (800) 242-2424 (toll free)

Ms. Nancy J. Avino
Customer Service Representative
Eckerd Drug Company
8333 Bryan Dairy Rd.
P.O. Box 4689
Clearwater, FL 34618
(813) 397-7461

Customer Service
Edmund Scientific Company
101 East Gloucester Pike
Barrington, NJ 08007-1380
(609) 573-6260

Electrolux Corporation
2300 Windy Ridge Parkway
Suite 900
Marietta, GA 30067
(404) 933-1000
1 (800) 243-9078 (toll free)

Customer Relations
Emery Worldwide
A CF Company
3350 West Bayshore Road
Palo Alto, CA 94303-0986
(415) 855-9100
1 (800) 443-6379 (toll free)

Ms. Martha S. Yocum
Director of Consumer Affairs
Encore Marketing International, Inc.
4501 Forbes Boulevard
Lanham, MD 20706
(301) 459-8020
1 (800) 638-0930 (toll free)

Mr. Norman Braun
Vice President, Public Affairs
Encyclopaedia Britannica, Inc.

310 South Michigan Avenue
Chicago, IL 60604-4293
(312) 347-7230

Mr. Labat R. Yancey
Assistant Vice President
Office of Consumer Affairs
Equifax
P.O. Box 4081
Atlanta, GA 30302
(404) 888-3500

Ms. Carolann V. Mathews
Vice President, Customer Relations
Equitable Life Assurance Society
135 West 50th Street
New York, NY 10020
(212) 641-7700 (collect calls accepted)

Retail Customer Service Department
Esprit de Corp.
900 Minnesota Street
San Francisco, CA 94107-3000
(415) 648-6900
1 (800) 777-8765 (toll free)

Ms. Theresa Sullivan
Vice President, Consumer Relations
Estee Lauder Companies
767 Fifth Avenue
New York, NY 10153-0003
(212) 572-4455

Ms. Carol Archer
Supervisor, Consumer Affairs
Ethan Allen, Inc.
Ethan Allen Drive
Danbury, CT 06811
(203) 743-8553

Mr. Rick Gremer
Consumer Relations Manager
The Eureka Company
1201 East Bell Street
Bloomington, IL 61701-6902
(309) 823-5735
1 (800) 282-2886 (toll free—warranty center)

Mr. Dan Evans, Chairman of the Board
Bob Evans Farms, Inc.
3776 South High Street
P.O. Box 07863
Columbus, OH 43207
(614) 491-2225
1 (800) 272-PORK (toll free outside OH)

Eveready Battery Company
Checkerboard Square
St. Louis, MO 63164
(314) 982-4078

Mr. W. D. Dermott, Manager
Consumer and Regulatory Affairs
Exxon Company U.S.A.
P.O. Box 2180
Houston, TX 77252-2180
(713) 656-3151

F

Ms. Erin Sparks
Consumer Affairs Coordinator
FMG/Tsumara
Jonathan Industrial Park
Chaska, MN 55318
(612) 448-4181

Ms. June Golden
Family Circle Magazine
110 Fifth Avenue
New York, NY 10011
(212) 463-1063

Consumer Affairs Department
Faultless Starch/Bon Ami Company
1025 West Eighth Street
Kansas City, MO 64101-1200
(816) 842-1230

Fayva Shoe Stores
see Morse Shoe Company

Mr. John R. West, Manager
Corporate Quality Improvement
Federal Express Corporation
P.O. Box 727, Department 2605
Memphis, TN 38194-2605
(901) 922-5454
1 (800) 238-5355 (toll free)

Ms. Patricia Ikeda, Director
Community Relations and Operations
Federated Department Stores
7 West Seventh Street
Cincinnati, OH 45202
(513) 579-7000

Ms. Cathy Sharkey
Manager, Consumer Relations
Fieldcrest Cannon, Inc.
60 West 40th Street
New York, NY 10018
(212) 536-1284
1 (800) 841-3336
(toll free—Fieldcrest Stores)
1 (800) 237-3209
(toll free—Cannon Stores)

Ms. Mary Luethmers
Customer Relations Manager
Fingerhut Corporation
11 McLeland Road
St. Cloud, MN 56395
(612) 259-2500

Consumer Affairs
Firestone Tire & Rubber Co.
205 North Michigan Avenue
Chicago, IL 60601-5965
1 (800) 367-3872 (toll free)

Mr. Lee Mann
Director, Consumer Affairs
First Brands Corporation
88 Long Hill Street
East Hartford, CT 06108
(203) 728-6000

Mr. Patrick J. Swanick
Senior Vice President, Customer Services
Customer Service Center
First Fidelity Bancorporation

100 Constitution Drive
Upper Darby, PA 19082-4603
(215) 734-5090
1 (800) 345-9042 (toll free)
(215) 734-5599 (TDD)

Consumer Affairs Department
First Interstate Bank of California
707 Wilshire Boulevard, W35-13
Los Angeles, CA 90017
(213) 614-3103
1 (800) 626-3400 (toll free)

Ms. Susan Alcorn, Director
Consumer, Government and Media Center
First National Supermarkets, Inc.
17000 Rockside Road
Cleveland, OH 44137-4390
(216) 587-7100

Mr. Michael Cisneros
Consumer Affairs Officer
First Nationwide Bank
135 Main Street, 4th Floor
San Francisco, CA 94105-1817
1 (800) 237-0756 (toll free)

Customer Service
First Union National Bank of Florida
P.O. Box 2870
Jacksonville, FL 32231-0010
(904) 361-6996
1 (800) 735-1012 (toll free)

Fisher
see SFS Corporation

Ms. Carol Steck
Manager, Consumer Affairs
Fisher Price
636 Girard Avenue
East Aurora, NY 14052-1880
1 (800) 432-5437 (toll free)

Ms. Kathryn McDonald
Consumer Affairs Manager
Florida Power and Light Co.
P.O. Box 029100
Miami, FL 33102-9100
(305) 227-4646
1 (800) 432-6554 (toll free TDD)

Ms. Monica Schmelter, Manager
Customer Relations
Florists' Transworld Delivery Association (FTD)
29200 Northwestern Highway
P.O. Box 2227
Southfield, MI 48037-4077
(313) 355-9300
1 (800) 788-9000 (toll free)

Florsheim Shoe Company
130 South Canal Street
Chicago, IL 60606-3999
(312) 559-2500

Mr. Heeth Varnedoe, President
Flowers Industries, Inc.
P.O. Box 1338
Thomasville, GA 31799-1338
(912) 226-9110

Mr. Leonard H. Yablon
Executive Vice President
Forbes Inc.
60 Fifth Avenue
New York, NY 10011
(212) 620-2248

Ford Motor Company
The American Rd.
Dearborn, MI 48126-2798
(313) 322-3000

Customer Service
Foster & Gallagher, Inc.
6523 North Galena Road
Peoria, IL 61632
(309) 691-4610
(Monday—Friday, 8:30 a.m.—5 p.m.)
(309) 691-3633
(Monday—Friday, after 5:15 p.m.)

Marketing and Customer Service
Fotomat Corporation
201 Prestige Park Road
East Hartford, CT 06108
(203) 291-0100
1 (800) 842-0001 (toll free in CT)
1 (800) 243-0003 (toll free outside CT)

Mr. David Listman, Vice President
Customer Service/Operations
The Franklin Mint
U.S. Route One
Franklin Center, PA 19091
(215) 459-6000

Frank's Nursery and Crafts, Inc.
A Division of General Host Corporation
6501 East Nevada
Detroit, MI 48234
(313) 366-8400

Customer Service Department
Freeman and French Shriner Shoes
1 Freeman Lane
Beloit, WI 53511-3989
1 (800) 456-9745 (toll free)

Customer Relations
Fretter Appliance Company
14985 Telegraph Road
Redford, MI 48239
(313) 537-3701
1 (800) 736-3430 (toll free)

Frigidaire Appliances
see White Consolidated Industries

Frito-Lay Inc.
6303 Forest Park Rd.
Dallas, TX 75235-5401
(214) 351-7000

Frontier Airlines
see Continental Airlines

Ms. Janet Rosati
Director, Consumer Services
Fruit of the Loom, Inc.
One Fruit of the Loom Drive
Bowling Green, KY 42102-9015
(502) 781-6400

Ms. Marianne Salembene
Associate Manager, Customer Service Department
Fuji Photo Film U.S.A., Inc.
800 Central Boulevard
Carlstadt, NJ 07072-3009

Customer Resource Center
Fuller Brush Company
P.O. Box 729
Great Bend, KS 67530-0729
1 (800) 523-3794 (toll free)

Funk and Wagnalls
70 Hilltop Rd.
Ramsey, NJ 07446

G

GTE Corporation
One Stamford Forum
Stamford, CT 06904
(203) 965-2000

Ms. Millie Roberson
Director, Consumer Relations
Ernest & Julio Gallo Winery
P.O. Box 1130
Modesto, CA 95353
(209) 579-3111

Ms. Jeannine Collins, Supervisor
Consumer Service Department
Lewis Galoob Toys, Inc.
500 Forbes Boulevard
San Francisco, CA 94080
(415) 952-1678
1 (800) 4-GALOOB (toll free outside CA)

Ms. Sheila Gibbons
Director, Public Affairs
Gannett Company, Inc.
1100 Wilson Boulevard
Arlington, VA 22234
(703) 284-6048

General Electric Company
For information on GE consumer products and services, call: GE ANSWER CENTER® service
1 (800) 626-2000 (toll free)

Mr. Donald L. Mayer
Director of Consumer Response and Information Center
General Foods Corporation
250 North Street
White Plains, NY 10625
1 (800) 431-1001 (toll free—desserts)
1 (800) 431-1002 (toll free—beverages)
1 (800) 431-1003 (toll free—meals and Post cereals)
1 (800) 431-1004 (toll free—Maxwell House and Bird's Eye)
1 (800) 424-BAKE (toll free—Entenmann's)
1 (800) 431-POST (toll free—Post cereals)
1 (800) FOR-WACKY (toll free—Kool Aid)

General Host Corporation
P.O. Box 10045
Stamford, CT 06904
(203) 357-9900

Ms. Sandy Weisenburger
Assistant Manager, Consumer Services
General Mills, Inc.
P.O. Box 1113
Minneapolis, MN 55440-1113
(612) 540-4295
1 (800) 328-6787 (toll free—bakery products)
1 (800) 231-0308 (toll free—cereals)
1 (800) 222-6846 (toll free—Gorton's)
1 (800) 231-0308 (toll free—snacks)

Customer Relations Department
General Motors Acceptance Corporation (GMAC)
3044 West Grand Boulevard, Room AX348
Detroit, MI 48202
(313) 556-0510
1 (800) 441-9234 (toll free)
1 (800) TDD-GMAC (toll free TDD)

Customer Service
General Tire Inc.
One General Street
Akron, OH 44329-0006
1 (800) 847-3349 (toll free)

Ms. Lori Thies, Vice President
Customer Service
Generra
278 Broad Street
Seattle, WA 98121
(206) 728-6888

Sales Department
Genesee Brewing Company, Inc.
445 St. Paul Street
Rochester, NY 14605
(716) 546-1030

Ms. Denise Irish (paper products)
Ms. Janet Folk (building products)
Georgia-Pacific Corp.
P.O. Box 105605
Atlanta, GA 30348-5605
(404) 521-4708 (building products)
(404) 527-0038 (paper products)

Mr. L. James Lovejoy, Director
Corporate Communications
Gerber Products Company
445 State Street
Fremont, MI 49413-1056
(616) 928-2000
1 (800) 4-GERBER (toll free—24 hours)
1 (800) 421-4221 (toll free, 24-hour breastfeeding advice)
1 (800) 828-9119 (toll free—baby formula)

Ms. Odonna Mathews
Vice President for Consumer Affairs
Giant Food Inc.

P.O. Box 1804, Department 597
Washington, DC 20013
(301) 341-4365
(301) 341-4327 (TDD)

Gibbons Greenvan
see Budget Rent-A-Car Corporation

Gibson Appliances
see White Consolidated Industries

Ms. Beverly Smart
Manager, Consumer Affairs
Gillette Company
P.O. Box 61
Boston, MA 02199
(617) 463-3337

Glenbrook Laboratories
see Sterling Drug Inc.

Mr. James Sainsbury
Manager, Product Regulation
The Glidden Company
925 Euclid Avenue
Cleveland, OH 44115
(216) 344-8818

Mr. M. F. Smithson, Director
Consumer Relations
Goodyear Tire & Rubber Co.
1144 East Market Street
Akron, OH 44316
(216) 796-4940
(216) 796-6055 (TDD)
1 (800) 321-2136 (toll free)

Mr. Michael Legrand
Vice President, Operations
Gordon's Jewelers
A Subsidiary of Zale Corporation
901 West Walnut Hill Lane
Irving, TX 75038-1003
(214) 580-4924

Consumer Affairs
Greensweep
800 North Lindbergh
St. Louis, MO 63167
1 (800) 225-2883 (toll free)

Ms. Janna Willardson
Manager, Customer Relations
Greyhound Lines, Inc.
901 Main Street, Suite 2500
Dallas, Texas 75202
(214) 744-6500

Guess? Inc.
1444 South Alameda Street
Los Angeles, CA 90021
(213) 231-2385

Guinness Import Company
Six Landmark Square
Stamford, CT 06901-2704
(203) 323-3311
1 (800) 521-1591 (toll free)

H

Ms. Marti Johnson
Director of Client Relations
H&R Block, Inc.
4410 Main Street
Kansas City, MO 64111-9986
(816) 753-6900
1 (800) 829-7733 (toll free)

HVR Company
see Clorox Company

Haggar Apparel Co., Inc.
6113 Lemmon Ave.
Dallas, TX 75209-5798
(214) 352-8481

Mr. Don Freberg
Manager of Consumer Affairs
Hallmark Cards, Inc.
P.O. Box 419034
Kansas City, MO 64141-6034
(816) 274-5697

Halston
see Revlon

Hanes
see L'eggs

Mr. Fred Gould
Director, Consumer Service
Hanover-Direct Inc.
340 Poplar Street
Hanover, PA 17333-9989
(717) 637-6000

Hardwick
see Maycor

Harley Davidson, Inc.
3700 W. Juneau Avenue
Milwaukee, WI 53208-2865
(414) 342-4680

Mr. Jim Round
Vice President, Advertising
Hartmarx Specialty Stores, Inc.
101 North Wacker Drive, 20th Floor
Chicago, IL 60606-7389
(312) 372-6300

Ms. Nancy Moland
Hartz Mountain Corporation
700 Frank E. Rodgers Blvd. South
Harrison, NJ 07029-9987
(201) 481-4800

Ms. Bonnie Fisher
Supervisor, Consumer Service
Hasbro, Inc.
P.O. Box 200
Pawtucket, RI 02861-0200
(401) 431-8697
1 (800) 237-0063 (toll free)

Hathaway Shirts
see Warnaco Men's Apparel

Mr. Jim Lytle, Vice President
Direct Marketing
Heath Company
Benton Harbor, MI 49022
(616) 982-3672

Mr. Thomas J. Rattigan
Chairman and CEO
G. Heileman Brewing Company
100 Harborview Plaza
La Crosse, WI 54602-0459
(608) 785-1000

Ms. Donna Elliott
Manager, Consumer Relations
Heinz U.S.A.
P.O. Box 57
Pittsburgh, PA 15230-0057
(412) 237-5740

Consumer Affairs Department
Consumer Products Division

Helene Curtis, Inc.
325 North Wells Street
Chicago, IL 60610-4713
(312) 661-0222

Ms. Lael M. Moynihan
Manager, Consumer Relations
Hershey Foods Corporation
P.O. Box 815
Hershey, PA 17033-0815
1 (800) 468-1714 (toll free)

Ms. Leslie Rotonda, Manager
Executive Customer Relations
Hertz Corporation
225 Brae Boulevard
Park Ridge, NJ 07656-0713
(201) 307-2000
1 (800) 654-3131 (toll free—reservations)
1 (800) 654-2280 (toll free TDD)

Customer Information Center
Hewlett-Packard Company
19310 Prune Ridge Avenue
Cupertino, CA 95014
(408) 973-1919

Mr. Tony Schwartz
Helpline
Highland Superstores, Inc.
909 North Sheldon Road
Plymouth, MI 48170
(313) 451-3200

Hilton Hotels Corporation
9336 Civic Center Drive
Beverly Hills, CA 90209-5567
(310) 278-4321

Ms. Casslyn Allen
Vice President, Human Resources
Hit or Miss
100 Campanelli Parkway
Stoughton, MA 02072
(617) 344-0800

Mr. Jim Drummond, Director
Advertising and Sales Promotion
Hitachi Home Electronics (America), Inc.
3890 Steve Reynolds Boulevard
Norcross, GA 30093
(404) 279-5600
1 (800) 241-6558 (toll free)

Mr. Bill Bellican
Holiday Inns
3796 Lamar Avenue
Memphis, TN 38195
(901) 362-4827
1 (800) 621-0555 (toll free)

Mr. Bill Sanders
Director, Consumer Affairs
Home Depot Inc.
2727 Paces Ferry Road
Atlanta, GA 30339
(404) 433-8211

Ms. Karen McKeever
Director of Marketing
Home Owners Warranty Corporation (HOW)
1110 North Glebe Road
Arlington, VA 22201
(703) 516-4100
1 (800) CALL-HOW (toll free)

Home Shopping Network
P.O. Box 9090
Clearwater, FL 34618-9090
(813) 572-8585
1 (800) 753-5353 (toll free TDD)

Honda Motor Company of America
100 W. Allondra Blvd.
Gardena, CA 90247
(310) 604-2518

Mr. Ray Gwin, Manager
Consumer Affairs
Residential Division
Honeywell, Inc.
1885 Douglas Drive
Golden Valley, MN 55422-4386
(612) 542-7354
1 (800) 468-1502 (toll free)

Mr. Larry Calder
Manager of Consumer Affairs
Hoover Company
101 East Maple
North Canton, OH 44720
(216) 499-9200, ext 2669

Customer Service Division
The Horchow Collection
13800 Diplomat Drive
Dallas, TX 75234
(214) 484-6600
1 (800) 395-5397 (toll free)

Mr. Allan Krejci
Director, Public Relations
George A. Hormel and Company
501 16th Avenue N.E.
Austin, MN 55912-9989
(507) 437-5355

Hostess
see Continental Baking Co.

Mrs. Joyce Bryant
Vice President, Consumer Affairs
Household International
2700 Sanders Road
Prospect Heights, IL 60070
(708) 564-5000

Ms. Judy McCray, Consumer Relations
Huffy Corporation
P.O. Box 1204
Dayton, OH 45401
(513) 866-6251

Customer Relations
Humana Inc.
500 West Main Street
P.O. Box 1438
Louisville, KY 40201-1438
(502) 580-1000

Hunt-Wesson, Inc.
Grocery Division
1645 West Balencia Drive
Fullerton, CA 92634
(714) 680-1430

Ms. Chris Buzanis
Director, Quality Assurance
Hyatt Hotels & Resorts
200 West Madison Street, 39th Floor
Chicago, IL 60606
(312) 750-1234
1 (800) 228-3336 (toll free)

I

Mr. John F. Akers, Chairman of the Board
IBM Corporation
Old Orchard Road
Armonk, NY 10504
(914) 765-5546

Consumer Affairs Department
Illinois Bell
225 West Randolph Street, Room 30-D
Chicago, IL 60606
(312) 727-9411

Mr. Stephen Powell
Community Affairs Manager
Indiana Bell
251 North Illinois Street, Room 1680
Indianapolis, IN 46204
(317) 265-5965
1 (800) 556-4949 (toll free)

Ingersoll-Rand Company
200 Chestnut Ridge Rd.
Woodcliff, NJ 07675-7700
(201) 573-0123

Mr. David Steadman
President and CEO
Integra
4441 West Airport Freeway
Irving, TX 75062
(214) 258-8500

Communications Department
International Dairy Queen, Inc.
5701 Green Valley Drive
Minneapolis, MN 55437-1089
(612) 830-0200

J

Mr. James Bennett
Customer Relations Manager
JVC Company of America
41 Slater Drive
Elmwood Park, NJ 07407
(201) 794-3900
1 (800) 252-5722 (toll free)

Mr. Murray Taylor
Manager, Customer Service
Jackson & Perkins Nursery Stock
2518 South Pacific Highway
Medford, OR 97501
(503) 776-2400
1 (800) 872-7673 (toll free)

Ms. Eileen Guernsey
Manager of Consumer Affairs
James River Corporation
Dixie Products
P.O. Box 6000
Norwalk, CT 06856-6000
(203) 854-2469
1 (800) 243-5384 (toll free)

Ms. Rita Topp
Manager of Consumer Affairs
James River Corporation
Towel and Tissue Products
P.O. Box 6000
Norwalk, CT 06856-6000
1 (800) 243-5384 (toll free)

Customer Service
James River Traders
5000 City Lane Road
Hampton, VA 23661
(804) 827-6000

Jenn-Air Company
see Maycor

Jhirmack
see Playtex Family Products Group

Ms. Barbara Short
Customer Relations
Jockey International, Inc.
2300 60th Street
Kenosha, WI 53140
(414) 658-8111

Consumer Affairs
John Hancock Financial Services
P.O. Box 111
Boston, MA 02117
(617) 572-6272

Johnny Appleseed's, Inc.
30 Tozer Road
Beverly, MA 01915-0720
1 (800) 225-5051 (toll free)

Johnson & Johnson Consumer Products, Inc.
Information Center
199 Grandview Road
Skillman, NJ 08558
1 (800) 526-2433 (toll free)
1 (800) 526-3967 (toll free)

Complaint Department
Johnson Publishing Company, Inc.
820 South Michigan Avenue
Chicago, IL 60605
(written complaints only)

Mr. Tom Conrardy
Consumer Affairs Director
S. C. Johnson and Sons
1525 Howe Street
Racine, WI 53403
1 (800) 558-5252 (toll free)

Ms. Denise Mori
Manager, Guest Services
Howard Johnson, Inc.
P.O. Box 29004
Phoenix, AZ 85038
(602) 389-5555

Mr. Jerry Taylor, Vice President
Advertising and Marketing
Jordache Enterprises, Inc.
226 West 37th Street
New York, NY 10018
(212) 279-7343
1 (800) 289-5326 (toll free)
1 (800) 442-2056 (toll free in NY)

K

Mr. Robert J. Clark
Manager, Customer Service
K mart Corporation
3100 West Big Beaver Road
Troy, MI 48084
(313) 643-1643
1 (800) 63-KMART (toll free)

Kaiser Aluminum and Chemical Corporation
300 Lakeside Dr.
Oakland, CA 94643
(415) 271-3300

Kal Kan Foods, Inc.
3250 E. 44th Street
Vernon, CA 90058-2499
(213) 587-2727

Ms. Annette Watkins-Habeski
Manager, Consumer Relations
Fieldcrest Cannon Carpet Division
Karastan/Bigelow
725 North Regional Rd.
Greensboro, NC 27409
(919) 665-4000
1 (800) 476-7113 (toll free)

Mr. Ray Perry
Vice President, Operations
Carl Karcher Enterprises
1200 North Harbor Boulevard
P.O. Box 4349
Anaheim, CA 92803
(714) 774-5796

Consumer Services
Kawasaki Motor Corporation, U.S.A.
P.O. Box 25252
Santa Ana, CA 92799-5252
(714) 770-0400

Ms. Sara C. Maness
Consumer Relations Manager
Kayser-Roth Corporation
612 South Main Street
Burlington, NC 27215
(919) 229-2224

Ms. Paige Riccio, Supervisor
Consumer Communications
Keebler Company, Inc.
One Hollow Tree Lane
Elmhurst, IL 60126
(708) 833-2900

Ms. Linda J. Pell
Manager, Consumer Affairs
Kellogg Company
P.O. Box CAMB
Battle Creek, MI 49016
(616) 961-2277

Mr. Don Diehl, Manager
Product Service
The Kelly Springfield Tire Company
Willowbrook Road
Cumberland, MD 21502-2599
(301) 777-6631
(301) 777-6017

Kelvinator Appliance Company
see White Consolidated Industries

Ms. Dee Atkinson
Consumer Relations Manager
Kemper National Insurance Company
Public Affairs and Communications
Long Grove, IL 60049-0001
(708) 540-2122
1 (800) 833-0355 (toll free)

Consumer Affairs
Kenner Products
1014 Vine Street
Cincinnati, OH 45202
(513) 579-4041
1 (800) 347-4613 (toll free)

Kentucky Fried Chicken Corporation
1441 Gardiner Lane
Louisville, KY 40213-1957
(502) 456-8300

Ms. Cindy Van Grinsven
Director, Consumer Services
Kimberly-Clark Corporation
P.O. Box 2020
Neenah, WI 54957-2020
(414) 721-5604
1 (800) 544-1847 (toll free)

Kingsford Products Company
see Clorox Company

Consumer Assistance Center
KitchenAid
701 Main Street
St. Joseph, MO 49085-1392
(616) 982-4500
1 (800) 422-1230 (toll free)

Mrs. Lori Masters
Assistant to the Senior Vice President
Public Relations and Communications
Calvin Klein Industries, Inc.
205 West 39th Street, 10th Floor
New York, NY 10018
(212) 719-2600
1 (800) 327-8731 (toll free)

Ms. Anita Davis, Director
Customer Relations
Kloster Cruise Ltd.
95 Merrick Way
Miami, FL 33134
(305) 447-9660

Kodiak Smokeless Tobacco
see Conwood Co., L.P.

Mr. Paul Scholten, Manager
Service and Technical Publications
Kohler Company
Kohler, WI 53044
(414) 457-4441

Mr. Allen Wilson, Manager
Sales Administration
Kohler Company
Kohler, WI 53044
(414) 457-4441

Mr. Mark Grunow, Manager
Consumer Affairs
Plumbing Products
Kohler Company
Kohler, WI 53044
(414) 457-4441

ATTN: Consumer Response Center
Kraft, Inc.
Kraftcourt
Glenview, IL 60025
1 (800) 323-0768 (toll free)

Ms. Judy Ball
Customer Relations Manager
Kroger Company
1014 Vine Street
Cincinnati, OH 45201
(513) 762-1589
1 (800) 632-6900
(toll free—product information)

Mr. Rody Davenport, IV
Vice President Operations
Krystal Company

One Union Square
Chattanooga, TN 37402
(615) 757-1550

L

Ms. Danielle King
Consumer Affairs
Coordinator
LA Gear
4221 Redwood Avenue
Los Angeles, CA 90066
(310) 822-1995

Mrs. Colleen Fogle
Manager of Consumer
Services
La-Z-Boy Chair Company
1284 North Telegraph Road
Monroe, MI 48161-3309
(313) 242-1444

Consumer Relations
L&F Products
225 Summit Avenue
Montvale, NJ 07645
(201) 573-5700

Ms. Marie Holen
Manager, Consumer Affairs
Land O'Lakes, Inc.
P.O. Box 116
Minneapolis, MN
55440-0116
1 (800) 328-4155 (toll free)

Customer Service
Land's End
One Land's End Lane
Dodgeville, WI 53595
1 (800) 356-4444 (toll free)

Mr. Donald Tucker
Manager, Customer Service
Lane Furniture
East Franklin Avenue
P.O. Box 151
Altavista, VA 24517
(804) 369-5641

Mr. John Gray, Director
Customer Services
Lechmere
275 Wildwood Street
Woburn, MA 01801
(617) 935-8340
1 (800) 733-4666 (toll free)

Ms. Barbara Distasi
Manager, Consumer Affairs
Lederle Consumer Health Products Division
697 Route 46
Clifton, NJ 07015
1 (800) 282-8805
(toll free 9 a.m.—4 p.m., M-F)

Ms. Christine Anderson
Customer Service
Lee Company
9001 West 67th Street
Marriam, KS 66202
(913) 384-4000

L'eggs Products, Inc.
Sara Lee Hosiery
Sara Lee Corporation
5660 University Parkway
Winston-Salem, NC 27105
(919) 768-9540

Customer Service
Leichtung, Inc.
4944 Commerce Parkway
Cleveland, OH 44128
(216) 831-7645
1 (800) 654-7817 (toll free)

Lennox Industries
P.O. Box 799900
Dallas, TX 75380-9000
(214) 497-5000

Consumer Service Manager
Lever Brothers Corporation
390 Park Avenue
New York, NY 10022-4698
1 (800) 451-6679 (toll free)

Consumer Affairs
Levi Strauss & Co.
1155 Battery Street
San Francisco, CA 94111
1 (800) USA-LEVI (toll free)

Ms. Eleanor Eckardt
Vice President, Consumer
Relations
Levitz Furniture Corporation
6111 Broken Sound Parkway, N.W.
Boca Raton, FL 33487-2799
1 (800) 523-2572 (toll free in FL)
1 (800) 631-4601 (toll free outside FL)

Customer Service
Levolor Corporation
7614 Business Park Drive
Greensboro, NC 27409
1 (800) LEVOLOR (toll free)

Mr. Edward T. Frackiewicz
Manager of Consumer
Affairs
Liberty Mutual Insurance Group
175 Berkeley Street
Boston, MA 02117
(617) 357-9500
1 (800) 225-2390 (toll free)

Customer Service
Life Fitness Products
10601 West Belmont
Franklin Park, IL 60131
1 (800) 351-3737 (toll free)

Customer Service
Lillian Vernon Corporation
2600 International Parkway
Virginia Beach, VA 23452
(804) 430-1500

Consumer Technical Services
Eli Lilly & Company
Lilly Corporate Center
Indianapolis, IN 46285
(317) 276-2339 (product information)
(For medical information, contact your physician)

Mr. Alfred Dietzel
Vice President
Financial and Public
Relations
The Limited, Inc.
Two Limited Parkway
P.O. Box 16000
Columbus, OH 43216
(614) 479-7000

Ms. Sharlene Ungar
Manager
Customer Service Center
Little Caesar Enterprises

2211 Woodward Avenue
Detroit, MI 48201
1 (800) 7-CAESAR

Lone Star Brewing Company
see G. Heileman Brewing Company

Long John Silver's
101 Jerrico Drive
P.O. Box 11988
Lexington, KY 40579
(606) 263-6000

L'Oreal
see Cosmair, Inc.

Mr. David Hicks
Customer Relations Manager
Lorillard Tobacco Company
2525 East Market Street
P.O. Box 21688
Greensboro, NC 27420-1688
(919) 373-6669

Public Relations Department
Los Angeles Times
Times Mirror Square
Los Angeles, CA 90053
(213) 237-5000

Ms. Judy Decker
Communications Coordinator
Lucky Stores, Inc.
P.O. Box BB
Dublin, CA 94568
(415) 833-6000

M

Ms. Marie A. Lentz
Director, Customer Services
MAACO Enterprises, Inc.
381 Brooks Road
King of Prussia, PA 19406
1 (800) 523-1180 (toll free outside PA)

Public Information
MCA, Inc.
100 Universal City Plaza
Universal City, CA 91608-1085
(818) 777-1000

Mr. Roy Gamse
Senior Vice President
Consumer Service
MCI Consumer Markets
1200 South Hayes Street, 12th Floor
Arlington, VA 22202
(703) 415-6726

Consumer Affairs Department
M&M/Mars, Inc.
High Street
Hackettstown, NJ 07840
(201) 852-1000
1 (800) 222-0293 (toll free)

MTV Networks, Inc.
see Viacom International, Inc.

Vice President
Customer Service
R. H. Macy & Company, Inc.
151 West 34th Street
New York, NY 10001
(212) 695-4400

Magic Chef
see Maycor

Magnavox
see Philips Company

Valli Zale, General Manager
I. Magnin
3050 Wilshire Boulevard
Los Angeles, CA 90010
(213) 382-6161

Mr. Ross DeMaris
Consumer Services Manager
Mannington Resilient Floors, Inc.
P.O. Box 30
Salem, NJ 08079
(609) 935-3000
1 (800) 356-6787 (toll free)

Professional Services Department
Manor Care Healthcare
10770 Columbia Pike
Silver Spring, MD 20901
(301) 681-9400
1 (800) 637-1400 (toll free outside MD)

Ms. Marie DeAngelo
Assistant Vice President
Manufacturers Hanover Trust Company
270 Park Avenue
New York, NY 10017
(212) 270-7370

Manville Corporation
P.O. Box 5108
Denver, CO 80217-5108
(303) 978-2000
1 (800) 654-3103
(toll free—product information)

Corporate Customer Relations
Marine Midland Bank, N.A.
One Marine Midland Center
Buffalo, NY 14203
(716) 841-2424

Mr. William Guinty
Manager, Regulatory Services
Marion Merrell Dow
Consumer Products Division
Marion Park Drive
Kansas City, MO 64134
(816) 966-5305

Consumer Affairs
Marriott Corporation
One Marriott Drive
Attn: Department 921-60
Washington, DC 20058
(301) 380-7600

Ms. Norma Vinick
Director of Customer Relations
Massachusetts Mutual Life Insurance Company
1295 State Street
Springfield, MA 01111
(413) 788-8411
1 (800) 828-4902 (toll free)

MasterCard International
(contact issuing bank)

Mr. Joseph Dillon, President
Matsushita Servicing Company
50 Meadowlands Parkway
Secaucus, NJ 07094
(201) 348-7000

Ms. Tammy Longworth
Director, Consumer Affairs
Mattel Toys, Inc.
333 Continental Boulevard
El Segundo, CA 90245-5012
(310) 524-2000
1 (800) 421-2887
(toll free outside CA)

Max Factor
see Revlon

Consumer Affairs
Maxicare Health Plans, Inc.
1149 South Broadway
Los Angeles, CA 90015
(213) 742-0900

Maxwell House
see General Foods

Mr. James F. Harner, Senior Vice President
Customer Service and Operations
May Department Stores Co.
611 Olive Street
St. Louis, MO 63101
(314) 342-4336

Maybelline
see Schering-Plough HealthCare Products, Inc.

Maycor Appliance, Parts, and Service Company
240 Edwards Street, S.E.
Cleveland, TN 37311
(615) 472-3333

Customer Service Department
Mayflower Transit, Inc.
P.O. Box 107
Indianapolis, IN 46206
(317) 875-1000
1 (800) 428-1200 (toll free)

Maytag
see Maycor

Mazda Motors of America, Inc.
77 Irvine Center Drive
Irvine, CA 92718-2906
(714) 727-1990

Ms. Mary Randisi, Director
Consumer Affairs
McCormick & Company, Inc.
211 Schilling Circle
Hunt Valley, MD 21031
(301) 527-6273
1 (800) 632-5847 (toll free)

McCrory Stores, Inc.
2955 East Market Street
York, PA 17402
(717) 757-8181

Ms. Beth Petersohn
Manager, Customer Relations
McDonald's Corporation
McDonald's Plaza
Oak Brook, IL 60521
(708) 575-6198

Ms. Mary Jo Oller
Customer Service
McGraw-Hill Company
Blue Ridge Summit, PA 17294
(717) 794-5461
1 (800) 262-4729 (toll free)

MCI Telecommunications Corporation
1133 19th St NW
Washington, DC 20036-3607
(202) 872-1600

Consumer Services
McKee Baking Company
P.O. Box 750
Collegedale, TN 37315
(615) 238-7111

Vice President Marketing
McKesson Water Products Company
4500 York Boulevard
Los Angeles, CA 90041
(213) 259-2000

Consumer Affairs
McNeil Consumer Products Company
Johnson & Johnson
Camp Hill Road
Fort Washington, PA 19034
(215) 233-7000

Mead Corporation
Courthouse Plaza, NE
Dayton, OH 45463
(513) 222-6323

Mr. Marshall Morton
Senior Vice President
Media General, Inc.
333 East Grace Street
Richmond, VA 23219
(804) 649-6000

Ms. Angela Cureton
Customer Service Representative
Meineke Discount Muffler
128 South Tryon Street, Suite 900
Charlotte, NC 28202
(704) 377-8855

Customer Service Department
Melitta USA, Inc.
1401 Berlin Road
Cherry Hill, NJ 08003
(609) 428-7202
1 (800) 451-1694 (toll free)

Ms. Sandra J. McLaughlin
Senior Vice President
Corporate Affairs
Mellon Bank Corporation
One Mellon Bank Center, 151-1840
Pittsburgh, PA 15258
(412) 234-4003

Ms. Diana Epstein
Consumer Affairs
Melville Corporation
1 Theall Road
Rye, NY 10580
(914) 925-4000

Mr. Otto Schmitt
Consumer Relations
Mem Company, Inc.
Union Street
Northvale, NJ 07647
(201) 767-0100

Ms. Mary Ann Molnar
Consumer Relations Administrator

Mennen Company
Hanover Avenue
Morristown, NJ 07962-1928
(201) 631-9000 (collect calls accepted)

Mr. Jim Dickson
Product Manager
Mentholatum Company Inc.
1360 Niagara Street
Buffalo, NY 14213
(716) 882-7660

Mercedes-Benz of North America
1 Mercedes Dr.
Montvale, NJ 07645-1833
(201) 573-0600

Consumer Affairs
Mercury Marine
P.O. Box 1939
Fond Du Lac, WI 54936-1939
(414) 929-5000

Mr. Dave Smith, Manager
Customer Service
Merillat Industries
5353 West U.S. 223
Adrian, MI 49221
(517) 263-0771

Customer Service Department
Merrill Lynch Pierce Fenner & Smith
265 Davidson Avenue, 4th Floor
Somerset, NJ 08873
(908) 563-8777

Ms. Colleen Dahle-Hong
Consumer Affairs Analyst
Mervyn's
25001 Industrial Boulevard
Hayward, CA 94545
(415) 786-8337

Office of the President
Metromedia Steakhouses, Inc.
P.O. Box 578
Dayton, OH 45401-0578
(513) 454-2400

Mr. Bruce C. Hemer
Director, Consumer Affairs
Metropolitan Life and Affiliated Companies
One Madison Avenue
Area 1-Z
New York, NY 10010-3690
(212) 578-2544

Mr. Martin J. Wertheim, Manager
Corporate Consumer Relations
Michelin Tire Corporation
One Parkway South
Greenville, SC 29615
(803) 458-5000

Mr. David E. Bassett
Senior Director, Community Relations
Michigan Bell Telephone Co.
1365 Cass Avenue, Room 1800
Detroit, MI 48226
(313) 223-7224
1 (800) 482-3141 (toll free TDD)

Ms. Darlene Snape
Customer Service Manager
Michigan Bulb Company
1950 Waldorf, N.W.
Grand Rapids, MI 49550
(616) 771-9500

Mr. Charles Ayers, Manager
Consumer Relations
Midas International
225 North Michigan Avenue
Chicago, IL 60601
(312) 565-7500
1 (800) 621-8545 (toll free outside IL)

Mid-Michigan Surgical Supply
360 Capitol Avenue, N.E.
Battlecreek, MI 49017
(616) 962-9541

Ms. Diane Ferri, Manager
Consumer Relations
Midway Airlines
5959 South Cicero Avenue
Chicago, IL 60638
(312) 838-4684
1 (800) 866-9000, ext. 4684 (toll free)

Customer Service
Miles Kimball
41 West 8
Oshkosh, WI 54906
(written inquiries only)

Ms. Debra K. Wood
Consumer Service Representative
Milton Bradley Company
443 Shaker Road
East Long Meadow, MA 01028
(413) 525-6411

Mr. George Manning, National Manager
Consumer Relations
Minolta Corporation
100 Williams Drive
Ramsey, NJ 07446
(201) 825-4000

Technical Services
Minwax, Inc.
15 Mercedes Drive
Montvale, NJ 07645
1 (800) 526-0495 (toll free)

Miracle Gro Products, Inc.
P.O. Box 800
Port Washington, NY 11050
(516) 883-6550

Consumer Relations
Mitsubishi Electric Sales of America, Inc.
5757 Plaza Drive
P.O. Box 6007
Cypress, CA 90630
(714) 220-2500

Mr. G. T. Cox, Manager
Customer Relations
Mobil Oil Corporation
3225 Gallows Road
Fairfax, VA 22037
(703) 849-3994

Mr. Al Kedora
Customer Services Manager
Mobil Oil Credit Corporation
210 West Tenth Street
Kansas City, MO 64105
(816) 391-9100

Customer Service
Crystal Brand Jewelry Group
Monet, Crisart and Marvella Jewelry
Number Two Lonsdale Avenue
Pawtucket, RI 02860
(401) 728-9800

Mr. Dan R. Bishop, Director
Corporate Communications
Monsanto Company
800 North Lindbergh Boulevard
St. Louis, MO 63167
(314) 694-2883

Mr. W. Andrew Werry
Consumer Affairs Manager
Montgomery Ward
One Montgomery Ward Plaza, 9-S
Chicago, IL 60671
(312) 467-2814

Mr. Kenneth C. Cummins
Vice President and General Counsel
Morse Shoe Company
555 Turnpike Street
Canton, MA 02021
(617) 828-9300
1 (800) 366-6773 (toll free)

Consumer Affairs
Morton International
Morton Salt Division
100 North Riverside Plaza
Chicago, IL 60606
(312) 807-2694

Director of Marketing
Motorola, Inc.
1303 East Algonquin Road
Schaumburg, IL 60196
(708) 576-5000

Mr. Paul Murphy
Vice President, Advertising
Murphy-Phoenix Co.
25800 Science Park Drive, Suite 200
P.O. Box 22930
Beachwood, OH 44122
(216) 831-0404

Mutual Life Insurance Company of New York (MONY)
Glenpoint Center West
500 Frank W. Burr Boulevard
Teaneck, NJ 07666
(201) 907-6669

Ms. Terry Calek
Second Vice President, Public Affairs
Mutual of Omaha Insurance Co.
Mutual of Omaha Plaza
Omaha, NE 68175
(402) 342-7600

N

Audience Services
NBC
30 Rockefeller Plaza
New York, NY 10112
(212) 664-2333

Mr. Greg VanZandt
Consumer Affairs Manager
NEC Technologies Inc.
1255 Michael Drive
Wood Dale, IL 60191-1094
(708) 860-0335

Ms. Alice Gabel, Manager
"800" Toll Free Center
Consumer Affairs
Nabisco Brands, Inc.
100 DeForest Ave.
East Hanover, NJ 07936
(201) 503-2659
1 (800) 932-7800 (toll free)

Mr. Dennis Dotson
Director, Theater Operations
National Amusements Inc.
200 Elm Street
Dedham, MA 02026
(617) 461-1600

Mr. Joel Martin
Divisional Vice President
Customer Services
National Car Rental System, Inc.
7700 France Avenue, South
Minneapolis, MN 55435
(612) 893-6209
1 (800) 627-7777 (toll free)

National Education Corporation
1732 Reynolds Street
Irvine, CA 92714
(714) 261-7606

Mr. Bill Campbell, Vice President
National Media Corporation
4360 Main Street
Philadelphia, PA 19127
(215) 482-9800

Mr. James Jenson, Controller
National Presto Industries, Inc.
3925 North Hastings Way
Eau Claire, WI 54703-3703
(715) 839-2121

Mr. Glenn W. Soden
Customer Relations Officer
Nationwide Insurance Companies
One Nationwide Plaza
Columbus, OH 43216
(614) 249-6985

NCR Corporation (National Cash Register)
1700 S. Patterson Blvd.
Dayton, OH 45479
(513) 445-5000

Customer Relations
Neighborhood Periodical Club, Inc.
One Crowne Point Court, #130
Cincinnati, OH 45241
(513) 771-9400

Customer Service Department
Neiman-Marcus
P.O. Box 64780
Dallas, TX 75206
(214) 761-2600
1 (800) 442-2274 (toll free in TX)
1 (800) 527-1767 (toll free outside TX)

Mrs. Andrea McLean
Manager, Consumer Affairs
Nestle Foods Corporation

100 Manhattanville Road
Purchase, NY 10577
(914) 251-3000
1 (800) NESTLES (toll free)

Mr. Dick L. Curd
Media Affairs Director
Corporate Communications
Nestle USA, Inc.
800 North Brand Boulevard
Glendale, CA 91203
(818) 549-6000

Ms. Alene Lain
Consumer Relations
Neutrogena Corporation
5760 West 96th Street
Los Angeles, CA 90045
(310) 642-1150
1 (800) 421-6857 (toll free outside CA)

Consumer Relations
Nevada Bell
645 East Plumb Lane
Reno, NV 89520
(702) 789-6000

Mr. Edward C. Hall
Executive Vice President
The New England
500 Boylston Street
Boston, MA 02117
(617) 578-2000

Mr. William H. Willett
Chairman, CEO
New Hampton, Inc.
5000 City Line Road
Hampton, VA 23661
(804) 827-7010

Customer Service
News America Publishing, Inc.
Four Radnor Corporate Center
Radnor, PA 19088
(215) 293-8500
1 (800) 345-8500 (toll free)

Ms. Barbara Fagnano
Assistant Vice President
New York Life Insurance Company
51 Madison Avenue
New York, NY 10010
(212) 576-5081 (collect calls accepted)

Mr. Robert P. Smith, Manager
Advertising Acceptability Department
New York Times Company
229 West 43rd Street
New York, NY 10036
(212) 556-7171

Customer Service Representative
Newsweek, Inc.
P.O. Box 403
Livingston, NJ 07039
(212) 350-4000
1 (800) 631-1040
(toll free—subscriber service only)

Customer Service
Nexxus Products
P.O. Box 1274
Santa Barbara, CA 93116-9976
(805) 968-6900

Ms. Nancy L. Testani
Director, Consumer Affairs
Niagara Mohawk Power Corporation
300 Erie Boulevard West
Syracuse, NY 13202
(315) 474-1511

Ms. Jackie Evey, Supervisor
Consumer Services
Nike, Inc.
Nike/World Campus
1 Bowerman Drive
Beaverton, OR 97005
(503) 671-6453
1 (800) 344-6453 (toll free outside OR)

Consumer Affairs
Nintendo of America Inc.
4820 150th Avenue NE
Redmond, WA 98052
1 (800) 255-3700 (toll free)

No Nonsense
see Kayser-Roth Corporation

Norge
see Maycor

Ms. Amy Grant
Marketing Servicing Manager
North American Watch Corporation
650 Fifth Avenue
New York, NY 10019
(212) 397-7800

Mr. G. C. Strickland
Supervisor, Consumer Affairs
Northern Electric Company
1621 Highway 15 North
P.O. Box 247
Laurel, MS 39441-0247
(601) 649-6170

Customer Relations
Northwest Airlines
A5270 Minneapolis/St. Paul International Airport
St. Paul, MN 55111-3034
(612) 726-2046
1 (800) 328-2298
(toll free TDD—reservations)

Mr. Thomas W. Towers
Associate Director, Public Relations
Northwestern Mutual Life Insurance Company
720 East Wisconsin Avenue
Milwaukee, WI 53202
(414) 271-1444

Norwegian Cruise Line
see Kloster Cruise Ltd.

Ms. Claire Lee, Product Manager
Nostril/Nostrilla
Boehringer Ingelheim
90 East Ridge
P.O. Box 368
Ridgefield, CT 06877
(203) 798-9988

Mr. E. R. Steinmeier
Director, Consumer Services
Noxell Corporation
11050 York Road
Hunt Valley, MD 21030-2098
(301) 785-4411
1 (800) 638-6204 (toll free)

Mr. Ralph Profitt
Director of Consumer Relations
Nu Tone, Inc.

Madison and Red Bank Roads
Cincinnati, OH 45227
(513) 527-5100
1 (800) 582-2030 (toll free in OH)
1 (800) 543-8687 (toll free outside OH)

The NutraSweet Company
1751 Lake Cook Road
Deerfield, IL 60015
1 (800) 321-7254 (toll free—NutraSweet)
1 (800) 323-5316 (toll free—Equal)

Ms. Nancy Moskowitz
Customer Relations
Nutri/System Inc.
380 Sentry Parkway
Blue Bell, PA 19422-2332
(215) 940-3000, ext. 3443

President's Help Line
Nynex/New York Telephone
1095 Avenue of the Americas
New York, NY 10036
1 (800) 722-2300 (toll free)
1 (800) 342-4181 (toll free TDD in NY)

O

Mrs. Linda Compton
Supervisor, Consumer Affairs
Ocean Spray Cranberries Inc.
One Ocean Spray Drive
Lakeville/Middleboro, MA 02349
(508) 946-1000

Ms. Gail Holmes, District Manager
Consumer Affairs
Ohio Bell Telephone Company
45 ErieView, Room 870
Cleveland, OH 44114
(216) 822-2124

O'Keefe & Merit Appliances
see White Consolidated Industries

Ms. Gay F. Gandrow
Director, Marketing Services
Olan Mills, Inc.
4325 Amnicola Highway
P.O. Box 23456
Chattanooga, TN 37422-3456
(615) 622-5141
1 (800) 251-6323 (toll free)

Mr. Ralph LePore
Manager, Camera Service
Olympus Optical Company, Ltd.
145 Crossways Park
Woodbury, NY 11797
(516) 364-3000

Ms. Bridget Burke
Consumer Relations Representative
Oneida, Ltd.
Kenwood Station
Oneida, NY 13421
(315) 361-3000
1 (800) 877-6667 (toll free)

Orkin
see Rollins, Inc.

Mr. Brodrick William Hill
Manager, Consumer Affairs
Ortho Consumer Products
Chevron Chemical Company
P.O. Box 5047
San Ramon, CA 94583-0947
(510) 842-5500

OSCO Drugs
see American Stores Company

Mr. Bob Schroer, Manager
Field and Customer Services
Outboard Marine Corporation
100 Sea Horse Drive
Waukegan, IL 60085
(708) 689-6200

Owens-Corning Fiberglas Corporation
Fiberglas Tower
Toledo, OH 43659
(419) 248-8000

P

Customer Appeals Group
Pacific Bell
140 New Montgomery Street
San Francisco, CA 94108
(415) 882-8000
1 (800) 592-6500 (toll free in CA)

Public Affairs
Pacific Enterprises
P.O. Box 60043
Los Angeles, CA 90060-0043
(213) 895-5000

Consumer Relations Department
Pacific Telesis Group
130 Kearny Street
San Francisco, CA 94108
(415) 882-8000

Mr. Frank S. Pluchino
Director and Vice President
Customer Services
PaineWebber, Inc.
Lincoln Harbor
1200 Harbor Boulevard, 10th Floor
Weehawken, NJ 07087
(201) 902-3000

Panasonic
see Matsushita Servicing Company

Paper Art Company
see Mennen Company

Mr. Rick Bates
Vice President
Customer Operations
Paramount Communications Inc.
200 Old Tappan Road
Old Tappan, NJ 07675
(201) 767-5000

Parke-Davis
see Warner-Lambert Company

Piedmont Airlines
see USAir

Ms. Pamela Lumpkin
Consumer Relations Manager
J.C. Penney Company, Inc.
P.O. Box 659000
Dallas, TX 75265-9000
(214) 591-8500

Mr. William E. Place
National Technical Service Manager
Pennzoil Products Company
P.O. Box 2967
Houston, TX 77252-2967
(713) 546-8783 (collect calls accepted)

Ms. Redon Forest
Director of Public Affairs
Peoples Drug Stores, Inc.
6315 Bren Mar Drive
Alexandria, VA 22312
(703) 750-6100
1 (800) 572-0267 (toll free in VA)
1 (800) 336-4990 (toll free outside VA)

Mrs. Ellie Eng
Manager, Consumer Services
Pepperidge Farm, Inc.
595 Westport Avenue
Norwalk, CT 06856
(203) 846-7276

Ms. Christine Jones
Manager, Consumer Affairs
Pepsi-Cola Company
1 Pepsi Way
Somers, NY 10589-2201
(914) 767-6000

Ms. Connie Littleton
Director of Advertising
Perdue Farms
P.O. Box 1537
Salisbury, MD 21802
(301) 543-3000
1 (800) 442-2034 (toll free outside MD)

Ms. Maria Cammarosano
Marketing Division
The Perrier Group
777 West Putnam Avenue
Greenwich, CT 06830
(203) 531-4100

Ms. Joyce Hofer
Consumer Affairs Correspondent
Dry Foods (Except Progresso)
Pet Incorporated
P.O. Box 66719
St. Louis, MO 63166-6719
(314) 622-6695

Ms. Janice Leidner
Consumer Affairs Correspondent
Progresso Line
Pet Incorporated
P.O. Box 66719
St. Louis, MO 63166-6719
(314) 622-6364

Ms. Mary Carich
Consumer Affairs Specialist
Frozen and Bakery Foods
Pet Incorporated
P.O. Box 66719
St. Louis, MO 63166-6719
(314) 622-6146

Marketing Department
Pfizer Inc.
235 East 42nd Street
New York, NY 10017
(212) 573-2323

Philco
see Philips Company

Ms. Anne T. Dowling, Director
Corporate Contributions
Philip Morris Companies Incorporated
120 Park Avenue
New York, NY 10017
(212) 880-3366

Department of Consumer Affairs
Philips Company
Consumer Electronics Division
P.O. Box 555
Jefferson City, TN 37760
(615) 475-0317

Ms. Toni J. Honkisz
Corporate Quality Administrator
Philips Lighting Company
200 Franklin Square Drive
P.O. Box 6800
Somerset, NJ 08875-6800
1 (800) 631-1259 (toll free)

Public Relations
Phillips Petroleum Company
16 Phillips Building
Bartlesville, OK 74004
(918) 661-1215

Piaget
see North American Watch Corporation

Pillsbury Company
Consumer Response
P.O. Box 550
Minneapolis, MN 55440
1 (800) 767-4466 (toll free)

Mr. Al Segaul, Division Manager
Customer Service
Pioneer Electronics Service, Inc.
P.O. Box 1760
Long Beach, CA 90810
1 (800) 421-1404 (toll free)

Mr. Fred Fuest
Manager, Consumer Affairs
Pirelli Tire
Pirelli/Armstrong Tire Corporation
500 Sargent Drive
New Haven, CT 06536-0201
1 (800) 327-2442 (toll free)

Pizza Hut Inc.
P.O. Box 428
911 E. Douglas
Wichita, KS 67201-0428
(316) 681-9000

Playskool
see Hasbro, Inc.

Ms. Theresa M. Boutin
Manager, Consumer Affairs
Playtex Apparel, Inc.
P.O. Box 631
MS 1526
Dover, DE 19903-0631
(302) 674-6000
1 (800) 537-9955 (toll free)

Playtex Family Products Corp.
215 College Rd.
P.O. Box 728
Paramus, NJ 07652

1 (800) 624-0825 (toll free in NJ)
1 (800) 222-0453 (toll free outside NJ)

Customer Service Department
Polaroid Corporation
784 Memorial Drive
Cambridge, MA 02139
(617) 577-2000
(collect calls accepted within MA)
1 (800) 343-5000 (toll free outside MA)

Mr. Richard Lugo
Consumer Relations Manager
Polo/Ralph Lauren Corporation
4100 Beechwood Drive
Greensboro, NC 27410
1 (800) 775-7656 (toll free)

Ponderosa
see Metromedia Steakhouses, Inc.

Operations Department
Popeye's/Church's Fried Chicken, Inc.
P.O. Box BH001
San Antonio, TX 78201
(512) 735-9392
1 (800) 222-5857 (toll free)

Premier Beverages
see Dr. Pepper

Prescriptives, Inc.
see Estee Lauder

Princeton Pharmaceutical Products
see Bristol-Myers Squibb Pharmaceutical Group

Ms. Patti Schively
Associate Director, Consumer Services
Procter & Gamble Co.
P.O. Box 599
Cincinnati, OH 45201-0599
(513) 983-2200
(toll free numbers appear on all Procter & Gamble product labels)

Mr. Joe Kenney
Asssociate Counsel and Secretary
Provident Mutual Life Insurance
1600 Market Street
P.O. Box 7378
Philadelphia, PA 19101
(215) 636-5000

Individual Insurance Services
Prudential Insurance Company of America
Executive Offices
Prudential Plaza, 24th Floor
Newark, NJ 07101
(201) 802-6000

Public Affairs
Prudential Property & Casualty Company
23 Main Street
P.O. Box 419
Holmdel, NJ 07733
(609) 653-3000

Client Relations
Prudential Securities Inc.
One Seaport Plaza
New York, NY 10292
(212) 214-1000

Ms. Patricia Kaufman
Director, Customer Operations
Publishers Clearing House
382 Channel Drive
Port Washington, NY 11050
(516) 883-5432
1 (800) 645-9242 (toll free outside NY)

Ms. Mary Ann Jones
Director of Customer Relations
Publix Super Markets
1936 George Jenkins Boulevard
P.O. Box 407
Lakeland, FL 33802
(813) 688-1188

Q

QVC Network
Goshen Corporate Park
1365 Enterprise Drive
West Chester, PA 19380
(215) 430-1000

Ms. Beverly Kloehn
Director of Consumer Response
Quaker Oats Company
P.O. Box 9003
Chicago, IL 60604-9003
(312) 222-7843

Mr. Benton H. Faulkner
Manager, Public Relations
Quaker State Corporation
P.O. Box 989
Oil City, PA 16301
(814) 676-7676

Quasar
see Matsushita Servicing Company

R

Radio Shack
see Tandy Corporation

Ms. Doris Hewkin, Director
Office of Consumer Affairs
Ralston Purina Company
Checkerboard Square
St. Louis, MO 63164
(314) 982-4566
1 (800) 345-5678 (toll free)

Ms. Judy Crawford
Director, Public Relations
Ramada International Hotels and Resorts
3838 East VanBuren
P.O. Box 29004
Phoenix, AZ 85038
(602) 273-4604

Rand Corporation
1700 Main St.
Santa Monica, CA 90401-3297
(310) 393-0411

Rand McNally & Company
8255 N. Central Park Avenue
Skokie, IL 60076-2970
(708) 673-9100

Rayovac Corporation
601 Rayovac Drive
Madison, WI 53711

Raytheon Company
141 Spring Street
Lexington, MA 02173-7899
(617) 862-6600

Mrs. Patricia Rosafort
Supervisor, Customer Services
Reader's Digest Association, Inc.
Pleasantville, NY 10570-7000
1 (800) 431-1246 (toll free)
1 (800) 735-4327 (toll free TDD)

Consumer Affairs Department
Reckitt & Colman Household Products
Division of Reckitt & Colman Inc.
P.O. Box 945
Wayne, NJ 07474-0945
(201) 633-6700

Orville Redenbacher
see Hunt-Wesson, Inc.

Consumer Relations
Reebok International, Ltd.
100 Technology Center Drive
Stoughton, MA 02072
1 (800) 843-4444 (toll free)

Mr. Richard Jones
Customer Service Manager
The Regina Company
P.O. Box 638
Long Beach, MS 39560
1 (800) 847-8336 (toll free)

Ms. Cass Carroll
Director of Consumer Relations
Reliance Insurance Company
Four Penn Center Plaza
Philadelphia, PA 19103
(215) 864-4445
1 (800) 441-1652 (toll free)

Mr. Mitch Maples, Manager
Consumer Affairs
Remco America, Inc.
P.O. Box 42946
Houston, TX 77242-2946
(713) 977-2288

Customer Relations Department
Remington Products, Inc.
60 Main Street
Bridgeport, CT 06004
(203) 367-4400

Remington Rifle
see E.I. duPont de Nemours & Co.

Ms. Natalie Korman
Director, Consumer Relations
Revlon
625 Madison Avenue
New York, NY 10022
(212) 527-5644

Ms. Carol Owen, Director
Consumer Services
Reynolds Metals Company
6603 West Broad Street
Richmond, VA 23230
(804) 281-4073 (collect calls accepted)

Rhone-Poulenc Rorer Pharmaceuticals Inc.
Consumer Affairs Information Center
500 Virginia Drive
Fort Washington, PA 19034
1 (800) 548-3708 (toll free 8:30—4:30 EST)

Ms. Kathleen M. Fitzsimmons
Manager, Consumer Services
Richardson-Vicks, Inc.
One Far Mill Crossing
Shelton, CT 06484-0925
(203) 925-6000

Mr. Marce Seim
Coordinator, Consumer Relations
A. H. Robins Company, Inc.
1405 Cummings Drive
Richmond, VA 23261-6609
(804) 257-2000

Rockwell International Corporation
600 Grant St.
Pittsburgh, PA 15219-2884
(412) 565-2000

Rockport
see Reebok

Mrs. Jean Dorney
Assistant Director of Fulfillment Services
Rodale Press, Inc.
33 East Minor Street
Emmaus, PA 18049
1 (800) 441-7761 (toll free)

Mr. Patrick Puton
Service Manager
Rolex Watch U.S.A., Inc.
665 Fifth Avenue
New York, NY 10022
(212) 758-7700

Ms. Jan Bell, Director
Customer Service
Rollins, Inc.
2170 Piedmont Road, N.E.
Atlanta, GA 30324
(404) 888-2151

Mr. Leo VanVark, Manager
Customer Service
Rolscreen Company
102 Main Street
Pella, IA 50219
(515) 628-1000

Ms. Joanne Taddeo, Manager
Customer Relations
Ross Laboratories
625 Cleveland Avenue
Columbus, OH 43215
(614) 229-7900

Mr. Paul W. Carter, Director
Franchise Administration
Roto-Rooter Corporation
300 Ashworth Road
West Des Moines, IA 50265
(515) 223-1343

Roundup Lawn and Garden
see Greensweep

Ms. Wynelle Sanders, Marketing Secretary
Royal Oak Enterprises, Inc.
900 Ashwood Parkway, Suite 800
Atlanta, GA 30338

(404) 393-1430
1 (800) 241-3955 (toll free)

Mrs. Denice Kaack
Manager
Customer Service
Royal Silk Ltd.
45 East Madison Avenue
Clifton, NJ 07011

Royal Viking Cruise Line
see Kloster Cruise Ltd.

Ms. Ruth A. Chambers
Supervisor, Consumer Services
Rubbermaid, Inc.
1147 Akron Road
Wooster, OH 44691-0800
(216) 264-6464

Rustler Jeans
see Blue Bell, Inc.

Mr. Donald Berryman
Director, Customer Service
Ryder Truck Rental
P.O. Box 020816
Miami, FL 33102-0816
1 (800) 327-7777 (toll free)

Administrative Assistant to the President
Ryland Building Company
Ryland Group, Inc.
P.O. Box 4000
Columbia, MD 21044
(301) 730-7222

S

7 Eleven Food Stores
see The Southland Corporation

SFS Corporation
Customer Information Center
1 (800) 421-5013 (toll free)

Mr. Brian Dowling
Public Affairs Department Manager
Safeway Inc.
Oakland, CA 94660
(415) 891-3267

Ms. Victoria Loesch
Director, Corporate Customer Relations
Saks & Companies NY
450 West 15th Street
New York, NY 10011
(212) 940-5027

Samsonite Corporation
11200 E 45th Avenue
Denver, CO 80239-3000
(303) 373-2000

Sandoz Company
Sandoz Pharmaceuticals
59 Route 10
East Hanover, NJ 07936
(201) 503-7500

Sanyo Electric Inc.
see SFS Corporation

Sara Lee Corporation
Three First National Plaza
70 West Madison Street
Chicago, IL 60602-4260
(312) 726-2600

Ms. Watson Brooks
Manager, Consumer Relations
Schering-Plough HealthCare Products, Inc.
3030 Jackson Avenue
Memphis, TN 38151-0001
(901) 320-2998

Scholl
see Schering-Plough HealthCare Products, Inc.

Consumer Relations Department
Schwinn Bicycle Company
217 North Jefferson Street
Chicago, IL 60661-1111
1 (800) 633-0231 (toll free)

Ms. Janet Jones, Manager
Consumer Relations Operations
Scott Paper Company
Scott Plaza Two
Philadelphia, PA 19113
(215) 522-6170
1 (800) 835-7268 (toll free outside PA)

Shareholder Services Representative
Scudder Funds Distributor
160 Federal Street
Boston, MA 02110
1 (800) 225-2470 (toll free)

Joseph E. Seagram & Sons, Inc.
375 Park Avenue
New York, NY 10152
(212) 572-7147

Customer Service Representative
Sealy Mattress Manufacturing Company
1228 Euclid Avenue, 10th Floor
Cleveland, OH 44115
(216) 522-1310
(216) 522-1366 (TDD)

Mr. Ken Waldhof
Customer Affairs Manager
Seamans Furniture Company, Inc.
70 Charles Lindbergh Boulevard
Uniondale, NY 11553
(516) 227-1563
1 (800) 445-2503 (toll free)

Customer Service
G. D. Searle and Company Pharmaceuticals
P.O. Box 5110
Chicago, IL 60680
1 (800) 323-1603 (toll free)

Mr. Jerry Hauber
National Consumer Relations Manager
Sears, Roebuck & Co.
Department 731 CR, BSC 39-33
Sears Tower
Chicago, IL 60684
(312) 875-5188

Sedgefield Jeans
see Blue Bell, Inc.

Coserv
Seiko Corporation of America
27 McKee Drive
Mahwah, NJ 07430
(201) 529-3311

Ms. Rosemarie Martinez
Customer Relations Department
Serta, Inc.
2800 River Road
Des Plaines, IL 60018
(708) 699-9300

Seventeen Magazine
see News America Publishing, Inc.

Seven-Up
see Dr. Pepper

Mr. Vernon Brisson, General Manager
Customer Relations
Sharp Electronics Corporation
Sharp Plaza
P.O. Box 650
Mahwah, NJ 07430-2135
(201) 529-9140
1 (800) 526-0264 (toll free)

Customer Relations
The Sharper Image
650 Davis Street
San Francisco, CA 94111
1 (800) 344-5555 (toll free)

Mr. T. J. McPhail, Manager
Customer Services
Shell Oil Company
P.O. Box 80
Tulsa, OK 74102
(918) 496-4500
1 (800) 331-3703
(toll free—credit card inquiries)

Sheraton Hotels Corporation
60 State Street
Boston, MA 02109-6002
(617) 367-3600

Mr. Dave Schutz
Wholesale Marketing Administrator
Sherwin-Williams Company
101 Prospect Avenue, N.W.
Cleveland, OH 44115-1075
(216) 566-2000

Shoppers Department
Shoney's Inc.
1727 Elm Hill Pike
Nashville, TN 37210
(615) 391-5201

ShowBiz Pizza
see Integra

Showtime Networks, Inc.
see Viacom International, Inc.

Ms. Elaine Deaver, Vice President
Consumer/Marketing Services
Simmons Company
P.O. Box 95465
Atlanta, GA 30347
(404) 321-3030

Consumer Affairs Department
Sewing Products Division
Singer Sewing Company
P.O. Box 1909
Edison, NJ 08818-1909
(908) 287-0707

Mr. Mike Minchin
Executive Vice President
Sizzler International, Inc.
12655 West Jefferson Boulevard
Los Angeles, CA 90066
(310) 827-2300, ext 3324

Skaggs Company
see American Stores Company

Skoal Chewing Tobacco
see UST

Consumer Services Department
Slim•Fast Foods Company
919 Third Avenue
New York, NY 10022-3898
1 (800) 862-4500 (toll free)

Smith & Wesson
2100 Roosevelt Avenue
Springfield, MA 01104-1698
(413) 781-8300

Law and Compliance Department
Smith Barney, Harris Upham & Co., Inc.
333 West 34th Street
New York, NY 10001
(212) 356-2800

Consumer/Public Affairs Department
SmithKline Beecham Consumer Brands
P.O. Box 1467
Pittsburgh, PA 15230-1467
(412) 928-1000
1 (800) 245-1040 (toll free)

Ms. Vickie Limbach
Manager of Communications
J. M. Smucker Company
Strawberry Lane
Orrville, OH 44667-0280
(216) 682-3000

Snapper Power Equipment
McDonough, GA 30253
(404) 957-9141

Solar Nutritionals
see Thompson Medical Company

Mr. Paul Sonnabend, President
Sonesta International Hotels Corporation
200 Clarendon Street
Boston, MA 02116
(617) 421-5413

Ms. Kathryn M. O'Brien
Director, National Customer Relations
Sony Corporation of America
Sony Service Company
Sony Drive
Park Ridge, NJ 07656
(201) 930-7669
(NJ Consumer Information Center) (714) 821-7669
(CA Consumer Information Center) (708) 250-7669
(IL Consumer Information Center)

South Central Bell
see BellSouth Telephone Operations

Southern Bell Corporation
see BellSouth Telephone Operations

Mr. Jerry Snearly
National Consumer Services Manager
The Southland Corporation
P.O. Box 711
Dallas, TX 75221-0711
(214) 841-6642
1 (800) 255-0711 (toll free)

Mr. Jim Ruppel, Director
Customer Relations
Southwest Airlines
Love Field
P.O. Box 36611
Dallas, TX 75235-1657
(214) 904-4223
1 (800) 533-1305
(toll free TDD—reservations)

Executive Director
Corporate Communications
Southwestern Bell Corporation
1667 K Street, N.W., Suite 1000
Washington, D.C. 20006
(202) 293-8550

Ms. Shirley Brisbois
Manager, Consumer Relations
Spalding & Evenflo, Inc.
425 Meadow Street
P.O. Box 901
Chicopee, MA 01021-0901
(413) 536-1200
1 (800) 225-6601 (toll free)

Mr. Paul Weiske
Customer Service Manager
Speed Queen Company
P.O. Box 990
Ripon, WI 54971-0990
(414) 748-3121
(414) 748-4053 (TDD)

Supervisor
Customer Service Department
Spencer Gifts
MCA, Inc.
1050 Black Horse Pike
Pleasantville, NJ 08232
(609) 645-3300

Customer Service
Spiegel, Inc.
P.O. Box 927
Oak Brook, IL 60522-0927
(708) 954-2772

Springs Industries Inc.
Springmaid Home Fashions
Consumer Fashions Division
787 7th Avenue
New York, NY 10019
(212) 903-2100

Squibb
see Bristol-Myers Squibb Pharmaceutical Group

Mr. Jack Gauthier, Marketing Manager
Stanley Hardware
Division Stanley Works
480 Myrtle Street
New Britain, CT 06050
(203) 225-5111
1 (800) 622-4393 (toll free)

Mr. Jim Stahly
Public Relations Director
State Farm Mutual Automobile Insurance Company
One State Farm Plaza
Bloomington, IL 61710
(309) 766-2714

Consumer Affairs Section
Sterling Drug, Inc.
90 Park Avenue, 8th Floor
New York, NY 10016
(212) 907-2000
1 (800) 331-4536
(toll free—Glenbrook, Winthrop Consumer Products)

J. P. Stevens
see WestPoint Pepperell

Ms. Esther Rasmussen
Director, Consumer Relations
Stokely USA, Inc.
626 East Wisconsin Avenue
P.O. Box 248
Oconomowoc, WI 53066-0248
(414) 567-1731
1 (800) 872-1110 (toll free)

Ms. Christine Filardo
Director, Consumer Affairs
Stop & Shop Supermarket Company Inc.
P.O. Box 1942
Boston, MA 02103
(617) 770-8895

Ms. Frances D. Karpowicz, Manager
Consumer Affairs Department
Stouffer Foods Corporation
5750 Harper Road
Solon, OH 44139-1880
(216) 248-3600

President
Stouffer Restaurant Company
30050 Chagrin Boulevard
Cleveland, OH 44124
(216) 464-6606

Mr. Matthew Cook
Director, Consumer Relations
Strawbridge & Clothier
801 Market Street
Philadelphia, PA 19107
(215) 629-6722

Ms. Kathy Hatfield, Coordinator
Quality Assurance Administration
The Stroh Brewery Company
100 River Place
Detroit, MI 48207-4291
(313) 446-2000

Consumer Affairs
Sunbeam/Oster Housewares
8989 North Deerwood Drive
Brown Deer, WI 53223
(written inquiries only)

Ms. Donna Samelson, Manager
Consumer Relations

Sun-Diamond Growers of California
P.O. Box 1727
Stockton, CA 95201
(209) 467-6000

Subscriber Service
Sunset Magazine
Box 2040
Harlan, IA 51593-0003
1 (800) 777-0117 (toll free)

Ms. Noreen MacConchie
Manager, Customer Relations
Supermarkets General Corporation
301 Blair Road
Woodbridge, NJ 07095
(908) 499-3500

Mr. Doug Williams, Customer Service
Swatch Watch USA
1817 William Penn Way
Lancaster, PA 17604
(717) 394-5288
1 (800) 8-SWATCH (toll free)

Swift-Eckrich, Inc.
2001 Butterfield Road
Downers Grove, IL 60515
(708) 512-1000
1 (800) 325-7424 (toll free)

The Swiss Colony
Customer Service
1112 Seventh Avenue
Monroe, WI 53566
(608) 324-4000

Sylvania Television
see Philips Company

T

Ms. Deedee Kindy, Supervisor
Consumer Affairs
3M
3M Center, Building 225-5N-04
St. Paul, MN 55144-1000
(612) 733-1871

TJX Companies (T. J. Maxx)
770 Cochituate Rd.
Framingham, MA 01701
(508) 390-1000
1 (800) 926-6299 (toll free)

National Consumer Assistance Center
TRW Information Services
12606 Greenville Avenue
P.O. Box 749029
Dallas, TX 75374-9029
(214) 699-6111

T.V. Guide
see News America Publishing, Inc.

Customer Service
Talbots
175 Beal Street
Hingham, MA 02043
1 (800) 992-9010 (toll free)
1 (800) 624-9179 (toll free TDD)

Ms. Cindy Nothe
Manager, Consumer Services
TAMBRANDS, Inc.
P.O. Box 271
Palmer, MA 01069
(413) 283-3431
1 (800) 523-0014 (toll free)

Ms. Lucille Frey, Director
Customer Relations
Tandy Corporation/Radio Shack
1600 One Tandy Center
Fort Worth, TX 76102
(817) 390-3218

Tappan Company, Inc.
see White Consolidated Industries

Consumer Relations and Quality Assurance
Target Stores
33 South 6th Street
P.O. Box 1392
Minneapolis, MN 55440-1392
(612) 370-6056

Technics
see Matsushita Servicing Company

Mr. Richard C. Keller
Director, Consumer Affairs
Teledyne Water Pik
1730 East Prospect Street
Fort Collins, CO 80553-0001
(303) 484-1352
1 (800) 525-2774 (toll free)

Ms. Kathy Laffin, Supervisor
Customer Service
Teleflora
12233 West Olympic, Suite 140
Los Angeles, CA 90064-0780
(310) 826-5253
1 (800) 421-2815 (toll free)

Mr. Charles Funk
Telesphere
6000 Executive Boulevard, Suite 400
Rockville, MD 20852-3902
1 (800) 864-4060 (toll free)

Public Affairs
Tenneco, Inc.
P.O. Box 2511
Houston, TX 77001-2511
(713) 757-2131

Consumer Affairs Department
Tetley Inc.
100 Commerce Drive
P.O. Box 856
Shelton, CT 06484-0856
(203) 929-9342

Mr. W. D. Kistler
Manager, Customer Relations
Texaco Refining and Marketing
P.O. Box 2000
Bellaire, TX 77401-2000
(713) 432-2235
1 (800) 552-7827 (toll free)

Mr. Tom Thomas, Consumer Products
Texas Instruments Incorporated
P.O. Box 53
Lubbock, TX 79408-0053
(806) 741-2000
1 (800) 842-2737 (toll free)

Customer Service Representative

Thom McAn Shoe Co.
67 Millbrook Street
Worcester, MA 01606-2804
(508) 791-3811

Thompson & Formby, Inc.
825 Crossover Lane, Suite 240
Memphis, TN 38117
1 (800) FORMBYS (toll free)

Consumer Services Department
Thompson Medical Company, Inc.
222 Lakeview Avenue
West Palm Beach, FL 33401-6112
(407) 820-9900
1 (800) 521-7857 (toll free)

Ms. Janice Meikle, Vice President
Professional & Public Affairs
Thrift Drug, Inc.
615 Alpha Drive
Pittsburgh, PA 15238
(412) 963-6600
1 (800) 2-THRIFT (toll free)

Customer Service
Time Inc.
1 North Dale Mabry
Tampa, FL 33609
(813) 878-6100
1 (800) 541-1000 (toll free)

Corporate Public Affairs
Time Warner Inc.
75 Rockefeller Plaza
New York, NY 10019
(212) 484-6630

Ms. Letha Watkins
Consumer Correspondent
Timex Corporation
P.O. Box 2740
Little Rock, AR 72203-2740
(501) 372-1111
1 (800) 367-9282 (toll free)

Mr. Jim Percherke and Mr. Jeff Cline
Golf Division
National Consumer Relations
Titleist
P.O. Box B 965
New Bedford, MA 02741
1 (800) 225-8500 (toll free)

Tonka Products
see Hasbro Inc.

Tootsie Roll Industries Inc.
7401 Cicero Avenue
Chicago, IL 60629-5885
(312) 838-3400

Ms. Mary Elliott, Director
Communications and Public Affairs
The Toro Company
8111 Lyndale Avenue South
Minneapolis, MN 55420
(612) 887-8900

Mr. John Newman
Vice President of Service
Mr. Dave Byrnes
Administrative Manager of Service
Toshiba America Consumer Products, Inc.
Consumer Products Business Sector
1420 Toshiba Drive
Lebanon, TN 37087
(615) 449-2360

Ms. Helen Baur
Administrative Assistant
Totes, Incorporated
10078 East Kemper Road
Loveland, OH 45140
(513) 583-2300

Director, Consumer Complaints
Tourneau, Inc.
488 Madison Avenue
New York, NY 10022
(212) 758-3265
1 (800) 223-1288 (toll free outside NY)

Corporate Spokesperson
Toys "R" Us
461 From Road
Paramus, NJ 07652
(201) 599-7897

Ms. Thompson, Manager
Control Center
Trak Auto
3300 75th Avenue
Landover, MD 20785
(301) 731-1200

Trane/CAC, Inc.
see American Standard, Inc.

Trans Union Corporation

Western Region
1561 E. Orangethorpe
Fullerton, CA 92631

Southern Region
222 S. First Street
Louisville, KY 40202

North Eastern Region
1211 Chestnut Street
Philadelphia, PA 19107

Midwest
212 S. Market Street
Wichita, KS 67202

North Eastern Ohio
25249 Country Club Boulevard
N. Olmstead, OH 44070

Ms. Rosemary Aurichio
Director, Customer Relations
Trans World Airlines (TWA)
110 South Bedford Road
Mt. Kisco, NY 10549
(914) 242-3000
1 (800) 421-8480
(toll free TDD—reservations)

Office of Consumer Information
The Travelers Companies
One Tower Square
Hartford, CT 06183-1060
1 (800) 243-0191 (toll free)

Tropicana Products Inc.
1001 13th Avenue E
Bradenton, FL 34208-2699
(813) 747-4461

True Value Hardware Stores
see Cotter & Company

Ms. Chris Clark, Manager
Customer Services Department
Tupperware

P.O. Box 2353
Orlando, Fl 32802
(407) 847-3111
1 (800) 858-7221 (toll free)

Ms. Terri Tingle
Director, Public Affairs
Turner Broadcasting System Inc.
One CNN Center
Atlanta, GA 30335
(404) 827-1690

Ms. Karen Hanik
Consumer Correspondence Representative
Turtle Wax, Inc.
5655 West 73rd Street
Chicago, IL 60638-6211
(708) 563-3600
1 (800) 323-9883 (toll free)

Mr. Jerry Rasor
Manager, Quality Control
Tyco Industries
540 Glenn Avenue
Moorestown, NJ 08057
(609) 234-7714

Mr. Jay Benham
Manager, Consumer Relations
Tyson Foods
P.O. Box 2020
Springdale, AR 72765-2020
(501) 756-4714
1 (800) 233-6332 (toll free)

U

Ms. Elaine De Shong, Vice President
Marketing Consumer Service
U-Haul International
2727 North Central Avenue
Phoenix, AZ 85004-1120
(602) 263-6771
1 (800) 528-0463 (toll free outside AZ)

Mr. Alan Kaiser, Director
Corporate Communications
UST
100 West Putnam Avenue
Greenwich, CT 06830
(203) 661-1100

Union Fidelity Life Insurance Company
see Aon Corporation

Mr. Stephen A. Colton
Manager, Consumer Affairs
Uniroyal Goodrich Tire Company
600 South Main Street
Akron, OH 44397-0001
(216) 374-3796
1 (800) 521-9796 (toll free)

UNISYS Corporation
P.O. Box 500
Blue Bell, PA 19424-0001
(215) 986-4011

Mr. Paul Tinebra
Director of Customer Relations
United Airlines
P.O. Box 66100
Chicago, IL 60666
(312) 952-6168
1 (800) 323-0170
(toll free TDD—reservations)

Mr. Dick Porter
National Consumer Relations Manager
United Parcel Service of America, Incorporated
51 Weaver Street, OPS
Greenwich, CT 06831
(203) 862-6000

United States Fidelity & Guarantee Corporation
100 Light Street
Baltimore, MD 21203-1138
(301) 547-3000

Bette Malone® Relocation Service
United Van Lines, Inc.
One United Drive
Fenton, MO 63026
1 (800) 325-3870 (toll free)

Ms. Hattie Amer
Supervisor, Customer Service
Unocal Corporation
Room 1405
P.O. Box 7600
Los Angeles, CA 90051-7600
(213) 977-6728
1 (800) 527-5476 (toll free)

Consumer Products Division (over-the-counter)
Customer Service Unit (prescriptions)
Upjohn Company
7000 Portage Road
Kalamazoo, MI 49001
1 (800) 253-8600 (toll free)

Mrs. Deborah Thompson
Director, Consumer Affairs
USAir
4001 North Liberty Street
Winston-Salem, NC 27105
(919) 661-8126 (collect calls accepted)

Consumer Services Representative
U.S. Shoe Corporation
One Eastwood Drive
Cincinnati, OH 45227-1197
(513) 527-7590

Mr. Slobodan B. Ajdukovic, Supervisor
Executive Consumer Services
U.S. Sprint
8001 Stemmons Freeway
Dallas, TX 75247
(214) 688-5707
1 (800) 877-4646 (toll free)

U S WEST, Inc.
Orchard Falls Building
7800 E. Orchard Rd.
Englewood, CO 80111-2533
(303) 793-6500
1 (800) USW-HELP (toll free)
1 (800) 955-5833 (toll free TDD)

V

Consumer Relations Department
Valvoline Oil Company
3499 Dabney Drive
P.O. Box 14000
Lexington, KY 40512
(606) 264-7777

Van Heusen Company
281 Centennial Avenue
Piscataway, NJ 08854
(908) 685-0050

Mr. John McAna
Executive Vice President
Van Munching and Co., Inc.
1270 Avenue of the Americas, 10th Floor
New York, NY 10020
(212) 265-2685

Ms. Jan Still-Lindeman
Vanity Fair
640 Fifth Avenue
New York, NY 10019
(212) 582-6767
1 (800) 832-8662 (toll free)

Ms. Hilary E. Condit
Director, Corporate Relations
Viacom International Inc.
1515 Broadway
New York, NY 10036
(212) 258-6346

Mr. Peter Doane
Vice President/Treasurer
Vicorp Restaurants
400 West 48th Avenue
Denver, CO 80216
(303) 296-2121

Customer Relations
Visa USA, Inc.
P.O. Box 8999
San Francisco, CA 94128-8999
(415) 570-2900

Volkswagen of America, Inc.
888 W. Big Beaver Rd.
Troy, MI 48084-4736
(313) 362-6000

Volvo North America Corporation
7 Volvo Drive
Rockleigh, NJ 07647-2507
(201) 768-7300

Customer Service
Vons Companies Inc.
P.O. Box 3338
Los Angeles, CA 90054
(818) 821-7000

W

Customer Service Representative
Wagner Spray Tech Corporation
1770 Fernbrook Lane
Plymouth, MN 55447
(612) 553-7000
1 (800) 328-8251 (toll free)

Mr. Edward H. King, Director
Government and Corporate Relations
Walgreen Co.
200 Wilmot Road
Deerfield, IL 60015
(708) 940-3500
1 (800) 289-2273 (toll free)

Customer Relations
Wal-Mart Stores, Inc.
702 S.W. Eighth Street
Bentonville, AR 72716-0117
(501) 273-4000

Ms. Rebecca Pierce
Consumer Affairs Manager
Wamsutta Pacific
1285 Avenue of the Americas
34th Floor
New York, NY 10019
(212) 903-2000
1 (800) 344-2142 (toll free)

Wang Direct
Wang Laboratories Inc.
1001 Pawtucket Boulevard
Lowell, MA 01854
(508) 656-8000

Mr. George A. Silva
Manufacturing Vice President
Warnaco Men's Apparel
10 Water Street
Waterville, ME 04901
(207) 873-4241

Mr. Mitch Rosalsky, Director
Consumer Affairs Division
Warner-Lambert Company
201 Tabor Road
Morris Plains, NJ 07950
(201) 540-2459
1 (800) 223-0182 (toll free)
1 (800) 524-2624 (toll free—Parke Davis Products/over-the-counter)
1 (800) 742-8377 (toll free—Schick Razor)
1 (800) 562-0266 (toll free—EPT)
1 (800) 223-0182 (toll free—Warner-Lambert products)
1 (800) 524-2854 (toll free—Trident)
1 (800) 343-7805 (toll free TDD)

Customer Service
Weider Health and Fitness
615 West Johnson Avenue, Suite 3
Cheshire, CT 06410
1 (800) 423-5713 (toll free)

Ms. Karen Wegmann
Executive Vice President
Corporate Community Development Group
Wells Fargo & Company
420 Montgomery Street
MAC 0101-111
San Francisco, CA 94163
(415) 396-3832
(916) 322-1700 (TDD)

Ms. Susan Kosling
Consumer Relations Manager
Wendy's International, Inc.
P.O. Box 256
Dublin, OH 43017-0256
(614) 764-6800

Ms. Joanne Turchany
Manager of Consumer Information
West Bend Company
400 Washington Street
West Bend, WI 53095
(414) 334-2311

Mr. Russ A. Phillips
Director, Consumer Affairs
Western Union Financial Services

One Lake Street
Upper Saddle River, NJ 07458
(201) 818-6041

Ms. Jackie McWhorter
Consumer Affairs Coordinator
WestPoint Pepperell
P.O. Box 609
West Point, GA 31833-0609
1 (800) 533-8229 (toll free)

Mr. Don Skinner, Director
Customer Relations Department
Whirlpool Corporation
Administrative Center, 2000 M-63
Benton Harbor, MI 49022
(616) 926-5000
1 (800) 253-1301 (toll free)

Mr. Brian Wooden
Manager, Consumer Relations
White Consolidated Industries
6000 Perimeter Drive
Dublin, OH 43017
(614) 792-4100
1 (800) 451-7007
(toll free—Frigidaire Appliances)
1 (800) 485-1445
(toll free—Gibson Appliances)
1 (800) 323-7773
(toll free—Kelvinator Appliance Company)
1 (800) 537-5530
(toll free—O'Keefe & Merit Appliances)
1 (800) 537-5530
(toll free—Tappan Company, Inc.)
1 (800) 245-0600
(toll free—White Westinghouse)

White Westinghouse
see White Consolidated Industries

Ms. Terese Kaminskas
Corporate Communicator
Wickes Companies, Inc.
3340 Ocean Park Boulevard, Suite 2000
Santa Monica, CA 90405
(310) 452-0160

Customer Service
Williams-Sonoma
100 North Point Street
San Francisco, CA 94133
(415) 421-7900

Mr. C. H. McKellar
Executive Vice President
Winn Dixie Stores Inc.
Box B
Jacksonville, Fl 32203
(904) 783-5000

Mr. Steven R. Evenson
Owner Relations Manager
Winnebago Industries
P.O. Box 152
Forest City, IA 50436-0152
(515) 582-6939

Winthrop Consumer Products
see Sterling Drug, Inc.

Corporate Communications
Wisconsin Bell
722 North Broadway, 13th Floor
Milwaukee, WI 53202-4396
(414) 678-0681
1 (800) 237-8576 (toll free)
1 (800) 242-9393 (toll free TDD in WI)

Wonderbread
see Continental Baking Company

Customer Service
F. W. Woolworth Company
233 Broadway
New York, NY 10279-0001
(212) 553-2000

Customer Service
World Book Educational Products
101 Northwest Point Boulevard
Elk Grove Village, IL 60007-1192
1 (800) 621-8202 (toll free)

Wrangler Jeans
see Blue Bell, Inc.

Ms. Barbara Zibell
Consumer Affairs Coordinator
William Wrigley Jr. Company
410 North Michigan Avenue
Chicago, IL 60611
(312) 645-4076

X

Customer Relations
Xerox Corporation
100 Clinton Avenue South
Rochester, NY 14644
(716) 423-5480

Y

Ms. Lindsey Bice, Manager
Customer Relations
Yamaha Motor Corporation
6555 Katella Avenue
Cypress, CA 90630-5101
(714) 761-7439

Z

Ms. Renee Hoke, Director
Communications
Zale Corporation
901 West Walnut Hill Lane
Irving, TX 75038-1003
(214) 580-5104

Zayre Corporation
see TJX Companies

Mr. Don Knutson
Vice President, Customer Service
Zenith Data Systems
2150 East Lake Cook Road
Buffalo Grove, IL 60089
(708) 808-4697

Vice President, Consumer Affairs
Zenith Electronics Corporation
1000 Milwaukee Avenue
Glenview, IL 60025-2493
(708) 391-8100

TELEVISION NETWORKS, CABLE CHANNELS, AND RADIO

Networks

Capital Cities/ABC Inc.
24 E. 51st St.
New York, NY 10022-6887
(212) 421-9595
(212) 308-1398 FAX

Columbia Broadcasting System, Inc.
51 W. 52nd St.
New York, NY 10019-6101
(212) 975-4321
(212) 975-3286 FAX

National Broadcasting Co., Inc.
30 Rockefeller Plaza
New York, NY 10112-0001
(212) 664-4444
(212) 765-1478 FAX

Public Broadcasting Service
1320 Braddock Pl.
Alexandria, VA 22314-1698
(703) 739-5380
(703) 739-0775 FAX

Lifetime
Customer Relations
36-12 Thirty-fifth Ave.
Astoria, NY 11106
(718) 482-4120

MTV (Music Television)
1515 Broadway
New York, NY 10036
(212) 258-8700

The Nashville Network
Public Relations
2806 Opryland Dr.
Nashville, TN 37214
(615) 889-6840 ext. 6996

Nickelodeon
1515 Broadway
New York, NY 10036
(212) 258-7500

QVC
Customer Service
1365 Enterprise Dr.
West Chester, PA 19380
1 (800) 367-9444

Showtime/Movie Channel
Public Relations
1633 Broadway
New York, NY 10019
(212) 708-1600

TNT, CNN, TBS, CNN Headline
Viewer Services
One CNN Center
P.O. Box 105366
Atlanta, GA 30348-5366
(404) 827-1500

USA Network
1230 Avenue of the Americas
New York, NY 10020
(212) 408-9100

The Weather Channel
Viewer Services
2600 Cumberland Parkway
Atlanta, GA 30339
(404) 434-6800 ext. 529

VH-1
1515 Broadway
New York, NY 10036
(212) 258-7840

Radio

Corporation for Public Broadcasting
901 E St. NW
Washington, DC 20004
(202) 879-9600

National Public Radio
2025 M St. NW
Washington, DC 20036-3348
(202) 822-2000
(202) 822-2329 FAX

PBS (Public Broadcasting Service)
609 5th Ave.
New York, NY 10017

MAGAZINES

Toll free numbers for subscription and customer service of some of the more popular magazines.

Business Week		**(800) 635-1200**
Entertainment Weekly	(orders)	**(800) 541-3000**
	(customer service)	**(800) 541-1000**
Fortune Magazine	(orders)	**(800) 541-3000**
	(customer service)	**(800) 541-1000**
Life Magazine	(orders)	**(800) 541-3000**
	(customer service)	**(800) 541-1000**
Money Magazine	(orders)	**(800) 541-3000**
	(customer service)	**(800) 541-1000**
National Geographic Society		**(800) 638-4077**
Newsweek Inc.		**(800) 631-1040**
People Magazine	(orders)	**(800) 541-3000**
	(customer service)	**(800) 541-1000**
Readers Digest		**(800) 431-1246**
Sports Illustrated	(orders)	**(800) 541-3000**
	(customer service)	**(800) 541-1000**
Time Magazine	(orders)	**(800) 541-3000**
	(customer service)	**(800) 541-1000**
US News & World Report		**(800) 334-1313**

NEW CAR BUYING GUIDE

Buying a new car is usually the second most expensive purchase many consumers make, after the purchase of their home. According to the U.S. Department of Commerce, the average cost of a new car sold in the United States in 1985—the latest figures available—was $11,860.

Buying Your New Car

Before you step into a dealer's showroom, it helps to know what car model and options you want and how much you are willing to spend. That way, you are less likely to feel pressured into making a hasty or expensive decision and more likely to get a better deal. To help you shop, you may want to consider the following suggestions:

- Check publications at a library or bookstore that discuss new car features and prices. These may provide information on the dealer's costs for specific models and options.
- Shop around to get the best possible price by comparing models and prices at dealer showrooms. You also may want to contact car buying services and broker buying services and make comparisons there.
- Plan to negotiate on price. Dealers may be willing to bargain on their profit margin, which is generally between 15 to 20 percent. This is usually the difference between the manufacturer's suggested retail price and the invoice price.
- Consider ordering your new car if you do not see the car you want on the dealer's lot. This usually involves a delay, but cars on the lot frequently have options you do not want—which add considerably to the cost.

Learning the Terms

To give you a better sense of the negotiating room you have when buying your car, it helps to understand the following terms, listed here in order of increasing price:

INVOICE PRICE is the manufacturer's initial charge to the dealer. This is usually higher than the dealer's final cost because dealers often receive rebates, allowances, discounts, and incentive awards. The invoice price always includes freight (also known as destination and delivery). If you are buying a car based on the invoice price (for example, "at invoice," "$100 below invoice," "two percent above invoice"), be sure freight is not added to the sales contract.

BASE PRICE is the cost of the car without options, but includes standard equipment, factory warranty, and freight. This price is printed on the Monroney sticker (see below).

MONRONEY STICKER PRICE, which appears on a label affixed to the car window and is required by federal law, shows the base price, the manufacturer's installed options with the manufacturer's suggested retail price, the manufacturer's transportation charge, and the fuel economy (mileage). The label may not be removed by anyone other than the purchaser.

DEALER STICKER PRICE, usually on a supplemental sticker, is the Monroney sticker price plus the suggested retail price of dealer-installed options, such as additional dealer mark-up (ADM) or additional dealer profit (ADP), dealer preparation, and undercoating.

Financing Your New Car

If you decide to finance your car, you have the option of checking the dealer's rate against banks, credit unions, savings and loans institutions, and other loan companies. Because interest rates vary, shop around for the best deal and compare the annual percentage rates (APR).

Sometimes, dealers offer very low financing rates for specific cars or models, but may not be willing to negotiate on the price of these cars. In addition, they may require you to make a large downpayment to qualify for these special interest rates. With these conditions, you may find that it is sometimes more affordable to pay higher financing charges on a car that is lower in price or to purchase a car that requires a smaller downpayment.

Some dealers and lenders may ask you to buy credit insurance, which pays off your loan if you should die or become disabled. Before you add this cost, you may want to consider the benefits available from existing policies you may have. Remember, buying credit insurance is not required for a loan.

Trading in Your Old Car

After getting your new car for the best possible price, only then discuss the possibility of a trade-in. First, however, find out the value of your old car. You may want to check the library for references and periodicals that can tell you how much your car is worth. This information may help you get a better overall price from the dealer. Remember, too, that though it may take longer, you generally will get more money by selling the car yourself.

Considering a Service Contract

Service contracts that you may buy with a new car provide for the repair of certain specified parts or problems. These contracts are offered by manufacturers, dealers, or independent companies and usually initially run concurrently with the manufacturer's warranty. Remember: a warranty is included in the price of the car; a service contract costs extra.

Before deciding to purchase a service contract, read it carefully and consider some of the following questions:

- What is the difference between the coverage under the warranty and the coverage under the service contract?
- What repairs are covered?
- Who pays for the labor? The parts?
- Who performs the repairs? Can repairs be made elsewhere?
- How long does the service contract last?
- What is the cancellation and refund policy?

For Further Information

In addition to checking publications about new car features and prices when buying a car, you may find it helpful to read Federal Trade Commission brochures. These include "Car Ads: Low Interest Loans and Other Offers," "Service Contracts," "Warranties," "Buying a Used Car," and "A Consumer Guide to Vehicle Leasing." For a free copy write Public Reference, Federal Trade Commission, Washington, D.C. 20580. For further information, you may want to write to Division of Marketing Practices, Federal Trade Commission, Washington, D.C. 20580. Although the FTC generally does not intervene in individual consumer disputes, it can take action if there is evidence of a pattern of deceptive or unfair practices.

Checklist for Buying a New Car

You are likely to get a better deal on a car if you know beforehand exactly what you are looking for and what you are willing to spend. Therefore, before signing a sales contract with a car dealer, you may want to:

- Decide which car model and specific options you want.
- Find out the invoice price (the lowest price) of the model and each option you want.
- Decide how much you are willing to pay the dealer, if anything, above the invoice price.
- Compare final sales prices with other dealers and buying services.
- Compare financing costs from various sources, such as credit unions and savings and loan institutions, with those of car dealers.
- Find out the value of your old car, independent of a dealer's trade-in offer.
- Decide if you need an optional service contract or credit insurance.

Car Ads: Low Interest Loans and Other Offers

Many new car dealers have been advertising unusually low interest rates and other special promotions such as high trade-in allowances and free or low-cost options. While these advertisements may help you shop, finding the best deal requires careful comparison.

There are many factors that determine whether a special offer provides genuine savings. The interest rate, for example, is only part of the car dealer's financing package. Other terms, such as the size of the downpayment, also affect the total financing cost. Be sure to consider *all* aspects of a financing plan before you sign a contract.

When considering an advertised special, read the ad carefully and call or visit the dealer to find out about all the terms and conditions of the offer. Then compare the specials advertised by other dealers.

Low Interest Loans

Listed below are some financing questions you should consider when talking to dealers.

- Will you be charged a higher price for the car to qualify for the low-rate financing? Would the price be lower if you paid cash, or supplied your own financing from your bank or credit union?

- Does the financing require a larger-than-usual downpayment? Perhaps 25 or 30 percent?
- Are there limits on the length of the loan? In other words, are you required to repay the loan in a short period of time, such as 24 or 36 months?
- Do you have to buy special or extra merchandise or services such as rustproofing, an extended warranty, or a service contract to qualify for a low interest loan?
- Is the financing available for a limited time only? Some merchants limit special deals to a few days or require that you take delivery by a specified date.
- Does the low rate apply to all cars in stock or only to certain models?
- Are you required to give the dealer the manufacturer's rebate (if one is offered) to qualify for financing?

Other Promotions

Other special promotions include high trade-in allowances and free or low-cost options. Some dealers also promise to sell you a car for a stated amount over the "dealer's invoice." The following questions can help you determine if such special promotions offer genuine value.

- Does the advertised trade-in allowance apply to all cars, regardless of their condition? Are there any deductions for high mileage, dents, or rust?
- Does the larger trade-in allowance make the cost of the new car higher than it would be without the trade-in? You might be giving back the big trade-in allowance by paying more for your new car.
- Is the dealer who offers high trade-in allowance and free or low-cost options actually giving you a better price on the car than another dealer who does not offer such promotions?
- Does the "dealer's invoice" reflect the actual amount that the dealer pays the manufacturer? You can consult consumer or automotive publications for information about what the dealer pays.
- Does the "dealer's invoice" include the cost of options, such as rustproofing or waterproofing, that have already been added to your car? Is the dealer charging more for these options than other dealers?
- Does the dealer have cars in stock without expensive added options? If not, will the dealer order one for you?
- Are the special offers available if you order a car instead of buying one off the lot?
- Can you take advantage of all special offers simultaneously?

Remember, you are not limited to financing offered by the dealer. You may wish to see what type of loan you can arrange with your bank or credit union.

Once you decide which dealer offers the car and financing you want, read the invoice and the installment contract carefully. Check to see that all the terms of the contract reflect the agreement you made with the dealer. If they differ, get a written explanation before you sign. Careful shopping will help you decide what financing, car, and options are best for you.

CAR MANUFACTURERS

If you have a problem with a car purchased from a local dealer, first try to work it out with the dealer. If an agreement cannot be reached, contact the manufacturer's regional or national office. Many of these offices are listed in this section.

If the regional office cannot resolve the problem, you might wish to contact one of the third-party dispute resolution programs.

All of the toll-free "800" numbers in the following list can be reached from anywhere in the continental United States.

ACURA

Customer Relations Department
ACURA
1919 Torrance Boulevard
Torrance, CA 90501-2746
1 (800) 382-2238 (toll free)

Alfa-Romeo Distributors of North America, Inc.

Customer Service Manager
Alfa-Romeo Distributors of North America, Inc.
8259 Exchange Drive
P.O. Box 598026
Orlando, FL 32859-8026
(407) 856-5000

American Honda Motor Company, Inc.

California
Customer Relations Department
American Honda Motor Company, Inc.
Western Zone
700 Van Ness Boulevard
Torrance, CA 90509-2260
(310) 781-4565

Utah, Arizona, Colorado, New Mexico, Nebraska, Kansas, Oklahoma, Nevada, Texas (El Paso)
Customer Relations Department
American Honda Motor Company, Inc.
West Central Zone
1600 South Abilene Street, Suite D
Aurora, CO 80012-5815
(303) 696-3935

Maine, Vermont, New Hampshire, New York State (excluding NY City, its five boroughs, Long Island, Westchester County), Connecticut (excluding Fairfield County), Massachusetts, Rhode Island
Customer Relations Department
American Honda Motor Company, Inc.
New England Zone
555 Old County Road
Windsor Locks, CT 06096-0465
(203) 623-3310

Tennessee, Alabama, Georgia, Florida
Customer Relations Department
American Honda Motor Company, Inc.
Southeastern Zone
1500 Morrison Parkway
Alpharetta, GA 30201-2199
(404) 442-2045 (collect calls accepted)

Minnesota, Iowa, Missouri, Wisconsin, Illinois, Michigan (Upper Peninsula)
Customer Relations Department
American Honda Motor Company, Inc.
North Central Zone
601 Campus Drive, Suite A-9
Arlington Heights, IL 60004-1407
(708) 870-5600

West Virginia, Maryland, Virginia, North Carolina, South Carolina, District of Columbia
Customer Relations Department
American Honda Motor Company, Inc.
Mid-Atlantic Zone Office
902 Wind River Lane, Suite 200
Gaithersburg, MD 20878-1974
(301) 990-2020

Ohio (Steubenville), West Virginia (Wheeling), Pennsylvania, New Jersey, Delaware, New York (NY City, its five boroughs, Long Island, Westchester County), Connecticut (Fairfield County)
Customer Relations Department
American Honda Motor Company, Inc.
Northeast Zone
115 Gaither Drive
Moorestown, NJ 08057-0337
(609) 235-5533

Michigan (except for Upper Peninsula), Indiana, Ohio, Kentucky
Customer Relations Department
American Honda Motor Company, Inc.
Central Zone
101 South Stanfield Road
Troy, OH 45373-8010
(513) 332-6250

Washington, Oregon, Idaho, Montana, Wyoming, North Dakota, South Dakota, Hawaii, Alaska
Customer Relations Department
American Honda Motor Company, Inc.
Northwest Zone
12439 N.E. Airport Way
Portland, OR 97220-0186
(503) 256-0943

Texas (excluding El Paso), Arkansas (excluding Fayetteville, Bentonville, Fort Smith, Jonesboro), Oklahoma (Lawton, Ardmore), Louisiana, Mississippi
Customer Relations Department
American Honda Motor Company, Inc.
South Central Zone
4529 Royal Lane
Irving, TX 75063-2583
(214) 929-5481

Corporate Office:
American Honda Motor Company, Inc.
Consumer Affairs Department
1919 Torrance Boulevard
Torrance, CA 90501-2746
(310) 783-3260

American Isuzu Motors, Inc.

California
Mr. Neil Wiggins
Regional Customer Relations Manager
American Isuzu Motors, Inc.
One Autry Street
Irvine, CA 92718-2785
(714) 770-2626

Alabama, Florida, Georgia, Mississippi, North Carolina, South Carolina
Regional Customer Relations Manager
American Isuzu Motors, Inc.
Southeast Region
205 Hembree Park Drive
P.O. Box 6250
Roswell, GA 30076
(404) 475-1995

Illinois, Indiana, Iowa, Michigan, Minnesota, Missouri, North Dakota, Ohio, Wisconsin
Regional Customer Relations Manager
American Isuzu Motors, Inc.
Central Region
1830 Jarvis Avenue
Elk Grove Village, IL 60007
(708) 952-8111

Connecticut, Maine, Massachusetts, New Hampshire, New Jersey (north of Toms River), New York, Rhode Island, Vermont
Regional Customer Relations Manager
American Isuzu Motors, Inc.
Northeast Region
156 Ludlow Avenue
P.O. Box 965
Northvale, NJ 07647-0965
(201) 784-1414

Arizona, Arkansas, Kansas, Louisiana, Nevada (southern), New Mexico, Oklahoma, Texas
Regional Customer Relations Manager
American Isuzu Motors, Inc.
Southwest Region
1150 Isuzu Parkway
Grand Prairie, TX 75050
(214) 647-2911

Alaska, Hawaii, Idaho, Montana, Nevada (Northern), Oregon, Utah, Washington, Wyoming, Colorado, Nebraska, South Dakota
Regional Customer Relations Manager
American Isuzu Motors, Inc.
Northwest Region
8727 148th Avenue, N.E.
Redmond, WA 98052
(206) 881-0203

New Jersey (south of Toms River), Pennsylvania, Maryland, Delaware, Kentucky, Tennessee, Virginia, West Virginia
Regional Customer Relations Manager
American Isuzu Motors, Inc.
1 Isuzu Way
Glen Burnie, MD 21061
(301) 761-2121

Headquarters:
American Isuzu Motors, Inc.
13181 Crossroads Parkway North
P.O. Box 2480
City of Industry, CA 91746-0480
(310) 699-0500
1 (800) 255-6727 (toll free)

American Motors Corporation
see **Jeep/Eagle Division of Chrysler Motors Corporation**

American Suzuki Motor Corporation

3251 E. Imperial Highway
Brea, CA 92621-6722
Attn: Customer Relations Department
Automobiles
1 (800) 934-0934, ext. 445 (toll free)
Motorcycles
(714) 996-7040, ext. 380

Audi of America, Inc.

Connecticut, New Jersey, New York
Director, Corporate Service

World-Wide Volkswagen Corp.
Greenbush Road
Orangeburg, NY 10962
(914) 578-5000

Corporate Office *(and all other states):*
Consumer Relations Manager
Audi of America, Inc.
888 West Big Beaver Road
Troy, MI 48007-3951
1 (800) 822-AUDI (toll free)

BMW of North America, Inc.

Arizona, California, Nevada, Oregon, Washington, Montana, Idaho, Arizona, Alaska, Hawaii, Colorado, Utah, New Mexico, Wyoming, Texas (El Paso)
Customer Relations Manager
BMW of North America, Inc.
Western Region
12541 Beatrice Street
P.O. Box 66916
Los Angeles, CA 90066
(310) 574-7300

Tennessee, North Carolina, Virginia (except northern), Mississippi, Alabama, Georgia, Florida, South Carolina, Louisiana, Oklahoma, Arkansas, Texas (except El Paso)
Customer Relations Manager
BMW of North America, Inc.
Southern Region
1280 Hightower Trail
Atlanta, GA 30350-2977
(404) 552-3800

North Dakota, South Dakota, Minnesota, Wisconsin, Iowa, Illinois, Michigan, Indiana, Ohio, Kentucky, Kansas, Missouri, Nebraska
Customer Relations Manager
BMW of North America, Inc.
Central Region
498 East Commerce Drive
Schaumburg, IL 60173
(708) 310-2700

Connecticut, Maine, Massachusetts, New Hampshire, New Jersey, New York, Rhode Island, Vermont, Washington, D.C., Virginia (northern), West Virginia, Delaware, Maryland, Pennsylvania
Customer Relations Manager
BMW of North America, Inc.
Eastern Region
BMW Plaza
Montvale, NJ 07645
(201) 573-2100

Corporate Office:
National Customer Relations Manager
BMW of North America, Inc.
P.O. Box 1227
Westwood, NJ 07675-1227
(201) 307-4000

Chrysler Motors Corporation

Phoenix Zone Office
Customer Relations Manager
Chrysler Motors Corporation
11811 N. Tatum Boulevard, Suite 4025
Phoenix, AZ 85028
(602) 953-6899

Los Angeles Zone Office
Customer Relations Manager
Chrysler Motors Corporation
P.O. Box 14112
Orange, CA 92668-4600
(714) 565-5111

San Francisco Zone Office
Customer Relations Manager
Chrysler Motors Corporation
P.O. Box 5009
Pleasanton, CA 94566-0509
(415) 463-1770

Denver Zone Office
Customer Relations Manager
Chrysler Motors Corporation
P.O. Box 39006
Denver, CO 80239
(303) 373-8888

Orlando Zone Office
Customer Relations Manager
Chrysler Motors Corporation
8000 South Orange Blossom Trail
Orlando, FL 32809
(407) 352-7402

Atlanta Zone Office
Customer Relations Manager
Chrysler Motors Corporation
900 Circle 75 Parkway, Suite 1600
Atlanta, GA 30339
(404) 953-8880

Chicago Zone Office
Customer Relations Manager
Chrysler Motors Corporation
650 Warrenville Road, Suite 502
Lisle, IL 60532
(708) 515-2450

Kansas City Zone Office
Customer Relations Manager
Chrysler Motors Corporation
P.O. Box 25668
Overland Park, KS 66225-5668
(913) 469-3090

New Orleans Zone Office
Customer Relations Manager
Chrysler Motors Corporation
P.O. Box 157
Metairie, LA 70004
(504) 838-8788

Washington, D.C. Zone Office
Customer Relations Manager
Chrysler Motors Corporation

P.O. Box 1900
Bowie, MD 20716
(301) 464-4040

Boston Zone Office
Customer Relations Manager
Chrysler Motors Corporation
550 Forbes Boulevard
Mansfield, MA 02048-2038
(508) 261-2299

Detroit Zone Office
Customer Relations Manager
Chrysler Motors Corporation
P.O. Box 3000
Troy, MI 48007-3000
(313) 952-1300

Minneapolis Zone Office
Customer Relations Manager
Chrysler Motors Corporation
P.O. Box 1231
Minneapolis, MN 55440
(612) 553-2546

St. Louis Zone Office
Customer Relations Manager
Chrysler Motors Corporation
P.O. Box 278
Hazelwood, MO 63042
(314) 895-0731

Syracuse Zone Office
Customer Relations Manager
Chrysler Motors Corporation
P.O. Box 603
Dewitt, NY 13214-0603
(315) 445-6941

New York Zone Office
Customer Relations Manager
Chrysler Motors Corporation
500 Route 303
Tappan, NY 10983-1592
(914) 359-0110

Charlotte Zone Office
Customer Relations Manager
Chrysler Motors Corporation
4944 Parkway Plaza Boulevard
Suite 470
Charlotte, NC 28217
(704) 357-7065

Cincinnati Zone Office
Customer Relations Manager
Chrysler Motors Corporation
P.O. Box 41902
Cincinnati, OH 45241
(513) 530-1500

Portland Zone Office
Customer Relations Manager
Chrysler Motors Corporation
P.O. Box 744
Beaverton, OR 97075
(503) 526-5555

Philadelphia Zone Office
Customer Relations Manager
Chrysler Motors Corporation
Valley Brook Corporate Center
101 Linden Wood Drive, Suite 320
Malvern, PA 19355
(215) 251-2990

Pittsburgh Zone Office
Customer Relations Manager
Chrysler Motors Corporation
Penn Center West 3, Suite 420
Pittsburgh, PA 15276
(412) 788-6622

Memphis Zone Office
Customer Relations Manager
Chrysler Motors Corporation
P.O. Box 18008
Memphis, TN 38181-0008
(901) 797-3870

Dallas Zone Office
Customer Relations Manager
Chrysler Motors Corporation
P.O. Box 110162
Carrollton, TX 75011-0162
(214) 242-8462

Houston Zone Office
Customer Relations Manager
Chrysler Motors Corporation
363 North Sam Houston Parkway East
Suite 590
Houston, TX 77060-2405
(713) 820-7062

Milwaukee Zone Office
Customer Relations Manager
Chrysler Motors Corporation
445 South Moorland Road, Suite 470
Brookfield, WI 53005
(414) 797-3750

Corporate Office:
Mr. R. T. Smith
National Owner Relations Manager
Chrysler Motors Corporation
P.O. Box 1086
Detroit, MI 48288-1086
1 (800) 992-1997 (toll free)

Ferrari North America, Inc.

Corporate Office:
Mr. Kenneth McCay
Director of Service and Parts
Ferrari North America, Inc.
250 Sylvan Avenue
Englewood Cliffs, NJ 07632
(201) 816-2650

Ford Motor Company

Customer Relations Manager
Ford Motor Company
300 Renaissance Center
P.O. Box 43360
Detroit, MI 48243
1 (800) 392-3673 (toll free—all makes)
1 (800) 521-4140
(toll free—Lincoln and Merkur only)
1 (800) 241-3673
(toll free—towing and dealer location service)
1 (800) 232-5952 (toll free TDD)

General Motors Corporation

Customer Assistance Center
Chevrolet/Geo Motor Division
General Motors Corporation
P.O. Box 7047
Troy, MI 48007-7047
1 (800) 222-1020 (toll free)
1 (800) TDD-CHEV (toll free TDD)

Customer Assistance Center
Pontiac Division
General Motors Corporation
One Pontiac Plaza
Pontiac, MI 48340-2952
1 (800) 762-2737 (toll free)
1 (800) TDD-PONT (toll free TDD)

Customer Assistance Network
Oldsmobile Division
General Motors Corporation
P.O. Box 30095
Lansing, MI 48909-7595
1 (800) 442-6537 (toll free)
1 (800) TDD-OLDS (toll free TDD)

Customer Assistance Center
Buick Motor Division
General Motors Corporation
902 East Hamilton Avenue
Flint, MI 48550
1 (800) 521-7300 (toll free)
1 (800) TD-BUICK (toll free TDD)

Consumer Relations Center
Cadillac Motor Car Division
General Motors Corporation
2860 Clark Street
Detroit, MI 48232
1 (800) 458-8006 (toll free)
1 (800) TDD-CMCC (toll free TDD)

Customer Service Department
GMC Truck Division
General Motors Corporation
Mail Code 1607-07
31 Judson Street
Pontiac, MI 48342
(313) 456-4547
1 (800) TDD-TKTD (toll free TDD)

Saturn Assistance Center
Saturn Corporation
General Motors Corporation
100 Saturn Parkway
Spring Hill, TN 37174
1 (800) 553-6000 (toll free)
1 (800) TDD-6000 (toll free TDD)

Mr. Duane E. Poole
Director, Public Relations
GM Service Parts Operations
6060 West Bristol Road
Flint, MI 48554-2110
(313) 635-5412

Honda
see American Honda Motor Company, Inc.

Hyundai Motor America

Customer Service
Hyundai Motor America
10550 Talbert Avenue
P.O. Box 20850
Fountain Valley, CA 92728-0850
1 (800) 633-5151 (toll free)

Isuzu
see American Isuzu

Jaguar Cars, Inc.

Alaska, Arizona, California, Colorado, Hawaii, Idaho, Montana, Nevada, New Mexico, Oregon, Utah, Washington, Wyoming, Texas (El Paso)
Western Zone
Customer Relations Manager
Jaguar Cars, Inc.
422 Valley Drive
Brisbane, CA 94005
(415) 467-9402

Eastern Zone *(all other states)*
Customer Relations Manager
Jaguar Cars, Inc.
555 MacArthur Boulevard
Mahwah, NJ 07430-2327
(201) 818-8500

Jeep/Eagle Division of Chrysler Motors Corporation
see Chrysler Zone and National Offices

Mazda Motor of America, Inc.

Corporate Headquarters:
Customer Relations Manager
Mazda Motor of America, Inc.
P.O. Box 19734
Irvine, CA 92718
1 (800) 222-5500 (toll free)

Mercedes-Benz of North America, Inc.

National Headquarters:
Mercedes-Benz of North America
1 Mercedes Drive
Montvale, NJ 07645-0350
(201) 573-0600 (Owner Service)

North Central Region Office
3333 Charles Street
Franklin Park, IL 60131-1469

Northeast Region Office
Baltimore Commons Business Park
1300 Mercedes Drive (2nd Floor)
Hanover, MD 21076-0348

Southern Region Office
8813 Western Way
Jacksonville, FL 32245-7604

Western Region Office
6357 Sunset Boulevard
Hollywood, CA 90093-0637

Mitsubishi Motor Sales of America, Inc.

Corporate Office:
National Consumer Relations Manager
Mitsubishi Motor Sales of America, Inc.
6400 West Katella Avenue
Cypress, CA 90630-0064
1 (800) 222-0037 (toll free)

Nissan Motor Corporation in USA

P.O. Box 191
Gardena, CA 90248-0191
1 (800) 647-7261
(toll free—all consumer inquiries)

Peugeot Motors of America, Inc.

Mr. William J. Atanasio
National Consumer Relations Manager
Peugeot Motors of America, Inc.
P.O. Box 607
One Peugeot Plaza
Lyndhurst, NJ 07071-3498
(201) 935-8400
1 (800) 345-5549 (toll free)

Porsche Cars North America, Inc.

Customer Relations Manager
Porsche Cars North America, Inc.
100 West Liberty Street
P.O. Box 30911
Reno, NV 89520-3911
(702) 348-3154

Saab Cars USA, Inc.

National Consumer Relations
P.O. Box 697
Orange, CT 06477
(203) 795-5671
1 (800) 955-9007 (toll free)

Subaru of America

Arizona, California, Nevada
Owner Service Manager
Subaru of America, Western Region
12 Whatney Drive
Irvine, CA 92718-2895
(714) 951-6592

Alabama, Georgia, North Carolina, South Carolina, Florida, Tennessee, West Virginia, Virginia, Maryland, Washington, D.C.
Owner Service Manager
Southeast Region Subaru
220 The Bluffs
Austell, GA 30001
(404) 732-3200

Illinois, Indiana, Iowa, Kentucky, Michigan, Minnesota, Missouri, Ohio, Wisconsin
Owner Service Manager
Subaru Mid-America Region
301 Mitchell Court
Addison, IL 60101
(708) 953-1188

Maine, Vermont, New Hampshire, Massachusetts, Rhode Island, Connecticut
Customer Relations Manager
Subaru of New England, Inc.
95 Morse Street
Norwood, MA 02062
(617) 769-5100

Southern New Jersey, Pennsylvania, Delaware
Customer Relations Manager
Penn Jersey Region
1504 Glen Avenue
Moorestown, NJ 08057
(609) 234-7600

New York, Northern New Jersey
Customer Relations Manager
Subaru Distributors Corporation
6 Ramland Road
Orangeburg, NY 10962
(914) 359-2500

Hawaii
Schuman-Carriage Co. Inc.
1234 South Beretania Street
P.O. Box 2420
Honolulu, HI 96804
(808) 533-6211

Alaska, Idaho, Montana, Nebraska, Oregon, Utah, Washington, North Dakota, South Dakota, Wyoming
Owner Service Manager
Subaru of America Northwest Region
8040 East 33rd Drive
Portland, OR 97211
1 (800) 878-6677 (toll free)

Arkansas, Colorado, Kansas, New Mexico, Mississippi, Oklahoma, Texas
Owner Service Manager
Subaru of America Southwest Region
1500 East 39th Avenue
Aurora, CO 80011
(303) 373-8895

Corporate Office:
Owner Service Department
Subaru of America
P.O. Box 6000
Cherry Hill, NJ 08034-6000
(609) 488-3278

Toyota Motor Sales, Inc.

Customer Assistance Center
Toyota Motor Sales USA, Inc.
Department A404
19001 South Western Avenue
Torrance, CA 90509
1 (800) 331-4331 (toll free)

Volkswagen United States, Inc.

Connecticut, New Jersey, New York
Director of Corporation Service
World-Wide Volkswagen, Inc.

Greenbush Road
Orangeburg, NY 10962
(914) 578-5000
1 (800) 822-8987 (toll free)

For all other locations:
Consumer Relations
Volkswagen United States, Inc.
888 West Big Beaver
Troy, MI 48007
General assistance and customer relations
1 (800) 822-8987 (toll free)

Volvo Cars of North America

Corporate Office:
Operations Manager
Volvo Cars of North America
15 Volvo Drive, Building D
P.O. Box 914
Rockleigh, NJ 07647-0914
(201) 767-4737

Yugo America, Inc.

Director, Customer Services
Yugo America, Inc.
120 Pleasant Avenue
P.O. Box 730
Upper Saddle River, NJ 07458-0730
(201) 825-4600

CONSUMER AND PUBLIC INFORMATION HOTLINES

This is a list of Consumer and Information hotlines for information and help both from private industry and nonprofit organizations.

Al-Anon Family Group Headquarters, Inc.
New York, NY
(800) 356-9996

Alcohol & Drug Treatment Prevention
College Park, MD
(800) 635-7619

American Council on Alcoholism
Towsen, MD
(800) 527-5344

Ford, Betty, Center
(800) 854-9211 (ex. CA)

National Council on Alcoholism
New York, NY
(800) 622-2255

Alexander Graham Bell Assoc. for the Deaf
(800) 225-4817 (ex DC)

AIDS
(800) 342-AIDS

Alzheimer's Disease & Related Disorders Assoc.
(800) 272-3900 (ex IL)
(800) 572-6037 (in IL)

American Cancer Society-Public Information
(800) 227-2345

American Council of Blind
(800) 424-8666 (ex DC)

American Sudden Infant Death Syndrome Institute
(800) 232-7437 (ex GA)

Arizona Heart Institute
(800) 345-4278

Arthritis Medical Center
(800) 327-3027

Asthma and allergy information
(800) 727-5400

Blind Children's Center
Los Angeles, CA
(800) 222-3566 (ex CA)

Chesebrough-Ponds
Consumer Information Center
(800) 243-5804

Cochlear implant information
(800) 458-4999 (TDD)

Childhelp National Child Abuse Hotline
(800) 422-4453

Coca-Cola Consumer Information
Atlanta, GA
(800) 438-2653

Duracell Inc. (Consumer Services)
(800) 551-2355 (ex CT)

Eating Disorders
(800) 382-2832

800 Cocaine Information
(800) 262-2463

Epilepsy Foundation of America
(800) 332-1000 (ex MD)

General Electric Answer Center
(Consumer Products Information)
(800) 626-2000

Hearing Aid Helpline
(800) 521-5247

Juvenile Diabetes Foundation Intl.
(800) 223-1138 (ex NY)
(212) 889-7575 (in NY)

Lactaid Inc. (for lactose intolerance)
(800) 522-8243

Levi Strauss & Co.
(800) 872-5384

National Council on Compulsive Gambling
(800) 522-4700

National Down Syndrome Congress
(800) 232-6372 (ex IL)

National Down Syndrome Society
(800) 221-4602 (ex NY)

National Food Addiction Hotline
(800) 872-0088

National Runaway Switchboard
(800) 621-4000

Pepsi Cola Bottling Group
(Consumer Affairs)
(800) 433-2652

Ragu
(800) 328-7248

Runaway Hotline
(800) 231-6946 (ex TX)
(800) 392-3352 (TX)

St. Jude Children's Research Hospital
(800) 341-5800 (ex MA)

Sexually transmitted diseases
(800) 227-8922

Spina Bifida Association
(800) 621-3141

United Sclerderma Foundation
(800) 722-4673 (ex CA)

U.S. Air Force Fraud, Waste, & Abuse Hotline
(800) 538-8429 (ex VA)

U.S. Coast Guard Boating Safety
(800) 368-5647 (ex DC)

Vietnam Veterans of America
(800) 424-7275 (ex DC)

Whirlpool Cool Line
(800) 253-1301

BETTER BUSINESS BUREAUS

Better Business Bureaus (BBBs) are non-profit organizations sponsored by local businesses. BBBs offer a variety of consumer services. They can provide consumer education materials, answer consumer questions, mediate and arbitrate complaints, and provide general information on companies' consumer complaint records.

Each BBB has its own policy about reporting information. It might or might not tell you the nature of the complaint against a business, but all will tell you if a complaint has been registered. Many of the BBBs accept written complaints and will contact a firm on your behalf. BBBs do not judge or rate individual products or brands, handle complaints concerning the prices of goods or services, or give legal advice. However, many bureaus do offer binding arbitration, a form of dispute resolution, to those who ask for it. If you need help with a consumer question or complaint, call your local BBB to ask about their services.

This list includes the local BBBs in the United States. The Council of Better Business Bureaus can give you the addresses for BBBs in Canada.

National Headquarters

Council of Better Business Bureaus, Inc.
4200 Wilson Boulevard
Arlington, VA 22203
(703) 276-0100

Local Bureaus

Alabama

P.O. Box 55268
Birmingham, AL 35255-5268
(205) 558-2222

118 Woodburn Street
Dothan, AL 36301
(205) 792-3804

P.O. Box 383
Huntsville, AL 35801
(205) 533-1640

707 Van Antwerp Building
Mobile, AL 36602
(205) 433-5494, 5495

Commerce Street, Suite 806
Montgomery, AL 36104
(205) 262-5606

Alaska

3380 C Street, Suite 103
Anchorage, AK 99503
(907) 562-0704

Arizona

4428 North 12th Street
Phoenix, AZ 85014-4585
(602) 264-1721

50 West Drachman Street
Suite 103
Tucson, AZ 85705
(602) 622-7651 (inquiries)
(602) 622-7654 (complaints)

Arkansas

1415 S. University
Little Rock, AR 72204
(501) 664-7274

California

705 Eighteenth Street
Bakersfield, CA 93301-4882
(805) 322-2074

P.O. Box 970
Colton, CA 92324-0522
(714) 825-7280

6101 Ball Rd., Suite 309
Cypress, CA 90630
(714) 527-0680

1398 West Indianapolis
Suite 102
Fresno, CA 93705
(209) 222-8111

494 Alvarado Street, Suite C
Monterey, CA 93940
(408) 372-3149

510 16th Street
Oakland, CA 94612
(415) 839-5900

400 S Street
Sacramento, CA 95814
(916) 443-6843

3111 Camino del Rio, North
Suite 600
San Diego, CA 92108-1729
(619) 281-6422

33 New Montgomery St. Tower
San Francisco, CA 94105
(415) 243-9999

1505 Meridian Avenue
San Jose, CA 95125
(408) 978-8700

P.O. Box 294
San Mateo, CA 94401
(415) 696-1240

P.O. Box 746
Santa Barbara, CA 93102
(805) 963-8657

300 B Street
Santa Rosa, CA 95401
(707) 577-0300

1111 North Center Street
Stockton, CA 95202-1383
(209) 948-4880, 4881

Colorado

P.O. Box 7970
Colorado Springs, CO 80933
(719) 636-1155

1780 South Bellaire, Suite 700
Denver, CO 80222
(303) 758-2100 (inquiries)
(303) 758-2212 (complaints)

1730 S. College Ave., Suite 303
Fort Collins, CO 80525
(303) 484-1348

119 West 6th Street, Suite 203
Pueblo, CO 81003-3119
(719) 542-6464

Connecticut

2345 Black Rock Turnpike
Fairfield, CT 06430
(203) 374-6161

2080 Silas Deane Highway
Rocky Hill, CT 06067-2311
(203) 529-3575

100 South Turnpike Road
Wallingford, CT 06492-4395
(203) 269-2700 (inquiries)
(203) 269-4457 (complaints)

Delaware

2055 Limestone Road
Suite 200
Wilmington, DE 19808
(302) 996-9200

District of Columbia

1012 14th Street, N.W.
14th Floor
Washington, DC 20005-3410
(202) 393-8000

Florida

In addition to the Better Business Bureaus, Florida has a number of Better Business Councils which are affiliated with local Chambers of Commerce throughout the state. The Better Business Councils are listed following the Better Business Bureaus.

Better Business Bureaus

P.O. Box 7950
Clearwater, FL 34618-7950
(813) 535-5522

2976-E Cleveland Avenue
Fort Myers, FL 33901
(813) 334-7331

3100 University Blvd., South
Suite 239
Jacksonville, FL 32216
(904) 721-2288

2605 Maitland Center Parkway
Maitland, FL 32751-7147
(407) 660-9500

16291 Northwest 57th Avenue
Miami, FL 33014-6709
(305) 625-0307
(inquiries for Dade County)
(305) 625-1302
(complaints for Dade County)
(305) 524-2803
(inquiries for Broward County)
(305) 527-1643
(complaints for Broward County)

P.O. Box 1511
Pensacola, FL 32597-1511
(904) 433-6111

1950 SE Port St. Lucie Blvd.
Suite 211
Port St. Lucie, FL 34952
(407) 878-2010
(407) 337-2083 (Martin County)

2247 Palm Beach Lakes Blvd.
Suite 211
West Palm Beach, FL 33409
(407) 686-2200

Better Business Councils

P.O. Box 3607
Lakeland, FL 33802-3607
(813) 680-1030 (Polk County)

P.O. Box 492426
Leesburg, FL 32749-2426
(904) 326-0770 (Lake County)

400 Fortenberry Road
Merritt Island, FL 32952
(407) 452-8869 (Central Brevard County)

13000 South Tamiami Trail
Suite 111
North Port, FL 34287
(813) 426-8744

4100 Dixie Highway, NE
Palm Bay, FL 32905
(407) 984-8454 (South Brevard County)

1819 Main Street, Suite 240
Sarasota, FL 34236
(813) 366-3144

P.O. Drawer 2767
Titusville, FL 32781-2767
(407) 268-2822 (North Brevard County)

257 Tamiami Trail, North
Venice, FL 34285-1534
(813) 485-3510

Georgia

1319-B Dawson Road
Albany, GA 31707
(912) 883-0744
1 (800) 868-4222 (toll free)

100 Edgewood Avenue
Suite 1012
Atlanta, GA 30303
(404) 688-4910

P.O. Box 2085
Augusta, GA 30903
(404) 722-1574

P.O. Box 2587
Columbus, GA 31902
(404) 324-0712

1765 Shurling Drive
Macon, GA 31211
(912) 742-7999

P.O. Box 13956
Savannah, GA 31416-0956
(912) 354-7521

Hawaii

1600 Kapiolani Boulevard
Suite 714
Honolulu, HI 96814
(808) 942-2355

Idaho

1333 West Jefferson
Boise, ID 83702
(208) 342-4649
(208) 467-5547
(Canyon County)

545 Shoup Avenue, Suite 210
Idaho Falls, ID 83402
(208) 523-9754

Illinois

211 W. Wacker Drive
Chicago, IL 60606
(312) 444-1188 (inquiries)
(312) 346-3313 (complaints)

3024 West Lake
Peoria, IL 61615
(309) 688-3741

810 East State Street, 3rd Floor
Rockford, IL 61104
(815) 963-2222

Indiana

P.O. Box 405
Elkhart, IN 46515-0405
(219) 262-8996

4004 Morgan Avenue, Suite 201
Evansville, IN 47715
(812) 473-0202

1203 Webster Street
Fort Wayne, IN 46802
(219) 423-4433

4231 Cleveland Street
Gary, IN 46408
(219) 980-1511

Victoria Centre
22 East Washington Street
Suite 200
Indianapolis, IN 46204
(317) 637-0197

Marion, IN
1 (800) 552-4631
(toll free in IN)

Consumer Education Council (non-BBB)
BSW WB 150
Muncie, IN 47306
(317) 285-5668

52303 Emmons Road, Suite 9
South Bend, IN 46637
(219) 277-9121

Iowa

852 Middle Road, Suite 290
Bettendorf, IA 52722-4100
(319) 355-6344

615 Insurance Exchange Building
Des Moines, IA 50309
(515) 243-8137

318 Badgerow Building
Sioux City, IA 51101
(712) 252-4501

Kansas

501 Jefferson, Suite 24
Topeka, KS 66607-1190
(913) 232-0454

300 Kaufman Building
Wichita, KS 67202
(316) 263-3146

Kentucky

311 West Short Street
Lexington, KY 40507
(606) 259-1008

844 South 4th Street
Louisville, KY 40203-2186
(502) 583-6546

Louisiana

1605 Murray St., Suite 117
Alexandria, LA 71301
(318) 473-4494

2055 Wooddale Boulevard
Baton Rouge, LA 70806-1519
(504) 926-3010

501 East Main Street
Houma, LA 70360
(504) 868-3456

P.O. Box 30297
Lafayette, LA 70593-0297
(318) 981-3497

P.O. Box 1681
Lake Charles, LA 70602
(318) 433-1633

141 De Siard Street, Suite 808
Monroe, LA 71201-7380
(318) 387-4600, 8421

1539 Jackson Avenue
New Orleans, LA 70130-3400
(504) 581-6222

1401 North Market Street
Shreveport, LA 71107-6525
(318) 221-8352

Maine

812 Stevens Avenue
Portland, ME 04103
(207) 878-2715

Maryland

2100 Huntingdon Avenue
Baltimore, MD 21211-3215
(301) 347-3990

Massachusetts

20 Park Plaza, Suite 820
Boston, MA 02116-4404
(617) 426-9000

Framingham, MA
1 (800) 422-2811
(toll free in MA)

78 North Street, Suite 1
Hyannis, MA 02601-3808
(508) 771-3022

Lawrence, MA
1 (800) 422-2811
(toll free in MA)

293 Bridge Street, Suite 320
Springfield, MA 01103
(413) 734-3114

P.O. Box 379
Worcester, MA 01601
(508) 755-2548

Michigan

620 Trust Building
Grand Rapids, MI 49503
(616) 774-8236

30555 Southfield Road
Suite 200
Southfield, MI 48076-7751
(313) 644-1012 (inquiries)
(313) 644-9136 (complaints)
(313) 644-9152 (Auto Line)
1 (800) 955-5100
(toll free nationwide auto line)

Minnesota

2706 Gannon Road
St. Paul, MN 55116
(612) 699-1111

Mississippi

460 Briarwood Drive, Suite 340
Jackson, MS 39206-3088
(601) 956-8282
1 (800) 274-7222
(toll free in MS)
(601) 957-2886
(automotive complaints only)

Missouri

306 East 12th Street
Suite 1024
Kansas City, MO 64106-2418
(816) 421-7800

5100 Oakland Avenue
Suite 200
St. Louis, MO 63110
(314) 531-3300

205 Park Central East
Suite 509
Springfield, MO 65806
(417) 862-9231

Nebraska

719 North 48th Street
Lincoln, NE 68504-3491
(402) 467-5261

1613 Farnam Street, Room 417
Omaha, NE 68102-2158
(402) 346-3033

Nevada

1022 E. Sahara Avenue
Las Vegas, NV 89104-1515
(702) 735-6900, 1969

P.O. Box 21269
Reno, NV 89515-1269
(702) 322-0657

New Hampshire

410 South Main Street
Concord, NH 03301
(603) 224-1991

New Jersey

494 Broad Street
Newark, NJ 07102
(201) 642-INFO

2 Forest Avenue
Paramus, NJ 07652
(201) 845-4044

1721 Route 37, East
Toms River, NJ 08753-8239
(201) 270-5577

1700 Whitehorse
Hamilton Square, Suite D-5
Trenton, NJ 08690
(609) 588-0808 (Mercer County)

P.O. Box 303
Westmont, NJ 08108-0303
(609) 854-8467

New Mexico

4600-A Montgomery NE
Suite 200
Albuquerque, NM 87109
(505) 884-0500
1 (800) 445-1461
(toll free in NM)

308 North Locke
Farmington, NM 87401
(505) 326-6501

2407 W. Picacho, Suite B-2
Las Cruces, NM 88005
(505) 524-3130

New York

346 Delaware Avenue
Buffalo, NY 14202
(716) 856-7180

266 Main Street
Farmingdale, NY 11735
(516) 420-0500
1 (800) 955-5100
(toll free—Auto Line)

257 Park Avenue South
New York, NY 10010
(900) 463-6222
($.85 per minute)

1122 Sibley Tower
Rochester, NY 14604-1084
(716) 546-6776

847 James Street, Suite 200
Syracuse, NY 13203
(315) 479-6635

1211 Route 9
Wappingers Falls, NY 12590
(914) 297-6550
1 (800) 955-5100
(toll free—Auto Line)

30 Glenn Street
White Plains, NY 10603
(914) 428-1230, 1231
1 (800) 955-5100
(toll free—Auto Line)

North Carolina

801 BB&T Building
Asheville, NC 28801
(704) 253-2392

1130 East Third Street
Suite 400
Charlotte, NC 28204-2626
(704) 332-7151

3608 West Friendly Avenue
Greensboro, NC 27410
(919) 852-4240, 4241, 4242

P.O. Box 1882
Hickory, NC 28603
(704) 464-0372

3120 Poplarwood Court
Suite 101
Raleigh, NC 27604-1080
(919) 872-9240

2110 Cloverdale Avenue
Suite 2-B
Winston-Salem, NC 27103
(919) 725-8348

Ohio

222 West Market Street
Akron, OH 44303-2111
(216) 253-4590

1434 Cleveland Avenue, NW
Canton, OH 44703
(216) 454-9401

898 Walnut Street
Cincinnati, OH 45202
(513) 421-3015

2217 East 9th St., Suite 200
Cleveland, OH 44115-1299
(216) 241-7678

527 South High Street
Columbus, OH 43215
(614) 221-6336

40 West Fourth Street
Suite 1250
Dayton, OH 45402
(513) 222-5825
1 (800) 521-8357
(toll free in OH)

P.O. Box 269
Lima, OH 45802
(419) 223-7010

130 West 2nd Street
Mansfield, OH 44902-1915
(419) 522-1700

425 Jefferson Avenue
Suite 909
Toledo, OH 43604-1055
(419) 241-6276

345 N. Market, Suite 202
Wooster, OH 44691
(216) 263-6444

P.O. Box 1495
Youngstown, OH
44501-1495
(216) 744-3111

Oklahoma

17 South Dewey
Oklahoma City, OK 73102
(405) 239-6860 (inquiries)
(405) 239-6081 (inquiries)
(405) 239-6083 (complaints)

6711 S. Yale, Suite 230
Tulsa, OK 74136-3327
(918) 492-1266

Oregon

610 S.W. Alder St., Suite
615
Portland, OR 97205
(503) 226-3981
1 (800) 488-4166
(toll free in OR)

Pennsylvania

528 North New Street
Bethlehem, PA 18018
(215) 866-8780

6 Marion Court
Lancaster, PA 17602
(717) 291-1151
(717) 232-2800 (Harrisburg)
(717) 846-2700 (York
County)
(717) 394-9318 (Auto Line)

P.O. Box 2297
Philadelphia, PA
19103-0297
(215) 496-1000

610 Smithfield Street
Pittsburgh, PA 15222
(412) 456-2700

P.O. Box 993
Scranton, PA 18501
(717) 342-9129, 655-0445

Puerto Rico

Condominium Olimpo Plaza
Suite 208
1002 Munoz Rivera Avenue
Rio Piedras, PR 00927
(809) 756-5400
(809) 767-0446

Rhode Island

Bureau Park
P.O. Box 1300
Warwick, RI 02887-1300
(401) 785-1212 (inquiries)
(401) 785-1213 (complaints)

South Carolina

1830 Bull Street
Columbia, SC 29201
(803) 254-2525

311 Pettigru Street
Greenville, SC 29601
(803) 242-5052

1310-G Azalea Court
Myrtle Beach, SC 29577
(803) 497-8667

Tennessee

P.O. Box 1178 TCAS
Blountville, TN 37617
(615) 323-6311

1010 Market Street, Suite 200
Chattanooga, TN 37402-2614
(615) 266-6144
(also serves Whitfield and Murray counties in GA)
(615) 479-6096
(Bradley County only)

900 East Hill Avenue, Suite 165
Knoxville, TN 37915-2525
(615) 522-2552

P.O. Box 750704
Memphis, TN 38175-0704
(901) 795-8771

Sovran Plaza, Suite 1830
Nashville, TN 37239
(615) 254-5872

Texas

3300 S. 14th St., Suite 307
Abilene, TX 79605
(915) 691-1533

P.O. Box 1905
Amarillo, TX 79105-1905
(806) 379-6222

708 Colorado, Suite 720
Austin, TX 78701-3028
(512) 476-1616

P.O. Box 2988
Beaumont, TX 77704-2988
(409) 835-5348

202 Varisco Building
Bryan, TX 77803
(409) 823-8148, 8149

4535 S. Padre Island Drive
Suite 28
Corpus Christi, TX 78411
(512) 854-2892

2001 Bryan Street, Suite 850
Dallas, TX 75201
(214) 220-2000
1 (800) 442-1456
(toll free in TX)

5160 Montana, Lower Level
El Paso, TX 79903
(915) 772-2727

512 Main Street, Suite 807
Fort Worth, TX 76102
(817) 332-7585

2707 North Loop West
Suite 900
Houston, TX 77008
(713) 868-9500

P.O. Box 1178
Lubbock, TX 79408-1178
(806) 763-0459

P.O. Box 60206
Midland, TX 79711-0206
(915) 563-1880
1 (800) 592-4433
(toll free in 915 area code)

P.O. Box 3366
San Angelo, TX 76902-3366
(915) 949-2989

1800 Northeast Loop 410
Suite 400
San Antonio, TX 78217
(512) 828-9441

P.O. Box 6652
Tyler, TX 75711-6652
(903) 581-5704

P.O. Box 7203
Waco, TX 76714-7203
(817) 772-7530

P.O. Box 69
Weslaco, TX 78596-0069
(512) 968-3678

1106 Brook Street
Wichita Falls, TX 76301-5079
(817) 723-5526

Utah

1588 South Main Street
Salt Lake City, UT 84115
(801) 487-4656

Virginia

4022B Plank Road
Fredericksburg, VA 22407
(703) 786-8397

3608 Tidewater Drive
Norfolk, VA 23509-1499
(804) 627-5651

701 East Franklin Street
Suite 712
Richmond, VA 23219
(804) 648-0016

31 W. Campbell Avenue
Roanoke, VA 24011-1301
(703) 342-3455

Washington

127 West Canal Drive
Kennewick, WA 99336-3819
(509) 582-0222

2200 Sixth Avenue, Suite 828
Seattle, WA 98121-1857
(206) 448-8888
(206) 448-6222 (24-hour business reporting system)

South 176 Stevens
Spokane, WA 99204-1393
(509) 747-1155

P.O. Box 1274
Tacoma, WA 98401-1274
(206) 383-5561

P.O. Box 1584
Yakima, WA 98907-1584
(509) 248-1326

Wisconsin

740 North Plankinton Avenue
Milwaukee, WI 53203
(414) 273-1600 (inquiries)
(414) 273-0123 (complaints)

Wyoming

BBB/Idaho Falls
(serves Teton, Park and Lincoln
counties in Wyoming)
545 Shoup Avenue, Suite 210
Idaho Falls, ID 83402
(208) 523-9754

BBB/Fort Collins
(serves all other Wyoming Counties)
1730 South College Avenue
Suite 303
Fort Collins, CO 80525
1 (800) 873-3222
(toll free in WY)

TRADE ASSOCIATION AND OTHER DISPUTE RESOLUTION PROGRAMS

Companies that manufacture similar products or offer similar services often belong to industry associations. These associations help resolve problems between their member companies and consumers. Depending on the industry, you might have to contact an association, service council, or consumer action program.

If you have a problem with a company and cannot get it resolved with the company, ask if the company is a member of an assocation. Then check this list to see if the association is listed. If the name of the association is not included on this list, check with a local library.

This list includes the names and addresses of the association and other dispute resolution programs that handle consumer complaints for their members. In some cases, the national organizations listed here can refer you to dispute resolution programs near you.

These programs are usually called alternative dispute resolution programs. Generally, there are three types of programs: arbitration, conciliation, and mediation. All three methods of dispute resolution vary. Ask for a copy of the rules of the program before you file your case. Generally, the decisions of the arbitrators are binding and must be accepted by both the customer and the business. However, in other forms of dispute resolution, only the business is required to accept the decision. In some programs, decisions are not binding on either party.

Remember, before contacting one of these programs, try to resolve the complaint by contacting the company.

Ms. Ann Lawrence, Director
Education and Conventions
American Apparel Manufacturers Association
2500 Wilson Boulevard, Suite 301
Arlington, VA 22201
(703) 524-1864
Membership: Manufacturers of clothing.

Ms. Donna Silberberg
Public Relations Director
American Arbitration Association
140 West 51st Street
New York, NY 10020-1203
(212) 484-4006
Private, non-profit organization with 35 regional offices across the country. Provides consumer information on request. Check local telephone directory for listing. If there is no office in your area, write or call the office listed above.

American Automobile Association
AUTOSOLVE
1000 AAA Drive
Heathrow, FL 32746-5064
1 (800) 477-6583 (toll free)
Third-party dispute resolution program for Toyota, Lexus, Hyundai and Subaru in selected areas of the United States.

American Bar Association
Standing Committee on Dispute Resolution
1800 M Street, N.W., Suite 790
Washington, DC 20036
(202) 331-2258
Publishes a directory of state and local alternative dispute resolution programs. Provides consumer information on request.

Mr. John W. Johnson
Executive Vice President
American Collectors Association
4040 West 70th Street
P.O. Box 39106
Minneapolis, MN 55439-0106
(612) 926-6547
Membership: Collection services handling overdue accounts for retail, professional and commercial credit grantors.

Information Department
American Council of Life Insurance
1001 Pennsylvania Avenue, N.W.
Washington, DC 20004-2599
1 (800) 942-4242 (toll free—
8 a.m.-8 p.m. EST, M-F)
Membership: Life insurance companies authorized to do business in the United States.

Ms. Jane Marden, Director Consumer Affairs
Ms. Linda Wood, Associate Director
Community Affairs
American Gas Association
1515 Wilson Boulevard
Arlington, VA 22209
(703) 841-8583
Membership: Distributors and transporters of natural gas.

American Health Care Association
1201 L Street, N.W.
Washington, DC 20005-4014
(202) 842-4444
1 (800) 321-0343
(toll free—publications only)
Membership: State associations of long-term health care facilities.

American Hotel and Motel Association
1201 New York Avenue, N.W. Suite 600
Washington, DC 20005-3931
(written inquiries only)
Membership: State and regional hotel associations.

Mr. Herbert A. Finkston, Director
Professional Ethics Division
American Institute of Certified Public Accountants
1211 Avenue of the Americas
New York, NY 10036-8775
(212) 575-6209
Membership: Professional society of accountants certified by the states and territories.

American Newspaper Publishers Assn. Credit Bureau, Inc.
P.O. Box 17022
Dulles International Airport
Washington, D.C. 20041
(703) 648-1038
Investigates fraudulent advertising published in newspapers.

American Orthotic and Prosthetic Association
1650 King Street, Suite 500
Alexandria, VA 22314-1885
(703) 836-7116
Represents member companies that custom fit or manufacture components for patients with prostheses or orthoses.

Mr. Ray Greenly, Vice President
Consumer Affairs
American Society of Travel Agents, Inc.
P.O. Box 23992
Washington, DC 20026-3992
(703) 739-2782
Membership: Travel agents.

Mr. James A. Morrissey, Director
Communications Division
American Textile Manufacturers Institute
1801 K Street, N.W., Suite 900
Washington, DC 20006
(202) 862-0552
Membership: Textile mills which produce a variety of textile products, e.g., clothing, using natural and man-made fibers.

Manager, Consumer Affairs
Automotive Consumer Action Program (AUTOCAP)
8400 Westpark Drive
McLean, VA 22102
(703) 821-7144
Third-party dispute resolution program administered through the National Automobile Dealers Association. Consumer information available on request.

BBB AUTO LINE
Council of Better Business Bureaus, Inc.
4200 Wilson Boulevard, Suite 800
Arlington, VA 22203-1804
(703) 276-0100
Third-party dispute resolution program for AMC, Audi, General Motors and its divisions, Honda, Jeep, Nissan, Peugeot, Porsche, Renault, SAAB and Volkswagen.

Better Hearing Institute
P.O. Box 1840
Washington, DC 20013
(703) 642-0580
1 (800) EAR-WELL (toll free)
Membership: Professionals and others who help persons with impaired hearing. Provides voluntary mediation between consumers and hearing aid dispensers.

Consumer Affairs
Blue Cross and Blue Shield Association
Metro Square—Phase II
655 15th Street, N.W., Suite 350F
Washington, DC 20005
(202) 626-4780
Membership: Local Blue Cross and Blue Shield plans in the United States, Canada and Jamaica.

Ms. Caroline C. Ortado
Administrator, Consumer Protection Bureau
Boat Owners Association of the United States (BOAT/U.S.)
880 South Pickett Street
Alexandria, VA 22304-0730
(703) 823-9550
Consumer Protection Bureau serves as a mediator in disputes between boat owners and the marine industry. BOAT/U.S. also works closely with the U.S. Coast Guard to monitor safety defect problems.

Mr. Richard N. "Ned" Hopper
Director of Governmental Affairs
Carpet and Rug Institute
1155 Connecticut Avenue, N.W., Suite 500
Washington, DC 20036
(written inquiries only)
Membership: Manufacturers of carpets, rugs, bath mats and bedspreads; suppliers of raw materials and services to the industry.

Mr. Robert M. Fells, Assistant Secretary
Cemetery Consumer Service Council
P.O. Box 3574
Washington, DC 20007
(703) 379-6426
Industry-sponsored dispute resolution program. Other consumer information about cemetery practices and rules available on request.

Children's Advertising Review Unit (CARU)
Council of Better Business Bureaus, Inc.
845 Third Avenue
New York, NY 10022
(212) 754-1354
Handles consumer complaints about fraudulent and deceptive advertising related to children.

Chrysler Motors
Customer Relations
National Office
26311 Lawrence Avenue
Center Line, MI 48288
1 (800) 992-1997 (toll free)

Department of Defense
Office of National Ombudsman
National Committee for Employer Support of the Guard and Reserve
1555 Wilson Boulevard, Suite 200
Arlington, VA 22209-2405
(703) 696-1391
1 (800) 336-4590 (toll free outside DC)
Provides assistance with employer/employee problems for members of the Guard and Reserve and their employers.

Ms. Lorna Christie, Director
Ethics and Consumer Affairs
Direct Marketing Association (DMA)
6 East 43rd Street
New York, NY 10017-4646
(written complaints only)
Membership: Members who market goods and services directly to consumers using direct mail, catalogs, telemarketing, magazine and newspaper ads, and broadcast advertising.

DMA operates the Mail Order Action Line, Mail Preference Service and Telephone Preference Service.

For problems with a mail order company, write:
Mail Order Action Line
6 East 43rd Street
New York, NY 10017

Mr. William Rogal
Code Administrator
Direct Selling Association
1776 K Street, N.W. Suite 600
Washington, DC 20006-2387
(202) 293-5760
Membership: Manufacturers and distributors selling consumer products door-to-door and through homc-party plans.

Ms. Sally Browne, Executive Director
Consumer Affairs
Electronic Industries Association
2001 Pennsylvania Avenue, N.W.
10th Floor
Washington, DC 2006
(202) 457-4977
Complaint assistance program, consumer education, etc., concerning televisions, video cassette recorders and other video systems, audio products, personal computers and communication electronic products.

Ford Consumer Appeals Board
P.O. Box 5120
Southfield, MI 48086-5120
1 (800) 392-3673 (toll free)

Funeral Service Consumer Arbitration Program (FSCAP)
1614 Central Street
Evanston, IL 60201
1 (800) 662-7666 (toll free)
Third-party dispute resolution program sponsored by the National Funeral Directors Association.

Ms. Carole M. Rogin, President
Market Development
Hearing Industries Association
1255 23rd Street, N.W.
Washington, DC 20037-1174
(202) 833-1411
Membership: Companies engaged in the manufacture and/or sale of electronic hearing aids, their components, parts and related products and services on a national basis.

Home Owners Warranty Corporation (HOW) Operation Center
P.O. Box 152087
Irving, TX 75015-2087
1 (800) 433-7657 (toll free)
Third-party dispute resolution program for new homes built by HOW-member home builders.

Ms. Jill A. Wolper, Manager
Consumer Affairs and Education
Insurance Information Institute
110 William Street
New York, NY 10038
1 (800) 942-4242 (toll free)
National Insurance Consumer Helpline is a resource for consumers with automobile and home insurance questions. The Helpline is open Monday through Friday from 8 a.m. to 8 p.m.

National Headquarters
International Association for Financial Planning
2 Concourse Parkway, Suite 800
Atlanta, GA 30328
(404) 395-1605
Membership: Individuals involved in financial planning.

Major Appliance Consumer Action Panel (MACAP)
20 North Wacker Drive
Chicago, IL 60606
(312) 984-5858
1 (800) 621-0477 (toll free)
Third-party dispute resolution program of the major appliance industry.

Mr. John E. Dianis
Executive Vice President
Monument Builders of North America
1740 Ridge Avenue
Evanston, IL 60201
(708) 869-2031
Membership: Cemetery monument retailers, manufacturers and wholesalers; bronze manufacturers and suppliers. Consumer brochures available on request.

Ms. Sharon McHale
Media Relations Coordinator/Consumer Affairs
Mortgage Bankers Association of America
1125 15th Street, N.W., 7th Floor
Washington, DC 20005
(202) 861-1929
Membership: Mortgage banking firms, commercial banks, life insurance companies, title companies, and savings and loan associations.

National Advertising Division (NAD)
A Division of the Council of Better Business Bureaus, Inc.
845 Third Avenue
New York, NY 10022
(212) 754-1320
Program: Handles consumer complaints about the truth and accuracy of national advertising.

Mr. William Young, Director
Consumer Affairs/Public Liaison
National Association of Home Builders
15th and M Streets, N.W.
Washington, DC 20005
(202) 822-0409
1 (800) 368-5242 (toll free outside D.C.)
Membership: Single and multi-family home builders, commercial builders and others associated with the building industry.

National Association of Personnel Consultants
3133 Mt. Vernon Avenue
Alexandria, VA 22305
(703) 684-0180
Membership: Private employment agencies.

Consumer Arbitration Center
National Association of Securities Dealers, Inc.
33 Whitehall Street, 10th Floor
New York, NY 10004
(212) 858-4000
Third-party dispute resolution for complaints about over-the-counter stocks and corporate bonds.

Accrediting Commission
National Association of Trade and Technical Schools
2251 Wisconsin Avenue, N.W.
Washington, DC 20007-4181
(202) 333-1021
(written inquiries only)
Membership: Private schools providing job training.

Mrs. Juanita Duggan
Government Affairs
National Food Processors Association
1401 New York Avenue, N.W.
Washington, DC 20005
(202) 639-5939
Membership: Commercial packers of such food products as fruit, vegetables, meat, poultry, seafood, and canned, frozen, dehydrated, pickled and other preserved food items.

Ms. Deb Deutsch
Manager, Compliance
National Futures Association
200 West Madison Street
Chicago, IL 60606-3447
(312) 781-1410
1 (800) 621-3570 (toll free outside IL)
Membership: Futures commission merchants; commodity trading advisers; commodity pool operators; introducing brokers; and brokers and associated individuals.

Ms. Cindy Donahue
Assistant to Executive Director
National Home Study Council
1601 18th Street, N.W.
Washington, DC 20009
(written inquiries only)
Membership: Home study (correspondence) schools.

National Tire Dealers and Retreaders Association
1250 Eye Street, N.W., Suite 400
Washington, DC 20005
(202) 789-2300
1 (800) 876-8372 (toll free)
Membership: Independent tire dealers and retreaders.

Department of Consumer Affairs
National Turkey Federation
11319 Sunset Hills Road
Reston, VA 22090-5205
(written inquiries only)
Membership: Turkey growers, turkey hatcheries, turkey breeders, processors, marketers, and allied industry firms and poultry distributors.

Mr. Craig Halverson
Assistant Executive Director
Photo Marketing Association
3000 Picture Place
Jackson, MI 49201
(written complaints only)
Membership: Retailers of photo equipment, film and supplies; firms developing and printing film.

Mrs. Jane Meyer
Director of Consumer Affairs
The Soap and Detergent Association
475 Park Avenue South
New York, NY 10016
(212) 725-1262
Membership: Manufacturers of soap, detergents, fatty acids and glycerine; raw materials suppliers.

Tele-Consumer Hotline
1910 K Street, N.W., Suite 610
Washington, D.C. 20006
(202) 223-4371 (voice/TDD)
Provides information on special telephone products and services for persons with disabilities, selecting a long distance company, money saving tips for people on low income, reducing unsolicited phone calls, telemarketing fraud, dealing with the phone company and other issues. All telephone assistance and publications are free of charge, and Spanish-speaking counselors are available.

Ms. Diane Cardinale
Assistant Communications Director
Toy Manufacturers of America
200 Fifth Avenue, Room 740
New York, NY 10010
(212) 675-1141
Membership: American toy manufacturers.

Mr. Robert E. Whitley, President
U.S. Tour Operators Association (USTOA)
211 East 51st Street, Suite 12-B
New York, NY 10022
(212) 944-5727
Membership: Wholesale tour operators, common carriers, suppliers and providers of travel services.

STATE, COUNTY, AND CITY GOVERNMENT CONSUMER PROTECTION OFFICES

City and county consumer offices can be helpful because they are easy to contact and are familiar with local businesses and laws. Some will investigate and help resolve consumer complaints. If there is no local consumer office in your area, contact a state consumer office. State consumer offices are set up differently across the nation. Some states have a separate department of consumer affairs, while others have a consumer affairs office as part of the governor's or attorney general's office. These offices will help or refer you to the proper agency.

If you have a consumer problem with a business outside the state where you live, you should contact the consumer office in the state where you made the purchase. When you contact any local or state consumer office, be sure to have handy copies of your sales receipts, other sales documents, and all correspondence with the company.

To save time, try to contact the office by telephone before sending a written complaint. Most consumer affairs offices that handle complaints have special forms or other requirements for filing complaints.

This list is arranged in alphabetical order by state name. The state name, city name, and any toll-free "800" and TDD numbers are printed in bold type.

Alabama

State Office
Mr. Dennis Wright, Director
Consumer Protection Division
Office of Attorney General
11 South Union Street
Montgomery, AL 36130
(205) 242-7334
1 (800) 392-5658 (toll free in AL)

Alaska

The Consumer Protection Section in the Office of the Attorney General has been closed. Consumers with complaints are being referred to the Better Business Bureau, small claims court, and private attorneys.

American Samoa

Mr. Tauivi Tuinei
Assistant Attorney General
Consumer Protection Bureau
P.O. Box 7
Pago Pago, AS 96799
011 (684) 633-4163
011 (684) 633-4164

Arizona

State Offices
Ms. H. Leslie Hall, Chief Counsel
Consumer Protection
Office of the Attorney General
1275 West Washington Street, Room 259
Phoenix, AZ 85007
(602) 542-3702
(602) 542-5763
(consumer information and complaints)
1 (800) 352-8431 (toll free in AZ)

Ms. Noreen Matts
Assistant Attorney General
Consumer Protection
Office of the Attorney General
402 West Congress Street, Suite 315
Tucson, AZ 85701
(602) 628-6504

County Offices
Mr. Stephen Udall, County Attorney
Apache County Attorney's Office
P.O. Box 637
St. Johns, AZ 85936
(602) 337-4364, ext. 240

Mr. Alan Polley, County Attorney
Cochise County Attorney's Office
P.O. Drawer CA
Bisbee, AZ 85603
(602) 432-9377

Mr. John Verkamp, County Attorney
Coconino County Attorney's Office
Coconino County Courthouse
100 East Birch
Flagstaff, AZ 86001
(602) 779-6518

Mr. Joe Albo, Jr., County Attorney
Gila County Attorney's Office
1400 East Ash Street
Globe, AZ 85501
(602) 425-3231

Mr. Paul H. McCullar, County Attorney
Graham County Attorney's Office
Graham County Courthouse
800 West Main
Safford, AZ 85546
(602) 428-3620

Mr. Charles E. Fletcher, County Attorney
Greenlee County Attorney's Office
P.O. Box 1387
Clifton, AZ 85533
(602) 865-3842

Mr. Steven P. Suskin, County Attorney
La Paz County Attorney's Office
1200 Arizona Avenue
P.O. Box 709
Parker, AZ 85344
(602) 669-6118

Mr. William Ekstrom, County Attorney
Mohave County Attorney's Office
315 North 4th Street
Kingman, AZ 86401
(602) 753-0719

Mr. Melvin Bowers, County Attorney
Navajo County Attorney's Office
Governmental Complex
Holbrook, AZ 86025
(602) 524-6161

Mr. Stephen D. Neely, County Attorney
Pima County Attorney's Office
1400 Great American Tower
32 North Stone
Tucson, AZ 85701
(602) 740-5733

Mr. Roy Mendoza, County Attorney
Pinal County Attorney's Office
P.O. Box 887
Florence, AZ 85232
(602) 868-5801

Mr. Jose L. Machado, County Attorney
Santa Cruz County Attorney's Office
2100 N. Congress Drive, Suite 201
Nogales, AZ 85621
(602) 281-4966

Mr. Charles Hastings, County Attorney
Yavapai County Attorney's Office
Yavapai County Courthouse
Prescott, AZ 86301
(602) 771-3344

Mr. David S. Ellsworth, County Attorney
Yuma County Attorney's Office
168 South Second Avenue
Yuma, AZ 85364
(602) 329-2270

City Office

Mr. Ronald M. Detrick
Supervising Attorney
Consumer Affairs Division
Tucson City Attorney's Office
110 East Pennington Street, 2nd Floor
P.O. Box 27210
Tucson, AZ 85726-7210
(602) 791-4886

Arkansas

State Office

Mr. Royce Griffin, Director
Consumer Protection Division
Office of Attorney General
200 Tower Building
323 Center Street
Little Rock, AR 72201
(501) 682-2007 (voice/TDD)
1 (800) 482-8982
(toll free voice/TDD in AR)

California

State Offices

Mr. James Conran, Director
California Department of Consumer Affairs
400 R Street, Suite 1040
Sacramento, CA 95814
(916) 445-0660 (complaint assistance)
(916) 445-1254 (consumer information)
(916) 522-1700 (TDD)
1 (800) 344-9940 (toll free in CA)

Office of Attorney General
Public Inquiry Unit
P.O. Box 944255
Sacramento, CA 94244-2550
(916) 322-3360
1 (800) 952-5225 (toll free in CA)
1 (800) 952-5548 (toll free TDD in CA)

Bureau of Automotive Repair
California Department of Consumer Affairs
10240 Systems Parkway
Sacramento, CA 95827
(916) 366-5100
1 (800) 952-5210
(toll free in CA—auto repair only)

County Offices

Ms. Lorraine K. Provost
Coordinator
Alameda County Consumer Affairs Commission
4400 MacArthur Boulevard
Oakland, CA 94619
(415) 530-8682

Mr. Gary Yancey, District Attorney
Contra Costa County
District Attorney's Office
725 Court Street, 4th Floor
P.O. Box 670
Martinez, CA 94553
(415) 646-4500

Mr. Alan Yengoyan
Senior Deputy District Attorney
Business Affairs
Fresno County District Attorney's Office
2220 Tulare Street, Suite 1000
Fresno, CA 93721
(209) 488-3156

Mr. Edward R. Jagels, District Attorney
Consumer and Major Business Fraud Section
Kern County District Attorney's Office
1215 Truxtun Avenue
Bakersfield, CA 93301
(805) 861-2421

Mr. Pastor Herrera, Jr., Director
Los Angeles County Department of Consumer Affairs
500 West Temple Street, Room B-96
Los Angeles, CA 90012
(213) 974-1452

Ms. Betty Times, Director
Citizens Service Office
Marin County Mediation Services
Marin County Civic Center, Room 412
San Rafael, CA 94903
(415) 499-6190

Mr. Jerry Herman, District Attorney
Marin County District Attorney's Office
Marin County Civic Center, Room 155
San Rafael, CA 94903
(415) 499-6482

Mr. Robert Nichols
Deputy District Attorney
Consumer Protection Division
Marin County District Attorney's Office
Hall of Justice, Room 183
San Rafael, CA 94903
(415) 499-6450

Ms. Susan Massini, District Attorney
Mendocino County District Attorney's Office
P.O. Box 1000
Ukiah, CA 95482
(707) 463-4211

Ms. Candice Chin, Coordinator
Monterey County Office of Consumer Affairs
P.O. Box 1369
Salinas, CA 93902
(408) 755-5073

Mr. Daryl A. Roberts
Deputy District Attorney
Consumer Affairs Division
Napa County District Attorney's Office
931 Parkway Mall
P.O. Box 720
Napa, CA 94559
(707) 253-4059

Mr. Guy Ormes
Deputy District Attorney in Charge
Major Fraud Unit
Orange County District Attorney's Office
801 Civic Center Drive West, Suite 120
Santa Ana, CA 92701
(714) 541-7600

Mr. Christopher P. Kralick
Deputy District Attorney in Charge
Consumer and Environmental Protection Unit
Orange County District Attorney's Office
801 Civic Center Drive West, Suite 120
Santa Ana, CA 92702-0808
(714) 541-7600

Mr. Paul Zellerbach
Deputy District Attorney
Economic Crime Division
Riverside County District Attorney's Office
4075 Main Street
Riverside, CA 92501
(714) 275-5400

Mr. M. Scott Prentice
Supervising Deputy District Attorney
Consumer and Environmental Protection Division
Sacramento County District Attorney's Office
P.O. Box 749
Sacramento, CA 95812-0749
(916) 440-6174

Mr. Anthony Samson, Director
Consumer Fraud Division
San Diego County District Attorney's Office
P.O. Box X-1011
San Diego, CA 92112
(619) 531-3507 (fraud complaint line)
(8:30 a.m.-11:30 a.m.; leave message at other times)

Mr. Robert H. Perez, Attorney
Consumer and Environmental Protection Unit
San Francisco County District Attorney's Office
732 Brannan Street
San Francisco, CA 94103
(415) 552-6400 (public inquiries)
(415) 553-1814 (complaints)

Mr. Stephen Taylor, Deputy District Attorney
Consumer and Business Affairs Division
San Joaquin County District Attorney's Office
222 East Weber, Room 202
P.O. Box 990
Stockton, CA 95202
(209) 468-2419

Ms. Leigh Lawrence
Director, Economic Crime Unit
Consumer Fraud Department
County Government Center
1050 Monterey Street, Room 235
San Luis Obispo, CA 93408
(805) 549-5800

Mr. John E. Wilson, Deputy in Charge
Consumer Fraud and Environmental Protection Unit
San Mateo County District Attorney's Office

401 Marshall Street
Hall of Justice and Records
Redwood City, CA 94063
(415) 363-4656

Mr. Alan Kaplan, Deputy District Attorney
Consumer Protection Unit
Santa Barbara County District Attorney's Office
1105 Santa Barbara Street
Santa Barbara, CA 93101
(805) 568-2300

Mr. Albert C. Bender
Deputy District Attorney
Consumer Fraud Unit
Santa Clara County District Attorney's Office
70 West Hedding Street, West Wing
San Jose, CA 95110
(408) 299-7400

Mr. Lawrence R. Sheahan, Director
Santa Clara County Department of Consumer Affairs
2175 The Alameda
San Jose, CA 95126
(408) 299-4211

Ms. Robin McFarland Gysin
Ms. Gloria Lorenzo
Coordinators, Division of Consumer Affairs
Santa Cruz County District Attorney's Office
701 Ocean Street, Room 200
Santa Cruz, CA 95060
(408) 425-2054

Mr. William Atkinson
Deputy District Attorney
Consumer Affairs Unit
Solano County District Attorney's Office
600 Union Avenue
Fairfield, CA 94533
(707) 421-6860

Mr. Thomas Quinlan
Deputy District Attorney
Consumer Fraud Unit
Stanislaus County District Attorney's Office
P.O. Box 442
Modesto, CA 95353
(209) 571-5550

Mr. Greg Brose, Deputy District Attorney
Consumer and Environmental Protection Division
Ventura County District Attorney's Office
800 South Victoria Avenue
Ventura, CA 93009
(805) 654-3110

Mr. Mark Jerome Jones
Supervising Deputy District Attorney
Special Services Unit—Consumer/Environmental
Yolo County District Attorney's Office
P.O. Box 245
Woodland, CA 95695
(916) 666-8424

City Offices

Ms. Sue Frauens
Supervising Deputy City Attorney
Consumer Protection Division
Los Angeles City Attorney's Office
200 North Main Street
1600 City Hall East
Los Angeles, CA 90012
(213) 485-4515

Ms. Teresa Bransfield
Consumer Affairs Specialist
Consumer Division
Santa Monica City Attorney's Office
1685 Main Street, Room 310
Santa Monica, CA 90401
(310) 458-8336

Colorado

State Offices

Consumer Protection Unit
Office of Attorney General
110 16th Street, 10th Floor
Denver, CO 80202
(303) 620-4500

Ms. Helen Davis
Consumer and Food Specialist
Department of Agriculture
700 Kipling Street, Suite 4000
Lakewood, CO 80215-5894
(303) 239-4114

County Offices

Mr. Victor Reichman, District Attorney
Archuleta, LaPlata and San Juan Counties
District Attorney's Office
P.O. Drawer 3455
Durango, CO 81302
(303) 247-8850

Mr. Alex Hunter, District Attorney
Boulder County District Attorney's Office
P.O. Box 471
Boulder, CO 80306
(303) 441-3700

Ms. Clair Villano, Executive Director
Denver County District Attorney's Consumer Fraud Office
303 West Colfax Avenue, Suite 1300
Denver, CO 80204
(303) 640-3555 (inquiries)
(303) 640-3557 (complaints)

Mr. David Zook
Chief Deputy District Attorney
Economic Crime Division
El Paso and Teller Counties District Attorney's Office
326 South Tejon
Colorado Springs, CO 80903-2083
(719) 520-6002

Mr. Gus Sandstrom, District Attorney
Pueblo County District Attorney's Office
Courthouse
215 West Tenth Street
Pueblo, CO 81003
(719) 546-6030

Mr. A. M. Dominguez, Jr., District Attorney
Mr. Tony Molocznik
Consumer Fraud Investigator
Weld County District Attorney's Consumer Office
P.O. Box 1167
Greeley, CO 80632
(303) 356-4000 ext. 4735

Connecticut

State Offices

Ms. Gloria Schaffer, Commissioner
Department of Consumer Protection
State Office Building
165 Capitol Avenue
Hartford, CT 06106
(203) 566-4999
1 (800) 842-2649 (toll free in CT)

Mr. Robert M. Langer
Assistant Attorney General
Antitrust/Consumer Protection
Office of Attorney General
110 Sherman Street
Hartford, CT 06105
(203) 566-5374

City Office

Mr. Guy Tommasi, Director
Middletown Office of Consumer Protection
City Hall
Middletown, CT 06457
(203) 344-3492

Delaware

State Offices

Mr. Donald E. Williams, Director
Division of Consumer Affairs
Department of Community Affairs
820 North French Street, 4th Floor
Wilmington, DE 19801
(302) 577-3250

Mr. Stuart Drowos, Deputy Attorney General for Economic Crime and Consumer Protection
Office of Attorney General
820 North French Street
Wilmington, DE 19801
(302) 577-3250

District of Columbia

Mr. Aubrey Edwards, Director
Department of Consumer and Regulatory Affairs
614 H Street, N.W.
Washington, DC 20001
(202) 727-7000

Florida

State Offices

Ms. Barbara Edwards, Assistant Director
Department of Agriculture and Consumer Services
Division of Consumer Services
218 Mayo Building
Tallahassee, FL 32399
(904) 488-2226
1 (800) 342-2176
(toll free TDD in FL)
1 (800) 327-3382
(toll free information and education in FL)
1 (800) 321-5366
(toll free lemon law in FL)

Mr. Jack A. Norris, Jr., Chief
Consumer Litigation Section
The Capitol
Tallahassee, FL 32399-1050
(904) 488-9105

Mr. Richard Scott, Chief
Consumer Division
Office of Attorney General
4000 Hollywood Boulevard
Suite 505 South
Hollywood, FL 33021
(305) 985-4780

County Offices

Mr. Stanley A. Kaufman, Director
Broward County Consumer Affairs Division
115 South Andrews Avenue, Room 119
Fort Lauderdale, FL 33301
(305) 357-6030

Mr. Leonard Elias, Consumer Advocate
Metropolitan Dade County Consumer Protection Division
140 West Flagler Street, Suite 902
Miami, FL 33130
(305) 375-4222

Mr. Frederic A. Kerstein, Chief
Dade County Economic Crime Unit
Office of State Attorney
1469 N.W. 13th Terrace, Room 600
Miami, FL 33125
(305) 324-3030

Mr. Henry Huerta, Manager
Hillsborough County Department of Consumer Affairs
412 East Madison Street, Room 1001
Tampa, FL 33602
(813) 272-6750

Mr. Larry F. Blalock, Chief
Orange County Consumer Fraud Unit
250 North Orange Avenue
P.O. Box 1673
Orlando, FL 32802
(407) 836-2490

Citizens Intake
Palm Beach County
Office of State Attorney
P.O. Drawer 2905
West Palm Beach, FL 33402
(407) 355-3560

Mr. Lawrence Breeden, Director
Palm Beach County Department of Consumer Affairs
3111 S. Dixie Highway, Suite 128
West Palm Beach, FL 33405
(407) 355-2670

Mr. Alfred J. Cortis, Administrator

Pasco County Consumer Affairs Division
7530 Little Road
New Port Richey, FL 34654
(813) 847-8110

Mr. William H. Richards, Director
Pinellas County Office of Consumer Affairs
P.O. Box 17268
Clearwater, FL 34622-0268
(813) 530-6200

Ms. Beth Rutberg, Coordinator
Seminole Economic Crime Unit
Office of State Attorney
100 East First Street
Sanford, FL 32771
(407) 322-7534

State Attorney
Consumer Fraud Unit
700 S. Park Avenue
Titusville, FL 32780
(407) 264-5230

City Offices
Ms. Rachel Marcus-Hendry
Chief of Consumer Affairs
City of Jacksonville
Division of Consumer Affairs
421 W. Church Street, Suite 404
Jacksonville, FL 32202
(904) 630-3667

Mr. Al Dezure, Chairman
Lauderhill Consumer Protection Board
1176 N.W. 42nd Way
Lauderhill, FL 33313
(305) 321-2450

Mr. Irving Lopatey, Chairman
Tamarac Board of Consumer Affairs
7525 N.W. 88th Avenue
Tamarac, FL 33321
(305) 722-5900, ext. 389
(Tuesday, Wednesday and Thursday—10 a.m. to Noon)

Georgia

State Office
Mr. Barry W. Reid, Administrator
Governor's Office of Consumer Affairs
2 Martin Luther King, Jr., Drive, S.E.
Plaza Level—East Tower
Atlanta, GA 30334
(404) 651-8600
(404) 656-3790
1 (800) 869-1123 (toll free in GA)

Hawaii

State Offices
Mr. Philip Doi, Director
Office of Consumer Protection
Department of Commerce and Consumer Affairs
828 Fort St. Mall, Suite 600B
P.O. Box 3767
Honolulu, HI 96812-3767
(808) 586-2630

Mr. Gene Murayama, Investigator
Office of Consumer Protection
Department of Commerce and Consumer Affairs
75 Aupuni Street
Hilo, HI 96720
(808) 933-4433

Mr. Glenn Ikemoto, Investigator
Office of Consumer Protection
Department of Commerce and Consumer Affairs
3060 Eiwa Street
Lihue, HI 96766
(808) 241-3365

Mr. James E. Radford, Investigator
Office of Consumer Protection
Department of Commerce and Consumer Affairs
54 High Street
P.O. Box 3767
Honolulu, HI 96812
(808) 586-2630

Idaho

State Office
Mr. Brett De Lange
Deputy Attorney General
Office of the Attorney General
Consumer Protection Unit
Statehouse, Room 113A
Boise, ID 83720-1000
(208) 334-2424
1 (800) 432-3545
(toll free in ID)

Illinois

State Offices
Ms. Drinda L. O'Connor, Director
Governors Office of Citizens Assistance
222 South College
Springfield, IL 62706
(217) 782-0244
1 (800) 642-3112
(toll free in IL)

Ms. Sally Saltzberg, Chief
Consumer Protection Division
Office of Attorney General
100 West Randolph, 12th Floor
Chicago, IL 60601
(312) 814-3580
(312) 793-2852 (TDD)

Ms. Elaine Hirsch, Director
Department of Citizen Rights
100 West Randolph, 13th Floor
Chicago, IL 60601
(312) 814-3289
(312) 814-7123 (TDD)

Regional Offices
Mr. Anthony Dyhrkopp
Assistant Attorney General
Carbondale Regional Office
Office of Attorney General

626A East Walnut Street
Carbondale, IL 62901
(618) 457-3505
(618) 457-4421 (TDD)

Ms. Regina Haasis
Assistant Attorney General
Champaign Regional Office
34 East Main Street
Champaign, IL 61820
(217) 333-7691 (voice/TDD)

Ms. Agather McKeel
Assistant Attorney General
East St. Louis Regional Office
Office of Attorney General
8712 State Street
East St. Louis, IL 62203
(618) 398-1006
(618) 398-1009 (TDD)

Mr. Dennis Orsey
Assistant Attorney General
Granite City Regional Office
Office of Attorney General
1314 Niedringhaus
Granite City, IL 62040
(618) 877-0404

Mr. Tony L. Brasel
Assistant Attorney General
Kankakee Regional Office
Office of Attorney General
1012 North 5th Avenue
Kankakee, IL 60901
(815) 935-8500

Ms. Cynthia Tracy
Assistant Attorney General
LaSalle Regional Office
Office of Attorney General
1222 Shooting Park Rd., Suite 106
Peru, IL 61354
(815) 224-4861
(815) 224-4864 (TDD)

Mt. Vernon Regional Office
Office of Attorney General
3405 Broadway
Mt. Vernon, IL 62864
(618) 242-8200 (voice/TDD)

Ms. Dianna Zimmerman
Assistant Attorney General
Peoria Regional Office
Office of Attorney General
323 Main Street
Peoria, IL 61602
(309) 671-3191
(309) 671-3089 (TDD)

Quincy Regional Office
Office of Attorney General
523 Main Street
Quincy, IL 62301
(217) 223-2221 (voice/TDD)

Mr. Joseph Bruscato
Assistant Attorney General
Rockford Regional Office
Office of Attorney General
119 North Church Street
Rockford, IL 61101
(815) 987-7580
(815) 987-7579 (TDD)

Mr. Herbert S. Schultz, Jr.
Assistant Attorney General
Rock Island Regional Office
Office of Attorney General
1614 2nd Avenue
Rock Island, IL 61201
(309) 793-0950
(309) 793-0956 (TDD)

Ms. Deborah Hagan
Assistant Attorney General and Chief
Consumer Protection Division
Office of Attorney General
500 South Second Street
Springfield, IL 62706
(217) 782-9011
1 (800) 252-8666 (toll free in IL)

Ms. Elizabeth Foran
Assistant Attorney General
Waukegan Regional Office
Office of Attorney General
12 South County Street
Waukegan, IL 60085
(708) 336-2207
(708) 336-2374 (TDD)

Mr. Michael Pasko
Assistant Attorney General
West Frankfort Regional Office
Office of Attorney General
222 East Main Street
West Frankfort, IL 62896
(618) 937-6453

Ms. Colleen McLaughlin
Assistant Attorney General
West Chicago Regional Office
Office of Attorney General
122A County Farm Road
Wheaton, IL 60187
(708) 653-5060 (voice/TDD)

County Offices

Mr. Allen Reissman, Supervisor
Consumer Fraud Division—303
Cook County Office of State's Attorney
303 Daley Center
Chicago, IL 60602
(312) 443-4600

Mr. William Haine, State's Attorney
Madison County Office of State's Attorney
325 E. Vandalia
Edwardsville, IL 62025
(618) 692-6280

Mr. Floyd Atkinson, Director
Consumer Protection Division
Rock Island County
State's Attorney's Office
County Courthouse
Rock Island, IL 61201
(309) 786-4451, ext. 229

City Offices

Ms. Mary Runion, Consumer Fraud
Wheeling Township
1616 North Arlington Heights Road
Arlington Heights, IL 60004
(708) 259-7730 (Wednesdays only)

Ms. Caroline O. Shoenberger
Commissioner
Chicago Department of Consumer Services
121 North LaSalle Street, Room 808
Chicago, IL 60602
(312) 744-4090
(312) 744-9385 (TDD)

Mr. Robert E. Hinde, Administrator
Des Plaines Consumer Protection Commission
1420 Miner Street
Des Plaines, IL 60016
(708) 391-5363

Indiana

State Office

Mr. David A. Miller
Chief Counsel and Director
Consumer Protection Division
Office of Attorney General
219 State House
Indianapolis, IN 46204
(317) 232-6330
1 (800) 382-5516 (toll free in IN)

County Offices

Ms. Gail Barus, Director
Consumer Protection Division
Lake County Prosecutors Office
2293 North Main Street
Crown Point, IN 46307
(219) 755-3720

Mr. Jeffrey Modisett
Marion County Prosecuting Attorney
560 City-County Building
200 East Washington Street
Indianapolis, IN 46204-3363
(317) 236-3522

Mr. Stanley Levco
Vanderburgh County Prosecuting Attorney
108 Administration Building
Civic Center Complex
Evansville, IN 47708
(812) 426-5150

City Office

Mr. Robert McCrady, Director
Gary Office of Consumer Affairs
Annex East
1100 Massachusetts Street
Gary, IN 46407
(219) 886-0145

Iowa

State Office
Mr. Steve St. Clair
Assistant Attorney General
Consumer Protection Division
Office of Attorney General
1300 East Walnut Street, 2nd Floor
Des Moines, IA 50319
(515) 281-5926

Kansas

State Office

Mr. Daniel P. Kolditz
Deputy Attorney General
Consumer Protection Division
Office of Attorney General
301 West 10th
Kansas Judicial Center
Topeka, KS 66612-1597
(913) 296-3751
1 (800) 432-2310 (toll free in KS)

County Offices

Mr. Roger A. Nordeen, Head
Consumer Fraud Division
Johnson County District Attorney's Office
Johnson County Courthouse
P.O. Box 728
Olathe, KS 66061
(913) 782-5000

Mr. Richard L. Schodorf, Chief Attorney
Consumer Fraud and Economic Crime Division
Sedgwick County District Attorney's Office
Sedgwick County Courthouse
Wichita, KS 67203
(316) 268-7921

Mr. James J. Welch
Assistant District Attorney
Shawnee County District Attorney's Office
Shawnee County Courthouse, Room 212
Topeka, KS 66603-3922
(913) 291-4330

City Office

Mr. Brenden Long
Assistant City Attorney
Topeka Consumer Protection Division
City Attorney's Office
215 East Seventh Street
Topeka, KS 66603
(913) 295-3883

Kentucky

State Offices

Ms. Nora K. McCormick, Director
Consumer Protection Division
Office of Attorney General
209 Saint Clair Street
Frankfort, KY 40601-1875
(502) 564-2200
1 (800) 432-9257 (toll free in KY)

Mr. Robert L. Winlock, Administrator
Consumer Protection Division
Office of Attorney General
107 S. 4th Street
Louisville, KY 40202
(502) 588-3262
1 (800) 432-9257 (toll free in KY)

Louisiana

State Office

Ms. Mary H. Travis, Chief
Consumer Protection Section
Office of Attorney General
State Capitol Building
P.O. Box 94005
Baton Rouge, LA 70804-9005
(504) 342-7373

County Office

Sgt. Albert H. Olsen, Chief
Consumer Protection Division
Jefferson Parish District Attorney's Office
200 Huey P. Long Avenue
Gretna, LA 70053
(504) 364-3644

Maine

State Offices

Mr. William N. Lund
Superintendent
Bureau of Consumer Credit Protection
State House Station No. 35
Augusta, ME 04333-0035
(207) 582-8718
1 (800) 332-8529 (toll free)

Mr. Stephen Wessler, Chief
Consumer and Antitrust Division
Office of Attorney General
State House Station No. 6
Augusta, ME 04333
(207) 289-3716 (9 a.m.-1 p.m.)

Maryland

State Offices

Mr. William Leibovici, Chief
Consumer Protection Division
Office of Attorney General
200 St. Paul Place
Baltimore, MD 21202-2021
(301) 528-8662 (9 a.m.–3 p.m.)
(301) 576-6372 (TDD in Baltimore area)
(301) 565-0451 (TDD in DC metro area)
1 (800) 969-5766 (toll free)

Mr. Ronald E. Forbes, Director
Licensing & Consumer Services
Motor Vehicle Administration
6601 Ritchie Highway, N.E.
Glen Burnie, MD 21062
(301) 768-7420

Ms. Emalu Myer
Consumer Affairs Specialist
Eastern Shore Branch Office
Consumer Protection Division
Office of Attorney General
Salisbury District Court/Multi-service Center
201 Baptist Street, Suite 30
Salisbury, MD 21801-4976
(301) 543-6620

Mr. Larry Munson, Director
Western Maryland Branch Office
Consumer Protection Division
Office of Attorney General
138 East Antietam Street, Suite 210
Hagerstown, MD 21740-5684
(301) 791-4780

County Offices

Mr. Stephen D. Hannan, Administrator
Howard County Office of Consumer Affairs
9250 Rumsey Rd.
Columbia, MD 21045
(301) 313-7220
(301) 313-7201, 2323 (TDD)

Ms. Barbara B. Gregg, Executive Director
Montgomery County Office of Consumer Affairs
100 Maryland Avenue, 3rd Floor
Rockville, MD 20850
(301) 217-7373

Ms. Michelle Tucker Rozner
Executive Director
Prince George's County Consumer Protection Commission
9201 Basil Court
Landover, MD 20785
(301) 925-5100
(301) 925-5167 (TDD)

Massachusetts

State Offices

Mr. Robert Sherman, Chief
Consumer Protection Division
Department of Attorney General
131 Tremont Street
Boston, MA 02111
(617) 727-8400
(information and referral to local consumer offices that work in conjunction with the Department of Attorney General)

Ms. Gloria Cordes Larson, Secretary
Executive Office of Consumer Affairs and Business Regulation
One Ashburton Place, Room 1411
Boston, MA 02108
(617) 727-7780
(information and referral only)

Mr. Carmen Picknally
Managing Attorney
Western Massachusetts Consumer Protection Division
Department of Attorney General
436 Dwight Street
Springfield, MA 01103
(413) 784-1240

County Offices

Ms. Margaret Platek, Complaint Supervisor
Consumer Fraud Prevention
Franklin County District Attorney's Office
238 Main Street
Greenfield, MA 01301
(413) 774-5102

Ms. Susan Grant, Director
Consumer Fraud Prevention
Hampshire County District Attorney's Office
1 Court Square
Northhampton, MA 01060
(413) 586-9225

Project Coordinator
Worcester County Consumer Rights Project
340 Main Street, Room 370
Worcester, MA 01608
(508) 754-7420 (9:30 a.m.–4 p.m.)

City Offices

Ms. Diane J. Modica, Commissioner
Mayor's Office of Consumer Affairs and Licensing
Boston City Hall, Room 613
Boston, MA 02201
(617) 725-3320

Ms. Jean Courtney, Director
Consumer Information Center
Springfield Action Commission
P.O. Box 1449 Main Office
Springfield, MA 01101
(413) 737-4376
(Hampton and Hampshire Counties)

Michigan

State Offices

Mr. Frederick H. Hoffecker
Assistant in Charge
Consumer Protection Division
Office of Attorney General
P.O. Box 30213
Lansing, MI 48909
(517) 373-1140

Mr. Kent Wilcox, Executive Director
Michigan Consumers Council
414 Hollister Building
106 West Allegan Street
Lansing, MI 48933
(517) 373-0947
(517) 373-0701 (TDD)

Mr. Rodger James, Acting Director
Bureau of Automotive Regulation
Michigan Department of State
Lansing, MI 48918
(517) 373-7858
1 (800) 292-4204 (toll free in MI)

County Offices

Mr. George Mullison, Prosecuting Attorney
Bay County Consumer Protection Unit
Bay County Building
Bay City, MI 48708-5994
(517) 893-3594

Ms. Margaret DeMuynck, Director
Consumer Protection Department
Macomb County
Office of the Prosecuting Attorney
Macomb Court Building, 6th Floor
Mt. Clemens, MI 48043
(313) 469-5350

Ms. Charleen Berels, Director
Washtenaw County Consumer Services
4133 Washtenaw Street
P.O. Box 8645
Ann Arbor, MI 48107-8645
(313) 971-6054

City Office

Ms. Esther K. Shapiro, Director
City of Detroit
Department of Consumer Affairs
1600 Cadillac Tower
Detroit, MI 48226
(313) 224-3508

Minnesota

State Offices

Mr. Curt Loewe, Director
Office of Consumer Services
Office of Attorney General
117 University Avenue
St. Paul, MN 55155
(612) 296-2331

Consumer Services Division
Office of Attorney General
320 West Second Street
Duluth, MN 55802
(218) 723-4891

County Office

Ms. Kate McPherson
Citizen Protection Unit
Hennepin County Attorney's Office
C2000 County Government Center
Minneapolis, MN 55487
(612) 348-4528

City Office

Mr. James Moncur, Director
Consumer Affairs Division
Minneapolis Department of Licenses & Consumer Services
One C City Hall
Minneapolis, MN 55415
(612) 348-2080

Mississippi

State Offices

Mr. Trey Bobinger
Special Assistant Attorney General
Chief, Consumer Protection Division
Office of Attorney General
P.O. Box 22947
Jackson, MS 39225-2947
(601) 354-6018

Mr. Joe B. Hardy, Director
Regulatory Services
Department of Agriculture and Commerce
500 Greymont Avenue
P.O. Box 1609
Jackson, MS 39215
(601) 354-7063

Ms. Mattie T. Stevens
Consumer Counselor
Gulf Coast Regional Office of the Attorney General
P.O. Box 1411
Biloxi, MS 39533
(601) 436-6000

Missouri

State Offices

Office of the Attorney General
Consumer Complaints or Problems
P.O. Box 899
Jefferson City, MO 65102
(314) 751-3321
1 (800) 392-8222 (toll free in MO)

Mr. Henry Herschel, Chief Counsel
Trade Offense Division
Office of Attorney General
P.O. Box 899
Jefferson City, MO 65102
(314) 751-3321
1 (800) 392-8222 (toll free in MO)

Montana

State Office
Consumer Affairs Unit
Department of Commerce
1424 Ninth Avenue
Helena, MT 59620
(406) 444-4312

Nebraska

State Office
Mr. Paul N. Potadle
Assistant Attorney General
Consumer Protection Division
Department of Justice
2115 State Capitol
P.O. Box 98920
Lincoln, NE 68509
(402) 471-2682

County Office
Mr. James Jansen
Douglas County Attorney
County Attorney's Office
428 Hall of Justice
17th and Farnam
Omaha, NE 68183
(402) 444-7040

Nevada

State Offices
Mr. Myram Borders
Commissioner of Consumer Affairs
Department of Commerce
State Mail Room Complex
Las Vegas, NV 89158
(702) 486-7355
1 (800) 992-0900 (toll free in NV)

Mr. Ray Trease, Consumer Services Officer
Consumer Affairs Division
Department of Commerce
4600 Kietzke Lane, M-245
Reno, NV 89502
(702) 688-1800
1 (800) 992-0900 (toll free in NV)

County Office
Mr. John Long, Investigator
Consumer Fraud Division
Washoe County District Attorney's Office
P.O. Box 11130
Reno, NV 89520
(702) 328-3456

New Hampshire

State Office
Chief
Consumer Protection and Antitrust Bureau
Office of Attorney General
State House Annex
Concord, NH 03301
(603) 271-3641

New Jersey

State Offices
Ms. Patricia A. Royer, Director
Division of Consumer Affairs
P.O. Box 45027
Newark, NJ 07101
(201) 648-4010

Mr. Wilfredo Caraballo, Commissioner
Department of the Public Advocate
CN 850, Justice Complex
Trenton, NJ 08625
(609) 292-7087
1 (800) 792-8600 (toll free in NJ)

Ms. Cindy K. Miller
Deputy Attorney General
New Jersey Division of Law
1207 Raymond Boulevard
P.O. Box 45029
Newark, NJ 07101
(201) 648-7579

County Offices
Mr. William H. Ross III, Director
Atlantic County Consumer Affairs
1333 Atlantic Avenue, 8th Floor
Atlantic City, NJ 08401
(609) 345-6700

Mary E. Courtney, Director
Bergen County Division of Consumer Affairs
21 Main Street, Room 101-E
Hackensack, NJ 07601-7000
(201) 646-2650

Mrs. Renee L. Borstad, Director
Burlington County Office of Consumer Affairs
49 Rancocas Road
Mount Holly, NJ 08060
(609) 265-5054

Ms. Patricia M. Tuck, Director
Camden County Office of Consumer Affairs
1800 Pavilion West
2101 Ferry Avenue, Suite 609
Camden, NJ 08104
(609) 757-8397

Mr. Mark Diederich, Director
Cape May County Consumer Affairs
DN-310, Central Mail Room
Cape May Court House
Cape May Court House, NJ 08210
(609) 465-1076

Mr. Louis G. Moreno, Director
Cumberland County Department of Consumer Affairs and Weights and Measures
788 East Commerce Street
Bridgeton, NJ 08302
(609) 453-2202

Director
Essex County Consumer Services
15 Southmunn Avenue, 2nd Floor
East Orange, NJ 07018
(201) 678-8071
(201) 678-8928

Mr. Edward McGoldrick, Director
Gloucester County Consumer Affairs
152 North Broad Street
Woodbury, NJ 08096
(609) 853-3349
(609) 848-6616 (TDD)

Ms. Barbara Donnelly, Director
Hudson County Division of Consumer Affairs
595 Newark Avenue
Jersey City, NJ 07306
(201) 795-6295

Ms. Helen Mataka, Director
Hunterdon County Consumer Affairs
P.O. Box 283
Lebanon, NJ 08833
(908) 236-2249

Ms. Donna Giovannetti, Division Chief
Mercer County Consumer Affairs
640 South Broad Street, Room 229
Trenton, NJ 08650-0068
(609) 989-6671

Mr. Lawrence Cimmino, Director
Middlesex County Consumer Affairs
149 Kearny Avenue
Perth Amboy, NJ 08861
(201) 324-4600

Ms. Dorothy H. Avallone, Director
Mommouth County Consumer Affairs
1 East Main Street
P.O. Box 1255
Freehold, NJ 07728-1255
(908) 431-7900

Ms. Janet Opiekun, Director
Morris County Consumer Affairs
P.O. Box 900
Morristown, NJ 07963-0900
(201) 285-6070
(201) 584-9189 (TDD)

Mr. Kenneth J. Leake, Director
Ocean County Consumer Affairs
P.O. Box 2191
County Administration Building
Room 130-1
Toms River, NJ 08754-2191
(908) 929-2105

Ms. Mary Ann Maloney, Director
Passaic County Consumer Affairs
County Administration Building
309 Pennsylvania Avenue
Paterson, NJ 07503
(201) 881-4547, 4499

Ms. Ruth A. Hotz
Somerset County Consumer Affairs
County Administration Building
P.O. Box 3000
Somerville, NJ 08876
(908) 231-7000, ext 7400

Mrs. Ollie Jones, Office Manager
Union County Consumer Affairs
300 North Avenue East
P.O. Box 186
Westfield, NJ 07091
(201) 654-9840

Ms. Barbara McHenry, Director
Warren County Consumer Affairs
Dumont Administration Bldg., Route 519
Belvedere, NJ 07823
(908) 475-6500

City Offices

Ms. Lorraine Sudia, Director
Brick Consumer Affairs
Municipal Building
401 Chambers Bridge Road
Brick, NJ 08723
(908) 477-3000, ext. 296

Mr. Lawrence A. Eleuteri, Director
Cinnaminson Consumer Affairs
Municipal Building
1621 Riverton Road
Cinnaminson, NJ 08077
(609) 829-6000

Ms. Theresa Ward, Director
Clark Consumer Affairs
430 Westfield Avenue
Clark, NJ 07066
(908) 388-3600

Ms. Mary Ann Pizzello, Director
Elizabeth Consumer Affairs
City Hall
60 West Scott Plaza
Elizabeth, NJ 07203
(908) 820-4183

Mr. H. Gerald Niemira, Director
Fort Lee Consumer Protection Board
Bourough Hall
309 Main Street
Fort Lee, NJ 07024
(201) 592-3579

Ms. Libby Saltzman, Director
Glen Rock Consumer Affairs
Municipal Building, Harding Plaza
Glen Rock, NJ 07452-2100
(201) 670-3956

Mr. Robert King
Consumer Advocate
City Hall
94 Washington Street
Hoboken, NJ 07030
(201) 420-2038

Ms. Bernadine Jacobs, Director
Livingston Consumer Affairs
357 South Livingston Avenue
Livingston, NJ 07039
(201) 535-7976

Ms. Genevieve Ross, Director
Middlesex Borough Consumer Affairs
1200 Mountain Avenue
Middlesex, NJ 08846
(908) 356-8090

Ms. Mildred Pastore, Director
Mountainside Consumer Affairs

1455 Coles Avenue
Mountainside, NJ 07092
(908) 232-6600

Mr. Max Moses
Department of Community Services
Municipal Building
North Bergen, NJ 07047
(201) 330-7292, 91

Ms. Annmarie Nicolette, Director
Nutley Consumer Affairs
City Hall
228 Chestnut Street
Nutley, NJ 07110
(201) 284-4936

Ms. Beth Jenkins, Director
Parsippany Consumer Affairs
Municipal Building, Room 101
1001 Parsippany Boulevard
Parsippany, NJ 07054
(201) 263-7011

Ms. Maria Jimenez, Director
Perth Amboy Consumer Affairs
City Hall
260 High Street
Perth Amboy, NJ 08861
(908) 826-0290, ext. 61, 62

Ms. Priscilla Castles, Director
Plainfield Action Services
510 Watchung Avenue
Plainfield, NJ 07060
(908) 753-3519

Michael B. Bukatman, Director
Secaucus Department of Consumer Affairs
Municipal Government Center
Secaucus, NJ 07094
(201) 330-2019

Ms. Marion Cramer, Director
Union Township Consumer Affairs
Municipal Building
1976 Morris Avenue
Union, NJ 07083
(908) 688-6763

Mr. Charles A. Stern, Director
Wayne Township Consumer Affairs
475 Valley Road
Wayne, NJ 07470
(201) 694-1800, ext. 290

Mr. John Weitzel, Director
Weehawken Consumer Affairs
400 Park Avenue
Weehawken, NJ 07087
(201) 319-6005

Mr. John Busuttil, Director
West New York Consumer Affairs
428 60th Street
West New York, NJ 07093
(201) 861-2522

New Mexico

State Office

Consumer Protection Division
Office of Attorney General
P.O. Drawer 1508
Santa Fe, NM 87504
(505) 827-6060
1 (800) 432-2070 (toll free in NM)

New York

State Offices

Mr. Richard M. Kessel
Chairperson and Executive Director
New York State Consumer Protection Board
99 Washington Avenue
Albany, NY 12210-2891
(518) 474-8583

Ms. Rachael Kretser
Assistant Attorney General
Bureau of Consumer Frauds and Protection
Office of Attorney General
State Capitol
Albany, NY 12224
(518) 474-5481

Mr. Richard M. Kessel
Chairperson and Executive Director
New York State Consumer Protection Board
250 Broadway, 17th Floor
New York, NY 10007-2593
(212) 417-4908 (complaints)
(212) 417-4482 (main office)

Mr. John Corwin
Assistant Attorney General
Bureau of Consumer Frauds and Protection
Office of Attorney General
120 Broadway
New York, NY 10271
(212) 341-2345

Regional Offices

Mr. John R. Marshall, Jr.
Assistant Attorney General in Charge
Binghamton Regional Office
Office of Attorney General
59-61 Court Street, 7th Floor
Binghamton, NY 13901
(607) 773-7877

Mr. Peter B. Sullivan
Assistant Attorney General in Charge
Buffalo Regional Office
Office of Attorney General
65 Court Street
Buffalo, NY 14202
(716) 847-7184

Mr. Alan J. Burczak
Assistant Attorney General in Charge
Plattsburgh Regional Office
Office of Attorney General
70 Clinton Street
Plattsburgh, NY 12901
(518) 563-8012

Mr. Kent L. Mardon
Assistant Attorney General in Charge
Poughkeepsie Regional Office
Office of Attorney General
235 Main Street
Poughkeepsie, NY 12601
(914) 485-3920

Mr. Eugene Welch
Assistant Attorney General in Charge
Rochester Regional Office

Office of Attorney General
144 Exchange Boulevard
Rochester, NY 14614
(716) 546-7430

Ms. Susan B. Blum
Assistant Attorney General in Charge
Suffolk Regional Office
Office of Attorney General
300 Motor Parkway
Hauppauge, NY 11788
(516) 231-2400

Mr. John R. Voninski
Assistant Attorney General in Charge
Syracuse Regional Office
Office of Attorney General
615 Erie Boulevard West
Syracuse, NY 13204-2465
(315) 448-4848

Ms. Aniela J. Carl
Assistant Attorney General in Charge
Utica Regional Office
Office of Attorney General
207 Genesee Street
Utica, NY 13501
(315) 793-2225

County Offices

Mr. Thomas M. Jablonowski
Deputy Director of General Services
Broome County Bureau of Consumer Affairs
Governmental Plaza, P.O. Box 1766
Binghamton, NY 13902
(607) 778-2168

Mr. Nelson Kranker, Director
Dutchess County Department of Consumer Affairs
38-A Dutchess Turnpike
Poughkeepsie, NY 12603
(914) 471-6322

Ms. Candace K. Vogel
Assistant District Attorney
Consumer Fraud Bureau
Erie County District Attorney's Office
25 Delaware Avenue
Buffalo, NY 14202
(716) 858-2424

Mr. James E. Picken, Commissioner
Nassau County Office of Consumer Affairs
160 Old Country Road
Mineola, NY 11501
(516) 535-2600

Mr. John McCullough, Executive Director
New Justice Conflict Resolution Services, Inc.
210 East Fayette Street, Suite 700
Syracuse, NY 13202
(315) 471-4676

Mr. Edward J. Brown, Commissioner
Orange County Department of Consumer Affairs and Weights and Measures
99 Main Street
Goshen, NY 10924
(914) 294-5151, ext. 1762

Mr. Francis D. Phillips II, District Attorney
Orange County District Attorney's Office
255 Main Street
County Government Center
Goshen, NY 10924
(914) 294-5471

Mr. Joseph LaBarbera
Putnam County Office Facility
Department of Consumer Affairs
Myrtle Avenue
Mahopac Falls, NY 10542-0368
(914) 621-2317

Mr. Alfred J. Stelzl, Director/Coordinator
Rockland County Office of Consumer Protection
County Office Building
18 New Hempstead Road
New City, NY 10956
(914) 638-5282

Mr. Dennis S. Abbey, Director
Steuben County Department of Weights, Measures and Consumer Affairs
3 East Pulteney Square
Bath, NY 14810
(607) 776-9631
(607) 776-9631 ext. 2101 (voice/TDD)

Ms. Jane Devine, Commissioner
Suffolk County Department of Consumer Affairs
Suffolk County Center
Hauppauge, NY 11788
(516) 360-4600

Mr. Jon Van Vlack, Director
Ulster County Consumer Fraud Bureau
285 Wall Street
Kingston, NY 12401
(914) 339-5680, ext. 240

Mr. Frank D. Castaldi, Jr.
Chief, Frauds Bureau
Westchester County District Attorney's Office
111 Grove Street
White Plains, NY 10601
(914) 285-3303

Mr. Jeffrey A. Conte, Acting Director
Westchester County Department of Consumer Affairs
Room 104, Michaelian Office Building
White Plains, NY 10601
(914) 285-2155

City Offices

Mr. Steven M. Nagel, Director
Babylon Consumer Protection Board
Town Hall Office Annex
281 Phelps Lane
North Babylon, NY 11703
(516) 422-7636

Town of Colonie Consumer Protection
Memorial Town Hall
Newtonville, NY 12128
(518) 783-2790

Mr. Stephen Pedone, Commissioner
Mt. Vernon Office of Consumer Affairs
City Hall
Mt. Vernon, NY 10550
(914) 665-2433

Mr. Mark Green, Commissioner
New York City Department of Consumer Affairs
42 Broadway
New York, NY 10004
(212) 487-4444

Bronx Neighborhood Office
New York City Department of Consumer Affairs
1932 Arthur Avenue, Room 104-A
Bronx, NY 10457
(212) 579-6766

Brooklyn Neighborhood Office
New York City Department of Consumer Affairs
1360 Fulton Street, Room 320
Brooklyn, NY 11216
(718) 636-7092

Ms. Isabel Butler, Director
Queens Neighborhood Office
New York City Department of Consumer Affairs
120-55 Queens Boulevard, Room 301A
Kew Gardens, NY 11424
(718) 261-2922

Ms. Johanna Kepley, Director
Staten Island Neighborhood Office
New York City Department of Consumer Affairs
Staten Island Borough Hall, Room 422
Staten Island, NY 10301
(718) 390-5154

Mr. Joseph Kapuscinski, Director
City of Oswego Office of Consumer Affairs
City Hall
West Oneida Street
Oswego, NY 13126
(315) 342-8150

Ms. Cathie Dworkin, Chairwoman
Ramapo Consumer Protection Board
Ramapo Town Hall
237 Route 59
Suffern, NY 10901-5399
(914) 357-5100

Schenectady Bureau of Consumer Protection
City Hall, Room 22
Jay Street
Schenectady, NY 12305
(518) 382-5061

Mr. Jack Casey, Director
White Plains Department of Weights and Measures
77 South Lexington Avenue
White Plains, NY 10601-2512
(914) 422-6359

Mr. Ralph A. Capozzi, Director
Yonkers Office of Consumer Protection, Weights and Measures
201 Palisade Avenue
Yonkers, NY 10703
(914) 377-6807

North Carolina

State Office

Mr. James C. Gulick
Special Deputy Attorney General
Consumer Protection Section
Office of Attorney General
Raney Building
P.O. Box 629
Raleigh, NC 27602
(919) 733-7741

North Dakota

State Offices

Mr. Nicholas J. Spaeth
Office of Attorney General
600 East Boulevard
Bismarck, ND 58505
(701) 224-2210
1 (800) 472-2600 (toll free in ND)

Mr. Tom Engelhardt, Director
Consumer Fraud Section
Office of Attorney General
600 East Boulevard
Bismarck, ND 58505
(701) 224-3404
1 (800) 472-2600 (toll free in ND)

County Office

Mr. Kent Keys, Executive Director
Quad County Community Action Agency
27½ South Third Street
Grand Forks, ND 58201
(701) 746-5431

Ohio

State Offices

Ms. Dianne Goss Paynter
Consumer Frauds and Crimes Section
Office of Attorney General
30 East Broad Street
State Office Tower, 25th Floor
Columbus, OH 43266-0410
(614) 466-4986 (complaints)
(614) 466-1393 (TDD)
1 (800) 282-0515 (toll free in OH)

Mr. William A. Spratley
Office of Consumers' Counsel
77 South High Street, 15th Floor
Columbus, OH 43266-0550
(614) 466-9605 (voice/TDD)
1 (800) 282-9448 (toll free in OH)

County Offices

Mr. Richard Whitehouse, Director
Economic Crime Division
Franklin County Office of Prosecuting Attorney

369 South High Street
Columbus, OH 43215
(614) 462-3555

Mr. Steven C. LaTourette
County Prosecutor
Consumer Protection Division
Lake County Office of Prosecuting Attorney
Lake County Court House
Painesville, OH 44077
(216) 357-2683
1 (800) 899-5253 (toll free in OH)

Mr. Robert A. Skinner
Assistant Prosecuting Attorney
Montgomery County Fraud Section
301 West 3rd Street
Dayton Montgomery
County Courts Building
Dayton, OH 45402
(513) 225-5757

Mr. David Norris, Prosecuting Attorney
Portage County Office of Prosecuting Attorney
466 South Chestnut Street
Ravenna, OH 44266-0671
(216) 296-4593

Mr. Lynn C. Slaby, Prosecuting Attorney
Summit County Office of Prosecuting Attorney
53 University Avenue
Akron, OH 44308-1680
(216) 379-2800

City Offices

Mr. Steven Kurtz, Chief
Cincinnati Office of Consumer Services
Division of Human Services
City Hall, Room 126
Cincinnati, OH 45202
(513) 352-3971

Mr. Anthony C. Julian, Director
Youngstown Office of Consumer Affairs and Weights and Measures
26 South Phelps Street
City Hall
Youngstown, OH 44503-1318
(216) 742-8884

Oklahoma

State Offices

Ms. Jane Wheeler
Assistant Attorney General
Office of Attorney General
420 West Main, Suite 550
Oklahoma City, OK 73102
(405) 521-4274

Mr. Prescott H. Cowley, Administrator
Department of Consumer Credit
4545 Lincoln Boulevard, Suite 104
Oklahoma City, OK 73105-3408
(405) 521-3653

Oregon

State Office

Mr. Timothy Wood, Attorney in Charge
Financial Fraud Section
Department of Justice
Justice Building
Salem, OR 97310
(503) 378-4320

Pennsylvania

State Offices

Mr. Renardo Hicks, Director
Bureau of Consumer Protection
Office of Attorney General
Strawberry Square, 14th Floor
Harrisburg, PA 17120
(717) 787-9707
1 (800) 441-2555 (toll free in PA)

Mr. Irwin A. Popowsky, Consumer Advocate
Office of Consumer Advocate—Utilities
Office of Attorney General
1425 Strawberry Square
Harrisburg, PA 17120
(717) 783-5048 (utilities only)

Mr. Michael Butler
Deputy Attorney General
Bureau of Consumer Protection
Office of Attorney General
27 North Seventh Street
Allentown, PA 18101
(215) 821-6690

Mr. Joseph Farrell, Director
Bureau of Consumer Services
Pennsylvania Public Utility Commission
203 North Office Building
Harrisburg, PA 17120
(717) 787-4970 (out-of-state calls only)
1 (800) 782-1110 (toll free in PA)

Mr. Daniel R. Goodemote
Deputy Attorney General
Bureau of Consumer Protection
Office of Attorney General
919 State Street, Room 203
Erie, PA 16501
(814) 871-4371

Mr. Robin David Bleecher
Attorney in Charge
Bureau of Consumer Protection
Office of Attorney General
132 Kline Village
Harrisburg, PA 17104
(717) 787-7109
1 (800) 441-2555 (toll free in PA)

Mr. Barry Creany, Deputy Attorney General
Bureau of Consumer Protection
Office of the Attorney General
IGA Building, Route 219 North
P.O. Box 716
Ebensburg, PA 15931
(814) 949-7900

Mr. John E. Kelly, Deputy Attorney General
Bureau of Consumer Protection
Office of Attorney General
21 South 12th Street, 2nd Floor
Philadelphia, PA 19107
(215) 560-2414
1 (800) 441-2555 (toll free in PA)

Ms. Caren L. Mariani
Deputy Attorney General
Bureau of Consumer Protection
Office of Attorney General
Manor Complex, 5th Floor
564 Forbes Avenue
Pittsburgh, PA 15219
(412) 565-5394

Mr. J. P. McGowan
Deputy Attorney General
Bureau of Consumer Protection
Office of Attorney General
State Office Building, Room 358
100 Lackawanna Avenue
Scranton, PA 18503
(717) 963-4913

County Offices

Mr. Sidney Elkin, Director
Beaver County Alliance for Consumer Protection
699 Fifth Street
Beaver, PA 15009-1997
(412) 728-7267

Mr. A. Courtney Yelle, Dircctor/Chief Sealer
Bucks County Consumer Protection, Weights and Measures
50 North Main
Doylestown, PA 18901
(215) 348-7442

Mr. Robert Taylor, Director
Chester County Bureau of Consumer Protection, Weights and Measures
Courthouse, 5th Floor, North Wing
High and Market Streets
West Chester, PA 19380
(215) 344-6150

Ms. Karen A. Koblish, Consumer Mediator
Cumberland County Consumer Affairs
One Courthouse Square
Carlisle, PA 17013-3387
(717) 240-6180

Ms. Evelyn Yancoskie, Director
Delaware County Office of Consumer Affairs, Weights and Measures
Government Center Building
Second and Olive Streets
Media, PA 19063
(215) 891-4865

Mrs. Helen Dunigan, Director
Montgomery County Consumer Affairs Department
County Courthouse
Norristown, PA 19404
(215) 278-3565

City Office

Mr. James Fitzpatrick, Chief
Economic Crime Unit
Philadelphia District Attorney's Office
1421 Arch Street
Philadelphia, PA 19102
(215) 686-8750

Puerto Rico

Mr. Luis Roberto Pinero, Sccrctary
Department of Consumer Affairs (DACO)
Minillas Station, P.O. Box 41059
Santurce, PR 00940
(809) 721-0940

Mr. Hector Rivera Cruz, Secretary
Department of Justice
P.O. Box 192
San Juan, PR 00902
(809) 721-2900

Rhode Island

State Offices

Ms. Lee Baker, Director
Consumer Protection Division
Department of Attorney General
72 Pine Street
Providence, RI 02903
(401) 277-2104
(401) 274-4400 ext. 354 (voice/TDD)
1 (800) 852-7776 (toll free in RI)

Mr. Edwin P. Palumbo, Executive Director
Rhode Island Consumers' Council
365 Broadway
Providence, RI 02909
(401) 277-2764

South Carolina

State Offices

Mr. Ken Moore
Assistant Attorney General
Consumer Fraud and Antitrust Section
Office of Attorney General
P.O. Box 11549
Columbia, SC 29211
(803) 734-3970

Mr. Steve Hamm, Administrator
Department of Consumer Affairs
P.O. Box 5757
Columbia, SC 29250-5757
(803) 734-9452
(803) 734-9455 (TDD)
1 (800) 922-1594 (toll free in SC)

Mr. W. Jefferson Bryson, Jr.
State Ombudsman
Office of Executive Policy and Program
1205 Pendleton Street, Room 308
Columbia, SC 29201
(803) 734-0457
(803) 734-1147 (TDD)

South Dakota

State Office

Mr. Jeff Hallem, Assistant Attorney General
Division of Consumer Affairs
Office of Attorney General
500 East Capitol
State Capitol Building
Pierre, SD 57501-5070
(605) 773-4400

Tennessee

State Offices

Mr. Perry A. Craft, Deputy Attorney General
Antitrust and Consumer Protection Division
Office of Attorney General
450 James Robertson Parkway
Nashville, TN 37243-0485
(615) 741-2672

Ms. Elizabeth Owen, Director
Division of Consumer Affairs
Department of Commerce and Insurance
500 James Robertson Parkway, 5th Floor
Nashville, TN 37243-0600
(615) 741-4737
1 (800) 342-8385 (toll free in TN)
1 (800) 422-CLUB (toll free health club hotline in TN)

Texas

State Offices

Mr. Joe Crews
Assistant Attorney General and Chief
Consumer Protection Division
Office of Attorney General
P.O. Box 12548
Austin, TX 78711
(512) 463-2070

Mr. Stephen Gardner
Assistant Attorney General
Consumer Protection Division
Office of Attorney General
714 Jackson Street, Suite 700
Dallas, TX 75202-4506
(214) 742-8944

Ms. Viviana Patino
Assistant Attorney General
Consumer Protection Division
Office of Attorney General
6090 Surety Drive, Room 260
El Paso, TX 79905
(915) 772-9476

Mr. Richard Tomlinson
Assistant Attorney General
Consumer Protection Division
Office of Attorney General
1019 Congress Street, Suite 1550
Houston, TX 77002-1702
(713) 223-5886

Mr. Robert E. Reyna
Assistant Attorney General
Consumer Protection Division
Office of Attorney General
1208 14th Street, Suite 900
Lubbock, TX 79401-3997
(806) 747-5238

Mr. Thomas M. Bernstein
Assistant Attorney General
Consumer Protection Division
Office of Attorney General
3600 North 23rd Street, Suite 305
McAllen, TX 78501-1685
(512) 682-4547

Mr. Aaron Valenzuela
Assistant Attorney General
Consumer Protection Division
Office of Attorney General
115 East Travis Street, Suite 925
San Antonio, TX 78205-1607
(512) 225-4191

Office of Consumer Protection
State Board of Insurance
816 Congress Avenue, Suite 1400
Austin, TX 78701-2430
(512) 322-4143

County Offices

Mr. Ted Steinke
Assistant District Attorney and Chief of Dallas County District Attorney's Office
Specialized Crime Division
133 North Industrial Boulevard, LB 19
Dallas, TX 75207-4313
(214) 653-3820

Mr. Russel Turbeville
Assistant District Attorney and Chief
Harris County Consumer Fraud Division
Office of District Attorney
201 Fannin, Suite 200
Houston, TX 77002-1901
(713) 221-5836

City Office

Ms. Adela Gonzalez, Director
Dallas Consumer Protection Division
Health and Human Services Department
320 East Jefferson Boulevard, Suite 312
Dallas, TX 75203
(214) 948-4400

Utah

State Offices

Mr. Gary R. Hansen, Director
Division of Consumer Protection
Department of Commerce
160 East 3rd South
P.O. Box 45802
Salt Lake City, UT 84145-0802
(801) 530-6601

Ms. Sheila Page
Assistant Attorney General for Consumer Affairs
Office of Attorney General

115 State Capitol
Salt Lake City, UT 84114
(801) 538-1331

Vermont

State Offices

Mr. J. Wallace Malley
Assistant Attorney General and
Chief, Public Protection Division
Office of Attorney General
109 State Street
Montpelier, VT 05609-1001
(802) 828-3171

Mr. Bruce Martell, Supervisor
Consumer Assurance Section
Department of Agriculture, Food and Market
120 State Street
Montpelier, VT 05620-2901
(802) 828-2436

Virgin Islands

Mr. Clement Magras, Commissioner
Department of Licensing and Consumer Affairs
Property and Procurement Building
Subbase #1, Room 205
St. Thomas, VI 00802
(809) 774-3130

Virginia

State Offices

Mr. Frank Seales, Jr., Chief
Antitrust and Consumer Litigation Section
Office of Attorney General
Supreme Court Building
101 North Eighth Street
Richmond, VA 23219
(804) 786-2116
1 (800) 451-1525 (toll free in VA)

Ms. Betty Blakemore, Director
Division of Consumer Affairs
Department of Agriculture and
Consumer Services
Room 101, Washington Building
1100 Bank Street
P.O. Box 1163
Richmond, VA 23219
(804) 786-2042

Mr. Robert Minnich, Investigator
Northern Virginia Branch
Office of Consumer Affairs
Department of Agriculture and
Consumer Services
100 North Washington St., Suite 412
Falls Church, VA 22046
(703) 532-1613

County Offices

Ms. Diane Jemmott, Section Chief
Office of Citizen and Consumer Affairs
#1 Court House Plaza, Suite 314
2100 Clarendon Boulevard
Arlington, VA 22201
(703) 358-3260

Mr. Ronald B. Mallard, Director
Fairfax County Department of
Consumer Affairs
3959 Pender Drive, Suite 200
Fairfax, VA 22030-6093
(703) 246-5949
(703) 591-3260 (TDD)

Mr. Hubert King, Administrator
Prince William County Office of Consumer Affairs
4370 Ridgewood Center Drive
Prince William, VA 22192-9201
(703) 792-7370

City Offices

Ms. Rose Boyd, Director
Alexandria Office of Citizens Assistance
City Hall
Alexandria, VA 22313
(703) 838-4350
(703) 838-5056 (TDD)

Mr. Robert L. Gill, Coordinator
Division of Consumer Affairs
City Hall
Norfolk, VA 23501
(804) 441-2821
(804) 441-2000 (TDD)

Ms. Dolores Daniels
Assistant to the City Manager
Roanoke Consumer Protection Division
364 Municipal Building
215 Church Avenue, S.W.
Roanoke, VA 24011
(703) 981-2583

Mr. J. N. McClanan
Director, Consumer Affairs Division
Office of the Commonwealth's Attorney
3500 Virginia Beach Boulevard, Suite 304
Virginia Beach, VA 23452
(804) 431-4610

Washington

State Offices

Ms. Renee Olbricht, Investigator
Consumer and Business Fair Practices Division
Office of the Attorney General
111 Olympia Avenue, NE
Olympia, WA 98501
(206) 753-6210

Ms. Sally Sterling
Director of Consumer Services
Consumer and Business Fair Practices Division
Office of the Attorney General
900 Fourth Avenue, Suite 2000
Seattle, WA 98164
(206) 464-6431
1 (800) 551-4636 (toll free in WA)

Mr. Owen Clarke, Chief
Consumer and Business Fair Practices Division
Office of the Attorney General
West 1116 Riverside Avenue
Spokane, WA 99201
(509) 456-3123

Ms. Cynthia Lanphear, Contact Person
Consumer and Business Fair Practices Division
Office of the Attorney General
1019 Pacific Avenue, 3rd Floor
Tacoma, WA 98402-4411
(206) 593-2904

City Offices

Ms. Kristie Anderson, Director
Department of Weights and Measures
3200 Cedar Street
Everett, WA 98201
(206) 259-8810

Mr. C. Patrick Sainsbury
Chief Deputy Prosecuting Attorney
Fraud Division
1002 Bank of California
900 4th Avenue
Seattle, WA 98164
(206) 296-9010

Mr. Dale H. Tiffany, Director
Seattle Department of Licenses and Consumer Affairs
102 Municipal Building
600 4th Avenue
Seattle, WA 98104-1893
(206) 684-8484

West Virginia

State Offices

Mr. Robert J. Lamont, Director
Consumer Protection Division
Office of Attorney General
812 Quarrier Street, 6th Floor
Charleston, WV 25301
(304) 348-8986
1 (800) 368-8808 (toll free in WV)

Mr. Stephen Casto, Director
Division of Weights and Measures
Department of Labor
1800 Washington Street, East
Bldg. #3, Room 319
Charleston, WV 25305
(304) 348-7890

City Office

Mrs. Carolyn Lawler, Director
Department of Consumer Protection
P.O. Box 2749
Charleston, WV 25330
(304) 348-8172

Wisconsin

State Offices

Mr. John Alberts, Administrator
Division of Trade and Consumer Protection
Department of Agriculture, Trade and Consumer Protection
801 West Badger Road
P.O. Box 8911
Madison, WI 53708
(608) 266-9836
1 (800) 422-7128 (toll free in WI)

Ms. Margaret Quaid, Regional Supervisor
Division of Trade and Consumer Protection
Department of Agriculture, Trade and Consumer Protection
927 Loring Street
Altoona, WI 54720
(715) 839-3848
1 (800) 422-7128 (toll free in WI)

Mr. Eugene E. Lindauer
Regional Supervisor
Division of Trade and Consumer Protection
Department of Agriculture, Trade and Consumer Protection
200 North Jefferson Street, Suite 146A
Green Bay, WI 54301
(414) 448-5111
1 (800) 422-7128 (toll free in WI)

Regional Supervisor
Consumer Protection Regional Office
Department of Agriculture, Trade and Consumer Protection
3333 N. Mayfair Rd., Suite 114
Milwaukee, WI 53222-3288
(414) 257-8956

Mr. James D. Jeffries
Assistant Attorney General
Office of Consumer Protection and Citizen Advocacy
Department of Justice
P.O. Box 7856
Madison, WI 53707-7856
(608) 266-1852
1 (800) 362-8189 (toll free)

Mr. Nadim Sahar
Assistant Attorney General
Office of Consumer Protection
Department of Justice
Milwaukee State Office Building
819 North 6th Street, Room 520
Milwaukee, WI 53203-1678
(414) 227-4948
1 (800) 362-8189 (toll free)

County Offices

Mr. Gregory Grau, District Attorney
Marathon County District Attorney's Office
Marathon County Courthouse
Wausau, WI 54401
(715) 847-5555

Mr. Darryl Nevers
Assistant District Attorney
Milwaukee County District
Attorney's Office
Consumer Fraud Unit
821 West State Street, Room 412
Milwaukee, WI 53233-1485
(414) 278-4792

Mr. James A. Dehne
Consumer Fraud Investigator
Racine County Sheriff's
Department
717 Wisconsin Avenue
Racine, WI 53403
(414) 636-3125

Wyoming

State Office

Mr. Mark Moran, Assistant
Attorney General
Office of Attorney General
123 State Capitol Building
Cheyenne, WY 82002
(307) 777-7874

AGENCIES ON AGING

Are there exercise programs designed especially for older people? How can I find a qualified hearing aid specialist? Who can tell me about my Social Security benefits? Which medical centers are studying new treatments for Alzheimer's disease? The answers to these and many other questions about resources and services for older Americans can be found in this list of organizations which was prepared by the National Institute on Aging (NIA). It is intended for a wide audience, including older people and their families, students of aging, health professionals, librarians, legal professionals, providers of social services, and others who have a special interest in the field of aging. The directory contains the names, addresses, and telephone numbers (toll-free whenever possible) of national organizations that offer health information, legal aid, self-help programs, educational opportunities, social services, consumer advice, or other assistance.

Included are federal government agencies, professional societies, private groups, and voluntary programs. Some of these organizations deal primarily with older people and their families. Some serve professionals who work with older adults. And many others assist people of all ages. We have tried to include as many groups as possible. **Please keep in mind, however, that the NIA does not recommend or endorse specific organizations.**

Many of the groups listed here produce and distribute materials (including many free or low-cost pamphlets and brochures) or offer information and referral services.

ACTION
1100 Vermont Avenue NW
Washington, DC 20525
(202) 606-4845

Administration on Aging
330 Independence Avenue SW
Washington, DC 20201
(202) 690-5641

Adult Education
400 Maryland Avenue NW
Room 4428
Washington, DC 20202
(202) 205-8270

Aging Network Services
Suite 907
4400 East-West Highway
Bethesda, MD 20814
(301) 657-4329

Alliance for Aging Research
Suite 305
2021 K Street NW
Washington, DC 20006
(202) 293-2856

Alzheimer's Association
Suite 600
70 East Lake Street
Chicago, IL 60601
(312) 335-8700

INFORMATION AND REFERRAL SERVICE
1 (800) 272-3900 (toll-free)
1 (800) 572-6037 (toll-free to residents of Illinois)

Alzheimer's Disease Education and Referral Center
Federal Building, Room 6C12
9000 Rockville Pike
Bethesda, MD 20892
(301) 496-1752

American Academy of Family Physicians
8880 Ward Parkway
Kansas City, MO 64114-2797
(816) 333-9700

American Academy of Neurology
Suite 335
2221 University Avenue SE
Minneapolis, MN 55414
(612) 623-8115

American Academy of Ophthalmology
P.O. Box 7424
San Francisco, CA 94120-7424
(415) 561-8500
NATIONAL EYE CARE PROJECT HELPLINE
1 (800) 222-3973 (toll-free)

American Academy of Orthopaedic Surgeons
222 South Prospect Avenue
Park Ridge, IL 60068
(708) 823-7186

American Academy of Otolaryngology—Head and Neck Surgery, Inc.
Suite 302
1101 Vermont Avenue NW
Washington, DC 20005
(703) 836-4444

American Academy of Physical Medicine and Rehabilitation
Suite 1300
122 South Michigan Avenue
Chicago, IL 60603-6107
(312) 922-9366

American Academy of Physician Assistants
950 North Washington Street
Alexandria, VA 22314
(703) 836-2272

American Association of Cardiovascular and Pulmonary Rehabilitation
Suite 201
7611 Elmwood Avenue
Middleton, WI 53562
(608) 831-6989

American Association for Geriatric Psychiatry
P.O. Box 376-A
Greenbelt, MD 20770
(301) 220-0952

American Association of Homes for the Aging
Suite 400
1129 20th Street NW
Washington, DC 20036-3489

American Association of Retired Persons
1909 K Street NW
Washington, DC 20049
(202) 434-2277

American Bar Association Commission on the Legal Problems of the Elderly
Second Floor, South Lobby
1800 M Street NW
Washington, DC 20036
(202) 331-2297

American Cancer Society
1599 Clifton Road NE
Atlanta, GA 30329
(404) 320-3333
INFORMATION SERVICE
1 (800) 227-2345 (toll-free)

American Chiropractic Association
1701 Clarendon Boulevard
Arlington, VA 22209
(703) 276-8800

American College of Obstetricians and Gynecologists
409 12th Street SW
Washington, DC 20024
(202) 638-5577

American College of Physicians
Independence Mall West
6th Street at Race
Philadelphia, PA 19106
(215) 351-2400
INFORMATION SERVICE
1 (800) 523-1546 (toll-free)

American College of Surgeons
55 East Erie Street
Chicago, IL 60611
(312) 664-4050

American Council of the Blind
Suite 1100
1010 Vermont Avenue NW
Washington, DC 20005
(202) 467-5081
INFORMATION SERVICE
1 (800) 424-8666 (toll-free)

American Dental Association
211 East Chicago Avenue
Chicago, IL 60611
(312) 440-2500

American Diabetes Association
1660 Duke Street
Alexandria, VA 22314
(703) 549-1500
INFORMATION SERVICE HOTLINE
1 (800) 232-3472 (toll-free)

American Dietetic Association
Suite 800
216 West Jackson Boulevard
Chicago, IL 60606
(312) 889-0040

American Federation for Aging Research
725 Park Avenue
New York, NY 10021
(212) 570-2090

American Foundation for the Blind
15 West 16th Street
New York, NY 10011
(212) 620-2147
INFORMATION SERVICE
1 (800) 232-5463 (toll-free)

American Geriatrics Society
Suite 400
770 Lexington Avenue
New York, NY 10021
(212) 308-1414

American Health Care Association
1201 L Street NW
Washington, DC 20005
(202) 842-4444

American Health Foundation
320 East 43rd Street
New York, NY 10017
(212) 953-1900

American Heart Association
7320 Greenville Avenue
Dallas, TX 75231
(214) 750-5397

American Hospital Association
840 North Lake Shore Drive
Chicago, IL 60611
(312) 280-6000
PUBLICATIONS SERVICE
1 (800) 242-2626 (toll-free)

American Lung Association
1740 Broadway
New York, NY 10019-4374
(212) 315-8700

American Medical Association
535 North Dearborn Street
Chicago, IL 60610
(312) 464-5000

American Mental Health Fund
Suite 302
2735 Hartland Road
Falls Church, VA 22043

American Nurses Association
2420 Pershing Road
Kansas City, MO 64108
(202) 554-4444

American Occupational Therapy Association, Inc.
P.O. Box 1725
1383 Piccard Drive
Rockville, MD 20850-4375
(301) 948-9626

American Optometric Association
243 North Lindbergh Boulevard
St. Louis, MO 63141
(314) 991-4100

American Osteopathic Association
142 East Ontario Street
Chicago, IL 60611
(312) 280-5800

American Parkinson's Disease Association
Suite 417
116 John Street
New York, NY 10038
(212) 732-9550
INFORMATION HOTLINE
1 (800) 223-2732

American Pharmaceutical Association
2215 Constitution Avenue NW
Washington, DC 20077-6718
(202) 628-4410

American Physical Therapy Association
1111 North Fairfax Street
Alexandria, VA 22314
(703) 684-2782

American Podiatric Medical Association
9312 Old Georgetown Road
Bethesda, MD 20814
(301) 571-9200

American Psychiatric Association
1400 K Street NW
Washington, DC 20005
(202) 682-6239

American Psychological Association
1200 17th Street NW
Washington, DC 20036
(202) 336-5500

American Red Cross
18th and D Streets NW
Washington, DC 20006
(202) 737-8300

American Society on Aging
Suite 512
833 Market Street
San Francisco, CA 94103
(415) 882-2910

American Society for Geriatric Dentistry
Suite 1616
211 East Chicago Avenue
Chicago, IL 60611
(312) 440-2660

American Society for Internal Medicine
Suite 500
1101 Vermont Avenue NW.
Washington, DC 20005
(202) 835-2746

American Society of Plastic and Reconstructive Surgeons
444 East Algonquin Road
Arlington Heights, IL 60005
(708) 228-9900
PATIENT REFERRAL SERVICE
1 (800) 635-0635 (toll-free)

American Speech-Language-Hearing Association
10801 Rockville Pike
Rockville, MD 20852
(301) 897-5700
HELPLINE
1 (800) 638-8255 (toll-free outside Maryland)
(301) 897-8682 (residents of Maryland)

American Tinnitus Association
P.O. Box 5
Portland, OR 97207
(503) 248-9985

Arthritis Foundation
1314 Spring Street NW
Atlanta, GA 30309
(404) 872-7100

Association for Brain Tumor Research
2910 West Montrose Avenue
Chicago, IL 60618
(312) 286-5571

Association for Gerontology in Higher Education
West Wing 204
600 Maryland Avenue SW
Washington, DC 20024
(202) 429-9277

Association of Sleep Disorders Centers
604 Second Street SW
Rochester, MN 55902
(507) 287-6006

Better Vision Institute
Suite 1310
1800 North Kent Street
Rosslyn, VA 22209
(703) 243-1528

Beverly Foundation
Suite 750
70 South Lake Avenue
Pasadena, CA 91101
(818) 792-2292

B'nai B'rith International
1640 Rhode Island Avenue NW
Washington, DC 20036
(202) 857-6600

Brookdale Center on Aging
425 East 25th Street
New York, NY 10010
(212) 481-4426
ALZHEIMER'S DISEASE RESPITE CARE INFORMATION
1 (800) 648-2673 (toll-free)

Catholic Charities
1319 F Street NW
Washington, DC 20004
(202) 526-4100

Catholic Golden Age
400 Lackawanna Avenue
Scranton, PA 18503
(717) 342-3294

Center for Social Gerontology
Suite 204
117 North First Street
Ann Arbor, MI 48104
(313) 665-1126

Center for the Study of Aging
706 Madison Avenue
Albany, NY 12208
(518) 465-6927

Children of Aging Parents
2761 Trenton Road
Levittown, PA 19056
(215) 945-6900

Concerned Relatives of Nursing Home Patients
3130 Mayfield Road
Cleveland Heights, OH 44118
(216) 321-0403

Consumer Information Center
P.O. Box 100
Pueblo, CO 81009

Consumer Product Safety Commission
Office of Information and Public Affairs
5401 Westbard Avenue
Bethesda, MD 20207
(301) 492-6580
CONSUMER PRODUCT SAFETY HOTLINE
1 (800) 638-2772 (toll-free)
1 (800) 638-8270 (toll-free TDD outside Maryland)
1-800-492-8104 (toll-free TDD for residents of Maryland)

Council of Better Business Bureaus
8th Floor
4200 Wilson Boulevard
Arlington, VA 22209
(703) 276-0133

Delta Society
P.O. Box 1080
Renton, WA 98057-1080
(206) 226-7357

Department of Labor
Consumer Affairs
Room S1032
200 Constitution Avenue NW
Washington, DC 20210
(202) 523-6060

DES Action
Long Island Jewish Medical Center
New Hyde Park, NY 11040
(516) 775-3450

Disabled American Veterans
P.O. Box 14301
Cincinnati, OH 45250
(606) 441-7300

Displaced Homemaker Network
Suite 930
1411 K Street NW
Washington, DC 20005
(202) 467-6346

Dizziness and Balance Disorders Association
Resource Center
Room 300
1015 Northwest 22nd Avenue
Portland, OR 97210
(503) 229-7348

Elder Craftsmen
135 East 65th Street
New York, NY 10021
(212) 861-5260

Elderhostel
Suite 400
80 Boylston Street
Boston, MA 02116
(617) 426-8056

Elvirita Lewis Foundation
P.O. Box 1539
La Quinta, CA 92253
(619) 564-1780

Environmental Protection Agency
Public Information Center
401 M Street SW
Washington, DC 20460
(202) 260-2090
ASBESTOS INFORMATION
(202) 260-5543
SAFE DRINKING WATER INFORMATION
(202) 382-5543
NATIONAL PESTICIDES TELECOMMUNICATIONS NETWORK
1 (800) 858-7378 (toll-free outside Texas)
(806) 743-3091 (for residents of Texas)

Episcopal Society for Ministry on Aging
317 Wyandotte Street
Bethlehem, PA 18015
(215) 868-5400

Equal Employment Opportunity Commission
1801 L Street NW
Washington, DC 20507
(202) 663-4264

Federal Council on Aging
Room 4280 HHS-N
330 Independence Avenue SW
Washington, DC 20201
(202) 619-2451

Federal Trade Commission
Office of Public Affairs
Room 421
Sixth Street and Pennsylvania Avenue NW
Washington, DC 20580
(202) 326-2180

Food and Drug Administration
5600 Fishers Lane
Rockville, MD 20857
(301) 443-3170

Food and Nutrition Information Center
Room 304
National Agricultural Library Building
Silver Spring, MD 20705
(301) 504-5755

Foundation for Hospice and Home Care
519 C Street NE
Washington, DC 20002
(202) 547-7424

Gerontological Society of America
Suite 350
1275 K Street NW
Washington, DC 20005-4006
(202) 842-1275

Gray Panthers
Suite 602
1424 16th St., NW
Washington, DC 20036
(202) 387-3111

Health Care Financing Administration
200 Independence Avenue SW
Washington, DC 20201
(202) 690-6145
SECOND SURGICAL OPINION HOTLINE
1 (800) 638-6833 (toll-free)
1 (800) 492-6603 (toll-free to residents of Maryland)

Health Insurance Association of America
Suite 1200
1025 Connecticut Avenue NW
Washington, DC 20036
(202) 223-7780
INFORMATION SERVICE
1 (800) 423-8000 (toll-free)

Help for Incontinent People
P.O. Box 544
Union, SC 29379
(803) 579-7900

Hill-Burton Program
Health Resources and Services Administration
5600 Fishers Lane
Rockville, MD 20857
(301) 443-5656
HOTLINE
1 (800) 638-0742 (toll-free)
1 (800) 492-0359 (toll-free to residents of Maryland)

Huntington's Disease Society of America
6th Floor
140 West 22nd Street
New York, NY 10011
(212) 242-1968
HOTLINE
1 (800) 345-4372 (toll-free)
(212) 242-1968 (residents of New York State)

Hysterectomy Educational Resources and Services Foundation
422 Bryn Mawr Avenue
Bala Cynwyd, PA 19004
(215) 667-7757

Japanese-American Citizens League
1765 Sutter Street
San Francisco, CA 94115
(415) 921-5225

John Douglas French Foundation for Alzheimer's Disease
11620 Wilshire Boulevard
Los Angeles, CA 90025
(310) 470-5462
INFORMATION SERVICE
1 (800) 537-3624 (toll-free)

Legal Services for the Elderly
3rd Floor
132 West 43rd Street
New York, NY 10036
(212) 391-0120

Leukemia Society of America
733 Third Avenue
New York, NY 10017
(212) 573-8484

Lupus Foundation of America
Suite 203
1717 Massachusetts Avenue NW
Washington, DC 20036
INFORMATION SERVICE
1 (800) 558-0121 (toll-free)

Make Today Count
101½ South Union Street
Alexandria, VA 22314-3323
(703) 548-9674

Medic Alert Foundation
P.O. Box 1009
Turlock, CA 95381-1009
(209) 668-3333
INFORMATION SERVICE
1 (800) 344-3226 (toll-free)

Mind's Eye
(Books on Tape)
Box 6727
San Francisco, CA 94101
1 (800) 227-2020 (toll-free)

National Action Forum for Midlife and Older Women
c/o Dr. Jane Porcino
P.O. Box 816
Stony Brook, NY 11790-0609

National AIDS Information Clearinghouse
P.O. Box 6003
Rockville, MD 20850
(301) 762-5111
AIDS INFORMATION CLEARINGHOUSE PUBLICATION ORDERS
1 (800) 458-5231 (toll-free)

AIDS HOTLINE
1 (800) 342-2437 (toll-free)
1 (800) 344-SIDA (toll-free for Spanish-speaking individuals)
1 (800) 243-7889 (toll-free TDD)

National Alliance of Senior Citizens
2525 Wilson Boulevard
Arlington, VA 22201

National Arthritis and Musculoskeletal and Skin Diseases Information Clearinghouse
P.O. Box AMS
Bethesda, MD 20892
(301) 468-3235

National Association on Area Agencies of Aging
Suite 208W
600 Maryland Avenue SW
Washington, DC 20024

National Association of Community Health Centers
Suite 122
1330 New Hampshire Avenue NW
Washington, DC 20036
(202) 659-8008

National Association for the Deaf
814 Thayer Avenue
Silver Spring, MD 20910
(301) 587-1788 (voice and TDD)

National Association for Hispanic Elderly Association Nacional Pro Personas Mayores
Suite 270
2727 West Sixth Street
Los Angeles, CA 90057
(213) 487-1922

National Association for Home Care
519 C Street NE
Washington, DC 20002
(202) 547-7424

National Association for Human Development
1424 16th Street NW
Washington, DC 20036
(202) 328-2191

National Association of Meal Programs
204 E Street NE
Washington, DC 20002
(202) 547-6340

National Association for Practical Nurse Education and Services
Suite 310
1400 Spring Street
Silver Spring, MD 20910
(301) 588-2491

National Association of Social Workers
7981 Eastern Avenue
Silver Spring, MD 20910
(202) 408-8600

National Association of State Units on Aging
Suite 304
2033 K Street NW
Washington, DC 20006
(202) 785-0707

National Cancer Institute
Office of Cancer Communications
Building 31, Room 10A24
9000 Rockville Pike
Bethesda, MD 20892
(301) 496-5583
CANCER INFORMATION SERVICE
1 (800) 4-CANCER (toll-free)
(In Hawaii, on Oahu, call 524-1234; call collect from neighboring islands.)

National Caucus and Center on Black Aged
Suite 500
1424 K Street NW
Washington, DC 20005
(202) 637-8400

National Center for Health Statistics
3700 East-West Highway
Hyattsville, MD 20782
(301) 436-8500

National Cholesterol Education Program
4733 Bethesda Avenue
Bethesda, MD 20814
(301) 951-3260

National Citizens Coalition for Nursing Home Reform
Suite L2
1424 16th Street NW
Washington, DC 20036

National Clearinghouse for Primary Care Information
Suite 600
8201 Greensboro Drive
McLean, VA 22102
(703) 821-8955

National Commission of Working Women
Lower Level
1325 G Street NW
Washington, DC 20005
(202) 737-5764

National Committee on the Treatment of Intractable Pain
P.O. Box 9553
Friendship Station
Washington, DC 20016
(202) 965-6717

National Consumers League
Suite 928-N
815 15th Street NW
Washington, DC 20005
(202) 639-8140

National Council on the Aging
West Wing 100
600 Maryland Avenue SW
Washington, DC 20024
(202) 479-1200

National Council on Alcoholism
8th Floor
12 West 21st Street
New York, NY 10010
(212) 206-6770

National Council on Patient Information and Education
Suite 810
666 11th Street NW
Washington, DC 20001
(202) 347-6711

National Council of Senior Citizens
925 15th Street NW
Washington, DC 20005
(202) 347-8800

National Diabetes Information Clearinghouse
Box NDIC
Bethesda, MD 20892
(301) 468-2162

National Digestive Diseases Information Clearinghouse
Box NDDIC
Bethesda, MD 20892
(301) 468-6344

National Eye Institute Information Office
Building 31, Room 6A29
Bethesda, MD 20892
(301) 496-5248

National Foundation for Long-Term Health Care
Suite 402
1200 15th Street NW
Washington, DC 20005
(202) 659-3148

National Geriatrics Society
212 West Wisconsin Avenue
Milwaukee, WI 53203

National Hearing Aid Society
20361 Middlebelt Street
Livonia, MI 48152
(313) 478-2610
HEARING AID HELPLINE
1 (800) 521-5247 (toll-free)

National Heart, Lung, and Blood Institute Information Office
Building 31, Room 4A21
9000 Rockville Pike
Bethesda, MD 20892
(301) 496-4236

National High Blood Pressure Information Center
4733 Bethesda Avenue
Bethesda, MD 20814
(301) 951-3260

National Hispanic Council on Aging
2713 Ontario Road NW
Washington, DC 20009
(202) 265-1288

National Hospice Organization
Suite 901
1901 North Moore Street
Arlington, VA 22209
(703) 243-5900

National Indian Council on Aging
P.O. Box 2088
Albuquerque, NM 87103
(505) 242-9505

National Information Center on Deafness
Gallaudet University
800 Florida Avenue NE
Washington, DC 20002
(202) 651-5051 (voice)
(202) 651-5052 (TDD)
INFORMATION SERVICE
1 (800) 672-6720 (toll-free voice and TDD)
(Ask for the National Information Center on Deafness.)

National Institute on Aging
Public Information Office
Federal Building, Room 6C12
9000 Rockville Pike
Bethesda, MD 20892
(301) 496-1752

National Information Center for Orphan Drugs and Rare Diseases
P.O. Box 1133
Washington, DC 20013
1 (800) 456-3505 (toll free)

National Institute on Alcohol Abuse and Alcoholism
Room 16–95
5600 Fishers Lane
Rockville, MD 20857
(301) 443-1677
NATIONAL CLEARINGHOUSE FOR ALCOHOL AND DRUG ABUSE INFORMATION
(301) 468-2600

National Institute of Allergy and Infectious Diseases
Office of Communications
Building 31, Room 7A32
9000 Rockville Pike
Bethesda, MD 20892
(301) 496-5717

National Institute of Arthritis and Musculoskeletal and Skin Diseases Information Office
Building 31, Room B2B15
9000 Rockville Pike
Bethesda, MD 20892
(301) 496-8188

National Institute on Deafness and Other Communication Disorders
Information Office
9000 Rockville Pike
Bethesda, MD 20892
(301) 496-5751

National Institute of Dental Research
Information Office
Building 31, Room 2C35
9000 Rockville Pike
Bethesda, MD 20892
(301) 496-4261

National Institute of Diabetes and Digestive and Kidney Diseases
Information Office
Building 31, Room 9A06
9000 Rockville Pike
Bethesda, MD 20892
(301) 496-3583

National Institute on Drug Abuse
Information Office
Room 10A46
5600 Fishers Lane
Rockville, MD 20857
(301) 443-6500

National Institute of General Medical Sciences
Office of Research Reports
Building 31, Room 4A52
9000 Rockville Pike
Bethesda, MD 20892
(301) 496-7301

National Institute of Mental Health
Public Inquiries Office
Room 15C-05
5600 Fishers Lane
Rockville, MD 20857
(301) 443-4513

National Institute of Neurological Disorders and Stroke
Information Office
Building 31, Room 8A06
9000 Rockville Pike
Bethesda, MD 20892
(301) 496-5751

National Interfaith Coalition on Aging
P.O. Box 1924
Athens, GA 30603
(706) 353-1331

National Kidney Foundation
30 East 33rd Street
New York, NY 10016
(212) 889-2210

National Kidney and Urologic Diseases Information Clearinghouse
Box NKUDIC
Bethesda, MD 20892
(301) 468-6345

National League for Nursing
10 Columbus Circle
New York, NY 10019-1350
(212) 989-9393
INFORMATION SERVICE
1 (800) 847-8480 (toll-free outside New York State)

National Library of Medicine
8600 Rockville Pike
Bethesda, MD 20894
(301) 496-5501
MEDLARS SERVICE DESK
1 (800) 638-8480 (toll-free outside Maryland)
(301) 496-6193 (for residents of Maryland)

National Multiple Sclerosis Society
205 East 42nd Street
New York, NY 10017
(212) 986-3240
INFORMATION SERVICE
1 (800) 624-8236 (toll-free)

National Organization for Rare Disorders
P.O. Box 8923
New Fairfield, CT 06812
(203) 746-6518
INFORMATION SERVICE
1 (800) 447-6673 (toll-free outside Connecticut)

National Organization for Victim Assistance
717 D Street NW
Washington, DC 20004

National Osteoporosis Foundation
Suite 822
1625 Eye Street NW
Washington, DC 20006
(202) 223-2226

National Pacific/Asian Resource Center on Aging
Melbourne Tower,
Suite 914
1511 Third Avenue
Seattle, WA 98101
(206) 624-1221

National Rehabilitation Association
633 South Washington Street
Alexandria, VA 22314
(703) 715-9090
(703) 715-9090 (TDD)

National Rehabilitation Information Center
Suite 935
8455 Colesville Road
Silver Spring, MD 20910-3319
(301) 588-9284 (Voice and TDD)
INFORMATION SERVICE
1 (800) 346-2742 (toll-free—Voice and TDD)

National Rural Health Care Association
Suite 420
301 East Armour Boulevard
Kansas City, MO 64111
(816) 756-3140

National Safety Council
444 North Michigan Avenue
Chicago, IL 60611-3991
(708) 285-1121

National Self-Help Clearinghouse
33 West 42nd Street
New York, NY 10036
(212) 642-2944

National Senior Citizens Law Center
Suite 400
2025 M Street NW
Washington, DC 20036
(202) 887-5380

National Senior Sports Association
Suite 205
10560 Main Street
Fairfax, VA 22030
(703) 385-7540

National Shut-In Society
P.O. Box 986
Village Station, NY 10014-1986
(212) 222-7699

National Society to Prevent Blindness
500 East Remington Road
Schaumburg, IL 60173
(708) 843-2020
INFORMATION SERVICE
1 (800) 221-3004 (toll-free)

National Stroke Association
Suite 240
300 East Hampden Avenue
Englewood, CO 80110
(303) 762-9922

National Technical Information Service
5285 Port Royal Road
Springfield, VA 22161
(703) 487-4600

National Urban League
500 East 62nd Street
New York, NY 10021
(212) 310-9000

National Women's Health Network
1325 G Street NW
Washington, DC 20005
(202) 347-1140

Office of Disease Prevention and Health Promotion
Mary Switzer Building, Room 2132
330 C Street SW
Washington, DC 20201
(202) 205-8660
HEALTHY OLDER PEOPLE HOTLINE
1 (800) 336-4797 (toll-free outside Maryland)
(301) 565-4167 (for residents of Maryland)
NATIONAL HEALTH INFORMATION CLEARINGHOUSE
1 (800) 336-4797 (toll-free outside Maryland)
(301) 565-4167 (for residents of Maryland)

Office on Smoking and Health
Park Building, Room 1–10
5600 Fishers Lane
Rockville, MD 20857
(301) 443-3825

Older Women's League
Suite 300
730 11th Street NW
Washington, DC 20001
(202) 783-6686

Opticians Association of America
10341 Democracy Lane
P.O. Box 10110
Fairfax, VA 22030
(703) 691-8355

Organization of Chinese Americans
Suite 926
2025 Eye Street NW
Washington, DC 20006
(202) 223-5500

President's Council on Physical Fitness and Sports
Suite 7103
450 Fifth Street NW
Washington, DC 20001
(202) 272-3430

Pride Long-Term Home Health Care Institute
153 West 11th Street
New York, NY 10011
(212) 790-8864

Public Affairs Committee
381 Park Avenue South
New York, NY 10016

Retirement Research Foundation
Suite 214
1300 West Higgins Road
Park Ridge, IL 60068
(312) 714-8080

The Robert Wood Johnson Foundation
P.O. Box 2316
Princeton, NJ 08543-2316
(609) 452-8701

Self-Help for Hard of Hearing People
7800 Wisconsin Avenue
Bethesda, MD 20814
(301) 657-2248 (voice)
(301) 657-2249 (TDD)

Simon Foundation
Box 835
Wilmette, IL 60091
(708) 864-3913
INFORMATION SERVICE
1 (800) 237-4666 (toll-free)

Skin Cancer Foundation
Suite 2402
245 Fifth Avenue
New York, NY 10016
(212) 725-5176

Social Security Administration
Office of Public Inquiries
6401 Security Boulevard
Baltimore, MD 21235
(301) 594-1234

United Ostomy Association
Suite 120
36 Executive Park
Irvine, CA 92714
(714) 660-8624

United Parkinson Foundation
360 West Superior Street
Chicago, IL 60610
(312) 664-2344

United Seniors Health Cooperative
Suite 500
1334 G Street NW
Washington, DC 20005
(202) 393-6222

U.S. Pharmacopeial Convention
12601 Twinbrook Parkway
Rockville, MD 20852
(301) 881-0666
PUBLICATIONS ORDERING SERVICE
1 (800) 227-8772 (toll-free)

United Way of America
701 North Fairfax Street
Alexandria, VA 22314-2045
(703) 836-7100

Veterans Administration Office of Public Affairs
810 Vermont Avenue NW
Washington, DC 20420
(202) 233-2843

Volunteers of America
3813 North Causeway Boulevard
Metairie, LA 70002
(504) 837-2652

Women's Equity Action League
Suite 305
1250 Eye Street NW
Washington, DC 20005
(202) 898-1588

Young Men's Christian Association
101 North Wacker Drive
Chicago, IL 60606
(312) 977-0031

Young Women's Christian Association
726 Broadway
New York, NY 10003
(212) 614-2700

STATE AGENCIES ON AGING

The offices listed in this section coordinate services for older Americans. They provide information on services, programs and opportunities for these consumers.

Alabama
Dr. Oscar D. Tucker
Executive Director
Commission on Aging
136 Catoma Street
Montgomery, AL 36130
(205) 242-5743
1 (800) 243-5463
(toll free in AL)

Alaska
Ms. Connie J. Sipe
Executive Director
Older Alaskans Commission
P.O. Box C
Juneau, AK 99811-0209
(907) 465-3250

American Samoa
Mr. Luavasa Tauala, Director
Territorial Administration on Aging
Government of American Samoa
Pago Pago, AS 96799
011 (684) 633-1251

Arizona
Mr. Richard Littler, Administrator
Aging and Adult Administration
1400 West Washington, 950A
Phoenix, AZ 85007
(602) 542-4446

Arkansas
Mr. Herb Sanderson, Director
Office of Aging and Adult Services
Department of Human Services
P.O. Box 1437
Little Rock, AR 72203-1437
(501) 682-2441
1 (800) 482-8049
(toll free in AR)

California
Ms. Chris Arnold, Director
Department of Aging
1600 K Street
Sacramento, CA 95814
(916) 322-5290
(916) 323-8913 (TDD)
1 (800) 231-4024
(toll free in CA)

Colorado
Ms. Irene M. Ibarra
Executive Director
Colorado Department of Social Services
1575 Sherman Street
Denver, CO 80203-1714
(303) 866-5700

Connecticut
Ms. Edith Prague, Commissioner
Department on Aging
175 Main Street
Hartford, CT 06106
(203) 566-3238
1 (800) 443-9946
(toll free voice/TDD in CT)

Delaware
Ms. Eleanor L. Cain, Director
Department of Health and Social Services
Division of Aging
1901 North DuPont Highway
New Castle, DE 19720
(302) 421-6791
1 (800) 223-9074
(toll free in DE)

District of Columbia
Ms. E. Veronica Pace
Executive Director
D.C. Office on Aging
1424 K Street, N.W., 2nd Floor
Washington, DC 20005
(202) 724-5623

Florida
Dr. Larry Polivka
Assistant Secretary
Aging and Adult Services
1321 Winewood Boulevard
Room 323
Tallahassee, FL 32399-0700
(904) 488-8922

Georgia
Mr. Fred McGinnis, Director
Office of Aging
878 Peachtree Street, N.E.
Suite 632
Atlanta, GA 30309
(404) 894-5333

Guam
Mr. Robert Kelley
Acting Administrator
Office of Aging
Government of Guam
P.O. Box 2816
Agana, GU 96910
011 (671) 734-2942

Hawaii
Ms. Jeanette Takamura, Director
Executive Office on Aging
335 Merchant Street, Room 241
Honolulu, HI 96813
(808) 548-2593
1 (800) 468-4644
(toll free in HI)

Idaho
Ms. Charlene W. Martindale Director
Idaho Office on Aging
Statehouse, Room 108
Boise, ID 83720
(208) 334-3833

Illinois

Mr. Victor L. Wirth,
Director
Department on Aging
421 East Capitol Avenue
Springfield, IL 62701
(217) 785-2870
1 (800) 252-8966
(toll free voice/TDD)

Indiana

Ms. Geneva Shedd, Director
Aging/In-Home Care
Services Division
Department of Human
Services
P.O. Box 7083
Indianapolis, IN 46207-7083
(317) 232-1139
1 (800) 545-7763
(toll free in IN)

Iowa

Ms. Betty Grandquist
Executive Director
Department of Elder Affairs
914 Grand Avenue, Suite 236
Des Moines, IA 50319
(515) 281-5187
1 (800) 532-3213
(toll free in IA)

Kansas

Ms. Joanne Hurst, Secretary
Department on Aging
Docking State Office
Building
Room 122 South
915 Southwest Harrison
Street
Topeka, KS 66612-1500
(913) 296-4986
1 (800) 432-3535
(toll free in KS)

Kentucky

Ms. Sue N. Tuttle, Director
Division for Aging Services
Department for Social
Services
275 East Main Street
6th Floor West
Frankfort, KY 40621
(502) 564-6930
(502) 564-5497 (TDD)
1 (800) 372-2991
(toll free in KY)
1 (800) 372-2973
(toll free TDD in KY)

Louisiana

Ms. Vicky Hunt, Director
Governor's Office of Elder
Affairs
P.O. Box 80374
Baton Rouge, LA 70898
(504) 925-1700

Maine

Ms. Christine Gianopoulos
Director
Bureau of Elder and Adult
Service
35 Anthony Avenue
Statehouse, Station 11
Augusta, ME 04333-0011
(207) 626-5335

Maryland

Ms. Rosalie S. Abrams,
Director
Office on Aging
301 West Preston Street
10th Floor
Baltimore, MD 21201
(301) 225-1100
(301) 383-7555 (TDD)
1 (800) 338-0153
(toll free in MD)

Massachusetts

Mr. Franklin P. Ollivierre,
Secretary
Executive Director of Elder
Affairs
38 Chauncy Street
Boston, MA 02111
(617) 727-7750
1 (800) 882-2003
(toll free in MA)
1 (800) 872-0166
(toll free TDD in MA)
1 (800) 922-2275
(toll free voice/TDD in
MA—Elder Abuse Hotline)

Michigan

Ms. Nancy Crandall,
Director
Office of Services to the
Aging
P.O. Box 30026
Lansing, MI 48909
(517) 373-8230

Minnesota

Mr. Gerald Bloedow
Executive Secretary
Minnesota Board on Aging
444 Lafayette Road
St. Paul, MN 55155-3843
(612) 296-2770
1 (800) 652-9747
(toll free in MN)

Mississippi

Ms. Billie J. Marshall, LSW
Director, Council on Aging
Division of Aging and Adult
Services
421 West Pascagoula Street
Jackson, MS 39203
(601) 949-2070
1 (800) 222-7622
(toll free in MS)

Missouri

Mr. Edwin L. Walker
Director, Division of Aging
P.O. Box 1337
Jefferson City, MO 65102
(314) 751-3082
1 (800) 235-5503
(toll free in MO)

Montana

Mr. Hank Hudson
Coordinator of Aging
Services
Governor's Office
State Capitol
Helena, MT 59620
(406) 444-3111
1 (800) 332-2272
(toll free in MT)

Nebraska

Ms. Connie Bratka
Acting Director
Nebraska Department on
Aging

State Office Building
P.O. Box 95044
Lincoln, NE 68509
(402) 471-2306

Nevada

Ms. Suzanne Ernst, Administrator
Division of Aging Services
Department of Human Resources
340 North 11th Street
Las Vegas, NV 89158
(702) 486-3545

New Hampshire

Mr. Richard A. Chevrefils, Director
Division of Elderly and Adult Services
6 Hazen Drive
Concord, NH 03301
(603) 271-4390
1 (800) 852-3311
(toll free in NH)

New Jersey

Ms. Lois Hull, Director
Division on Aging
Department of Community Affairs
101 South Broad Street, CN 807
Trenton, NJ 08625
(609) 292-0920
1 (800) 792-8820
(toll free in NJ)

New Mexico

Ms. Michelle Lujan Grisham
Director, State Agency on Aging
224 East Palace Avenue
4th Floor
Santa Fe, NM 87501
(505) 827-7640 (voice/TDD)
1 (800) 432-2080
(toll free in NM)

New York

Ms. Jane Gould, Director
New York State Office for the Aging
Agency Building 2, ESP
Albany, NY 12223
(518) 474-5731
1 (800) 342-9871
(toll free in NY)

North Carolina

Ms. Bonnie M. Cramer, Director
Division of Aging
Department of Human Resources
Caller Box No. 2953
693 Palmer Drive
Raleigh, NC 27626-0531
(919) 733-3983
1 (800) 662-7030
(toll free voice/TDD in NC)

North Dakota

Mr. Larry Brewster, Administrator
Aging Services
Department of Human Service
600 East Boulevard
Bismarck, ND 58505
(701) 224-2577
1 (800) 472-2622
(toll free in ND)

Ohio

Ms. Judith Y. Brachman, Director
Ohio Department of Aging
50 West Broad Street, 9th Floor
Columbus, OH 43266-0501
(614) 466-5500
(614) 466-6191 (TDD)
1 (800) 282-1206
(toll free in OH—nursing home information)

Oklahoma

Mr. Roy R. Keen
Division Administrator
Special Unit on Aging
P.O. Box 25352
Oklahoma City, OK 73125
(405) 521-2327
(405) 521-2327 (TDD)

Oregon

Mr. Richard Ladd, Administrator
Senior Services Division
Department of Human Resources
State of Oregon
313 Public Service Building
Salem, OR 97310
(503) 378-4728
1 (800) 232-3020
(toll free voice/TDD in OR)

Pennsylvania

Ms. Linda M. Rhodes, Secretary
Department of Aging
231 State Street
Harrisburg, PA 17101
(717) 783-1550

Puerto Rico

Dr. Celia Cintron
Executive Director
Office of Elder Affairs
Call Box 563
Old San Juan Station, PR 00902
(809) 721-0753

Rhode Island

Ms. Maureen Maigret, Director
Department of Elderly Affairs
160 Pine Street
Providence, RI 02903
(401) 277-2858 (voice/TDD)
1 (800) 752-8088
(toll free in RI)

South Carolina

Ms. Ruth Q. Seigler
Executive Director
South Carolina Commission on Aging
400 Arbor Lake Drive
Suite B-500
Columbia, SC 29223
(803) 735-0210
1 (800) 922-1107 (toll free)

South Dakota
Ms. Gail Ferris,
Administrator
Office of Adult Services and Aging
700 Governors Drive
Pierre, SD 57501
(605) 773-3656

Tennessee
Ms. Emily Wiseman,
Director
Commission on Aging
706 Church Street, Suite 201
Nashville, TN 37243-0860
(615) 741-2056

Texas
Ms. Polly S. Owell
Executive Director
Texas Department on Aging
P.O. Box 12786, Capitol Station
Austin, TX 78711
(512) 444-2727 (voice/TDD)
1 (800) 252-9240
(toll free in TX)

Utah
Mr. Percy Devine, III,
Director
Division of Aging and Adult Services
P.O. Box 45500
Salt Lake City, UT 84145-0500
(801) 538-3910

Vermont
Mr. Lawrence G. Crist,
Commissioner
Department of Aging and Disabilities
103 South Main Street
Waterbury, VT 05671-2301
(802) 241-2400 (voice/TDD)
1 (800) 642-5119 (toll free in VT)

Virgin Islands
Ms. Juel C. Rhymer Molloy
Commissioner
Department of Human Services
Barbel Plaza South
Charlotte Amalie
St. Thomas, VI 00802
(809) 774-0930

Virginia
Ms. Thelma E. Bland,
Commissioner
Department for the Aging
700 East Franklin Street
10th Floor
Richmond, VA 23219
(804) 225-2271 (voice/TDD)
1 (800) 552-4464
(toll free in VA)
1 (800) 552-3402
(toll free in VA—Ombudsman Hotline)

Washington
Mr. Charles Reed
Assistant Secretary
Aging and Adult Services Administration
OB-44A
Olympia, WA 98504
(206) 586-3768
1 (800) 422-3263
(toll free in WA)

West Virginia
Dr. David K. Brown
Executive Director
Commission on Aging
State Capitol
Charleston, WV 25305
(304) 348-3317

Wisconsin
Ms. Donna McDowell,
Director
Bureau on Aging
P.O. Box 7851
Madison, WI 53707
(608) 266-2536

Wyoming
Mr. E. Scott Sessions,
Director
Division on Aging
139 Hathaway Building
Cheyenne, WY 82002-0480
(307) 777-7986
1 (800) 442-2766
(toll free in WY)

STATE BANKING AUTHORITIES

The officials listed below regulate and supervise state-chartered banks. Many of them handle or refer problems and complaints about other types of financial institutions as well. Some also answer general questions about banking and consumer credit.

Alabama

Mr. Zack Thompson
Superintendent of Banks
101 South Union Street
Montgomery, AL 36130
(205) 242-3452

Alaska

Mr. Willis F. Kirkpatrick
Director of Banking, Securities and Corporations
P.O. Box D
Juneau, AK 99811-0800
(907) 465-2521

Arizona

Mr. William H. Rivoir
Superintendent of Banks
3225 North Central, Suite 815
Phoenix, AZ 85012
(602) 255-4421
1 (800) 544-0708
(toll free in AZ)

Arkansas

Mr. Bill J. Ford
Bank Commissioner
Tower Building
323 Center Street, Suite 500
Little Rock, AR 72201-2613
(501) 324-9019

California

Mr. James E. Gilleran
Superintendent of Banks
111 Pine Street, Suite 1100
San Francisco, CA 94111-5613
(415) 557-3535
1 (800) 622-0620
(toll free in CA)

Colorado

Ms. Barbara M.A. Walker
State Bank Commissioner
Division of Banking
First West Plaza, Suite 650
303 West Colfax
Denver, CO 80204
(303) 866-6440

Connecticut

Mr. Ralph Shulansky
Banking Commissioner
44 Capitol Avenue
Hartford, CT 06106
(203) 566-4560
1 (800) 842-2220
(toll free in CT)

Delaware

Mr. Keith H. Ellif
State Bank Commissioner
555 E. Loockerman Street
Suite 210
Dover, DE 19901
(302) 739-4235

District of Columbia

Ms. Fè Morales Marks
Acting Superintendent of Banking and Financial Institutions
1250 I Street, N.W.
Suite 1003
Washington, DC 20005
(202) 727-1563

Florida

Mr. Gerald Lewis
State Comptroller
State Capitol Building
Tallahassee, FL 32399-0350
(904) 488-0286
1 (800) 848-3792
(toll free in FL)

Georgia

Mr. Edward D. Dunn
Commissioner
Banking and Finance
2990 Brandywine Road
Suite 200
Atlanta, GA 30341-5565
(404) 986-1633
1 (800) 932-6246
(toll free in GA)

Guam

Mr. Joaquin Blaz
Director
Department of Revenue and Taxation
P.O. Box 2796
Agana, GU 96910
011 (671) 734-2942

Hawaii

Mr. Clifford Higa
Commissioner
Financial Institutions
P.O. Box 2054
Honolulu, HI 96805
(808) 586-2820

Idaho

Mr. Belton J. Patty
Director
Department of Finance
700 West State Street
2nd Floor
Boise, ID 83720-2700
(208) 334-3319

Illinois

Mr. Bob Piel
Commissioner of Banks and Trust Companies
117 South Fifth Street
Room 100
Springfield, IL 62701
(217) 785-2837

1 (800) 634-5452
(toll free in IL)
(credit card rate information only)

Indiana

Mr. Charles W. Phillips
Director
Department of Financial Institutions
Indiana State Office Building
Room 1024
Indianapolis, IN 46204-2294
(317) 232-3955
1 (800) 382-4880
(toll free in IN)

Iowa

Mr. Robert R. Rigler
Superintendent of Banking
200 East Grand, Suite 300
Des Moines, IA 50309
(515) 281-4014

Kansas

Mr. Frank D. Dunnick
State Bank Commissioner
700 Jackson Street, Suite 300
Topeka, KS 66603-3714
(913) 296-2266

Kentucky

Mr. Edward B. Hatchett, Jr.
Commissioner, Department of Financial Institutions
911 Leawood Drive
Frankfort, KY 40601
(502) 564-3390

Louisiana

Mr. A. Bridger Eglin
Commissioner
Financial Institutions
P.O. Box 94095
Baton Rouge, LA 70804
(504) 925-4660

Maine

Mr. H. Donald DeMatteis
Superintendent of Banking
State House Station #36
Augusta, ME 04333-0036
(207) 582-8713

Maryland

Ms. Margie H. Muller
Bank Commissioner
501 St. Paul Place
13th Floor
Baltimore, MD 21202
(301) 333-6262
1 (800) 492-7521
(toll free in MD)

Massachusetts

Mr. Michael C. Hanson
Commissioner of Banks
100 Cambridge Street
Boston, MA 02202
(617) 727-3120

Michigan

Mr. Russell Kropschot
Acting Commissioner
Financial Institutions Bureau
P.O. Box 30224
Lansing, MI 48909
(517) 373-3460

Minnesota

Mr. James G. Miller
Deputy Commissioner of Commerce
133 East 7th Street
St. Paul, MN 55101
(612) 296-2135

Mississippi

Mr. Thomas L. Wright
Commissioner
Department of Banking and Consumer Finance
P.O. Box 23729
Jackson, MS 39225
(601) 359-1031
1 (800) 826-2499
(toll free in MS)

Missouri

Mr. Earl L. Manning
Commissioner of Finance
P.O. Box 716
Jefferson City, MO 65102
(314) 751-3242

Montana

Mr. Donald W. Hutchinson
Commissioner
Financial Institutions
1520 East Sixth Avenue
Room 50
Helena, MT 59620-0542
(406) 444-2091

Nebraska

Mr. James A. Hansen
Director of Banking and Finance
301 Centennial Mall, South
Lincoln, NE 68509
(402) 471-2171

Nevada

Mr. L. Scott Walshaw
Commissioner
Financial Institutions
406 East Second Street
Carson City, NV 89710
(702) 687-4260

New Hampshire

Mr. A. Roland Roberge
Bank Commissioner
169 Manchester Street
Concord, NH 03301
(603) 271-3561

New Jersey

Mr. Jeff Connor
Commissioner of Banking
20 West State Street CN-040
Trenton, NJ 08625
(609) 292-3421

New Mexico

Mr. Kenneth J. Carson, Jr.
Director
Financial Institutions Division
P.O. Box 25101
Sante Fe, NM 87504
(505) 827-7100

New York

Ms. Jill M. Considine
Superintendent of Banks

Two Rector Street
New York, NY 10006-1894
(212) 618-6642
1 (800) 522-3330
(toll free in NY—general consumer information)
1 (800) 832-1838
(toll free in NY—Community Reinvestment Unit)

North Carolina

Mr. William T. Graham
Commissioner of Banks
P.O. Box 29512
Raleigh, NC 27626-0512
(919) 733-3016

North Dakota

Mr. Gary D. Preszler
Commissioner of Banking and Financial Institutions
600 East Boulevard, 13th Floor
Bismarck, ND 58505
(701) 224-2256

Ohio

Mr. John L. Burns
Acting Superintendent of Banks
77 South High Street
21st Floor
Columbus, OH 43266-0549
(614) 466-2932

Oklahoma

Mr. Wayne Osborn
Bank Commissioner
4100 North Lincoln Boulevard
2nd Floor
Oklahoma City, OK 73105
(405) 521-2783

Oregon

Mr. Cecil R. Monroe
Administrator
Division of Finance and Corporate Securities
21 Labor and Industries Building
Salem, OR 97310
(503) 378-4140

Pennsylvania

Ms. Sarah W. Hargrove
Secretary of Banking
333 Market Street, 16th Floor
Harrisburg, PA 17101
(717) 787-6991
1 (800) PA-BANKS
(toll free in PA)

Puerto Rico

Mr. Angel L. Rosas
Commissioner of Banking
G.P.O. Box 70324
San Juan, PR 00936
(809) 781-0545

Rhode Island

Mr. Edward D. Pare Jr.
Acting Associate Director and Superintendent of Banking and Securities
233 Richmond Street
Suite 231
Providence, RI 02903-4231
(401) 277-2405
(401) 277-2223 (TDD)

South Carolina

Mr. Robert C. Cleveland
Commissioner of Banking
1015 Sumter Street, Room 309
Columbia, SC 29201
(803) 734-2001

South Dakota

Mr. Richard A. Duncan
Director of Banking
State Capitol Building
500 East Capitol Avenue
Pierre, SD 57501-5070
(605) 773-3421

Tennessee

Mr. Talmadge Gilley
Commissioner
Financial Institutions
John Sevier Building
4th Floor
Nashville, TN 37243-0705
(615) 741-2236

Texas

Mr. Kenneth W. Littlefield
Banking Commissioner
2601 North Lamar
Austin, TX 78705
(512) 479-1200

Utah

Mr. George Sutton
Commissioner
Financial Institutions
P.O. Box 89
Salt Lake City, UT 84110
(801) 538-8830

Vermont

Mr. Jeffrey Johnson
Commissioner
Banking and Insurance
120 State Street
Montpelier, VT 05620-3101
(802) 828-3301

Virgin Islands

Mr. Derek M. Hodge
Lieutenant Governor
Chairman of the Banking Board
Kongens Garde 18
St. Thomas, VI 00802
(809) 774-2991

Virginia

Mr. Sidney A. Bailey
Commissioner
Financial Institutions
P.O. Box 2-AE
Richmond, VA 23205
(804) 786-3657
1 (800) 552-7945
(toll free in VA)

Washington

Mr. Thomas H. Oldfield
Supervisor of Banking
P.O. Box 9032
Olympia, WA 98504
(206) 753-6520

West Virginia

Mr. James H. Paige III
Commissioner of Banking
State Capitol Complex
Building 3, Room 311
Charleston, WV 25305
(304) 348-2294
1 (800) 642-9056
(toll free in WV)

Wisconsin

Mr. Toby Sherry
Commissioner of Banking
131 West Wilson, 8th Floor
Madison, WI 53703
(608) 266-1621
1 (800) 452-3328
(toll free in WI—complaints only)

Wyoming

Ms. Sue E. Mecca
Manager
Division of Banking
Herschler Building
3rd Floor East
Cheyenne, WY 82002
(307) 777-6600

FEDERAL RESERVE BANKS

Board of Governors of the Federal Reserve System
20th and C Streets, N.W.
Washington, D.C. 20551
(202) 452-3000

Atlanta, Georgia
104 Marietta Street, N.W.
ZIP 30303
(404) 521-8500

Boston, Massachusetts
600 Atlantic Avenue
ZIP 02106
(617) 973-3000

Chicago, Illinois
230 South LaSalle Street
ZIP 60690
(312) 322-5322

Cleveland, Ohio
1455 East Sixth Street
ZIP 44101
(216) 579-2000

Dallas, Texas
400 South Akard Street
ZIP 75222
(214) 651-6111

Kansas City, Missouri
925 Grand Avenue
ZIP 64198
(816) 881-2000

Minneapolis, Minnesota
250 Marquette Avenue
ZIP 55480
(612) 340-2345

New York, New York
33 Liberty Street
ZIP 10045
(212) 720-5000

Philadelphia, Pennsylvania
10 Independence Mall
ZIP 19106
(215) 574-6000

Richmond, Virginia
701 East Byrd Street
ZIP 23219
(804) 697-8000

St. Louis, Missouri
411 Locust Street
ZIP 63102
(314) 444-8444

San Francisco, California
101 Market Street
ZIP 94105
(415) 974-2000

STATE INSURANCE REGULATORS

Each state has its own laws and regulations for all types of insurance, including car, homeowner, and health insurance. The officials listed below enforce these laws. Many of these offices can provide you with information to help you make informed insurance buying decisions. Your local library also will have information that can help you compare insurance companies before making a purchase.

If you have a question or complaint about your insurance company's policies, contact the company before you contact the state insurance regulator.

Alabama

Mr. Mike Weaver
Insurance Commissioner
135 South Union Street #181
Montgomery, AL 36130
(205) 269-3550

Alaska

The Honorable David J. Walsh
Director of Insurance
P.O. Box D
Juneau, AK 99811
(907) 465-2515

American Samoa

Insurance Commissioner
Office of the Governor
Pago Pago, AS 96799

Arizona

Ms. Susan Gallinger
Director of Insurance
3030 North Third Street
Suite 1100
Phoenix, AZ 85012
(602) 255-5400

Arkansas

Mr. Lee Douglass
Insurance Commissioner
400 University Tower Building
Little Rock, AR 72204-1699
(501) 371-1325

California

Mr. John Garamendi
Commissioner of Insurance
100 Van Ness Avenue
San Francisco, CA 94102
(415) 557-3245 (San Francisco)
(213) 736-2551 (Los Angeles)
1 (800) 233-9045
(toll free in CA—complaints)
1 (800) 927-HELP
(toll free in CA—complaints)

Colorado

Mr. John Kezer
Commissioner of Insurance
303 West Colfax Avenue
Suite 500
Denver, CO 80204
(303) 620-4300

Connecticut

Mr. Robert R. Googins
Insurance Commissioner
P.O. Box 816
Hartford, CT 06142-0816
(203) 297-3800

Delaware

Mr. David N. Levinson
Insurance Commissioner
841 Silver Lake Boulevard
Dover, DE 19901
(302) 739-4251
1 (800) 282-8611
(toll free in DE)

District of Columbia

Mr. Patrick E. Kelly
Acting Superintendent of Insurance
614 H Street, N.W.
North Potomac Building
Suite 516
Washington, DC 20001
(202) 727-8017

Florida

Mr. Tom Gallagher
Insurance Commissioner
Plaza Level Eleven—The Capitol
Tallahassee, FL 32399-0300
(904) 488-3440
1 (800) 342-2762
(toll free in FL)

Georgia

Mr. Tim Ryles
Insurance Commissioner
2 Martin L. King, Jr. Drive
Atlanta, GA 30334
(404) 656-2056

Guam

Mr. Joaquin Blaz
Insurance Commissioner
P.O. Box 2796
Agana, GU 96910

Hawaii

Mr. Robin Campaniano
Insurance Commissioner
P.O. Box 3614
Honolulu, HI 96811
(808) 548-2790

Idaho

Mr. George Neumayer
Acting Director of Insurance
500 South 10th Street
Boise, ID 83720
(208) 334-2250

Illinois

Mr. James W. Schacht
Acting Director of Insurance
320 West Washington Street
Springfield, IL 62767
(217) 782-4515
(217) 524-4872 (TDD)

Indiana

Mr. John J. Dillon III
Commissioner of Insurance
311 West Washington Street
Suite 300
Indianapolis, IN 46204-2787
(317) 232-2385
1 (800) 622-4461
(toll free in IN—complaints)

Iowa

Mr. David Lyons
Insurance Commissioner
Lucas State Office Building
6th Floor
Des Moines, IA 50319
(515) 281-5705

Kansas

Mr. Ron Todd
Commissioner of Insurance
420 S.W. 9th Street
Topeka, KS 66612
(913) 296-7801
1 (800) 432-2484
(toll free in KS)

Kentucky

Ms. Elizabeth Wright
Insurance Commissioner
229 West Main Street
P.O. Box 517
Frankfort, KY 40602
(502) 564-3630

Louisiana

Mr. Hunter O. Wagner
Acting Commissioner of Insurance
P.O. Box 94214
Baton Rouge, LA 70804-9214
(504) 342-5900

Maine

Mr. Joseph A. Edwards
Superintendent of Insurance
State House Station 34
Augusta, ME 04333-0034
(207) 582-8707

Maryland

Mr. John A. Donaho
Insurance Commissioner
501 St. Paul Place
7th Floor South
Baltimore, MD 21202
(301) 333-2520
(301) 383-7555 (TDD)
1 (800) 492-7521
(toll free in MD)

Massachusetts

Ms. Susan Scott
Acting Commissioner of Insurance
280 Friend Street
Boston, MA 02114
(617) 727-7189, ext. 300

Michigan

Mr. David Dykhouse
Commissioner of Insurance
Insurance Bureau
P.O. Box 30220
Lansing, MI 48909
(517) 373-9273

Minnesota

Mr. Bert J. McKasy
Commissioner of Commerce
133 East 7th Street
St. Paul, MN 55101
(612) 296-2594

Mississippi

Mr. George Dale
Commissioner of Insurance
1804 Walter Sillers Building
Jackson, MS 39201
(601) 359-3569
1 (800) 562-2957
(toll free in MS—claims only)

Missouri

Mr. Lewis E. Melahn
Director of Insurance
301 West High Street
Room 630
P.O. Box 690
Jefferson City, MO 65102
(314) 751-4126
1 (800) 726-7390
(toll free in MO)

Montana

Ms. Andy Bennett
Commissioner of Insurance
P.O. Box 4009
Helena, MT 59604-4009
(406) 444-2040
1 (800) 332-6148
(toll free in MT)

Nebraska

Mr. William H. McCartney
Director of Insurance
941 "O" Street, Suite 400
Lincoln, NE 68508
(402) 471-2201

Nevada

Ms. Theresa Rankin
Acting Commissioner of Insurance
1665 Hot Springs Road
Capitol Complex 152
Carson City, NV 89710
(702) 687-4270
1 (800) 992-0900
(toll free in NV)

New Hampshire

Mr. Louis E. Bergeron
Insurance Commissioner
169 Manchester Street
Concord, NH 03301
(603) 271-2261
1 (800) 852-3416
(toll free in NH—consumer services)

New Jersey

Mr. Samuel F. Fortunato
Commissioner
Department of Insurance
20 West State Street
CN325
Trenton, NJ 08625
(609) 292-5363

New Mexico

Mr. Fabian Chavez
Superintendent of Insurance
PERA Building, Room 428
P.O. Drawer 1269
Santa Fe, NM 87504-1269
(505) 827-4500

New York

Mr. Salvatore R. Curiale
Superintendent of Insurance
160 West Broadway
New York, NY 10013-3393
(212) 602-0429
1 (800) 342-3736
(toll free in NY—consumer services)

North Carolina

Mr. James E. Long
Commissioner of Insurance
Dobbs Building
P.O. Box 26387
Raleigh, NC 27611
(919) 733-7343
1 (800) 662-7777
(toll free in NC)

North Dakota

Mr. Earl R. Pomeroy
Commissioner of Insurance
Capitol Building, 5th Floor
600 East Boulevard Avenue
Bismarck, ND 58505-0320
(701) 224-2440
1 (800) 247-0560
(toll free in ND)

Ohio

Mr. Harold T. Duryee
Director of Insurance
2100 Stella Court
Columbus, OH 43266-0566
(614) 644-2651

Consumer Services
(614) 644-2673
1 (800) 686-1526
(toll free in OH)

Fraud Division
(614) 644-2671
1 (800) 686-1527
(toll free in OH)

Oklahoma

Mr. Gerald Grimes
Insurance Commissioner
P.O. Box 53408
Oklahoma City, OK 73152
(405) 521-2828
1 (800) 522-0071
(toll free in OK)

Oregon

Mr. Gary K. Weeks
Insurance Commissioner
21 Labor and Industries Bldg.
Salem, OR 97310-0765
(503) 378-4271

Pennsylvania

Ms. Constance B. Foster
Insurance Commissioner
Strawberry Square, 13th Floor
Harrisburg, PA 17120
(717) 787-5173

Puerto Rico

Mr. Billafane Nerix
Commissioner of Insurance
Fernandez Juncos Station
P.O. Box 8330
Santurce, PR 00910
(809) 722-8686

Rhode Island

Mr. Maurice C. Paradis
Insurance Commissioner
233 Richmond Street
Providence, RI 02903
(401) 277-2246

South Carolina

Mr. John G. Richards V
Chief Insurance Commissioner
P.O. Box 100105
Columbia, SC 29202-3105
(803) 737-6117
1 (800) 768-3467
(toll free in SC—consumer department)

South Dakota

Ms. Mary Jane Cleary
Director of Insurance
Insurance Building
910 East Sioux Avenue
Pierre, SD 57501-3940
(605) 773-3563

Tennessee

Ms. Elaine A. McReynolds
Commissioner of Insurance
500 James Robertson Parkway
Nashville, TN 37243-0565
(615) 741-2241
1 (800) 342-4029
(toll free in TN)

Texas

Mr. Ray Marek
Director
Claims and Compliance Division
State Board of Insurance
P.O. Box 149091
Austin, TX 78714-9091
(512) 463-6501
1 (800) 252-3439
(toll free in TX—complaints)

Utah

Mr. Harold C. Yancey
Commissioner of Insurance
3110 State Office Building
Salt Lake City, UT 84114
(801) 530-6400

Vermont

Mr. Jeffrey Johnson
Commissioner of Banking and Insurance
120 State Street
Montpelier, VT 05620-3101
(802) 828-3301

Virgin Islands

Mr. Derek M. Hodge
Commissioner of Insurance
Kongens Garde 18
St. Thomas, VI 00802
(809) 774-2991

Virginia

Mr. Steven T. Foster
Commissioner of Insurance
700 Jefferson Building
P.O. Box 1157
Richmond, VA 23209
(804) 786-3741
(804) 225-3806 (TDD)
1 (800) 552-7945
(toll free in VA)

Washington

Mr. Richard G. Marquardt
Insurance Commissioner
Insurance Building AQ21
Olympia, WA 98504-0321
(206) 753-7301
1 (800) 562-6900
(toll free in WA)

West Virginia

Mr. Hanley C. Clark
Insurance Commissioner
2019 Washington Street, East
Charleston, WV 25305
(304) 348-3394
1 (800) 642-9004
(toll free in WV)

Wisconsin

Mr. Robert D. Haase
Commissioner of Insurance
P.O. Box 7873
Madison, WI 53707-7873
(608) 266-3585
1 (800) 236-8517
(toll free in WI—complaints)

Wyoming

Mr. Kenneth Erickson
Commissioner of Insurance
Herschler Building
122 West 25th Street
Cheyenne, WY 82002-0440
(307) 777-7401
1 (800) 442-4333
(toll free in WY)

STATE UTILITY COMMISSIONS

State utility commissions regulate consumer service and rates for gas, electricity and a variety of other services within your state. These services include rates for telephone calls and moving household goods. In some states, the utility commissions regulate water and transportation rates. Rates for utilities and services provided between states are regulated by the Federal government.

Many utility commissions handle consumer complaints. Sometimes, if a number of complaints are received about the same utility matter, they will conduct investigations.

If you have a consumer question or complaint about a utility matter, write or call the commission in your state.

Alabama

Mr. James Sullivan
President
Public Service Commission
P.O. Box 991
Montgomery, AL
36101-0991
(205) 242-5207
1 (800) 392-8050
(toll free in AL)

Alaska

Mr. Don Schroer
Commissioner
Public Utilities Commission
1016 West 6th
Anchorage, AK 99501
(907) 276-6222

Arizona

Mr. Renz Jennings
Chairman
Corporation Commission
1200 West Washington Street
Phoenix, AZ 85007
(602) 542-3935
(602) 255-2105 (TDD)
1 (800) 222-7000
(toll free in AZ)

Arkansas

Mr. Sam I. Bratton, Jr.
Chairman
Public Service Commission
P.O. Box 400
Little Rock, AR 72203-0400
(501) 682-1453
1 (800) 482-1164
(toll free in AR—complaints)

California

Ms. Patricia Eckert
President
Public Utilities Commission
505 Van Ness Avenue
Room 5207
San Francisco, CA 94102
(415) 557-3700
(415) 557-0798 (TDD)
1 (800) 548-9919
(toll free in Northern CA—complaints)
1 (800) 648-6967
(toll free in Southern CA—complaints)

Colorado

Mr. Arnold H. Cook
Chairman
Public Utilities Commission
1580 Logan Street
Logan Tower—Office Level 2
Denver, CO 80203
(303) 894-2021
1 (800) 888-0170
(toll free in CO)

Connecticut

Mr. Clifton Leonhardt
Chairperson
Department of Public Utility Control
1 Central Park Plaza
New Britain, CT 06051
(203) 827-1553
1 (800) 382-4586
(toll free in CT)

Delaware

Ms. Nancy M. Norling
Chairman
Public Service Commission
1560 South DuPont Highway
P.O. Box 457
Dover, DE 19903
(302) 739-4247
1 (800) 282-8574
(toll free in DE)

District of Columbia

Mr. Edward M. Meyers
Acting Chairperson
Public Service Commission
450 Fifth Street, N.W.
Washington, DC 20001
(202) 626-5110

Florida

Mr. Thomas M. Beard
Chairman
Public Service Commission
101 East Gaines Street
Tallahassee, FL 32399-0850
(904) 488-7001
1 (800) 342-3552
(toll free in FL)

Georgia

Mr. Bob Durden
Commissioner
Public Service Commission
244 Washington Street, S.W.
Atlanta, GA 30334
(404) 656-4512
1 (800) 282-5813
(toll free in GA)

Hawaii

Mr. Wukio Naito
Chairman
Public Utilities Commission
465 South King Street
Room 103
Honolulu, HI 96813
(808) 548-3990

Idaho

Mr. Dean J. (Joe) Miller
President
Public Utilities Commission
State House
Boise, ID 83720
(208) 334-3427

Illinois

Mr. Terrence L. Barnich
Chairman
Commerce Commission
527 East Capitol Avenue
P.O. Box 19280
Springfield, IL 62794
(217) 782-7295
(217) 782-7434 (TDD)

Indiana

Mr. James Monk
Chairman
Utility Regulatory Commission
913 State Office Building
Indianapolis, IN 46204
(317) 232-2701

Iowa

Mr. Dennis J. Nagel
Chairman
Iowa Utilities Board
Lucas State Office Bldg.
5th Floor
Des Moines, IA 50319
(515) 281-5979

Kansas

Mr. Jim Robinson
Chairman
State Corporation Commission
1500 SW Arrowhead Road
Topeka, KS 66604-4027
(913) 271-3100
1 (800) 662-0027
(toll free in KS)

Kentucky

Mr. George E. Overby, Jr.
Chairman
Public Service Commission
730 Schenkel Lane
P.O. Box 615
Frankfort, KY 40602
(502) 564-3940

Louisiana

Mr. Louis J. Lambert, Jr.
Chairman
Public Service Commission
P.O. Box 1026
Gonzales, LA 70707
(504) 342-4404
1 (800) 256-2413
(toll free in LA)

Maine

Mr. Kenneth Gordon
Chairman
Public Utilities Commission
State House Station 18
Augusta, ME 04333
(207) 289-3831
1 (800) 452-4699
(toll free in ME)

Maryland

Mr. Frank O. Heintz, Jr.
Chairman
Public Service Commission
231 East Baltimore Street
Baltimore, MD 21202
(301) 333-6000
1 (800) 492-0474
(toll free in MD)

Massachusetts

Mr. Robert Yargler Jr.
Chairman
Department of Public Utilities
100 Cambridge Street
12th Floor
Boston, MA 02202
(617) 727-3500

Michigan

Mr. Steven Fetter
Chairperson
Public Service Commission
6545 Mercantile Way
P.O. Box 30221
Lansing, MI 48909
(517) 334-6445
1 (800) 292-9555
(toll free in MI)
1 (800) 443-8926
(toll free TDD in MI)

Minnesota

Mr. Darrel L. Peterson
Chairman
Public Utilities Commission
780 American Center Building
160 East Kellogg Boulevard
St. Paul, MN 55101-1471
(612) 296-7124
(612) 297-1200 (TDD)
1 (800) 652-9747
(toll free in MN)

Mississippi

Mr. Neilson Cochran
Chairman
Public Service Commission
P.O. Box 1174
Jackson, MS 39215
(601) 961-5400
Northern District
1 (800) 356-6428
(toll free in MS)
Central District
1 (800) 356-6430
(toll free in MS)
Southern District
1 (800) 356-6429
(toll free in MS)

Missouri

Mr. William D. Steinmeier
Chairman
Public Service Commission
P.O. Box 360
Jefferson City, MO 65102
(314) 751-3234
1 (800) 392-4211
(toll free in MO)

Montana

Mr. Howard Ellis
Chairman
Public Service Commission

2701 Prospect Avenue
Helena, MT 59620-2601
(406) 444-6199

Nebraska

Mr. Frank Landis
Chairman
Public Service Commission
300 The Atrium
1200 "N" Street
P.O. Box 94927
Lincoln, NE 68509
(402) 471-3101
1 (800) 526-0017
(toll free in NE)

Nevada

Mr. Thomas E. Stephens
Chairman
Public Service Commission
727 Fairview Drive
Carson City, NV 89710
(702) 687-6000

New Hampshire

Mr. Larry M. Smukler
Chairman
Public Utilities Commission
8 Old Suncook Road
Building No. 1
Concord, NH 03301
(603) 271-2431
1 (800) 852-3793
(toll free in NH)

New Jersey

Mr. George Barbour
Mr. Jeremiah F. O'Connor
Commissioners
Board of Public Utilities
Two Gateway Center
Newark, NJ 07102
(201) 648-2027
(201) 648-7983 (TDD)
1 (800) 824-0241
(toll free in NJ)

New Mexico

Mr. Laurence B. Ingram
Chairman
New Mexico Public Service Commission
Marian Hall
224 East Palace Avenue
Sante Fe, NM 87501-2013
(505) 827-6940

New York

Mr. Peter A. Bradford
Chairman
Public Service Commission
3 Empire State Plaza
Albany, NY 12223
(518) 474-5527
1 (800) 342-3377
(toll free in NY—complaints)
1 (800) 342-3355
(toll free in NY—emergency service cutoff
7:30 a.m.—7:30 p.m.
Monday—Friday)

North Carolina

Mr. William Redman
Chairman
Utilities Commission
P.O. Box 29510
Raleigh, NC 27626-0510
(919) 733-4249
(919) 733-9277
(consumer services and complaints)

North Dakota

Mr. Bruce Hagen
President
Public Service Commission
State Capitol Building
Bismarck, ND 58505-0480
(701) 224-2400
1 (800) 932-2400
(toll free in ND)

Ohio

Mr. Craig A. Glazer
Chairman
Public Utilities Commission
180 East Broad Street
Columbus, OH 43266-0573
(614) 466-3016
(614) 466-8180 (TDD)
1 (800) 686-7826
(toll free in OH—consumer services)

Oklahoma

Mr. Bob Hopkins
Chairman
Corporation Commission
Jim Thorpe Office Building
2101 Lincoln Boulevard
Oklahoma City, OK 73105
(405) 521-2264
1 (800) 522-8154
(toll free in OK)

Oregon

Mr. Myron B. Katz
Chairman
Public Utility Commission
300 Labor and Industries Bldg.
Salem, OR 97310-0335
(503) 378-6611
1 (800) 522-2404
(toll free in OR)

Pennsylvania

Mr. William H. Smith
Chairman
Public Utility Commission
P.O. Box 3265
Harrisburg, PA 17120
(717) 783-1740
1 (800) 782-1110
(toll free in PA)

Puerto Rico

Mr. Enrique Rodriguez
Chairman
Public Service Commission
Call Box 870
Hato Rey, PR 00919-0870
(809) 751-5050

Rhode Island

Mr. James J. Malachowski
Chairman
Public Utilities Commission
100 Orange Street
Providence, RI 02903
(401) 277-3500 (voice/TDD)
1 (800) 341-1000
(toll free in RI)

South Carolina

Ms. Marjorie Amos-Frazier
Chairman
Public Service Commission

P.O. Drawer 11649
Columbia, SC 29211
(803) 737-5100
1 (800) 922-1531
(toll free in SC)

South Dakota

Mr. James A. Burg
Chairman
Public Utilities Commission
500 East Capitol Avenue
Pierre, SD 57501-5070
(605) 773-3201
1 (800) 332-1782
(toll free in SD)

Tennessee

Mr. Steve Hewlett
Chairman
Public Service Commission
460 James Robertson Parkway
Nashville, TN 37243-0505
(615) 741-2904
1 (800) 342-8359
(toll free voice/TDD in TN)

Texas

Mr. Paul D. Meek
Chairman
Public Utility Commission
7800 Shoal Creek Boulevard
Suite 400N
Austin, TX 78757
(512) 458-0100
(512) 458-0221 (TDD)

Utah

Mr. Brian T. Stewart
Chairman
Public Service Commission
160 East 300 South
Salt Lake City, UT 84111
(801) 530-6716
(801) 530-6706 (TDD)

Vermont

Mr. Richard H. Cowart
Chairman
Public Service Board
120 State Street
Montpelier, VT 05602-2701
(802) 828-2358
1 (800) 622-4496
(toll free in VT)

Virgin Islands

Mr. George C. Parrott
Chairman
Public Services Commission
P.O. Box 40
Charlotte Amalie
St. Thomas, VI 00804
(809) 776-1291

Virginia

Mr. Theodore V. Morrison Jr.
Chairman
State Corporation Commission
P.O. Box 1197
Richmond, VA 23209
(804) 786-3608
1 (800) 552-7945
(toll free in VA)

Washington

Ms. Sharon Nelson
Chairman
Utilities and Transportation Commission
1300 Evergreen Park Dr. South
Olympia, WA 98504
(206) 753-6423
1 (800) 562-6150
(toll free in WA)

West Virginia

Mr. Boyce Griffith
Chairman
Public Service Commission
P.O. Box 812
Charleston, WV 25323
(304) 340-0300
1 (800) 344-5113
(toll free in WV)

Wisconsin

Mr. Charles H. Thompson
Chairman
Public Service Commission
4802 Sheboygan Avenue
P.O. Box 7854
Madison, WI 53707
(608) 266-2001

Wyoming

Mr. Bill Tucker
Chairman
Public Service Commission
700 West 21st Street
Cheyenne, WY 82002
(307) 777-7427

STATE VOCATIONAL AND REHABILITATION AGENCIES

State vocational and rehabilitation agencies coordinate and provide a number of services for disabled persons. These services can include counseling, evaluation, training, and job placement. There are also services for the sight and hearing impaired. For more information, call or write the office nearest you.

Alabama

Ms. Lamona H. Lucas
Director
Rehabilitation Services
P.O. Box 11586
Montgomery, AL 36111-0586
(205) 281-8780

Alaska

Mr. Keith J. Anderson, Director
Division of Vocational Rehabilitation
Box F, M.S. 0581
Juneau, AK 99811-0500
(907) 465-2814
(907) 465-2440 (TDD)

American Samoa

Mr. Peter Galeai
Director
Vocational Rehabilitation
Department of Manpower Resources
Pago Pago, AS 96799
011 (684) 633-2336

Arizona

Mr. James B. Griffith
Administrator
Rehabilitation Services Administration
1789 West Jefferson, North Wing
Phoenix, AZ 85007
(602) 542-3332
(602) 542-6049 (voice/TDD)

Arkansas

Mr. Bobby C. Simpson
Deputy Director
Division of Rehabilitation Services
Department of Human Services
P.O. Box 3781
Little Rock, AR 72203
(501) 682-6709
(501) 682-6669 (TDD)

Mr. James C. Hudson
Commissioner
Division of Services for the Blind
Department of Human Services
P.O. Box 3237
Little Rock, AR 72203
(501) 324-9270

California

Mr. Bill Tainter
Director
Department of Rehabilitation
830 K Street Mall
Sacramento, CA 95814
(916) 445-3971 (voice/TDD)

Colorado

Mr. Anthony Francavilla
Manager
Department of Social and Rehabilitation Services
1575 Sherman Street, 4th Floor
Denver, CO 80203-1714
(303) 866-2866 (voice/TDD)

Connecticut

Mr. Richard Carlson
Acting Bureau Chief
Bureau of Client Services
State Department of Education
Division of Rehabilitation Services
10 Griffin Road North
Windsor, CT 06095
(203) 298-2000
1 (800) 537-2549
(toll free in CT)

Mr. George Precourt
Director
Board of Education and Services for the Blind
170 Ridge Road
Wethersfield, CT 06109
(203) 566-5800
1 (800) 842-4510
(toll free in CT)

Delaware

Mr. Tony Sokolowski
Director
Division of Vocational Rehabilitation
Delaware Elwyn Institutes
321 East 11th Street, 4th Floor
Wilmington, DE 19801
(302) 577-2851 (voice/TDD)

Ms. Diane Post
Acting Director
Division for the Visually Impaired
Department of Health and Social Services
305 West 8th Street
Wilmington, DE 19801
(302) 421-5730

District of Columbia

Ms. Ruth Royall Hill
Acting Administrator
D.C. Rehabilitation Services Administration
Department of Human Services
605 G Street NW, Suite 1111
Washington, DC 20001
(202) 727-3227
(202) 727-0981 (TDD)

Florida

Calvin Melton, Ph.D.
Director

Division of Vocational Rehabilitation
Department of Labor and Employment Security
1709 "A" Mahan Drive
Tallahassee, FL 32399-0696
(904) 488-6210
(904) 488-2867 (voice/TDD)

Mr. Carl F. McCoy
Director
Division of Blind Services
Department of Education
2540 Executive Center Circle West
Douglas Building, Room 203
Tallahassee, FL 32399
(904) 488-1330 (voice/TDD)
1 (800) 342-1828
(toll free in FL)

Georgia

Ms. Darlene Taylor
Director
Division of Rehabilitation Services
Department of Human Resources
878 Peachtree Street, NE, Room 706
Atlanta, GA 30309
(404) 894-6670
(404) 894-8558 (voice/TDD)
1 (800) 822-9727
(toll free in GA)

Guam

Mr. Norbert Ungacto
Acting Director
Department of Vocational Rehabilitation
122 Harmon Plaza, Room B201
Harmon Industrial Park, GU 96911
011 (671) 646-9468

Hawaii

Mr. Neil Shim
Administrator
Division of Vocational Rehabilitation and Services for the Blind
Department of Human Services
P.O. Box 339
Honolulu, HI 96809
(808) 586-5355
1 (800) 586-5366
(toll free in HI)

Idaho

Mr. George Pelletier, Jr.
Administrator
Division of Vocational Rehabilitation
Len B. Jordan Building, Room 150
650 West State
Boise, ID 83720-3650
(208) 334-3390
(208) 334-2520 (voice/TDD)

Mr. Edward McHugh
Administrator
Idaho Commission for the Blind
341 West Washington
Boise, ID 83702
(208) 334-3220
1 (800) 542-8688
(toll free in ID)

Illinois

Ms. Audrey McCrimon
Director
Department of Rehabilitation Services
623 East Adams Street
Springfield, IL 62794
(217) 785-0218
(217) 782-5734 (TDD)

Indiana

Mr. Jeff Richardson
Commissioner
Department of Human Services
402 West Washington Street
P.O. Box 7083
Indianapolis, IN 46207-7083
(317) 232-6500
(317) 232-1427 (TDD)
1 (800) 545-7763
(toll free in IN)

Iowa

Mr. Jerry L. Starkweather
Administrator
Division of Vocational Rehabilitation Services
Department of Education
510 East 12th Street
Des Moines, IA 50319
(515) 281-4311 (voice/TDD)

Mr. R. Creig Slayton
Director
Department for the Blind
524 4th Street
Des Moines, IA 50309
(515) 281-1333
1 (800) 362-2587
(toll free in IA)

Kansas

Mr. Glen Yancey
Commissioner
Rehabilitation Services
Department of Social and Rehabilitation Services
300 S.W. Oakley
Biddle Building, 1st Floor
Topeka, KS 66606
(913) 296-3911
(913) 296-7029 (TDD)

Kentucky

Mr. Carroll Burchett
Commissioner
Department of Vocational Rehabilitation
Capital Plaza Tower, 9th floor
Frankfort, KY 40601
(502) 564-4566
(502) 564-4440 (voice/TDD)
1 (800) 372-7172
(toll free in KY)

Mr. Charles W. McDowell
Director
Department for the Blind
Workforce Development Cabinet
427 Versailles Road
Frankfort, KY 40601
(502) 564-4754

Louisiana

Mr. Alton Toms
Director
Louisiana Rehabilitation Services

Department of Social Services
P.O. Box 94371
Baton Rouge, LA 70804-9071
(504) 342-2285
(504) 342-2266 (voice/TDD)

Maine

Ms. Pamela A. Tetley
Director
Bureau of Rehabilitation Services
Department of Human Services
35 Anthony Avenue
Augusta, ME 04333-0011
(207) 626-5300
(207) 626-5321 (voice/TDD)

Mariana Islands

Mr. Manny Villagomez
Chief
Vocational Rehabilitation Division
Commonwealth of Northern Mariana Islands
P.O. Box 1521
SaiPan, Mariana Islands 96950
011 (670) 234-6538

Maryland

Mr. James S. Jeffers
Assistant State Superintendent
Division of Vocational Rehabilitation
State Department of Education
2301 Argonne Drive
Baltimore, MD 21218
(301) 554-3276
(301) 554-3277 (TDD)

Massachusetts

Mr. Charles Crawford
Commissioner
Commission for the Blind
88 Kingston Street
Boston, MA 02111-2227
(617) 727-5550
1 (800) 392-6556
(toll free TDD in MA)
1 (800) 392-6450
(toll free voice in MA)

Mr. Elmer C. Bartels
Commissioner
Rehabilitation Commission
4 Point Place
27–43 Wormwood Street
Boston, MA 02210
(617) 727-2172
(617) 727-9063 (TDD)

Michigan

Ivan Cotman, Ed.D.
Associate Superintendent
Bureau of Rehabilitation and Disability Determination
Department of Education
P.O. Box 30010
Lansing, MI 48909
(517) 373-3390
(517) 373-3979 (voice/TDD)

Mr. Philip E. Peterson
Director
Commission for the Blind
Department of Labor
201 North Washington Square
Lansing, MI 48909
(517) 373-2062
(517) 335-4592 (voice/TDD)
(517) 373-4025 (voice/TDD)
1 (800) 292-4200
(toll free in MI)

Mr. Peter Griswold
State Director
Michigan Rehabilitation Services
Department of Education
P.O. Box 30010
Lansing, MI 48909
(517) 373-3391
(517) 373-4031 (voice/TDD)
1 (800) 292-5896
(toll free in MI)

Mr. Charles Jones
State Director
Disability Determination Service
Department of Education
P.O. Box 30011
Lansing, MI 48909
(517) 373-7830
1 (800) 366-3404
(toll free in MI)

Minnesota

Ms. Mary Shortall
Acting Assistant Commissioner
Department of Jobs and Training
Division of Rehabilitation Services
390 North Robert Street
5th Floor
St. Paul, MN 55101
(612) 296-1822
(612) 296-3900 (TDD)

Mr. Rick Hokanson
Director
Services for the Blind
1745 University Avenue West
St. Paul, MN 55104
(612) 642-0500
(612) 642-0506 (voice/TDD)
1 (800) 652-9000

Mississippi

Mr. Joe Carballo
Interim Director
Vocational Rehabilitation for the Blind
P.O. Box 4872
Jackson, MS 39296
(601) 354-6411

Mr. Morris Selby
Director
Vocational Rehabilitation Division
Department of Rehabilitation Services
P.O. Box 1698
Jackson, MS 39215
(601) 354-6825
(601) 354-6830 (voice/TDD)
1 (800) 943-1000
(toll free in MS)

Missouri

Mr. Don L. Gann, Ed.
Assistant Commissioner
Division of Vocational Rehabilitation
State Department of Education
2401 East McCarty
Jefferson City, MO 65101
(314) 751-3251 (voice/TDD)

Mr. David S. Vogel
Deputy Director
Bureau for the Blind
Division of Family Services
619 East Capitol
Jefferson City, MO 65101
(314) 751-4249

Montana

Mr. Joe A. Mathews
Administrator
Department of Social and Rehabilitation Services
Rehabilitative/Visual Services Divisions
P.O. Box 4210
Helena, MT 59604
(406) 444-2590 (voice/TDD)

Nebraska

Jason D. Andrew, Ph.D.
Associate Commissioner
Division of Rehabilitation Services
State Department of Education
P.O. Box 94987
Lincoln, NE 68509
(402) 471-3649
(402) 471-3659 (voice/TDD)

James S. Nyman, Ph.D.
Director
Services for the Visually Impaired
Department of Public Institutions
4600 Valley Road
Lincoln, NE 68510
(402) 471-2891
(402) 471-3593 (voice/TDD)

Nevada

Mr. Stephen A. Shaw
Administrator
Department of Human Resources
Rehabilitation Division
505 East King Street
Room 502
Carson City, NV 89710
(702) 687-4440 (voice/TDD)

New Hampshire

Mr. Bruce A. Archambault
Director
Division of Vocational Rehabilitation
State Department of Education
78 Regional Drive
Concord, NH 03301
(603) 271-3800
(603) 271-3471 (voice/TDD)

New Jersey

Mrs. Jamie Casabianca Hilton
Executive Director
New Jersey Commission for the Blind and Visually Impaired
P.O. Box 47017
153 Halsey Street, 6th Floor
Newark, NJ 07101
(201) 648-3333
(201) 648-4559 (voice/TDD)
(201) 648-6276 (TDD)
1 (800) 962-1233
(toll free in NJ)

Mr. Stephen Janick
Director
Division of Vocational Rehabilitation Services
Labor Building
CN 398—Room 612
Trenton, NJ 08625
(609) 292-5987
(609) 292-2919 (voice/TDD)

New Mexico

Mr. Ross Sweat
Director
Department of Education
Division of Vocational Rehabilitation
604 West San Mateo
Santa Fe, NM 87503
(505) 827-3500 (voice/TDD)
1 (800) 235-5387 (complaints)

New York

Mr. Lawrence C. Gloeckler
Deputy Commissioner
Office of Vocational and Educational Services for Individuals with Disabilities
New York State Education Department
One Commerce Plaza
Room 1606
Albany, NY 12234
(518) 474-2714
(518) 473-9333 (voice/TDD)
1 (800) 222-JOBS
(toll free in NY—employment hotline)

Mr. Jack L. Ryan, Jr.
Director
State Department of Social Services
Commission for the Blind and Visually Handicapped
10 Eyck Office Building
40 North Pearl Street
Albany, NY 12243
(518) 473-1801
1 (800) 342-3715
(toll free in NY)

North Carolina

Mr. Claude A. Myer
Director
Division of Vocational Rehabilitation Services
Department of Human Resources
State Office
P.O. Box 26053
Raleigh, NC 27611
(919) 733-3364
(919) 733-5920 (voice/TDD)

Mr. Herman O. Gruber
Director
Division of Services for the Blind
Department of Human Resources
309 Ashe Avenue
Raleigh, NC 27606
(919) 733-9822
(919) 733-5199 (voice/TDD)

North Dakota

Mr. Gene Hysjulien
Associate Director

Office of Vocational Rehabilitation
Department of Human Services
600 East Boulevard
State Capitol Building
Bismarck, ND 58505
(701) 224-2907
(701) 224-2699 (voice/TDD)
1 (800) 472-2622
(toll free in ND)

Ohio

Mr. Robert L. Rabe
Administrator
Rehabilitation Services Commission
400 East Campus View Boulevard
Columbus, OH 43235-4604
(614) 438-1210 (voice/TDD)
1 (800) 282-4536, ext. 1210
(toll free in OH)

Oklahoma

Mr. Jerry Dunlap
Administrator
Department of Human Services
Division of Rehabilitation Services
P.O. Box 25352
Oklahoma City, OK 73125
(405) 424-6647
(405) 424-2794 (voice/TDD)

Oregon

Mr. Charles Young
Administrator
Commission for the Blind
535 S.E. 12th Avenue
Portland, OR 97214
(503) 238-8380 (voice/TDD)

Mr. Joil Southwell
Administrator
Division of Vocational Rehabilitation
Department of Human Resources
2045 Silverton Road Northeast
Salem, OR 97310
(503) 378-3850 (voice/TDD)

Pennsylvania

Mr. Gil Selders
Executive Director
Office of Vocational Rehabilitation
Labor and Industry Building
7th and Forster Streets
Harrisburg, PA 17120
(717) 787-5244
(717) 783-8917 (voice/TDD)
1 (800) 442-6351
(toll free in PA)

Mr. Norman E. Witman
Director
Bureau of Blindness and Visual Services
Department of Public Welfare
P.O. Box 2675
Harrisburg, PA 17105-2675
(717) 787-6176
(717) 787-6280 (voice/TDD)
1 (800) 622-2842
(toll free in PA)

Puerto Rico

Mr. Angel L. Jimerez
Assistant Secretary for Vocational Rehabilitation
Department of Social Services
Vocational Rehabilitation Program
P.O. Box 1118, Building 10
Hato Rey, PR 00919
(809) 725-1792

Rhode Island

Mr. William Messore
Administrator
Department of Human Services
Division of Community Services
Vocational Rehabilitation Services
40 Fountain Street
Providence, RI 02903
(401) 421-7005
(401) 421-7016 (TDD)

Mr. John T. Thompson
Acting Administrator
Rhode Island Services for the Blind and Visually Impaired
Department of Human Services
275 Westminister Street
Providence, RI 02903
(401) 277-2300
(401) 277-3010 (voice/TDD)
1 (800) 752-8088
(toll free in RI)

South Carolina

Mr. Donald Gist
Commissioner
Commission for the Blind
1430 Confederate Avenue
Columbia, SC 29201
(803) 734-7522
1 (800) 922-2222
(toll free in SC)

Mr. Joseph S. Dusenbury
Commissioner
Vocational Rehabilitation Department
1410 Boston Avenue
P.O. Box 15
West Columbia, SC 29171
(803) 822-4300
(803) 822-5313 (voice/TDD)

South Dakota

Mr. David L. Miller
Division Director
Division of Rehabilitation Services
Department of Human Services
700 Governors Drive
Pierre, SD 57501-2291
(605) 773-3195
(605) 773-4544 (TDD)

Mr. Grady Kickul
Division Director
Division of Service to the Blind and Visually Impaired
700 Governors Drive
Pierre, SD 57501-2291
(605) 773-3195
(605) 773-4544 (TDD)

Tennessee

Ms. Patsy Mathews
Assistant Commissioner
Rehabilitation Services
Department of Human Services
Citizens Plaza State Office Bldg. 15th Floor
400 Deaderick Street
Nashville, TN 37248-0060
(615) 741-2019
(615) 741-5644 (voice/TDD)

Texas

Mr. Vernon M. Arrell
Commissioner
Rehabilitation Commission
4900 North Lamar
Austin, TX 78751
(512) 445-8100
1 (800) 735-2988 (voice)
1 (800) 735-2989 (TDD)
1 (800) 628-5115
(toll free in TX)

Mr. Pat D. Westbrook
Executive Director
Commission for the Blind
P.O. Box 12866 Capitol Station
Austin, TX 78711
(512) 459-2500
(512) 459-2608 (voice/TDD)
1 (800) 252-5204
(toll free in TX)

Utah

Judy Ann Buffmire, Ph.D.
Director
Division of Rehabilitation Services
State Office of Education
250 East Fifth South
Salt Lake City, UT 84111
(801) 538-7530 (voice/TDD)

Mr. William G. Gibson
Director
Services for the Visually Handicapped
State Office of Rehabilitation
309 East First South
Salt Lake City, UT 84111
(801) 533-9393
1 (800) 284-1823

Vermont

Ms. Diane Dalmasse, Director
Vocational Rehabilitation Division
103 South Main Street
Waterbury, VT 05671-2303
(802) 241-2189 (voice/TDD)

Mr. David Mentasti
Director
Division for the Blind and Visually Impaired
103 South Main Street
Waterbury, VT 05676
(802) 241-2211

Virgin Islands

Ms. Sedonie Halbert
Administrator
Division for Disabilities and Rehabilitation Services
Virgin Islands Department of Human Services
Barbel Plaza South
St. Thomas, VI 00802
(809) 774-0930

Virginia

Ms. Susan Urofsky
Commissioner
Department of Rehabilitative Services
4901 Fitzhugh Avenue
P.O. Box 11045
Richmond, VA 23230
(804) 367-0316
(804) 367-0315 (voice/TDD)
1 (800) 552-5019
(toll free in VA)

Mr. Donald Cox, Commissioner
Department for the Visually Handicapped
397 Azalea Avenue
Richmond, VA 23227
(804) 371-3140 (voice/TDD)
1 (800) 622-2155
(toll free in VA)

Washington

Ms. Jeanne Munro
Director
Division of Vocational Rehabilitation
Department of Social and Health Services
OB 21-C
Olympia, WA 98504
(206) 753-0293
(206) 753-5473 (voice/TDD)
1 (800) 637-5627
(toll free in WA)

Ms. Shirley Smith
Director
Department of Services for the Blind
521 East Legion Way
Olympia, WA 98501
(206) 586-1224
(206) 721-6437 (TDD)

West Virginia

Mr. John Panza
Director
Division of Rehabilitation Services
State Board of Rehabilitation
State Capitol
Charleston, WV 25305
(304) 766-4600
(304) 766-4970 (voice/TDD)
1 (800) 642-3021
(toll free in WV)

Wisconsin

Ms. Judy R. Norman-Nunnery, Ph.D.
Administrator
Division of Vocational Rehabilitation
Department of Health and Social Services
1 West Wilson, 8th Floor
Madison, WI 53707-7852
(608) 266-5466
(608) 266-9599 (voice/TDD)
1 (800) 362-7433
(toll free in WI)

Wyoming

Ms. Joan B. Watson
Administrator
Division of Vocational Rehabilitation
Department of Employment
1 East Herschler Building
Cheyenne, WY 82002
(307) 777-7385
(307) 777-7389 (voice/TDD)

STATE WEIGHTS AND MEASURES OFFICES

State Weights and Measures offices enforce laws and regulations about the weights of such packaged items as food and household products. These offices also check the accuracy of weighing and measuring devices, for example, supermarket scales, gasoline pumps, taxicab meters, and rental car odometers.

Contact the Weights and Measures office nearest you if you think you have purchased a product that weighed less than it should or you think a scale or meter is inaccurate.

Alabama

Mr. Donald E. Stagg
Director
Weights and Measures Division
Department of Agriculture
P.O. Box 3336
Montgomery, AL 36109-0336
(205) 242-2613
1 (800) 321-0018
(toll free in AL)

Alaska

Mr. Edward Moses
Director
Mr. Aves D. Thompson
Chief Inspector
Weights and Measures
Department of Commerce and Economic Development
Division of Measurement Standards
12050 Industry Way
Huffman Business Park
Building O
Anchorage, AK 99515
(907) 345-7750
1 (800) 478-7636
(toll free in AK)

Arizona

Mr. Raymond Helmick
Director
Weights and Measures Division
Department of Administration
1951 West North Lane
Phoenix, AZ 85021
(602) 255-5211

Arkansas

Mr. Sam F. Hindsman
Director
Bureau of Standards
4608 West 61st Street
Little Rock, AR 72209
(501) 324-9681

California

Mr. Darrell A. Guensler
Assistant Director
Division of Measurement Standards
Department of Food and Agriculture
8500 Fruitridge Road
Sacramento, CA 95826
(916) 366-5119

Colorado

Mr. David Wallace
Chief
Measurements Standards Section
Department of Agriculture
3125 Wyandot Street
Denver, CO 80211
(303) 866-2845

Connecticut

Mr. Allan M. Nelson
Director
Weights and Measures Division
Department of Consumer Protection
State Office Building
Room G-17
165 Capitol Avenue
Hartford, CT 06106
(203) 566-5230

Delaware

Supervisor
Office of Weights and Measures
Department of Agriculture
2320 South DuPont Highway
Dover, DE 19901-9999
(302) 739-4811

District of Columbia

Acting Chief
Weights and Measures
Market Branch
Department of Consumer and Regulatory Affairs
1110 U Street, SE
Washington, DC 20020
(202) 767-7923

Florida

Mr. Max Gray
Chief
Bureau of Weights and Measures
Department of Agriculture and Consumer Services
3125 Conner Boulevard
Building #2
Tallahassee, FL 32399-1650
(904) 488-9140

Georgia

Mr. Bill Truby
Assistant Commissioner
Division of Weights and Measures
Department of Agriculture
Agriculture Building
Atlanta, GA 30334
(404) 656-3605

Hawaii

Mr. James E. Maka
Administrator
Measurement Standards
Department of Agriculture
725 Ilalo Street
Honolulu, HI 96813-5524
(808) 548-7152

Idaho

Mr. Glen H. Jex
Chief
Bureau of Weights and Measures
Department of Agriculture
2216 Kellogg Lane
Boise, ID 83712
(208) 334-2345

Illinois

Mr. Sidney A. Colbrook
Manager
Weights and Measures Program
Department of Agriculture
801 East Sangamon Avenue
P.O. Box 19281
Springfield, IL 62794-9281
(217) 782-3817

Indiana

Ms. Sharon S. Rhoades
Program Administrator
Weights and Measures
State Board of Health
1330 West Michigan Street
Indianapolis, IN 46206-1964
(317) 633-0350

Iowa

Mr. Jerry L. Bane
Bureau Chief
Weights and Measures
Department of Agriculture and Land Stewardship
H.A. Building
Des Moines, IA 50319
(515) 281-5716

Kansas

Mr. DeVern H. Phillips
State Sealer
Weights and Measures Division
State Board of Agriculture
2016 South West 37th Street
Topeka, KS 66611-2570
(913) 267-4641

Kentucky

Mr. Charles Prebble
Director
Division of Weights and Measures
Department of Agriculture
106 West Second Street
Frankfort, KY 40601-2882
(502) 564-4870

Louisiana

Mr. Ronald Harrell
Director
Weights and Measures
Department of Agriculture
P.O. Box 3098
Baton Rouge, LA 70821-3098
(504) 925-3780

Maine

Mr. Clayton F. Davis
Director
Division of Regulations
State House Station 28
Augusta, ME 04333
(207) 289-3841
(207) 289-4470 (TDD)

Maryland

Mr. Kenneth S. Butcher
Chief
Weights and Measures Section
Maryland Department of Agriculture
50 Harry S. Truman Parkway
Annapolis, MD 21401
(301) 841-5790

Massachusetts

Mr. Charles H. Carroll
Assistant Director of Standards
Division of Standards
One Ashburton Place
McCormick Building
Room 1115
Boston, MA 02108
(617) 727-3480

Michigan

Mr. Edward Heffron
Chief
Food Division
Department of Agriculture
Ottawa Building North
4th Floor
P.O. Box 30017
Lansing, MI 48909
(517) 373-1060

Minnesota

Mr. Michael F. Blacik
Director
Division of Weights and Measures
Department of Public Service
2277 Highway 36
St. Paul, MN 55113
(612) 341-7200

Mississippi

Mr. William P. Eldridge
Director
Weights and Measures Division
Department of Agriculture
500 Greymont Avenue
Jackson, MS 39215-1609
(601) 354-7077

Missouri

Mr. Lester Barrows
Director
Weights and Measures Division
Department of Agriculture
P.O. Box 630
Jefferson City, MO 65102-0630
(314) 751-4278

Montana

Mr. W. James Kembel
Bureau Chief
Bureau of Weights and Measures
Department of Commerce
Capitol Station
Helena, MT 59620
(406) 444-3164

Nebraska

Mr. Steven A. Malone
Director
Division of Weights and Measures
Department of Agriculture
301 Centennial Mall South
4th Floor
P.O. Box 94757
Lincoln, NE 68509
(402) 471-4292

Nevada

Mr. William H. McCrea
State Supervisor
Department of Agriculture
Weights and Measures
P.O. Box 11100
Reno, NV 89510-1100
(702) 688-1166

New Hampshire

Mr. Stephen Taylor
Commissioner
Department of Agriculture
Bureau of Weights and Measures
Caller Box 2042
Concord, NH 03302-2042
(603) 271-3700

New Jersey

Mr. William J. Wolfe
State Superintendent
State Office of Weights and Measures
1261 Routes 1 and 9 South
Avenel, NJ 07001
(201) 815-4840

New Mexico

Mr. Fred A. Gerk
Director
Division of Standards and Consumer Services
Department of Agriculture
P.O. Box 30005, Dept. 3170
Las Cruces, NM 88003-0005
(505) 646-1616
1 (800) 458-0179
(toll free in NM)

New York

Mr. John J. Bartfai
Director
Bureau of Weights and Measures
Department of Agriculture
Building 7-A
1220 Washington Avenue
Albany, NY 12235
(518) 457-3452

North Carolina

Mr. N. David Smith
Director, Standards Division
Department of Agriculture
P.O. Box 27647—Dept. SD
Raleigh, NC 27611
(919) 733-3313

North Dakota

Mr. Curtis Roberts
Director
Division of Weights and Measures
State Capitol
Bismarck, ND 58505-0480
(701) 224-2400
1 (800) 932-2400
(toll free in ND)

Ohio

Chief
Division of Weights and Measures
Department of Agriculture
8995 East Main Street, Bldg. 5
Reynoldsburg, OH 43068
(614) 866-6361

Oklahoma

Mr. O. Ray Elliott
Director
Agricultural Products Division
Department of Agriculture
2800 North Lincoln Boulevard
Oklahoma City, OK 73105
(405) 521-3864, ext. 301

Oregon

Mr. Kendrick J. Simila
Administrator
Measurement Standards
Department of Agriculture
635 Capitol Street, N.E.
Salem, OR 97310-0110
(503) 378-3792

Pennsylvania

Mr. Neil E. Cashman Jr.
Director
Bureau of Weights and Measures
Department of Agriculture
2301 North Cameron Street
Harrisburg, PA 17110
(717) 787-6772

Puerto Rico

Mr. Hector Niedes
Auxiliary Secretary for Complaints
Department of Consumer Affairs
P.O. Box 41059
Minillas Station
Santurce, PR 00940
(809) 722-7555

Rhode Island

Ms. Lynda L. Maurer
Supervising Metrologist
Mercantile Division
Department of Labor
220 Elmwood Avenue
Providence, RI 02907
(401) 457-1867
(401) 457-1888 (TDD)

South Carolina

Mr. Carol P. Fulmer
Assistant Commissioner of Consumer Services Division
Department of Agriculture
P.O. Box 11280
Columbia, SC 29211-1280
(803) 737-2080

South Dakota

Mr. James Melgaard
Director
Division of Commercial Inspection and Regulation
118 West Capitol
Pierre, SD 57501-2036
(605) 773-3697

Tennessee

Mr. Robert Williams
Standards Administrator
Weights and Measures
Department of Agriculture
P.O. Box 40627
Melrose Station
Nashville, TN 37204
(615) 360-0109

Texas

Mr. Ed Price
Administrator
Weights and Measures Program
Department of Agriculture
P.O. Box 12847
Austin, TX 78711
(512) 463-7602
1 (800) 835-5832
(toll free in TX)

Utah

Mr. Robert Smoot
Director
Division of Weights and Measures
State Department of Agriculture
350 North Redwood Road
Salt Lake City, UT 84116
(801) 538-7159

Vermont

Mr. Phil Benedict
Director
Consumer Assurance Section
Department of Agriculture
116 State Street
State Office Building
Montpelier, VT 05620
(802) 828-2436

Virgin Islands

Ms. Joycelyn Encarnacion
Director
Weights and Measures Division
Dept. of Licensing and Consumer Affairs
Golden Rock Shopping Center
Christiansted
St. Croix, VI 00820
(809) 773-2226

Virginia

Mr. J. Alan Rogers
Program Manager
Office of Weights and Measures
Department of Agriculture and Consumer Services
P.O. Box 1163, Room 403
Richmond, VA 23209-1163
(804) 786-2476

Washington

Ms. Dannie McQueen
Acting Program Manager
Weights and Measures
Department of Agriculture
406 General Administration Bldg.
Olympia, WA 98504-0641
(206) 753-5042

West Virginia

Mr. Stephen L. Casto
Director
Division of Weights and Measures
Department of Labor
1800 Washington Street, East
Building 3, Room 319
Charleston, WV 25305
(304) 348-7890

Wisconsin

Ms. Merry Fran Tryon
Director
Bureau of Weights and Measures
Department of Agriculture, Trade and Consumer Protection
801 West Badger Road
P.O. Box 8911
Madison, WI 53708
(608) 266-9836
1 (800) 362-3020
(toll free in WI)

Wyoming

Mr. Jim Bigelow
Technical Services Manager
Consumer/Compliance Division
Department of Agriculture
2219 Carey Avenue
Cheyenne, WY 82002-0100
(307) 777-6591

MILITARY COMMISSARY AND EXCHANGE OFFICES

Consumers who shop at military commissaries and exchanges and who have a question or problem should contact the local manager before contacting the regional offices in this section. If your problem is not resolved at the local level, then write or call the regional office nearest you. Be sure to discuss the problem with the local and regional offices before contacting the national headquarters of a commissary or exchange.

Defense Commissary Agency

Northwest/Pacific Region
Commander
Defense Commissary Agency
Northwest Pacific Region
Fort Lewis, WA 98433-7300
(206) 967-4222

Southwest Region
Director
Defense Commissary Agency
Southwest Region
Building 329
MCAS El Toro
Santa Ana, CA 92709-5002
(714) 726-4276

Midwest Region
Commander
Defense Commissary Agency
Midwest Region
Building 3030
Kelly AFB, TX 78241-6290
(512) 925-3948

Central Region
Director
Defense Commissary Agency
Central Region
Building 3345
NAB Little Creek
Norfolk, VA 23521-5330
(804) 460-3779

Southern Region
Director
Defense Commissary Agency
Southern Region
Building 678
Maxwell AFB, AL 36112
(205) 953-2026

Northeast Region
Director
Defense Commissary Agency
Northeast Region
Building 2257
Fort Meade, MD 20755-5220
(301) 677-4932

European Region
Director
Defense Commissary Agency
European Region
Ramstein AB, Germany
APO New York 09094-5001
(011) 49 6371 42896

DeCA Headquarters
Director
Defense Commissary Agency
38th and E Streets
Building P11200
Fort Lee, VA 23801-6300
(804) 734-2227

Army and Air Force Exchange Service

AAFES Operations Centers
Central Operations
AAFES
P.O. Box 650455
Dallas, TX 75265-0455
(214) 280-7100

Eastern Operations
AAFES
P.O. Box 650454
Dallas, TX 75265-0454
(214) 280-7200

Southern Operations
AAFES
P.O. Box 650447
Dallas, TX 75265-0447
(214) 280-7300

Western Operations
AAFES
P.O. Box 650429
Dallas, TX 75265-0429
(214) 280-7400

U.S. Headquarters
Army and Air Force Exchange
Service Headquarters
Customer Relations (PA-R)
P.O. Box 660202
Dallas, TX 75266-0202
(214) 780-3531

Marine Corps Exchange Service

Regional Headquarters
Marine Corps Exchange
Marine Corps Logistics Support Base, Atlantic
Albany, GA 31704
(912) 435-1471

Marine Corps Exchange
Headquarters Battalion, HQMC
Henderson Hall
Arlington, VA 22214
(703) 979-8420

Marine Corps Exchange
Marine Corps Logistics Base
Barstow, CA 92311
(714) 256-8971

Marine Corps Exchange
Marine Corps Base
Camp Lejeune, NC 28547
(919) 451-2481

Marine Corps Exchange
Marine Corps Base
Camp Pendleton, CA 92055
(619) 725-6233

Marine Corps Exchange
Marine Corps Air Station
Cherry Point, NC 28533
(919) 447-7041

Marine Corps Exchange
Marine Corps Air Station
Kaneohe Bay, HI 96863
(808) 254-5871

Marine Corps Exchange
Camp Elmore
U.S. Marine Corps
Norfolk, VA 23511
(804) 423-1187

Marine Corps Exchange
Marine Corps Recruit Depot
Parris Island, SC 29905
(803) 525-3301

Marine Corps Exchange
Marine Corps Development and Education Command
Quantico, VA 22134
(703) 640-7171

Marine Corps Exchange
Marine Corps Recruit Depot
San Diego, CA 92140
(619) 297-2500

Marine Corps Exchange
Marine Corps Air Station—El Toro
Santa Ana, CA 92709
(714) 726-3340

Marine Corps Exchange
Marine Corps Air/Ground Combat Center
Building 1533
Twentynine Palms, CA 92278
(619) 368-6163

Marine Corps Exchange
Marine Corps Air Station
Yuma, AZ 85364
(602) 726-2363

U.S. Headquarters
Head
Marine Corps Exchange
Service Branch
P.O. Box 1834
Quantico, VA 22134
(703) 640-6156

Navy Exchange Service

Regional Headquarters
Executive Officer
NAVRESSO
Field Support Office
2801 "C" Street, SW
Naval Supply Center
Auburn, WA 98001-7499
(201) 931-7665

Executive Officer
NAVRESSO
Field Support Office
P.O. Box 13—Naval Air Station
Jacksonville, FL 32212-0013
(904) 777-7075

Executive Officer
NAVRESSO
Field Support Office
P.O. Box 15037
Norfolk, VA 23511-0799
(804) 440-2399

Executive Officer
NAVRESSO
Field Support Office
P.O. Box 23330
Oakland, CA 94623
(415) 466-7020

Office in Charge
Navy Resale Activity
Naval Base
Pearl Harbor, HI 96860-6000
(808) 471-0263

Executive Officer
NAVRESSO
Field Support Office
P.O. Box 150—Naval Station
San Diego, CA 92136-5150
(619) 237-5601

U.S. Headquarters
Customer Service Representative
Navy Resale and Services Support Office
Naval Station, New York
Staten Island, NY 10305-5097
(718) 390-3868

FEDERAL INFORMATION CENTER

The Federal Information Center (FIC), administered by the General Services Administration, can help you find information about Federal government services, programs, and regulations. The FIC also can tell you which Federal agency to contact for help with problems.

Simply call the telephone number listed below for your metropolitan area or state. All the "800" numbers on this list are toll free. These "800" numbers can be called only from within the states and cities listed. If your area is not listed, please call **(301) 722-9098.** If you would prefer to write, please mail your inquiry to:

Federal Information Center
P.O. Box 600
Cumberland, MD 21502

Users of Telecommunications Devices for the Deaf (TDD/TTY) may call toll free from any point in the United States by dialing **1 (800) 326-2996.**

Akron	**(800) 347-1997**
Albany	**(800) 347-1997**
Albuquerque	**(800) 359-3997**
Anchorage	**(800) 729-8003**
Atlanta	**(800) 347-1997**
Austin	**(800) 366-2998**
Baltimore	**(800) 347-1997**
Birmingham	**(800) 366-2998**
Boston	**(800) 347-1997**
Buffalo	**(800) 347-1997**
Charlotte	**(800) 347-1997**
Chattanooga	**(800) 347-1977**
Chicago	**(800) 366-2998**
Cincinnati	**(800) 347-1997**
Cleveland	**(800) 347-1997**
Colorado Springs	**(800) 359-3997**
Columbus	**(800) 347-1997**
Dallas	**(800) 366-2998**
Dayton	**(800) 347-1997**
Denver	**(800) 359-3997**
Detroit	**(800) 347-1997**
Fort Lauderdale	**(800) 347-1997**
Fort Worth	**(800) 366-2998**
Gary	**(800) 366-2998**
Grand Rapids	**(800) 347-1997**
Hartford	**(800) 347-1997**
Honolulu	**(800) 733-5996**
Houston	**(800) 366-2998**
Indianapolis	**(800) 347-1997**
Iowa	**(800) 753-8004**
Jacksonville	**(800) 347-1997**
Kansas	**(800) 735-8004**
Little Rock	**(800) 366-2998**
Los Angeles	**(800) 726-4995**
Louisville	**(800) 347-1997**
Memphis	**(800) 366-2998**
Miami	**(800) 347-1997**
Milwaukee	**(800) 366-2998**
Minneapolis	**(800) 366-2998**
Missouri	**(800) 735-8004**
Mobile	**(800) 366-2998**
Nashville	**(800) 366-2998**
Nebraska	**(800) 735-8004**
New Haven	**(800) 347-1997**
New Orleans	**(800) 366-2998**
New York	**(800) 347-1997**
Newark	**(800) 347-1997**
Norfolk	**(800) 347-1997**
Oklahoma City	**(800) 366-2998**
Omaha	**(800) 366-2998**
Orlando	**(800) 347-1997**
Philadelphia	**(800) 347-1997**
Phoenix	**(800) 359-3997**
Pittsburgh	**(800) 347-1997**
Portland	**(800) 726-4995**
Providence	**(800) 347-1997**
Pueblo	**(800) 359-3997**
Richmond	**(800) 347-1997**
Roanoke	**(800) 347-1997**
Rochester	**(800) 347-1997**
Sacramento	**(800) 726-4995**
Saint Louis	**(800) 366-2998**
Saint Petersburg	**(800) 347-1997**
Salt Lake City	**(800) 359-3997**
San Antonio	**(800) 366-2998**
San Diego	**(800) 726-4995**
San Francisco	**(800) 726-4995**
Santa Ana	**(800) 726-4995**

Seattle	(800) 726-4995
Syracuse	(800) 347-1997
Tacoma	(800) 726-4995
Tampa	(800) 347-1997
Toledo	(800) 347-1997
Trenton	(800) 347-1997
Tulsa	(800) 366-2998
West Palm Beach	(800) 347-1997

SELECTED FEDERAL AGENCIES

Many Federal agencies have enforcement and/or complaint-handling duties for products and services used by the general public. Others act for the benefit of the public, but do not resolve individual consumer problems.

Agencies also have fact sheets, booklets and other information which might be helpful in making purchase decisions and dealing with consumer problems. If you need help in deciding where to go with your consumer problem, call the nearest Federal Information Center. The Federal agencies listed below respond to consumer complaints and inquiries.

Commission on Civil Rights
Look in your telephone directory under "U.S. Government, Civil Rights Commission." If it does not appear, call the appropriate FIC number, or contact:
Commission on Civil Rights
1121 Vermont Avenue, N.W.
Suite 800
Washington, DC 20425
1 (800) 552-6843
(toll free—complaint referral outside DC)
(202) 376-8512
(complaint referral in DC)
(202) 376-8116
(TDD—nationwide complaint referral)
(202) 376-8105 (publications)
(202) 376-8312 (public affairs)

Commodity Futures Trading Commission (CFTC)
2033 K Street, N.W.
Washington, DC 20581
(202) 254-3067
(complaints only)
(202) 254-8630 (information)

Consumer Information Center (CIC)
Pueblo, CO 81009
You can obtain a free *Consumer Information Catalog* by writing to the above address or by calling (719) 948-4000.

Department of Agriculture (USDA)

Agricultural Marketing Service
Department of Agriculture
Washington, DC 20250
(202) 447-8998

Animal and Plant Health Inspection Service
Public Information
Department of Agriculture
Federal Building, Room 700
6505 Belcrest Road
Hyattsville, MD 20782
(301) 436-7799

Cooperative Extension Service
Department of Agriculture
Washington, DC 20250
(202) 447-3029
(202) 755-2799 (TDD)
Or consult county or city government listings in your local telephone directory for the number of your local Cooperative Extension Service office.

Farmers Home Administration
Department of Agriculture
Washington, DC 20250
(202) 447-4323

Food and Nutrition Service
Department of Agriculture
3101 Park Center Drive
Alexandria, VA 22302
(703) 756-3276

Human Nutrition Information Service
Department of Agriculture
Federal Building
Rooms 360 and 364
6505 Belcrest Road
Hyattsville, MD 20782
(301) 436-8617, 7725

Inspector General's Hotline
Office of the Inspector General
Department of Agriculture
P.O. Box 23399
Washington, DC 20026
1 (800) 424-9121 (toll free)

Meat and Poultry Hotline Food Safety and Inspection Service
Department of Agriculture
Washington, DC 20250
(202) 447-3333
(voice/TDD)
1 (800) 535-4555
(toll free voice/TDD outside DC)

Office of the Consumer Advisor
Department of Agriculture
Washington, DC 20250
(202) 382-9681

Office of Public Affairs
Visitor Information Center
Department of Agriculture
Washington, DC 20250
(202) 447-2791

Department of Commerce

Bureau of the Census
Customer Services
Data User Services Division
Department of Commerce
Washington, DC 20233
(301) 763-4100

Office of Consumer Affairs
Department of Commerce
Room 5718
Washington, DC 20230
(202) 377-5001

National Institute of Standards and Technology
Office of Weights and Measures
Department of Commerce
Washington, DC 20234
(301) 975-4004

National Marine Fisheries Service
Office of Trade and Industry Services
Department of Commerce
1335 East-West Highway
Silver Spring, MD 20910
(301) 427-2355
(inspection and safety)
(301) 427-2358
(nutrition information)

Constituent Affairs
National Weather Service
Department of Commerce
Washington, DC 20901
(301) 427-7258

Metric Program Office
Department of Commerce
Room H4845
Washington, DC 20230
(202) 377-0944

Patent and Trademark Office
Department of Commerce
Washington, DC 20231
(703) 557-3341

Department of Defense

Office of National Ombudsman
National Committee for Employer Support of the Guard and Reserve
1555 Wilson Boulevard
Suite 200
Arlington, VA 22209-2405
(703) 696-1400
1 (800) 336-4590
(toll free outside DC metropolitan area)
Provides assistance with employer/employee problems for members of the Guard and Reserve and their employers.

Department of Education

Clearinghouse on Disability Information
OSERS
Department of Education
Room 330 C Street, SW
Washington, DC 20202-2524
(202) 732-1241
(202) 732-1265 (TDD)

Consumer Affairs Staff
OIIA
Department of Education
Room 3061
Washington, DC 20202
(202) 401-3679

Federal Student Financial Aid Programs
Public Documents Distribution Center
31451 United Avenue
Pueblo, CO 81009-8109
(202) 708-8391

National Clearinghouse on Bilingual Education Hotline
Department of Education
1118 22nd Street, NW
Washington, DC 20037
(202) 467-0867
1 (800) 321-NCBE
(toll free outside DC)

Office of Public Affairs
Department of Education
400 Maryland Avenue, SW
Washington, DC 20202
(202) 401-3020

Center for Choice in Education
400 Maryland Avenue, SW
Room 3077
Washington, DC 20202
1 (800) 442-PICK (toll free)

Department of Energy

For information about conservation and renewable energy:

National Appropriate Technology Assistance Service
Department of Energy
P.O. Box 2525
Butte, MT 59702-2525
1 (800) 428-1718
(toll free in MT)
1 (800) 428-2525
(toll free outside MT)

Conservation and Renewable Energy Inquiry and Referral Service
Department of Energy
P.O. Box 8900
Silver Spring, MD 20907
1 (800) 523-2929 (toll free)

Office of Scientific and Technical Information
Department of Energy
P.O. Box 62
Oak Ridge, TN 37831
(written inquiries only)

Office of Consumer and Public Liaison
Department of Energy
Washington, DC 20585
(202) 586-5373

Office of Conservation and Renewable Energy
Weatherization Assistance Inquiries:
Department of Energy
Washington, DC 20585
(202) 586-2204

Department of Health and Human Services (HHS)

AIDS Hotline
Acquired Immune Deficiency Syndrome
1 (800) 342-AIDS (toll free)

Cancer Hotline
1 (800) 4-CANCER (toll free)
During daytime hours, callers in California, Florida, Georgia, Illinois, Northern New Jersey, New York, and Texas may ask for Spanish-speaking staff members.

Food and Drug Administration (FDA)
Look in your telephone directory under "U.S. Government, Health and Human Services Department, Food and Drug Administration." If it does not appear, call the appropriate FIC number or contact:

Consumer Affairs and Information Staff
Food and Drug Administration (HFE–88)
Department of Health and Human Services
5600 Fishers Lane
Room 16-85
Rockville, MD 20857
(301) 443-3170

Division of Beneficiary Services Health Care Financing Administration (HCFA)
Department of Health and Human Services
6325 Security Boulevard
Baltimore, MD 21207
1 (800) 638-6833 (toll free)
(This is a taped answering service; a specialist will return your call.)

Hill-Burton Free Hospital Care Hotline
1 (800) 492-0359
(toll free in MD)
1 (800) 638-0742
(toll free outside MD)

Inspector General's Hotline
HHS/OIG/Hotline
P.O. Box 17303
Baltimore, MD 21203-7303
1 (800) 368-5779 (toll free)

National Center on Child Abuse and Neglect
Department of Health and Human Services
330 C Street, S.W.
Washington, DC 20201
(202) 245-0586

National Health Information Center
Department of Health and Human Services
P.O. Box 1133
Washington, DC 20013-1133
(301) 565-4167
(Washington Metro Area)
1 (800) 336-4797 (toll free)

National Runaway Switchboard
1 (800) 621-4000 (toll free)

Office of Child Support Enforcement
Department of Health and Human Services
Washington, DC 20201
(202) 401-9387

Office for Civil Rights
Department of Health and Human Services
Washington, DC 20201
(202) 376-8177
(202) 368-1019 (TDD)

Office of Prepaid Health Care
Operations and Oversight
HCFA
Department of Health and Human Services
Washington, DC 20201
(202) 619-3555

President's Council on Physical Fitness and Sports
Department of Health and Human Services
450 5th Street, NW
Suite 7103
Washington, DC 20001
(202) 272-3430

Second Surgical Opinion Program
Department of Health and Human Services
Washington, DC 20201
1 (800) 838-6833 (toll free outside DC)

Social Security Administration
1 (800) SSA-1213 (toll free)

Department of Housing and Urban Development (HUD)

HUD Fraud Hotline
(202) 708-4200
1 (800) 347-3735 (toll free outside DC)

Interstate Land Sales Registration Division
Department of Housing and Urban Development
Room 6278
Washington, DC 20410
(202) 708-0502

Manufactured Housing and Construction Standards Division
Department of Housing and Urban Development
Room 9158
Washington, DC 20410
(202) 708-2210

Office of Fair Housing and Equal Opportunity
Department of Housing and Urban Development
Room 5100
Washington, DC 20410
(202) 708-4252

Office of Single Family Housing
Department of Housing and Urban Development
Room 9282
Washington, DC 20410
(202) 708-3175

Office of Urban Rehabilitation
Department of Housing and Urban Development
Room 7168
Washington, DC 20410
(202) 708-2685

Title I Insurance Division
Department of Housing and Urban Development
Room 9156
Washington, DC 20410
(202) 708-1590

Department of the Interior

Bureau of Indian Affairs
Department of the Interior
Washington, DC 20240
(202) 208-4190

Bureau of Land Management
Department of the Interior
Washington, DC 20240
(202) 208-5717

Consumer Affairs Administrator
Office of the Secretary
Department of the Interior
Washington, DC 20240
(202) 208-5521

National Park Service
Department of the Interior
Washington, DC 20240
(202) 208-4917

United States Fish and Wildlife Service
Department of the Interior
Washington, DC 20240
(703) 358-2156

United States Geological Survey
Department of the Interior
12201 Sunrise Valley Drive
Reston, VA 22092
(703) 648-4427

Department of Justice

Antitrust Division
Department of Justice
Washington, DC 20530
(202) 514-2401

Civil Rights Division
Look in your telephone directory under "U.S. Government, Justice Department, Civil Rights Division." If it does not appear, call the appropriate FIC number or contact:
Civil Rights Division
Department of Justice
Washington, DC 20530
(202) 514-2151
(202) 514-0716 (TDD)

Drug Enforcement Administration (DEA)
Look in your telephone directory under "U.S. Government, Justice Department, Drug Enforcement Administration." If it does not appear, call the appropriate FIC number or contact:
Drug Enforcement Administration (DEA)
Department of Justice
Washington, DC 20537
(202) 307-8000

Federal Bureau of Investigation (FBI)
Look inside the front cover of your telephone directory for the number of the nearest FBI office. If it does not appear, look under "U.S. Government, Justice Department, Federal Bureau of Investigation." You may also contact:
Federal Bureau of Investigation
Department of Justice
Washington, DC 20535
(202) 324-3000

Immigration and Naturalization Service (INS)
Look in your telephone directory under "U.S. Government, Justice Department, Immigration and Naturalization Service." If it does not appear, call the appropriate FIC number or contact:
Immigration and Naturalization Service
Department of Justice
425 I Street, NW
Washington, DC 20536
(202) 514-4316

Department of Labor

Bureau of Labor-Management Relations and Cooperative Programs
Department of Labor
Washington, DC 20210
(202) 523-6098

Coordinator of Consumer Affairs
Department of Labor
Washington, DC 20210
(202) 523-6060
(general inquiries)

Employment and Training Administration
Look in your telephone directory under "U.S. Government, Labor Department, Employment and Training Administration." If it does not appear, call the appropriate FIC number or contact:
Employment and Training Administration
Director, Office of Public Affairs
Department of Labor
Washington, DC 20210
(202) 523-6871

Employment Standards Administration
Office of Public Affairs
Department of Labor
Washington, DC 20210
(202) 523-8743

Mine Safety and Health Administration
Office of Information and Public Affairs
Department of Labor
Ballston Towers #3
Arlington, VA 22203
(703) 235-1452

Occupational Safety and Health Administration (OSHA)
Look in your telephone directory under "U.S. Government, Labor Department, Occupational Safety and Health Administration." If it does not appear, call the appropriate FIC number or contact:
Occupational Safety and Health Administration
Office of Information and Consumer Affairs
Department of Labor
Washington, DC 20210
(202) 523-8151

Office of the Assistant Secretary for Veterans' Employment and Training
Department of Labor
Washington, DC 20210
(202) 523-9116
1 (800) 442-2VET
(toll free—Veterans' Job Rights Hotline)

Office of Labor-Management Standards
Department of Labor
Washington, DC 20210
(202) 523-7343

Pension and Welfare Benefits Administration
Office of Program Services
Department of Labor
Washington, DC 20210
(202) 523-8776

Women's Bureau
The Work and Family Clearinghouse
Department of Labor
Washington, DC 20210
1 (800) 827-5335 (toll free)
Employers may contact this office for information about dependent care (child and/or elder care) policies.

Women's Bureau
The Workforce Quality Clearinghouse
Department of Labor
Washington, DC 20210
(202) 523-8913
1 (800) 523-0525
(toll free outside DC)
Employers may contact this office for information about workplace quality resources, e.g., employee training and skills development.

Department of State

Overseas Citizen Services
Department of State
Washington, DC 20520
(202) 647-3666
(nonemergencies)
(202) 647-5225
(emergencies)

Passport Services
Washington Passport Agency
1425 K Street, NW
Washington, DC 20524
(202) 647-0518

Visa Services
Department of State
Washington, DC 20520
(202) 647-0510

Department of Transportation (DOT)

Air Safety:
Federal Aviation Administration (FAA)
Community and Consumer Liaison Division
FAA (APA-200)
Washington, DC 20591
(202) 267-3479, 8592
1 (800) FAA-SURE
(toll free outside DC)

Airline Service Complaints:
Office of Intergovernmental and Consumer Affairs (I–25)
Department of Transportation
Washington, DC 20590
(202) 366-2220

Auto Safety Hotline:
National Highway Traffic Safety Administration (NHTSA) (NEF-11)
Department of Transportation
Washington, DC 20690
(202) 366-0123
(202) 755-8919 (TDD)
1 (800) 424-9393
(toll free outside DC)
1 (800) 424-9153
(toll free TDD outside DC)

Boating Safety Classes:
United States Coast Guard
Office of Boating, Public and Consumer Affairs (G-NAB-5)
Department of Transportation
Washington, DC 20593
(202) 267-0972

Boating Safety Hotline:
United States Coast Guard
Department of Transportation
Washington, DC 20593
(202) 267-0780
1 (800) 368-5647 (toll free)

Oil and Chemical Spills:
National Response Center
United States Coast Guard
Headquarters, G-TGC-2
Department of Transportation
Washington, DC 20593
(202) 267-2675
1 (800) 424-8802
(toll free outside DC)

Railway Safety:
Federal Railroad Administration
Office of Safety (RRS-20)
Department of Transportation
Washington, DC 20590
(202) 366-0522

Department of the Treasury

Bureau of Alcohol, Tobacco and Firearms
Department of the Treasury
Look in your telephone directory under "U.S. Government, Treasury Department, Bureau of Alcohol, Tobacco and Firearms." If it does not appear, call the appropriate FIC number or contact:
Bureau of Alcohol, Tobacco and Firearms
Department of the Treasury
Room 5500
650 Massachusetts Avenue, NW
Washington, DC 20226
(202) 535-6379

To report lost or stolen explosives, or to report explosive incidents or bombings, call:
(202) 566-7777
1 (800) 424-9555
(toll free outside DC)
(202) 789-3000

Bureau of Engraving and Printing
Congressional and Media Affairs Division
Department of the Treasury
14th and C Streets, SW, Room 533M
Washington, DC 20228
(202) 447-0193

Bureau of the Public Debt
Public Affairs Officer
Office of the Commissioner
Department of the Treasury
999 E Street, NW, Room 553
Washington, DC 20239-0001
(202) 376-4302

Comptroller of the Currency
The Comptroller of the Currency handles complaints about national banks, i.e., banks that have the word "National" in their names or the initials "N.A." after their names. For assistance, look in your telephone directory under "U.S. Government, Treasury Department, Comptroller of the Currency." If it does not appear, call the appropriate FIC number or contact:
Comptroller of the Currency
Director, Compliance Policy
Department of the Treasury
250 E Street, SW
Washington, DC 20219
(202) 874-4820

Financial Management Service
Office of Legislative and Public Affairs
Department of the Treasury
401 14th Street, SW
Room 555
Washington, DC 20227
(202) 287-0669

Internal Revenue Service (IRS)
Look in your telephone directory under "U.S. Government, Treasury Department, Internal Revenue Service." If it does not appear, call the appropriate FIC number.

Office of Thrift Supervision
(formerly Federal Home Loan Bank Board)
The Office of Thrift Supervision handles complaints about savings and loan associations and savings banks.

For assistance contact:
Office of Thrift Supervision
Consumer Affairs
1700 G Street, NW
Washington, DC 20552
(202) 906-6237
1 (800) 842-6929
(toll free outside DC)

United States Customs Service
Look in your telephone directory under "U.S. Government, Treasury Department, U.S. Customs Service." If it does not appear, call the appropriate FIC number.

To report fraudulent import practices, call U.S. Customs Service's **Fraud Hotline: 1 (800) USA-FAKE** (toll free)

To report drug smuggling activity, call U.S. Customs Service's **Narcotics Hotline: 1 (800) BE-ALERT** (toll free)

United States Mint
Customer Relations Division
Department of the Treasury
10001 Aerospace Road
Lanham, MD 20706
(301) 436-7400

United States Savings Bonds Division
Office of Public Affairs
Department of the Treasury
Washington, DC 20220
(202) 634-5389
1 (800) US-BONDS
(toll free recording)

Department of Veterans Affairs (VA)
For information about VA medical care or benefits, write, call, or visit your nearest VA facility. Your telephone directory will list a VA medical center or regional office under "U.S. Government, Department of Veterans Affairs," or under "U.S. Government, Veterans Administration." You may

also contact the offices listed below.

For information about benefits:
Veterans Benefits Administration (27)
Department of Veterans Affairs
810 Vermont Avenue, NW
Washington, DC 20420
(202) 233-2576

For information about medical care:
Veterans Health Administration (184C)
810 Vermont Avenue, NW
Washington, DC 20420
(202) 535-7208

For information about burials, headstones, or markers, and presidential memorial certificates:
National Cemetery System (40H)
Department of Veterans Affairs
810 Vermont Avenue, NW
Washington, DC 20420
(202) 535-7856

For consumer information or general assistance:
Consumer Affairs Service
Department of Veterans Affairs
810 Vermont Avenue, NW
Washington, DC 20420
(202) 535-8962

Environmental Protection Agency (EPA)

Asbestos Action Program
(202) 382-3949

Emergency Planning and Community Right-to-Know Information Hotline
Environmental Protection Agency
Washington, DC 20460
(202) 479-2449
1 (800) 535-0202
(toll free outside AK and DC)

Inspector General's Whistle Blower Hotline
(202) 382-4977
1 (800) 424-4000
(toll free outside DC)

National Pesticides Telecommunications Network (NPTN)
(806) 743-3091
1 (800) 858-PEST
(toll free outside TX)

Office of External Relations
Environmental Protection Agency
Washington, DC 20460
(202) 382-4454

Public Information Center
PIC (PM-211B)
Environmental Protection Agency
Washington, DC 20460
(202) 382-2080
(general information)

Resource Conservation and Recovery Act
RCRA/Superfund Hotline
Environmental Protection Agency
Washington, DC 20460
(703) 920-9810
1 (800) 424-9346
(toll free outside DC)

Safe Drinking Water Hotline
(202) 382-5533
1 (800) 426-4791
(toll free outside DC)

Toxic Substances Control Act Assistance Information Service
Environmental Protection Agency
Washington, DC 20024
(202) 554-1404

Equal Employment Opportunity Commission

Look in your telephone directory under "U.S. Government, Equal Employment Opportunity Commission." If it does not appear, call the appropriate FIC number or contact:
Office of Communications and Legislative Affairs
Equal Employment Opportunity Commission
1801 L Street, NW
Washington, DC 20507
(202) 663-4900
(202) 663-4494 (TDD)
1 (800) 800-3302
(toll free TDD)

Federal Communications Commission (FCC)

Complaints about telephone systems:
Common Carrier Bureau
Informal Complaints Branch
Federal Communications Commission
2025 M Street, NW
Room 6202
Washington, DC 20554
(202) 632-7553
(202) 634-1855 (TDD)

General Information:
Consumer Assistance and Small Business Office
Federal Communications Commission
1919 M Street, NW
Room 254
Washington, DC 20554
(202) 632-7000
(202) 632-6999 (TDD)

Complaints about radio or television:
Mass Media Bureau
Complaints and Investigations
Federal Communications Commission
2025 M Street, NW
Room 8210
Washington, DC 20554
(202) 632-7048

Federal Deposit Insurance Corporation (FDIC)

FDIC handles questions about deposit insurance coverage

and complaints about FDIC-insured state banks which are not members of the Federal Reserve System. For assistance, look in your telephone directory under "U.S. Government, Federal Deposit Insurance Corporation." If it does not appear, call the appropriate FIC number or contact:

Office of Consumer Affairs
Federal Deposit Insurance Corporation
550 17th Street, NW
Washington, DC 20429
(202) 898-3536
(202) 898-3535 (voice/TDD)
1 (800) 424-5488
(toll free outside DC)

Federal Emergency Management Agency

Look in your telephone directory under "U.S. Government, Federal Emergency Management Agency." If it does not appear, call the appropriate FIC number or contact:

Emergency Preparedness and Response
Office of the External Affairs Directorate
Federal Emergency Management Agency
Washington, DC 20472
(202) 646-4000

Federal Insurance Administration
Federal Emergency Management Agency
Washington, DC 20472
(202) 646-2781
1 (800) 638-6620 (toll free)

Office of Disaster Assistance Programs
Federal Emergency Management Agency
Washington, DC 20472
(202) 646-3615

U.S. Fire Administration
Federal Emergency Management Agency
NETC
16825 South Seton Avenue
Emmitsburg, MD 21727
(301) 447-1080
(202) 646-2449

Federal Maritime Commission

Office of Informal Inquiries and Complaints
1100 L Street, NW
Washington, DC 20573
(202) 523-5807

Federal Reserve System

The Board of Governors handles consumer complaints about state-chartered banks and trust companies which are members of the Federal Reserve System. For assistance, look in your telephone directory under "U.S. Government, Federal Reserve System, Board of Governors," or "Federal Reserve Bank." If neither appears, call the appropriate FIC number or contact:

Board of Governors of the Federal Reserve System
Division of Consumer and Community Affairs
Washington, DC 20551
(202) 452-3946
(202) 452-3544 (TDD)

Federal Trade Commission (FTC)

Look in your telephone directory under "U.S. Government, Federal Trade Commission." If it does not appear, call the appropriate FIC number or contact:

Correspondence Branch
Federal Trade Commission
Washington, DC 20580
(written complaints only)

Public Reference Section
Federal Trade Commission
6th & Pennsylvania Ave., NW
Room 130
Washington, DC 20580
(202) 326-2222 (publications)

General Services Administration (GSA)

Business Service Centers
Look in your telephone directory under "U.S. Government, General Services Administration." If this does not appear, call the appropriate FIC number.

Federal Information Relay Service
7th & D Streets, SW
Room 6040
Washington, DC 20407
(202) 708-9300 (TDD)
1 (800) 877-8339
(toll free voice/TDD outside DC)

Surplus Federal Property Sales
Look in your telephone directory under "U.S. Government, General Services Administration." If it does not appear, call the appropriate FIC number.

Government Printing Office (GPO)

Government Publications:
Publications Service Section
Government Printing Office
Washington, DC 20402
(202) 275-3050

Subscriptions to Government Periodicals:
Subscription Research Section
Government Printing Office
Washington, DC 20402
(202) 275-3054

Interstate Commerce Commission (ICC)

Office of Compliance and Consumer Assistance
Washington, DC 20423
(202) 275-7148

National Archives and Records Administration

Reference Services Branch
National Archives and Records Administration
Washington, DC 20408
(202) 501-5400
(202) 501-5404 (TDD)

Federal Register
National Archives and Records Administration
Washington, DC 20408
(202) 523-5240
(202) 523-5229 (TDD)

Publications Services
National Archives and Records Administration
Washington, DC 20408
(202) 501-5240
(202) 501-5404 (TDD)

National Credit Union Administration

Look in your telephone directory under "U.S. Government, National Credit Union Administration." If it does not appear, call the appropriate FIC number or contact:

National Credit Union Administration
1776 G Street, NW
Washington, DC 20456
(202) 682-9640

National Labor Relations Board

Office of the Executive Secretary
1717 Pennsylvania Ave., NW
Room 701
Washington, DC 20570
(202) 254-9430

Nuclear Regulatory Commission (NRC)

Office of Governmental and Public Affairs
Washington, DC 20555
(301) 492-0240

Pension Benefit Guaranty Corporation

2020 K Street, NW
Washington, DC 20006-1860
(202) 778-8800
(202) 778-8859 (TDD)

Postal Rate Commission

Office of the Consumer Advocate
Postal Rate Commission
1333 H Street, NW
Suite 300
Washington, DC 20268
(202) 789-6830

President's Committee on Employment of People with Disabilities

1111 20th Street, NW
Suite 636
Washington, DC 20036-3470
(202) 653-5044
(202) 653-5050 (TDD)

Railroad Retirement Board

844 Rush Street
Chicago, IL 60611
(312) 751-4500

Securities and Exchange Commission (SEC)

Office of Filings, Information and Consumer Services
450 5th Street, NW
(Mail Stop 2-6)
Washington, DC 20549
(202) 272-7440
(investor complaints)
(202) 272-7450
(filings by corporations and other regulated entities)
(202) 272-5624
(SEC Information Line—general topics and sources of assistance)

Small Business Administration (SBA)

Office of Consumer Affairs
409 Third Street, SW
Washington, DC 20416
(202) 205-6948
(complaints only)
1 (800) U-ASK-SBA
(toll free—information)

Tennessee Valley Authority (TVA)

Regional Communications
400 West Summit Hill Drive
Knoxville, TN 37902
(615) 632-7196
(615) 751-8500 (TDD)

U.S. Consumer Product Safety Commission (CPSC)

To report a hazardous product or a product-related injury, or to inquire about product recalls, call or write:

Product Safety Hotline
U.S. Consumer Product Safety Commission
Washington, DC 20207
1 (800) 638-CPSC (toll free)
1 (800) 638-8270
(toll free TDD outside MD)
1 (800) 492-8104
(toll free TDD in MD)

United States Postal Service

If you experience difficulty when ordering merchandise or conducting business transactions through the mail, or suspect that you have been the victim of a mail fraud or misrepresentation scheme, contact your postmaster or local Postal Inspector. Look in your telephone directory under "U.S. Government, Postal Service U.S." for these local listings. If they do not appear, contact:

Chief Postal Inspector
United States Postal Service
Washington, DC 20260-2100
(202) 268-4267
For consumer convenience, all post offices and letter

carriers have postage-free Consumer Service Cards available for reporting mail problems and submitting comments and suggestions. If the problem cannot be resolved using the Consumer Service Card or through direct contact with the local post office, write or call:

Consumer Advocate
United States Postal Service
Washington, DC 20260-6720
(202) 268-2284
(202) 268-2310 (TDD)

FEDERAL TDD DIRECTORY

This section lists Federal government offices that have Telecommunications Devices for the Deaf (TDDs). These offices can respond to questions and complaints from persons with speech and hearing impairments. If you are a voice user, the Federal Information Relay Service (FIRS) will relay the call for you. Call FIRS on **1 (800) 877-8339** (toll free) or (202) 708-9300 in Washington, DC, and a relay operator will come on the line. Additional TDD numbers are published in the *U.S. Government TDD Directory,* available free by writing the Consumer Information Center, Item 573X, Pueblo, CO 81009.

Architectural and Transportation Barriers Compliance Board
1111 18th Street, NW
Room 501
Washington, DC 20036-3894
(202) 653-7834 (voice/TDD)
(202) 653-7848 (voice/TDD)
(202) 653-7951 (voice/TDD)

Central Intelligence Agency
Handicapped Program Office
Washington, DC 20505
(202) 874-4449 (voice/TDD)

Commission on Civil Rights
1121 Vermont Avenue, NW
Washington, DC 20425
(202) 376-8116 (voice/TDD)

Congressional TDD Numbers

United States House of Representatives
Congressional Telecommunications for the Deaf (TDD message relay service—to leave messages for Representatives)
(202) 225-1904 (TDD)

Subcommittee on Select Education
Majority Office, Rep. Owens
(202) 226-7532 (voice/TDD)

United States Senate
Senate Special Services
(202) 224-4049 (TDD)

Senate Human Resources
(202) 224-7806 (TDD)

Committee on Labor and Human Resources
(202) 224-1975 (voice/TDD)

Subcommittee on the Handicapped
Majority Office
Sen. Harkin
(202) 224-3457 (TDD)

Minority Office
Sen. Durenberger
(202) 224-9522 (voice/TDD)

United States Capitol Switchboard
(202) 224-3091 (TDD)

U.S. Consumer Product Safety Commission
5401 Westbard Avenue
Bethesda, MD 20207
1 (800) 638-8270 (TDD)

Department of Agriculture
14th Street and Independence Avenue, SW
Washington, DC 20250

Central Employment and Selective Placement Office
(202) 447-2436 (voice/TDD)

Meat and Poultry Hotline
(202) 447-3333 (voice/TDD)
1 (800) 535-4555
(toll free voice/TDD)

Department of the Army

Civilian Personnel Office
Arlington, VA 22212
(703) 697-3887 (voice/TDD)

Department of Commerce
14th Street and Constitution Avenue, NW
Washington, DC 20230

Bureau of the Census
Population Division
Statistical Information Staff
Suitland and Silver Hill Roads
Federal Building #3
Room 2375
Suitland, MD 20233
(301) 763-5020 (voice/TDD)

International Trade Administration
Office of Commercial Information Management
Herbert C. Hoover Building
Room 1848
Washington, DC 20230
(202) 377-1669 (TDD)

National Institute of Standards and Technology (NIST)
Office of Information Services
Room E106
Gaithersburg, MD 20899
(301) 975-2812 (TDD)

NIST Personnel Office
Administration Building
Room A123
Gaithersburg, MD 20899
(301) 975-3007 (voice/TDD)

National Weather Service
National Meteorological Center

World Weather Building
Room 307
Washington, DC 20233
(301) 427-4409 (voice/TDD)
(official business—no forecasts)

Office of the Secretary
Office of Civil Rights
Programs, Planning and Systems Division
Herbert C. Hoover Building
Room 6010
Washington, DC 20230
(202) 377-5691 (voice/TDD)

Department of Education
330 C Street, SW
Washington, DC 20202

Captioning and Media Services
330 C Street, SW
Washington, DC 20202
(202) 732-1177 (voice)
(202) 732-1169 (TDD)

National Institute on Disability and Rehabilitation Research
330 C Street, SW
Washington, DC 20202
(202) 732-1198 (TDD)

Office of Civil Rights
330 C Street, SW
Washington, DC 20202
(202) 732-1663 (TDD)

Office of Deafness and Communicative Disorders
330 C Street, SW
Washington, DC 20202
(202) 732-1398 (voice/TDD)

Rehabilitation Services Administration
330 C Street, SW
Washington, DC 20202
(202) 732-1298, 2848 (TDD)

Department of Health and Human Services

Handicapped Employment Program
200 Independence Ave., SW
Washington, DC 20201
(202) 475-0073 (TDD)

Food and Drug Administration
5600 Fishers Lane
Parklawn Building
Rockville, MD 20857
Personnel
(301) 443-1970 (voice/TDD)

Equal Employment Opportunity Office
(301) 443-1818 (TDD)

Office of the Secretary
Personnel Office
(202) 619-3540 (voice/TDD)

Office for Civil Rights
200 Independence Ave., SW
Washington, DC 20201
(202) 472-2916 (TDD)

Social Security Administration
6401 Security Boulevard
Baltimore, MD 21235
(301) 965-4404 (TDD)

Department of Housing and Urban Development
451 Seventh Street, SW
Washington, DC 20410
(202) 755-5965 (TDD)
1 (800) 424-8590
(toll free TDD)

Department of Interior
18th and C Streets, NW
Washington, DC 20240

Personnel Office
(202) 208-4817 (TDD)

Department of Justice
10th Street and Constitution Avenue, NW
Washington, DC 20530

Immigration and Naturalization
(202) 514-4012 (voice/TDD)

Civil Rights Division
(202) 307-2678 (voice/TDD)

FBI Tours
(202) 324-3553 (TDD)

FBI Identification Division
(202) 324-2334 (voice/TDD)

Department of Labor
200 Constitution Avenue, NW
Washington, DC 20210

Office of Civil Rights
(202) 523-7090 (voice/TDD)

Department of the Navy

Civilian Personnel Office
Washington, DC 20376
(202) 692-2658 (TDD)

Department of State
2201 C Street NW
Washington, DC 20520

Personnel Office
(202) 647-7256 (voice/TDD)

Department of Transportation

National Highway Traffic Safety Administration
400 7th Street, SW
Washington, DC 20590
(202) 366-2602 (voice/TDD)

Department of the Treasury

Bureau of the Public Debt
13th and C Streets, SW
Washington, DC 20590
(202) 287-4097 (TDD)

Internal Revenue Service
1111 Constitution Avenue, NW
Washington, DC 20224
(202) 708-9300 (TDD)

Department of Veterans Affairs
810 Vermont Avenue, NW
Washington, DC 20420

Personnel Office
(202) 233-3225 (voice/TDD)

Environmental Protection Agency
401 M Street, SW
Washington, DC 20460
(202) 382-4565 (voice/TDD)

Equal Employment Opportunity Commission
2401 E Street, NW
Washington, DC 20507
(202) 663-4494 (TDD)
1 (800) 800-3302 (toll free TDD)

Executive Office of the President
The White House
1600 Pennsylvania Ave., NW
Washington, DC 20500
(202) 456-6213 (TDD)

Federal Communications Commission
1919 M Street, NW
Washington, DC 20554
(202) 632-6999 (voice/TDD)

Federal Deposit Insurance Corporation
1776 F Street, NW
Washington, DC 20429
(202) 898-3537 (voice/TDD)
1 (800) 442-5488
(toll free voice/TDD)

Federal Reserve Board
20th and C Streets, NW
Washington, DC 20551
(202) 452-3544 (voice/TDD)

General Services Administration
18th & F Streets, NW
Washington, DC 20405

Clearinghouse on Computer Accommodation
(202) 501-4906 (voice/TDD)

Council on Accessible Technology (COAT)
(202) 501-2296 (TDD)

Federal Information Relay Service
(202) 708-9300 (TDD)
1 (800) 877-8339
(toll free voice/TDD outside DC)

Interstate Commerce Commission
Constitution Avenue and 12th Street, NW
Washington, DC 20011
(202) 275-1721 (TDD)

Library of Congress
1291 Taylor St., NW
Washington, DC 20542
(202) 707-6200 (TDD)

Merit Systems Protection Board
1120 Vermont Avenue, NW
Washington, DC 20419
(202) 653-8896 (voice/TDD)

National Aeronautics and Space Administration
400 Maryland Avenue, SW
Washington, DC 20546

Personnel Office
(202) 426-1436 (voice/TDD)

Greenbelt Personnel Office
(301) 286-3729 (voice/TDD)

National Archives and Records Service
8th and Pennsylvania Ave., NW
Washington, DC 20408
(202) 501-5404 (voice/TDD)

National Council on Disability
800 Independence Ave., SW
Suite 814
Washington, DC 20591
(202) 267-3232 (voice/TDD)

National Endowment for the Arts
1100 Pennsylvania Ave., NW
Washington, DC 20506
(202) 682-5496 (voice/TDD)

National Science Foundation
1800 G Street, NW,
Room 212
Washington, DC 20550
(202) 357-7492 (voice/TDD)

Nuclear Regulatory Commission
Washington, DC 20555
(301) 492-4626 (voice/TDD)

Office of Personnel Management
1900 E Street, NW
Washington, DC 20415

Equal Employment Opportunity Division
(202) 606-2460 (voice/TDD)

Job Information Center
(202) 606-0591 (TDD)

President's Committee on Employment of People with Disabilities
1111 20th Street, NW
Washington, DC 20036
(202) 653-5050 (TDD)

Securities and Exchange Commission
450 Fifth Street, NW
Washington, DC 20549
(202) 272-2552 (voice/TDD)

Small Business Administration
409 Third Street, SW
Washington, DC 20416
(202) 205-7333 (TDD)

Smithsonian Institution
Special Education Program
Washington, DC 20560
(202) 357-1696 (TDD)

Tennessee Valley Authority
400 West Summit Hill Drive
Knoxville, TN 37902
(615) 751-8500 (TDD)

United States House of Representatives
Washington, DC 20215
(202) 225-1904 (TDD)

United States Information Agency
301 4th Street, SW
Washington, DC 20547
(202) 485-7157 (voice/TDD)

United States Postal Service
475 L'Enfant Plaza West, SW
Washington, DC 20260
(202) 268-2310 (voice/TDD)

United States Senate
Washington, DC 20510
(202) 224-4049, 4075 (TDD)

TDD Operator Services

Hearing or speech impaired individuals who use a Telecommunications Device for the Deaf (TDD or TTY) can get assistance with calls made to and from a telecommunications device by calling:

TDD/TTY Operator Services
1 (800) 855-1155 (toll free) or
(202) 708-9300 (D.C. Metro Area)

If you need assistance and you have TDD equipment, the TDD Operator can help you make any of the following:

- credit card calls (with valid telephone calling card);
- collect calls (paid for by the person you are calling);
- person-to-person calls (to a specific person);
- third party calls (calls billed to a number other than the one you are calling to or from);
- calls from a hotel or motel; and
- calls from a pay phone (only credit card, collect, or third-party calls).

Federal Information Relay Service

- If you use a TDD and need to reach a Federal agency or program that does not have a TDD,
- If you are a Federal employee who uses a TDD and your job requires you to contact an office that does not have a TDD, or
- If you do not have a TDD, but need to get in touch with a Federal employee who uses a TDD,

Call the Federal Information Relay Service (FIRS) on **1 (800) 877-8339** (toll free) or **(202) 708-9300** (D.C. Metropolitan Area)

Books for Blind and Physically Handicapped Persons

The Library of Congress has a free reading program for blind and physically handicapped individuals. Books, magazines, and other publications are available in Braille and/or audio recordings to persons who cannot hold a book or see to read regular print.

Special playback equipment is available on loan from the Library of Congress. Cassettes and records can be ordered from about 158 cooperating libraries. Anyone who is medically certified as unable to hold a book or who is unable to read ordinary print because of a visual handicap, may borrow and return these materials, postage-free. For more information, send name and address to:

National Library Service for the
Blind and Physically Handicapped
The Library of Congress
Washington, DC 20542

Recording for the Blind (RFB) is a national, nonprofit organization providing recorded textbooks, library services, and other educational resources to people who cannot read standard print because of a visual, physical, or perceptual disability.

RFB's educational library has more than 78,000 titles. Reference assistance is available, along with individually tailored subject bibliographies. RFB also provides an "on-demand" recording service through which new recordings are produced from books sent to RFB by the people they serve.

Anyone with a documented print disability (blindness, low vision, learning disabilities, or other physical impairment that affects reading) is eligible for RFB services.

An application for service form must be completed. RFB does charge a one-time registration fee of $25. For more information or to request an application, call or write:

Recording for the Blind
20 Roszel Road
Princeton, NJ 08540
(609) 452-0606
1 (800) 221-4792 (toll free)

Part III

Recreation, Travel and Leisure

INTERNATIONAL TRAVEL

American consuls at U.S. embassies and consulates abroad are there to help if you encounter serious difficulties in your travels. They are happy to meet you if you come in to register your passport at the consular section of the U.S. embassy or consulate. But it is also their duty to assist American citizens abroad in times of emergency—at hospitals or police stations, for instance. This is written in the hope that it will help you to prevent such emergencies from arising.

Useful Travel Publications

For the official word on immunizations, customs, and what you can legally bring into the United States, you may order one of the following U.S. Government publications:

Health Information for International Travel is a comprehensive listing of immunization requirements of foreign governments. In addition, it gives the U.S. Public Health Service's recommendations on immunizations and other health precautions for the international traveler. Copies are available for $4.75 from the Superintendent of Documents, U.S. Government Printing Office, Washington, DC 20402; tel. (202) 783-3238.

Know Before You Go, Customs Hints for Returning U.S. Residents gives detailed information on U.S. Customs regulations, including duty rates. Single copies are available free from any local customs office or by writing to the Department of the Treasury, U.S. Customs Service, P.O. Box 7407, Washington, DC 20044.

Travelers Tips on Bringing Food, Plant, and Animal Products Into the United States lists the regulations on bringing these items into the United States from most parts of the world. Fresh fruits and vegetables, meat, potted plants, pet birds, and other items are prohibited or restricted. Obtain the publication free from the Animal and Plant Health Inspection Service, U.S. Department of Agriculture, 732 Federal Bldg., 6505 Belcrest Road, Hyattsville, Maryland 20782.

The following publication is prepared by the World Wildlife Fund:

Buyer Beware! tells about restrictions on importing wildlife and wildlife products. For a free copy, write to the Publications Unit, U.S. Fish and Wildlife Service, Department of the Interior, Washington, DC 20240; (202) 343-5634.

The following three publications from the Department of State may be ordered for $1 each from the Superintendent of Documents, U.S. Government Printing Office, Washington, DC 20402; tel. (202) 783-3238:

Your Trip Abroad provides basic travel information—tips on passports, visas, immunizations, and more. It will help you prepare for your trip and make it as trouble-free as possible.

A Safe Trip Abroad gives travel security advice for any traveler, but particularly for those who plan trips to areas of high crime or terrorism.

Tips for Americans Residing Abroad is prepared for the more than 2 million Americans who live in foreign countries.

The following three publications are also from the Department of State (see ordering information below):

Foreign Entry Requirements lists visa and other entry requirements of foreign countries and tells you how to apply for visas and tourist cards. Order this publication for 50¢ from the Consumer Information Center, Dept. 438T, Pueblo, CO 81009.

Key Officers of Foreign Service Posts gives addresses and telephone, telex, and FAX numbers for all U.S. embassies and consulates abroad. (NOTE: When writing to a U.S. embassy or consulate, address the envelope to the appropriate section, such as Consular Section, rather than to a specific individual.) This publication is updated 3 times a year and may be purchased from the Superintendent of Documents, U.S. Government Printing Office, Washington, DC 20402; tel. (202) 783-3238.

Background Notes are brief, factual pamphlets on each of 170 countries. They give current information on each country's people, culture, geography, history, government, economy, and political conditions. They also include a factual profile, brief travel notes, a country map, and a suggested reading list. For information on their price and to order copies, contact: Superintendent of Documents, U.S. Government Printing Office, Washington, DC 20402; tel. (202) 783-3238.

Passport Agencies

Apply Early for Your Passport!

Boston Passport Agency
Thomas P. O'Neill Federal Building, Room 247
10 Causeway Street
Boston, Massachusetts 02222
*Recording: 617-565-6998
Public Inquiries: 617-565-6990

Chicago Passport Agency
Kluczynski Federal Building, Suite 380
230 South Dearborn Street
Chicago, Illinois 60604-1564
Public Inquiries: 312-353-7155 or 7163

Honolulu Passport Agency
New Federal Building, Room C-106
300 Ala Moana Boulevard
Honolulu, Hawaii 96850
*Recording: 808-541-1919
Public Inquiries: 808-541-1918

Houston Passport Agency
Concord Towers
1919 Smith Street, Suite 1100
Houston, Texas 77002
*Recording: 713-653-3159
Public Inquiries: 713-653-3153

Los Angeles Passport Agency
11000 Wilshire Boulevard, Room 13100
Los Angeles, California 90024-3615
*Recording: 310-209-7070
Public Inquiries: 310-209-7075

Miami Passport Agency
Federal Office Building, 16th Floor
51 Southwest First Avenue
Miami, Florida 33130-1680
*Recording: 305-536-5395 (English)
305-536-4448 (Spanish)
Public Inquiries: 305-536-4681

New Orleans Passport Agency
Postal Services Building, Room T-12005
701 Loyola Avenue
New Orleans, Louisiana 70113-1931
*Recording: 504-589-6728
Public Inquiries: 504-589-6161

New York Passport Agency
Rockefeller Center, Room 270
630 Fifth Avenue
New York, New York 10111-0031
*Recording: 212-541-7700
Public Inquiries: 212-541-7710

Philadelphia Passport Agency
Federal Office Building, Room 4426
600 Arch Street
Philadelphia, Pennsylvania 19106-1684
*Recording: 215-597-7482
Public Inquiries: 215-597-7480

San Francisco Passport Agency
525 Market Street, Suite 200
San Francisco, California 94105-2773
*Recording: 415-974-7972
Public Inquiries: 415-974-9941

Seattle Passport Agency
Federal Office Building, Room 992
915 Second Avenue
Seattle, Washington 98174-1091
*Recording: 206-442-7941
Public Inquiries: 206-442-7945

Stamford Passport Agency
One Landmark Square
Broad and Atlantic Streets
Stamford, Connecticut 06901-2767
*Recording: 203-325-4401
Public Inquiries: 203-325-3538 or 3530

Washington Passport Agency
1425 K Street, N.W.
Washington, D.C. 20524-0002
*Recording: 202-647-0518
Public Inquiries: (M-F 8 a.m.-4:45 p.m. EST): 202-647-0518

*The twenty-four hour recording includes general passport information, passport agency location, and hours of operation.

TRAVEL/TOURISM

Included in this section are addresses and telephone numbers for the major tourism bureau of each state, Puerto Rico, Mexico, and Canada. Where available, toll-free 800 numbers have been included so you may contact them at no cost.

These bureaus will be able to answer the majority of your questions and will provide you with free information such as travel brochures, maps, attractions guides, lodging, camping, and restaurant directories.

ALABAMA

Alabama Tourism and Travel
532 South Perry St.
Montgomery, AL 36104
205-242-4169
(800) ALABAMA (252-2262)
(800) 392-8096 (In Alabama)

Department of State Parks
Alabama Department of Conservation & Natural Resources
64 North Union St.
Montgomery, AL 36130
Reservations: **(800) ALA-PARK**

ALASKA

Alaska Division of Tourism
P.O. Box E-301
Juneau, AK 99811
907-465-2010

ARIZONA

Arizona Office of Tourism
1100 W. Washington Ave.
Phoenix, AZ 85007
602-542-8687

ARKANSAS

Arkansas Department of Parks & Tourism
One Capitol Mall
Little Rock, AR 72201
501-682-7777
(800) 828-8974

CALIFORNIA

California Office of Tourism
1121 L St., Suite 103
Sacramento, CA 95814

California Department of Parks & Recreation
P.O. Box 942896
Sacramento, CA 94296-0838
916-445-6477

COLORADO

Colorado Tourism Board
1625 Broadway, Suite 1700
Denver, CO 80202
303-592-5410
(800) 433-2656

CONNECTICUT

Department of Economic Development Tourism Division
865 Brook St.
Rocky Hill, CT 06067-3405
(800) 282-6863 (800-CT-Bound)
(Outside CT)

DELAWARE

Delaware Tourism Office
99 Kings Hwy, Box 1401
Dover, DE 19903
302-736-4271
(800) 441-8846
(800) 282-8667 (in Delaware)

WASHINGTON, DC

Washington DC Convention & Visitors Association
1212 New York Ave. NW
Washington, DC 20005
202-789-7000

Washington Visitor Information Center
1455 Pennsylvania Ave., NW
202-789-7000

Smithsonian Information Center
Smithsonian Building (The Castle)
Visitor Information and Associates' Reception Center
1000 Jefferson Dr., SW
202-357-2700 (All 14 museums)

FLORIDA

Florida Department of Commerce
Division of Tourism
126 W Van Buren St.
Tallahassee, FL 32399-2000
904-487-1462

GEORGIA

Georgia Department of Industry and Trade
P.O. Box 1776
Atlanta, GA 30301
404-656-3590
(800) 847-4842

HAWAII

Hawaii Visitors Bureau
Suite 801
Waikiki Business Plaza
2270 Kalakaua Avenue
Honolulu, HI 96815
808-923-1811

IDAHO

The Idaho Travel Council
700 W State St.
Boise, ID 83720
208-334-2470
(800) 635-7820

ILLINOIS

Illinois Department of Commerce and Community Affairs
Office of Tourism
Tourist Information Center

310 S Michigan Ave., Suite 108
Chicago, IL 60604
312-793-2094
(800) 223-0121 (For Literature)

INDIANA

Indiana Department of Commerce
Tourism Development Division
One North Capitol, Suite 700
Indianapolis, IN 46204-2288
(800) 289-ON IN
Hotline: **(800) 2-WANDER**

IOWA

Bureau of Tourism and Visitors
Iowa Department of Economic Development
200 E Grand Ave.
Des Moines, IA 50309
(800) 345-4692
515-281-3100

KANSAS

Kansas Department of Commerce
Division of Travel & Tourism Development
400 W 8th, 5th Floor
Topeka, KS 66603
913-296-2009
(800) 2KANSAS (In Kansas)

KENTUCKY

Kentucky Department of Travel Development
Capital Plaza Tower
Frankfort, KY 40601
502-564-4930
(800) 225-TRIP

LOUISIANA

Louisiana Office of Tourism
P.O. Box 94291
Baton Rouge, LA 70804
504-342-8119
(800) 33-GUMBO

MAINE

Maine Publicity Bureau
97 Winthrop St.
Hallowell, ME 04347-2300
207-289-6070

MARYLAND

Maryland Department of Economic & Employment Development
Office of Tourism Development
217 East Redwood St.
Baltimore, MD 21202
301-333-6611
(800) 543-1036

MASSACHUSETTS

Massachusetts Travel and Tourism
100 Cambridge St., 13th Floor
Boston, MA 02202
617-727-3201
(800) 447-MASS

MICHIGAN

Michigan Travel Bureau
P.O. Box 30226
Lansing, MI 48909
(800) 5432-YES

MINNESOTA

Minnesota Office of Tourism
375 Jackson St.
250 Skyway Level
St. Paul, MN 55101
612-296-5029
(800) 657-3700
(800) 652-9747 (in Minnesota)

MISSISSIPPI

Division of Tourism Development
P.O. Box 22825
Jackson, MS 39205
(800) 647-2290
601-359-3297

MISSOURI

Division of Tourism
P.O. Box 1055
Jefferson City, MO 65102
314-751-4133
(800) 877-1234

MONTANA

Travel Montana
1424 9th Ave.
Helena, MT 59620
(800) 541-1447 (Outside Montana)
406-444-2654

NEBRASKA

Nebraska Department of Economic Development
Division of Travel and Tourism
P.O. Box 94666
Lincoln, NE 68509
(800) 228-4307
(800) 742-7595 (In Nebraska)

NEVADA

Nevada Commission on Tourism
Capitol Complex
Carson City, NV 89710
702-885-4322
(800) 638-2328 or **237-0774**

NEW HAMPSHIRE

New Hampshire Office of Vacation Travel
P.O. Box 856
Concord, NH 03301
603-271-2666

NEW JERSEY

New Jersey Division of Travel and Tourism
20 West State St.
Trenton, NJ 08625
609-292-2470

NEW MEXICO

New Mexico Travel Division
Joseph Montoya Building
1100 St. Francis Drive
Santa Fe, NM 87503
505-827-0291
(800) 545-2040 (Outside New Mexico)

NEW YORK
Department of Economic Development
Division of Tourism
One Commerce Plaza Complex
Albany, NY 12245
518-474-4116
(800) 225-5697

NORTH CAROLINA
North Carolina Division of Travel and Tourism
430 N. Salisbury St.
Raleigh, NC 27611
919-733-4171
(800) VISIT-NC

NORTH DAKOTA
North Dakota Tourism Promotion
Liberty Memorial Building
State Capitol Grounds
Bismarck, ND 58505
701-224-2525
(800) 437-2077
(800) 472-2100 (In North Dakota)
(800) 537-8879 (In Canada)

OHIO
Ohio Division of Travel and Tourism
P.O. Box 1001
Columbus, OH 43266-0101
(800) BUCKEYE

OKLAHOMA
Oklahoma Tourism and Recreation Department
Literature Distribution Center
P.O. Box 60000
Oklahoma City, OK 73146
(800) 654-8240
405-521-2464

OREGON
State of Oregon
Economic Development Department
Tourism Division
595 Cottage St. NE
Salem, OR 97810
(800) 547-7842
(800) 543-8838 (In Oregon)

PENNSYLVANIA
Pennsylvania Department of Commerce
Bureau of Travel Marketing
453 Forum Building
Harrisburg, PA 17120
717-787-5453
(800) VISIT-PA

RHODE ISLAND
Rhode Island Tourism Division
7 Jackson Walkway
Providence, RI 02903
401-277-2601
(800) 556-2484

SOUTH CAROLINA
South Carolina Division of Tourism
P.O. Box 71
Columbia, SC 29202
803-734-0235

SOUTH DAKOTA
South Dakota Tourism
P.O. Box 1000
Pierre, SD 57501
(800) 843-1930
(800) 952-2217 (In South Dakota)

TENNESSEE
Tennessee Tourism Development
P.O. Box 23170
Nashville, TN 37202
615-741-2158

TEXAS
Texas Department of Commerce
Tourism Division
P.O. Box 12728
Austin, TX 78711
512-462-9191
512-463-8585
Brochure: **(800) 8888-TEX**

UTAH
Utah Travel Council
Council Hall/Capitol Hill
Salt Lake City, UT 84114
801-538-1030

VERMONT
Vermont Travel Division
134 State St.
Montpelier, VT 05602
802-828-3236

VIRGINIA
Virginia Division of Tourism
202 N Ninth St., Suite 500
Richmond, VA 23219
804-786-4484

WASHINGTON
Washington State Department of Trade and Economic Development
Tourism Development Division
101 General Administration Building
Olympia, WA 98504-0613
206-753-5600

WEST VIRGINIA
West Virginia Department of Commerce
State Capitol
Charleston, WV 25305
(800) CALL-WVA

WISCONSIN
Wisconsin Tourism Development
Box 7606
Madison, WI 53707
608-266-2161
(800) 372-2737

WYOMING
Wyoming Travel Commission
I-25 at College Dr.
Cheyenne, WY 82002
307-777-7777
(800) 225-5996 (Outside Wyoming)

PUERTO RICO
Puerto Rico Tourism
P.O. Box 5268
Miami, FL 33102
(800) 866-STAR

CANADA

Travel ALBERTA
P.O. Box 2500
Edmonton, Alberta
Canada T5J 2Z4
403-427-4321
(800) 661-8888

Tourism BRITISH COLUMBIA
Parliament Buildings
Victoria, B.C.
Canada V8V 1X4
714-852-1054
(800) 663-6000

Travel MANITOBA
7-155 Carlton St.
Winnipeg, Manitoba
Canada R3C 3H8
(800) 665-0040

Tourism NEW BRUNSWICK
P.O. Box 12345
Fredericton, New Brunswick
Canada E3B 5C3
(800) 561-0123

NEWFOUNDLAND and LABRADOR
Department of Development and Tourism
P.O. Box 2016
St. Johns, Newfoundland
Canada A1C 5R8
709-576-2830
(800) 563-6353

NORTHWEST TERRITORY
(800) 661-0788

NOVA SCOTIA
Department of Tourism and Culture
P.O. Box 130
Halifax, Nova Scotia
Canada B3J 2M7
902-425-5781
(800) 341-6096
(800) 492-0643 (In Maine)

ONTARIO Travel
Queen's Park
Toronto, Ontario
Canada M7A 2E5
(800) ONTARIO

PRINCE EDWARD ISLAND
Visitor Services
PO Box 940
Charlottetown, P.E.I.
Canada C1A 7M5
902-368-4444
(800) 565-9060 (Eastern US)

Tourism QUEBEC
P.O. Box 20,000
Quebec (Quebec)
Canada G1K 7X2
(800) 443-7000

Tourism SASKATCHEWAN
Trade & Convention Center
1919 Saskatchewan Dr.
Regina, Saskatchewan
Canada S4P 3V7
306-787-2300
(800) 667-7191

Tourism YUKON
P.O. Bag 2745
Yukon, Canada Y1A 5B9
403-667-5340

While visiting Canada U.S. citizens will need proof of citizenship (birth certificate or passport), proof of international auto insurance coverage and vehicle registration (or car rental agreement).

MEXICO

Any Mexican Consulate, Mexican government Tourism Office or Office of Mexican Immigration can provide tourism information about Mexico.

Consulates (C) and Consulates General (CG)

Ciudad Juarez (CG)
011-52-161-34048 (day US)
915-525-6066 (night US)

Guadalajara (CG)
011-52-362-52700
011-52-362-52998 (US)

Hermosillo (C)
011-32-621-72375
011-52-621-72585 (night US)

Matamoros (C)
011-52-891-25251
011-52-891-25252 (US)

Mazatlan (C)
011-52-678-12905
011-52-678-12685
011-52-678-12687 (US)

Merida (C)
011-52-992-55409
011-52-992-55011 (day US)

Monterrey (CG)
011-52-83-452120 (US)

Nuevo Laredo (C)
011-52-871-40512 (day US)
512-727-9661 (night US)

Tijuana (CG)
706-681-7400 (day US)
619-585-2000 (night US)

U.S. citizens visiting Mexico for 72 hours or less and remaining within 20 kilometers (about 12 miles) of the Mexican border need no type of permit to enter. All other visits by U.S. citizens require a tourist card (FMT).

Many states bordering Mexico cover entry and exit requirements in their tourism brochures. Chambers of Commerce in U.S. border towns also provide information on entering Mexico. The Government Printing Office offers "Tips for Travelers to Mexico" which should answer any other questions you may have.

Travel

Toll-free 800 numbers for airlines, car rental, cruise lines, resorts, and hotel and motel accommodations.

Airlines

Alaska Airlines	**(800) 426-0333**
America West	**(800) 247-5692**
American Airlines	**(800) 433-7300**
American Eagle	**(800) 351-3337** (ex TX)
British Airways	**(800) 247-9297**
Continental Airlines	**(800) 231-0856** **(800) 343-9195** (TDD)
Delta Air Lines	**(800) 221-1212**
Hawaiian Airlines	**(800) 367-5320**
Midway Airlines	**(800) 621-5700**
Midwest Express	**(800) 452-2022**
Northwest Airlines	**(800) 225-2525**
Piedmont Airlines	**(800) 251-5720**
TWA	**(800) 221-2000**
United Airlines	**(800) 241-6522**
USAir	**(800) 428-4322**

Automobile Rental and Leasing

Action Auto Rental	**(800) 759-4440**
Agency Rent-A-Car	**(800) 321-1972**
Airways Rent-A-Car	**(800) 952-9200**
Alamo Rent-A-Car	**(800) 327-9633**
Amerex Rent-A-Car	**(800) 843-1143**
American International	**(800) 527-0202**
Avis Rent-A-Car	**(800) 331-1212**
Budget Car & Truck Rental	**(800) 527-0700** **(800) 826-5510** (TDD)
Dollar Rent-A-Car	**(800) 421-6878**
Enterprise Rent-A-Car	**(800) 325-8007**
General Rent-A-Car	**(800) 327-7607**
Hertz Rent-A-Car	**(800) 654-3131**
National Car Rental	**(800) 227-7368**
Payless Car Rental	**(800) PAYLESS**
Rent-a-Wreck	**(800) 423-2158**
Sears Car & Truck Rental	**(800) 527-0770**
Thrifty Car Rental	**(800) 367-2277**
U-Drive America Car Rental	**(800) 433-5111** (ex. NV)

Railroads

AMTRAK	**(800) USA-RAIL**

Cruises

American Hawaii Cruise Lines	**(800) 227-3666**
Carnival Cruise Lines	**(800) 327-7373**
Custom Cruises Inc.	**(800) 621-6010**
Delta Queen Steamboat	**(800) 543-7637** (ex LA)
Holland America Line	**(800) 426-0327**
Westours Inc. (Brochure)	**(800) 626-9900**
Norwegian Cruise Lines	**(800) 262-4625**
Windjammer Barefoot Cruises	**(800) 327-2601** (ex FL)

Hotel, Motels, Resorts

Best Western	**(800) 528-1234**
Budget Motels of America	**(800) 624-1257**
Budgetel Inns	**(800) 428-3438**
Clarion	**(800) 221-2222**
Clubhouse Inns	**(800) CLUB-INN**
Comfort Inns	**(800) 221-2222**
Courtyard by Marriott	**(800) 321-2211**
Days Inns of America	**(800) 325-2525**
Dillon Inn	**(800) 253-7503**

Disney World Area Hotels and Resorts

Grand Floridian	**(800) 647-7900**
Disney's Polynesian Resort	**(800) 647-7900**
Disney's Caribbean Beach Resort	**(800) 647-7900**
Disney's Fort Wilderness Resort and Campground	**(800) 647-7900**
Disney's Inn	**(800) 647-7900**
Disney's Village Resort	**(800) 647-7900**
Disney's Beach Club & Yacht Club Resort	**(800) 647-7900**
Disney's Village Hotel Plaza	**(800) 647-7900**

(includes Hotel Plaza, Buena Vista Palace, Gorszenor Resort, Hilton Hotel, Royal Plaza, and Howard Johnson Ticket Suite Resorts)

Walt Disney World Swan EPCOT)	**(800) 647-7900**
Walt Disney World Dolphin EPCOT)	**(800) 647-7900**
Guest Quarter Suite Resorts	**(800) 647-7900**
Doubletree Hotels	**(800) 528-0444**
Drury Inn	**(800) 325-8300**
Econo Lodge	**(800) 446-6900**
Economy Inns of America	**(800) 826-0778**
Embassy Suites Hotel	**(800) 362-2779**
Excel Inn	**(800) 356-8013**
Fairfield Inn by Marriott	**(800) 228-2800**
Four Seasons Hotels	**(800) 332-3442**
Guest Quarters	**(800) 424-2900**
Hampton Inns	**(800) 426-7866** **(800) 451-4833** (TDD)
Harley Hotels	**(800) 321-2323**
Hilton Reservation Service	**(800) 445-8667**
Holiday Inn	**(800) 465-4329**
Holiday Inn Crowne Plaza	**(800) 521-2762**
Hotel Royal Plaza Walt Disney World Village	**(800) 248-7890**
Howard Johnson Hotels & Lodges	**(800) 654-2000**
Hyatt	**(800) 228-9000**
Inter-Continental Hotels	**(800) 332-4246**
Knights Inn	**(800) 722-7220**
La Quinta	**(800) 531-5900**
Lexington Hotel Suites	**(800) 53-SUITE**
Loews Hotels	**(800) 223-0888**
Marriott Hotels & Resorts	**(800) 228-9290**
Motel 6	505-891-6161
Nendel's	**(800) 547-0106**
Omni International	**(800) 843-6664**
Parks Inns	**(800) 437-PARK**
Park Suite	**(800) 432-7272**
Pickett Suite	**(800) 742-5388**
Quality International	**(800) 221-2222**
Radisson	**(800) 333-3333**
Ramada Inns	**(800) 2-RAMADA**
Red Carpet Inns	**(800) 251-1962**
Red Lion/Thunderbird	**(800) 547-8010**
Red Roof Inns	**(800) 843-7663**
Residence Inn by Marriott	**(800) 331-3131**
Ritz-Carlton	**(800) 241-3333**
Rodeway Inns	**(800) 228-2660**
Scottish Inns	**(800) 251-1962**
Sheraton Hotels	**(800) 325-3535**
Shoney's Inn	**(800) 222-2222**
Sonesta	**(800) 343-7170**
Stouffer Hotels & Resorts	**(800) 468-3571**
Super 8 Motels	**(800) 843-1991**
Susse Chalet	**(800) 258-1980**
Travelodge/Viscount	**(800) 222-6081**
Vagabond Inn	**(800) 522-1555**
Westin Hotels	**(800) 228-3000**

TV Show Tickets

While in the Los Angeles, California, area, you may wish to enquire about network television shows which have audiences.
(Tickets for all TV shows are free)

ABC . . . 310-557-7777
CBS . . . 213-852-2624
NBC . . . 818-840-3537
Paramount . . . 213-468-5575
20th Century Fox . . . 310-277-2211

Theme Parks

Listed here are the ten most popular theme parks in the U.S. You will find other parks and attractions listed by state and also a list of national parks follows.

Busch Gardens
Busch Blvd. and 40th St.
Tampa, FL 33602
813-971-8282

Cedar Point
Sandusky, OH

Disneyland
1313 Harbor Blvd.
Anaheim, CA 92802
714-999-4565

King's Island
Cincinnati, OH

Knott's Berry Farm
8039 N. Beach Blvd.
Buena Park, CA 90621
714-220-5200

Sea World
7007 Sea World Drive
Orlando, FL 32819
407-351-3600

Six Flags/Great Adventure
Jackson, NJ
201-928-2000

Six Flags/Great America
Gurnee, IL

Universal City Studios Tour
100 Universal City Plaza
Universal City, CA 91608
Tour: 818-508-9600
Reservations: 818-777-3801

Walt Disney World
Lake Buena Vista, FL
407-824-4321

National Parks

Acadia National Park
P.O. Box 177
Bar Harbor, ME 04609

Arches National Park
P.O. Box 907
Moab, UT 84532

Badlands National Park
P.O. Box 6
Interior, SD 57750

Big Bend National Park
Big Bend National Park, TX 79834

Biscayne National Park
P.O. Box 1369
Homestead, FL 33090

Bryce Canyon National Park
Bryce Canyon, UT 84717

Canyonlands National Park
446 S. Main St.
Moab, UT 84532

Capitol Reef National Park
Torrey, UT 84775

Carlsbad Caverns National Park
3225 National Parks Highway
Carlsbad, NM 88220

Channel Islands National Park
1699 Anchors Way Dr.
Ventura, CA 93003

Crater Lake National Park
Box 7
Crater Lake, OR 97604

Denali National Park
Anderson, AK

Everglades National Park
P.O. Box 279
Homestead, FL 33030

Gates of the Arctic National Park
Wiseman, AK

Glacier Bay National Park
Yakutat, AK

Glacier National Park
West Glacier, MT 59936

Grand Canyon National Park
P.O. Box 129
Grand Canyon, AZ 86023

Grand Teton National Park
Drawer 170
Moose, WY 83012

Great Smoky Mountains National Park
Gatlinburg, TN 37738

Guadalupe Mountains National Park
Pine Springs, TX
c/o Superintendent
Carlsbad Caverns National Park
3225 Nat'l Parks Highway
Carlsbad, NM 88220

Haleakala National Park
Kahului, Maui, HI

Hawaii Volcanoes National Park
Island of Hawaii

Hot Springs National Park
P.O. Box 1860
Hot Springs, AR 71901

Isle Royale National Park
87 N. Ripley St.
Houghton, MI 49931

Katmai National Park
King Salmon, AK

Kenai Fjords National Park
Kenai, AK

Kings Canyon National Park
Three Rivers, CA 93271

Kobuk Valley National Park
Kotzebue, AK

Lake Clark National Park
Anchorage, AK

Lassen Volcanic National Park
Mineral, CA 96063

Mammoth Cave National Park
Mammoth Cave, KY 42259

Mesa Verde National Park
Mesa Verde, CO 81330

Mount Rainier National Park
Tahoma Woods
Star Route
Ashford, WA 98304

North Cascades National Park
2105 Washington 20
Sedro Woolley, WA 98284

Olympic National Park
600 East Park Ave.
Port Angeles, WA 98362

Petrified Forest National Park
P.O. Box 247
Petrified Forest National Park, AZ 86028

Platt National Park
Sulphur, OK

Redwood National Park
1111 Second St.
Crescent City, CA 95531

Rocky Mountain National Park
Estes Park, CO 80517

Sequoia National Park
Three Rivers, CA

Shenandoah National Park
Rte. 4, Box 348
Luray, VA 22835

Theodore Roosevelt Memorial National Park
P.O. Box 7
Medora, ND 58645

Virgin Islands National Park
St. John, U.S. Virgin Islands

Voyageurs National Park
P.O. Box 50
International Falls, MN 56649

Wind Cave National Park
Hot Springs, SD 57747

Wrangell-St. Elias National Park
Cordova, AK

Yellowstone National Park
P.O. Box 168
Yellowstone National Park, WY 82190

Yosemite National Park
P.O. Box 577
Yosemite Village, CA

Zion National Park
Springdale, UT 84767

Places of Interest Along the USA's Highways and By-ways

ALABAMA

Alabama Space and Rocket Center
Huntsville, AL 35807
205 837-3400

ARIZONA

Saguaro National Monument
3693 S. Old Spanish Trail
Tucson, AZ 85730
602 296-8576

Tombstone
P.O. Box 917
Tombstone, AZ 85638
602 457-2211

CALIFORNIA

America's Cup
Sail America
1904 Hotel Circle North
San Diego, CA 92108

Alcatraz
Powell St. at Fisherman's Wharf
San Francisco, CA

Death Valley National Monument
National Park Service
Death Valley, CA 92328
619 786-2331

Hearst-San Simeon Historical Monument
P.O. Box 8
San Simeon, CA 93452
800 444-7275

Hollywood Walk of Fame
c/o Hollywood Chamber of Commerce
6290 Sunset Blvd.
Hollywood, CA 90028

COLORADO

Dinosaur National Monument

P.O. Box 210
Dinosaur, CO 81610

WASHINGTON, D.C. MALL ATTRACTIONS

Jefferson Memorial
Tidal Basin (West Bank)
West Potomac Park

Lincoln Memorial
West end of the Mall at 23rd St., NW

U.S. Capitol
East End of the Mall
202-224-3121
202-225-6827 (Tours)

Vietnam Veterans Memorial
Constitution Ave. Between Henry Bacon Dr. and 21st St., NW
202-426-6841

Washington Monument
Mall at 15th St.
202-426-6841

The White House
1600 Pennsylvania Ave.
202-456-7041

FLORIDA

NASA Kennedy Space Center
Spaceport USA Visitor Center
Kennedy Space Center, FL 32899
407 452-2121

The Ringling Museums
U.S. Hwy. 41
Sarasota, FL
813 355-5101

GEORGIA

Chickamauga and Chattanooga National Military Park
P.O. Box 2128
Fort Oglethorpe, GA 30742

Martin Luther King, Jr. Historic Site
522 Auburn Ave. NE
Atlanta, GA
Center: 404 524-1956
Church: 404 688-7263
Home: 404 331-3919

IDAHO

Sun Valley Tourism
800 786-8259

INDIANA

Indianapolis Motor Speedway
Hall of Fame and Museum
4790 W. 16th St.
Indianapolis, IN 46222

KANSAS

Boot Hill Museum
Dodge City, KS
316 227-3119

KENTUCKY

Land Between the Lakes
Golden Pond, KY 42231
502 924-5602

Churchill Downs
700 Central Avenue
Louisville, KY 40208

LOUISIANA

French Quarter Walking Tour
751 Chartres St. on Jackson Square
New Orleans, LA
504 523-3939

MARYLAND

Antietam National Battlefield
P.O. Box 158
Sharpsburg, MD 21782
301 432-5124

MASSACHUSETTS

Faneuil Hall/Quincy Market
Congress St.
Boston, MA
617 725-3105

Naismith Memorial Basketball Hall of Fame
150 W. Columbus Ave.
Springfield, MA 01101

MICHIGAN

Motown Museum
2648 W. Grand Blvd.
Detroit, MI 48208

MISSISSIPPI

Vicksburg National Military Park
3201 Clay St.
Vicksburg, MS 39180
601 636-0583

MISSOURI

Branson Lakes Area Chamber of Commerce
P.O. Box 220, Hwy. 65N
Branson, MO 65616
417 334-4136

Anheuser-Busch Brewery
1 Busch Place
St. Louis, MO
314 577-2626

Gateway Arch
St. Louis Riverfront
St. Louis, MO
314 425-4465

Six Flags Over Mid-America
I-44
Eureka, MO
314 938-5300

MONTANA

Custer Battlefield National Monument
P.O. Box 39
Crow Agency, MT 59022
406 638-2622

NEBRASKA

Boys Town
138th & W. Dodge Rd.
Omaha, NE
402 498-1140

NEVADA

Lake Mead
601 Nevada Hwy.
Boulder City, NV 89005-2426
702 293-4041

Las Vegas Convention and Visitors Bureau
Las Vegas, NV
702 733-2323

NEW JERSEY

Atlantic City Boardwalk
Atlantic City, NJ
609 348-7044

NEW MEXICO

White Sands National Monument
P.O. Box 458
Alamogordo, NM 88310

NEW YORK

Central Park
59th St. to 110th St.
New York, NY
212 397-3156

Club Med
40 West 57th St.
New York, NY 10019

Madison Square Garden
Seventh Ave., 31st-33rd Sts.
New York, NY

Metropolitan Museum of Art
Fifth Ave. at 82nd St.
New York, NY 10028

Metropolitan Opera House
Columbus Ave. & 63rd-64th Sts.
New York, NY
212 362-6000

Museum of Modern Art (MOMA)
11 W. 53rd St.
New York, NY 10019

National Baseball Hall of Fame
P.O. Box 590
Cooperstown, NY 13326

New York Aquarium
Boardwalk and W. 8th St.
Brooklyn, NY 11224

Statue of Liberty
Liberty Island, NY
Circle Line Boat: 212 269-5755

Whitney Museum of American Art
945 Madison Ave.
New York, NY 10021

OHIO

United States Air Force Museum
Wright-Patterson AFB, OH 45433
513 255-3286

Pro Football Hall of Fame
2121 George Halas Dr. NW
Canton, OH 44708

OKLAHOMA

National Cowboy Hall of Fame
1700 NE 63rd St.
Oklahoma City, OK
405 478-2250

OREGON

Oregon Museum of Science and Industry
4015 SW Canyon Rd.
Portland, OR
503 222-2828

PENNSYLVANIA

Independence Hall
Chestnut St. between 5th & 6th Sts.
Philadelphia, PA

Liberty Bell
Independence National Historical Park
313 Walnut St.
Philadelphia, PA 19106

Valley Forge National Historical Park
Valley Forge, PA 19481

RHODE ISLAND

The Breakers
Ochre Point Ave.
Newport, RI
401 847-1000

SOUTH CAROLINA

Fort Sumter National Monument
1214 Middle St.
Sullivans Island, SC 29482
803 883-3123

SOUTH DAKOTA

Mt. Rushmore National Memorial
P.O. Box 268
Keystone, SD 57751
605 574-2523

TENNESSEE

Country Music Hall of Fame & Museum
4 Music Square East
Nashville, TN
615 256-1639

Graceland
3717 Elvis Presley Blvd.
Memphis, TN
800 238-2000 (ex TN)

Grand Ole Opry House
2804 Opryland Dr.
Nashville, TN 37214

Lookout Mountain Incline Railway
827 East Brow Rd.
Chattanooga, TN
615 821-4224

Opryland USA
2802 Opryland Dr.
Nashville, TN 37214
615 889-6611

TEXAS

The Alamo
Alamo Plaza
San Antonio, TX
512 225-1391

John F. Kennedy Memorial
Market St. between Commerce & Main Sts.
Dallas, TX

Six Flags Over Texas
I-30 at State Hwy. 360
Arlington, TX
817 640-8900

Southfork Ranch
Parker Rd. at FM 2551
Parker, TX
214 442-6536

UTAH

Historic Temple Square
50 W. North Temple
Salt Lake City, UT

VIRGINIA

Busch Gardens, The Old Country
Williamsburg, VA
804 253-3350

Jamestown Festival Park
(Jamestown Settlement)
Rt. 31 & Colonial Parkway
Jamestown, VA
804 229-1607

Mount Vernon
Mount Vernon, VA 22121
703 780-2000

WASHINGTON

Coulee Dam National Recreation Area
P.O. Box 37
Coulee Dam, WA 99116
509 633-0881

Mount Rainier National Park
Tahoma Woods, Star Route
Ashford, WA 98304
206 569-2211

Mount St. Helens Visitors Center
I-5 on S.R. 504
Soutle, WA
206 274-4038

WEST VIRGINIA

Harpers Ferry National Historical Park
P.O. Box 65
Harpers Ferry, WV 25425
304 535-6371

WYOMING

Buffalo Bill Historical Center
P.O. Box 1000
Cody, WY 82414
307 587-4771

Sports

Major league baseball, basketball, football, and hockey teams are listed by state with addresses and phone numbers for tickets and information.

ARIZONA

Phoenix Suns Basketball
2910 N. Central Ave.
Phoenix, AZ 85102

CALIFORNIA

California Angels Baseball
2000 State College Blvd. at Katella Ave.
Anaheim, CA 92802
Information: 714-937-6700
Tickets: 714-634-2000

Golden State Warriors Basketball
Oakland Coliseum Arena
Oakland, CA 94621

Los Angeles Clippers Basketball
Los Angeles Sports Arena
3939 S Figueroa St. at Martin Luther King Blvd.
Los Angeles, CA 90037-1292
213-748-0500

Los Angeles Dodgers Baseball
Dodgers Stadium
1000 Elysian Park Ave. at Stadium Way
Los Angeles, CA 90012-1199
Information: 213-224-1400
Tickets: 213-224-1471

Los Angeles Kings Hockey
The Forum
3900 W. Manchester Ave. at Prairie Ave.
Inglewood, CA 90306
Information: 310-419-3182
Tickets: 310-419-3160

Los Angeles Lakers Basketball
The Forum
3900 W. Manchester at Prairie Ave.
Inglewood, CA 90306
213-637-1300

Los Angeles Raiders Football
Memorial Coliseum Exposition Park
3911 Figueroa St. at Exposition Blvd.
Los Angeles, CA 90245
Information: 310-322-3341
Tickets: 310-322-5901

Los Angeles Rams Football
Anaheim Stadium
2000 State College Blvd. at Katella Ave.
Anaheim, CA 92806
714-937-6767

Sacramento Kings Basketball
One Sports Parkway
Sacramento, CA 95834

San Diego Chargers Football
Jack Murphy Stadium
9449 Friars Rd. off Stadium Way & I-8
San Diego, CA 92108
619-563-8281

San Diego Padres Baseball
9449 Friars Road
P.O. Box 2000
San Diego, CA 92108
Information: 619-280-4636
Tickets: 619-283-4494

Oakland Athletics Baseball
Oakland Coliseum
Nimitz Fwy. & Hegenberger Rd.
Oakland, CA 94621
415-638-0500

San Francisco 49ers
Candlestick Park
Giants Dr. & Gilman Ave.
San Francisco, CA 94061
415-468-2249

San Francisco Giants
Candlestick Park
Giants Dr. & Gilman Ave.
San Francisco, CA 94124
415-467-8000

COLORADO

Denver Broncos Football
Mile High Stadium
1805 Bryant Street
Denver, CO 80216
303-433-7466

Denver Nuggets Basketball
McNichols Sports Arena
1635 Clay Street
Denver, CO 80204
303-893-DUNK

WASHINGTON, D.C.

Washington Redskins Football
Robert F. Kennedy Memorial Stadium
East Capitol and 22nd Streets, NE
Washington, DC 17247
Stadium Box Office: 202-546-3337
Ticket Office: 202-546-2222

FLORIDA

Miami Dolphins Football
Joe Robbie Stadium
NW 27th Ave. at NW 199th St.
North Miami, FL
305-623-6100

Miami Heat Basketball
Miami Arena
Miami, FL 33136

Tampa Bay Buccaneers
Tampa Stadium/Tampa Bay Performing Arts Center
4201 Dale Mabry
Tampa, FL 33607
813-872-7977

GEORGIA

Atlanta Braves Baseball
521 Capitol Ave., SW
Atlanta, GA 30312
Information: 404-522-7630
Tickets: 404-249-6400

Atlanta Falcons Football
One Atlanta Plaza
950 E Paces Ferry Rd., Suite 2920
Atlanta, GA 30326
404-261-5400

Atlanta Hawks Basketball
Omni Sports Arena
100 Techwood Dr.
Atlanta, GA 30303
404-827-DUNK (3865)

ILLINOIS

Chicago Bears Football
Soldier Field
425 E McFetridge Dr.
Chicago, IL 60605
Tickets: 312-663-5408

Chicago Blackhawks Hockey
Chicago Stadium
1800 Madison St.
Chicago, IL 60612
312-733-5300

Chicago Bulls Basketball
Chicago Stadium
1800 Madison St.
Chicago, IL 60612
Information: 312-902-1919
Tickets: 312-733-5300

Chicago Cubs Baseball
Wrigley Field
1060 W Addison St.
Chicago, IL 60613
312-404-CUBS (2827)
Ticketmaster: 312-347-CUBS (2827)

Chicago White Sox Baseball
Comiskey Park
333 W 35th St.
Chicago, IL 60616
312-942-1000
Ticketmaster: 312-559-1212

INDIANA

Indianapolis Colts Football
7001 W 56th St.
Indianapolis, IN 46254
317-297-7000

Indiana Pacers Basketball
300 E Market St.
Indianapolis, IN 46204
Information: 317-263-2100
Tickets: 317-639-2112

LOUISIANA

New Orleans Saints Football
1599 Poydras
New Orleans, LA
504-522-2600

MARYLAND

Baltimore Bullets Basketball
Capital Centre
1 Harry S. Truman Dr.
off Beltway Exits 15A or 17A
Landover, MD
Information: 301-350-3400
Ticketron: 301-432-0200

Baltimore Orioles Baseball
Memorial Stadium
33rd St. and Ellerslie Ave.
Baltimore, MD
Information: 301-243-9800
Tickets: 301-338-1300

Washington Bullets Basketball
Capital Centre
Landover, MD 20785

Washington Capitals Hockey
Capital Centre
Landover, MD 20785

MASSACHUSETTS

Boston Bruins Hockey
Boston Garden
150 Causeway
Boston, MA
617-227-3206

Boston Celtics Basketball
Boston Garden
150 Causeway
Boston, MA
617-227-3206

Boston Red Sox Baseball
Fenway Park
Kenmore Sq.
Boston, MA
617-267-8661

New England Patriots
Sullivan Stadium
Route 1
Foxboro, MA
800-543-1776

MICHIGAN

Detroit Lions Football
1200 Featherstone
P.O. Box 4200
Pontiac, MI 48057
313-335-4131

Detroit Pistons Basketball
3700 Lapeer Rd.
Auburn Hills, MI 48057
313-377-8600

Detroit Red Wings Hockey
600 Civic Center Dr.
Detroit, MI 48226
313-567-7333

Detroit Tigers Baseball
Tiger Stadium
Trumbull and Michigan Avenues
Detroit, MI 48216
313-962-4000

MINNESOTA

Minnesota North Stars Hockey
Met Center
7901 Cedar Ave. S.
Minneapolis, MN 55420
612-853-9300

Minnesota Timberwolves Basketball
730 Hennepin Ave.
Minneapolis, MN 55403

Minnesota Twins Baseball
501 Chicago Ave., S.
Minneapolis, MN 55415
612-375-7444
Hubert H. Humphrey Metrodome
Minneapolis, MN
Information: 612-375-7444
Tickets: 612-375-1116

Minnesota Vikings Football
9520 Viking Drive
Eden Prairie, MN 55344
612-828-6500

Hubert H. Humphrey Metrodome
900 S 5th St.
Minneapolis, MN
Information: 612-332-0386
Tickets: 612-333-8828

MISSOURI

Kansas City Royals Baseball
P.O. Box 419969
Kansas City, MO 64141
Tickets: 816-921-8000

Kansas City Chiefs Football
One Arrowhead Dr.
Kansas City, MO 64129
816-924-9300

St. Louis Blues Hockey
5700 Oakland
St. Louis, MO 63110
Information: 314-781-5300
Tickets: 314-781-2583

St. Louis Cardinals Baseball
250 Stadium Plaza
St. Louis, MO 63102
314-421-2400

NEW JERSEY

Meadowlands Sports Complex
(Giants Stadium, Meadowlands Racetrack and Brendan Byrne Arena)
East Rutherford, NJ
201-935-8500

New Jersey Nets Basketball
New Jersey Devils Hockey
Byrne Meadowlands Arena
Meadowlands Sports Complex
East Rutherford, NJ
201-935-3900

NEW YORK

Buffalo Bills Football
One Bills Drive
Orchard Park, NY 14127

Buffalo Sabres Hockey
Memorial Auditorium
Buffalo, NY 14202

New York Giants Football
New York Jets Football
Giants Stadium
Meadowlands Sports Complex
East Rutherford, NJ
201-935-3900

New York Islanders Hockey
Nassau Coliseum
Hempstead Turnpike
Uniondale, NY
516-794-9300

New York Mets Baseball
Shea Stadium
126th St. and Roosevelt Ave.
Flushing, NY
718-507-8499

New York Rangers Hockey
New York Knickerbockers Basketball
Ticket Information: 212-563-8300
Charge Cards: 212-307-7171
516-888-9000,
201-507-8900,
914-965-2700

New York Yankees Baseball
Yankee Stadium
161st St. and River Ave.
Bronx, NY
212-293-6000

NORTH CAROLINA

Charlotte Hornets Basketball
Two First Union Center (#2600)
Charlotte, NC 28282

OHIO

Cincinnati Bengals Football
Riverfront Stadium
Cincinnati, OH 45202
513-621-3550

Cincinnati Reds Baseball
205 W 4th
Cincinnati, OH 45202
Hot Line: 513-421-7887
Tickets: 513-221-7337

Cleveland Browns Football
Cleveland Stadium
434 Eastland
Cleveland, OH 44114
Information: 216-234-3838
Tickets: 216-696-3800

Cleveland Cavaliers Basketball
2923 Streetsboro
Richfield, OH 44286
Information: 216-659-9100
Tickets: 216-659-2140

Cleveland Indians Baseball
Cleveland Stadium
Cleveland, OH 44114
216-861-1200
800-729-6464

OREGON

Portland Trailblazers Basketball
Lloyd Building
700 N.E. Multnomah St. (#600)
Portland, OR 97232

PENNSYLVANIA

Philadelphia Eagles Football
Veteran's Stadium
Broad St. & Pattison Ave.
Philadelphia, PA 19148-5201
Tickets: 215-463-5500

Philadelphia Phillies Baseball
Veteran's Stadium
Broad St. & Pattison Ave.
Philadelphia, PA 19101
Tickets: 215-463-1000

Philadelphia 76ers Basketball
The Spectrum
Broad St. & Pattison Ave.
Philadelphia, PA 19147
215-339-7676

Philadelphia Flyers Hockey
The Spectrum
Broad St. & Pattison Ave.
Philadelphia, PA 19148-5290
215-755-9700

Pittsburgh Penguins Hockey
Civic Arena
Auditorium Place
Pittsburgh, PA 15219
412-323-7328

Pittsburgh Pirates Baseball
Three Rivers Stadium
600 Stadium Circle
Pittsburgh, PA 15212
412-321-2827

Pittsburgh Steelers Football
Three Rivers Stadium
600 Stadium Circle
Pittsburgh, PA 15212
412-323-1200

TEXAS

Texas Rangers Baseball
Arlington Stadium
1700 Copeland Rd.
Arlington, TX 76010
214-273-5000 or 5100

Dallas Cowboys Football
Cowboys Center
One Cowboy Parkway
Irving, TX 75063-4727
214-566-2500
(800) 877-8587

Dallas Mavericks Basketball
Reunion Arena
777 Sports St.
Dallas, TX 75207
214-658-7068

San Antonio Spurs Basketball
600 East Market (#102)
San Antonio, TX 78205

Texas Rangers Baseball
Arlington Stadium
1700 Copeland Rd.
Arlington, TX 76010
214-273-5000 or 5100

Houston Astros Baseball
8400 Kirby Drive
Houston, TX 72054
713-526-1709
Information: 713-799-9555
Teletron: **(800) 284-5780**

Houston Oilers Football
6910 Fannin St.
Houston, TX 77030
713-797-1000

Houston Rockets Basketball
10 Greenway Plaza
Houston, TX 77046
Tickets: 713-627-0600

UTAH

Utah Jazz Basketball
5 Triad Center
Salt Palace Convention Center
Salt Lake City, UT 84180
801-355-3865

WASHINGTON

Seattle Mariners Baseball
P.O. Box 4100
Seattle, WA 98104
206-628-3555

Seattle Seahawks Football
5305 Lake Washington Boulevard
Kirkland, WA 98033
206-827-9777

Seattle Supersonics Basketball
P.O. Box 900911
Seattle, WA 98109-9711
206-281-5800

Kingdome (Mariners and Seahawks)
201 S King
Seattle, WA
206-296-3111

WISCONSIN

Green Bay Packers Football
Milwaukee County Stadium
201 S 46th St.
Milwaukee, WI 54307
414-933-1818

Milwaukee Admirals Hockey
Bradley Center
1001 N 4th St.
Milwaukee, WI
414-227-0400

Milwaukee Brewers Baseball
Milwaukee County Stadium
201 S 46th St.
Milwaukee, WI 53214
414-342-2717

Milwaukee Bucks Basketball
Bradley Center
1001 N 4th St.
Milwaukee, WI 53203
414-227-0400

CANADA

Toronto Blue Jays Baseball
Exhibition Stadium
Toronto, ON
Canada M5C 2K7

Toronto Maple Leafs Hockey
60 Carlton St.
Toronto, ON
Canada M5B 1L1

Calgary Flames Hockey
P.O. Box 1540, Station M
Calgary, AL
Canada T2P 3B9

Montreal Canadien's Hockey
2313 St. Catherine St. West
Montreal, QU
Canada H3H 1N2

Montreal Expos Baseball
Olympic Stadium
Montreal, QU
Canada

Quebec Nordiques Hockey
2205 Ave. du Colisee
Quebec, QU
Canada G1L 4W7

Vancouver Canucks Hockey
100 North Renfrew St.
Vancouver, BC
Canada V5K 3N7

Winnipeg Jets Hockey
15-1430 Maroons Rd.
Winnipeg, MB
Canada R3G 0L5

Part IV

Where to Write for Vital Records

Births, Deaths, Marriages, and Divorces

INTRODUCTION

As part of its mission to provide access to data and information relating to the health of the Nation, the National Center for Health Statistics produces a number of publications containing reference and statistical materials. The purpose of this publication is solely to provide information about individual vital records maintained only on file in State or local vital statistics offices.

An official certificate of every birth, death, marriage, and divorce should be on file in the locality where the event occurred. The Federal Government does not maintain files or indexes of these records. These records are filed permanently either in a State vital statistics office or in a city, county, or other local office.

To obtain a certified copy of any of the certificates, write or go to the vital statistics office in the State or area where the event occurred. Addresses and fees are given for each event in the State or area concerned.

To ensure that you receive an accurate record for your request and that your request is filled expeditiously, please follow the steps outlined below for the information in which you are interested:

- Write to the appropriate office to have your request filled.
- Under the appropriate office, information has been included for birth and death records concerning whether the State will accept checks or money orders and to whom they should be made payable. This same information would apply when marriage and divorce records are available from the State office. However, it is impossible for us to list fees and addresses for all county offices where marriage and divorce records may be obtained.
- For all certified copies requested, make check or money order payable for the correct amount for the number of copies you want to obtain. Cash is not recommended because the office cannot refund cash lost in transit.
- Because all fees are subject to change, a telephone number has been included in the information for each State for use in verifying the current fee.
- Type or print all names and addresses in the letter.
- Give the following facts when writing for **birth or death records:**

1. Full name of person whose record is being requested.
2. Sex.
3. Parents' names, including maiden name of mother.
4. Month, day, and year of birth or death.
5. Place of birth or death (city or town, county, and State; and name of hospital, if known).
6. Purpose for which copy is needed.
7. Relationship to person whose record is being requested.

- Give the following facts when writing for **marriage records:**

1. Full names of bride and groom.
2. Month, day, and year of marriage.
3. Place of marriage (city or town, county, and State).

4. Purpose for which copy is needed.
5. Relationship to persons whose record is being requested.

- Give the following facts when writing for **divorce records:**

1. Full names of husband and wife.
2. Date of divorce or annulment.
3. Place of divorce or annulment.
4. Type of final decree.
5. Purpose for which copy is needed.
6. Relationship to persons whose record is being requested.

State/Event	Cost	Where to Write	Remarks
Alabama			
Birth or Death	$5.00	Center for Health Statistics State Department of Public Health 434 Monroe Street Montgomery, AL 36130-1701	State office has had records since January 1908. Additional copies at same time are $2.00 each. Fee for special searches is $5.00 per hour. Money order or certified check should be made payable to **Center for Health Statistics.** Personal checks are not accepted. To verify current fees, the telephone number is **(205) 242-5033.**
Marriage	$5.00	Same as Birth or Death	State office has had records since August 1936.
	Varies	See remarks	Probate Judge in county where license was issued.
Divorce	$5.00	Same as Birth or Death	State office has had records since January 1950.
	Varies	See remarks	Clerk or Register of Court of Equity in county where divorce was granted.
Alaska			
Birth or Death	$7.00	Department of Health and Social Services Bureau of Vital Statistics P.O. Box H-02G Juneau, AK 99811-0675	State office has had records since January 1913. Money order should be made payable to **Bureau of Vital Statistics.** Personal checks are not accepted. To verify current fees, the telephone number is **(907) 465-3391.** This will be a **recorded** message.
Marriage	$7.00	Same as Birth or Death	State office has had records since 1913.
Divorce	$7.00	Same as Birth or Death	State office has had records since 1950.
	Varies	See remarks	Clerk of Superior Court in judicial district where divorce was granted. Juneau and Ketchikan (First District), Nome (Second District), Anchorage (Third District), Fairbanks (Fourth District).
American Samoa			
Birth or Death	$2.00	Registrar of Vital Statistics Vital Statistics Section Government of American Samoa Pago Pago, AS 96799	Registrar has had records since 1900. Money order should be made payable to **ASG Treasurer.** Personal checks are not accepted. To verify current fees, the telephone number is **(684) 633-1222, extension 214.** Personal identification required before record will be sent.
Marriage	$2.00	Same as Birth or Death	
Divorce	$1.00	High Court of American Samoa Tutuila, AS 96799	
Arizona			
Birth (long form) Birth (short form) Death	$8.00 $5.00 $5.00	Vital Records Section Arizona Department of Health Services P.O. Box 3887 Phoenix, AZ 85030	State office has had records since July 1909 and abstracts of records filed in counties before then. Check or money order should be made payable to **Office of Vital Records.** Personal checks are accepted. To verify current fees, the telephone number is **(602) 542-1080.** This will be a **recorded** message. Applicants must submit a copy of picture identification or have their request notarized.
Marriage	Varies	See remarks	Clerk of Superior Court in county where license was issued.
Divorce	Varies	See remarks	Clerk of Superior Court in county where divorce was granted.

State/Event	Cost	Where to Write	Remarks
Arkansas			
Birth Death	$5.00 $4.00	Division of Vital Records Arkansas Department of Health 4815 West Markham Street Little Rock, AR 72201	State office has had records since February 1914 and some original Little Rock and Fort Smith records from 1881. Additional copies of death record, when requested at the same time, are $1.00 each. Check or money order should be made payable to **Arkansas Department of Health.** Personal checks are accepted. To verify current fees, the telephone number is **(501) 661-2336.** This will be a **recorded** message.
Marriage	$5.00	Same as Birth or Death	Coupons since 1917.
	Varies	See remarks	Full certified copy may be obtained from County Clerk in county where license was issued.
Divorce	$5.00	Same as Birth or Death	Coupons since 1923.
	Varies	See remarks	Full certified copy may be obtained from Circuit or Chancery Clerk in county where divorce was granted.
California			
Birth Death	$11.00 $7.00	Vital Statistics Section Department of Health Services 410 N Street Sacramento, CA 95814	State office has had records since July 1905. For earlier records, write to County Recorder in county where event occurred. Check or money order should be made payable to **State Registrar, Department of Health Services** or **Vital Statistics.** Personal checks are accepted. To verify current fees, the telephone number is **(916) 445-2684.**
Heirloom Birth	$30.00	Same as Birth or Death	Decorative birth certificate (11″ x 14″) suitable for framing.
Marriage	$11.00	Same as Birth or Death	State office has had records since July 1905. For earlier records, write to County Recorder in county where event occurred.
Divorce	$11.00	Same as Birth or Death	Fee is for search and identification of county where certified copy can be obtained. Certified copies are not available from State Health Department.
	Varies	See remarks	Clerk of Superior Court in county where divorce was granted.
Canal Zone			
Birth or Death	$2.00	Panama Canal Commission Vital Statistics Clerk APO Miami, FL 34011	Records available from May 1904 to September 1979.
Marriage	$1.00	Same as Birth or Death	Records available from May 1904 to September 1979.
Divorce	$0.50	Same as Birth or Death	Records available from May 1904 to September 1979.
Colorado			
Birth or Death	$6.00 Regular service $10.00 Priority service	Vital Records Section Colorado Department of Health 4210 East 11th Avenue Denver, CO 80220	State office has had death records since 1900 and birth records since 1910. State office also has birth records for some counties for years before 1910. Regular service means the record is mailed within 3 weeks. Priority service means the record is mailed within 5 days. Check or money order should be made payable to **Colorado Department of Health.** Personal checks are accepted. To verify current fees, the telephone number is **(303) 320-8474.** This will be a **recorded** message.
Marriage	See remarks	Same as Birth or Death	Certified copies are not available from State Health Department. Statewide index of records for 1900–39 and 1975 to present. Fee for verification is $6.00.

State/Event	Cost	Where to Write	Remarks
	Varies	See remarks	Copies available from County Clerk in county where license was issued.
Divorce	See remarks	Same as Birth or Death	Certified copies are not available from State Health Department. Statewide index of records for 1900–39 and 1968 to present. Fee for verification is $6.00.
	Varies	See remarks	Copies available from Clerk of District Court in county where divorce was granted.
Connecticut			
Birth or Death	$5.00	Vital Records Department of Health Services 150 Washington Street Hartford, CT 06106	State office has had records since July 1897. For earlier records, write to Registrar of Vital Statistics in town or city where event occurred. Check or money order should be made payable to **Department of Health Services.** Personal checks are accepted. FAX requests are not accepted. Must have original signature on request. To verify current fees, the telephone number is **(203) 566-2334.** This will be a **recorded** message.
Marriage	$5.00	Same as Birth or Death	Records since July 1897.
		See remarks	Registrar of Vital Statistics in town where license was issued.
Divorce		See remarks	Index of records since 1947. Applicant must contact Clerk of Superior Court where divorce was granted. State office does not have divorce decrees and cannot issue certified copies.
Delaware			
Birth or Death	$5.00	Office of Vital Statistics Division of Public Health P.O. Box 637 Dover, DE 19903	State office has death records since 1930 and birth records since 1920. Additional copies of the same record requested at the same time are $3.00 each. Check or money order should be made payable to **Office of Vital Statistics.** Personal checks are accepted. To verify current fees, the telephone number is **(302) 736-4721.**
Marriage	$5.00	Same as Birth or Death	Records since 1930. Additional copies of the same record requested at the same time are $3.00 each.
Divorce	See remarks	Same as Birth or Death	Records since 1935. Inquiries will be forwarded to appropriate office. Fee for search and verification of essential facts of divorce is $5.00 for each 5-year period searched. Certified copies are not available from State office.
	$2.00	See remarks	Prothonotary in county where divorce was granted up to 1975. For divorces granted after 1975 the parties concerned should contact Family Court in county where divorce was granted.
District of Columbia			
Birth or Death	$8.00	Vital Records Branch Room 3009 425 I Street, NW Washington, DC 20001	Office has had death records since 1855 and birth records since 1874 but no death records were filed during the Civil War. Cashiers check or money order should be made payable to **DC Treasurer.** To verify current fees, the telephone number is **(202) 727-9281.**
Marriage	$5.00	Marriage Bureau 515 5th Street, NW Washington, DC 20001	
Divorce	$2.00	Clerk, Superior Court for the District of Columbia, Family Division	Records since September 16, 1956.

State/Event	Cost	Where to Write	Remarks
		500 Indiana Avenue, NW Washington, DC 20001	
	Varies	Clerk, U.S. District Court for the District of Columbia Washington, DC 20001	Records before September 16, 1956.
Florida			
Birth Death	$8.00 $4.00	Department of Health and Rehabilitative Services Office of Vital Statistics 1217 Pearl Street Jacksonville, FL 32202	State office has some birth records dating back to April 1865 and some death records dating back to August 1877. The majority of records date from January 1917. (If the exact date is unknown, the fee is $8.00 [births] or $4.00 [deaths] for the first year searched and $2.00 for each additional year up to a maximum of $50.00. Fee includes one certification of record if found or certified statement stating record not on file.) Additional copies are $3.00 each when requested at the same time. Check or money order should be made payable to **Office of Vital Statistics.** Personal checks are accepted. To verify current fees, the telephone number is **(904) 359-6900.** This will be a **recorded** message.
Marriage	$4.00	Same as Birth or Death	Records since June 6, 1927. (If the exact date is unknown, the fee is $4.00 for the first year searched and $2.00 for each additional year up to a maximum of $50.00. Fee includes one copy of record if found or certified statement stating record not on file.) Additional copies are $3.00 each when requested at the same time.
Divorce	$4.00	Same as Birth or Death	Records since June 6, 1927. (If the exact date is unknown, the fee is $4.00 for the first year searched and $2.00 for each additional year up to a maximum of $50.00. Fee includes one copy of record if found or certified statement stating record not on file.) Additional copies are $3.00 each when requested at the same time.
Georgia			
Birth or Death	$3.00	Georgia Department of Human Resources Vital Records Unit Room 217-H 47 Trinity Avenue, SW Atlanta, GA 30334	State office has had records since January 1919. For earlier records in Atlanta or Savannah, write to County Health Department in county where event occurred. Additional copies of same record ordered at same time are $1.00 each except birth cards, which are $4.00 each. Money order should be made payable to **Vital Records, GA. DHR.** Personal checks are not accepted. To verify current fees, the telephone number is **(404) 656-4900.** This is a **recorded** message.
Marriage	$3.00	Same as Birth or Death	Centralized State records since June 9, 1952. Certified copies are issued at State office. Inquiries about marriages occurring before June 9, 1952, will be forwarded to appropriate Probate Judge in county where license was issued.
	$3.00	See remarks	Probate Judge in county where license issued.
Divorce	Varies	See remarks	Centralized State records since June 9, 1952. Certified copies are not issued at State office. Inquiries will be forwarded to appropriate Clerk of Superior Court in county where divorce was granted.
	$3.00	See remarks	Clerk of Superior Court in county where divorce was granted.
Guam			
Birth or Death	$5.00	Office of Vital Statistics Department of Public Health and Social Services Government of Guam	Office has had records since October 16, 1901. Money order should be made payable to **Treasurer of Guam.** Personal checks are not accepted. To verify current fees, the telephone number is **(671) 734-7292.**

State/Event	Cost	Where to Write	Remarks
		P.O. Box 2816 Agana, GU, M.I. 96910	
Marriage	$5.00	Same as Birth or Death	
Divorce	Varies	Clerk, Superior Court of Guam Agana, GU, M.I. 96910	
Hawaii			
Birth or Death	$2.00	Office of Health Status Monitoring State Department of Health P.O. Box 3378 Honolulu, HI 96801	State office has had records since 1853. Check or money order should be made payable to **State Department of Health.** Personal checks are accepted for the correct amount only. To verify current fees, the telephone number is **(808) 548-5819.** This is a **recorded** message.
Marriage	$2.00	Same as Birth or Death	
Divorce	$2.00	Same as Birth or Death	Records since July 1951.
	Varies	See remarks	Circuit Court in county where divorce was granted.
Idaho			
Birth or Death	$8.00	Vital Statistics Unit Idaho Department of Health and Welfare 450 West State Street Statehouse Mail Boise, ID 83720-9990	State office has had records since 1911. For records from 1907 to 1911, write to County Recorder in county where event occurred. Check or money order should be made payable to **Idaho Vital Statistics.** Personal checks are accepted. To verify current fees, the telephone number is **(208) 334-5988.** This is a **recorded** message.
Marriage	$8.00	Same as Birth or Death	Records since 1947. Earlier records are with County Recorder in county where license was issued.
	Varies	See remarks	County Recorder in county where license was issued.
Divorce	$8.00	Same as Birth or Death	Records since January 1947. Earlier records are with County Recorder in county where divorce was granted.
	Varies	See remarks	County records in county where divorce was granted.
Illinois			
Birth or Death	$15.00 certified copy $10.00 certification	Division of Vital Records Illinois Department of Public Health 605 West Jefferson Street Springfield, IL 62702-5079	State office has had records since January 1916. For earlier records and for copies of State records since January 1916, write to County Clerk in county where event occurred (county fees vary). The fee for a search of the State files is $10.00. If the record is found, one certified copy is issued at no additional charge. Additional certified copies of the same record ordered at the same time are $2.00 each. The fee for a full certified copy is $15.00. Additional certified copies of the same record ordered at the same time are $2.00 each. Money orders, certified checks, or personal checks should be made payable to **Illinois Department of Public Health.** To verify current fees, the telephone number is **(217) 782-6553.** This will be a **recorded** message.
Marriage	$5.00	Same as Birth or Death	Records since January 1962. All items may be verified (fee $5.00). For certified copies, inquiries will be forwarded to appropriate office. Certified copies are NOT available from State office.
Divorce	$5.00	Same as Birth or Death	Records since January 1962. Selected items may be verified (fee $5.00). Certified copies are NOT available from State office. For certified copies, write to the Clerk of Circuit Court in county where divorce was granted.

State/Event	Cost	Where to Write	Remarks
Indiana			
Birth Death	$6.00 $4.00	Vital Records Section State Board of Health 1330 West Michigan Street P.O. Box 1964 Indianapolis, IN 46206-1964	State office has had birth records since October 1907 and death records since 1900. Additional copies of the same record ordered at the same time are $1.00 each. For earlier records, write to Health Officer in city or county where event occurred. Check or money order should be made payable to **Indiana State Board of Health.** Personal checks are accepted. To verify current fees, the telephone number is **(317) 633-0274.**
Marriage	See remarks	Same as Birth or Death	Marriage index since 1958. Certified copies are not available from State Health Department.
	Varies	See remarks	Clerk of Circuit Court or Clerk of Superior Court in county where license was issued.
Divorce	Varies	See remarks	County Clerk in county where divorce was granted.
Iowa			
Birth or Death	$6.00	Iowa Department of Public Health Vital Records Section Lucas Office Building 321 East 12th Street Des Moines, IA 50319	State office has had records since July 1880. Check or money order should be made payable to **Iowa Department of Public Health.** To verify current fees, the telephone number is **(515) 281-5871.** This will be a **recorded** message.
Marriage	$6.00	Same as Birth or Death	State office has had records since July 1880.
Divorce	See remarks	Same as Birth or Death	Brief statistical record only since 1906. Inquiries will be forwarded to appropriate office. Certified copies are not available from State Health Department.
	$6.00	See remarks	Clerk of District Court in county where divorce was granted.
Kansas			
Birth or Death	$6.00	Office of Vital Statistics Kansas State Department of Health and Environment 900 Jackson Street Topeka, KS 66612-1290	State office has had records since July 1911. For earlier records, write to County Clerk in county where event occurred. Additional copies of same record ordered at same time are $3.00 each. Check or money order should be made payable to **State Registrar of Vital Statistics.** Personal checks are accepted. To verify current fees, the telephone number is **(913) 296-1400.** This will be a **recorded** message.
Marriage	$6.00	Same as Birth or Death	State office has had records since May 1913.
	Varies	See remarks	District Judge in county where license was issued.
Divorce	$6.00	Same as Birth or Death	State office has had records since July 1951.
	Varies	See remarks	Clerk of District Court in county where divorce was granted.
Kentucky			
Birth Death	$5.00 $4.00	Office of Vital Statistics Department for Health Services 275 East Main Street Frankfort, KY 40621	State office has had records since January 1911 and some records for the cities of Louisville, Lexington, Covington, and Newport before then. Check or money order should be made payable to **Kentucky State Treasurer.** Personal checks are accepted. To verify current fees, the telephone number is **(502) 564-4212.**
Marriage	$4.00	Same as Birth or Death	Records since June 1958.
	Varies	See remarks	Clerk of County Court in county where license was issued.
Divorce	$4.00	Same as Birth or Death	Records since June 1958.
	Varies	See remarks	Clerk of Circuit Court in county where decree was issued.

State/Event	Cost	Where to Write	Remarks
Louisiana			
Birth (long form)	$8.00	Vital Records Registry Office of Public Health 325 Loyola Avenue New Orleans, LA 70112	State office has had records since July 1914. Birth records for City of New Orleans are available from 1790, and death records from 1803. Check or money order should be made payable to **Vital Records.** Personal checks are accepted. To verify current fees, the telephone number is **(504) 568-2561.**
Birth (short form)	$5.00		
Death	$5.00		
Marriage			
Orleans Parish	$5.00	Same as Birth or Death	
Other Parishes	Varies	See remarks	Certified copies are issued by Clerk of Court in parish where license was issued.
Divorce	Varies	See remarks	Clerk of Court in parish where divorce was granted.
Maine			
Birth or Death	$5.00	Office of Vital Records Human Services Building Station 11 State House Augusta, ME 04333	State office has had records since 1892. For earlier records, write to the municipality where the event occurred. Additional copies of same record ordered at same time are $2.00 each. Check or money order should be made payable to **Treasurer, State of Maine.** Personal checks are accepted. To verify current fees, the telephone number is **(207) 289-3184.**
Marriage	$5.00	Same as Birth or Death	Additional copies of same record ordered at same time are $2.00 each.
Divorce	$5.00	Same as Birth or Death	Records since January 1892.
	Varies	See remarks	Clerk of District Court in judicial division where divorce was granted.
Maryland			
Birth or Death	$4.00	Division of Vital Records Department of Health and Mental Hygiene Metro Executive Building 4201 Patterson Avenue P.O. Box 68760 Baltimore, MD 21215-0020	State office has had records since August 1898. Records for City of Baltimore are available from January 1875. Will not do research for genealogical studies. Must apply to State of Maryland Archives, 350 Rowe Blvd., Annapolis, MD 21401, (301) 974-3914. Check or money order should be made payable to **Division of Vital Records.** Personal checks are accepted. To verify current fees, the telephone number is **(301) 225-5988.** This will be a **recorded** message.
Marriage	$4.00	Same as Birth or Death	Records since June 1951.
	Varies	See remarks	Clerk of Circuit Court in county where license was issued or Clerk of Court of Common Pleas of Baltimore City (for licenses issued in City of Baltimore).
Divorce Verification only	$4.00	Same as Birth or Death	Records since January 1961. Certified copies are not available from State office. Some items may be verified.
	Varies	See remarks	Clerk of Circuit Court in county where divorce was granted.
Massachusetts			
Birth or Death	$6.00	Registry of Vital Records and Statistics 150 Tremont Street, Room B-3 Boston, MA 02111	State office has records since 1896. For earlier records, write to The Massachusetts Archives at Columbia Point, 220 Morrissey Boulevard, Boston, MA 02125, (617) 727-2816. Check or money order should be made payable to **Commonwealth of Massachusetts.** Personal checks are accepted. To verify current fees, the telephone number is **(617) 727-7388.** This will be a **recorded** message.

State/Event	Cost	Where to Write	Remarks
Marriage	$6.00	Same as Birth or Death	Records since 1896.
Divorce	See remarks	Same as Birth or Death	Index only since 1952. Inquirer will be directed where to send request. Certified copies are not available from State office.
	$3.00	See remarks	Registrar of Probate Court in county where divorce was granted.
Michigan			
Birth or Death	$10.00	Office of the State Registrar and Center for Health Statistics Michigan Department of Public Health 3423 North Logan Street Lansing, MI 48909	State office has had records since 1867. Copies of records since 1867 may also be obtained from County Clerk in county where event occurred. Fees vary from county to county. Detroit records may be obtained from the City of Detroit Health Department for births occurring since 1893 and for deaths since 1897. Check or money order should be made payable to **State of Michigan.** Personal checks are accepted. To verify current fees, the telephone number is **(517) 335-8655.** This will be a **recorded** message.
Marriage	$10.00	Same as Birth or Death	Records since April 1867.
	Varies	See remarks	County Clerk in county where license was issued.
Divorce	$10.00	Same as Birth or Death	Records since 1897.
	Varies	See remarks	County Clerk in county where divorce was granted.
Minnesota			
Birth Death	$11.00 $8.00	Minnesota Department of Health Section of Vital Statistics 717 Delaware Street, SE P.O. Box 9441 Minneapolis, MN 55440	State office has had records since January 1908. Copies of earlier records may be obtained from Court Administrator in county where event occurred or from the St. Paul City Health Department if the event occurred in St. Paul. Additional copies of the birth record when ordered at the same time are $5.00 each. Additional copies of the death record when ordered at the same time are $2.00 each. Check or money order should be made payable to **Treasurer, State of Minnesota.** Personal checks are accepted. To verify current fees, the telephone number is **(612) 623-5121.**
Marriage	See remarks	Same as Birth or Death	Statewide index since January 1958. Inquiries will be forwarded to appropriate office. Certified copies are not available from State Department of Health.
	$8.00	See remarks	Court Administrator in county where license was issued. Additional copies of the marriage record when ordered at the same time are $2.00 each.
Divorce	See remarks	Same as Birth or Death	Index since January 1970. Certified copies are not available from State office.
	$8.00	See remarks	Court Administrator in county where divorce was granted.
Mississippi			
Birth Birth (short form) Death	$11.00 $6.00 $5.00	Vital Records State Department of Health 2423 North State Street Jackson, MS 39216	State office has had records since 1912. Full copies of birth certificates obtained within 1 year after the event are $5.00. Additional copies of same record ordered at same time are $2.00 each for birth; $1.00 each for death. For out-of-State requests only bank or postal money orders are accepted and should be made payable to **Mississippi State Department of Health.** Personal checks are accepted only for in-State requests. To verify current fees, the telephone number is **(601) 960-7981.** A **recorded** message may be reached on **(601) 960-7450.**
Marriage	$5.00	Same as Birth or Death	Statistical records only from January 1926 to July 1, 1938, and since January 1942.

State/Event	Cost	Where to Write	Remarks
	$3.00	See remarks	Circuit Clerk in county where license was issued.
Divorce	See remarks $0.50 per page plus $1.00 for certification	Same as Birth or Death	Records since January 1926. Certified copies are not available from State office. Inquiries will be forwarded to appropriate office.
	Varies	See remarks	Chancery Clerk in county where divorce was granted.
Missouri			
Birth or Death	$4.00	Department of Health Bureau of Vital Records 1730 East Elm P.O. Box 570 Jefferson City, MO 65102	State office has had records since January 1910. If event occurred in St. Louis (City), St. Louis County, or Kansas City before 1910, write to the City or County Health Department. Copies of these records are $3.00 each in St. Louis City and $5.00 each in St. Louis County. In Kansas City, $6.00 for first copy and $3.00 for each additional copy ordered at same time. Check or money order should be made payable to **Missouri Department of Health.** Personal checks are accepted. To verify current fees on birth records, the telephone number is **(314) 751-6387;** for death records, **(314) 751-6376.**
Marriage	No fee	Same as Birth or Death	Indexes since July 1948. Correspondent will be referred to appropriate Recorder of Deeds in county where license was issued.
	Varies	See remarks	Recorder of Deeds in county where license was issued.
Divorce	No fee	Same as Birth or Death	Indexes since July 1948. Certified copies are not available from State Health Department. Inquiries will be forwarded to appropriate office.
	Varies	See remarks	Clerk of Circuit Court in county where divorce was granted.
Montana			
Birth or Death	$5.00	Bureau of Records and Statistics State Department of Health and Environmental Sciences Helena, MT 59620	State office has had records since late 1907. Check or money order should be made payable to **Montana Department of Health and Environmental Sciences.** Personal checks are accepted. To verify current fees, the telephone number is **(406) 444-2614.**
Marriage	See remarks	Same as Birth or Death	Records since July 1943. Some items may be verified. Inquiries will be forwarded to appropriate office. Apply to county where license was issued if known. Certified copies are not available from State office.
	Varies	See remarks	Clerk of District Court in county where license was issued.
Divorce	See remarks	Same as Birth or Death	Records since July 1943. Some items may be verified. Inquiries will be forwarded to appropriate office. Apply to court where divorce was granted if known. Certified copies are not available from State office.
	Varies	See remarks	Clerk of District Court in county where divorce was granted.
Nebraska			
Birth Death	$6.00 $5.00	Bureau of Vital Statistics State Department of Health	State office has had records since late 1904. If birth occurred before then, write the State office for information.

State/Event	Cost	Where to Write	Remarks
		301 Centennial Mall South P.O. Box 95007 Lincoln, NE 68509-5007	Check or money order should be made payable to **Bureau of Vital Statistics.** Personal checks are accepted. To verify current fees, the telephone number is **(402) 471-2871.**
Marriage	$5.00	Same as Birth or Death	Records since January 1909.
	Varies	See remarks	County Court in county where license was issued.
Divorce	$5.00	Same as Birth or Death	Records since January 1909.
	Varies	See remarks	Clerk of District Court in county where divorce was granted.
Nevada			
Birth or Death	$7.00	Division of Health-Vital Statistics Capitol Complex 505 East King Street #102 Carson City, NV 89710	State office has records since July 1911. For earlier records, write to County Recorder in county where event occurred. Check or money order should be made payable to **Section of Vital Statistics.** Personal checks are accepted. To verify current fees, the telephone number is **(702) 885-4480.**
Marriage	See remarks	Same as Birth or Death	Indexes since January 1968. Certified copies are not available from State Health Department. Inquiries will be forwarded to appropriate office.
	Varies	See remarks	County Recorder in county where license was issued.
Divorce	See remarks	Same as Birth or Death	Indexes since January 1968. Certified copies are not available from State Health Department. Inquiries will be forwarded to appropriate office.
	Varies	See remarks	County Clerk in county where divorce was granted.
New Hampshire			
Birth or Death	$3.00	Bureau of Vital Records Health and Human Services Building 6 Hazen Drive Concord, NH 03301	State office has had records since 1640. Copies of records may be obtained from State office or from City or Town Clerk in place where event occurred. Check or money order should be made payable to **Treasurer, State of New Hampshire.** Personal checks are accepted. To verify current fees, the telephone number is **(603) 271-4654.** This will be a **recorded** message.
Marriage	$3.00	Same as Birth or Death	Records since 1640.
	Varies	See remarks	Town Clerk in town where license was issued.
Divorce	$3.00	Same as Birth or Death	Records since 1808.
	Varies	See remarks	Clerk of Superior Court where divorce was granted.
New Jersey			
Birth or Death	$4.00	State Department of Health Bureau of Vital Statistics South Warren and Market Streets CN 370 Trenton, NJ 08625	State office has had records since June 1878. Additional copies of same record ordered at same time are $2.00 each. If the exact date is unknown, the fee is an additional $1.00.
		Archives and History Bureau State Library Division State Department of Education Trenton, NJ 08625	For records from May 1848 to May 1878. Check or money order should be made payable to **New Jersey State Department of Health.** Personal checks are accepted. To verify current fees, the telephone number is **(609) 292-4087.** This will be a **recorded** message.
Marriage	$4.00	Same as Birth or Death	If the exact date is unknown, the fee is an additional $1.00 per year searched.

State/Event	Cost	Where to Write	Remarks
	$2.00	Archives and History Bureau State Library Division State Department of Education Trenton, NJ 08625	For records from May 1848 to May 1878.
Divorce	$2.00	Superior Court Chancery Division State House Annex Room 320 CN 971 Trenton, NJ 08625	The fee is for the first four pages. Additional pages cost $0.50 each.

New Mexico

State/Event	Cost	Where to Write	Remarks
Birth Death	$10.00 $5.00	Vital Statistics New Mexico Health Services Division 1190 St. Francis Drive Santa Fe, NM 87503	State office has had records since 1920 and delayed records since 1880. Check or money order should be made payable to **Vital Statistics.** Personal checks are accepted. To verify current fees, the telephone number is **(505) 827-2338.** This will be a **recorded** message.
Marriage	Varies	See remarks	County Clerk in county where license was issued.
Divorce	Varies	See remarks	Clerk of Superior Court where divorce was granted.

New York

(except New York City)

State/Event	Cost	Where to Write	Remarks
Birth or Death	$15.00	Vital Records Section State Department of Health Empire State Plaza Tower Building Albany, NY 12237-0023	State office has had records since 1880. For records before 1914 in Albany, Buffalo, and Yonkers, or before 1880 in any other city, write to Registrar of Vital Statistics in city where event occurred. For the rest of the State, except New York City, write to State office. Check or money order should be made payable to **New York State Department of Health.** Personal checks are accepted. To verify current fees, the telephone number is **(518) 474-3075.** This will be a **recorded** message.
Marriage	$5.00	Same as Birth or Death	Records from 1880 to present.
	$5.00	See remarks	For records from 1880–1907 and licenses issued in the cities of Albany, Buffalo, or Yonkers, apply to—Albany: City Clerk, City Hall, Albany, NY 12207; Buffalo: City Clerk, City Hall, Buffalo, NY 14202; Yonkers: Registrar of Vital Statistics, Health Center Building, Yonkers, NY 10701.
Divorce	$15.00	Same as Birth or Death	Records since January 1963.
	Varies	See remarks	County Clerk in county where divorce was granted.

New York City

State/Event	Cost	Where to Write	Remarks
Birth or Death	$5.00	Bureau of Vital Records Department of Health of New York City 125 Worth Street New York, NY 10013	Office has birth records since 1898 and death records since 1930. For Old City of New York (Manhattan and part of the Bronx) birth records for 1865-97 and death records for 1865–1929 write to Archives Division, Department of Records and Information Services, 31 Chambers Street, New York, NY 10007. Money order should be made payable to **New York City Department of Health.** To verify current fees, the telephone number is **(212) 619-4530.** This will be a **recorded** message.

State/Event	Cost	Where to Write	Remarks
Marriage			
Bronx Borough	$10.00	City Clerk's Office 1780 Grand Concourse Bronx, NY 10457	Records from 1847 to 1865: Archives Division, Department of Records and Information Services, 31 Chambers Street, New York, NY 10007, except Brooklyn records for this period which are filed with County Clerk's Office, Kings County, Supreme Court Building, Brooklyn, NY 11201. Additional copies of same record ordered at same time are $5.00 each. Records from 1866 to 1907: City Clerk's Office in borough where marriage was performed. Records from 1908 to May 12, 1943: New York City residents write to City Clerk's Office in the borough of bride's residence; nonresidents write to City Clerk's Office in borough where license was obtained. Records since May 13, 1943: City Clerk's Office in borough where license was issued.
Brooklyn Borough	$10.00	City Clerk's Office Municipal Building Brooklyn, NY 11201	
Manhattan Borough	$10.00	City Clerk's Office Municipal Building New York, NY 10007	
Queens Borough	$10.00	City Clerk's Office 120-55 Queens Boulevard Kew Gardens, NY 11424	
Staten Island Borough (no longer called Richmond)	$10.00	City Clerk's Office Staten Island Borough Hall Staten Island, NY 10301	
Divorce			See New York State.

North Carolina

State/Event	Cost	Where to Write	Remarks
Birth or Death	$5.00	Department of Environment, Health, and Natural Resources Division of Epidemiology Vital Records Section 225 North McDowell Street P.O. Box 27687 Raleigh, NC 27611-7687	State office has had birth records since October 1913 and death records since January 1, 1930. Death records from 1913 through 1929 are available from Archives and Records Section, State Records Center, 215 North Blount Street, Raleigh, NC 27602. Check or money order should be made payable to **Vital Records Section.** Personal checks are accepted. To verify current fees, the telephone number is **(919) 733-3526.**
Marriage	$5.00	Same as Birth or Death	Records since January 1962.
	$3.00	See remarks	Registrar of Deeds in county where marriage was performed.
Divorce	$5.00	Same as Birth or Death	Records since January 1958.
	Varies	See remarks	Clerk of Superior Court where divorce was granted.

North Dakota

State/Event	Cost	Where to Write	Remarks
Birth Death	$7.00 $5.00	Division of Vital Records State Capitol 600 East Boulevard Avenue Bismarck, ND 58505	State office has had some records since July 1893. Years from 1894 to 1920 are incomplete. Additional copies of birth records are $4.00 each; death records are $2.00 each. Money order should be made payable to **Division of Vital Records.** To verify current fees, the telephone number is **(701) 224-2360.**
Marriage	$5.00	Same as Birth or Death	Records since July 1925. Requests for earlier records will be forwarded to appropriate office. Additional copies are $2.00 each.
	Varies	See remarks	County Judge in county where license was issued.
Divorce	See remarks	Same as Birth or Death	Index of records since July 1949. Some items may be verified. Certified copies are not available from State Health Department. Inquiries will be forwarded to appropriate office.
	Varies	See remarks	Clerk of District Court in county where divorce was granted.

Northern Mariana Islands

State/Event	Cost	Where to Write	Remarks
Birth or Death	$3.00	Office of Vital Statistics Superior Court	No information available on years for which records are available. If any questions, contact the address shown.

State/Event	Cost	Where to Write	Remarks
		Commonwealth of the Northern Mariana Islands Saipan, MP 96950	
Marriage	$3.00	Same as Birth or Death	Money order or Bank Cashiers Check should be made payable to **Treasurer, CNMI.** Personal checks are not accepted. To verify current fees, the telephone number is **(670) 234-6401.**
Divorce	$2.50 plus $0.50 per page for Divorce Decree	Same as Birth or Death	
Ohio			
Birth or Death	$7.00	Division of Vital Statistics Ohio Department of Health G-20 Ohio Department Building 65 South Front Street Columbus, OH 43266-0333	State office has had birth records since December 20, 1908. For earlier birth and death records, write to the Probate Court in the county where the event occurred. The State Office has death records which occurred less than 50 years ago. Death records which occurred 50 or more years ago—through December 20, 1908—can be obtained from the Ohio Historical Society, Archives Library Division, 1985 Velma Avenue, Columbus, OH 43211-2497. Check or money order should be made payable to **State Treasury.** Personal checks are accepted. To verify current fees, the telephone number is **(614) 466-2531.** This will be a **recorded** message.
Marriage	See remarks	Same as Birth or Death	Records since September 1949. All items may be verified. Certified copies are not available from State Health Department. Inquiries will be referred to appropriate office.
	Varies	See remarks	Probate Judge in county where license was issued.
Divorce	See remarks	Same as Birth or Death	Records since September 1949. All items may be verified. Certified copies are not available from State Health Department. Inquiries will be forwarded to appropriate office.
	Varies	See remarks	Clerk of Court of Common Pleas in county where divorce was granted.
Oklahoma			
Birth or Death	$5.00	Vital Records Section State Department of Health 1000 Northeast 10th Street P.O. Box 53551 Oklahoma City, OK 73152	State office has had records since October 1908. Check or money order should be made payable to **Oklahoma State Department of Health.** Personal checks are accepted. To verify current fees, the telephone number is **(405) 271-4040.**
Marriage	Varies	See remarks	Clerk of Court in county where license was issued.
Divorce	Varies	See remarks	Clerk of Court in county where divorce was granted.
Oregon			
Birth or Death	$8.00	Oregon Health Division Vital Statistics Section P.O. Box 116 Portland, OR 97207	State office has had records since January 1903. Some earlier records for the City of Portland since approximately 1880 are available from the Oregon State Archives, 1005 Broadway, NE, Salem, OR 97310.
Heirloom Birth	$25.00	Same as Birth or Death	Presentation-style calligraphy certificate suitable for framing. Check or money order should be made payable to **Oregon Health Division.** To verify current fees, the telephone number is **(503) 229-5710.** This will be a **recorded** message.

State/Event	Cost	Where to Write	Remarks
Marriage	$8.00	Same as Birth or Death	Records since January 1906.
	Varies	See remarks	County Clerk in county where license was issued. County Clerks also have some records before 1906.
Divorce	$8.00	Same as Birth or Death	Records since 1925.
	Varies	See remarks	County Clerk in county where divorce was granted. County Clerks also have some records before 1925.
Pennsylvania			
Birth Wallet card Death	$4.00 $5.00 $3.00	Division of Vital Records State Department of Health Central Building 101 South Mercer Street P.O. Box 1528 New Castle, PA 16103	State office has had records since January 1906. For earlier records, write to Register of Wills, Orphans Court, in county seat of county where event occurred. Persons born in Pittsburgh from 1870 to 1905 or in Allegheny City, now part of Pittsburgh, from 1882 to 1905 should write to Office of Biostatistics, Pittsburgh Health Department, City-County Building, Pittsburgh, PA 15219. For events occurring in City of Philadelphia from 1860 to 1915, write to Vital Statistics, Philadelphia Department of Public Health, City Hall Annex, Philadelphia, PA 19107. Check or money order should be made payable to **Division of Vital Records.** Personal checks are accepted. To verify current fees, the telephone number is **(412) 656-3147.** This will be a **recorded** message.
Marriage	See remarks	Same as Birth or Death	Records since January 1906. Certified copies are not available from State Health Department. Inquiries will be forwarded to appropriate office.
	Varies	See remarks	Marriage License Clerks, County Court House, in county where license was issued.
Divorce	Varies	Same as Birth or Death	Records since January 1946. Certified copies are not available from State Health Department. Inquiries will be forwarded to appropriate office.
	Varies	See remarks	Prothonotary, Court House, in county seat of county where divorce was granted.
Puerto Rico			
Birth or Death	$2.00	Department of Health Demographic Registry P.O. Box 11854 Fernández Juncos Station San Juan, PR 00910	Central office has had records since July 22, 1931. Copies of earlier records may be obtained by writing to local Registrar (Registrador Demografico) in municipality where event occurred or by writing to central office for information. Money order should be made payable to **Secretary of the Treasury.** Personal checks are not accepted. To verify current fees, the telephone number is **(809) 728-7980.**
Marriage	$2.00	Same as Birth or Death	
Divorce	$2.00	Same as Birth or Death See remarks	Superior Court where divorce was granted.
Rhode Island			
Birth or Death	$5.00	Division of Vital Records Rhode Island Department of Health Room 101, Cannon Building 3 Capitol Hill Providence, RI 02908-5097	State office has had records since 1853. For earlier records, write to Town Clerk in town where event occurred. Additional copies of the same record ordered at the same time are $3.00 each. Money order should be made payable to **General Treasurer, State of Rhode Island.** To verify current fees, the telephone number is **(401) 277-2811.** This will be a **recorded** message.

State/Event	Cost	Where to Write	Remarks
Marriage	$5.00	Same as Birth or Death	Records since January 1853. Additional copies of the same record ordered at the same time are $3.00 each.
Divorce	$1.00	Clerk of Family Court 1 Dorrance Plaza Providence, RI 02903	
South Carolina			
Birth or Death	$6.00	Office of Vital Records and Public Health Statistics South Carolina Department of Health and Environmental Control 2600 Bull Street Columbia, SC 29201	State office has had records since January 1915. City of Charleston births from 1877 and deaths from 1821 are on file at Charleston County Health Department. Ledger entries of Florence City births and deaths from 1895 to 1914 are on file at Florence County Health Department. Ledger entries of Newberry City births and deaths from the late 1800s are on file at Newberry County Health Department. These are the only early records obtainable. Check or money order should be made payable to **Office of Vital Records.** Personal checks are accepted. To verify current fees, the telephone number is **(803) 734-4830.**
Marriage	$6.00	Same as Birth or Death	Records since July 1950.
	Varies	See remarks	Records since July 1911: Probate Judge in county where license was issued.
Divorce	$6.00	Same as Birth or Death	Records since July 1962.
	Varies	See remarks	Records since April 1949: Clerk of county where petition was filed.
South Dakota			
Birth or Death	$5.00	State Department of Health Center for Health Policy and Statistics Vital Records 523 E. Capitol Pierre, SD 57501	State office has had records since July 1905 and access to other records for some events that occurred before then. Money order should be made payable to **South Dakota Department of Health.** Personal checks are accepted. To verify current fees, the telephone number is **(605) 773-3355.** This will be a **recorded** message.
Marriage	$5.00	Same as Birth or Death	Records since July 1905.
		See remarks	County Treasury in county where license was issued.
Divorce	$5.00	Same as Birth or Death	Records since July 1905.
	Varies	See remarks	Clerk of Court in county where divorce was granted.
Tennessee			
Birth (long form) Birth (short form) Death	$10.00 $5.00 $5.00	Tennessee Vital Records Department of Health and Environment Cordell Hull Building Nashville, TN 37219-5402	State office has had birth records for entire State since January 1914, for Nashville since June 1881, for Knoxville since July 1881, and for Chattanooga since January 1882. State office has had death records for entire State since January 1914, for Nashville since July 1874, for Knoxville since July 1887, and for Chattanooga since March 6, 1872. Birth and death enumeration records by school district are available for July 1908 through June 1912. For Memphis birth records from April 1874 through December 1887 and November 1898 to January 1, 1914, and for Memphis death records from May 1848 to January 1, 1914, write to Memphis-Shelby County Health Department, Division of Vital Records, Memphis, TN 38105. Additional copies of the same birth, marriage, or divorce record, requested at the same time, are $2.00 each. Check or money order should be made payable to **Tennessee Vital Records.** Personal checks are accepted. To verify current fees, the telephone number is **(615) 741-1763.** In Tennessee call **1-800-423-1901.**

State/Event	Cost	Where to Write	Remarks
Marriage	$10.00	Same as Birth or Death	Records since July 1945.
	Varies	See remarks	County Clerk in county where license was issued.
Divorce	$10.00	Same as Birth or Death	Records since July 1945.
	Varies	See remarks	Clerk of Court in county where divorce was granted.
Texas			
Birth or Death	$8.00	Bureau of Vital Statistics Texas Department of Health 1100 West 49th Street Austin, TX 78756-3191	State office has had records since 1903. State office has had records since 1903. Additional copies of same record ordered at same time are $2.00 each. Check or money order should be made payable to **Texas Department of Health.** Personal checks are accepted. To verify current fees, the telephone number is **(512) 458-7451.** This is a **recorded** message.
Marriage	See remarks	Same as Birth or Death	Records since January 1966. Certified copies are not available from State office. Fee for search and verification of essential facts of marriage is $8.00.
	Varies	See remarks	County Clerk in county where license was issued.
Divorce	See remarks	Same as Birth or Death	Records since January 1968. Certified copies are not available from State office. Fee for search and verification of essential facts of divorce is $8.00.
	Varies	See remarks	Clerk of District Court in county where divorce was granted.
Utah			
Birth Death	$11.00 $8.00	Bureau of Vital Records Utah Department of Health 288 North 1460 West P.O. Box 16700 Salt Lake City, UT 84116-0700	State office has had records since 1905. If event occurred from 1890 to 1904 in Salt Lake City or Ogden, write to City Board of Health. For records elsewhere in the State from 1898 to 1904, write to County Clerk in county where event occurred. Additional copies, when requested at the same time, are $4.00 each. Check or money order should be made payable to **Utah Department of Health.** Personal checks are accepted. To verify current fees, the telephone number is **(801) 538-6105.** This is a **recorded** message.
Marriage	$8.00	Same as Birth or Death	State office has had records since 1978. Only short form certified copies are available.
	Varies	See remarks	County Clerk in county where license was issued.
Divorce	$8.00	Same as Birth or Death	State office has had records since 1978. Only short form certified copies are available.
	Varies	See remarks	County Clerk in county where divorce was granted.
Vermont			
Birth or Death	$5.00	Vermont Department of Health Vital Records Section Box 70 60 Main Street Burlington, VT 05402	State has had records since 1955. Check or money order should be made payable to **Vermont Department of Health.** Personal checks are accepted. To verify current fees, the telephone number is **(802) 863-7275.**
Birth, Death, or Marriage	$5.00	Division of Public Records 6 Baldwin Street Montpelier, VT 05602	Records prior to 1955.
	$5.00	See remarks	Town or City Clerk of town where birth or death occurred.

State/Event	Cost	Where to Write	Remarks
Marriage	$5.00	Same as Birth or Death	State has had records since 1955.
	$5.00	See remarks	Town Clerk in town where license was issued.
Divorce	$5.00	Same as Birth or Death	State has had records since 1968.
	$5.00	See remarks	Town Clerk in town where divorce was granted.

Virginia

State/Event	Cost	Where to Write	Remarks
Birth or Death	$5.00	Division of Vital Records State Health Department P.O. Box 1000 Richmond, VA 23208-1000	State office has had records from January 1853 to December 1896 and since June 14, 1912. For records between those dates, write to the Health Department in the city where event occurred. Check or money order should be made payable to **State Health Department.** Personal checks are accepted. To verify current fees, the telephone number is **(804) 786-6228.**
Marriage	$5.00	Same as Birth or Death	Records since January 1853.
	Varies	See remarks	Clerk of Court in county or city where license was issued.
Divorce	$5.00	Same as Birth or Death	Records since January 1918.
	Varies	See remarks	Clerk of Court in county or city where divorce was granted.

Virgin Islands

State/Event	Cost	Where to Write	Remarks
Birth or Death St. Croix	$10.00	Registrar of Vital Statistics Charles Harwood Memorial Hospital St. Croix, VI 00820	Registrar has had birth and death records on file since 1840.
St. Thomas and St. John	$10.00	Registrar of Vital Statistics Knud Hansen Complex Hospital Ground Charlotte Amalie St. Thomas, VI 00802	Registrar has had birth records on file since July 1906 and death records since January 1906. Money order for birth and death records should be made payable to **Bureau of Vital Statistics.** Personal checks are not accepted. To verify current fees, the telephone number is **(809) 774-9000 ext. 218 or 298.**
Marriage	See remarks	Bureau of Vital Records and Statistical Services Virgin Islands Department of Health Charlotte Amalie St. Thomas, VI 00801	Certified copies are not available. Inquiries will be forwarded to the appropriate office.
St. Croix	$2.00	Chief Deputy Clerk Family Division Territorial Court of the Virgin Islands P.O. Box 929 Christiansted St. Croix, VI 00820	
St. Thomas and St. John	$2.00	Clerk of the Territorial Court of the Virgin Islands Family Division P.O. Box 70 Charlotte Amalie St. Croix, VI 00801	
Divorce	See remarks	Same as Marriage	Certified copies are not available. Inquiries will be forwarded to appropriate office.

State/Event	Cost	Where to Write	Remarks
St. Croix	$5.00	Same as Marriage	Money order for marriage and divorce records should be made payable to **Territorial Court of the Virgin Islands.** Personal checks are not accepted.
St. Thomas and St. John	$5.00	Same as Marriage	
Washington			
Birth or Death	$11.00	Vital Records 1112 South Quince P.O. Box 9709, ET-11 Olympia, WA 98504-9709	State office has had records since July 1907. For King, Pierce, and Spokane counties copies may also be obtained from county health departments. County Auditor of county of birth has registered births prior to July 1907. Money order should be made payable to **Vital Records.** To verify current fees, the telephone number is **(206) 753-5936.** Recorded messages for out of State, call **1-800-551-0562;** in State, call **1-800-331-0680.**
Marriage	$11.00	Same as Birth or Death	State office has had records since January 1968.
	$2.00	See remarks	County Auditor in county where license was issued.
Divorce	$11.00	Same as Birth or Death	State office has had records since January 1968.
	Varies	See remarks	County Clerk in county where divorce was granted.
West Virginia			
Birth or Death	$5.00	Vital Registration Office Division of Health State Capitol Complex Bldg. 3 Charleston, WV 25305	State office has had records since January 1917. For earlier records, write to Clerk of County Court in county where event occurred. Check or money order should be made payable to **Vital Registration.** Personal checks are accepted. To verify current fees, the telephone number is **(304) 348-2931.**
Marriage	$5.00	Same as Birth or Death	Records since 1921. Certified copies available from 1964.
	Varies	See remarks	County Clerk in county where license was issued.
Divorce	See remarks	Same as Birth or Death	Index since 1968. Some items may be verified (fee $5.00). Certified copies are not available from State office.
	Varies	See remarks	Clerk of Circuit Court, Chancery Side, in county where divorce was granted.
Wisconsin			
Birth Death	$8.00 $5.00	Vital Records 1 West Wilson Street P.O. Box 309 Madison, WI 53701	State office has scattered records earlier than 1857. Records before October 1, 1907, are very incomplete. Additional copies of the same record ordered at the same time are $2.00 each. Check or money order should be made payable to **Center for Health Statistics.** Personal checks are accepted. To verify current fees, the telephone number is **(608) 266-1371.** This will be a **recorded** message.
Marriage	$5.00	Same as Birth or Death	Records since April 1836. Records before October 1, 1907, are incomplete. Additional copies of the same record ordered at the same time are $2.00 each.
Divorce	$5.00	Same as Birth or Death	Records since October 1907. Additional copies of the same record ordered at the same time are $2.00 each.

State/Event	Cost	Where to Write	Remarks
Wyoming			
Birth Death	$5.00 $3.00	Vital Records Services Hathaway Building Cheyenne, WY 82002	State office has had records since July 1909. Money order should be made payable to **Vital Records Services.** To verify current fees, the telephone number is **(307) 777-7591.**
Marriage	$5.00	Same as Birth or Death	Records since May 1941.
	Varies	See remarks	County Clerk in county where license was issued.
Divorce	$5.00	Same as Birth or Death	Records since May 1941.
	Varies	See remarks	Clerk of District Court where divorce took place.

FOREIGN OR HIGH-SEA BIRTHS AND DEATHS AND CERTIFICATES OF CITIZENSHIP

Birth records of persons born in foreign countries who are U.S. citizens at birth

Births of U.S. citizens in foreign countries should be reported to the nearest American consular office as soon after the birth as possible on the Consular Report of Birth (Form FS-240). This report should be prepared and filed by one of the parents. However, the physician or midwife attending the birth or any other person having knowledge of the facts may prepare the report.

Documentary evidence is required to establish citizenship. Consular offices provide complete information on what evidence is needed. The Consular Report of Birth is a sworn statement of facts of birth. When approved, it establishes in documentary form the child's acquisition of U.S. citizenship. It has the same value as proof of citizenship as the Certificate of Citizenship issued by the Immigration and Naturalization Service.

A $13.00 fee is charged for reporting the birth. The original document is filed in Passport Services, Correspondence Branch, U.S. Department of State, Washington, DC 20524. The parents are given a certified copy of the Consular Report of Birth (Form FS-240) and a short form, Certification of Birth (Form DS-1350 or Form FS-545).

To obtain a copy of a report of the birth in a foreign country of a U.S. citizen, write to Passport Services, Correspondence Branch, U.S. Department of State, Washington, DC 20524. State the full name of the child at birth, date of birth, place of birth, and names of parents. Also include any information about the U.S. passport on which the child's name was first included. Sign the request and state the relationship to the person whose record is being requested and the reason for the request.

The fee for each copy is $4.00. Enclose a check or money order made payable to the U.S. Department of State. Fee may be subject to change.

The Department of State issues two types of copies from the Consular Report of Birth (Form FS-240):

1. A full copy of Form FS-240 as it was filed.
2. A short form, Certification of Birth (Form DS-1350), which shows only the name and sex of child, the date and place of birth, and date of recording.

The information on both forms is valid. The Certification of Birth may be obtained in a name subsequently acquired by adoption or legitimation after proof is submitted to establish that such an action legally took place.

Birth records of alien children adopted by U.S. citizens

Birth certifications for alien children adopted by U.S. citizens and lawfully admitted to the United States may be obtained from the Immigration and Naturalization Service (INS) if the birth information is on file.

Certification may be issued for children under 21 years of age who were born in a foreign country. Requests must be submitted on INS Form G-641, which can be obtained from any INS office. (Address can be found in a telephone directory.) For Certification of Birth Data (INS Form G-350), a $15.00 search fee, paid by check or money order, should accompany INS Form G-641.

Certification can be issued in the new name of an adopted or legitimated child after proof of an adoption or legitimation is submitted to INS. Because it may be issued for a child who has not yet become a U.S. citizen, this certification (Form G-350) is not proof of U.S. nationality.

Certificate of citizenship

U.S. citizens who were born abroad and later naturalized or who were born in a foreign country to a U.S. citizen (parent or parents) may apply for a certificate of citizenship pursuant to the provisions of Section 341 of the Immigration and Nationality Act. Application can be made for this document in the United States at the nearest office of the Immigration and Naturalization Service (INS). The INS will issue a certification of citizenship for the person if proof of citizenship is submitted and the person is within the United States. The decision whether to apply for a certificate of citizenship is optional; its possession is not mandatory because a valid U.S. passport or a Form FS-240 has the same evidentiary status.

Death records of U.S. citizens who die in foreign countries

The death of a U.S. citizen in a foreign country is normally reported to the nearest U.S. consular office. The consul prepares the official "Report of the Death of an American Citizen Abroad" (Form OF-180), and a copy of the Report of Death is filed permanently in the U.S. Department of State (see exceptions below).

To obtain a copy of a report, write to Passport Services, Correspondence Branch, U.S. Department of State, Washington, DC 20524. The fee for a copy is $4.00. Fee may be subject to change.

Exception: Reports of deaths of members of the Armed Forces of the United States are made only to the branch of the service to which the person was attached at the time of death—Army, Navy, Air Force, Marines, or Coast Guard. In these cases, requests for copies of records should be directed as follows.

For members of the Army:

Commander USTAPA
Attention: TAPC-PED
Alexandria, VA 22331-0482

For members of the Navy (Active Duty and Civilian Employees):

Navy Bureau of Medicine and Surgery
Code 3134
23rd and E Streets, NW
Washington, DC 20372

For members of the Air Force:

HQ AFESC/DEHM
Tyndall AFB, FL 32403-6001

For members of the Marine Corps:

HQ Marine Corps
Line 3 MSPA-1
Washington, DC 20380

For members of the Coast Guard:

Commandant GPE
U.S. Coast Guard Headquarters
2100 2nd Street, SW
Washington, DC 20593

For Civilian Employees of DOD (Except for Navy):

National Personnel Records Center
111 Winnebago Street
St. Louis, MO 63118

Records of birth and death occurring on vessels or aircraft on the high seas

When a birth or death occurs on the high seas, whether in an aircraft or on a vessel, the determination of where the record is filed is decided by the direction in which the vessel or aircraft was headed at the time the event occurred.

1. If the vessel or aircraft was outbound or docked or landed at a foreign port, requests for copies of the record should be made to the U.S. Department of State, Washington, DC 20520.
2. If the vessel or aircraft was inbound and the first port of entry was in the United States, write to the registration authority in the city where the vessel or aircraft docked or landed in the United States.
3. If the vessel was of U.S. registry, contact the U.S. Coast Guard facility at the port of entry.

Records maintained by foreign countries

Most, but not all, foreign countries record births and deaths. It is not feasible to list in this publication all foreign vital records offices, the charges they make for copies of records, or the information they may require to locate a record. However, most foreign countries will provide certifications of births and deaths occurring within their boundaries.

U.S. citizens who need a copy of a foreign birth or death record may obtain assistance by writing to the Office of Overseas Citizens Services, U.S. Department of State, Washington, DC 20520.

Aliens residing in the United States who seek records of these events should contact their nearest consular office.

Part V

Personal Finance and Complete Amortization Guide

CONSUMER CREDIT

The Consumer Credit Protection Act of 1968—which launched Truth in Lending—was a landmark piece of legislation. For the first time, creditors had to state the cost of borrowing in a common language so that you—the customer—could figure out exactly what the charges would be, compare costs, and shop around for the credit deal best for you.

Since 1968, credit protections have multiplied rapidly. The concepts of "fair" and "equal" credit have been written into laws that outlaw unfair discrimination in credit transactions; require that consumers be told the reason when credit is denied; let borrowers find out about their credit records; and set up a way to settle billing disputes.

Each law was meant to reduce the problems and confusion surrounding consumer credit which, as it became more widely used in our economy, also grew more complex. Together, these laws set a standard for how individuals are to be treated in their financial dealings.

The laws say, for instance:

—that you cannot be turned down for a credit card just because you're a single woman;
—that you can limit your risk if a credit card is lost or stolen;
—that you can straighten out errors in your monthly bill without damage to your credit rating; and
—that you won't find credit shut off just because you've reached the age of 65.

But, let the buyer **be aware!** It is important to know your rights and how to use them. The consumer credit laws can help you shop for credit, apply for it, keep up your credit standing, and—if need be—complain about an unfair deal. Become aware of what you should look for when using credit and what creditors look for before extending it. You will also learn about the laws' solutions to discriminatory practices that have made it difficult for women and minorities to get credit in the past.

Shopping Is the First Step

You get credit by promising to pay in the future for something you receive in the present.

Credit is a convenience. It lets you charge a meal on your credit card, pay for an appliance on the installment plan, take out a loan to buy a house, or pay for schooling or vacations. With credit, you can enjoy your purchase while you're paying for it—or you can make a purchase when you're lacking ready cash.

But there are strings attached to credit too. It usually costs something. And of course what is borrowed must be paid back.

If you are thinking of borrowing or opening a credit account, your first step should be to figure out how much it will cost you and whether you can afford it. Then you should shop around for the best terms.

What Laws Apply?

Two laws help you compare costs:

TRUTH IN LENDING requires creditors to give you certain basic information about the cost of buying on credit or taking out a loan. These "disclosures" can help you shop around for the best deal.

CONSUMER LEASING disclosures can help you compare the cost and terms of one lease with another and with the cost and terms of buying for cash or on credit.

The Finance Charge and Annual Percentage Rate (APR)

Credit costs vary. By remembering two terms, you can compare credit prices from different sources. Under Truth in Lending, the creditor must tell you—in writing and before you sign any agreement—the finance charge and the annual percentage rate.

The *finance charge* is the total dollar amount you pay to use credit. It includes interest costs, and other costs, such as service charges and some credit-related insurance premiums.

For example, borrowing $100 for a year might cost you $10 in interest. If there were also a service charge of $1, the finance charge would be $11.

The *annual percentage rate* (APR) is the percentage cost (or relative cost) of credit on a yearly basis. This is your key to comparing costs, regardless of the amount of credit or how long you have to repay it:

Again, suppose you borrow $100 for one year and pay a finance charge of $10. If you can keep the entire $100 for the whole year and then pay back $110 at the end of the year, you are paying an APR of 10 percent. But, if you repay the $100 and finance charge (a total of $110) in twelve equal monthly installments, you don't really get to use $100 for the whole year. In fact, you get to use less and less of that $100 each month. In this case, the $10 charge for credit amounts to an APR of 18 percent

All creditors—banks, stores, car dealers, credit card companies, finance companies—must state the cost of their credit in terms of the finance charge and the APR. Federal law does not set interest rates or other credit charges. But it does require their disclosure so that you can compare credit costs. The law says these two pieces of information must be shown to you before you sign a credit contract or before you use a credit card.

A Comparison

Even when you understand the terms a creditor is offering, it's easy to underestimate the difference in dollars that different terms can make. Suppose you're buying a $7,500 car. You put $1,500 down, and need to borrow $6,000. Compare these three credit arrangements.

	APR	Length of Loan	Monthly Payment	Total Finance Charge	Total of Payments
Creditor A	14%	3 years	$205.07	$1,382.52	$7,382.52
Creditor B	14%	4 years	$163.96	$1,870.08	$7,870.08
Creditor C	15%	4 years	$166.98	$2,015.04	$8,015.04

How do these choices stack up? The answer depends partly on what you need. The *lowest cost loan* is available from Creditor A.

If you were looking for *lower monthly payments,* you could get them by paying the loan off over a longer period of time. However, you would have to pay more in total costs. A loan from Creditor B—also at a 14 percent APR, but for four years—will add about $488 to your finance charge.

If that four-year loan were available only from Creditor C, the *APR of 15 percent* would add another $145 or so to your finance charges as compared with Creditor B.

Other terms—such as the size of the down payment—will also make a difference. Be sure to look at all the terms before you make your choice.

Cost of Open-end Credit

Open-end credit includes bank and department store credit cards, gasoline company cards, home equity lines, and check-overdraft accounts that let you write checks for more than your actual balance with the bank. Open-end credit can be used again and again, generally until you reach a certain prearranged borrowing limit. Truth in Lending requires that open-end creditors tell you the terms of the credit plan so that you can shop and compare the costs involved.

When you're shopping for an open-end plan, the APR you're told represents only the periodic rate that you will be charged—figured on a yearly basis. (For instance, a creditor that charges 1 1/2 percent interest each month would quote you an APR of 18 percent.) Annual membership fees, transaction charges, and points, for example, are listed separately; they are not included in the APR. Keep this in mind and compare all the costs involved in the plans, not just the APR.

Creditors must tell you when finance charges begin on your account, so you know how much time you have to pay your bill before a finance charge is added. Creditors may give you a 25-day grace period, for example, to pay your balance in full before making you pay a finance charge.

Creditors also must tell you the method they use to figure the balance on which you pay a finance charge; the interest rate they charge is applied to this balance to come up with the finance charge. Creditors use a number of different methods to arrive at the balance. Study them carefully; they can significantly affect your finance charge.

Some creditors, for instance, take the amount you owed at the beginning of the billing cycle, and subtract any payments you made during that cycle. Purchases are not counted. This is called the *adjusted balance method.*

Another is the *previous balance method.* Creditors simply use the amount owed at the beginning of the billing cycle to come up with the finance charge.

Under one of the most common methods—the *average daily balance method*—creditors add your balances for each day in the billing cycle and then divide that total by the number of days in the cycle. Payments made during the cycle are subtracted in arriving at the daily amounts, and, depending on the plan, new purchases may or may not be included. Under another method—the *two-cycle average daily balance method*—creditors use the average daily balances for two billing cycles to compute your finance charge. Again, payments will be taken into account in figuring the balances, but new purchases may or may not be included.

The amount of the finance charge may vary considerably depending on the method used, even for the same pattern of purchases and payments.

If you receive a credit card offer or an application, the creditor must give you information about the APR and other important terms of the plan at that time. Likewise, with a home equity plan: information must be given to you with an application.

Truth in Lending does not set the rates or tell the creditor how to calculate finance charges—it only requires that the creditor tell you the method that it uses. You should ask for an explanation of any terms you don't understand.

Leasing Costs and Terms

Leasing gives you temporary use of property in return for periodic payments. It has become a popular alternative to buying—under certain circumstances. For instance, you might consider leasing furniture for an apartment you'll use only for a year. The Consumer Leasing law requires leasing companies to give you the facts about the costs and terms of their contracts to help you decide whether leasing is a good idea.

The law applies to *personal property* leased to you for more than *four months* for *personal, family,* or *household use*. It covers, for example, long-term rentals of cars, furniture, and appliances, but not daily car rentals or leases for apartments.

Before you agree to a lease, the leasing company must give you a written statement of *costs,* including the amount of any security deposit, the amount of your monthly payments, and the amount you must pay for licensing, registration, taxes, and maintenance.

The company must also give you a written statement about *terms,* including any insurance you need, any guarantees, information about who is responsible for servicing the property, any standards for its wear and tear, and whether or not you have an option to buy the property.

Open-end Leases and Balloon Payments

Your costs will depend on whether you choose an open-end lease or a closed-end lease. Open-end leases usually mean lower monthly payments than closed-end leases, but you may owe a large extra payment—often called a balloon payment—based on the value of the property when you return it.

> Suppose you lease a car under a three-year open-end lease. The leasing company estimates the car will be worth $4,000 after three years of normal use. If you bring back the car in a condition that makes it worth only $3,500, you may owe a balloon payment of $500.

The leasing company must tell you whether you may owe a balloon payment and how it will be calculated. You should also know that:

—you have the right to an independent appraisal of the property's worth at the end of the lease. *You* must pay the appraiser's fee, however.

—a balloon payment is usually limited to *no more than three times the average monthly payment*. If your monthly payment is $100, your balloon payment wouldn't be more than $300—unless, for example, the property has received more than average wear and tear (for instance, if you drove a car more than average mileage).

Closed-end leases usually have a higher monthly payment than open-end leases, but there is no balloon payment at the end of the lease.

Costs of Settlement on a House

A house is probably the single largest credit purchase for most consumers—and one of the most complicated. The Real Estate Settlement Procedures Act, like Truth in Lending, is a disclosure law. The Act, administered by the Department of Housing and Urban Development, requires the lender to give you, in advance, certain information about the costs you will pay when you close the loan.

This event is called settlement or closing, and the law helps you shop for lower settlement costs. To find out more about it, write to:

Assistant Secretary for Housing
Office of Insured Single Family Housing
Attention: RESPA
U.S. Department of Housing and
Urban Development
451 7th Street, S.W.
Room 9266
Washington, D.C. 20410

Applying for Credit

When you're ready to apply for credit, you should know what creditors think is important in deciding whether you're credit-worthy. You should also know what they cannot legally consider in their decisions.

The Equal Credit Opportunity Act requires that all credit applicants be considered on the basis of their actual qualifications for credit and not be turned away because of certain personal characteristics.

What Creditors Look For

Creditors look for an ability to repay debt and a willingness to do so—and sometimes for a little extra security to protect their loans. They speak of the three C's of credit—capacity, character, and collateral.

Capacity. Can you repay the debt? Creditors ask for employment information: your occupation, how long you've worked, and how much you earn. They also want to know your expenses: how many dependents you have, whether you pay alimony or child support, and the amount of your other obligations.

Character. Will you repay the debt? Creditors will look at your credit history: How much you owe, how often you borrow, whether you pay bills on time, and whether you live within your means. They also look for signs of stability: how long you've lived at your present address, whether you own or rent, and length of your present employment.

Collateral. Is the creditor fully protected if you fail to repay? Creditors want to know what you may have that could be used to back up or secure your loan, and what sources you have for repaying debt other than income, such as savings, investments, or property.

Creditors use different combinations of these facts in reaching their decisions. Some set unusually high standards and others simply do not make certain kinds of loans. Creditors also use different kinds of rating systems. Some rely strictly on their own instinct and experience. Others use a "credit-scoring" or statistical system to predict whether you're a good credit risk. They assign a certain number of points to each of the various characteristics that have proved to be reliable signs that a borrower will repay. Then, they rate you on this scale.

And so, different creditors may reach different conclusions based on the same set of facts. One may find you an acceptable risk, while another may deny you a loan.

The Equal Credit Opportunity Act does not guarantee that you will get credit. You must still pass the creditor's tests of creditworthiness. But the creditor must apply these tests fairly, impartially, and without discriminating against you on any of the following grounds: age, sex, marital status, race, color, religion, national origin, because you receive public income such as veterans benefits, welfare or Social Security, or because you exercise your rights under Federal credit laws such as filing a billing error notice with a creditor. This means that a creditor may not use any of those grounds as a reason to:

- discourage you from applying for a loan;
- refuse you a loan if you qualify; or
- lend you money on terms different from those granted another person with similar income, expenses, credit history, and collateral.

In the past, many older persons have complained about being denied credit just because they were over a certain age. Or when they retired, they often found their credit suddenly cut off or reduced. So the law is very specific about how a person's age may be used in credit decisions.

A creditor may ask your age, but if you're old enough to sign a binding contract (usually 18 or 21 years old depending on state law), a creditor *may not:*

- turn you down or offer you less credit just because of your age;
- ignore your retirement income in rating your application;
- close your credit account or require you to reapply for it just because you reach a certain age or retire; or
- deny you credit or close your account because credit life insurance or other credit-related insurance is not available to persons your age.

Creditors may "score" your age in a credit-scoring system, but:

- if you are 62 or older you must be given at least as many points for age as any person under 62.

Because individuals' financial situations can change at different ages, the law lets creditors consider certain information related to age—such as how long until you retire or how long your income will continue. An older applicant might not qualify for a large loan with a 5 percent down payment on a risky venture, but might qualify for a smaller loan—with a bigger down payment—secured by good çollateral. Remember that while declining income may be a handicap if you are older, you can usually offer a solid credit history to your advantage. The creditor has to look at all the facts and apply the usual standards of creditworthiness to your particular situation.

You may not be denied credit just because you receive Social Security or public assistance (such as Aid to Families with Dependent Children). But—as is the case with age—certain information related to this source of income could clearly affect creditworthiness. So, a creditor may consider such things as:

- how old your dependents are (because you may lose benefits when they reach a certain age); or
- whether you will continue to meet the residency requirements for receiving benefits.

This information helps the creditor determine the likelihood that your public assistance income will continue.

The Equal Credit Opportunity Act covers your application for a mortgage or home improvement loan. It bans discrimination because of such characteristics as your race, color, sex, or because of the race or national origin of the people in the neighborhood where you live or want to buy your home. Nor may creditors use any appraisal of the value of the property that considers the race of the people in the neighborhood.

Discrimination Against Women

Both men and women are protected from discrimination based on sex or marital status. But many of the law's provisions were designed to stop particular abuses that generally made it difficult for women to get credit. For example, the idea that single women ignore their debts when they marry, or that a woman's income "doesn't count" because she'll leave work to have children, now is unlawful in credit transactions.

The general rule is that *you may not be denied credit just because you are a woman, or just because you are married, single, widowed, divorced, or separated.* Here are some important protections:

Sex and Marital Status. Usually, creditors may not ask your sex on an application form (one exception is a loan to buy or build a home).

You do not have to use Miss, Mrs., or Ms. with your name on a credit application. But, in some cases, a creditor may ask whether you are married, unmarried, or separated (unmarried includes single, divorced, and widowed).

Child-bearing Plans. Creditors may not ask about your birth control practices or whether you plan to have children, and they may not assume anything about those plans.

Income and Alimony. The creditor must count all of your income, even income from part-time employment.

Child support and alimony payments are a primary source of income for many women. You don't have to disclose these kinds of income, but if you do creditors must count them.

Telephones. Creditors may not consider whether you have a telephone listing in your name because this would discriminate against most married women. (You may be asked if there's a telephone in your home.)

A creditor *may* consider whether income is steady and reliable, so be prepared to show that you can count on uninterrupted income—particularly if the source is alimony payments or part-time wages.

Many married women used to be turned down when they asked for credit in their own name. Or, a husband had to cosign an account—agree to pay if the wife didn't—even when a woman's own income could easily repay the loan. Single women couldn't get loans because they were thought to be somehow less reliable than other applicants. You now have a right to your own credit, based on your own credit records and earnings. Your own credit means a separate account or loan in your own name—not a joint account with your husband or a duplicate card on his account. Here are the rules:

- Creditors may not refuse to open an account just because of your sex or marital status.
- You can choose to use your first name and maiden name (Mary Smith); your first name and husband's last name (Mary Jones); or a combined last name (Mary Smith-Jones).
- If you're creditworthy, a creditor may not ask your husband to cosign your account, with certain exceptions when property rights are involved.
- Creditors may not ask for information about your husband or ex-husband when you apply for your own credit based on your own income—unless that income is alimony, child support, or separate maintenance payments from your spouse or former spouse.

This last rule, of course, does not apply if your husband is going to use your account or be responsible for paying your debts on the account, or if you live in a community property state. (Community property states are Arizona, California, Idaho, Louisiana, Nevada, New Mexico, Texas, Washington, and Wisconsin.)

Married women have sometimes faced severe hardships when cut off from credit after their husbands died. Single women have had accounts closed when they married, and married women have had accounts closed after a divorce. The law says that creditors may not make you reapply for credit just because you marry or become widowed or divorced. Nor may they close your account or change the terms of your account on these grounds. There must be some sign that your creditworthiness has changed. For example, creditors *may* ask you to reapply if you relied on your ex-husband's income to get credit in the first place.

Setting up your own account protects you by giving you your own history of how you handle debt, to rely on if your financial situation changes because you are widowed or divorced. If you're getting married and plan to take your husband's surname, write to your creditors and tell them if you want to keep a separate account.

Remember, your sex or race may not be used to discourage you from applying for a loan. And creditors may not hold up or otherwise delay your application on those grounds. Under the Equal Credit Opportunity Act, you must be notified within 30 days after your application has been completed whether your loan has been approved or not. If credit is denied, this notice must be in writing and it must explain the specific reasons why you were denied credit or tell you of your right to ask for an explanation. You have the same rights if an account you have had is closed.

If you are denied credit, be sure to find out why. Remember, you may have to ask the creditor for this explanation. It may be that the creditor thinks you have requested more money than you can repay on your income. It may be that you have not been employed or lived long enough in the community. You can discuss terms with the creditor and ways to improve your creditworthiness.

If you think you have been discriminated against, cite the law to the lender. If the lender still says no without a satisfactory explanation, you may contact a Federal enforcement agency for assistance or bring legal action.

Credit History and Records

On your first attempt to get credit, you may face a common frustration: sometimes it seems you have to already have credit to get credit. Some creditors will look only at your salary and job and the other financial information you put on your application. But most also want to know about your track record in handling credit—how reliably you've repaid past debts. They turn to the records kept by credit bureaus or credit reporting agencies whose business is to collect and store information about borrowers that is routinely supplied by many lenders. These records include the amount of credit you have received and how faithfully you've paid it back.

Here are several ways you can begin to build up a good credit history:

- Open a checking account or a savings account, or both. These do not begin your credit file, but may be checked as evidence that you have money and know how to manage it. Cancelled checks can be used to show you pay utilities or rent bills regularly, a sign of reliability.
- Apply for a department store credit card. Repaying credit card bills on time is a plus in credit histories.
- Ask whether you may deposit funds with a financial institution to serve as collateral for a credit card; some institutions will issue a credit card with a credit limit usually no greater than the amount on deposit.
- If you're new in town, write for a summary of any credit record kept by a credit bureau in your former town. (Ask the bank or department store in your old hometown for the name of the agency it reports to.)
- If you don't qualify on the basis of your own credit standing, offer to have someone cosign your application.
- If you're turned down, find out why and try to clear up any misunderstandings.

The following laws can help you start your credit history and keep your record accurate:

The Equal Credit Opportunity Act gives women a way to start their own credit history and identity.

The Fair Credit Reporting Act sets up a procedure for correcting mistakes on your credit record.

Credit Histories for Women. Under the Equal Credit Opportunity Act, reports to credit bureaus must be made in the names of both husband and wife if both use an account or are responsible for repaying the debt. Some women who are divorced or widowed might not have separate credit histories because in the past credit accounts were listed in their husband's name only. But they can still benefit from this record. Under the Equal Credit Opportunity Act, creditors must consider the credit history of accounts women have held jointly with their husbands. Creditors must also look at the record of any account held only in the husband's name if a woman can show it also reflects her own creditworthiness. If the record is unfavorable—if an ex-husband was a bad credit risk—she can try to show that the record does not reflect her own reputation. Remember that a wife may also open her own account to be sure of starting her own credit history.

Keeping Up Credit Records. Mistakes on your credit record—sometimes mistaken identities—can cloud your credit future. Your credit rating is important, so be sure credit bureau records are complete and accurate.

The Fair Credit Reporting Act says that you must be told what's in your credit file and have any errors corrected.

If a lender refuses you credit because of unfavorable information in your credit report, you have a right to the name and address of the agency that keeps your report. Then, you may either request information from the credit bureau by mail or in person. You will not get an exact copy of the file, but you will at least learn what's in the report. The law also says that the credit bureau must help you interpret the data—because it's raw data that takes experience to analyze. If you're questioning a credit refusal made within the past 30 days, the bureau is not allowed to charge a fee for giving you information.

Any error that you find must be investigated by the credit bureau with the creditor who supplied the data. The bureau will remove from your credit file any errors the creditor admits are there. If you disagree with the findings, you can file a short statement in your record giving your side of the story. Future reports to creditors must include the statement or a summary of it.

Sometimes credit information is too old to give a good picture of your financial reputation. There is a limit on how long certain kinds of information may be kept in your file:

- Bankruptcies must be taken off your credit history after 10 years.
- Suits and judgments, tax liens, arrest records, and most other kinds of unfavorable information must be dropped after 7 years.

Your credit record may not be given to anyone who does not have a legitimate business need for it. Stores to which you are applying for credit or prospective employers may examine your record; curious neighbors may not.

Other Aspects of Using Credit

The best way to keep up your credit standing is to repay all debts on time. But there may be complications. To protect your credit rating, you should learn how to correct mistakes and misunderstandings that can tangle up your credit accounts.

When there's a snag, first try to deal directly with the creditor. The credit laws can help you settle your complaints without a hassle.

The Fair Credit Billing Act sets up procedures requiring creditors to promptly correct billing mistakes; allowing you to withhold credit card payments on defective goods; and requiring creditors to promptly credit your payments.

Truth In Lending gives you three days to change your mind about certain credit transactions that use your home as collateral; it also limits your risk on lost or stolen credit cards.

The Fair Credit Billing Act requires creditors to correct errors promptly and without damage to your credit rating.

The law defines a billing error as any charge:

- for something you didn't buy or for a purchase made by someone not authorized to use your account;
- that is not properly identified on your bill or is for an amount different from the actual purchase price or was entered on a date different from the purchase date; or
- for something that you did not accept on delivery or that was not delivered according to agreement.

Billing errors also include:

- errors in arithmetic;
- failure to show a payment or other credit to your account;
- failure to mail the bill to your current address, if you told the creditor about an address change at least 20 days before the end of the billing period; or
- a questionable item, or an item for which you need more information.

If you think your bill is wrong, or want more information about it, follow these steps:

1. Notify the creditor *in writing* within 60 days after the first bill was mailed that showed the error. Be sure to write to the address the creditor lists for billing inquiries and to tell the creditor:

- your name and account number;
- that you believe the bill contains an error and *why* you believe it is wrong; and
- the date and suspected amount of the error or the item you want explained.

2. Pay all parts of the bill that are not in dispute. But, while waiting for an answer,

you do not have to pay the amount in question (the "disputed amount") or any minimum payments or finance charges that apply to it.

The creditor must acknowledge your letter within 30 days, unless the problem can be resolved within that time. Within two billing periods—but in no case longer than 90 days—either your account must be corrected or you must be told why the creditor believes the bill is correct.

If the creditor made a mistake, you do not pay any finance charges on the disputed amount. Your account must be corrected, and you must be sent an explanation of any amount you still owe.

If no error is found, the creditor must send you an explanation of the reasons for that finding and promptly send a statement of what you owe, which may include any finance charges that have accumulated and any minimum payments you missed while you were questioning the bill. You then have the time usually given on your type of account to pay any balance, but not less than 10 days.

3. If you still are not satisfied, you should notify the creditor in writing within the time allowed to pay your bill.

Maintaining Your Credit Rating. A creditor may not threaten your credit rating while you're resolving a billing dispute.

Once you have written about a possible error, a creditor must not give out information to other creditors or credit bureaus that would hurt your credit reputation. And, until your complaint is answered, the creditor also may not take any action to collect the disputed amount.

After the creditor has explained the bill, if you do not pay in the time allowed, you may be reported as delinquent on the amount in dispute and the creditor may take action to collect. Even so, you can still disagree in writing. Then the creditor must report that you have challenged your bill and give you the name and address of each person who has received information about your account. When the matter is settled, the creditor must report the outcome to each person who has received information. Remember that you may also place your own side of the story in your credit report.

Defective Goods or Services. The Fair Credit Billing Act allows you to withhold payment on any damaged or poor quality goods or services purchased with a credit card, as long as you have made a real attempt to solve the problem with the merchant.

This right may be limited if the card was a bank or travel and entertainment card or any card *not* issued by the store where you made your purchase. In such cases, the sale:

- must have been for more than $50; and
- must have taken place in your home state or within 100 miles of your home address.

Some creditors will not charge a finance charge if you pay your account within a certain period of time. In this case, it is especially important that you get your bills, and get credit for paying them, promptly. Check your statements to make sure your creditor follows these rules:

Prompt Billing. Look at the date on the postmark. If your account is one on which no finance or other charge is added before a certain due date, then creditors must mail their statements at least 14 days before payment is due.

Prompt Crediting. Look at the payment date entered on the statement. Creditors must credit payments on the day they arrive, as long as you pay according to payment instructions. This means, for example, sending your payment to the address listed on the bill.

Credit Balances. If a credit balance results on your account (for example, because you pay more than the amount you owe, or you return a purchase and the purchase price is credited to your account), the creditor must make a refund to you. The refund must be made within seven business days after your written request, or automatically if the credit balance is still in existence after six months.

Cancelling a Mortgage. Truth in Lending gives you a chance to change your mind on one important kind of transaction—when you use your home as security for a credit transaction. For example, when you are financing a major repair or remodeling and use your home as security, you have three business days, usually after you sign a contract, to think about the transaction and to cancel it if you wish. The creditor must give you written notice of your right to cancel, and, if you decide to cancel, you must notify the creditor in writing within the three-day period. The creditor must then return all fees paid and cancel the security interest in your home. No contractor may start work on your home, and no lender may pay you or the contractor until the three days are up. If you must have the credit immediately to meet a financial emergency, you may give up your right to cancel by providing a written explanation of the circumstances.

The right to cancel (or right of rescission) was provided to protect you against hasty decisions—or decisions made under pressure—that might put your home at risk if you are unable to repay the loan. The law does not apply to a mortgage to finance the purchase of your home; for that, you commit yourself as soon as you sign the mortgage contract. And, if you use your home to secure an open-end credit line—a home equity line, for instance—you have the right to cancel only when you open the account or when your security interest or credit limit is increased. (In the case of an increase, only the increase would be cancelled.)

Lost or Stolen Credit Cards. If your wallet is stolen, your greatest cost may be inconvenience, because your liability on lost or stolen cards is limited under Truth in Lending.

You do not have to pay for *any* unauthorized charges made *after* you notify the card company of loss or theft of your card. So keep a list of your credit card numbers and notify card issuers immediately if your card is lost or stolen. The most you will have to pay for unauthorized charges is $50 on each card—even if someone runs up several hundred dollars worth of charges before you report a card missing.

Unsolicited Cards. It is illegal for card issuers to send you a credit card unless you ask for or agree to receive one. However, a card issuer may send, without your request, a new card to replace an expiring one.

Complaining About Credit

First try to solve your problem directly with a creditor. Only if that fails should you bring more formal complaint procedures. Here's the way to file a complaint with the Federal agencies responsible for carrying out consumer credit protection laws.

Complaints About Banks. If you have a complaint about a bank in connection with any of the Federal credit laws—or if you think any part of your business with a bank has been handled in an unfair or deceptive way—you may get advice and help from the Federal Reserve. The practice you complain about does not have to be covered by Federal law. Furthermore, you don't have to be a customer of the bank to file a complaint.

You should submit your complaint—in writing whenever possible—to

Division of Consumer and Community Affairs
Board of Governors of the Federal Reserve System
Washington, D.C. 20551

or to the Reserve Bank nearest you. Be sure to describe the bank practice you are complaining about and give the name and address of the bank involved.

The Federal Reserve will write back within 15 days—sometimes with an answer, sometimes telling you that more time is needed to handle your complaint. The additional time is required when complex issues are involved or when the complaint will be investigated by a Federal Reserve Bank. When this is the case, the Federal Reserve will try to keep you informed about the progress being made.

The Board supervises only state-chartered banks that are members of the Federal Reserve System. It will refer complaints about other institutions to the appropriate Federal regulatory agency and let you know where your complaint has been referred. Or you may write directly to the appropriate agency.

You may also take legal action against a creditor. If you decide to bring a lawsuit, here are the penalties a creditor must pay if you win.

Truth in Lending and Consumer Leasing Acts. If any creditor fails to disclose information required under these Acts, or gives inaccurate information, or does not comply with the rules about credit cards or the right to cancel, you as an individual may sue for actual damages—any money loss you suffer. In addition, you can sue for twice the finance charge in the case of certain credit disclosures, or, if a lease is concerned, 25 percent of total monthly payments. In either case, the least the court may award you if you win is $100, and the most is $1,000. In any lawsuit that you win, you are entitled to reimbursement for court costs and attorney's fees.

Class action suits are also permitted. A class action suit is one filed on behalf of a group of people with similar claims.

Equal Credit Opportunity Act. If you think you can prove that a creditor has discriminated against you for any reason prohibited by the Act, you as an individual may sue for actual damages plus punitive damages—that is, damages for the fact that the law has been violated—of up to $10,000. In a successful lawsuit, the court will award you court costs and a reasonable amount for attorney's fees. Class action suits are also permitted.

Fair Credit Billing Act. A creditor who breaks the rules for the correction of billing errors automatically loses the amount owed on the item in question and any finance charges on it, up to a combined total of $50—even if the bill was correct. You as an individual may also sue for actual damages plus twice the amount of any finance charges, but in any case not less than $100 nor more than $1,000. You are also entitled to court costs and attorney's fees in a successful lawsuit. Class action suits are also permitted.

Fair Credit Reporting Act. You may sue any credit reporting agency or creditor for breaking the rules about who may see your credit records and for not correcting errors in your file. Again, you are entitled to actual damages, plus punitive damages that the court may allow if the violation is proved to have been intentional. In any successful lawsuit, you will also be awarded court costs and attorney's fees. A person who obtains a credit report without proper authorization—or an employee of a credit reporting agency who gives a credit report to unauthorized persons—may be fined up to $5,000 or imprisoned for one year, or both.

Complaints About Other Institutions. The following is a list of the names of the regulatory agencies for other financial institutions and for businesses other than banks. Many of these agencies do not handle individual complaints; however, they will use information about your credit experiences to help enforce the credit laws.

National Banks
Comptroller of the Currency
Consumer Activities Division
Washington, D.C. 20219

State Member Banks of the Federal Reserve System
Federal Reserve Bank serving the district in which the State member bank is located.

Federally Insured Nonmember State Chartered Banks and Savings Banks
Federal Deposit Insurance Corporation Regional Director for the region in which the nonmember insured bank is located.

Federally Insured Savings and Loan Institutions and Federally Chartered Savings Banks
Manager, Consumer Affairs at the Office of Thrift Supervision in the district in which the institution is located.

Federal Credit Unions
Regional Office of the National Credit Union Administration serving the area in which the Federal credit union is located.

Creditors Subject to Aviation Enforcement
Assistant General Counsel for Aviation Enforcement and Proceedings
Department of Transportation
400 Seventh Street, S.W.
Washington, D.C. 20590

Creditors Subject to Interstate Commerce Commission
Office of Proceedings
Interstate Commerce Commission
Washington, D.C. 20523

Creditors Subject to Packers and Stockyards Act
Nearest Packers and Stockyards Administration area supervisor.

Small Business Investment Companies
U.S. Small Business Administration
1441 L Street, N.W.
Washington, D.C. 20416

Brokers and Dealers
Securities and Exchange Commission
Washington, D.C. 20549

Federal Land Banks, Federal Land Bank Associations, Federal Intermediate Credit Banks and Production Credit Associations
Farm Credit Administration
1501 Farm Credit Drive
McLean, Virginia 22102-5090

Mortgage Bankers, Consumer Finance Companies, and All Other Creditors
FTC Regional Office for region in which the creditor operates or
Division of Credit Practices
Bureau of Consumer Protection
Federal Trade Commission
Washington, D.C. 20580

OBTAINING STUDENT LOANS

When you apply for a loan to attend a college, university, trade, or proprietary institution, you make a commitment. Honoring that commitment will strengthen these programs, which will allow others to have the same type of assistance that was available to you for the pursuit of higher education. You also uphold the faith of working Americans who make these programs possible.

Financial assistance opens the door to higher education for many who could not otherwise afford its cost. Do your share to support these programs by repaying your loans after graduation. You owe it to those who will follow.

No person in the United States shall, on the ground of race, color, or national origin, be excluded from participation in, be denied the benefits of, or be subjected to discrimination under, any program or activity receiving Federal financial assistance, or be so treated on the basis of sex under most education programs or activities receiving Federal assistance.

Education or training after high school costs more than ever, and you need to learn about as many sources of aid as you can. The steps below will help.

Contact the financial aid administrator at each school you're interested in. He or she can tell you what aid programs are available there, and how much the total cost of education will be. If you're in high school, also talk to your guidance counselor. He or she can tell you about financial aid in general and where to look for help.

Ask the State higher education agency in your home State for information about State aid—including aid from a program jointly funded by individual States and the U.S. Department of Education. Each State has its own name for this program, as well as its own award levels, eligibility criteria, and application procedures. (At the Federal level, this program is called the State Student Incentive Grant Program.)

Your State agency can also give you information about the Paul Douglas Teacher Scholarship Program. These scholarships are for outstanding high school graduates who want to pursue teaching careers after they finish college. A Douglas scholarship provides up to $5,000 a year to students who graduate from high school in the top 10 percent of their class, and who meet other selection criteria their State agency may establish. Generally, students are required to teach two years for each year of scholarship assistance they receive.

The agency in your State responsible for public elementary and secondary schools can give you information on the Robert C. Byrd Honors Scholarship Program. Students who demonstrate outstanding academic achievement and show promise of continued excellence may receive $1,500 for their first year of postsecondary education.

Your public library has information on State and private sources of aid. Your financial need is usually considered, but other factors may also be taken into account.

Many companies, as well as labor unions, have programs to help pay the cost of postsecondary education for employees or members (or for their children).

Check foundations, religious organizations, fraternities or sororities, and town or city clubs. Include community organizations and civic groups such as the American Legion, YMCA, 4-H Clubs, Kiwanis, Jaycees, Chamber of Commerce, and the Girl or Boy Scouts.

Scholarships from the National Honor Society and National Merit Scholarships are available to students with high grades who qualify.

Don't overlook aid from organizations connected with your field of interest (for example, the American Medical Association or the American Bar Association). These organizations are listed in the U.S. Department of Labor's *Occupational Outlook Handbook* and can also be found in various directories of associations available at your public library.

If you're a veteran, veterans benefits may be available. Check with your local Veterans' Affairs office.

Choosing a School Carefully

Education after high school costs you time, money, and effort. It's a big investment, and you should carefully evaluate the school you're considering. You ought to know what you'll be getting for your money. When you enroll in school, you expect to learn certain subjects, or maybe certain skills that will help you get a specific job.

Ask for the names of the school's accrediting and licensing organizations. You also have the right to ask for a copy of the documents describing the institution's accreditation or licensing. Accreditation means a private educational agency or association has evaluated a school and found it meets certain minimum requirements that agency has set. But don't assume that if a school is accredited that's all you need to know.

A school can be very good but still not meet your individual needs. You have the right to ask a school about its programs, its faculty, and its instructional, laboratory, and other physical facilities (including what special facilities and services are available to the handicapped). What is the size of most classes? Will you have enough contact with your instructors? If you're attending a school that offers training using equipment, make sure the classes are not so large you never get to use it. If a school advertises a certain kind of equipment, make sure it actually has that equipment. Is it modern and what you'll actually be using in your field later on?

Find out how many credits you need to graduate or complete the course work. Ask how many students finish. A high dropout rate could mean students weren't satisfied with the education they were receiving.

It's also a good idea to talk to recent graduates about the school's courses, its professors or instructors, even its social life and living facilities, if applicable. And remember, just because a school participates in the U.S. Department of Education's student aid programs does *NOT* mean the Department has endorsed the quality of the education the school offers. The Department *does not approve* a school's curriculum, policies, or administrative practices, *except* as they relate to how the school operates Federal student aid programs. It's up to you to check out the school.

Many students are concerned about being able to get a job in their chosen field after they leave school. What is the school's job placement rate? Check with former graduates or prospective employers, not just the school. What is the placement rate of your chosen profession in general? If the school advertises its job placement rates, it must also publish the most recent available data about employment statistics, graduation statistics, and any other information necessary to back up its claims. This information must be available at or before the time you apply for admission to the school.

Does the school provide instruction on topics necessary for State or professional certification of graduates? If a school says it will help you find a job, what does this include? Will the school contact potential employers and set up interviews? Will you receive counseling on how to obtain and keep a job?

You have the right to ask the school the following:

- What financial assistance is available, including information on all Federal, State, local, private, and institutional financial aid programs. You also have the right to know how a school selects financial aid recipients.
- What the procedures and deadlines are for submitting applications for each available financial aid program.
- How the school determines your financial need. This process includes how costs for tuition and fees, room and board, travel, books and supplies, and personal and miscellaneous expenses are considered in your cost of education. It also includes the resources considered in calculating your need (such as parental contribution, other financial aid, assets, etc.). You also have the right to know how much of your financial need, as determined by the school, has been met and how and when you'll receive your aid.
- How the school determines each type and amount of assistance in your financial aid package. You also have the right to ask the school to reconsider your aid package if you believe a mistake has been made, or if your enrollment or financial circumstances have changed.
- How the school determines whether you're making satisfactory academic progress, and what happens if you're not. Whether you continue to receive Federal financial aid depends, in part, on whether you're making satisfactory progress.
- What the interest rate is on any student loan you may receive, the total amount you must repay, the length of time you have to repay, when you must start repaying, and what cancellation or deferment (postponement) provisions apply.
- If you're offered a College Work-Study job—what kind of job it is, what hours you must work, what your duties will be, what the rate of pay will be, and how and when you'll be paid.
- Who the school's financial aid personnel are, where they're located, and how to contact them for information.

You have the right to know what your school's refund policy is. If something happens and you never register for classes, or if you drop out of school within a short time after you start, you may be able to get a part of your educational expenses returned to you. But after a certain date, you won't get any money back. Check with your school to find out what expenses you may have to pay if you drop out. Keep in mind that if you receive Federal student aid from any of the programs mentioned other than College Work-Study—some or all of that aid will be returned to those programs or to your lender.

If you have a Stafford Loan or a Supplemental Loan for Students (SLS), or if your parents have a PLUS loan for you, the school must explain its refund policy, in writing, to you and to all prospective students. The school must also make its refund policy known to students who are currently enrolled. The school must include examples of how its policy applies and must explain the procedures you must follow to obtain a refund. If the school changes its refund policy, it must make sure all students are made aware of the new policy.

For specific information about the refund policy at your school, contact your financial aid administrator.

Check several sources to find out the answers to questions you may have about a school. Talk to high school counselors, local employers, and the State Department of Education that has jurisdiction over the school. See if any complaints have been filed about the school with the local Better Business Bureau, Chamber of Commerce, or consumer protection division of the State Attorney General's office. And contact these organizations if you have a complaint about a school.

You're paying for an education. Make sure you get it.

General Information

The U.S. Department of Education offers the following major student financial aid programs:

Grants are financial aid you don't have to pay back.

Work-Study gives you the chance to work and earn money to help pay for school.

Loans are borrowed money that you must repay with interest.

Undergraduates may receive all three types of financial aid. Graduate students may apply for loans or Work-Study, but not for Pell Grants or SEOG.

Not all schools take part in all the programs. To find out which ones are available at a school, contact the school's financial aid administrator.

Financial Need

Aid from most of the Federal student aid programs, except for PLUS and SLS loans is awarded on the basis of financial need. Of course, you must first meet the eligibility criteria. The information you report on an aid application is used in certain formulas that calculate your need and eligibility.

Eligibility for the Pell Grant Program is determined by a formula passed into law by Congress and depends on a number called the "Pell Grant Index (PGI)." If this number is low enough, you're eligible for a Pell Grant. And the lower the number, the larger your award will be. If your PGI is higher than a certain number, you're not eligible.

There isn't a minimum or maximum number in determining eligibility for the "campus-based" and Stafford Loan programs. Instead, your financial need is determined by the following subtraction: *Cost of Education – Family Contribution (FC) = Financial Need*

In other words, your financial aid administrator takes the cost of education at your school and subtracts the amount you and your family are expected to pay toward that cost (the Family Contribution [FC]). If there's anything left over, you are considered to have financial need.

Cost of education—your educational expenses such as tuition, fees, room, board, books, supplies, and other related expenses.

Family contribution (FC)—the amount you and your family are expected to pay toward your education. This amount is determined by a standard formula somewhat different from that used for the Pell Grant Program, although the FC formula has also been passed into law by Congress. (The formula is called the "Congressional Methodology.") Factors such as taxable and nontaxable income, assets (such as savings), and benefits (for example, unemployment or Social Security) are all considered in this calculation, which determines your family's financial strength. You can get a booklet describing the Family Contribution formula in detail by writing to—

Federal Student Aid Information Center
Box 84
Washington, DC 20044

Note that although need is determined by formula, the financial aid administrator can adjust—up or down—your Family Contribution (FC) or your cost of education, if he or she believes your family's financial circumstances warrant it. However, the aid administrator does not *have* to make such an adjustment.

Dependency Status

Certain questions on your student aid application will determine whether you're considered dependent on your parents and must report their income and assets as well as your own (and your spouse's, if you're married), or whether you're independent and must report only your own income and assets (and those of a spouse). Income and asset information will be used in determining your eligibility for Federal student aid, so answer the questions on your student financial aid application carefully.

Students are classified as dependent or independent because Federal student aid programs are based on the idea that students' parents have the primary responsibility of paying for their children's education. Students who have access to parental support—dependent students—should not receive Federal funds at the expense of students who don't have that access—independent students.

If you claim to be an independent student, your school may ask you to submit proof before you can receive any Federal student aid. If you think you have unusual circumstances that would make you independent even though you normally would be considered dependent, talk to the financial aid administrator at your school. The aid administrator can change your status to independent if he or she thinks your circumstances warrant it. But remember, the aid administrator won't automatically do this. That decision is based on his or her judgment, and it's *final*—you cannot appeal it to the U.S. Department of Education.

Forms

You can use any of the forms listed below to apply for Federal aid including a Pell Grant. To consider you for aid from non-Federal sources as well, your school may specify which of the forms listed below you should complete. Your school will have the form you need.

- *"Application for Federal Student Aid" (AFSA)*—The U.S. Department of Education's form

- *"Application for Pennsylvania State Grant and Federal Student Aid"*—The Pennsylvania Higher Education Assistance Agency's (PHEAA'S) form
- *"Application for Federal and State Student Aid (AFSSA)"*—CSX's form
- *"Singlefile Form"*—United Student Aid Funds' (USAF's) form
- *"Family Financial Statement" (FFS)*—The American College Testing (ACT) Program's form
- *"Financial Aid Form (FAF)"*—The College Scholarship Service's (CSS's) form

If you want to apply for Federal aid *only,* all the forms are free. (You will need to fill out only certain Federal "core" sections of the form. Your application will tell you which sections those are.) Then you must check a box to have your information forwarded to the Federal processing center. The box is in the middle of the form.

If you want to apply for non-Federal aid as well, you will have to fill out some additional information that all the forms except the AFSA collect. ACT and CSS charge a fee for processing that extra information. So, while applying for Federal aid is always free, you may have to pay a fee to apply for non-Federal aid—depending on which form your school asks you to use.

READ THE INSTRUCTIONS when you apply for financial aid. Most mistakes are made because students do not read the instructions on the application. Pay special attention to any questions on dependency status and income, since these areas are where most mistakes are made.

Send your application to the address given in your application booklet. It will take approximately 4 weeks for your application to be processed, and you may have to confirm or correct information and return it for reprocessing. Reprocessing takes another 2 to 3 weeks. Also, you may have to prove the information you reported is correct. You need to complete each step in the process promptly, so that you don't miss any deadlines. Missing a deadline means you will lose out on student aid.

If it's been more than 4 weeks since you applied and you haven't heard anything, you can check the status of your application by writing to—

Federal Student Aid Information Center
P.O. Box 84
Washington, DC 20044

When you write, make sure you include in your letter your full name, permanent address, Social Security number, date of birth, and signature.

NOTE: Aid from Federal programs is not guaranteed from one year to the next. You must reapply every year. Also, if you change schools, your aid doesn't automatically go with you. Check with your new school to find out what steps you must take.

Records Needed

When you fill out an application, you should have certain records on hand.

The most recent U.S. Income Tax Return is the most important one, since you must use specific numbers from specific lines on the tax return to fill out your application. You'll need to refer to—

- your tax return,
- your parents' return (if you apply as a dependent student), and
- your spouse's return (if you're married and your spouse filed a separate return).

Referring to the tax form will make it easier for you to complete your application and get it through the processing system.

You may apply even if the tax return is not yet completed. However, this means you'll have to estimate the financial information on your application, and you may have to prove the accuracy of your estimate before you're awarded aid. Also, you'll have to change later any figures that prove to be incorrect.

Other useful records to have on hand—

- W-2 forms and other records of income received the previous year
- current bank statements and mortgage information
- records of benefits received from the Social Security Administration, Department of Veterans' Affairs, and other agencies

You should save all records and all other materials used to prepare your application because you'll need them later if either the Department of Education or your school selects you for a process called "verification." This means you'll have to prove that what you reported on your application is correct. (Many schools require all financial aid applicants to verify the information they reported on their aid applications.) As part of the verification process, you'll have to give your financial aid administrator certain information or documents, such as the ones mentioned in this section. So make sure you keep these documents, and make sure the information you report is accurate.

Student Aid Report (SAR)

After you apply for Federal student aid, you'll receive a Student Aid Report (SAR) in approximately 4 weeks. The SAR will contain the information you gave on your application plus numbers that tell you about your eligibility for Federal student aid:

- a Pell Grant Index (PGI) number, which determines your Pell Grant eligibility, and a
- Family Contribution (FC) number, used in determining your eligibility for the campus-based and Stafford Loan programs

Unlike the FC, the PGI is a fixed number (below a certain number, you're eligible for a Pell Grant; above a certain number, you're not eligible). This means your SAR can tell you right away about your Pell Grant eligibility. That's why the SAR is most often associated with Pell Grant eligibility, even though it can be used in determining your eligibility for other Federal student aid programs.

If your Student Aid Report says:

You May Receive a Pell Grant

Your SAR will have 3 parts:

Part 1—Information Summary—Contains instructions to review your SAR to make sure it's correct, and will give you other information about the results of your application.

Part 2—Information *Review* Form—The part you use to change any information on the SAR that's incorrect—review this part carefully! If you need to make changes, put the correct information in the "The correct answer is" column. Then, sign the Certification statement on the back of Part 2 and return Part 2 only to the address given on the back of Part 2. You'll receive a new SAR in 2 to 3 weeks.

Part 3—Pell Grant Payment Voucher—This part is for your school's use.

If all the information on your SAR is correct as it is, submit all three parts of the SAR to your financial aid administrator right away. Your aid administrator will use the information on your SAR to determine the amount of your Pell Grant.

You're Ineligible For a Pell Grant

Your SAR will have 2 parts—Parts 1 and 2 only.

Even if your SAR says you're not eligible for a Pell Grant, contact your financial aid administrator. He or she may use the Family Contribution (FC) number on the SAR in determining whether you're eligible for other Federal student aid. If you are, your school will send you a letter telling you the amount and kinds of financial aid you'll get.

Your Eligibility Has Not Been Determined

This means you did not correctly or completely fill out your student aid application, and no PGI could be calculated. You'll receive a 2-part SAR—Parts 1 and 2 only.

Part 1, the Information Summary, will contain comments asking you to confirm, correct, or add information on . . .

Part 2—Information *Request* Form—review this part carefully! After you've made any necessary changes or additions, sign the Certification statement on the back of this part and return Part 2 only to the address given on the back of Part 2. You'll get a new SAR in 2 to 3 weeks.

If you have any trouble understanding what you're supposed to do after you get your SAR or how you're supposed to make corrections, your financial aid administrator can help you and can answer any questions you have.

To request a copy of your SAR or to correct your address for the records, write to the agency where you sent your application or write

Federal Student Aid Information Center
P.O. Box 84
Washington, DC 20044

When you write, make sure you include in your letter your full name, permanent address, Social Security number, date of birth, and signature.

Special Circumstances

Although the process of determining a student's eligibility for Federal student aid is generally the same for all applicants, there is some flexibility.

For instance, when you apply, if you indicate on your student aid application that you, your spouse, or either of your parents is a "dislocated worker" or "displaced homemaker," special consideration will be given your and/or their financial status when your application is processed. (For definitions of "dislocated worker" and "displaced homemaker," see your financial aid application.) And certain applicants with incomes of $15,000 or less can skip some of the questions on the application.

Some students may have special financial considerations that can't be described adequately on an application. If you feel you have special circumstances that might affect the amount you and your family are expected to contribute toward your education, see your financial aid administrator. Remember, if the aid administrator believes it's appropriate, he or she can change a student's dependency status from dependent to independent. And, for the campus-based and Stafford Loan programs, the aid administrator may adjust your cost of education or your Family Contribution (FC) if he or she feels your circumstances warrant it. For example, if you believe the amount you and your family are expected to contribute toward your education is too high, you can ask your aid administrator to review your case. But remember, the aid administrator does not have to make any of these changes—there have to be very good reasons for doing so. Also remember that the aid administrator's decision is *final* and cannot be appealed to the U.S. Department of Education.

The Pell Grant Program does not allow for *individualized* adjustments. However, there are certain special conditions that would make the family's financial circumstances worse. If one of the conditions listed below applies to you or your family, estimated income information for the following year will be used to calculate your Pell Grant eligibility, instead of the previous year's income.

The conditions are—

- Death
- Separation or divorce
- Loss of a full-time job
- Loss of nontaxable income or benefits such as Social Security, child support, Aid to Families with Dependent Children (AFDC or ADC), welfare, unemployment benefits, etc.

If you think you meet one of the special conditions, see your financial aid administrator. If you qualify, the aid administrator will explain what steps to take so that estimated income will be used.

Telephone Numbers

You may have questions about your application, your SAR, or other Federal student aid matters, and you need an answer right away. If so, you may call the number below at the Federal Student Aid Information Center between the hours of 9:00 a.m. and 5:30 p.m. (Eastern Standard Time), Monday through Friday:

1 (800) 4 FED AID—if calling on or after May 1, 1991

The Information Center provides the following services at the toll-free number listed above:

- Helping you file an application or correct a SAR
- Checking on whether a school takes part in Federal student aid programs
- Explaining student eligibility requirements

- Explaining the process of determining financial aid awards
- Mailing publications

1 (301) 722-9200
You must call this number at the Information Center if you want to find out if your application has been processed, or if you want a copy of your Student Aid Report (SAR). Please note that you will have to pay for this call. The Center cannot accept collect calls.

1 (301) 369-0518 (TDD)
If you are hearing impaired, you may call this TDD number at the Information Center for help with any Federal student aid questions you may have. This number is not toll-free, and the Center cannot accept collect calls.

If you have reason to suspect any fraud, waste, or abuse involving Federal student aid funds, you may call the following toll-free number:

1 (800) MIS-USED
This number is the hotline to the U.S. Department of Education's Inspector General's office. You may remain anonymous, if you wish.

Grants, Work-Study, and Loans

Pell Grants

A Pell Grant is an award to help undergraduates pay for their education after high school. For the Pell Grant Program, an undergraduate is one who has not earned a bachelor's or first professional degree. (A professional degree would include a degree in such fields as pharmacy or dentistry, for example.)

Eligibility for those who receive a Pell Grant for the first time is usually limited to 5 to 6 years of undergraduate study. For more information, see your financial aid administrator.

For many students, Pell Grants provide a "foundation" of financial aid, to which aid from other Federal and non-Federal sources may be added. Unlike loans, grants don't have to be paid back.

How do I qualify?

You must be attending school at least half-time.

To determine if you're eligible, the Department of Education uses a standard formula, passed into law by Congress, to evaluate the information you report on your student aid application. The formula produces a Pell Grant Index (PGI) number. Your Student Aid Report contains this number and will tell you whether you're eligible.

The formula used to determine your Pell Grant Index (PGI) is too long to be included here. However, you can get a booklet that describes it in detail by writing to—

Federal Student Aid Information Center
Box 84
Washington, DC 20044

How much money can I get?

How much you get will depend not only on your Pell Grant Index (PGI) number, but on the cost of education at your school, whether you're a full-time or part-time student, and whether you attend school for a full academic year, or less than that.

How will I be paid?

You must submit all 3 parts of your Student Aid Report (SAR) to your school by the deadline. Your school will then credit your award to your account, pay you directly, or use a combination of these methods.

The school must tell you in writing how and when you'll be paid and how much your award will be. You should acknowledge the school's notification in writing, for the school's records. Schools must pay at least once per term (semester, trimester, or quarter). Schools that do not use formally defined, traditional terms must pay at least twice per academic year.

Campus-based Programs

The three programs you'll read about in this section are called "campus-based" programs because they're administered by the financial aid administrator at each participating school. Your financial aid package may contain aid from one or more of these programs.

Even though each program is different—SEOG offers grants, CWS offers jobs, and Perkins provides loans—they have these characteristics in common:

- You can go to school less than half-time and still be able to receive aid.
- How much aid you receive from the campus-based programs depends on your financial need, the amount of other aid you'll receive, and the availability of funds at your school. Unlike the Pell Grant Program, which provides funds to every eligible student, each school participating in any of the campus-based programs receives a certain amount of funds for each program. When that money is gone, there are no more awards from that program for that year.
- There's no one deadline for applying as there is for the Pell Grant Program—each school sets its own. But most deadlines are quite early in each calendar year. Be sure to check with the financial aid administrator at your school to find out what its deadlines are. You'll probably miss out on receiving aid from the campus-based programs if you don't apply early!

SEOG

A Supplemental Educational Opportunity Grant (SEOG) is for undergraduates with exceptional financial need (with priority given to Pell Grant recipients), and it doesn't have to be paid back. You can get up to $4,000 a year, depending on the restrictions noted on the preceding page.

The Department of Education guarantees that each participating school will receive enough money to pay the Pell Grants of its eligible students. As noted on the preceding page, there's no guarantee every eligible student will be able to receive an SEOG.

Your school will credit your SEOG to your account, pay you directly, or use a combination of these methods. Schools must pay students at least once per term (semester, trimester, or quarter). Schools that do not use traditional terms must pay at least twice during the academic year. (There's one exception: If the total SEOG aid you receive is $500 or less, the school may pay you just once during the academic year, if it chooses.)

CWS

The College Work-Study (CWS) Program provides jobs for undergraduate and graduate students who need financial aid. CWS gives you a chance to earn money to help pay your educational expenses. Your pay will be at least the current Federal minimum wage, but it may also be related to the type of work you do and the skills required.

If you're an undergraduate, you'll be paid by the hour. If you're a graduate student, you may be paid by the hour or you may receive a salary. No CWS student may be paid by commission or fee. Your school must pay you at least once a month.

If you work on campus, you'll usually work for your school. If you work off campus, your job will usually involve work that is in the public interest, and your employer will usually be a private or public nonprofit organization, or a local, State, or Federal agency. However, some schools may have agreements with private sector employers for CWS jobs. These jobs must be related to your course of study.

Your school sets your work schedule. In arranging a job and assigning work hours, your financial aid administrator will take into account your class schedule, your health, and your academic progress. And remember, the amount you earn can't exceed your total CWS award.

Perkins Loans

A Perkins Loan is a low-interest (5 percent) loan to help you pay for your education after high school. These loans are for both undergraduate and graduate students and are made through a school's financial aid office. Your school is your lender. You must repay this loan.

Depending on the restrictions noted, you may borrow up to—

- $4,500 if you're enrolled in a vocational program, or if you have completed less than 2 years of a program leading to a bachelor's degree.
- $9,000 if you're an undergraduate student who has already completed 2 years of study toward a bachelor's degree and has achieved third-year status. (This total includes any amount you borrowed under Perkins [or under the National Direct Student Loan Program, its former name] for your first 2 years of study.)
- $18,000 for graduate or professional study. (This total includes any amount you borrowed under Perkins/NDSL for your undergraduate study.)

After you sign a promissory note agreeing to repay the loan, your school will either pay you directly or credit your account. You'll receive the loan in at least two payments during the academic year. (There's one exception: If the total Perkins Loan you receive is $500 or less, the school may pay you just once during the academic year, if it chooses.)

You have a certain period of time before you have to begin repayment, called a "grace period." If you're attending at least half-time, you have a grace period of 9 months after you graduate, leave school, or drop below half-time. If you're a less-than-half-time student, your grace period may be different. Check with your financial aid administrator.

If you borrowed under the old National Direct Student Loan (NDSL) Program ***on or after*** October 1, 1980, your grace period is 6 months. If you borrowed ***before*** October 1, 1980, your grace period is 9 months. At the end of your grace period, you must begin repaying your loan. You may be allowed up to 10 years to repay.

The amount of each payment depends on the size of your debt and on the length of your repayment period. Usually, you must pay at least $30 per month. In special cases—for example, if you're unemployed or ill for a long period of time—your school may allow you to make payments that are less than $30 per month or may extend your repayment period.

Under certain conditions, you can defer repayment of a Perkins Loan after you leave school, as long as you're not in default. However, deferments aren't automatic. You have to apply for one through your school, using a deferment request form that you must get from your school.

Even though you may have *applied* for a deferment, you still must continue to make payments until your deferment is processed. If you don't, you may end up in default.

Your loan will be cancelled if you die or become totally and permanently disabled. Your loan can be cancelled if you're a teacher (under certain circumstances), or if you're a Head Start or a Peace Corps or VISTA volunteer. For more information, read your promissory note or contact your financial aid administrator.

If you have any questions about the terms of your Perkins Loan, repayment obligations, deferment, or cancellation, check with the school that made you the loan. Remember, only that school can grant deferment or cancellation, or make decisions concerning your loan.

Stafford Loans

Stafford Loans are low-interest loans made to students attending school at least half-time. Loans are made by a lender such as a bank, credit union, or savings and loan association. Sometimes a school acts as a lender. These loans are insured by the guarantee agency in each State and reinsured by the Federal Government. You must repay this loan.

For new borrowers who receive loans for periods of enrollment beginning *on* or *after* July 1, 1988, the interest rate is generally 8 percent for the first 4 years of repayment and 10 percent after that. For new borrowers who took out a loan *between* July 1, 1987, and June 30, 1988, the interest rate is 8 percent.

Students who are *not* new borrowers should check their promissory note for the interest rate.

Depending on your financial need, you may borrow up to—

- $2,625 a year, if you're a first- or second-year undergraduate student.

- $4,000 a year, if you have completed 2 years of study and have achieved third-year status.
- $7,500 a year, if you're a graduate student.

The total debt you can have outstanding as an undergraduate is $17,250. This includes any amount you may have borrowed under the Guaranteed Student Loan (GSL) Program—the former name for the Stafford Loan Program. The total debt for graduate or professional study is $54,750 including any Stafford Loans and GSL's made at the undergraduate level.

You can't borrow more than the cost of education at your school, minus your FC and any other financial aid you receive.

You can get an application from a lender, a school, or your State guarantee agency. After you fill out your part of the application, the school you plan to attend must complete its part, certifying your enrollment, your cost of education, your academic standing, any other financial aid you'll receive, and your financial need.

Before you can receive a Stafford Loan, your school must first determine your eligibility for a Pell Grant, if you're an undergraduate and your school participates in the Pell Grant Program. If you're eligible, the amount of your Pell Grant will be considered in determining your financial aid package, so that you won't be over-awarded.

When the school's portion of the application is completed, you or your school submits it to the lender you've chosen. If the lender agrees to make the loan and gets the approval of the guarantee agency, the lender will send the loan amount to your school.

Since not every lender participates in the Stafford Loan Program, you should begin looking for one as soon as you're accepted by your school. Give yourself as much time as possible to complete the application process.

Your lender sends your loan proceeds to your school. Your loan proceeds will be made payable either to you or to both you and your school.

For loans made on or after January 1, 1990, for periods of enrollment beginning on or after that date, your school must issue your loan proceeds to you in two or more payments.

Contact your State guarantee agency. It's the best source of information on the Stafford Loan Program in your State. To find out your State guarantee agency's address and phone number and to find out more information about borrowing, call the Federal Student Aid Information Center (toll-free): **1 (800) 4 FED AID,** if calling on or after May 1, 1991.

There is an "origination fee" of **5 percent** for making a Stafford Loan, which will be deducted proportionately from each loan disbursement made to you. The money is passed on to the Federal Government to help reduce the Government's cost of subsidizing these low-interest loans.

Your lender may also charge you an insurance premium of up to 3 percent of the loan principle. This premium must be deducted proportionately from each disbursement.

After you graduate, leave school, or drop below half-time, you have a certain period of time before you have to begin repayment, called a "grace period." The length of this period depends on when you took out your loan, but it is usually 6 to 12 months. Check your promissory note or ask your lender what your grace period is.

When you graduate, leave school, or drop below half-time, you must notify your lender.

The amount of each payment depends on the size of your debt and on the length of your repayment period. Usually, you'll have to pay at least $50 per month or $600 per year. You should ask your lender what your monthly payments will be before you take out the loan, so you'll know what to expect.

For more detail about deferment and repayment of Stafford Loans, contact your financial aid administrator, your lender, or the guarantee agency in your State.

If you serve as an enlisted person in certain selected specialties of the U.S. Army, the Army Reserves, the Army National Guard, or the Air National Guard, the Department of Defense will, as an enlistment incentive, repay a portion of your Stafford Loan. If you think you may qualify, contact your recruiting officer.

If you have any questions about the terms of your Stafford Loan, repayment obligations, deferment, or cancellation, check with your lender. Remember, only your lender can grant deferment or cancellation, or make decisions concerning your loan.

PLUS/SLS

PLUS loans are for parents who want to borrow to help pay for their children's education; Supplemental Loans for Students (SLS) are for student borrowers. Both loans provide additional funds for educational expenses and, like Stafford Loans, are made by a lender such as a bank, credit union, or savings and loan association.

The interest rate for each loan is shown on the promissory note, signed by the borrower when the loan is made.

- PLUS enables parents to borrow up to $4,000 per year, to a total of $20,000, for each child who is enrolled at least half-time and is a dependent student.
- Under SLS, graduate students and independent undergraduates who are enrolled in a program whose length is a full academic year may borrow up to $4,000 per academic year, to a total of $20,000. This amount is in addition to the Stafford Loan limits. (In exceptional circumstances, the financial aid administrator may authorize dependent undergraduates to apply for an SLS.

First-year undergraduates enrolled in a program of less than a full academic year have different annual borrowing limits for SLS:

- $2,500 is the limit for those enrolled in a program that is at least ²⁄₃ of an academic year but less than a full academic year.
- $1,500 is the limit for those enrolled in a program that is less than ²⁄₃ but at least ¹⁄₃ of an academic year. (SLS loans are not made to first-year undergraduates enrolled in a program that is less than ¹⁄₃ of an academic year.)

Before you can receive an SLS, your school must determine your eligibility for a Stafford Loan and for a Pell Grant (if you're an undergraduate and your school participates in the Pell Grant Program). If you're eligible for aid from either or both of those programs, the amount you're eligible for may affect the amount you can borrow under SLS: Under SLS—as under the Stafford Loan Program—you can't borrow more than the cost of education at your school minus any other financial aid you receive.

If your parent(s) takes out a PLUS loan for you, the lender sends the full amount of the loan proceeds in the form of a check directly to your parent(s).

If you take out an SLS, the lender sends the loan proceeds to your school. Your loan proceeds will be made payable either to you or to both you and your school.

For loans made on or after January 1, 1990, for periods of enrollment beginning on or after that date, your school must issue your loan proceeds to you in two or more payments. If you're a first-year undergraduate student, you cannot receive your first payment until 30 days after the first day of your program of study.

Your lender may charge an insurance premium of up to 3 percent of the loan principal. This premium must be deducted proportionately from each loan disbursement made to you. There is no origination fee for these loans.

PLUS and SLS borrowers generally must begin repaying both principal and interest within sixty days after the last loan disbursement. However, if a deferment applies (including a deferment for being in school), borrowers do not begin repaying any *principal* until the deferment ends. Deferments do not apply to *interest,* although the lender may let the interest accumulate until the deferment ends.

SLS borrowers get the same deferments as Stafford Loan borrowers except that, as mentioned above, under SLS the deferments apply only to loan *principal*. PLUS deferments are much more limited and also apply only to principal. For more details about specific repayment and deferment conditions, contact your financial aid administrator, your lender, or the guarantee agency in your State.

Unlike Stafford Loans, there are no grace periods for PLUS and SLS loans.

Borrower Responsibilities, Borrower Rights

Responsibilities

When you take out any student loan, you have certain responsibilities you must live up to. Here are a few of them:

- When you sign a promissory note, you are agreeing to repay according to the terms of the note. This note is a *legally binding* document. This commitment to repay means that, except in cases of cancellation, *you will have to pay back the loan*—even if you don't complete your education, aren't able to get a job after you complete the program, or you're dissatisfied with, or don't receive, the educational or other services you purchased from your school. Think about what this obligation means before you take out a loan. If you don't pay back your loan on time or according to the terms in your promissory note, you may go into default. If you do, your school, lender, or guarantee agency can require you to repay immediately the entire amount you owe, including all interest, collection, and late payment charges. They can sue you to collect that amount, and they can ask the Federal Government for help in collecting from you.
- You must make payments on your loan even if you don't receive a bill. Billing statements (or coupon books) are sent as a convenience to the borrower, but not

receiving them doesn't relieve you of your obligation to make payments.

- You must notify your lender if you graduate, withdraw from school, or drop below half-time status; change your name, address, or Social Security number; or transfer to another school.
- Before you leave school, you must attend an exit interview.

Rights

You have certain rights as a borrower. Listed below are some of them.

- You have the right to a grace period before your repayment period begins, if your loan provides for one. The grace period begins when you leave school or drop below half-time status. The exact length of your grace period is shown on your promissory note.
- You must be given a loan repayment schedule, which lets you know when your first payment is due, and the number, frequency, and amount of all payments.
- You must be given a list of deferment conditions and the conditions under which the Department of Defense will repay your loan.

Before your school gives you your first loan disbursement, your school/lender must give you the following information about your loan:

- The full amount of the loan, the interest rate, and when you must start repaying.
- The effect borrowing will have on your eligibility for other types of financial aid.
- A complete list of any charges you must pay (loan fees), and information on how those charges are collected.
- The yearly and total amounts you can borrow, and the maximum and minimum repayment periods.
- A current description of loans you owe your school and/or lender, an estimate of what your total debt will be, and what your monthly payments will be.
- An explanation of default and its consequences.
- An explanation of options for prepaying your loan at any time without penalty, for refinancing your loan, and for taking advantage of loan consolidation.

Before your repayment period begins, your school/lender must tell you—

- The amount of your total debt (principal and interest), what your interest rate is, and the total interest charges on your loan.
- The name of your lender, where to send your payments, and where to write if you have questions about your loan.
- What fees you should expect during the repayment period.
- About prepayment, refinancing, and consolidation options.

There are some specific rights and information you're entitled to if you have a Stafford Loan or an SLS:

Before your school gives you your first loan disbursement, the school must counsel you about your loan. This includes emphasizing the seriousness of the repayment obligation you're assuming, describing in forceful terms the likely consequences of default, and emphasizing that you must repay even if you drop out, can't find employment after you've finished school, or don't like the quality of education you received.

In addition, the school must make sure that someone with expertise in *all* the Federal student aid programs is available shortly after this initial counseling session to answer any questions you may have about those programs.

Your school must also counsel you again shortly before you leave school or drop below half-time status. In this session, the exit interview, your school must again cover the topics it covered in the initial session. In addition, your school must—

- give you general information on the average indebtedness of those who have received Stafford Loans or SLS loans at the school.
- tell you what your average expected monthly repayment is, based on that average indebtedness.
- review available repayment options (for example, loan consolidation or refinancing).
- give you debt management advice that the school feels would help you in making your payments.

Before You Borrow

If you plan to apply for student loans each year you're in school, try to estimate how much your monthly payments will be when you leave school. The amount you'll have to repay will add up fast! If you need more information on debt management, contact your financial aid administrator, your lender, or the guarantee agency in your State.

A change in career goals, loss of a job, or some other unexpected change in your school or work situation could make loan repayment more difficult than you expected. Deferment may help in some cases (for example, if you want to return to school or decide to enter the Armed Forces), but the extended repayment period will be a long-term financial obligation.

If you're willing but unable to meet your repayment schedule because of unusual circumstances, and you have a Perkins Loan (or National Direct Student Loan [NDSL]), you may request a hardship deferment. If you have a Stafford Loan (or Guaranteed Student Loan [GSL]), PLUS, or SLS, you may request forbearance if you're willing but unable to meet your repayment schedule and you're not eligible for a deferment. "Forbearance" means permitting payments to be stopped temporarily, allowing a longer time for making smaller payments, or making smaller payments than were previously scheduled. Your lender does not have to grant forbearance, however.

Loan consolidation or refinancing might also be of help to you if you have multiple loans and if you qualify. Your lender can provide more information about consolidation and refinancing options. If you have a Stafford Loan or SLS (or if your parents have a PLUS for you) and you need to borrow again, try applying to the lender who made you (or your parents) the first loan. This will make future loan refinancing easier. To find out more, contact your lender.

Important Terms

Ability to Benefit: Applies to students who do not have a high school diploma, or its equivalent, or a GED (General Education Development Certificate). These students can still receive Federal student aid if they take a test measuring their ability to benefit from the education offered. The test must be administered independently and must be approved by the U.S. Department of Education. Students should check with their financial aid administrator for more information.

Anti-Drug Abuse Act Certification: To receive a Pell Grant, you must sign a statement certifying that you will not make, distribute, dispense, possess, or use illegal drugs during the period covered by the Grant. In addition, you are also certifying that if you are convicted of a drug-related offense committed during that period, you will report the conviction in writing to the U.S. Department of Education. Your Student Aid Report (SAR) will contain this certification statement although, in some cases, your school may ask you to sign instead a separate statement it has prepared.

Your eligibility for *any* of the programs covered may be suspended or terminated by a court as part of a conviction for possessing or distributing illegal drugs.

Assets: Savings and checking accounts, the value of a business, stocks, bonds, money market funds, mutual funds, real estate, trust funds, etc. Cars are not considered assets, nor are possessions such as stamp collections or musical instruments.

Citizen/Eligible Non-Citizen: You must be one of the following to receive Federal student aid:

- U.S. citizen
- U.S. national (includes natives of American Samoa or Swain's Island)
- U.S. permanent resident who has an I-151, I-551, or I-551C (Alien Registration Receipt Card)

If you're not in one of these categories, you must have an Arrival-Departure Record (I-94) from the U.S. Immigration and Naturalization Service (INS) showing one of the following designations:

- "Refugee"
- "Asylum Granted"
- "Indefinite Parole" and/or "Humanitarian Parole"
- "Cuban-Haitian Entrant, Status Pending"
- "Conditional Entrant" (valid only if issued before April 1, 1980)
- Other eligible non-citizen with a Temporary Resident Card (I-688)

Also, you're eligible for Federal student aid if you have a suspension of deportation case pending before Congress.

If you're in the U.S. on an F1 or F2 student visa only, or on a J1 or J2 exchange visitor visa only, you cannot get Federal student aid. Also, persons with G series visas (pertaining to international organizations) are not eligible for Federal student aid.

Only citizens and non-citizen nationals can receive a Stafford Loan, PLUS, or SLS for study at a foreign institution.

Permanent residents of the Trust Territory of the Pacific (Palau) may be eligible for all the student aid programs mentioned. Citizens of the Federated States of Micronesia and the Marshall Islands are eligible for Pell Grants, Supplemental Educational Opportunity Grants (SEOG's), or College Work-Study *only.* All of these citizens should check with their financial aid administrators for more information.

Cost of Education (or **Cost of Attendance**): The total amount it will cost a student to go to school—usually expressed as a yearly figure. The cost of education covers tuition and fees; on-campus room and board (or a housing and food allowance for off-campus students); and allowances for books, supplies, transportation, child care, costs related to a handicap, and miscellaneous expenses. Talk to the financial aid administrator at the school you're planning to attend if you have any unusual expenses that may affect your cost of education or your ability to pay that cost.

Default: Failure to repay a student loan according to the terms agreed to when you signed a promissory note. Default also means failure to submit requests for deferment or cancellation on a timely basis. If you default on a student loan, your school, lender, State, and the Federal Government all can take action to recover the money, including notifying national credit bureaus of your default. This may affect your future credit rating for a long time. For example, you may find it very difficult to borrow from a bank to buy a car or a house. Also, you may be liable for expenses incurred in collecting the loan. If you decide to return to school, you're not entitled to receive additional Federal aid or a deferment of your loan repayments. Finally, the Internal Revenue Service may withhold your income tax refund. The amount of your refund will be applied toward the amount you owe.

Eligible Program: A course of study that leads to a degree or certificate at a school that takes part in one or more of the student aid programs described. To get a Pell Grant, SEOG, Perkins Loan, or a College Work-Study job, you must be enrolled in an eligible program. The same is true for a Stafford Loan, PLUS, or SLS, with two exceptions:

–If a school has told you that you must take certain coursework to qualify for admission into one of its eligible programs, you can get a Stafford Loan or an SLS (or your parent[s] can get a PLUS for you) for up to 12 consecutive months while you're completing that coursework. You must be enrolled at least half-time, and you must meet the usual student aid eligibility requirements.

—If you're enrolled at least half-time in a program to obtain a professional credential or certification that is required for employment as an elementary or secondary school teacher in a particular State, you can get a Stafford Loan or an SLS (or your parent[s] can get a PLUS for you) while you're enrolled in the program.

Exit Interview: A counseling session you must attend before you leave your school, if you have any of the loans described. At this session, your school will give you information on the average amount borrowers owe, the amount of your monthly repayment, and information about deferment, refinancing, and loan consolidation options.

Family Contribution (FC): An amount that indicates how much of your family's financial resources should be available to help pay for school. This amount, determined by a formula called the Congressional Methodology, is used in determining your eligibility for aid from the Supplemental Educational Opportunity Grant (SEOG), College Work-Study (CWS), Perkins Loan, and Stafford Loan programs. If you have any unusual expenses that may affect your Family Contribution, make sure you notify your financial aid administrator.

Financial Aid Package: The total amount of financial aid a student receives. Federal and non-Federal aid such as loans, grants, or work-study are combined in a "package" to help meet the student's need. Using available resources to give each student the best possible package of aid is one of the major responsibilities of a school's financial aid administrator.

Guarantee Agency: The organization that administers the Stafford Loan, PLUS, and SLS programs in your State. The Federal Government sets loan limits and interest rates, but each State is free to set its own additional limitations, within Federal guidelines. This agency is the best source of information on Stafford Loans, PLUS loans, and SLS loans in your State. To find out the name, address, and telephone number of the agency in your State, as well as information about borrowing, call the Federal Student Aid Information Center at **1 (800) 4 FED AID.**

Half-Time: At schools measuring progress by credit hours and academic terms (semesters, trimesters, or quarters), "half-time" means at least 6 semester hours or quarter hours per term. At schools measuring progress by credit hours but not using academic terms, "half-time" means at least 12 semester hours or 18 quarter hours per year. At schools measuring progress by clock hours, "half-time" means at least 12 hours per week. Note that schools may choose to set higher minimums than these. Also, Stafford Loan, PLUS, and SLS requirements may be slightly different.

You must be attending school at least half-time to be eligible to receive a Pell Grant, Stafford Loan, a PLUS, or an SLS. Half-time enrollment is not a requirement to receive aid from the Supplemental Educational Opportunity Grant, College Work-Study, and Perkins Loan programs.

Internship Deferment: A period during which loan payments can be deferred (postponed) if a borrower is participating in a program required to begin professional practice or service. An internship deferment *also* includes participation in an internship or residency program leading to a degree or certificate awarded by an institution of higher education, hospital, or health care facility offering postgraduate training. (*Note to Perkins Loan borrowers:* This second aspect of an internship deferment applies only if your period of enrollment in school began on or after July 1, 1977, and you had no outstanding [unpaid] National Direct/Defense Student Loan [NDSL] on that date.) If you're in an eligible internship program, you may defer repayment of your Perkins Loan/NDSL, Stafford Loan, or SLS for up to 2 years.

Loan Consolidation: A plan that allows certain eligible lenders to pay off your existing student loans and to create one new loan. You're eligible for loan consolidation if you have loans totalling at least $5,000. You must be in repayment (or have entered your grace period) before your loans can be consolidated. You cannot be more than 90 days delinquent on any loan being consolidated. The interest rate on the consolidated loan will be 9 percent or more, depending on the interest rates of the loans consolidated. The repayment period will be from 10 to 25 years, depending on the amount to be repaid. Except for PLUS loans, the student loans described are eligible for consolidation.

New Borrower: A term that applies to the Stafford Loan, PLUS, or SLS programs. You're a "new borrower" under these programs if you had no outstanding (unpaid) Stafford Loans, PLUS, SLS, or consolidation loans on the date you signed your promissory note, *and* if your loan was either disbursed on or after July 1, 1987, or was for a period of enrollment that began on or after July 1, 1987. Once you qualify as a new borrower, the loan conditions that apply to "new borrowers" automatically apply to any future Stafford Loans, PLUS loans, or SLS loans you may receive.

Parental Leave Deferment: A period of up to 6 months when loan payments can be postponed if a borrower is pregnant, or if a borrower is taking care of a newborn or newly adopted child. The borrower must be unemployed and not attending school. To get this deferment, you must apply within 6 months after you leave school or drop below half-time status.

Pell Grant Index (PGI): The number that appears on your Student Aid Report (SAR), telling you about your Pell Grant eligibility. The PGI is calculated by a standard formula that uses the financial information you reported when you applied for Federal student aid.

Promissory Note: The legal document you sign when you get a student loan. It lists the conditions under which you're borrowing and the terms under which you agree to pay back the loan. It's very important to **READ AND SAVE** this document because you'll need to refer to it later when you begin repaying your loan.

Regular Student: One who is enrolled in an institution to obtain a degree or certificate. Generally, to receive aid from the programs discussed, you must be a regular student. (For the Stafford, PLUS, and SLS programs, there are two exceptions to this requirement.)

Satisfactory Academic Progress: To be eligible to receive Federal student aid, you must be maintaining satisfactory academic progress toward a degree or certificate. You must meet your school's written standard of satisfactory progress. Check with your school to find out what its standard is.

If you received Federal student aid for the first time on or after July 1, 1987 *and* you're enrolled in a program that's longer than 2 years, the following definition of satisfactory progress ***also*** applies to you: You must be maintaining a "C" average by the end of your second academic year of study, or have an academic standing consistent with your institution's graduation requirements. You must continue to maintain satisfactory academic progress for the rest of your course of study.

Statement of Educational Purpose/Certification Statement on Refunds and Default: You must sign this statement in order to receive Federal student aid. By signing it, you're stating that you do not owe a refund on a Pell Grant or SEOG, that you're not in default on a Perkins Loan, Stafford Loan, or SLS, and that the amount you've borrowed under those loan programs doesn't exceed the allowable limits. You're also agreeing to use your student aid only for education-related expenses. Part 1 of the 1991–92 Student Aid Report (SAR) contains such a statement. You must sign either this one or a similar one prepared by your school.

If your parent wants to borrow a PLUS loan for you, neither you nor your parent can owe a refund or be in default. Your parent will also have to sign a statement of educational purpose/certification statement on refunds and default that your school will prepare.

Statement of Registration Status: If you're required to register with the Selective Service, you must sign a statement indicating you have done so before you can receive any Federal student aid. This requirement applies to males who were born on or after January 1, 1960, are at least 18, are citizens or eligible non-citizens, and are not currently on active duty in the Armed Forces. (Citizens of the Federated States of Micronesia, the Marshall Islands, or the Trust Territory of the Pacific [Palau] are exempt from registering.)

Part 1 of the 1991–92 Student Aid Report contains a statement of registration status. You must sign either that one or a similar one prepared by your school. (Some schools require all students to sign a statement, indicating that the student either has registered with the Selective Service or is not required to do so.)

Statement of Updated Information: You must sign a statement certifying that certain Student Aid Report (SAR) items are correct *at the time you submit your SAR to your school*. If information for any of those items changes after you submit your application, you must update the information so that it's correct on the date you sign your SAR. Otherwise, you won't be able to receive Federal student aid. Read the Statement of Updated Information on the back of Part 1 of your SAR for the information that must be updated.

The only exception to the requirement to update is when changes occur because your marital status changes. In that case, you cannot update.

CAR LEASING: AN ALTERNATIVE

Originally an option offered to businesses, over the past few years, leasing a new automobile has become a popular alternative to purchasing. Offering lower monthly payments as the main advantage, leasing attracts consumers by promising the use of a new car with fewer hassles than owning.

Leasing is similar to renting, but for a much longer time. A leasing company buys a car from a dealership (even if the leasing is done *through* the dealer; many dealers own separate leasing operations), finances the purchase through a bank, then passes the costs on to the consumer.

Types of Leases

There are two basic types of leases. The first—and most popular—is the *closed-end lease,* also called a net, fixed-cost, or end lease. With this type, a consumer signs a contract to use an automobile for a specified time for a maximum number of miles, and agrees to pay a monthly fee based on the vehicle's resale value. The leasing company disposes of the car at the end of the lease, and may add charges for damage or excess mileage. In addition, some companies may negotiate with the consumer for an extension of the lease at a reduced rate or offer the driver the first choice to buy the car.

An *open-ended lease,* also known as an equity or finance lease, runs for a fixed time with payments based on the resale of the car. These payments are usually lower than a closed-end lease, however, since the consumer assumes some of the risks. When an open-ended lease expires, some options available include renegotiation of the lease at a reduced rate, first choice to buy, selling the car to a third party, or letting the leasing company sell the car.

Both types of leases specify who is responsible for service and repairs and to what degree. A lease *with* a maintenance contract includes an additional monthly fee, allowing the leasing company to handle the maintenance. *Without* a maintenance contract, the consumer will be responsible. Remember, too, that leasing companies are required by law to disclose any manufacturer's warranties which may cover some maintenance and repairs.

Advantages and Disadvantages

Leasing a car is simpler and often more convenient than financing. The use of a new car can be had as often as every three years, and a customer can avoid the tedium of disposing of the used car. Since the monthly payments are lower, a driver can often afford a larger car, or one with more options, than if the auto were purchased. The disadvantages of leasing, however, can far outweigh the advantages, especially if a consumer does not consider all the aspects of the leasing contract.

Leases are iron-clad contracts with many variables to consider. A consumer attracted by lower payments who opts for a more expensive car may find himself in a longer lease or with a higher end sum, either of which can add up to 40 percent to the overall price of a car. In addition, although some states cover leasing agreements under their lemon laws, many do not, and a driver with a faulty car may be stuck with the car and repair bills—and the inconvenience—or have to pay an additional fee for the premature end to the lease.

Check List for Leasing

If a consumer does decide on leasing, there are many options that should be considered:

- Is a security deposit or advance payment needed? How much? Will it be returned? When? If not, would it be enough for a down payment on the same car?
- What is the schedule of payments? Are taxes, title, registration, and insurance included? What late fees are charged?
- What are the restrictions on mileage and conditions of premature termination or renewal of the lease? Who is allowed to drive the car?
- What are the procedures to follow if the car is a lemon? Can the car be test driven before the agreement is signed?

As with financing a car, several comparisons should be made. Check at least three leasing companies and compare their prices, not only to each other but to the costs involved with purchasing the same car. When calling to check, be as specific as possible as to the type car wanted, number of months on a lease, amount of payments, etc. Ask questions about any aspect of the contract that is troubling.

Be Cautious

Leasing can be a simple, convenient way to afford a new car every three or four years, but it can also be a gamble to a consumer who does not take the time to consider all the options and read the fine print.

HOME MORTGAGE GUIDELINES

A home purchase is the largest investment most families undertake. When you settle in the community of your choice, you gain a stake in its future, its plans and problems. You will develop a sense of responsibility and pride in homeownership and, with your neighbors, will have a strong voice in determining the policies the community adopts and the direction it takes.

If you choose a home in the city, you'll enjoy close proximity to shopping areas and convenient transportation, but you may want to check on noise levels. Life in a quiet suburb offers lots of room in peaceful surroundings, but there may be limited transportation to shopping areas and schools. Take time to weigh all the possibilities before you reach a decision to purchase a home in a particular location.

Homeownership involves practical benefits. You can deduct interest paid on a mortgage loan from your income when you pay Federal income taxes. This also is true of taxes paid on the property. These advantages give the home buyer a good inflation hedge.

If properly and cautiously handled, the home buying process can be a pleasant experience resulting in a lifetime of genuine satisfaction. If your purchase is made in a hasty and unbusinesslike manner, the result may be a regrettable or even a disastrous financial error.

Are You Ready to Buy?

There are some key questions to ask when making up your mind about buying a house. To make a realistic choice you must determine how much you can spend on the property, based on your income and family expenses.

First, you must decide whether you are likely to live in the home for several years. In the early life of a mortgage, the bulk of your mortgage payment goes to interest and you are acquiring very little equity. The longer you hold the property, the more equity you acquire.

Perhaps your next consideration is the matter of paying for a new home. Here are two ways many people use to estimate ability to meet house payments.

1. The price of the home generally should not exceed two times your annual family income.

2. A homeowner usually should not pay more than 38 percent of income after Federal tax for monthly housing expense (payment on the mortgage loan plus average cost of heat, utilities, repair and maintenance).

The buyer should have the cash necessary to meet the down payment and other expenses at closing time, when the sale is completed. Ask your real estate sales person or lender to provide an estimate of all closing costs you will need at the time of settlement. Quite often the expenses are more than a new home purchaser expects. Congress passed the Real Estate Settlement Procedures Act (RESPA) to protect homebuyers from unnecessarily high settlement costs. It requires advance estimates of settlement costs, limits the size of escrow accounts and prohibits referral fees and kickbacks.

RESPA requires that all borrowers of federally related mortgage loans receive from the lender a HUD-prepared booklet containing information about real estate transactions, settlement services, cost comparisons and relevant consumer protection laws when applying for a loan.

One day before the settlement, the borrower may request that the person who will conduct the settlement provide information on the known actual settlement costs. At settlement, both the buyer and seller are entitled to a statement itemizing the costs they paid in connection with the transaction.

RESPA applies to all lenders and persons conducting settlement of federally related home mortgages.

RESPA prohibits certain abusive practices: kickbacks and referral fees are outlawed; sellers may not designate borrowers' title insurance companies; and excessively large escrow accounts cannot be established or maintained. If you feel a provider of settlement services has violated RESPA, you can address your complaint to the agency or association which has supervisory responsibility over the provider. For the names of such agencies or associations, you will have to check with local and State Governments or consumer agencies operating in your area. You are also encouraged to forward a copy of complaints regarding RESPA violations to the HUD Office of Single Family Housing, which has the primary responsibility for administering the RESPA program. Your complaints can lay the foundation for future legislative or administrative actions.

Send copies of complaints, and inquiries, to:

U.S. Department of Housing and Urban Development
Office of Single Family Housing
451 7th Street S.W.
Washington, D.C. 20410

How to Find the Right House

There are various ways to shop for the house that is right for your family. Houses are sold chiefly through real estate advertising and real estate brokers. Sometimes they can be purchased directly from the owners.

- Read the advertisements in real estate sections of local newspapers.
- Tell your friends and neighbors that you are house hunting. Then take your time in shopping the market. Don't quit until you have a clear idea of the cost and quality of homes currently offered for sale.
- Take a Sunday afternoon drive or walk through neighborhoods you find attractive. You may locate houses that are offered for sale and model homes on display.
- Don't trust to memory when you find an appealing house, but keep a record listing the asking price, owner's name, location, number of bedrooms, taxes, heating bills, and any special features.
- An inexpensive notebook is all you need to avoid ending your search with a blurred impression of houses and neighborhoods you've seen.

What Real Estate Brokers Do

In most cases using a real estate broker will be to your advantage. A good real estate broker provides a clearing center for marketable houses and his screening process will save you many a wild goose chase. Multiple listing services offered by a broker will give a better understanding of housing areas and price ranges.

A good broker will give you general information about a community and specific information about schools, churches, and stores. He may be able to help you get financing and may know how to eliminate much red tape.

The broker's commission is usually 6–7 percent of the sales price but may range up to 10 percent. This commission is paid by the party or parties who engage the broker, usually the seller of the house.

To find a good real estate broker, ask your friends or call the mortgage officers of local banks and savings-and-loan associations. Notice which brokers run the most newspaper advertisements for houses in the neighborhoods you prefer. Often brokers will specialize in a particular neighborhood.

One bit of cautious advice: do not rely too heavily on oral promises or agreements. Remember, the broker is usually working principally for a seller, not a buyer.

New House or Used

Statistics show that two out of every three buyers select a used house. The one person out of three who buys a new house is likely to purchase one that is already built rather than to build his own house or have one built. This is a choice each home buyer must make for himself. Usually one of the biggest advantages that an older house offers is more space for the money. The lot may have been planted with trees and shrubs by previous owners and therefore presents relatively few landscaping problems. In an established neighborhood taxes are usually stable. And, don't fail to weigh the possibility of shorter commuting times and distances from older neighborhoods to schools, offices, and other frequent destinations. Future road construction also could affect the value of a home, so you may wish to check plans for construction with local authorities.

Before purchasing a house in an older neighborhood, be sure that you check on any future plans for neighborhood improvement, urban renewal, or land appropriation for new highways or other projects.

Many older homes have ample bedroom space and this is an important factor in choosing a house. Observe how the floor space has been used by the builder. Most buyers will prefer a house containing fewer rooms that are spacious and livable to a house with a larger number of small cell-like rooms.

Once you've found a house you like, evaluate it carefully. You are buying the property "as is" and you must literally live in as well as with your mistakes.

Inspecting Your Selection

An Older Home

What first appears to be a bargain home may turn out to be a headache. A thorough inspection may reveal hidden defects and obvious remodeling needs. Few people make a full-time business of checking house construction. If you have doubts about the soundness of the house you have selected, obtain an expert appraisal of the property to establish its value and point out deficiencies.

In many cities there are reputable inspection firms that will examine the home and give you a detailed report. The $50 or $100 fee may be well spent. Some buyers face the expense of replacing basic equipment within the first year of ownership. If you have doubts about the wiring, plumbing or heating plant, the owner may permit you to have it checked by an expert. If the plumbing system includes a septic tank, an expert should check the equipment before you purchase.

The age of a house should not necessarily limit your choice. While older homes may require work, many have received excellent care from previous, long-term owners and will compare favorably with new structures.

If you must call in experts, first check their reputations and beware of unscrupulous operators who may justify their fee by exaggerating flaws, which they may want to repair at inflated costs. If it appears that repairs and improvements are needed, be sure to secure estimates in advance of the cost of the work and find out who will pay for it—you or the seller.

Older houses deserve special attention in nine areas before a prospective buyer signs on the dotted line. So check these items carefully.

1. *Termite infestation and wood rot.* The importance of a check by a termite specialist cannot be overemphasized, particularly in those areas of the country that have a history of infestation. It is generally wise to include a termite clause in the contract which gives certification of termite inspection and guarantee.
2. *Structural failure.* Examine the construction for a sagging roof, cracked walls or slabs, uneven floors or other evidence of supporting soil of poor bearing capacity or inadequate structural members of fastenings.
3. *Inadequate wiring.* Be sure that there is sufficient amperage and enough electric outlets. Request inspection by the local government for code compliance to make sure the wiring is not dilapidated, exposed, and dangerous.
4. *Run-down heating plant.* Check the general condition of the heating system. What kind of repairs are needed and how long will the system last?
5. *Inadequate insulation.* Ask if the attic and the space between interior and exterior walls has been filled with an insulating material. What material was used and how was it installed?
6. *Faulty plumbing.* Choose a home that is connected to a public sewer system in preference to one served by a septic tank or a cesspool. Check with the plumber who last serviced the house to determine condition of the plumbing and ask him to test for water pressure.
7. *Hot-water heater.* Check the type and capacity of the tank to determine if there will be sufficient hot water for family needs. Look for any signs of rust or leaks. Obtain any guarantee held by the present owner, if it is still in effect.
6. *Roof and gutters.* What kind of roofing material was used and how old is it? Check inside the attic for water stains and discolorations. Ask the owner for a guarantee if one exists.
9. *Wet basements.* A basement that looks dry in summer may be four inches under water in the spring. Are there signs around the foundation walls of water penetration?

Inadequacies in the above items can and should reduce the price of the house.

Examine the conditions of the outside paint and the paint and wall-paper inside the house. Be sure all windows and doors operate and are in repair. If there is a fireplace it should have a workable damper. Inspect floor and wall tile and fixtures in the bathroom. Determine if the attic has sufficient storage area.

Remember, there is no perfect house. Just be sure you know in advance the shortcomings of the house you are buying. Don't wait to be shocked after you move in.

A New House

If, after weighing all the factors, you decide that a new home will best meet your needs, make certain that you make the best buy by following these helpful rules.

The reliability of the builder is an important consideration in choosing a new home. A reputable builder is in business for life. Arrange to talk with people who are living in houses constructed by the builder you are considering. When you've decided on the builder, consider these points:

1. Don't be overwhelmed by the appearance of a glittering model home. Pin down exactly which features are provided with your new house and which are "extras" displayed in the model.
2. Be sure the contract is complete and that there is agreement on all the details of the transactions. Don't assume an item is included and later discover you've misunderstood.
3. If the community is to have new street paving, water and sewer lines and sidewalks, make sure you know whether you or the builder will assume the costs. Find out about charges for water and trash collection.
4. Check the lot site in advance. Is it the size and setting you want for your home? After the bulldozer has arrived it may be too late.
5. Don't take anyone else's word about the zoning uses permitted for the area in which you plan to buy a home. The neighborhood may be strictly residential or zoned for certain commercial uses. This information could affect future property values. The city, county, or township clerk's office can tell you where to inquire about zoning.
6. The contract with the builder should set forth the total sales price. If possible, try to locate a lender who will allow you to take advantage of lower interest rates which may apply at the time of closing. In any event, avoid an arrangement which would allow the lender to increase the mortgage interest rate if market conditions change between the date of mortgage commitment and the closing date.
7. Be sure your contract with the builder definitely stipulates the completion date of your new house.
8. Don't be afraid to check construction progress regularly while the house is being built.
9. Any extra features that are to be included in the finished house should be described in writing.
10. The day before you take title to the house (closing day) make a thorough in-

spection trip. Check all equipment, windows and doors. This is your last chance to request changes.

11. *Insist on these papers when you take possession:* (a) warranties from all manufacturers for equipment in the house; (b) certificate of occupancy; and (c) certificates from the Health Department clearing plumbing and sewer installations. It would also be best to obtain all applicable certificates of code compliance.

Financing and Purchasing

There are a number of ways to finance the purchase of a home. One, of course, is payment of the whole price in cash, but most people purchase by obtaining a long-term mortgage loan requiring a down-payment usually 5 to 10 percent of the price, followed by monthly mortgage payments of principal, interest, taxes and property insurance.

Also, you may assume and agree to pay the remaining mortgage debt on an existing house. This method has several advantages. The closing cost will be considerably lower, the interest rate on the old mortgage may be lower than the current rate for a new mortgage, and the transaction can be closed faster.

When placing a sales contract on a home, the buyer is usually required to deposit a nominal sum as earnest money. The house is then taken off the selling market until approved financing can be arranged. This earnest money deposit is forfeited to the seller if the purchaser defaults in carrying out the contract.

When a home purchase is financed through a mortgage loan, the title is passed to the buyer upon closing the sale, but is subject to payment on the mortgage. Failure to make monthly payments when due may result in the lender taking title to the property through legal means, such as foreclosure of the mortgage.

How to Shop for Mortgage Money

In very simple terms a mortgage loan is a special loan for purchasing a piece of property. The lender supplies cash to buy the house. The borrower (mortgagor) signs a legal document which obligates and binds him to repay the lender (mortgagee) regular payments, including interest for a specified number of years. The house and lot are pledged as security and the borrower promises to pay the taxes, keep the house insured and maintain the property in good condition. If the borrower fails to make payments (defaults), the lender has the legal right to take over the property and the borrower may lose any equity he has acquired.

In recent years major changes in home financing have introduced several alternative mortgage instruments. Although the traditional fixed-rate mortgage remains very popular, Graduated Payment Mortgages (GPM), Growing Equity Mortgages (GEM), and Adjustable Rate Mortgages (ARM) are gaining wide acceptance.

When selecting a mortgage be sure you understand the terms of your mortgage loan. Will your monthly payment change? If it does change, is it according to a predetermined schedule or are changes dependent upon a certain index? Find out how often the monthly payments can change and whether or not there is a maximum amount it can be increased or decreased. You should understand what effect the changes in monthly payments might have on the mortgage amount you are obligated to pay.

Sometimes the seller of the house will offer to provide financing by holding or "taking back" a mortgage. In such a situation, the term of the mortgage is often less than the amortization period, requiring you to obtain financing to pay the seller when the note is due.

Mortgage loans are obtained from savings banks, commercial banks, savings-and-loan associations, mortgage bankers, insurance companies, and relatives. Shop around, compare and find where you can secure a mortgage loan on the best terms for your financial condition. You will find the banking and savings-and-loan institutions ready to work with you. This is their business. Local mortgage-brokers and insurance company offices are also possibilities.

But, if you contact your relatives be sure to keep the deal on a firm business basis. It is important that you leave nothing to verbal agreement. The fine print is just as important in dealing with a relative or friend as in dealing with a stranger or a large, impersonal firm.

Each of the mortgage sources mentioned may provide a conventional mortgage loan, or one insured by HUD or guaranteed by the Veterans Administration, if you are an eligible veteran.

Federally Insured Mortgage Loans

In some instances a conventional mortgage may be best for you. This may be true if you are able to make a fairly sizable down payment. On the other hand, HUD-insured financing generally enables the borrower to make a smaller down payment and, frequently, to make lower monthly payments. If, after consideration, you decide to apply for a mortgage loan insured by the Department of Housing and Urban Development there are certain things you should know about HUD and its method of doing business.

The U.S. Department of Housing and Urban Development supports financing for home building, purchase, and improvement. Under HUD a homebuyer makes a designated down payment and obtains a mortgage loan for the balance of the purchase price. The mortgage loan is made by a bank, savings-and-loan association, mortgage banker, insurance company or other HUD-approved lender and is insured by HUD. It is important to note that HUD does not lend money or build homes. It does insure mortgages.

HUD mortgage insurance is a contractual arrangement between the mortgage lender which provides that, should the lender convey the property or assign the mortgage to HUD in accordance with specific requirements, HUD will honor the lender's claim for insurance benefits. HUD mortgage insurance will not pay off a loan on behalf of a borrower in the event of his death.

The cost of the mortgage insurance is paid by the borrower. For most of the HUD programs, the borrower is required to pay a single mortgage insurance premium when the loan is closed. This premium can be paid in cash or financed in the mortgage. A few of the HUD programs require the premium to be collected on a monthly basis as part of the regular payments to the lender. The premium is one-half of one percent of the unpaid principal balance.

A borrower must have an acceptable credit record, the cash needed at the closing of the mortgage agreement, and enough income to make the monthly payments without difficulty, in addition to the income required for recurring bills and other family needs. The house must meet HUD's applicable property standards. These standards can be checked at your local field office. The loan application is made to any lender that HUD has approved to make insured mortgage loans. The property is appraised to determine the amount of mortgage loan which HUD will insure.

If the lender is willing to make the loan, he provides the proper forms and helps the purchaser complete them. The lender forwards these papers to the HUD field office serving the area where the property is located. HUD reviews the borrower's credit history to judge whether the loan would be a reasonable debt for him to assume. If HUD approves the application, the lender arranges with the borrower to close the loan. The borrower deals directly with the lender. The lender handles the transaction with HUD. Certain lenders are eligible to process the loan and determine borrower eligibility without prior HUD approval.

Many people believe that when a property has been appraised and inspected for HUD, that the property is warranted against latent defects. This is not true. The appraisal is made solely to determine the maximum amount of mortgage HUD would be willing to insure for an acceptable buyer. HUD does not warrant the house being purchased. If the house is new, HUD requires the builder to warrant that it conforms substantially to the plans and specifications on which HUD based its appraisal.

HUD does not approve or disapprove a house in the sense that the design and construction get a stamp of approval. Some builders advertise "FHA Approval" to imply that their houses are superior. This is false advertising and could result in a criminal charge.

In some cases involving one- to four-family dwellings constructed under HUD inspection, the HUD Secretary may authorize payment to (1) correct the structural defect, (2) reimburse the owner's claims arising from the defect, or (3) to acquire the property. This will be done only if the owner asks for aid not later than four years after the mortgage is issued and if the mortgage was insured by HUD after September 2, 1964.

The Buyer's Obligation

The home buyer who contracts for a loan obligates himself to make monthly payments on time. Like other debts, he is required to meet these payments whether or not he likes certain features of the home. If the home is new, he can contact the builder to remedy defects reasonably soon after occupancy.

In addition, the buyer is obligated to maintain the property satisfactorily. Usually, there is a clause in the mortgage under which the buyer agrees to perform proper maintenance and it is in the buyer's own interest to do this. Some mortgages provide that the holder of the mortgage can have repairs made and add the expense to the mortgage debt if a great deal of deterioration occurs through lack of good maintenance.

Know What You're Signing

It would be to your advantage to have the advice of a qualified real estate attorney before you sign any documents, especially the sales contract. You may also want this attorney to represent you at the closing. Choose an attorney who specializes in the field of real estate. Many good lawyers are not real estate experts and one who is experienced in these matters may save you money and problems in year to come. You will be responsible for paying his fee.

Be sure there is a builder's guarantee and that you know the exact dimensions of your lot. A copy of a recent survey is often provided at the closing. However, you may be responsible for paying for this survey.

Find out what the taxes will be on the property and review the facts about your financial obligation. After purchase, make sure the payments are made promptly each month.

Beware of fraud. Make sure your title of ownership is clear and that there are no liens or claims against the property. It is a good idea to purchase a title insurance policy insuring you against defects in the chain of title.

. . . And Now You're the Owner

When you become the owner of a used or new home, you agree in your mortgage to keep the property in good condition. This is only common sense. Why sacrifice to buy an expensive house and then allow it to lose value through your neglect? Regularly put aside an amount for annual upkeep, allowing for the fact that maintenance costs will vary from year to year.

A house is a complicated mechanism and you can't expect to know how to keep everything in good working order. If you are handy with tools, you may be able to do some of the repair and improvement work. But don't tamper with expensive equipment and appliances unless you are sure that you know what you are doing. You may void the warranty on such equipment if you attempt to do repairs yourself. When the plumbing, electric, or heating system needs more than minor repairs, it's time to call in an expert.

Keep all the guarantees, service agreements, and instructions that come with your various appliances in one safe place. Read the instructions carefully before you operate any appliance. If anything goes wrong that you cannot correct, call the local utility company or the servicing agent.

Financing Rehabilitation

If you decide to buy an older house that needs repairs, it may be possible for you to buy and renovate the house by obtaining a HUD insured mortgage loan in an amount that will include the necessary repairs. The HUD commitment will be based on the value of the house as improved.

Money Troubles

If you encounter temporary financial problems that will prevent prompt payment on your mortgage, inform your lender immediately. Don't delay. Often, if your payment record is a good one, an arrangement can be worked out to help you through your difficulties. If your lender will not offer you assistance, contact the nearest HUD field office. They may be able to help.

Don't forget that once the closing has taken place you must continue to make payments according to the terms of the mortgage, no matter what defects you find in the house or who is legally responsible for correcting them.

Fair Housing and Equal Opportunity

The Fair Housing law, Title VIII of the Civil Rights Act of 1968, prohibits discrimination on the basis of race, color, religion, sex or national origin. It is unlawful to refuse to sell or rent, to deal or negotiate with any person; discriminate in terms or conditions for buying or renting housing; discriminate by advertising that housing is available only to persons of a certain race, color, religion, sex or national origin; deny that housing is available for inspection, sale or rent when it really is available; engage in "blockbusting" for profit, persuading owners to sell or rent housing by telling them that minority groups are moving into the neighborhoods; deny or make different terms or conditions for home loans by commercial lenders, such as banks, savings and loan associations and insurance companies; deny to anyone the use of or participation in any real estate services, such as brokers' organizations, multiple listing services or other facilities related to the selling or renting of housing.

Discrimination on the basis of race, sex, color, religion and national origin are expressly prohibited by law. Forbidden practices include discrimination in the sale or rental of housing or residential lots, in advertising the sale or rental of housing, in the financing of housing and in the provision of real estate brokerage services.

Those who believe that such discrimination has occurred have a choice of remedies, including filing a civil action in Federal court (or in some cases State courts), or complaining to the Department of Housing and Urban Development.

Complaints can be sent to:

Department of Housing and Urban Development
Office of Fair Housing and Equal Opportunity
c/o the nearest HUD Regional Office

Complaints can also be reported to the Regional Field Offices in your area listed below.

Field Office Jurisdictions of HUD

Region I

Regional Administrator
Rm. 800, John F. Kennedy Federal Building
Boston, Massachusetts 02203-0801

Connecticut, Hartford 06106-1860
330 Main Street
First Floor

Maine, Bangor 04401-1357
U.S. Federal and Post Office Building
202 Harlow Street

Massachusetts, Boston 02114-2598
Bulfinch Building
15 New Chardon Street

New Hampshire, Manchester 03101-2487
Norris Cotton Federal Building
275 Chestnut Street

Rhode Island, Providence 02903-1785
Rm. 330 John O. Pastore Federal Building, U.S. Post Office
Kennedy Plaza

Vermont, Burlington 05401-8420
110 Main Street
Fairchild Square

Region II

Regional Administrator
26 Federal Plaza
New York, New York 10278-0068

New Jersey, Camden 08103-9998
The Parkade Building
519 Federal Street

New Jersey, Newark 07102-5504
Military Park Building
60 Park Place

New York, Albany 12207-2395
Leo W. O'Brien Federal Building
North Pearl Street and Clinton Avenue

New York, Buffalo 14202-2986
Suite 800, Statler Building
107 Delaware Avenue

New York, New York 10278-0068
26 Federal Plaza

Caribbean Office

Puerto Rico, San Juan
Federico Degetau Federal Building
U.S. Courthouse
Room 428 Carlos E. Chardon Avenue
Hato Rey, Puerto Rico 00918-2276

Region III

Regional Administrator
Liberty Square Building
105 S. 7th Street
Philadelphia, Pennsylvania 19106-3392

District of Columbia Washington 20410-5500
HUD Building
451 7th Street, Room 3156

Maryland, Baltimore 21202-1865
Equitable Building
10 North Calvert Street

Pennsylvania, Philadelphia 19106-3392
Curtis Building
625 Walnut Street

Pennsylvania, Pittsburgh 15219-1906
412 Old Post Office Courthouse Bldg.
7 and Grant Streets

Virginia, Richmond 23219-2591
701 East Franklin Street

West Virginia, Charleston 25301-1795
405 Capitol Street
Suite 708

Delaware, Wilmington 19801-1387
IBM Building
800 Delaware Avenue
Room 101

Region IV

Regional Administrator
Richard B. Russell Federal Building
75 Spring Street, SW
Atlanta, Georgia 30303-3109

Alabama, Birmingham 35233-2096
Daniel Building
15 South 20th Street

Florida, Jacksonville 32202-4303
325 West Adams Street

Florida, Coral Gables 33146-2911
1320 South Dixie Highway

Florida, Orlando 32801-2226
Federal Office Building
80 North Hughey

Florida, Tampa 33601-4017
700 Twiggs Street
Post Office Box 2097

Georgia, Atlanta 30303-3109
Richard B. Russell Federal Building
75 Spring Street, SW

Kentucky, Louisville 40201-1044
601 W. Broadway
Post Office Box 1044

Mississippi, Jackson 39269-1016
Federal Building, Suite 1096
100 Capitol Street

North Carolina, Greensboro 27401-2107
415 North Edgeworth Street

South Carolina, Columbia 29201-2480
Strom Thurmond Federal Building
1835–45 Assembly Street

Tennessee, Knoxville 37919-4090
One Northshore Building
1111 Northshore Drive

Tennessee, Memphis 38103-5080
100 North Main Street, 28th Floor

Tennessee, Nashville 37239-1600
One Commerce Place
Suite 1600

Region V

Regional Administrator
300 South Wacker Drive
Chicago, Illinois 60606-6765

Illinois, Chicago 60606-5760
547 West Jackson Blvd.

Illinois, Springfield 62701-1774
Lincoln Tower Plaza
524 South Second Street

Indiana, Indianapolis 46204-2526
151 North Delaware Street

Michigan, Grand Rapids 49505-3409
Northbrook Building Number II
2922 Fuller Avenue, NE

Michigan, Flint 48502-1953
Gil Sabuco Building
352 South Saginaw Street
Room 200

Michigan, Detroit 48226-2592
Patrick V. McNamara Federal Building
477 Michigan Avenue

Minnesota, Minneapolis-St. Paul 55401-2195
220 South Second Street
Bridge Place Bldg.

Ohio, Columbus 43215-2499
New Federal Building
200 North High Street

Ohio, Cincinnati 45202-3253
Federal Office Building
550 Main Street, Room 9002

Ohio, Cleveland 44114-1832
One Playhouse Square
1375 Euclid Avenue, Room 420

Wisconsin, Milwaukee 53203-2290
Henry S. Reuss Federal Plaza
310 West Wisconsin Avenue, Suite 1380

Region VI

Regional Administrator
1600 Throckmorton
Post Office Box 2905
Fort Worth, Texas 76113-2905

Arkansas, Little Rock 72201-3523
320 West Capitol
Suite 700

Louisiana, New Orleans 70172-0288
P.O. Box 70288
1661 Canal Street

Louisiana, Shreveport 71101-3077
New Federal Building
500 Fannin Street

New Mexico, Albuquerque 87110-6443
625 Truman Street, NE

Oklahoma, Oklahoma City 73102-3202
Murrah Federal Building
200 N.W. 5th Street

Oklahoma, Tulsa 74127-8923
Robert S. Kerr Building
440 South Houston Avenue

Texas, Dallas 75207-5007
555 Griffin Square Office Building
525 Griffin Street, Room 106

Texas, San Antonio 78285-3301
Washington Square
800 Dolorosa
Post Office Box 9163

Texas, Fort Worth 76113-2905
221 W. Lancaster Avenue
P.O. Box 2905

Texas, Houston 77098-4096
National Bank of Texas Building
2211 Norfolk, Suite 300

Texas, Lubbock 79401-4001
Federal Office Building
1205 Texas Avenue

Region VII

Regional Administrator
Professional Building
1103 Grand Avenue
Kansas City, Missouri 64106-2496

Iowa, Des Moines 50309-2155
Room 259 Federal Building
210 Walnut Street

Kansas, Topeka 66683-3588
444 S.E. Quincy Street, Room 297

Missouri, Kansas City 64106-2496
Professional Building
1103 Grand Avenue

Missouri, St. Louis 63101-1997
210 North Tucker Boulevard

Nebraska, Omaha 68102-1622
Braiker/Brandeis Building
210 South 16th Street

Region VIII

Regional Administrator
Executive Tower Building
1405 Curtis Street
Denver, Colorado 80202-2349

Colorado, Denver 80202-2349
Executive Tower
1405 Curtis Street

Montana, Helena 59626-0095
Federal Office Building Drawer 10095
301 S. Park, Room 340

Utah, Salt Lake City 84111-2321
324 South State Street, Suite 220

North Dakota, Fargo 58108-2483
Federal Building
653 2nd Avenue North
Post Office Box 2483

South Dakota, Sioux Falls 57102-0983
Courthouse Plaza
300 N. Dakota Avenue, Suite 108

Wyoming, Casper 82602-1918
4225 Federal Office Building
100 East B Street
Post Office Box 580

Region IX

Regional Administrator
450 Golden Gate Avenue
Post Office Box 36003
San Francisco, California 94102-3448

Arizona, Phoenix 85002-3468
One North First Street, 3rd Floor
Post Office Box 13468

Arizona, Tucson 86701-1467
Pioneer Plaza
100 North Stone Avenue
Suite 410

California, Los Angeles 90015-3801
1615 W. Olympic Boulevard

California, San Francisco 94111-5494
1 Embarcadero Center
Suite 1600

California, Fresno 93710-8193
1630 E. Shaw Avenue, Suite 138

California, Sacramento 95809-1978
777 12th Street, Suite 200

California, San Diego 92188-0100
880 Front Street, Room 553

California, Santa Ana 92712-2850
34 Civic Center Plaza
Box 12850

Hawaii, Honolulu 96850-4991
300 Ala Moana Boulevard
Room 3318

Nevada, Reno 89505-4700
1050 Bible Way
Post Office Box 4700

Nevada, Las Vegas 89101-6930
720 South 7th Street

Region X

Regional Administrator
Arcade Plaza Building
1321 Second Avenue
Seattle, Washington 98101-2054

Alaska, Anchorage 99513-0001
701 C Street
Module G Box 64

Oregon, Portland 97204-1596
520 Southwest 6th Avenue

Idaho, Boise 83724-0420
Box 042, FB/USCH
550 West Fort Street

Washington, Seattle 98101-2054
Arcade Plaza Building
1321 Second Avenue

Washington, Spokane 99201-1075
West 920 Riverside Avenue

SECOND MORTGAGE FINANCING

If you are like most homeowners, you probably have a first mortgage loan on your home. Typically, such loans are for 25 to 30 years, with the monthly payments adjusted so that the loan is paid in full at the end of the term.

As you make monthly payments and the value of the home increases, your interest in the property (called "equity") grows. After a while, some homeowners may wish to borrow against the equity in their home to get cash, to make home improvements, to educate their children, or to consolidate personal debts. Because such loans are in addition to the first mortgage on the home, they are commonly called "second mortgage" loans.

Second mortgage loans are different from first mortgages in several ways. They often carry a higher interest rate, and they usually are for a shorter time, 15 years or less. In addition, they may require a large single payment at the end of the term, commonly known as a balloon payment.

Traditionally, second mortgage loans are offered with a fixed loan amount and a predetermined repayment schedule. Some lenders now offer lines of credit that allow you to obtain cash advances with a credit card or to write checks up to a certain credit limit. These often are called "home equity lines" because the equity in your home is collateral for the amount of credit you request. As you pay off the outstanding balance, you can reuse the line of credit during the loan period.

How Do I Choose a Lender?

When you are looking for a lender, shop around and make comparisons. Interest rates, repayment terms, and origination fees may vary substantially. Ask your local banks, savings and loans, credit unions, or finance companies about their loan terms. Although you will want to select the lender who offers you terms most suited to your needs, be sure to ask and compare the annual percentage rates (APR) because they will give you the total cost of the loan, including financing charges.

If you have not done business with the lender before, or if the lender is unfamiliar to you, you may wish to ask your local Better Business Bureau or consumer protection office if they have any complaints against the lender.

How Long Will I Have to Repay the Loan?

Some second mortgage loans may extend for as long as 15 or 20 years; others may require repayment in one year. You will need to discuss the repayment terms with the lenders and select one who offers terms that best suit your needs. For example, if you need to borrow $20,000 to make repairs on your home, you may not want a loan that requires you to repay the entire amount in one or two years because the monthly payments may be too high.

Will My Interest Rate Change?

If you have a fixed-rate loan, the interest rate is set for the life of the loan. However, many lenders offer variable rate mortgages, also known as adjustable rate mortgages or ARMs. These provide for periodic interest-rate adjustments. If your loan contract allows the lender to adjust or change the interest rate, be sure you understand when the lender has the right to change the interest rate, whether there are any limits on how much the interest or payments can change, and how often the lender can change the rate. You also should know what basis the lender will use to determine the new rate of interest.

How Much Will My Monthly Payments Be and Will They Pay Off the Loan?

Be sure you understand how much your monthly payments will be and what they cover. Your lender should be able to give you this information in advance. With some loans, you will be required to make monthly payments on the principal and interest. With other loans, you may be required to pay interest only on the borrowed amount; in these loans, your monthly payments will not reduce the principal amount of the loan. With such a loan, you will be required to pay back the entire borrowed amount at the end of the loan period. These loans are popularly known as "balloon loans." If your loan has a balloon payment, you should consider how you will arrange to repay the entire amount when it becomes due.

On "home equity lines," the lender does not have to give you the exact amount of the monthly payment, but must explain how it is figured. This is because the borrowed amount will vary and your outstanding balance will change if you use the line of credit. However, if your monthly payment term is 5% of the outstanding balance and your outstanding balance is $5,000, your minimum monthly payments would be $250.

Will I Have to Pay Any Fees to Get This Loan?

Many companies will charge a fee for lending you money. The fee is usually a percentage of the loan and is sometimes referred to as "points." One point is equal to one percent of the amount you borrow. For example, if you were to borrow $10,000 with a fee of eight points, you would pay $800 in "points." The number of points lenders charge varies, so it may be worthwhile to shop around. If the fee seems too high, you may be able to bargain for or find a lower fee. Be sure to get the amount of the fee in writing before you take the loan.

Many states limit the amount of fees a lender may charge on a second mortgage loan. You may want to check with your state's consumer protection office or banking commissioner to determine whether there is a limit in your state.

What Should I Get in Writing?

If your loan is primarily for personal, family, or household purposes, the lender is required to give you a federal Truth in Lending disclosure form before you sign the customary loan documents, such as a note or deed of trust. This Truth in Lending form will tell you the actual cost of the loan. It includes the annual percentage rate, the finance charge, and the fees included in the loan. For "home equity lines," your lender also is required to send you a periodic statement, usually monthly.

The lender also is required to give you a notice of your right of rescission. The right of rescission gives you three business days after signing for the loan and receiving the Truth in Lending Act disclosures to reconsider whether you want to take the loan. For additional information about the right of rescission, ask for the free FTC factsheet, "Getting a Loan: Your Home as Security," at the address listed below.

If your lender makes any promises, such as saying you can "automatically" get the loan refinanced at the end of the term, be sure your lender puts these promises in writing. In this way, you may avoid any future disputes.

What Should I Do If I Have a Problem?

If you ever have a problem making your loan payments, talk to your lender as soon as possible. Some lenders will work with you to arrange a temporary payment plan. Also, call the lender if you have any questions about your loan.

However, if you have problems with your lender, you may want to contact your state, county, or local consumer protection office. If they cannot help you, they can refer you to the office that can.

The Federal Trade Commission is responsible for enforcing laws such as the Truth in Lending Act, the Equal Credit Opportunity Act, the Fair Credit Reporting Act, and the Fair Debt Collection Practices Act. It also provides free factsheets explaining these laws. For these or credit-related publications, such as *Escrow Accounts for Home Mortgages, Using Ads to Shop for Home Financing,* and *Refinancing Your Home,* write to:

Public Reference
Federal Trade Commission
Washington, D.C. 20580.

If you believe your lender may be violating a law that the FTC administers, you can send complaints or questions to: Division of Credit Practices, Federal Trade Commission, Washington, D.C. 20580. Although the FTC cannot resolve individual consumer disputes, it can take action if there is evidence of a pattern of deceptive or unfair practices.

MORTGAGE REFINANCINGS

If you are a homeowner who was lucky enough to buy when mortgage rates were low, you may have no interest in refinancing your present loan. But perhaps you bought your home when rates were higher. Or perhaps you have an adjustable-rate loan and would like to obtain different terms.

Should you refinance? This section will answer some questions that may help you decide. If you do refinance, the process will remind you of what you went through in obtaining the original mortgage. That's because, in reality, refinancing a mortgage is simply taking out a new mortgage. You will encounter many of the same procedures—and the same types of costs—the second time around.

Would Refinancing Be Worth It?

Refinancing can be worthwhile, but it does not make good financial sense for everyone. A general rule of thumb is that refinancing becomes worth your while if the current interest rate on your mortgage is at least 2 percentage points higher than the prevailing market rate. This figure is generally accepted as the safe margin when balancing the costs of refinancing a mortgage against the savings.

There are other considerations, too, such as how long you plan to stay in the house. Most sources say that it takes at least three years to realize fully the savings from a lower interest rate, given the costs of the refinancing. (Depending on your loan amount and the particular circumstances, however, you might choose to refinance a loan that is only 1.5 percentage points higher than the current rate. You may even find you could recoup the refinancing costs in a shorter time.)

Refinancing can be a good idea for homeowners who:

- want to get out of a high interest rate loan to take advantage of lower rates. This is a good idea only if they intend to stay in the house long enough to make the additional fees worthwhile.
- have an adjustable-rate mortgage (ARM) and want a fixed-rate loan to have the certainty of knowing exactly what the mortgage payment will be for the life of the loan.
- want to convert to an ARM with a lower interest rate or more protective features (such as a better rate and payment caps) than the ARM they currently have.
- want to build up equity more quickly by converting to a loan with a shorter term.
- want to draw on the equity built up in their house to get cash for a major purchase or for their children's education.

If you decide that refinancing is not worth the costs, ask your lender whether you may be able to obtain all or some of the new terms you want by agreeing to a modification of your existing loan instead of a refinancing.

Should You Refinance Your ARM?

In deciding whether to refinance an ARM you should consider these questions:

- Is the next interest rate adjustment on your existing loan likely to increase your monthly payments substantially? Will the new interest rate be two or three percentage points higher than the prevailing rates being offered for either fixed-rate loans or other ARMs?

- If the current mortgage sets a cap on your monthly payments, are those payments large enough to pay off your loan by the end of the original term? Will refinancing to a new ARM or a fixed-rate loan enable you to pay your loan in full by the end of the term?

What Are the Costs of Refinancing?

The fees described below are the charges that you are most likely to encounter in a refinancing.

- **Application Fee.** This charge imposed by your lender covers the initial costs of processing your loan request and checking your credit report.
- **Title Search and Title Insurance.** This charge will cover the cost of examining the public record to confirm ownership of the real estate. It also covers the cost of a policy, usually issued by a title insurance company, that insures the policy holder in a specific amount for any loss caused by discrepancies in the title to the property.

  Be sure to ask the company carrying the present policy if it can re-issue your policy at a re-issue rate. You could save up to 70 percent of what it would cost you for a new policy.

Because costs may vary significantly from area to area and from lender to lender, the following are estimates only. Your actual closing costs may be higher or lower than the ranges indicated below.

Application Fee	**$ 75 to $300**
Appraisal Fee	**$150 to $400**
Survey Costs	**$125 to $300**
Homeowner's Hazard Insurance	**$300 to $600**
Lender's Attorney's Review Fees	**$ 75 to $200**
Title Search and Title Insurance	**$450 to $600**
Home Inspection Fees	**$175 to $350**
Loan Origination Fees	**1% of loan**
Mortgage Insurance	**0.5% to 1.0%**
Points	**1% to 3%**

- **Lender's Attorney's Review Fees.** The lender will usually charge you for fees paid to the lawyer or company that conducts the closing for the lender. Settlements are conducted by lending institutions, title insurance companies, escrow companies, real estate brokers, and attorneys for the buyer and seller. In most situations, the person conducting the settlement is providing a service to the lender. You may also be required to pay for other legal services relating to your loan which are provided to the lender. You may want to retain your own attorney to represent you at all stages of the transaction including settlement.

- **Loan Origination Fees and Points.** The origination fee is charged for the lender's work in evaluating and preparing your mortgage loan. Points are prepaid finance charges imposed by the lender at closing to increase the lender's yield beyond the stated interest rate on the mortgage note. One point equals one percent of the loan amount. For example, one point on a $75,000 loan would be $750. In some cases, the points you pay can be financed by adding them to the loan amount. The total number of points a lender charges will depend on market conditions and the interest rate to be charged.
- **Appraisal Fee.** This fee pays for an appraisal which is a supportable and defensible estimate or opinion of the value of the property.
- **Prepayment Penalty.** A prepayment penalty on your present mortgage could be the greatest deterrent to refinancing. The practice of charging money for an early pay-off of the existing mortgage loan varies by state, type of lender, and type of loan. Prepayment penalties are forbidden on various loans including loans from federally chartered credit unions, FHA and VA loans, and some other home-purchase loans. The mortgage documents for your existing loan will state if there is a penalty for prepayment. In some loans, you may be charged interest for the full month in which you prepay your loan.
- **Miscellaneous.** Depending on the type of loan you have and other factors, another major expense you might face is the fee for a VA loan guarantee, FHA mortgage insurance, or private mortgage insurance. There are a few other closing costs in addition to these.

In conclusion, a homeowner should plan on paying an average of 3 to 6 percent of the outstanding principal in refinancing costs, plus any prepayment penalties and the costs of paying off any second mortgages that may exist.

One way of saving on some of these costs is to check first with the lender who holds your current mortgage. The lender may be willing to waive some of them, especially if the work relating to the mortgage closing is still current. This could include the fees for the title search, surveys, inspections, and so on.

This information is intended to help you ask the right questions when considering a possible refinancing of your loan. It is not a replacement for professional advice. Talk with mortgage lenders, real estate agents, attorneys, and other advisors about lending practices, mortgage instruments, and your own interests before you commit to any specific loan.

Ask your lender or real estate agent for the following related pamphlets:

- A Consumer's Guide to Mortgage Settlement Costs
- A Consumer's Guide to Mortgage Lock-Ins
- Consumer Handbook on Adjustable Rate Mortgages

SECTION ONE

Monthly Payment Schedules

The tables in this section show the monthly payments of combined principal and interest that are necessary to repay a mortgage. Find the page with the amount of interest charged on your loan, go down the column to the amount borrowed, and across to the number of years of the repayment period. This will give you the monthly payment necessary to repay your loan.

MONTHLY PAYMENT
Needed to repay a loan

5%

TERM AMOUNT	1 YEAR	2 YEARS	3 YEARS	4 YEARS	5 YEARS	6 YEARS
500	42.80	21.94	14.99	11.51	9.44	8.05
1000	85.61	43.87	29.97	23.03	18.87	16.10
2000	171.21	87.74	59.94	46.06	37.74	32.21
3000	256.82	131.61	89.91	69.09	56.61	48.31
4000	342.43	175.49	119.88	92.12	75.48	64.42
5000	428.04	219.36	149.85	115.15	94.36	80.52
6000	513.64	263.23	179.83	138.18	113.23	96.63
7000	599.25	307.10	209.80	161.21	132.10	112.73
8000	684.86	350.97	239.77	184.23	150.97	128.84
9000	770.47	394.84	269.74	207.26	169.84	144.94
10000	856.07	438.71	299.71	230.29	188.71	161.05
11000	941.68	482.59	329.68	253.32	207.58	177.15
12000	1027.29	526.46	359.65	276.35	226.45	193.26
13000	1112.90	570.33	389.62	299.38	245.33	209.36
14000	1198.50	614.20	419.59	322.41	264.20	225.47
15000	1284.11	658.07	449.56	345.44	283.07	241.57
16000	1369.72	701.94	479.53	368.47	301.94	257.68
17000	1455.33	745.81	509.51	391.50	320.81	273.78
18000	1540.93	789.69	539.48	414.53	339.68	289.89
19000	1626.54	833.56	569.45	437.56	358.55	305.99
20000	1712.15	877.43	599.42	460.59	377.42	322.10
21000	1797.76	921.30	629.39	483.62	396.30	338.20
22000	1883.36	965.17	659.36	506.64	415.17	354.31
23000	1968.97	1009.04	689.33	529.67	434.04	370.41
24000	2054.58	1052.91	719.30	552.70	452.91	386.52
25000	2140.19	1096.78	749.27	575.73	471.78	402.62
30000	2568.22	1316.14	899.13	690.88	566.14	483.15
35000	2996.26	1535.50	1048.98	806.03	660.49	563.67
40000	3424.30	1754.86	1198.84	921.17	754.85	644.20
45000	3852.34	1974.21	1348.69	1036.32	849.21	724.72
50000	4280.37	2193.57	1498.54	1151.46	943.56	805.25
55000	4708.41	2412.93	1648.40	1266.61	1037.92	885.77
60000	5136.45	2632.28	1798.25	1381.76	1132.27	966.30
65000	5564.49	2851.64	1948.11	1496.90	1226.63	1046.82
70000	5992.52	3071.00	2097.96	1612.05	1320.99	1127.35
75000	6420.56	3290.35	2247.82	1727.20	1415.34	1207.87
80000	6848.60	3509.71	2397.67	1842.34	1509.70	1288.39
85000	7276.64	3729.07	2547.53	1957.49	1604.05	1368.92
90000	7704.67	3948.43	2697.38	2072.64	1698.41	1449.44
95000	8132.71	4167.78	2847.24	2187.78	1792.77	1529.97
100000	8560.75	4387.14	2997.09	2302.93	1887.12	1610.49
200000	17121.50	8774.28	5994.18	4605.86	3774.25	3220.99
300000	25682.24	13161.42	8991.27	6908.79	5661.37	4831.48
400000	34242.99	17548.56	11988.36	9211.72	7548.49	6441.97
500000	42803.74	21935.69	14985.45	11514.65	9435.62	8052.47

5%

MONTHLY PAYMENT
Needed to repay a loan

TERM AMOUNT	7 YEARS	8 YEARS	9 YEARS	10 YEARS	11 YEARS	12 YEARS
500	7.07	6.33	5.76	5.30	4.93	4.62
1000	14.13	12.66	11.52	10.61	9.86	9.25
2000	28.27	25.32	23.03	21.21	19.73	18.50
3000	42.40	37.98	34.55	31.82	29.59	27.75
4000	56.54	50.64	46.07	42.43	39.46	37.00
5000	70.67	63.30	57.59	53.03	49.32	46.24
6000	84.80	75.96	69.10	63.64	59.19	55.49
7000	98.94	88.62	80.62	74.25	69.05	64.74
8000	113.07	101.28	92.14	84.85	78.92	73.99
9000	127.21	113.94	103.66	95.46	88.78	83.24
10000	141.34	126.60	115.17	106.07	98.64	92.49
11000	155.47	139.26	126.69	116.67	108.51	101.74
12000	169.61	151.92	138.21	127.28	118.37	110.99
13000	183.74	164.58	149.72	137.89	128.24	120.24
14000	197.87	177.24	161.24	148.49	138.10	129.48
15000	212.01	189.90	172.76	159.10	147.97	138.73
16000	226.14	202.56	184.28	169.70	157.83	147.98
17000	240.28	215.22	195.79	180.31	167.70	157.23
18000	254.41	227.88	207.31	190.92	177.56	166.48
19000	268.54	240.54	218.83	201.52	187.43	175.73
20000	282.68	253.20	230.35	212.13	197.29	184.98
21000	296.81	265.86	241.86	222.74	207.15	194.23
22000	310.95	278.52	253.38	233.34	217.02	203.48
23000	325.08	291.18	264.90	243.95	226.88	212.72
24000	339.21	303.84	276.41	254.56	236.75	221.97
25000	353.35	316.50	287.93	265.16	246.61	231.22
30000	424.02	379.80	345.52	318.20	295.93	277.47
35000	494.69	443.10	403.10	371.23	345.26	323.71
40000	565.36	506.40	460.69	424.26	394.58	369.96
45000	636.03	569.70	518.28	477.29	443.90	416.20
50000	706.70	633.00	575.86	530.33	493.22	462.45
55000	777.36	696.30	633.45	583.36	542.55	508.69
60000	848.03	759.60	691.04	636.39	591.87	554.93
65000	918.70	822.89	748.62	689.43	641.19	601.18
70000	989.37	886.19	806.21	742.46	690.51	647.42
75000	1060.04	949.49	863.80	795.49	739.84	693.67
80000	1130.71	1012.79	921.38	848.52	789.16	739.91
85000	1201.38	1076.09	978.97	901.56	838.48	786.16
90000	1272.05	1139.39	1036.55	954.59	887.80	832.40
95000	1342.72	1202.69	1094.14	1007.62	937.13	878.65
100000	1413.39	1265.99	1151.73	1060.66	986.45	924.89
200000	2826.78	2531.98	2303.45	2121.31	1972.90	1849.78
300000	4240.17	3797.98	3455.18	3181.97	2959.35	2774.67
400000	5653.56	5063.97	4606.91	4242.62	3945.80	3699.56
500000	7066.95	6329.96	5758.64	5303.28	4932.24	4624.45

MONTHLY PAYMENT
Needed to repay a loan

5%

TERM AMOUNT	15 YEARS	20 YEARS	25 YEARS	30 YEARS	35 YEARS	40 YEARS
500	3.95	3.30	2.92	2.68	2.52	2.41
1000	7.91	6.60	5.85	5.37	5.05	4.82
2000	15.82	13.20	11.69	10.74	10.09	9.64
3000	23.72	19.80	17.54	16.10	15.14	14.47
4000	31.63	26.40	23.38	21.47	20.19	19.29
5000	39.54	33.00	29.23	26.84	25.23	24.11
6000	47.45	39.60	35.08	32.21	30.28	28.93
7000	55.36	46.20	40.92	37.58	35.33	33.75
8000	63.26	52.80	46.77	42.95	40.38	38.58
9000	71.17	59.40	52.61	48.31	45.42	43.40
10000	79.08	66.00	58.46	53.68	50.47	48.22
11000	86.99	72.60	64.30	59.05	55.52	53.04
12000	94.90	79.19	70.15	64.42	60.56	57.86
13000	102.80	85.79	76.00	69.79	65.61	62.69
14000	110.71	92.39	81.84	75.16	70.66	67.51
15000	118.62	98.99	87.69	80.52	75.70	72.33
16000	126.53	105.59	93.53	85.89	80.75	77.15
17000	134.43	112.19	99.38	91.26	85.80	81.97
18000	142.34	118.79	105.23	96.63	90.84	86.80
19000	150.25	125.39	111.07	102.00	95.89	91.62
20000	158.16	131.99	116.92	107.36	100.94	96.44
21000	166.07	138.59	122.76	112.73	105.98	101.26
22000	173.97	145.19	128.61	118.10	111.03	106.08
23000	181.88	151.79	134.46	123.47	116.08	110.91
24000	189.79	158.39	140.30	128.84	121.13	115.73
25000	197.70	164.99	146.15	134.21	126.17	120.55
30000	237.24	197.99	175.38	161.05	151.41	144.66
35000	276.78	230.98	204.61	187.89	176.64	168.77
40000	316.32	263.98	233.84	214.73	201.88	192.88
45000	355.86	296.98	263.07	241.57	227.11	216.99
50000	395.40	329.98	292.30	268.41	252.34	241.10
55000	434.94	362.98	321.52	295.25	277.58	265.21
60000	474.48	395.97	350.75	322.09	302.81	289.32
65000	514.02	428.97	379.98	348.93	328.05	313.43
70000	553.56	461.97	409.21	375.78	353.28	337.54
75000	593.10	494.97	438.44	402.62	378.52	361.65
80000	632.63	527.96	467.67	429.46	403.75	385.76
85000	672.17	560.96	496.90	456.30	428.98	409.87
90000	711.71	593.96	526.13	483.14	454.22	433.98
95000	751.25	626.96	555.36	509.98	479.45	458.09
100000	790.79	659.96	584.59	536.82	504.69	482.20
200000	1581.59	1319.91	1169.18	1073.64	1009.38	964.39
300000	2372.38	1979.87	1753.77	1610.46	1514.06	1446.59
400000	3163.17	2639.82	2338.36	2147.29	2018.75	1928.79
500000	3953.97	3299.78	2922.95	2684.11	2523.44	2410.98

5.5% MONTHLY PAYMENT
Needed to repay a loan

TERM AMOUNT	1 YEAR	2 YEARS	3 YEARS	4 YEARS	5 YEARS	6 YEARS
500	42.92	22.05	15.10	11.63	9.55	8.17
1000	85.84	44.10	30.20	23.26	19.10	16.34
2000	171.67	88.19	60.39	46.51	38.20	32.68
3000	257.51	132.29	90.59	69.77	57.30	49.01
4000	343.35	176.38	120.78	93.03	76.40	65.35
5000	429.18	220.48	150.98	116.28	95.51	81.69
6000	515.02	264.57	181.18	139.54	114.61	98.03
7000	600.86	308.67	211.37	162.80	133.71	114.37
8000	686.69	352.77	241.57	186.05	152.81	130.70
9000	772.53	396.86	271.76	209.31	171.91	147.04
10000	858.37	440.96	301.96	232.56	191.01	163.38
11000	944.20	485.05	332.15	255.82	210.11	179.72
12000	1030.04	529.15	362.35	279.08	229.21	196.05
13000	1115.88	573.24	392.55	302.33	248.32	212.39
14000	1201.71	617.34	422.74	325.59	267.42	228.73
15000	1287.55	661.43	452.94	348.85	286.52	245.07
16000	1373.39	705.53	483.13	372.10	305.62	261.41
17000	1459.23	749.63	513.33	395.36	324.72	277.74
18000	1545.06	793.72	543.53	418.62	343.82	294.08
19000	1630.90	837.82	573.72	441.87	362.92	310.42
20000	1716.74	881.91	603.92	465.13	382.02	326.76
21000	1802.57	926.01	634.11	488.39	401.12	343.10
22000	1888.41	970.10	664.31	511.64	420.23	359.43
23000	1974.25	1014.20	694.51	534.90	439.33	375.77
24000	2060.08	1058.30	724.70	558.16	458.43	392.11
25000	2145.92	1102.39	754.90	581.41	477.53	408.45
30000	2575.10	1322.87	905.88	697.69	573.03	490.14
35000	3004.29	1543.35	1056.86	813.98	668.54	571.83
40000	3433.47	1763.83	1207.84	930.26	764.05	653.52
45000	3862.66	1984.30	1358.82	1046.54	859.55	735.20
50000	4291.84	2204.78	1509.80	1162.82	955.06	816.89
55000	4721.02	2425.26	1660.77	1279.11	1050.56	898.58
60000	5150.21	2645.74	1811.75	1395.39	1146.07	980.27
65000	5579.39	2866.22	1962.73	1511.67	1241.58	1061.96
70000	6008.57	3086.70	2113.71	1627.95	1337.08	1143.65
75000	6437.76	3307.17	2264.69	1744.24	1432.59	1225.34
80000	6866.94	3527.65	2415.67	1860.52	1528.09	1307.03
85000	7296.13	3748.13	2566.65	1976.80	1623.60	1388.72
90000	7725.31	3968.61	2717.63	2093.08	1719.10	1470.41
95000	8154.49	4189.09	2868.61	2209.37	1814.61	1552.10
100000	8583.68	4409.57	3019.59	2325.65	1910.12	1633.79
200000	17167.36	8819.13	6039.18	4651.30	3820.23	3267.58
300000	25751.04	13228.70	9058.77	6976.94	5730.35	4901.37
400000	34334.71	17638.26	12078.36	9302.59	7640.46	6535.15
500000	42918.39	22047.83	15097.95	11628.24	9550.58	8168.94

MONTHLY PAYMENT 5.5%
Needed to repay a loan

TERM AMOUNT	7 YEARS	8 YEARS	9 YEARS	10 YEARS	11 YEARS	12 YEARS
500	7.19	6.45	5.88	5.43	5.06	4.75
1000	14.37	12.90	11.76	10.85	10.11	9.50
2000	28.74	25.80	23.52	21.71	20.23	19.00
3000	43.11	38.70	35.28	32.56	30.34	28.51
4000	57.48	51.60	47.04	43.41	40.46	38.01
5000	71.85	64.50	58.80	54.26	50.57	47.51
6000	86.22	77.40	70.56	65.12	60.68	57.01
7000	100.59	90.30	82.32	75.97	70.80	66.51
8000	114.96	103.19	94.08	86.82	80.91	76.01
9000	129.33	116.09	105.84	97.67	91.03	85.52
10000	143.70	128.99	117.60	108.53	101.14	95.02
11000	158.07	141.89	129.36	119.38	111.25	104.52
12000	172.44	154.79	141.12	130.23	121.37	114.02
13000	186.81	167.69	152.88	141.08	131.48	123.52
14000	201.18	180.59	164.64	151.94	141.60	133.02
15000	215.55	193.49	176.40	162.79	151.71	142.53
16000	229.92	206.39	188.16	173.64	161.82	152.03
17000	244.29	219.29	199.92	184.49	171.94	161.53
18000	258.66	232.19	211.68	195.35	182.05	171.03
19000	273.03	245.09	223.44	206.20	192.16	180.53
20000	287.40	257.99	235.20	217.05	202.28	190.03
21000	301.77	270.89	246.96	227.91	212.39	199.54
22000	316.14	283.79	258.72	238.76	222.51	209.04
23000	330.51	296.68	270.48	249.61	232.62	218.54
24000	344.88	309.58	282.24	260.46	242.73	228.04
25000	359.25	322.48	294.00	271.32	252.85	237.54
30000	431.10	386.98	352.80	325.58	303.42	285.05
35000	502.95	451.48	411.60	379.84	353.99	332.56
40000	574.80	515.97	470.40	434.11	404.56	380.07
45000	646.65	580.47	529.20	488.37	455.13	427.58
50000	718.50	644.97	588.00	542.63	505.70	475.09
55000	790.35	709.46	646.80	596.89	556.27	522.59
60000	862.20	773.96	705.60	651.16	606.84	570.10
65000	934.05	838.46	764.40	705.42	657.41	617.61
70000	1005.90	902.95	823.20	759.68	707.98	655.12
75000	1077.75	967.45	882.00	813.95	758.54	712.63
80000	1149.60	1031.95	940.80	868.21	809.11	760.14
85000	1221.45	1096.44	999.60	922.47	859.68	807.65
90000	1293.30	1160.94	1058.40	976.74	910.25	855.15
95000	1365.15	1225.44	1117.20	1031.00	960.82	902.66
100000	1437.00	1289.93	1176.00	1085.26	1011.39	950.17
200000	2874.01	2579.86	2352.00	2170.53	2022.79	1900.34
300000	4311.01	3869.80	3528.00	3255.79	3034.18	2850.52
400000	5748.02	5159.73	4704.00	4341.05	4045.57	3800.69
500000	7185.02	6449.66	5880.00	5426.31	5056.97	4750.86

5.5%

MONTHLY PAYMENT
Needed to repay a loan

TERM AMOUNT	15 YEARS	20 YEARS	25 YEARS	30 YEARS	35 YEARS	40 YEARS
500	4.09	3.44	3.07	2.84	2.69	2.58
1000	8.17	6.88	6.14	5.68	5.37	5.16
2000	16.34	13.76	12.28	11.36	10.74	10.32
3000	24.51	20.64	18.42	17.03	16.11	15.47
4000	32.68	27.52	24.56	22.71	21.48	20.63
5000	40.85	34.39	30.70	28.39	26.85	25.79
6000	49.03	41.27	36.85	34.07	32.22	30.95
7000	57.20	48.15	42.99	39.75	37.59	36.10
8000	65.37	55.03	49.13	45.42	42.96	41.26
9000	73.54	61.91	55.27	51.10	48.33	46.42
10000	81.71	68.79	61.41	56.78	53.70	51.58
11000	89.88	75.67	67.55	62.46	59.07	56.73
12000	98.05	82.55	73.69	68.13	64.44	61.89
13000	106.22	89.43	79.83	73.81	69.81	67.05
14000	114.39	96.30	85.97	79.49	75.18	72.21
15000	122.56	103.18	92.11	85.17	80.55	77.37
16000	130.73	110.06	98.25	90.85	85.92	82.52
17000	138.90	116.94	104.39	96.52	91.29	87.68
18000	147.08	123.82	110.54	102.20	96.66	92.84
19000	155.25	130.70	116.68	107.88	102.03	98.00
20000	163.42	137.58	122.82	113.56	107.40	103.15
21000	171.59	144.46	128.96	119.24	112.77	108.31
22000	179.76	151.34	135.10	124.91	118.14	113.47
23000	187.93	158.21	141.24	130.59	123.51	118.63
24000	196.10	165.09	147.38	136.27	128.88	123.78
25000	204.27	171.97	153.52	141.95	134.25	128.94
30000	245.13	206.37	184.23	170.34	161.10	154.73
35000	285.98	240.76	214.93	198.73	187.96	180.52
40000	326.83	275.15	245.63	227.12	214.81	206.31
45000	367.69	309.55	276.34	255.51	241.66	232.10
50000	408.54	343.94	307.04	283.89	268.51	257.89
55000	449.40	378.34	337.75	312.28	295.36	283.67
60000	490.25	412.73	368.45	340.67	322.21	309.46
65000	531.10	447.13	399.16	369.06	349.06	335.25
70000	571.96	481.52	429.86	397.45	375.91	361.04
75000	612.81	515.92	460.57	425.84	402.76	386.83
80000	653.67	550.31	491.27	454.23	429.61	412.62
85000	694.52	584.70	521.97	482.62	456.46	438.40
90000	735.38	619.10	552.68	511.01	483.31	464.19
95000	776.23	653.49	583.38	539.40	510.17	489.98
100000	817.08	687.89	614.09	567.79	537.02	515.77
200000	1634.17	1375.77	1228.17	1135.58	1074.03	1031.54
300000	2451.25	2063.66	1842.26	1703.37	1611.05	1547.31
400000	3268.33	2751.55	2456.35	2271.16	2148.07	2063.08
500000	4085.42	3439.44	3070.44	2838.95	2685.08	2578.85

MONTHLY PAYMENT
Needed to repay a loan

6%

TERM AMOUNT	1 YEAR	2 YEARS	3 YEARS	4 YEARS	5 YEARS	6 YEARS
500	43.03	22.16	15.21	11.74	9.67	8.29
1000	86.07	44.32	30.42	23.49	19.33	16.57
2000	172.13	88.64	60.84	46.97	38.67	33.15
3000	258.20	132.96	91.27	70.46	58.00	49.72
4000	344.27	177.28	121.69	93.94	77.33	66.29
5000	430.33	221.60	152.11	117.43	96.66	82.86
6000	516.40	265.92	182.53	140.91	116.00	99.44
7000	602.47	310.24	212.95	164.40	135.33	116.01
8000	688.53	354.56	243.38	187.88	154.66	132.58
9000	774.60	398.89	273.80	211.37	174.00	149.16
10000	860.66	443.21	304.22	234.85	193.33	165.73
11000	946.73	487.53	334.64	258.34	212.66	182.30
12000	1032.80	531.85	365.06	281.82	231.99	198.87
13000	1118.86	576.17	395.49	305.31	251.33	215.45
14000	1204.93	620.49	425.91	328.79	270.66	232.02
15000	1291.00	664.81	456.33	352.28	289.99	248.59
16000	1377.06	709.13	486.75	375.76	309.32	265.17
17000	1463.13	753.45	517.17	399.25	328.66	281.74
18000	1549.20	797.77	547.59	422.73	347.99	298.31
19000	1653.26	842.09	578.02	446.22	367.32	314.88
20000	1721.33	886.41	608.44	469.70	386.66	331.46
21000	1807.40	930.73	638.86	493.19	405.99	348.03
22000	1893.46	975.05	669.28	516.67	425.32	364.60
23000	1979.53	1019.37	699.70	540.16	444.65	381.18
24000	2065.59	1063.69	730.13	563.64	463.99	397.75
25000	2151.66	1108.02	760.55	587.13	483.32	414.32
30000	2581.99	1329.62	912.66	704.55	579.98	497.19
35000	3012.33	1551.22	1064.77	821.98	676.65	580.05
40000	3442.66	1772.82	1216.88	939.40	773.31	662.92
45000	3872.99	1994.43	1368.99	1056.83	869.98	745.78
50000	4303.32	2216.03	1521.10	1174.25	966.64	828.64
55000	4733.65	2437.63	1673.21	1291.68	1063.30	911.51
60000	5163.99	2659.24	1825.32	1409.10	1159.97	994.37
65000	5594.32	2880.84	1977.43	1526.53	1256.63	1077.24
70000	6024.65	3102.44	2129.54	1643.95	1353.30	1160.10
75000	6454.98	3324.05	2281.65	1761.38	1449.96	1242.97
80000	6885.31	3545.65	2433.75	1878.80	1546.62	1325.83
85000	7315.65	3767.25	2585.86	1996.23	1643.29	1408.70
90000	7745.98	3988.85	2737.97	2113.65	1739.95	1491.56
95000	8176.31	4210.46	2890.08	2231.08	1836.62	1574.42
100000	8606.64	4432.06	3042.19	2348.50	1933.28	1657.29
200000	17213.29	8864.12	6084.39	4697.01	3866.56	3314.58
300000	25819.93	13296.18	9126.58	7045.51	5799.84	4971.87
400000	34426.57	17728.24	12168.77	9394.01	7733.12	6629.16
500000	43033.21	22160.31	15210.97	11742.51	9666.40	8286.44

MONTHLY PAYMENT
Needed to repay a loan

TERM AMOUNT	7 YEARS	8 YEARS	9 YEARS	10 YEARS	11 YEARS	12 YEARS
500	7.30	6.57	6.00	5.55	5.18	4.88
1000	14.61	13.14	12.01	11.10	10.37	9.76
2000	29.22	26.28	24.01	22.20	20.73	19.52
3000	43.83	39.42	36.02	33.31	31.10	29.28
4000	58.43	52.57	48.02	44.41	41.47	39.03
5000	73.04	65.71	60.03	55.51	51.84	48.79
6000	87.65	78.85	72.03	66.61	62.20	58.55
7000	102.26	91.99	84.04	77.71	72.57	68.31
8000	116.87	105.13	96.05	88.82	82.94	78.07
9000	131.48	118.27	108.05	99.92	93.30	87.83
10000	146.09	131.41	120.06	111.02	103.67	97.59
11000	160.69	144.56	132.06	122.12	114.04	107.34
12000	175.30	157.70	144.07	133.22	124.40	117.10
13000	189.91	170.84	156.07	144.33	134.77	126.86
14000	204.52	183.98	168.08	155.43	145.14	136.62
15000	219.13	197.12	180.09	166.53	155.51	146.38
16000	233.74	210.26	192.09	177.63	165.87	156.14
17000	248.35	223.40	204.10	188.73	176.24	165.89
18000	262.95	236.55	216.10	199.84	186.61	175.65
19000	277.56	249.69	228.11	210.94	196.97	185.41
20000	292.17	262.83	240.11	222.04	207.34	195.17
21000	306.78	275.97	252.12	233.14	217.71	204.93
22000	321.39	289.11	264.13	244.25	228.07	214.69
23000	336.00	302.25	276.13	255.35	238.44	224.45
24000	350.61	315.39	288.14	266.45	248.81	234.20
25000	365.21	328.54	300.14	277.55	259.18	243.96
30000	438.26	394.24	360.17	333.06	311.01	292.76
35000	511.30	459.95	420.20	388.57	362.85	341.55
40000	584.34	525.66	480.23	444.08	414.68	390.34
45000	657.38	591.36	540.26	499.59	466.52	439.13
50000	730.43	657.07	600.29	555.10	518.35	487.93
55000	803.47	722.78	660.32	610.61	570.19	536.72
60000	876.51	788.49	720.34	666.12	622.02	585.51
65000	949.56	854.19	780.37	721.63	673.86	634.30
70000	1022.60	919.90	840.40	777.14	725.69	683.10
75000	1095.64	985.61	900.43	832.65	777.53	731.89
80000	1168.68	1051.31	960.46	888.16	829.36	780.68
85000	1241.73	1117.02	1020.49	943.67	881.20	829.47
90000	1314.77	1182.73	1080.52	999.18	933.03	878.27
95000	1387.81	1248.44	1140.55	1054.69	984.87	927.06
100000	1460.86	1314.14	1200.57	1110.21	1036.70	975.85
200000	2921.71	2628.29	2401.15	2220.41	2073.41	1951.70
300000	4382.57	3942.43	3601.72	3330.62	3110.11	2927.55
400000	5843.42	5256.57	4802.30	4440.82	4146.81	3903.40
500000	7304.28	6570.72	6002.87	5551.03	5183.52	4879.25

MONTHLY PAYMENT
Needed to repay a loan

6%

TERM AMOUNT	15 YEARS	20 YEARS	25 YEARS	30 YEARS	35 YEARS	40 YEARS
500	4.22	3.58	3.22	3.00	2.85	2.75
1000	8.44	7.16	6.44	6.00	5.70	5.50
2000	16.88	14.33	12.89	11.99	11.40	11.00
3000	25.32	21.49	19.33	17.99	17.11	16.51
4000	33.75	28.66	25.77	23.98	22.81	22.01
5000	42.19	35.82	32.22	29.98	28.51	27.51
6000	50.63	42.99	38.66	35.97	34.21	33.01
7000	59.07	50.15	45.10	41.97	39.91	38.51
8000	67.51	57.31	51.54	47.96	45.62	44.02
9000	75.95	64.48	57.99	53.96	51.32	49.52
10000	84.39	71.64	64.43	59.96	57.02	55.02
11000	92.82	78.81	70.87	65.95	62.72	60.52
12000	101.26	85.97	77.32	71.95	68.42	66.03
13000	109.70	93.14	83.76	77.94	74.12	71.53
14000	118.14	100.30	90.20	83.94	79.83	77.03
15000	126.58	107.46	96.65	89.93	85.53	82.53
16000	135.02	114.63	103.09	95.93	91.23	88.03
17000	143.46	121.79	109.53	101.92	96.93	93.54
18000	151.89	128.96	115.97	107.92	102.63	99.04
19000	160.33	136.12	122.42	113.91	108.34	104.54
20000	168.77	143.29	128.86	119.91	114.04	110.04
21000	177.21	150.45	135.30	125.91	119.74	115.54
22000	185.65	157.61	141.75	131.90	125.44	121.05
23000	194.09	164.78	148.19	137.90	131.14	126.55
24000	202.53	171.94	154.63	143.89	136.85	132.05
25000	210.96	179.11	161.08	149.89	142.55	137.55
30000	253.16	214.93	193.29	179.87	171.06	165.06
35000	295.35	250.75	225.51	209.84	199.57	192.57
40000	337.54	286.57	257.72	239.82	228.08	220.09
45000	379.74	322.39	289.94	269.80	256.59	247.60
50000	421.93	358.22	322.15	299.78	285.09	275.11
55000	464.12	394.04	354.37	329.75	313.60	302.62
60000	506.31	429.86	386.58	359.73	342.11	330.13
65000	548.51	465.68	418.80	389.71	370.62	357.64
70000	590.70	501.50	451.01	419.69	399.13	385.15
75000	632.89	537.32	483.23	449.66	427.64	412.66
80000	675.09	573.14	515.44	479.64	456.15	440.17
85000	717.28	608.97	547.66	509.62	484.66	467.68
90000	759.47	644.79	579.87	539.60	513.17	495.19
95000	801.66	680.61	612.09	569.57	541.68	522.70
100000	843.86	716.43	644.30	599.55	570.19	550.21
200000	1687.71	1432.86	1288.60	1199.10	1140.38	1100.43
300000	2531.57	2149.29	1932.90	1798.65	1710.57	1650.64
400000	3375.43	2865.72	2577.21	2398.20	2280.76	2200.85
500000	4219.28	3582.16	3221.51	2997.75	2850.95	2751.07

6.5%

MONTHLY PAYMENT
Needed to repay a loan

TERM AMOUNT	1 YEAR	2 YEARS	3 YEARS	4 YEARS	5 YEARS	6 YEARS
500	43.15	22.27	15.32	11.86	9.78	8.40
1000	86.30	44.55	30.65	23.71	19.57	16.81
2000	172.59	89.09	61.30	47.43	39.13	33.62
3000	258.89	133.64	91.95	71.14	58.70	50.43
4000	345.19	178.19	122.60	94.86	78.26	67.24
5000	431.48	222.73	153.25	118.57	97.83	84.05
6000	517.78	267.28	183.89	142.29	117.40	100.86
7000	604.07	311.82	214.54	166.00	136.96	117.67
8000	690.37	356.37	245.19	189.72	156.53	134.48
9000	776.67	400.92	275.84	213.43	176.10	151.29
10000	862.96	445.46	306.49	237.15	195.66	168.10
11000	949.26	490.01	337.14	260.86	215.23	184.91
12000	1035.56	534.56	367.79	284.58	234.79	201.72
13000	1121.85	579.10	398.44	308.29	254.36	218.53
14000	1208.15	623.65	429.09	332.01	273.93	235.34
15000	1294.45	668.19	459.74	355.72	293.49	252.15
16000	1380.74	712.74	490.38	379.44	313.06	268.96
17000	1467.04	757.29	521.03	403.15	332.62	285.77
18000	1553.34	801.83	551.68	426.87	352.19	302.58
19000	1639.63	846.38	582.33	450.58	371.76	319.39
20000	1725.93	890.93	612.98	474.30	391.32	336.20
21000	1812.22	935.47	643.63	498.01	410.89	353.01
22000	1898.52	980.02	674.28	521.73	430.46	369.82
23000	1984.82	1024.56	704.93	545.44	450.02	386.63
24000	2071.11	1069.11	735.58	569.16	469.59	403.44
25000	2157.41	1113.66	766.23	592.87	489.15	420.25
30000	2588.89	1336.39	919.47	711.45	586.98	504.30
35000	3020.37	1559.12	1072.72	830.02	684.82	588.35
40000	3451.86	1781.85	1225.96	948.60	782.65	672.40
45000	3883.34	2004.58	1379.21	1067.17	880.48	756.45
50000	4314.82	2227.31	1532.45	1185.75	978.31	840.50
55000	4746.30	2450.04	1685.70	1304.32	1076.14	924.55
60000	5177.79	2672.78	1838.94	1422.90	1173.97	1008.60
65000	5609.27	2895.51	1992.19	1541.47	1271.80	1092.65
70000	6040.75	3118.24	2145.43	1660.05	1369.63	1176.70
75000	6472.23	3340.97	2298.68	1778.62	1467.46	1260.74
80000	6903.71	3563.70	2451.92	1897.20	1565.29	1344.79
85000	7335.20	3786.43	2605.17	2015.77	1663.12	1428.84
90000	7766.68	4009.16	2758.41	2134.35	1760.95	1512.89
95000	8198.16	4231.89	2911.66	2252.92	1858.78	1596.94
100000	8629.64	4454.63	3064.90	2371.50	1956.61	1680.99
200000	17259.28	8909.25	6129.80	4742.99	3913.23	3361.99
300000	25888.93	13363.88	9194.70	7114.49	5869.84	5042.98
400000	34518.57	17818.50	12259.60	9485.98	7826.46	6723.97
500000	43148.21	22273.13	15324.50	11857.48	9783.07	8404.96

MONTHLY PAYMENT
Needed to repay a loan

6.5%

TERM AMOUNT	7 YEARS	8 YEARS	9 YEARS	10 YEARS	11 YEARS	12 YEARS
500	7.42	6.69	6.13	5.68	5.31	5.01
1000	14.85	13.39	12.25	11.35	10.62	10.02
2000	29.70	26.77	24.51	22.71	21.25	20.04
3000	44.55	40.16	36.76	34.06	31.87	30.06
4000	59.40	53.54	49.02	45.42	42.50	40.08
5000	74.25	66.93	61.27	56.77	53.12	50.10
6000	89.10	80.32	73.53	68.13	63.74	60.12
7000	103.95	93.70	85.78	79.48	74.37	70.13
8000	118.80	107.09	98.04	90.84	84.99	80.15
9000	133.64	120.48	110.29	102.19	95.61	90.17
10000	148.49	133.86	122.55	113.55	106.24	100.19
11000	163.34	147.25	134.80	124.90	116.86	110.21
12000	178.19	160.63	147.05	136.26	127.49	120.23
13000	193.04	174.02	159.31	147.61	138.11	130.25
14000	207.89	187.41	171.56	158.97	148.73	140.27
15000	222.74	200.79	183.82	170.32	159.36	150.29
16000	237.59	214.18	196.07	181.68	169.98	160.31
17000	252.44	227.57	208.33	193.03	180.60	170.33
18000	267.29	240.95	220.58	204.39	191.23	180.35
19000	282.14	254.34	232.84	215.74	201.85	190.37
20000	296.99	267.72	245.09	227.10	212.48	200.38
21000	311.84	281.11	257.34	238.45	223.10	210.40
22000	326.69	294.50	269.60	249.81	233.72	220.42
23000	341.54	307.88	281.85	261.16	244.35	230.44
24000	356.39	321.27	294.11	272.52	254.97	240.46
25000	371.24	334.66	306.36	283.87	265.59	250.48
30000	445.48	401.59	367.64	340.64	318.71	300.58
35000	519.73	468.52	428.91	397.42	371.83	350.67
40000	593.98	535.45	490.18	454.19	424.95	400.77
45000	668.22	602.38	551.45	510.97	478.07	450.86
50000	742.47	669.31	612.73	567.74	531.19	500.96
55000	816.72	736.24	674.00	624.51	584.31	551.06
60000	890.97	803.17	735.27	681.29	637.43	601.15
65000	965.21	870.11	796.54	738.06	690.54	651.25
70000	1039.46	937.04	857.82	794.84	743.66	701.34
75000	1113.71	1003.97	919.09	851.61	796.78	751.44
80000	1187.95	1070.90	980.36	908.38	849.90	801.54
85000	1262.20	1137.83	1041.63	965.16	903.02	851.63
90000	1336.45	1204.76	1102.91	1021.93	956.14	901.73
95000	1410.70	1271.69	1164.18	1078.71	1009.26	951.83
100000	1484.94	1338.62	1225.45	1135.48	1062.38	1001.92
200000	2969.89	2677.25	2450.90	2270.96	2124.75	2003.84
300000	4454.83	4015.87	3676.35	3406.44	3187.13	3005.76
400000	5939.77	5354.49	4901.81	4541.92	4249.51	4007.68
500000	7424.72	6693.12	6127.26	5677.40	5311.88	5009.61

6.5%

MONTHLY PAYMENT
Needed to repay a loan

TERM AMOUNT	15 YEARS	20 YEARS	25 YEARS	30 YEARS	35 YEARS	40 YEARS
500	4.36	3.73	3.38	3.16	3.02	2.93
1000	8.71	7.46	6.75	6.32	6.04	5.85
2000	17.42	14.91	13.50	12.64	12.08	11.71
3000	26.13	22.37	20.26	18.96	18.12	17.56
4000	34.84	29.82	27.01	25.28	24.17	23.42
5000	43.56	37.28	33.76	31.60	30.21	29.27
6000	52.27	44.73	40.51	37.92	36.25	35.13
7000	60.98	52.19	47.26	44.24	42.29	40.98
8000	69.69	59.65	54.02	50.57	48.33	46.84
9000	78.40	67.10	60.77	56.89	54.37	52.69
10000	87.11	74.56	67.52	63.21	60.42	58.55
11000	95.82	82.01	74.27	69.53	66.46	64.40
12000	104.53	89.47	81.02	75.85	72.50	70.25
13000	113.24	96.92	87.78	82.17	78.54	76.11
14000	121.96	104.38	94.53	88.49	84.58	81.96
15000	130.67	111.84	101.28	94.81	90.62	87.82
16000	139.38	119.29	108.03	101.13	96.66	93.67
17000	148.09	126.75	114.79	107.45	102.71	99.53
18000	156.80	134.20	121.54	113.77	108.75	105.38
19000	165.51	141.66	128.29	120.09	114.79	111.24
20000	174.22	149.11	135.04	126.41	120.83	117.09
21000	182.93	156.57	141.79	132.73	126.87	122.95
22000	191.64	164.03	148.55	139.05	132.91	128.80
23000	200.35	171.48	155.30	145.38	138.96	134.66
24000	209.07	178.94	162.05	151.70	145.00	140.51
25000	217.78	186.39	168.80	158.02	151.04	146.36
30000	261.33	223.67	202.56	189.62	181.25	175.64
35000	304.89	260.95	236.32	221.22	211.45	204.91
40000	348.44	298.23	270.08	252.83	241.66	234.18
45000	392.00	335.51	303.84	284.43	271.87	263.46
50000	435.55	372.79	337.60	316.03	302.08	292.73
55000	479.11	410.07	371.36	347.64	332.28	322.00
60000	522.66	447.34	405.12	379.24	362.49	351.27
65000	566.22	484.62	438.88	410.84	392.70	380.55
70000	609.78	521.90	472.65	442.45	422.91	409.82
75000	653.33	559.18	506.41	474.05	453.12	439.09
80000	696.89	596.46	540.17	505.65	483.32	468.37
85000	740.44	633.74	573.93	537.26	513.53	497.64
90000	784.00	671.02	607.69	568.86	543.74	526.91
95000	827.55	708.29	641.45	600.46	573.95	556.18
100000	871.11	745.57	675.21	632.07	604.15	585.46
200000	1742.21	1491.15	1350.41	1264.14	1208.31	1170.91
300000	2613.32	2236.72	2025.62	1896.20	1812.46	1756.37
400000	3484.43	2982.29	2700.83	2528.27	2416.62	2341.83
500000	4355.54	3727.87	3376.04	3160.34	3020.77	2927.28

MONTHLY PAYMENT
Needed to repay a loan

7%

TERM AMOUNT	1 YEAR	2 YEARS	3 YEARS	4 YEARS	5 YEARS	6 YEARS
500	43.26	22.39	15.44	11.97	9.90	8.52
1000	86.53	44.77	30.88	23.95	19.80	17.05
2000	173.05	89.55	61.75	47.89	39.60	34.10
3000	259.58	134.32	92.63	71.84	59.40	51.15
4000	346.11	179.09	123.51	95.78	79.20	68.20
5000	432.63	223.86	154.39	119.73	99.01	85.25
6000	519.16	268.64	185.26	143.68	118.81	102.29
7000	605.69	313.41	216.14	167.62	138.61	119.34
8000	692.21	358.18	247.02	191.57	158.41	136.39
9000	778.74	402.95	277.89	215.52	178.21	153.44
10000	865.27	447.73	308.77	239.46	198.01	170.49
11000	951.79	492.50	339.65	263.41	217.81	187.54
12000	1038.32	537.27	370.53	287.35	237.61	204.59
13000	1124.85	582.04	401.40	311.30	257.42	221.64
14000	1211.37	626.82	432.28	335.25	277.22	238.69
15000	1297.90	671.59	463.16	359.19	297.02	255.74
16000	1384.43	716.36	494.03	383.14	316.82	272.78
17000	1470.95	761.13	524.91	407.09	336.62	289.83
18000	1557.48	805.91	555.79	431.03	356.42	306.88
19000	1644.01	850.68	586.66	454.98	376.22	323.93
20000	1730.53	895.45	617.54	478.92	396.02	340.98
21000	1817.06	940.22	648.42	502.87	415.83	358.03
22000	1903.59	985.00	679.30	526.82	435.63	375.08
23000	1990.12	1029.77	710.17	550.76	455.43	392.13
24000	2076.64	1074.54	741.05	574.71	475.23	409.18
25000	2163.17	1119.31	771.93	598.66	495.03	426.23
30000	2595.80	1343.18	926.31	718.39	594.04	511.47
35000	3028.44	1567.04	1080.70	838.12	693.04	596.72
40000	3461.07	1790.90	1235.08	957.85	792.05	681.96
45000	3893.70	2014.77	1389.47	1077.58	891.05	767.21
50000	4326.34	2238.63	1543.85	1197.31	990.06	852.45
55000	4758.97	2462.49	1698.24	1317.04	1089.07	937.70
60000	5191.60	2686.35	1852.63	1436.77	1188.07	1022.94
65000	5624.24	2910.22	2007.01	1556.51	1287.08	1108.19
70000	6056.87	3134.08	2161.40	1676.24	1386.08	1193.43
75000	6489.51	3357.94	2315.78	1795.97	1485.09	1278.68
80000	6922.14	3581.81	2470.17	1915.70	1584.10	1363.92
85000	7354.77	3805.67	2624.55	2035.43	1683.10	1449.17
90000	7787.41	4029.53	2778.94	2155.16	1782.11	1534.41
95000	8220.04	4253.40	2933.32	2274.89	1881.11	1619.66
100000	8652.67	4477.26	3087.71	2394.62	1980.12	1704.90
200000	17305.35	8954.52	6175.42	4789.25	3960.24	3409.80
300000	25958.02	13431.77	9263.13	7183.87	5940.36	5114.70
400000	34610.70	17909.03	12350.84	9578.50	7920.48	6819.60
500000	43263.37	22386.29	15438.55	11973.12	9900.60	8524.50

7% MONTHLY PAYMENT
Needed to repay a loan

TERM AMOUNT	7 YEARS	8 YEARS	9 YEARS	10 YEARS	11 YEARS	12 YEARS
500	7.55	6.82	6.25	5.81	5.44	5.14
1000	15.09	13.63	12.51	11.61	10.88	10.28
2000	30.19	27.27	25.01	23.22	21.77	20.57
3000	45.28	40.90	37.52	34.83	32.65	30.85
4000	60.37	54.53	50.03	46.44	43.54	41.14
5000	75.46	68.17	62.53	58.05	54.42	51.42
6000	90.56	81.80	75.04	69.67	65.30	61.70
7000	105.65	95.44	87.54	81.28	76.19	71.99
8000	120.74	109.07	100.05	92.89	87.07	82.27
9000	135.83	122.70	112.56	104.50	97.96	92.55
10000	150.93	136.34	125.06	116.11	108.84	102.84
11000	166.02	149.97	137.57	127.72	119.73	113.12
12000	181.11	163.60	150.08	139.33	130.61	123.41
13000	196.20	177.24	162.58	150.94	141.49	133.69
14000	211.30	190.87	175.09	162.55	152.38	143.97
15000	226.39	204.51	187.59	174.16	163.26	154.26
16000	241.48	218.14	200.10	185.77	174.15	164.54
17000	256.58	231.77	212.61	197.38	185.03	174.82
18000	271.67	245.41	225.11	209.00	195.91	185.11
19000	286.76	259.04	237.62	220.61	206.80	195.39
20000	301.85	272.67	250.13	232.22	217.68	205.68
21000	316.95	286.31	262.63	243.83	228.57	215.96
22000	332.04	299.94	275.14	255.44	239.45	226.24
23000	347.13	313.58	287.64	267.05	250.33	236.53
24000	362.22	327.21	300.15	278.66	261.22	246.81
25000	377.32	340.84	312.66	290.27	272.10	257.10
30000	452.78	409.01	375.19	348.33	326.52	308.51
35000	528.24	477.18	437.72	406.38	380.94	359.93
40000	603.71	545.35	500.25	464.43	435.36	411.35
45000	679.17	613.52	562.78	522.49	489.78	462.77
50000	754.63	681.69	625.31	580.54	544.21	514.19
55000	830.10	749.85	687.85	638.60	598.63	565.61
60000	905.56	818.02	750.38	696.65	653.05	617.03
65000	981.02	886.19	812.91	754.71	707.47	668.45
70000	1056.49	954.36	875.44	812.76	761.89	719.87
75000	1131.95	1022.53	937.97	870.81	816.31	771.29
80000	1207.41	1090.70	1000.50	928.87	870.73	822.70
85000	1282.88	1158.87	1063.03	986.92	925.15	874.12
90000	1358.34	1227.03	1125.56	1044.98	979.57	925.54
95000	1433.80	1295.20	1188.10	1103.03	1033.99	976.96
100000	1509.27	1363.37	1250.63	1161.08	1088.41	1028.38
200000	3018.54	2726.74	2501.26	2322.17	2176.82	2056.76
300000	4527.80	4090.12	3751.88	3483.25	3265.23	3085.14
400000	6037.07	5453.49	5002.51	4644.34	4353.64	4113.52
500000	7546.34	6816.86	6253.14	5805.42	5442.05	5141.91

MONTHLY PAYMENT 7%
Needed to repay a loan

TERM AMOUNT	15 YEARS	20 YEARS	25 YEARS	30 YEARS	35 YEARS	40 YEARS
500	4.49	3.88	3.53	3.33	3.19	3.11
1000	8.99	7.75	7.07	6.65	6.39	6.21
2000	17.98	15.51	14.14	13.31	12.78	12.43
3000	26.96	23.26	21.20	19.96	19.17	18.64
4000	35.95	31.01	28.27	26.61	25.55	24.86
5000	44.94	38.76	35.34	33.27	31.94	31.07
6000	53.93	46.52	42.41	39.92	38.33	37.29
7000	62.92	54.27	49.47	46.57	44.72	43.50
8000	71.91	62.02	56.54	53.22	51.11	49.71
9000	80.89	69.78	63.61	59.88	57.50	55.93
10000	89.88	77.53	70.68	66.53	63.89	62.14
11000	98.87	85.28	77.75	73.18	70.27	68.36
12000	107.86	93.04	84.81	79.84	76.66	74.57
13000	116.85	100.79	91.88	86.49	83.05	80.79
14000	125.84	108.54	98.95	93.14	89.44	87.00
15000	134.82	116.29	106.02	99.80	95.83	93.21
16000	143.81	124.05	113.08	106.45	102.22	99.43
17000	152.80	131.80	120.15	113.10	108.61	105.64
18000	161.79	139.55	127.22	119.75	114.99	111.86
19000	170.78	147.31	134.29	126.41	121.38	118.07
20000	179.77	155.06	141.36	133.06	127.77	124.29
21000	188.75	162.81	148.42	139.71	134.16	130.50
22000	197.74	170.57	155.49	146.37	140.55	136.71
23000	206.73	178.32	162.56	153.02	146.94	142.93
24000	215.72	186.07	169.63	159.67	153.33	149.14
25000	224.71	193.82	176.69	166.33	159.71	155.36
30000	269.65	232.59	212.03	199.59	191.66	186.43
35000	314.59	271.35	247.37	232.86	223.60	217.50
40000	359.53	310.12	282.71	266.12	255.54	248.57
45000	404.47	348.88	318.05	299.39	287.49	279.64
50000	449.41	387.65	353.39	332.65	319.43	310.72
55000	494.36	426.41	388.73	365.92	351.37	341.79
60000	539.30	465.18	424.07	399.18	383.31	372.86
65000	584.24	503.94	459.41	432.45	415.26	403.93
70000	629.18	542.71	494.75	465.71	447.20	435.00
75000	674.12	581.47	530.08	498.98	479.14	466.07
80000	719.06	620.24	565.42	532.24	511.09	497.15
85000	764.00	659.00	600.76	565.51	543.03	528.22
90000	808.95	697.77	636.10	598.77	574.97	559.29
95000	853.89	736.53	671.44	632.04	606.91	590.36
100000	898.83	775.30	706.78	665.30	638.86	621.43
200000	1797.66	1550.60	1413.56	1330.60	1277.71	1242.86
300000	2696.48	2325.90	2120.34	1995.91	1916.57	1864.29
400000	3595.31	3101.20	2827.12	2661.21	2555.43	2485.73
500000	4494.14	3876.49	3533.90	3326.51	3194.28	3107.16

7.25%

MONTHLY PAYMENT
Needed to repay a loan

TERM AMOUNT	1 YEAR	2 YEARS	3 YEARS	4 YEARS	5 YEARS	6 YEARS
500	43.32	22.44	15.50	12.03	9.96	8.58
1000	86.64	44.89	30.99	24.06	19.92	17.17
2000	173.28	89.77	61.98	48.12	39.84	34.34
3000	259.93	134.66	92.97	72.19	59.76	51.51
4000	346.57	179.54	123.97	96.25	79.68	68.68
5000	433.21	224.43	154.96	120.31	99.60	85.85
6000	519.85	269.32	185.95	144.37	119.52	103.02
7000	606.49	314.20	216.94	168.44	139.44	120.19
8000	693.14	359.09	247.93	192.50	159.35	137.35
9000	779.78	403.97	278.92	216.56	179.27	154.52
10000	866.42	448.86	309.92	240.62	199.19	171.69
11000	953.06	493.75	340.91	264.69	219.11	188.86
12000	1039.70	538.63	371.90	288.75	239.03	206.03
13000	1126.35	583.52	402.89	312.81	258.95	223.20
14000	1212.99	628.40	433.88	336.87	278.87	240.37
15000	1299.63	673.29	464.87	360.94	298.79	257.54
16000	1386.27	718.18	495.86	385.00	318.71	274.71
17000	1472.91	763.06	526.86	409.06	338.63	291.88
18000	1559.56	807.95	557.85	433.12	358.55	309.05
19000	1646.20	852.83	588.84	457.19	378.47	326.22
20000	1732.84	897.72	619.83	481.25	398.39	343.39
21000	1819.48	942.61	650.82	505.31	418.31	360.56
22000	1906.12	987.49	681.81	529.37	438.23	377.72
23000	1992.77	1032.38	712.81	553.44	458.15	394.89
24000	2079.41	1077.26	743.80	577.50	478.06	412.06
25000	2166.05	1122.15	774.79	601.56	497.98	429.23
30000	2599.26	1346.58	929.75	721.87	597.58	515.08
35000	3032.47	1571.01	1084.70	842.18	697.18	600.93
40000	3465.68	1795.44	1239.66	962.50	796.77	686.77
45000	3898.89	2019.87	1394.62	1082.81	896.37	772.62
50000	4332.10	2244.30	1549.58	1203.12	995.97	858.47
55000	4765.31	2468.73	1704.53	1323.43	1095.56	944.31
60000	5198.52	2693.16	1859.49	1443.74	1195.16	1030.16
65000	5631.73	2917.59	2014.45	1564.06	1294.76	1116.00
70000	6064.94	3142.02	2169.41	1684.37	1394.36	1201.85
75000	6498.15	3366.45	2324.36	1804.68	1493.95	1287.70
80000	6931.36	3590.88	2479.32	1924.99	1593.55	1373.54
85000	7364.57	3815.31	2634.28	2045.30	1693.15	1459.39
90000	7797.78	4039.74	2789.24	2165.62	1792.74	1545.24
95000	8230.99	4264.17	2944.20	2285.93	1892.34	1631.08
100000	8664.20	4488.60	3099.15	2406.24	1991.94	1716.93
200000	17328.41	8977.20	6198.31	4812.48	3983.87	3433.86
300000	25992.61	13465.80	9297.46	7218.72	5975.81	5150.79
400000	34656.82	17954.40	12396.61	9624.96	7967.74	6867.72
500000	43321.02	22443.00	15495.76	12031.20	9959.68	8584.65

MONTHLY PAYMENT
Needed to repay a loan

7.25%

TERM AMOUNT	7 YEARS	8 YEARS	9 YEARS	10 YEARS	11 YEARS	12 YEARS
500	7.61	6.88	6.32	5.87	5.51	5.21
1000	15.22	13.76	12.63	11.74	11.02	10.42
2000	30.43	27.52	25.27	23.48	22.03	20.84
3000	45.65	41.28	37.90	35.22	33.05	31.25
4000	60.86	55.03	50.53	46.96	44.06	41.67
5000	76.08	68.79	63.17	58.70	55.08	52.09
6000	91.29	82.55	75.80	70.44	66.09	62.51
7000	106.51	96.31	88.43	82.18	77.11	72.92
8000	121.72	110.07	101.07	93.92	88.12	83.34
9000	136.94	123.83	113.70	105.66	99.14	93.76
10000	152.15	137.58	126.33	117.40	110.16	104.18
11000	167.37	151.34	138.97	129.14	121.17	114.59
12000	182.58	165.10	151.60	140.88	132.19	125.01
13000	197.80	178.86	164.23	152.62	143.20	135.43
14000	213.01	192.62	176.87	164.36	154.22	145.85
15000	228.33	206.38	189.50	176.10	165.23	156.26
16000	243.44	220.14	202.13	187.84	176.25	166.68
17000	258.66	233.89	214.77	199.58	187.27	177.10
18000	273.87	247.65	227.40	211.32	198.28	187.52
19000	289.09	261.41	240.03	223.06	209.30	197.93
20000	304.30	275.17	252.67	234.80	220.31	208.35
21000	319.52	288.93	265.30	246.54	231.33	218.77
22000	334.73	302.69	277.93	258.28	242.34	229.19
23000	349.95	316.44	290.57	270.02	253.36	239.60
24000	365.16	330.20	303.20	281.76	264.37	250.02
25000	380.38	343.96	315.83	293.50	275.39	260.44
30000	456.46	412.75	379.00	352.20	330.47	312.53
35000	532.53	481.55	442.16	410.90	385.55	364.61
40000	608.61	550.34	505.33	469.60	440.62	416.70
45000	684.68	619.13	568.50	528.30	495.70	468.79
50000	760.76	687.92	631.66	587.01	550.78	520.88
55000	836.84	756.72	694.83	645.71	605.86	572.97
60000	912.91	825.51	758.00	704.41	660.94	625.05
65000	988.99	894.30	821.16	763.11	716.01	677.14
70000	1065.06	963.09	884.33	821.81	771.09	729.23
75000	1141.14	1031.88	947.50	880.51	826.17	781.32
80000	1217.21	1100.68	1010.66	939.21	881.25	833.40
85000	1293.29	1169.47	1073.83	997.91	936.33	885.49
90000	1369.37	1238.26	1136.99	1056.61	991.40	937.58
95000	1445.44	1307.05	1200.16	1115.31	1046.48	989.67
100000	1521.52	1375.85	1263.33	1174.01	1101.56	1041.76
200000	3043.04	2751.69	2526.66	2348.02	2203.12	2083.51
300000	4564.56	4127.54	3789.98	3522.03	3304.68	3125.27
400000	6086.07	5503.38	5053.31	4696.04	4406.24	4167.02
500000	7607.59	6879.23	6316.64	5870.05	5507.80	5208.78

7.25%

MONTHLY PAYMENT
Needed to repay a loan

TERM AMOUNT	15 YEARS	20 YEARS	25 YEARS	30 YEARS	35 YEARS	40 YEARS
500	4.56	3.95	3.61	3.41	3.28	3.20
1000	9.13	7.90	7.23	6.82	6.56	6.40
2000	18.26	15.81	14.46	13.64	13.13	12.79
3000	27.39	23.71	21.68	20.47	19.69	19.19
4000	36.51	31.62	28.91	27.29	26.26	25.59
5000	45.64	39.52	36.14	34.11	32.82	31.98
6000	54.77	47.42	43.37	40.93	39.39	38.38
7000	63.90	55.33	50.60	47.75	45.95	44.78
8000	73.03	63.23	57.82	54.57	52.52	51.17
9000	82.16	71.13	65.05	61.40	59.08	57.57
10000	91.29	79.04	72.28	68.22	65.65	63.97
11000	100.41	86.94	79.51	75.04	72.21	70.36
12000	109.54	94.85	86.74	81.86	78.78	76.76
13000	118.67	102.75	93.96	88.68	85.34	83.16
14000	127.80	110.65	101.19	95.50	91.91	89.55
15000	136.93	118.56	108.42	102.33	98.47	95.95
16000	146.06	126.46	115.65	109.15	105.03	102.35
17000	155.19	134.36	122.88	115.97	111.60	108.74
18000	164.32	142.27	130.11	122.79	118.16	115.14
19000	173.44	150.17	137.33	129.61	124.73	121.54
20000	182.57	158.08	144.56	136.44	131.29	127.93
21000	191.70	165.98	151.79	143.26	137.86	134.33
22000	200.83	173.88	159.02	150.08	144.42	140.73
23000	209.96	181.79	166.25	156.90	150.99	147.12
24000	219.09	189.69	173.47	163.72	157.55	153.52
25000	228.22	197.59	180.70	170.54	164.12	159.92
30000	273.86	237.11	216.84	204.65	196.94	191.90
35000	319.50	276.63	252.98	238.76	229.76	223.89
40000	365.15	316.15	289.12	272.87	262.59	255.87
45000	410.79	355.67	325.26	306.98	295.41	287.85
50000	456.43	395.19	361.40	341.09	328.23	319.84
55000	502.07	434.71	397.54	375.20	361.06	351.82
60000	547.72	474.23	433.68	409.31	393.88	383.80
65000	593.36	513.74	469.82	443.41	426.70	415.79
70000	639.00	553.26	505.96	477.52	459.53	447.77
75000	684.65	592.78	542.11	511.63	492.35	479.75
80000	730.29	632.30	578.25	545.74	525.17	511.74
85000	775.93	671.82	614.39	579.85	558.00	543.72
90000	821.58	711.34	650.53	613.96	590.82	575.70
95000	867.22	750.86	686.67	648.07	623.64	607.69
100000	912.86	790.38	722.81	682.18	656.47	639.67
200000	1825.73	1580.75	1445.61	1364.35	1312.93	1279.34
300000	2738.59	2371.13	2168.42	2046.53	1969.40	1919.02
400000	3651.45	3161.50	2891.23	2728.71	2625.87	2558.69
500000	4564.31	3951.88	3614.03	3410.88	3282.34	3198.36

MONTHLY PAYMENT
Needed to repay a loan

7.5%

TERM AMOUNT	1 YEAR	2 YEARS	3 YEARS	4 YEARS	5 YEARS	6 YEARS
500	43.38	22.50	15.55	12.09	10.02	8.65
1000	86.76	45.00	31.11	24.18	20.04	17.29
2000	173.51	90.00	62.21	48.36	40.08	34.58
3000	260.27	135.00	93.32	72.54	60.11	51.87
4000	347.03	180.00	124.42	96.72	80.15	69.16
5000	433.79	225.00	155.53	120.89	100.19	86.45
6000	520.54	270.00	186.64	145.07	120.23	103.74
7000	607.30	315.00	217.74	169.25	140.27	121.03
8000	694.06	360.00	248.85	193.43	160.30	138.32
9000	780.82	405.00	279.96	217.61	180.34	155.61
10000	867.57	450.00	311.06	241.79	200.38	172.90
11000	954.33	495.00	342.17	265.97	220.42	190.19
12000	1041.09	540.00	373.27	290.15	240.46	207.48
13000	1127.85	584.99	404.38	314.33	260.49	224.77
14000	1214.60	629.99	435.49	338.50	280.53	242.06
15000	1301.36	674.99	466.59	362.68	300.57	259.35
16000	1388.12	719.99	497.70	386.86	320.61	276.64
17000	1474.88	764.99	528.81	411.04	340.65	293.93
18000	1561.63	809.99	559.91	435.22	360.68	311.22
19000	1648.39	854.99	591.02	459.40	380.72	328.51
20000	1735.15	899.99	622.12	483.58	400.76	345.80
21000	1821.91	944.99	653.23	507.76	420.80	363.09
22000	1908.66	989.99	684.34	531.94	440.83	380.38
23000	1995.42	1034.99	715.44	556.11	460.87	397.67
24000	2082.18	1079.99	746.55	580.29	480.91	414.96
25000	2168.94	1124.99	777.66	604.47	500.95	432.25
30000	2602.72	1349.99	933.19	725.37	601.14	518.70
35000	3036.51	1574.99	1088.72	846.26	701.33	605.15
40000	3470.30	1799.98	1244.25	967.16	801.52	691.60
45000	3904.08	2024.98	1399.78	1088.05	901.71	778.06
50000	4337.87	2249.98	1555.31	1208.95	1001.90	864.51
55000	4771.66	2474.98	1710.84	1329.84	1102.09	950.96
60000	5205.45	2699.98	1866.37	1450.73	1202.28	1037.41
65000	5639.23	2924.97	2021.90	1571.63	1302.47	1123.86
70000	6073.02	3149.97	2177.44	1692.52	1402.66	1210.31
75000	6506.81	3374.97	2332.97	1813.42	1502.85	1296.76
80000	6940.59	3599.97	2488.50	1934.31	1603.04	1383.21
85000	7374.38	3824.97	2644.03	2055.21	1703.23	1469.66
90000	7808.17	4049.96	2799.56	2176.10	1803.42	1556.11
95000	8241.95	4274.96	2955.09	2297.00	1903.61	1642.56
100000	8675.74	4499.96	3110.62	2417.89	2003.79	1729.01
200000	17351.48	8999.92	6221.24	4835.78	4007.59	3458.02
300000	26027.23	13499.88	9331.87	7253.67	6011.38	5187.03
400000	34702.97	17999.84	12442.49	9671.56	8015.18	6916.04
500000	43378.71	22499.80	15553.11	12089.45	10018.97	8645.06

7.5% MONTHLY PAYMENT
Needed to repay a loan

TERM AMOUNT	7 YEARS	8 YEARS	9 YEARS	10 YEARS	11 YEARS	12 YEARS
500	7.67	6.94	6.38	5.94	5.57	5.28
1000	15.34	13.88	12.76	11.87	11.15	10.55
2000	30.68	27.77	25.52	23.74	22.30	21.10
3000	46.01	41.65	38.28	35.61	33.44	31.66
4000	61.35	55.54	51.04	47.48	44.59	42.21
5000	76.69	69.42	63.81	59.35	55.74	52.76
6000	92.03	83.30	76.57	71.22	66.89	63.31
7000	107.37	97.19	89.33	83.09	78.04	73.87
8000	122.71	111.07	102.09	94.96	89.18	84.42
9000	138.04	124.95	114.85	106.83	100.33	94.97
10000	153.38	138.84	127.61	118.70	111.48	105.52
11000	168.72	152.72	140.37	130.57	122.63	116.07
12000	184.06	166.61	153.13	142.44	133.78	126.63
13000	199.40	180.49	165.89	154.31	144.92	137.18
14000	214.74	194.37	178.65	166.18	156.07	147.73
15000	230.07	208.26	191.42	178.05	167.22	158.28
16000	245.41	222.14	204.18	189.92	178.37	168.84
17000	260.75	236.03	216.94	201.79	189.52	179.39
18000	276.09	249.91	229.70	213.66	200.66	189.94
19000	291.43	263.79	242.46	225.53	211.81	200.49
20000	306.77	277.68	255.22	237.40	222.96	211.05
21000	322.10	291.56	267.98	249.27	234.11	221.60
22000	337.44	305.45	280.74	261.14	245.26	232.15
23000	352.78	319.33	293.50	273.01	256.40	242.70
24000	368.12	333.21	306.26	284.88	267.55	253.25
25000	383.46	347.10	319.03	296.75	278.70	263.81
30000	460.15	416.52	382.83	356.11	334.44	316.57
35000	536.84	485.94	446.64	415.46	390.18	369.33
40000	613.53	555.35	510.44	474.81	445.92	422.09
45000	690.22	624.77	574.25	534.16	501.66	474.85
50000	766.91	694.19	638.05	593.51	557.40	527.61
55000	843.61	763.61	701.86	652.86	613.14	580.37
60000	920.30	833.03	765.66	712.21	668.88	633.14
65000	996.99	902.45	829.47	771.56	724.62	685.90
70000	1073.68	971.87	893.27	830.91	780.36	738.66
75000	1150.37	1041.29	957.08	890.26	836.10	791.42
80000	1227.06	1110.71	1020.88	949.61	891.84	844.18
85000	1303.75	1180.13	1084.69	1008.97	947.58	896.94
90000	1380.44	1249.55	1148.49	1068.32	1003.32	949.70
95000	1457.14	1318.97	1212.30	1127.67	1059.06	1002.46
100000	1533.83	1388.39	1276.10	1187.02	1114.80	1055.23
200000	3067.66	2776.77	2552.20	2374.04	2229.60	2110.45
300000	4601.48	4165.16	3828.30	3561.05	3344.40	3165.68
400000	6135.31	5553.55	5104.41	4748.07	4459.20	4220.91
500000	7669.14	6941.94	6380.51	5935.09	5574.00	5276.13

MONTHLY PAYMENT 7.5%
Needed to repay a loan

TERM AMOUNT	15 YEARS	20 YEARS	25 YEARS	30 YEARS	35 YEARS	40 YEARS
500	4.64	4.03	3.69	3.50	3.37	3.29
1000	9.27	8.06	7.39	6.99	6.74	6.58
2000	18.54	16.11	14.78	13.98	13.48	13.16
3000	27.81	24.17	22.17	20.98	20.23	19.74
4000	37.08	32.22	29.56	27.97	26.97	26.32
5000	46.35	40.28	36.95	34.96	33.71	32.90
6000	55.62	48.34	44.34	41.95	40.45	39.48
7000	64.89	56.39	51.73	48.95	47.20	46.06
8000	74.16	64.45	59.12	55.94	53.94	52.65
9000	83.43	72.50	66.51	62.93	60.68	59.23
10000	92.70	80.56	73.90	69.92	67.42	65.81
11000	101.97	88.62	81.29	76.91	74.17	72.39
12000	111.24	96.67	88.68	83.91	80.91	78.97
13000	120.51	104.73	96.07	90.90	87.65	85.55
14000	129.78	112.78	103.46	97.89	94.39	92.13
15000	139.05	120.84	110.85	104.88	101.14	98.71
16000	148.32	128.89	118.24	111.87	107.88	105.29
17000	157.59	136.95	125.63	118.87	114.62	111.87
18000	166.86	145.01	133.02	125.86	121.36	118.45
19000	176.13	153.06	140.41	132.85	128.11	125.03
20000	185.40	161.12	147.80	139.84	134.85	131.61
21000	194.67	169.17	155.19	146.84	141.59	138.19
22000	203.94	177.23	162.58	153.83	148.33	144.78
23000	213.21	185.29	169.97	160.82	155.08	151.36
24000	222.48	193.34	177.36	167.81	161.82	157.94
25000	231.75	201.40	184.75	174.80	168.56	164.52
30000	278.10	241.68	221.70	209.76	202.27	197.42
35000	324.45	281.96	258.65	244.73	235.98	230.32
40000	370.80	322.24	295.60	279.69	269.70	263.23
45000	417.16	362.52	332.55	314.65	303.41	296.13
50000	463.51	402.80	369.50	349.61	337.12	329.04
55000	509.86	443.08	406.45	384.57	370.83	361.94
60000	556.21	483.36	443.39	419.53	404.55	394.84
65000	602.56	523.64	480.34	454.49	438.26	427.75
70000	648.91	563.92	517.29	489.45	471.97	460.65
75000	695.26	604.19	554.24	524.41	505.68	493.55
80000	741.61	644.47	591.19	559.37	539.39	526.46
85000	787.96	684.75	628.14	594.33	573.11	559.36
90000	834.31	725.03	665.09	629.29	606.82	592.26
95000	880.66	765.31	702.04	664 25	640.53	625.17
100000	927.01	805.59	738.99	699.21	674.24	658.07
200000	1854.02	1611.19	1477.98	1398.43	1348.49	1316.14
300000	2781.04	2416.78	2216.97	2097.64	2022.73	1974.21
400000	3708.05	3222.37	2955.96	2796.86	2696.97	2632.28
500000	4635.06	4027.97	3694.96	3496.07	3371.21	3290.35

7.75%

MONTHLY PAYMENT
Needed to repay a loan

TERM AMOUNT	1 YEAR	2 YEARS	3 YEARS	4 YEARS	5 YEARS	6 YEARS
500	43.44	22.56	15.61	12.15	10.08	8.71
1000	86.87	45.11	31.22	24.30	20.16	17.41
2000	173.75	90.23	62.44	48.59	40.31	34.82
3000	260.62	135.34	93.66	72.89	60.47	52.23
4000	347.49	180.45	124.88	97.18	80.63	69.65
5000	434.36	225.57	156.11	121.48	100.78	87.06
6000	521.24	270.68	187.33	145.77	120.94	104.47
7000	608.11	315.79	218.55	170.07	141.10	121.88
8000	694.98	360.91	249.77	194.37	161.26	139.29
9000	781.86	406.02	280.99	218.66	181.41	156.70
10000	868.73	451.13	312.21	242.96	201.57	174.11
11000	955.60	496.25	343.43	267.25	221.73	191.53
12000	1042.47	541.36	374.65	291.55	241.88	208.94
13000	1129.35	586.47	405.88	315.84	262.04	226.35
14000	1216.22	631.59	437.10	340.14	282.20	243.76
15000	1303.09	676.70	468.32	364.44	302.35	261.17
16000	1389.97	721.81	499.54	388.73	322.51	278.58
17000	1476.84	766.93	530.76	413.03	342.67	295.99
18000	1563.71	812.04	561.98	437.32	362.83	313.41
19000	1650.58	857.15	593.20	461.62	382.98	330.82
20000	1737.46	902.27	624.42	485.91	403.14	348.23
21000	1824.33	947.38	655.64	510.21	423.30	365.64
22000	1911.20	992.49	686.87	534.51	443.45	383.05
23000	1998.08	1037.61	718.09	558.80	463.61	400.46
24000	2084.95	1082.72	749.31	583.10	483.77	417.87
25000	2171.82	1127.83	780.53	607.39	503.92	435.29
30000	2606.19	1353.40	936.63	728.87	604.71	522.34
35000	3040.55	1578.97	1092.74	850.35	705.49	609.40
40000	3474.92	1804.53	1248.85	971.83	806.28	696.46
45000	3909.28	2030.10	1404.95	1093.31	907.06	783.51
50000	4343.64	2255.67	1561.06	1214.79	1007.85	870.57
55000	4778.01	2481.23	1717.16	1336.27	1108.63	957.63
60000	5212.37	2706.80	1873.27	1457.74	1209.42	1044.69
65000	5646.74	2932.37	2029.38	1579.22	1310.20	1131.74
70000	6081.10	3157.93	2185.48	1700.70	1410.99	1218.80
75000	6515.47	3383.50	2341.59	1822.18	1511.77	1305.86
80000	6949.83	3609.07	2497.69	1943.66	1612.56	1392.91
85000	7384.19	3834.64	2653.80	2065.14	1713.34	1479.97
90000	7818.56	4060.20	2809.90	2186.62	1814.13	1567.03
95000	8252.92	4285.77	2966.01	2308.10	1914.91	1654.09
100000	8687.29	4511.34	3122.12	2429.57	2015.70	1741.14
200000	17374.58	9022.67	6244.23	4859.15	4031.39	3482.28
300000	26061.86	13534.01	9366.35	7288.72	6047.09	5223.43
400000	34749.15	18045.34	12488.47	9718.30	8062.78	6964.57
500000	43436.44	22556.68	15610.58	12147.87	10078.48	8705.71

MONTHLY PAYMENT
Needed to repay a loan

7.75%

TERM AMOUNT	7 YEARS	8 YEARS	9 YEARS	10 YEARS	11 YEARS	12 YEARS
500	7.73	7.00	6.44	6.00	5.64	5.34
1000	15.46	14.01	12.89	12.00	11.28	10.69
2000	30.92	28.02	25.78	24.00	22.56	21.38
3000	46.39	42.03	38.67	36.00	33.84	32.06
4000	61.85	56.04	51.56	48.00	45.13	42.75
5000	77.31	70.05	64.45	60.01	56.41	53.44
6000	92.77	84.06	77.34	72.01	67.69	64.13
7000	108.23	98.07	90.23	84.01	78.97	74.82
8000	123.70	112.08	103.12	96.01	90.25	85.50
9000	139.16	126.09	116.01	108.01	101.53	96.19
10000	154.62	140.10	128.89	120.01	112.81	106.88
11000	170.08	154.11	141.78	132.01	124.09	117.57
12000	185.54	168.12	154.67	144.01	135.38	128.26
13000	201.01	182.13	167.56	156.01	146.66	138.94
14000	216.47	196.14	180.45	168.01	157.94	149.63
15000	231.93	210.15	193.34	180.02	169.22	160.32
16000	247.39	224.16	206.23	192.02	180.50	171.01
17000	262.85	238.17	219.12	204.02	191.78	181.69
18000	278.32	252.18	232.01	216.02	203.06	192.38
19000	293.78	266.19	244.90	228.02	214.34	203.07
20000	309.24	280.20	257.79	240.02	225.63	213.76
21000	324.70	294.21	270.68	252.02	236.91	224.45
22000	340.16	308.22	283.57	264.02	248.19	235.13
23000	355.62	322.23	296.46	276.02	259.47	245.82
24000	371.09	336.24	309.35	288.03	270.75	256.51
25000	386.55	350.25	322.24	300.03	282.03	267.20
30000	463.86	420.30	386.68	360.03	338.44	320.64
35000	541.17	490.35	451.13	420.04	394.85	374.08
40000	618.48	560.40	515.58	480.04	451.25	427.52
45000	695.79	630.45	580.03	540.05	507.66	480.96
50000	773.10	700.50	644.47	600.05	564.06	534.40
55000	850.41	770.55	708.92	660.06	620.47	587.84
60000	927.72	840.60	773.37	720.06	676.88	641.28
65000	1005.03	910.65	837.82	780.07	733.28	694.71
70000	1082.34	980.70	902.26	840.07	789.69	748.15
75000	1159.65	1050.75	966.71	900.08	846.10	801.59
80000	1236.96	1120.80	1031.16	960.09	902.50	855.03
85000	1314.27	1190.85	1095.61	1020.09	958.91	908.47
90000	1391.58	1260.89	1160.05	1080.10	1015.32	961.91
95000	1468.89	1330.94	1224.50	1140.10	1071.72	1015.35
100000	1546.20	1400.99	1288.95	1200.11	1128.13	1068.79
200000	3092.39	2801.99	2577.90	2400.21	2256.26	2137.58
300000	4638.59	4202.98	3866.85	3600.32	3384.39	3206.38
400000	6184.78	5603.98	5155.80	4800.43	4512.51	4275.17
500000	7730.98	7004.97	6444.75	6000.53	5640.64	5343.96

7.75%

MONTHLY PAYMENT
Needed to repay a loan

TERM AMOUNT	15 YEARS	20 YEARS	25 YEARS	30 YEARS	35 YEARS	40 YEARS
500	4.71	4.10	3.78	3.58	3.46	3.38
1000	9.41	8.21	7.55	7.16	6.92	6.77
2000	18.83	16.42	15.11	14.33	13.84	13.53
3000	28.24	24.63	22.66	21.49	20.77	20.30
4000	37.65	32.84	30.21	28.66	27.69	27.06
5000	47.06	41.05	37.77	35.82	34.61	33.83
6000	56.48	49.26	45.32	42.98	41.53	40.60
7000	65.89	57.47	52.87	50.15	48.45	47.36
8000	75.30	65.68	60.43	57.31	55.37	54.13
9000	84.71	73.89	67.98	64.48	62.30	60.90
10000	94.13	82.09	75.53	71.64	69.22	67.66
11000	103.54	90.30	83.09	78.81	76.14	74.43
12000	112.95	98.51	90.64	85.97	83.06	81.19
13000	122.37	106.72	98.19	93.13	89.98	87.96
14000	131.78	114.93	105.75	100.30	96.90	94.73
15000	141.19	123.14	113.30	107.46	103.83	101.49
16000	150.60	131.35	120.85	114.63	110.75	108.26
17000	160.02	139.56	128.41	121.79	117.67	115.03
18000	169.43	147.77	135.96	128.95	124.59	121.79
19000	178.84	155.98	143.51	136.12	131.51	128.56
20000	188.26	164.19	151.07	143.28	138.44	135.32
21000	197.67	172.40	158.62	150.45	145.36	142.09
22000	207.08	180.61	166.17	157.61	152.28	148.86
23000	216.49	188.82	173.73	164.77	159.20	155.62
24000	225.91	197.03	181.28	171.94	166.12	162.39
25000	235.32	205.24	188.83	179.10	173.04	169.15
30000	282.38	246.28	226.60	214.92	207.65	202.99
35000	329.45	287.33	264.37	250.74	242.26	236.82
40000	376.51	328.38	302.13	286.56	276.87	270.65
45000	423.57	369.43	339.90	322.39	311.48	304.48
50000	470.64	410.47	377.66	358.21	346.09	338.31
55000	517.70	451.52	415.43	394.03	380.70	372.14
60000	564.77	492.57	453.20	429.85	415.31	405.97
65000	611.83	533.62	490.96	465.67	449.91	439.80
70000	658.89	574.66	528.73	501.49	484.52	473.63
75000	705.96	615.71	566.50	537.31	519.13	507.46
80000	753.02	656.76	604.26	573.13	553.74	541.30
85000	800.08	697.81	642.03	608.95	588.35	575.13
90000	847.15	738.85	679.80	644.77	622.96	608.96
95000	894.21	779.90	717.56	680.59	657.57	642.79
100000	941.28	820.95	755.33	716.41	692.18	676.62
200000	1882.55	1641.90	1510.66	1432.82	1384.35	1353.24
300000	2823.83	2462.85	2265.99	2149.24	2076.53	2029.86
400000	3765.10	3283.79	3021.32	2865.65	2768.70	2706.48
500000	4706.38	4104.74	3776.64	3582.06	3406.88	3383.10

MONTHLY PAYMENT
Needed to repay a loan

8%

TERM AMOUNT	1 YEAR	2 YEARS	3 YEARS	4 YEARS	5 YEARS	6 YEARS
500	43.49	22.61	15.67	12.21	10.14	8.77
1000	86.99	45.23	31.34	24.41	20.28	17.53
2000	173.98	90.45	62.67	48.83	40.55	35.07
3000	260.97	135.68	94.01	73.24	60.83	52.60
4000	347.95	180.91	125.35	97.65	81.11	70.13
5000	434.94	226.14	156.68	122.06	101.38	87.67
6000	521.93	271.36	188.02	146.48	121.66	105.20
7000	608.92	316.59	219.35	170.89	141.93	122.73
8000	695.91	361.82	250.69	195.30	162.21	140.27
9000	782.90	407.05	282.03	219.72	182.49	157.80
10000	869.88	452.27	313.36	244.13	202.76	175.33
11000	956.87	497.50	344.70	268.54	223.04	192.87
12000	1043.86	542.73	376.04	292.96	243.32	210.40
13000	1130.85	587.95	407.37	317.37	263.59	227.93
14000	1217.84	633.18	438.71	341.78	283.87	245.47
15000	1304.83	678.41	470.05	366.19	304.15	263.00
16000	1391.81	723.64	501.38	390.61	324.42	280.53
17000	1478.80	768.86	532.72	415.02	344.70	298.07
18000	1565.79	814.09	564.05	439.43	364.98	315.60
19000	1652.78	859.32	595.39	463.85	385.25	333.13
20000	1739.77	904.55	626.73	488.26	405.53	350.66
21000	1826.76	949.77	658.06	512.67	425.80	368.20
22000	1913.75	995.00	689.40	537.08	446.08	385.73
23000	2000.73	1040.23	720.74	561.50	466.36	403.26
24000	2087.72	1085.45	752.07	585.91	486.63	420.80
25000	2174.71	1130.68	783.41	610.32	506.91	438.33
30000	2609.65	1356.82	940.09	732.39	608.29	526.00
35000	3044.60	1582.96	1096.77	854.45	709.67	613.66
40000	3479.54	1809.09	1253.45	976.52	811.06	701.33
45000	3914.48	2035.23	1410.14	1098.58	912.44	789.00
50000	4349.42	2261.36	1566.82	1220.65	1013.82	876.66
55000	4784.36	2487.50	1723.50	1342.71	1115.20	964.33
60000	5219.31	2713.64	1880.18	1464.78	1216.58	1051.99
65000	5654.25	2939.77	2036.86	1586.84	1317.97	1139.66
70000	6089.19	3165.91	2193.55	1708.90	1419.35	1227.33
75000	6524.13	3392.05	2350.23	1830.97	1520.73	1314.99
80000	6959.07	3618.18	2506.91	1953.03	1622.11	1402.66
85000	7394.02	3844.32	2663.59	2075.10	1723.49	1490.33
90000	7828.96	4070.46	2820.27	2197.16	1824.88	1577.99
95000	8263.90	4296.59	2976.95	2319.23	1926.26	1665.66
100000	8698.84	4522.73	3133.64	2441.29	2027.64	1753.32
200000	17397.69	9045.46	6267.27	4882.58	4055.28	3506.65
300000	26096.53	13568.19	9400.91	7323.88	6082.92	5259.97
400000	34795.37	18090.92	12534.55	9765.17	8110.56	7013.30
500000	43494.21	22613.65	15668.18	12206.46	10138.20	8766.62

8%

MONTHLY PAYMENT
Needed to repay a loan

TERM AMOUNT	7 YEARS	8 YEARS	9 YEARS	10 YEARS	11 YEARS	12 YEARS
500	7.79	7.07	6.51	6.07	5.71	5.41
1000	15.59	14.14	13.02	12.13	11.42	10.82
2000	31.17	28.27	26.04	24.27	22.83	21.65
3000	46.76	42.41	39.06	36.40	34.25	32.47
4000	62.34	56.55	52.07	48.53	45.66	43.30
5000	77.93	70.68	65.09	60.66	57.08	54.12
6000	93.52	84.82	78.11	72.80	68.49	64.95
7000	109.10	98.96	91.13	84.93	79.91	75.77
8000	124.69	113.09	104.15	97.06	91.32	86.60
9000	140.28	127.23	117.17	109.19	102.74	97.42
10000	155.86	141.37	130.19	121.33	114.15	108.25
11000	171.45	155.50	143.21	133.46	125.57	119.07
12000	187.03	169.64	156.22	145.59	136.99	129.89
13000	202.62	183.78	169.24	157.73	148.40	140.72
14000	218.21	197.91	182.26	169.86	159.82	151.54
15000	233.79	212.05	195.28	181.99	171.23	162.37
16000	249.38	226.19	208.30	194.12	182.65	173.19
17000	264.97	240.32	221.32	206.26	194.06	184.02
18000	280.55	254.46	234.34	218.39	205.48	194.84
19000	296.14	268.60	247.36	230.52	216.89	205.67
20000	311.72	282.73	260.37	242.66	228.31	216.49
21000	327.31	296.87	273.39	254.79	239.72	227.32
22000	342.90	311.01	286.41	266.92	251.14	238.14
23000	358.48	325.14	299.43	279.05	262.56	248.96
24000	374.07	339.28	312.45	291.19	273.97	259.79
25000	389.66	353.42	325.47	303.32	285.39	270.61
30000	467.59	424.10	390.56	363.98	342.46	324.74
35000	545.52	494.78	455.66	424.65	399.54	378.86
40000	623.45	565.47	520.75	485.31	456.62	432.98
45000	701.38	636.15	585.84	545.97	513.70	487.10
50000	779.31	706.83	650.94	606.64	570.77	541.23
55000	857.24	777.52	716.03	667.30	627.85	595.35
60000	935.17	848.20	781.12	727.97	684.93	649.47
65000	1013.10	918.88	846.22	788.63	742.00	703.59
70000	1091.04	989.57	911.31	849.29	799.08	757.72
75000	1168.97	1060.25	976.40	909.96	856.16	811.84
80000	1246.90	1130.93	1041.50	970.62	913.24	865.96
85000	1324.83	1201.62	1106.59	1031.28	970.31	920.08
90000	1402.76	1272.30	1171.68	1091.95	1027.39	974.21
95000	1480.69	1342.98	1236.78	1152.61	1084.47	1028.33
100000	1558.62	1413.67	1301.87	1213.28	1141.54	1082.45
200000	3117.24	2827.34	2603.74	2426.55	2283.09	2164.91
300000	4675.86	4241.00	3905.61	3639.83	3424.63	3247.36
400000	6234.49	5654.67	5207.49	4853.10	4566.18	4329.81
500000	7793.11	7068.34	6509.36	6066.38	5707.72	5412.26

MONTHLY PAYMENT
Needed to repay a loan

8%

TERM AMOUNT	15 YEARS	20 YEARS	25 YEARS	30 YEARS	35 YEARS	40 YEARS
500	4.78	4.18	3.86	3.67	3.55	3.48
1000	9.56	8.36	7.72	7.34	7.10	6.95
2000	19.11	16.73	15.44	14.68	14.21	13.91
3000	28.67	25.09	23.15	22.01	21.31	20.86
4000	38.23	33.46	30.87	29.35	28.41	27.81
5000	47.78	41.82	38.59	36.69	35.51	34.77
6000	57.34	50.19	46.31	44.03	42.62	41.72
7000	66.90	58.55	54.03	51.36	49.72	48.67
8000	76.45	66.92	61.75	58.70	56.82	55.62
9000	86.01	75.28	69.46	66.04	63.92	62.58
10000	95.57	83.64	77.18	73.38	71.03	69.53
11000	105.12	92.01	84.90	80.71	78.13	76.48
12000	114.68	100.37	92.62	88.05	85.23	83.44
13000	124.23	108.74	100.34	95.39	92.33	90.39
14000	133.79	117.10	108.05	102.73	99.44	97.34
15000	143.35	125.47	115.77	110.06	106.54	104.30
16000	152.90	133.83	123.49	117.40	113.64	111.25
17000	162.46	142.19	131.21	124.74	120.74	118.20
18000	172.02	150.56	138.93	132.08	127.85	125.16
19000	181.57	158.92	146.65	139.42	134.95	132.11
20000	191.13	167.29	154.36	146.75	142.05	139.06
21000	200.69	175.65	162.08	154.09	149.15	146.02
22000	210.24	184.02	169.80	161.43	156.26	152.97
23000	219.80	192.38	177.52	168.77	163.36	159.92
24000	229.36	200.75	185.24	176.10	170.46	166.87
25000	238.91	209.11	192.95	183.44	177.57	173.83
30000	286.70	250.93	231.54	220.13	213.08	208.59
35000	334.48	292.75	270.14	256.82	248.59	243.36
40000	382.26	334.58	308.73	293.51	284.10	278.12
45000	430.04	376.40	347.32	330.19	319.62	312.89
50000	477.83	418.22	385.91	366.88	355.13	347.66
55000	525.61	460.04	424.50	403.57	390.64	382.42
60000	573.39	501.86	463.09	440.26	426.16	417.19
65000	621.17	543.69	501.68	476.95	461.67	451.95
70000	668.96	585.51	540.27	513.64	497.18	486.72
75000	716.74	627.33	578.86	550.32	532.70	521.48
80000	764.52	669.15	617.45	587.01	568.21	556.25
85000	812.30	710.97	656.04	623.70	603.72	591.01
90000	860.09	752.80	694.63	660.39	639.23	625.78
95000	907.87	794.62	733.23	697.08	674.75	660.55
100000	955.65	836.44	771.82	733.76	710.26	695.31
200000	1911.30	1672.88	1543.63	1467.53	1420.52	1390.62
300000	2866.96	2509.32	2315.45	2201.29	2130.78	2085.94
400000	3822.61	3345.76	3087.26	2935.06	2841.04	2781.25
500000	4778.26	4182.20	3859.08	3668.82	3551.30	3476.56

8.25% MONTHLY PAYMENT
Needed to repay a loan

TERM AMOUNT	1 YEAR	2 YEARS	3 YEARS	4 YEARS	5 YEARS	6 YEARS
500	43.55	22.67	15.73	12.27	10.20	8.83
1000	87.10	45.34	31.45	24.53	20.40	17.66
2000	174.21	90.68	62.90	49.06	40.79	35.31
3000	261.31	136.02	94.36	73.59	61.19	52.97
4000	348.42	181.37	125.81	98.12	81.59	70.62
5000	435.52	226.71	157.26	122.65	101.98	88.28
6000	522.62	272.05	188.71	147.18	122.38	105.93
7000	609.73	317.39	220.16	171.71	142.77	123.59
8000	696.83	362.73	251.61	196.24	163.17	141.24
9000	783.94	408.07	283.07	220.77	183.57	158.90
10000	871.04	453.41	314.52	245.30	203.96	176.56
11000	958.14	498.76	345.97	269.83	224.36	194.21
12000	1045.25	544.10	377.42	294.37	244.76	211.87
13000	1132.35	589.44	408.87	318.90	265.15	229.52
14000	1219.46	634.78	440.33	343.43	285.55	247.18
15000	1306.56	680.12	471.78	367.96	305.94	264.83
16000	1393.67	725.46	503.23	392.49	326.34	282.49
17000	1480.77	770.80	534.68	417.02	346.74	300.14
18000	1567.87	816.15	566.13	441.55	367.13	317.80
19000	1654.98	861.49	597.58	466.08	387.53	335.46
20000	1742.08	906.83	629.04	490.61	407.93	353.11
21000	1829.19	952.17	660.49	515.14	428.32	370.77
22000	1916.29	997.51	691.94	539.67	448.72	388.42
23000	2003.39	1042.85	723.39	564.20	469.11	406.08
24000	2090.50	1088.19	754.84	588.73	489.51	423.73
25000	2177.60	1133.53	786.30	613.26	509.91	441.39
30000	2613.12	1360.24	943.55	735.91	611.89	529.67
35000	3048.64	1586.95	1100.81	858.57	713.87	617.94
40000	3484.16	1813.66	1258.07	981.22	815.85	706.22
45000	3919.68	2040.36	1415.33	1103.87	917.83	794.50
50000	4355.20	2267.07	1572.59	1226.52	1019.81	882.78
55000	4790.72	2493.78	1729.85	1349.17	1121.79	971.06
60000	5226.24	2720.48	1887.11	1471.83	1223.78	1059.33
65000	5661.76	2947.19	2044.37	1594.48	1325.76	1147.61
70000	6097.28	3173.90	2201.63	1717.13	1427.74	1235.89
75000	6532.80	3400.60	2358.89	1839.78	1529.72	1324.17
80000	6968.33	3627.31	2516.15	1962.44	1631.70	1412.44
85000	7403.85	3854.02	2673.40	2085.09	1733.68	1500.72
90000	7839.37	4080.73	2830.66	2207.74	1835.66	1589.00
95000	8274.89	4307.43	2987.92	2330.39	1937.64	1677.28
100000	8710.41	4534.14	3145.18	2453.04	2039.63	1765.56
200000	17420.81	9068.28	6290.36	4906.09	4079.25	3531.11
300000	26131.22	13602.42	9435.55	7359.13	6118.88	5296.67
400000	34841.63	18136.56	12580.73	9812.18	8158.50	7062.22
500000	43552.03	22670.70	15725.91	12265.22	10198.13	8827.78

MONTHLY PAYMENT 8.25%
Needed to repay a loan

TERM AMOUNT	7 YEARS	8 YEARS	9 YEARS	10 YEARS	11 YEARS	12 YEARS
500	7.86	7.13	6.75	6.13	5.78	5.48
1000	15.71	14.26	13.15	12.27	11.55	10.96
2000	31.42	28.53	26.30	24.53	23.10	21.92
3000	47.13	42.79	39.45	36.80	34.65	32.89
4000	62.84	57.06	52.59	49.06	46.20	43.85
5000	78.56	71.32	65.74	61.33	57.75	54.81
6000	94.27	85.58	78.89	73.59	69.30	65.77
7000	109.98	99.85	92.04	85.86	80.85	76.73
8000	125.69	114.11	105.19	98.12	92.40	87.70
9000	141.40	128.38	118.34	110.39	103.95	98.66
10000	157.11	142.64	131.49	122.65	115.50	109.62
11000	172.82	156.90	144.64	134.92	127.06	120.58
12000	188.53	171.17	157.78	147.18	138.61	131.54
13000	204.24	185.43	170.93	159.45	150.16	142.51
14000	219.95	199.70	184.08	171.71	161.71	153.47
15000	235.67	213.96	197.23	183.98	173.26	164.43
16000	251.38	228.23	210.38	196.24	184.81	175.39
17000	267.09	242.49	223.53	208.51	196.36	186.36
18000	282.80	256.75	236.68	220.77	207.91	197.32
19000	298.51	271.02	249.82	233.04	219.46	208.28
20000	314.22	285.28	262.97	245.31	231.01	219.24
21000	329.93	299.55	276.12	257.57	242.56	230.20
22000	345.64	313.81	289.27	269.84	254.11	241.17
23000	361.35	328.07	302.42	282.10	265.66	252.13
24000	377.07	342.34	315.57	294.37	277.21	263.09
25000	392.78	356.60	328.72	306.63	288.76	274.05
30000	471.33	427.92	394.46	367.96	346.51	328.86
35000	549.89	499.24	460.20	429.28	404.27	383.67
40000	628.44	570.56	525.95	490.61	462.02	438.48
45000	707.00	641.88	591.69	551.94	519.77	493.29
50000	785.55	713.20	657.43	613.26	577.52	548.10
55000	864.11	784.52	723.18	674.59	635.28	602.91
60000	942.66	855.84	788.92	735.92	693.03	657.72
65000	1021.22	927.16	854.66	797.24	750.78	712.53
70000	1099.77	989.49	920.41	858.57	808.53	767.35
75000	1178.33	1069.81	986.15	919.89	866.29	822.16
80000	1256.88	1141.13	1051.89	981.22	924.04	876.97
85000	1335.44	1212.45	1117.64	1042.55	981.79	931.78
90000	1414.00	1283.77	1183.38	1103.87	1039.54	986.59
95000	1492.55	1355.09	1249.12	1165.20	1097.30	1041.40
100000	1571.11	1426.41	1314.87	1226.53	1155.05	1096.21
200000	3142.21	2852.81	2629.73	2453.05	2310.10	2192.41
300000	4713.32	4279.22	3944.60	3679.58	3465.15	3288.62
400000	6284.42	5705.63	5259.47	4906.11	4620.19	4384.83
500000	7855.53	7132.04	6574.33	6132.63	5775.24	5481.04

8.25%

MONTHLY PAYMENT
Needed to repay a loan

TERM AMOUNT	15 YEARS	20 YEARS	25 YEARS	30 YEARS	35 YEARS	40 YEARS
500	4.85	4.26	3.94	3.76	3.64	3.57
1000	9.70	8.52	7.88	7.51	7.28	7.14
2000	19.40	17.04	15.77	15.03	14.57	14.28
3000	29.10	25.56	23.65	22.54	21.85	21.42
4000	38.81	34.08	31.54	30.05	29.14	28.57
5000	48.51	42.60	39.42	37.56	36.42	35.71
6000	58.21	51.12	47.31	45.08	43.71	42.85
7000	67.91	59.64	55.19	52.59	50.99	49.99
8000	77.61	68.17	63.08	60.10	58.28	57.13
9000	87.31	76.69	70.96	67.61	65.56	64.27
10000	97.01	85.21	78.85	75.13	72.85	71.41
11000	106.72	93.73	86.73	82.64	80.13	78.56
12000	116.42	102.25	94.61	90.15	87.42	85.70
13000	126.12	110.77	102.50	97.66	94.70	92.84
14000	135.82	119.29	110.38	105.18	101.99	99.98
15000	145.52	127.81	118.27	112.69	109.27	107.12
16000	155.22	136.33	126.15	120.20	116.56	114.26
17000	164.92	144.85	134.04	127.72	123.84	121.40
18000	174.63	153.37	141.92	135.23	131.13	128.54
19000	184.33	161.89	149.81	142.74	138.41	135.69
20000	194.03	170.41	157.69	150.25	145.70	142.83
21000	203.73	178.93	165.57	157.77	152.98	149.97
22000	213.43	187.45	173.46	165.28	160.27	157.11
23000	223.13	195.98	181.34	172.79	167.55	164.25
24000	232.83	204.50	189.23	180.30	174.84	171.39
25000	242.54	213.02	197.11	187.82	182.12	178.53
30000	291.04	255.62	236.54	225.38	218.55	214.24
35000	339.55	298.22	275.96	262.94	254.97	249.95
40000	388.06	340.83	315.38	300.51	291.40	285.66
45000	436.56	383.43	354.80	338.07	327.82	321.36
50000	485.07	426.03	394.23	375.63	364.25	357.07
55000	533.58	468.64	433.65	413.20	400.67	392.78
60000	582.08	511.24	473.07	450.76	437.09	428.48
65000	630.59	553.84	512.49	488.32	473.52	464.19
70000	679.10	596.45	551.92	525.89	509.94	499.90
75000	727.61	639.05	591.34	563.45	546.37	535.60
80000	776.11	681.65	630.76	601.01	582.79	571.31
85000	824.62	724.26	670.18	638.58	619.22	607.02
90000	873.13	766.86	709.61	676.14	655.64	642.72
95000	921.63	809.46	749.03	713.70	692.07	678.43
100000	970.14	852.07	788.45	751.27	728.49	714.14
200000	1940.28	1704.13	1576.90	1502.53	1456.98	1428.28
300000	2910.42	2556.20	2365.35	2253.80	2185.47	2142.42
400000	3880.56	3408.26	3153.80	3005.07	2913.96	2856.56
500000	4850.70	4260.33	3942.25	3756.33	3642.46	3570.69

MONTHLY PAYMENT
Needed to repay a loan

8.5%

TERM AMOUNT	1 YEAR	2 YEARS	3 YEARS	4 YEARS	5 YEARS	6 YEARS
500	43.61	22.73	15.78	12.32	10.26	8.89
1000	87.22	45.46	31.57	24.65	20.52	17.78
2000	174.44	90.91	63.14	49.30	41.03	35.56
3000	261.66	136.37	94.70	73.94	61.55	53.34
4000	348.88	181.82	126.27	98.59	82.07	71.11
5000	436.10	227.28	157.84	123.24	102.58	88.89
6000	523.32	272.73	189.41	147.89	123.10	106.67
7000	610.54	318.19	220.97	172.54	143.62	124.45
8000	697.76	363.65	252.54	197.19	164.13	142.23
9000	784.98	409.10	284.11	221.83	184.65	160.01
10000	872.20	454.56	315.68	246.48	205.17	177.78
11000	959.42	500.01	347.24	271.13	225.68	195.56
12000	1046.64	545.47	378.81	295.78	246.20	213.34
13000	1133.86	590.92	410.38	320.43	266.71	231.12
14000	1221.08	636.38	441.95	345.08	287.23	248.90
15000	1308.30	681.84	473.51	369.72	307.75	266.68
16000	1395.52	727.29	505.08	394.37	328.26	284.45
17000	1482.74	772.75	536.65	419.02	348.78	302.23
18000	1569.96	818.20	568.22	443.67	369.30	320.01
19000	1657.18	863.66	599.78	468.32	389.81	337.79
20000	1744.40	909.11	631.35	492.97	410.33	355.57
21000	1831.62	954.57	662.92	517.61	430.85	373.35
22000	1918.84	1000.02	694.49	542.26	451.36	391.12
23000	2006.05	1045.48	726.05	566.91	471.88	408.90
24000	2093.27	1090.94	757.62	591.56	492.40	426.68
25000	2180.49	1136.39	789.19	616.21	512.91	444.46
30000	2616.59	1363.67	947.03	739.45	615.50	533.35
35000	3052.69	1590.95	1104.86	862.69	718.08	622.24
40000	3488.79	1818.23	1262.70	985.93	820.66	711.14
45000	3924.89	2045.51	1420.54	1109.17	923.24	800.03
50000	4360.99	2272.78	1578.38	1232.42	1025.83	888.92
55000	4797.09	2500.06	1736.21	1355.66	1128.41	977.81
60000	5233.19	2727.34	1894.05	1478.90	1230.99	1066.70
65000	5669.29	2954.62	2051.89	1602.14	1333.57	1155.59
70000	6105.38	3181.90	2209.73	1725.38	1436.16	1244.49
75000	6541.48	3409.18	2367.57	1848.62	1538.74	1333.38
80000	6977.58	3636.45	2525.40	1971.86	1641.32	1422.27
85000	7413.68	3863.73	2683.24	2095.11	1743.91	1511.16
90000	7849.78	4091.01	2841.08	2218.35	1846.49	1600.05
95000	8285.88	4318.29	2998.92	2341.59	1949.07	1688.95
100000	8721.98	4545.57	3156.75	2464.83	2051.65	1777.84
200000	17443.96	9091.13	6313.51	4929.66	4103.31	3555.68
300000	26165.93	13636.70	9470.26	7394.49	6154.96	5333.52
400000	34887.91	18182.27	12627.01	9859.32	8206.61	7111.35
500000	43609.89	22727.84	15783.77	12324.15	10258.27	8889.19

8.5% MONTHLY PAYMENT
Needed to repay a loan

TERM AMOUNT	7 YEARS	8 YEARS	9 YEARS	10 YEARS	11 YEARS	12 YEARS
500	7.92	7.20	6.64	6.20	5.84	5.55
1000	15.84	14.39	13.28	12.40	11.69	11.10
2000	31.67	28.78	26.56	24.80	23.37	22.20
3000	47.51	43.18	39.84	37.20	35.06	33.30
4000	63.35	57.57	53.12	49.59	46.75	44.40
5000	79.18	71.96	66.40	61.99	58.43	55.50
6000	95.02	86.35	79.68	74.39	70.12	66.60
7000	110.86	100.74	92.96	86.79	81.80	77.70
8000	126.69	115.14	106.23	99.19	93.49	88.80
9000	142.53	129.53	119.51	111.59	105.18	99.91
10000	158.36	143.92	132.79	123.99	116.86	111.01
11000	174.20	158.31	146.07	136.38	128.55	122.11
12000	190.04	172.71	159.35	148.78	140.24	133.21
13000	205.87	187.10	172.63	161.18	151.92	144.31
14000	221.71	201.49	185.91	173.58	163.61	155.41
15000	237.55	215.88	199.19	185.98	175.30	166.51
16000	253.38	230.27	212.47	198.38	186.98	177.61
17000	269.22	244.67	225.75	210.78	198.67	188.71
18000	285.06	259.06	239.03	223.17	210.36	199.81
19000	300.89	273.45	252.31	235.57	222.04	210.91
20000	316.73	287.84	265.59	247.97	233.73	222.01
21000	332.57	302.23	278.87	260.37	245.41	233.11
22000	348.40	316.63	292.15	272.77	257.10	244.21
23000	364.24	331.02	305.43	285.17	268.79	255.31
24000	380.08	345.41	318.70	297.57	280.47	266.41
25000	395.91	359.80	331.98	309.96	292.16	277.51
30000	475.09	431.76	398.38	371.96	350.59	333.02
35000	554.28	503.72	464.78	433.95	409.02	388.52
40000	633.46	575.69	531.17	495.94	467.46	444.02
45000	712.64	647.65	597.57	557.94	525.89	499.53
50000	791.82	719.61	663.97	619.93	584.32	555.03
55000	871.01	791.57	730.36	681.92	642.75	610.53
60000	950.19	863.53	796.76	743.91	701.18	666.03
65000	1029.37	935.49	863.16	805.91	759.62	721.54
70000	1108.55	1007.45	929.55	867.90	818.05	777.04
75000	1187.74	1079.41	995.95	929.89	876.48	832.54
80000	1266.92	1151.37	1062.35	991.89	934.91	888.04
85000	1346.10	1223.33	1128.74	1053.88	993.34	943.55
90000	1425.28	1295.29	1195.14	1115.87	1051.78	999.05
95000	1504.47	1367.25	1261.54	1177.86	1110.21	1054.55
100000	1583.65	1439.21	1327.94	1239.86	1168.64	1110.06
200000	3167.30	2878.43	2655.87	2479.71	2337.28	2220.11
300000	4750.95	4317.64	3983.81	3719.57	3505.92	3330.17
400000	6334.59	5756.85	5311.74	4959.43	4674.56	4440.22
500000	7918.24	7196.06	6639.68	6199.28	5843.20	5550.28

MONTHLY PAYMENT 8.5%
Needed to repay a loan

TERM AMOUNT	15 YEARS	20 YEARS	25 YEARS	30 YEARS	35 YEARS	40 YEARS
500	4.92	4.34	4.03	3.84	3.73	3.67
1000	9.85	8.68	8.05	7.69	7.47	7.33
2000	19.69	17.36	16.10	15.38	14.94	14.66
3000	29.54	26.03	24.16	23.07	22.41	21.99
4000	39.39	34.71	32.21	30.76	29.87	29.32
5000	49.24	43.39	40.26	38.45	37.34	36.65
6000	59.08	52.07	48.31	46.13	44.81	43.99
7000	68.93	60.75	56.37	53.82	52.28	51.32
8000	78.78	69.43	64.42	61.51	59.75	58.65
9000	88.63	78.10	72.47	69.20	67.22	65.98
10000	98.47	86.78	80.52	76.89	74.69	73.31
11000	108.32	95.46	88.57	84.58	82.15	80.64
12000	118.17	104.14	96.63	92.27	89.62	87.97
13000	128.02	112.82	104.68	99.96	97.09	95.30
14000	137.86	121.50	112.73	107.65	104.56	102.63
15000	147.71	130.17	120.78	115.34	112.03	109.96
16000	157.56	138.85	128.84	123.03	119.50	117.30
17000	167.41	147.53	136.89	130.72	126.97	124.63
18000	177.25	156.21	144.94	138.40	134.43	131.96
19000	187.10	164.89	152.99	146.09	141.90	139.29
20000	196.95	173.56	161.05	153.78	149.37	146.62
21000	206.80	182.24	169.10	161.47	156.84	153.95
22000	216.64	190.92	177.15	169.16	164.31	161.28
23000	226.49	199.60	185.20	176.85	171.78	168.61
24000	236.34	208.28	193.25	184.54	179.25	175.94
25000	246.18	216.96	201.31	192.23	186.72	183.27
30000	295.42	260.35	241.57	230.67	224.06	219.93
35000	344.66	303.74	281.83	269.12	261.40	256.58
40000	393.90	347.13	322.09	307.57	298.74	293.24
45000	443.13	390.52	362.35	346.01	336.09	329.89
50000	492.37	433.91	402.61	384.46	373.43	366.55
55000	541.61	477.30	442.87	422.90	410.77	403.20
60000	590.84	520.69	483.14	461.35	448.12	439.86
65000	640.08	564.09	523.40	499.79	485.46	476.51
70000	689.32	607.48	563.66	538.24	522.80	513.17
75000	738.55	650.87	603.92	576.69	560.15	549.82
80000	787.79	694.26	644.18	615.13	597.49	586.48
85000	837.03	737.65	684.44	653.58	634.83	623.13
90000	886.27	781.04	724.70	692.02	672.17	659.78
95000	935.50	824.43	764.97	730.47	709.52	696.44
100000	984.74	867.82	805.23	768.91	746.86	733.09
200000	1969.48	1735.65	1610.45	1537.83	1493.72	1466.19
300000	2954.22	2603.47	2415.68	2306.74	2240.58	2199.28
400000	3938.96	3471.29	3220.91	3075.65	2987.44	2932.38
500000	4923.70	4339.12	4026.14	3844.57	3734.30	3665.47

8.75% MONTHLY PAYMENT
Needed to repay a loan

TERM AMOUNT	1 YEAR	2 YEARS	3 YEARS	4 YEARS	5 YEARS	6 YEARS
500	43.67	22.79	15.84	12.38	10.32	8.95
1000	87.34	45.57	31.68	24.77	20.64	17.90
2000	174.67	91.14	63.37	49.53	41.27	35.80
3000	262.01	136.71	95.05	74.30	61.91	53.71
4000	349.34	182.28	126.73	99.07	82.55	71.61
5000	436.68	227.85	158.42	123.83	103.19	89.51
6000	524.01	273.42	190.10	148.60	123.82	107.41
7000	611.35	318.99	221.78	173.37	144.46	125.31
8000	698.68	364.56	253.47	198.13	165.10	143.21
9000	786.02	410.13	285.15	222.90	185.74	161.12
10000	873.36	455.70	316.84	247.67	206.37	179.02
11000	960.69	501.27	348.52	272.43	227.01	196.92
12000	1048.03	546.84	380.20	297.20	247.65	214.82
13000	1135.36	592.41	411.89	321.96	268.28	232.72
14000	1222.70	637.98	443.57	346.73	288.92	250.62
15000	1310.03	683.55	475.25	371.50	309.56	268.53
16000	1397.37	729.12	506.94	396.26	330.20	286.43
17000	1484.70	774.69.	538.62	421.03	350.83	304.33
18000	1572.04	820.26	570.30	445.80	371.47	322.23
19000	1659.38	865.83	601.99	470.56	392.11	340.13
20000	1746.71	911.40	633.67	495.33	412.74	358.03
21000	1834.05	956.97	665.35	520.10	433.38	375.94
22000	1921.38	1002.54	697.04	544.86	454.02	393.84
23000	2008.72	1048.11	728.72	569.63	474.66	411.74
24000	2096.05	1093.68	760.40	594.40	495.29	429.64
25000	2183.39	1139.25	792.09	619.16	515.93	447.54
30000	2620.07	1367.10	950.51	743.00	619.12	537.05
35000	3056.75	1594.95	1108.92	866.83	722.30	626.56
40000	3493.42	1822.80	1267.34	990.66	825.49	716.07
45000	3930.10	2050.66	1425.76	1114.49	928.68	805.58
50000	4366.78	2278.51	1584.18	1238.33	1031.86	895.09
55000	4803.46	2506.36	1742.59	1362.16	1135.05	984.59
60000	5240.14	2734.21	1901.01	1485.99	1238.23	1074.10
65000	5676.81	2962.06	2059.43	1609.82	1341.42	1163.61
70000	6113.49	3189.91	2217.85	1733.66	1444.61	1253.12
75000	6550.17	3417.76	2376.26	1857.49	1547.79	1342.63
80000	6986.85	3645.61	2534.68	1981.32	1650.98	1432.14
85000	7423.52	3873.46	2693.10	2105.15	1754.16	1521.65
90000	7860.20	4101.31	2851.52	2228.99	1857.35	1611.15
95000	8296.88	4329.16	3009.93	2352.82	1960.54	1700.66
100000	8733.56	4557.01	3168.35	2476.65	2063.72	1790.17
200000	17467.12	9114.02	6336.70	4953.30	4127.45	3580.34
300000	26200.68	13671.04	9505.05	7429.95	6191.17	5370.51
400000	34934.23	18228.05	12673.40	9906.60	8254.89	7160.68
500000	43667.79	22785.06	15841.75	12383.25	10318.62	8950.86

MONTHLY PAYMENT 8.75%
Needed to repay a loan

TERM AMOUNT	7 YEARS	8 YEARS	9 YEARS	10 YEARS	11 YEARS	12 YEARS
500	7.98	7.26	6.71	6.27	5.91	5.62
1000	15.96	14.52	13.41	12.53	11.82	11.24
2000	31.92	29.04	26.82	25.07	23.65	22.48
3000	47.89	43.56	40.23	37.60	35.47	33.72
4000	63.85	58.08	53.64	50.13	47.29	44.96
5000	79.81	72.60	67.05	62.66	59.12	56.20
6000	95.77	87.13	80.46	75.20	70.94	67.44
7000	111.74	101.65	93.88	87.73	82.76	78.68
8000	127.70	116.17	107.29	100.26	94.59	89.92
9000	143.66	130.69	120.70	112.79	106.41	101.16
10000	159.62	145.21	134.11	125.33	118.23	112.40
11000	175.59	159.73	147.52	137.86	130.05	123.64
12000	191.55	174.25	160.93	150.39	141.88	134.88
13000	207.51	188.77	174.34	162.92	153.70	146.12
14000	223.47	203.29	187.75	175.46	165.52	157.36
15000	239.44	217.81	201.16	187.99	177.35	168.60
16000	255.40	232.33	214.57	200.52	189.17	179.84
17000	271.36	246.85	227.98	213.06	200.99	191.08
18000	287.32	261.38	241.39	225.59	212.82	202.32
19000	303.29	275.90	254.80	238.12	224.64	213.56
20000	319.25	290.42	268.22	250.65	236.46	224.80
21000	335.21	304.94	281.63	263.19	248.29	236.04
22000	351.17	319.46	295.04	275.72	260.11	247.28
23000	367.14	333.98	308.45	288.25	271.93	258.52
24000	383.10	348.50	321.86	300.78	283.76	269.76
25000	399.06	363.02	335.27	313.32	295.58	281.00
30000	478.87	435.63	402.32	375.98	354.70	337.20
35000	558.69	508.23	469.38	438.64	413.81	393.40
40000	638.50	580.83	536.43	501.31	472.93	449.60
45000	718.31	653.44	603.48	563.97	532.04	505.80
50000	798.12	726.04	670.54	626.63	591.16	562.00
55000	877.94	798.65	737.59	689.30	650.27	618.20
60000	957.75	871.25	804.65	751.96	709.39	674.40
65000	1037.56	943.85	871.70	814.62	768.51	730.60
70000	1117.37	1016.46	938.75	877.29	827.62	786.80
75000	1197.19	1089.06	1005.81	939.95	886.74	843.00
80000	1277.00	1161.67	1072.86	1002.61	945.85	899.20
85000	1356.81	1234.27	1139.92	1065.28	1004.97	955.40
90000	1436.62	1306.88	1206.97	1127.94	1064.09	1011.60
95000	1516.44	1379.48	1274.02	1190.60	1123.20	1067.80
100000	1596.25	1452.08	1341.08	1253.27	1182.32	1124.00
200000	3192.50	2904.17	2682.15	2506.54	2364.63	2247.99
300000	4788.75	4356.25	4023.23	3759.80	3546.95	3371.99
400000	6385.00	5808.34	5364.31	5013.07	4729.27	4495.99
500000	7981.25	7260.42	6705.38	6266.34	5911.58	5619.98

8.75%

MONTHLY PAYMENT
Needed to repay a loan

TERM AMOUNT	15 YEARS	20 YEARS	25 YEARS	30 YEARS	35 YEARS	40 YEARS
500	5.00	4.42	4.11	3.93	3.83	3.76
1000	9.99	8.84	8.22	7.87	7.65	7.52
2000	19.99	17.67	16.44	15.73	15.31	15.04
3000	29.98	26.51	24.66	23.60	22.96	22.57
4000	39.98	35.35	32.89	31.47	30.61	30.09
5000	49.97	44.19	41.11	39.34	38.27	37.61
6000	59.97	53.02	49.33	47.20	45.92	45.13
7000	69.96	61.86	57.55	55.07	53.58	52.65
8000	79.96	70.70	65.77	62.94	61.23	60.17
9000	89.95	79.53	73.99	70.80	68.88	67.70
10000	99.94	88.37	82.21	78.67	76.54	75.22
11000	109.94	97.21	90.44	86.54	84.19	82.74
12000	119.93	106.05	98.66	94.40	91.84	90.26
13000	129.93	114.88	106.88	102.27	99.50	97.78
14000	139.92	123.72	115.10	110.14	107.15	105.30
15000	149.92	132.56	123.32	118.01	114.80	112.83
16000	159.91	141.39	131.54	125.87	122.46	120.35
17000	169.91	150.23	139.76	133.74	130.11	127.87
18000	179.90	159.07	147.99	141.61	137.77	135.39
19000	189.90	167.91	156.21	149.47	145.42	142.91
20000	199.89	176.74	164.43	157.34	153.07	150.43
21000	209.88	185.58	172.65	165.21	160.73	157.96
22000	219.88	194.42	180.87	173.07	168.38	165.48
23000	229.87	203.25	189.09	180.94	176.03	173.00
24000	239.87	212.09	197.31	188.81	183.69	180.52
25000	249.86	220.93	205.54	196.68	191.34	188.04
30000	299.83	265.11	246.64	236.01	229.61	225.65
35000	349.81	309.30	287.75	275.35	267.88	263.26
40000	399.78	353.48	328.86	314.68	306.15	300.87
45000	449.75	397.67	369.96	354.02	344.41	338.48
50000	499.72	441.86	411.07	393.35	382.68	376.09
55000	549.70	486.04	452.18	432.69	420.95	413.69
60000	599.67	530.23	493.29	472.02	459.22	451.30
65000	649.64	574.41	534.39	511.36	497.49	488.91
70000	699.61	618.60	575.50	550.69	535.75	526.52
75000	749.59	662.78	616.61	590.03	574.02	564.13
80000	799.56	706.97	657.71	629.36	612.29	601.74
85000	849.53	751.15	698.82	668.70	650.56	639.34
90000	899.50	795.34	739.93	708.03	688.83	676.95
95000	949.48	839.53	781.04	747.37	727.09	714.56
100000	999.45	883.71	822.14	786.70	765.36	752.17
200000	1998.90	1767.42	1644.29	1573.40	1530.73	1504.34
300000	2998.35	2651.13	2466.43	2360.10	2296.09	2256.51
400000	3997.79	3534.84	3288.57	3146.80	3061.45	3008.68
500000	4997.24	4418.55	4110.72	3933.50	3826.82	3760.85

MONTHLY PAYMENT
Needed to repay a loan

9%

TERM AMOUNT	1 YEAR	2 YEARS	3 YEARS	4 YEARS	5 YEARS	6 YEARS
500	43.73	22.84	15.90	12.44	10.38	9.01
1000	87.45	45.68	31.80	24.89	20.76	18.03
2000	174.90	91.37	63.60	49.77	41.52	36.05
3000	262.35	137.05	95.40	74.66	62.28	54.08
4000	349.81	182.74	127.20	99.54	83.03	72.10
5000	437.26	228.42	159.00	124.43	103.79	90.13
6000	524.71	274.11	190.80	149.31	124.55	108.15
7000	612.16	319.79	222.60	174.20	145.31	126.18
8000	699.61	365.48	254.40	199.08	166.07	144.20
9000	787.06	411.16	286.20	223.97	186.83	162.23
10000	874.51	445.85	318.00	248.85	207.58	180.26
11000	961.97	502.53	349.80	273.74	228.34	198.28
12000	1049.42	548.22	381.60	298.62	249.10	216.31
13000	1136.87	593.90	413.40	323.51	269.86	234.33
14000	1224.32	639.59	445.20	348.39	290.62	252.36
15000	1311.77	685.27	477.00	373.28	311.38	270.38
16000	1399.22	730.96	508.80	398.16	332.13	288.41
17000	1486.68	776.64	540.60	423.05	352.89	306.43
18000	1574.13	822.33	572.40	447.93	373.65	324.46
19000	1661.58	868.01	604.19	472.82	394.41	342.49
20000	1749.03	913.69	635.99	497.70	415.17	360.51
21000	1836.48	959.38	667.79	522.59	435.93	378.54
22000	1923.93	1005.06	699.59	547.47	456.68	396.56
23000	2011.38	1050.75	731.39	572.36	477.44	414.59
24000	2098.84	1096.43	763.19	597.24	498.20	432.61
25000	2186.29	1142.12	794.99	622.13	518.96	450.64
30000	2623.54	1370.54	953.99	746.55	622.75	540.77
35000	3060.80	1598.97	1112.99	870.98	726.54	630.89
40000	3498.06	1827.39	1271.99	995.40	830.33	721.02
45000	3935.32	2055.81	1430.99	1119.83	934.13	811.15
50000	4372.57	2284.24	1589.99	1244.25	1037.92	901.28
55000	4809.83	2512.66	1748.99	1368.68	1141.71	991.40
60000	5247.09	2741.08	1907.98	1493.10	1245.50	1081.53
65000	5684.35	2969.51	2066.98	1617.53	1349.29	1171.66
70000	6121.60	3197.93	2225.98	1741.95	1453.08	1261.79
75000	6558.86	3426.36	2384.98	1866.38	1556.88	1351.92
80000	6996.12	3654.78	2543.98	1990.80	1660.67	1442.04
85000	7433.38	3883.20	2702.98	2115.23	1764.46	1532.17
90000	7870.63	4111.63	2861.98	2239.65	1868.25	1622.30
95000	8307.89	4340.05	3020.97	2364.08	1972.04	1712.43
100000	8745.15	4568.47	3179.97	2488.50	2075.84	1802.55
200000	17490.30	9136.95	6359.95	4977.01	4151.67	3605.11
300000	26235.44	13705.42	9539.92	7465.51	6227.51	5407.66
400000	34980.59	18273.90	12719.89	9954.02	8303.34	7210.21
500000	43725.74	22842.37	15899.87	12442.52	10379.18	9012.77

9% MONTHLY PAYMENT
Needed to repay a loan

TERM AMOUNT	7 YEARS	8 YEARS	9 YEARS	10 YEARS	11 YEARS	12 YEARS
500	8.04	7.33	6.77	6.33	5.98	5.69
1000	16.09	14.65	13.54	12.67	11.96	11.38
2000	32.18	29.30	27.09	25.34	23.92	22.76
3000	48.27	43.95	40.63	38.00	35.88	34.14
4000	64.36	58.60	54.17	50.67	47.84	45.52
5000	80.45	73.25	67.71	63.34	59.80	56.90
6000	96.53	87.90	81.26	76.01	71.76	68.28
7000	112.62	102.55	94.80	88.67	83.73	79.66
8000	128.71	117.20	108.34	101.34	95.69	91.04
9000	144.80	131.85	121.89	114.01	107.65	102.42
10000	160.89	146.50	135.43	126.68	119.61	113.80
11000	176.98	161.15	148.97	139.34	131.57	125.18
12000	193.07	175.80	162.51	152.01	143.53	136.56
13000	209.16	190.45	176.06	164.68	155.49	147.94
14000	225.25	205.10	189.60	177.35	167.45	159.32
15000	241.34	219.75	203.14	190.01	179.41	170.70
16000	257.43	234.40	216.69	202.68	191.37	182.08
17000	273.51	249.05	230.23	215.35	203.33	193.47
18000	289.60	263.70	243.77	228.02	215.29	204.85
19000	305.69	278.35	257.32	240.68	227.26	216.23
20000	321.78	293.00	270.86	253.35	239.22	227.61
21000	337.87	307.65	284.40	266.02	251.18	238.99
22000	353.96	322.30	297.94	278.69	263.14	250.37
23000	370.05	336.95	311.49	291.35	275.10	261.75
24000	386.14	351.60	325.03	304.02	287.06	273.13
25000	402.23	366.26	338.57	316.69	299.02	284.51
30000	482.67	439.51	406.29	380.03	358.82	341.41
35000	563.12	512.76	474.00	443.37	418.63	398.31
40000	643.56	586.01	541.72	506.70	478.43	455.21
45000	724.01	659.26	609.43	570.04	538.24	512.11
50000	804.45	732.51	677.15	633.38	598.04	569.02
55000	884.90	805.76	744.86	696.72	657.84	625.92
60000	965.34	879.01	812.57	760.05	717.65	682.82
65000	1045.79	952.26	880.29	823.39	777.45	739.72
70000	1126.24	1025.51	948.00	886.73	837.26	796.62
75000	1206.68	1098.77	1015.72	950.07	897.06	853.52
80000	1287.13	1172.02	1083.43	1013.41	956.86	910.42
85000	1367.57	1245.27	1151.15	1076.74	1016.67	967.33
90000	1448.02	1318.52	1218.86	1140.08	1076.47	1024.23
95000	1528.46	1391.77	1286.58	1203.42	1136.28	1081.13
100000	1608.91	1465.02	1354.29	1266.76	1196.08	1138.03
200000	3217.82	2930.04	2708.58	2533.52	2392.16	2276.06
300000	4826.72	4395.06	4062.87	3800.27	3588.24	3414.09
400000	6435.63	5860.08	5417.16	5067.03	4784.32	4552.12
500000	8044.54	7325.10	6771.45	6333.79	5980.40	5690.15

MONTHLY PAYMENT 9%
Needed to repay a loan

TERM AMOUNT	15 YEARS	20 YEARS	25 YEARS	30 YEARS	35 YEARS	40 YEARS
500	5.07	4.50	4.20	4.02	3.92	3.86
1000	10.14	9.00	8.39	8.05	7.84	7.71
2000	20.29	17.99	16.78	16.09	15.68	15.43
3000	30.43	26.99	25.18	24.14	23.52	23.14
4000	40.57	35.99	33.57	32.18	31.36	30.85
5000	50.71	44.99	41.96	40.23	39.20	38.57
6000	60.86	53.98	50.35	48.28	47.04	46.28
7000	71.00	62.98	58.74	56.32	54.88	54.00
8000	81.14	71.98	67.14	64.37	62.72	61.71
9000	91.28	80.98	75.53	72.42	70.56	69.42
10000	101.43	89.97	83.92	80.46	78.40	77.14
11000	111.57	98.97	92.31	88.51	86.24	84.85
12000	121.71	107.97	100.70	96.55	94.08	92.56
13000	131.85	116.96	109.10	104.60	101.92	100.28
14000	142.00	125.96	117.49	112.65	109.76	107.99
15000	152.14	134.96	125.88	120.69	117.60	115.70
16000	162.28	143.96	134.27	128.74	125.44	123.42
17000	172.43	152.95	142.66	136.79	133.28	131.13
18000	182.57	161.95	151.06	144.83	141.12	138.85
19000	192.71	170.95	159.45	152.88	148.96	146.56
20000	202.85	179.95	167.84	160.92	156.80	154.27
21000	213.00	188.94	176.23	168.97	164.64	161.99
22000	223.14	197.94	184.62	177.02	172.48	169.70
23000	233.28	206.94	193.02	185.06	180.32	177.41
24000	243.42	215.93	201.41	193.11	188.16	185.13
25000	253.57	224.93	209.80	201.16	196.00	192.84
30000	304.28	269.92	251.76	241.39	235.20	231.41
35000	354.99	314.90	293.72	281.62	274.40	269.98
40000	405.71	359.89	335.68	321.85	313.60	308.54
45000	456.42	404.88	377.64	362.08	352.80	347.11
50000	507.13	449.86	419.60	402.31	392.00	385.68
55000	557.85	494.85	461.56	442.54	431.20	424.25
60000	608.56	539.84	503.52	482.77	470.40	462.82
65000	659.27	584.82	545.48	523.00	509.60	501.38
70000	709.99	629.81	587.44	563.24	548.80	539.95
75000	760.70	674.79	629.40	603.47	587.99	578.52
80000	811.41	719.78	671.36	643.70	627.19	617.09
85000	862.13	764.77	713.32	683.93	666.39	655.66
90000	912.84	809.75	755.28	724.16	705.59	694.23
95000	963.55	854.74	797.24	764.39	744.79	732.79
100000	1014.27	899.73	839.20	804.62	783.99	771.36
200000	2028.53	1799.45	1678.39	1609.25	1567.99	1542.72
300000	3042.80	2699.18	2517.59	2413.87	2351.98	2314.08
400000	4057.07	3598.90	3356.79	3218.49	3135.97	3085.45
500000	5071.33	4498.63	4195.98	4023.11	3919.96	3856.81

9.25% MONTHLY PAYMENT
Needed to repay a loan

TERM AMOUNT	1 YEAR	2 YEARS	3 YEARS	4 YEARS	5 YEARS	6 YEARS
500	43.78	22.90	15.96	12.50	10.44	9.07
1000	87.57	45.80	31.92	25.00	20.88	18.15
2000	175.13	91.60	63.83	50.01	41.76	36.30
3000	262.70	137.40	95.75	75.01	62.64	54.45
4000	350.27	183.20	127.66	100.02	83.52	72.60
5000	437.84	229.00	159.58	125.02	104.40	90.75
6000	525.40	274.80	191.50	150.02	125.28	108.90
7000	612.97	320.60	223.41	175.03	146.16	127.05
8000	700.54	366.40	255.33	200.03	167.04	145.20
9000	788.11	412.20	287.25	225.04	187.92	163.35
10000	875.67	458.00	319.16	250.04	208.80	181.50
11000	963.24	503.79	351.08	275.04	229.68	199.65
12000	1050.81	549.59	382.99	300.05	250.56	217.80
13000	1138.38	595.39	414.91	325.05	271.44	235.95
14000	1225.94	641.19	446.83	350.05	292.32	254.10
15000	1313.51	686.99	478.74	375.06	313.20	272.25
16000	1401.08	732.79	510.66	400.06	334.08	290.40
17000	1488.65	778.59	542.58	425.07	354.96	308.55
18000	1576.21	824.39	574.49	450.07	375.84	326.70
19000	1663.78	870.19	606.41	475.07	396.72	344.85
20000	1751.35	915.99	638.32	500.08	417.60	363.00
21000	1838.92	961.79	670.24	525.08	438.48	381.15
22000	1926.48	1007.59	702.16	550.09	459.36	399.30
23000	2014.05	1053.39	734.07	575.09	480.24	417.45
24000	2101.62	1099.19	765.99	600.09	501.12	435.60
25000	2189.19	1144.99	797.91	625.10	522.00	453.75
30000	2627.02	1373.99	957.49	750.12	626.40	544.50
35000	3064.86	1602.98	1117.07	875.14	730.80	635.25
40000	3502.70	1831.98	1276.65	1000.16	835.20	725.99
45000	3940.54	2060.98	1436.23	1125.18	939.60	816.74
50000	4378.37	2289.98	1595.81	1250.20	1043.99	907.49
55000	4816.21	2518.97	1755.39	1375.22	1148.39	998.24
60000	5254.05	2747.97	1914.97	1500.24	1252.79	1088.99
65000	5691.88	2976.97	2074.55	1625.25	1357.19	1179.74
70000	6129.72	3205.97	2234.13	1750.27	1461.59	1270.49
75000	6567.56	3434.96	2393.72	1875.29	1565.99	1361.24
80000	7005.40	3663.96	2553.30	2000.31	1670.39	1451.99
85000	7443.23	3892.96	2712.88	2125.33	1774.79	1542.74
90000	7881.07	4121.96	2872.46	2250.35	1879.19	1633.49
95000	8318.91	4350.96	3032.04	2375.37	1983.59	1724.24
100000	8756.75	4579.95	3191.62	2500.39	2087.99	1814.99
200000	17513.49	9159.91	6383.24	5000.78	4175.98	3629.97
300000	26270.24	13739.86	9574.86	7501.18	6263.97	5444.96
400000	35026.98	18319.81	12766.49	10001.57	8351.96	7259.95
500000	43783.73	22899.77	15958.11	12501.96	10439.95	9074.93

MONTHLY PAYMENT 9.25%
Needed to repay a loan

TERM AMOUNT	7 YEARS	8 YEARS	9 YEARS	10 YEARS	11 YEARS	12 YEARS
500	8.11	7.39	6.84	6.40	6.05	5.76
1000	16.22	14.78	13.68	12.80	12.10	11.52
2000	32.43	29.56	27.35	25.61	24.20	23.04
3000	48.65	44.34	41.03	38.41	36.30	34.56
4000	64.86	59.12	54.70	51.21	48.40	46.09
5000	81.08	73.90	68.38	64.02	60.50	57.61
6000	97.30	88.68	82.05	76.82	72.60	69.13
7000	113.51	103.46	95.73	89.62	84.70	80.65
8000	129.73	118.24	109.41	102.43	96.79	92.17
9000	145.95	133.02	123.08	115.23	108.89	103.69
10000	162.16	147.80	136.76	128.03	120.99	115.22
11000	178.38	162.58	150.43	140.84	133.09	126.74
12000	194.59	177.36	164.11	153.64	145.19	138.26
13000	210.81	192.14	177.79	166.44	157.29	149.78
14000	227.03	206.92	191.46	179.25	169.39	161.30
15000	243.24	221.70	205.14	192.05	181.49	172.82
16000	259.46	236.48	218.81	204.85	193.59	184.35
17000	275.68	251.26	232.49	217.66	205.69	195.87
18000	291.89	266.04	246.16	230.46	217.79	207.39
19000	308.11	280.82	259.84	243.26	229.89	218.91
20000	324.32	295.60	273.52	256.07	241.99	230.43
21000	340.54	310.38	287.19	268.87	254.09	241.95
22000	356.76	325.16	300.87	281.67	266.18	253.47
23000	372.97	339.95	314.54	294.48	278.28	265.00
24000	389.19	354.73	328.22	307.28	290.38	276.52
25000	405.41	369.51	341.89	320.08	302.48	288.04
30000	486.49	443.41	410.27	384.10	362.98	345.65
35000	567.57	517.31	478.65	448.11	423.48	403.25
40000	648.65	591.21	547.03	512.13	483.97	460.86
45000	729.73	665.11	615.41	576.15	544.47	518.47
50000	810.81	739.01	683.79	640.16	604.96	576.08
55000	891.89	812.91	752.17	704.18	665.46	633.69
60000	972.97	886.81	820.55	768.20	725.96	691.29
65000	1054.06	960.71	888.93	832.21	786.45	748.90
70000	1135.14	1034.62	957.30	896.23	846.95	806.51
75000	1216.22	1108.52	1025.68	960.25	907.45	864.12
80000	1297.30	1182.42	1094.06	1024.26	967.94	921.73
85000	1378.38	1256.32	1162.44	1088.28	1028.44	979.33
90000	1459.46	1330.22	1230.82	1152.29	1088.94	1036.94
95000	1540.54	1404.12	1299.20	1216.31	1149.43	1094.55
100000	1621.62	1478.02	1367.58	1280.33	1209.93	1152.16
200000	3243.25	2956.04	2735.15	2560.65	2419.86	2304.31
300000	4864.87	4434.07	4102.73	3840.98	3629.79	3456.47
400000	6486.50	5912.09	5470.31	5121.31	4839.72	4608.63
500000	8108.12	7390.11	6837.89	6401.64	6049.65	5760.78

9.25%

MONTHLY PAYMENT
Needed to repay a loan

TERM AMOUNT	15 YEARS	20 YEARS	25 YEARS	30 YEARS	35 YEARS	40 YEARS
500	5.15	4.58	4.28	4.11	4.01	3.95
1000	10.29	9.16	8.56	8.23	8.03	7.91
2000	20.58	18.32	17.13	16.45	16.05	15.81
3000	30.88	27.48	25.69	24.68	24.08	23.72
4000	41.17	36.63	34.26	32.91	32.11	31.63
5000	51.46	45.79	42.82	41.13	40.14	39.53
6000	61.75	54.95	51.38	49.36	48.16	47.44
7000	72.04	64.11	59.95	57.59	56.19	55.35
8000	82.34	73.27	68.51	65.81	64.22	63.25
9000	92.63	82.43	77.07	74.04	72.25	71.16
10000	102.92	91.59	85.64	82.27	80.27	79.07
11000	113.21	100.75	94.20	90.49	88.30	86.97
12000	123.50	109.90	102.77	98.72	96.33	94.88
13000	133.79	119.06	111.33	106.95	104.36	102.79
14000	144.09	128.22	119.89	115.17	112.38	110.69
15000	154.38	137.38	128.46	123.40	120.41	118.60
16000	164.67	146.54	137.02	131.63	128.44	126.51
17000	174.96	155.70	145.58	139.85	136.47	134.41
18000	185.25	164.86	154.15	148.08	144.49	142.32
19000	195.55	174.01	162.71	156.31	152.52	150.23
20000	205.84	183.17	171.28	164.54	160.55	158.13
21000	216.13	192.33	179.84	172.76	168.58	166.04
22000	226.42	201.49	188.40	180.99	176.60	173.95
23000	236.71	210.65	196.97	189.22	184.63	181.85
24000	247.01	219.81	205.53	197.44	192.66	189.76
25000	257.30	228.97	214.10	205.67	200.69	197.67
30000	308.76	274.76	256.91	246.80	240.82	237.20
35000	360.22	320.55	299.73	287.94	280.96	276.73
40000	411.68	366.35	342.55	329.07	321.10	316.26
45000	463.14	412.14	385.37	370.20	361.23	355.80
50000	514.60	457.93	428.19	411.34	401.37	395.33
55000	566.06	503.73	471.01	452.47	441.51	434.86
60000	617.52	549.52	513.83	493.61	481.65	474.40
65000	668.97	595.31	556.65	534.74	521.78	513.93
70000	720.43	641.11	599.47	575.87	561.92	553.46
75000	771.89	686.90	642.29	617.01	602.06	593.00
80000	823.35	732.69	685.11	658.14	642.20	632.53
85000	874.81	778.49	727.92	699.27	682.33	672.06
90000	926.27	824.28	770.74	740.41	722.47	711.59
95000	977.73	870.07	813.56	781.54	762.61	751.13
100000	1029.19	915.87	856.38	822.68	802.74	790.66
200000	2058.38	1831.73	1712.76	1645.35	1605.49	1581.32
300000	3087.58	2747.60	2569.15	2468.03	2408.23	2371.98
400000	4116.77	3663.47	3425.53	3290.70	3210.98	3162.64
500000	5145.96	4579.33	4281.91	4113.38	4013.72	3953.30

9.5%

MONTHLY PAYMENT
Needed to repay a loan

TERM AMOUNT	1 YEAR	2 YEARS	3 YEARS	4 YEARS	5 YEARS	6 YEARS
500	43.84	22.96	16.02	12.56	10.50	9.14
1000	87.68	45.91	32.03	25.12	21.00	18.27
2000	175.37	91.83	64.07	50.25	42.00	36.55
3000	263.05	137.74	96.10	75.37	63.01	54.82
4000	350.73	183.66	128.13	100.49	84.01	73.10
5000	438.42	229.57	160.16	125.62	105.01	91.37
6000	526.10	275.49	192.20	150.74	126.01	109.65
7000	613.78	321.40	224.23	175.86	147.01	127.92
8000	701.47	367.32	256.26	200.99	168.01	146.20
9000	789.15	413.23	288.30	226.11	189.02	164.47
10000	876.84	459.14	320.33	251.23	210.02	182.75
11000	964.52	505.06	352.36	276.35	231.02	201.02
12000	1052.20	550.97	384.40	301.48	252.02	219.30
13000	1139.89	596.89	416.43	326.60	273.02	237.57
14000	1227.57	642.80	448.46	351.72	294.03	255.85
15000	1315.25	688.72	480.49	376.85	315.03	274.12
16000	1402.94	734.63	512.53	401.97	336.03	292.40
17000	1490.62	780.55	544.56	427.09	357.03	310.67
18000	1578.30	826.46	576.59	452.22	378.03	328.94
19000	1665.99	872.38	608.63	477.34	399.04	347.22
20000	1753.67	918.29	640.66	502.46	420.04	365.49
21000	1841.35	964.20	672.69	527.59	441.04	383.77
22000	1929.04	1010.12	704.72	552.71	462.04	402.04
23000	2016.72	1056.03	736.76	577.83	483.04	420.32
24000	2104.40	1101.95	768.79	602.96	504.04	438.59
25000	2192.09	1147.86	800.82	628.08	525.05	456.87
30000	2630.51	1377.43	960.99	753.69	630.06	548.24
35000	3068.92	1607.01	1121.15	879.31	735.07	639.61
40000	3507.34	1836.58	1281.32	1004.93	840.07	730.99
45000	3945.76	2066.15	1441.48	1130.54	945.08	822.36
50000	4384.18	2295.72	1601.65	1256.16	1050.09	913.73
55000	4822.59	2525.30	1761.81	1381.77	1155.10	1005.11
60000	5261.01	2754.87	1921.98	1507.39	1260.11	1096.48
65000	5699.43	2984.44	2082.14	1633.00	1365.12	1187.85
70000	6137.85	3214.01	2242.31	1758.62	1470.13	1279.23
75000	6576.26	3443.59	2402.47	1884.24	1575.14	1370.60
80000	7014.68	3673.16	2562.64	2009.85	1680.15	1461.98
85000	7453.10	3902.73	2722.80	2135.47	1785.16	1553.35
90000	7891.52	4132.30	2882.97	2261.08	1890.17	1644.72
95000	8329.93	4361.88	3043.13	2386.70	1995.18	1736.10
100000	8768.35	4591.45	3203.29	2512.31	2100.19	1827.47
200000	17536.70	9182.90	6406.59	5024.63	4200.37	3654.94
300000	26305.05	13774.35	9609.88	7536.94	6300.56	5482.41
400000	35073.40	18365.80	12813.18	10049.25	8400.74	7309.88
500000	43841.76	22957.25	16016.47	12561.57	10500.93	9137.35

9.5%

MONTHLY PAYMENT
Needed to repay a loan

TERM AMOUNT	7 YEARS	8 YEARS	9 YEARS	10 YEARS	11 YEARS	12 YEARS
500	8.17	7.46	6.90	6.47	6.12	5.83
1000	16.34	14.91	13.81	12.94	12.24	11.66
2000	32.69	29.82	27.62	25.88	24.48	23.33
3000	49.03	44.73	41.43	38.82	36.72	34.99
4000	65.38	59.64	55.24	51.76	48.95	46.65
5000	81.72	74.55	69.05	64.70	61.19	58.32
6000	98.06	89.47	82.86	77.64	73.43	69.98
7000	114.41	104.38	96.67	90.58	85.67	81.65
8000	130.75	119.29	110.47	103.52	97.91	93.31
9000	147.10	134.20	124.28	116.46	110.15	104.97
10000	163.44	149.11	138.09	129.40	122.39	116.64
11000	179.78	164.02	151.90	142.34	134.63	128.30
12000	196.13	178.93	165.71	155.28	146.86	139.96
13000	212.47	193.84	179.52	168.22	159.10	151.63
14000	228.82	208.75	193.33	181.16	171.34	163.29
15000	245.16	223.66	207.14	194.10	183.58	174.96
16000	261.50	238.57	220.95	207.04	195.82	186.62
17000	277.85	253.49	234.76	219.98	208.06	198.28
18000	294.19	268.40	248.57	232.92	220.30	209.95
19000	310.54	283.31	262.38	245.86	232.53	221.61
20000	326.88	298.22	276.19	258.80	244.77	233.27
21000	343.22	313.13	290.00	271.73	257.01	244.94
22000	359.57	328.04	303.81	284.67	269.25	256.60
23000	375.91	342.95	317.62	297.61	281.49	268.27
24000	392.26	357.86	331.42	310.55	293.73	279.93
25000	408.60	372.77	345.23	323.49	305.97	291.59
30000	490.32	447.33	414.28	388.19	367.16	349.91
35000	572.04	521.88	483.33	452.89	428.35	408.23
40000	653.76	596.44	552.37	517.59	489.55	466.55
45000	735.48	670.99	621.42	582.29	550.74	524.87
50000	817.20	745.54	690.47	646.99	611.93	583.19
55000	898.92	820.10	759.51	711.69	673.13	641.51
60000	980.64	894.65	828.56	776.39	734.32	699.82
65000	1062.36	969.21	897.61	841.08	795.51	758.14
70000	1144.08	1043.76	966.66	905.78	856.71	816.46
75000	1225.80	1118.32	1035.70	970.48	917.90	874.78
80000	1307.52	1192.87	1104.75	1035.18	979.09	933.10
85000	1389.24	1267.43	1173.80	1099.88	1040.28	991.42
90000	1470.96	1341.98	1242.84	1164.58	1101.48	1049.74
95000	1552.68	1416.53	1311.89	1229.28	1162.67	1108.05
100000	1634.40	1491.09	1380.94	1293.98	1223.86	1166.37
200000	3268.80	2982.18	2761.87	2587.95	2447.73	2332.75
300000	4903.19	4473.27	4142.81	3881.93	3671.59	3499.12
400000	6537.59	5964.35	5523.74	5175.90	4895.46	4665.49
500000	8171.99	7455.44	6904.68	6469.88	6119.32	5831.87

MONTHLY PAYMENT
Needed to repay a loan

9.5%

TERM AMOUNT	15 YEARS	20 YEARS	25 YEARS	30 YEARS	35 YEARS	40 YEARS
500	5.22	4.66	4.37	4.20	4.11	4.05
1000	10.44	9.32	8.74	8.41	8.22	8.10
2000	20.88	18.64	17.47	16.82	16.43	16.20
3000	31.33	27.96	26.21	25.23	24.65	24.30
4000	41.77	37.29	34.95	33.63	32.86	32.40
5000	52.21	46.61	43.68	42.04	41.08	40.50
6000	62.65	55.93	52.42	50.45	49.30	48.60
7000	73.10	65.25	61.16	58.86	57.51	56.70
8000	83.54	74.57	69.90	67.27	65.73	64.80
9000	93.98	83.89	78.63	75.68	73.95	72.91
10000	104.42	93.21	87.37	84.09	82.16	81.01
11000	114.86	102.53	96.11	92.49	90.38	89.11
12000	125.31	111.86	104.84	100.90	98.59	97.21
13000	135.75	121.18	113.58	109.31	106.81	105.31
14000	146.19	130.50	122.32	117.72	115.03	113.41
15000	156.63	139.82	131.05	126.13	123.24	121.51
16000	167.08	149.14	139.79	134.54	131.46	129.61
17000	177.52	158.46	148.53	142.95	139.67	137.71
18000	187.96	167.78	157.27	151.35	147.89	145.81
19000	198.40	177.10	166.00	159.76	156.11	153.91
20000	208.84	186.43	174.74	168.17	164.32	162.01
21000	219.29	195.75	183.48	176.58	172.54	170.11
22000	229.73	205.07	192.21	184.99	180.75	178.21
23000	240.17	214.39	200.95	193.40	188.97	186.31
24000	250.61	223.71	209.69	201.81	197.19	194.41
25000	261.06	233.03	218.42	210.21	205.40	202.52
30000	313.27	279.64	262.11	252.26	246.48	243.02
35000	365.48	326.25	305.79	294.30	287.56	283.52
40000	417.69	372.85	349.48	336.34	328.64	324.02
45000	469.90	419.46	393.16	378.38	369.73	364.53
50000	522.11	466.07	436.85	420.43	410.81	405.03
55000	574.32	512.67	480.53	462.47	451.89	445.53
60000	626.53	559.28	524.22	504.51	492.97	486.04
65000	678.75	605.89	567.90	546.56	534.05	526.54
70000	730.96	652.49	611.59	588.60	575.13	567.04
75000	783.17	699.10	655.27	630.64	616.21	607.55
80000	835.38	745.70	698.96	672.68	657.29	648.05
85000	887.59	792.31	742.64	714.73	698.37	688.55
90000	939.80	838.92	786.33	756.77	739.45	729.06
95000	992.01	885.52	830.01	798.81	780.53	769.56
100000	1044.22	932.13	873.70	840.85	821.61	810.06
200000	2088.45	1864.26	1747.39	1681.71	1643.22	1620.12
300000	3132.67	2796.39	2621.09	2522.56	2464.83	2430.18
400000	4176.90	3728.52	3494.79	3363.42	3286.45	3240.25
500000	5221.12	4660.66	4368.48	4204.27	4108.06	4050.31

9.75% MONTHLY PAYMENT

Needed to repay a loan

TERM AMOUNT	1 YEAR	2 YEARS	3 YEARS	4 YEARS	5 YEARS	6 YEARS
500	43.90	23.01	16.07	12.62	10.56	9.20
1000	87.80	46.03	32.15	25.24	21.12	18.40
2000	175.60	92.06	64.30	50.49	42.25	36.80
3000	263.40	138.09	96.45	75.73	63.37	55.20
4000	351.20	184.12	128.60	100.97	84.50	73.60
5000	439.00	230.15	160.75	126.21	105.62	92.00
6000	526.80	276.18	192.90	151.46	126.75	110.40
7000	614.60	322.21	225.05	176.70	147.87	128.80
8000	702.40	368.24	257.20	201.94	168.99	147.20
9000	790.20	414.27	289.35	227.18	190.12	165.60
10000	878.00	460.30	321.50	252.43	211.24	184.00
11000	965.80	506.33	353.65	277.67	232.37	202.40
12000	1053.60	552.36	385.80	302.91	253.49	220.80
13000	1141.40	598.39	417.95	328.15	274.62	239.20
14000	1229.20	644.41	450.10	353.40	295.74	257.60
15000	1316.99	690.44	482.25	378.64	316.86	276.00
16000	1404.79	736.47	514.40	403.88	337.99	294.40
17000	1492.59	782.50	546.55	429.13	359.11	312.80
18000	1580.39	828.53	578.70	454.37	380.24	331.20
19000	1668.19	874.56	610.85	479.61	401.36	349.60
20000	1755.99	920.59	643.00	504.85	422.48	368.00
21000	1843.79	966.62	675.15	530.10	443.61	386.40
22000	1931.59	1012.65	707.30	555.34	464.73	404.80
23000	2019.39	1058.68	739.45	580.58	485.86	423.20
24000	2107.19	1104.71	771.60	605.82	506.98	441.60
25000	2194.99	1150.74	803.75	631.07	528.11	460.00
30000	2633.99	1380.89	964.50	757.28	633.73	552.00
35000	3072.99	1611.04	1125.25	883.49	739.35	644.00
40000	3511.99	1841.18	1286.00	1009.71	844.97	736.00
45000	3950.98	2071.33	1446.75	1135.92	950.59	828.00
50000	4389.98	2301.48	1607.50	1262.13	1056.21	920.00
55000	4828.98	2531.63	1768.25	1388.35	1161.83	1012.00
60000	5267.98	2761.78	1929.00	1514.56	1267.45	1104.00
65000	5706.98	2991.93	2089.75	1640.77	1373.08	1196.00
70000	6145.98	3222.07	2250.50	1766.99	1478.70	1288.00
75000	6584.97	3452.22	2411.25	1893.20	1584.32	1380.00
80000	7023.97	3682.37	2572.00	2019.42	1689.94	1472.00
85000	7462.97	3912.52	2732.74	2145.63	1795.56	1564.00
90000	7901.97	4142.67	2893.49	2271.84	1901.18	1656.00
95000	8340.97	4372.81	3054.24	2398.06	2006.80	1748.00
100000	8779.97	4602.96	3214.99	2524.27	2112.42	1840.00
200000	17559.93	9205.92	6429.99	5048.54	4224.85	3680.00
300000	26339.90	13808.89	9644.98	7572.81	6337.27	5520.00
400000	35119.86	18411.85	12859.98	10097.08	8449.70	7360.01
500000	43899.83	23014.81	16074.97	12621.35	10562.12	9200.01

MONTHLY PAYMENT 9.75%

Needed to repay a loan

TERM AMOUNT	7 YEARS	8 YEARS	9 YEARS	10 YEARS	11 YEARS	12 YEARS
500	8.24	7.52	6.97	6.54	6.19	5.90
1000	16.47	15.04	13.94	13.08	12.38	11.81
2000	32.94	30.08	27.89	26.15	24.76	23.61
3000	49.42	45.13	41.83	39.23	37.14	35.42
4000	65.89	60.17	55.77	52.31	49.52	47.23
5000	82.36	75.21	69.72	65.39	61.89	59.03
6000	98.83	90.25	83.66	78.46	74.27	70.84
7000	115.31	105.30	97.61	91.54	86.65	82.65
8000	131.78	120.34	111.55	104.62	99.03	94.45
9000	148.25	135.38	125.49	117.69	111.41	106.26
10000	164.72	150.42	139.44	130.77	123.79	118.07
11000	181.20	165.46	153.38	143.85	136.17	129.87
12000	197.67	180.51	167.32	156.92	148.55	141.68
13000	214.14	195.55	181.27	170.00	160.92	153.49
14000	230.61	210.59	195.21	183.08	173.30	165.30
15000	247.08	225.63	209.15	196.16	185.68	177.10
16000	263.56	240.68	223.10	209.23	198.06	188.91
17000	280.03	255.72	237.04	222.31	210.44	200.72
18000	296.50	270.76	250.99	235.39	222.82	212.52
19000	312.97	285.80	264.93	248.46	235.20	224.33
20000	329.45	300.84	278.87	261.54	247.58	236.14
21000	345.92	315.89	292.82	274.62	259.96	247.94
22000	362.39	330.93	306.76	287.69	272.33	259.75
23000	378.86	345.97	320.70	300.77	284.71	271.56
24000	395.34	361.01	334.65	313.85	297.09	283.36
25000	411.81	376.06	348.59	326.93	309.47	295.17
30000	494.17	451.27	418.31	392.31	371.37	354.20
35000	576.53	526.48	488.03	457.70	433.26	413.24
40000	658.89	601.69	557.75	523.08	495.15	472.27
45000	741.25	676.90	627.46	588.47	557.05	531.31
50000	823.61	752.11	697.18	653.85	618.94	590.34
55000	905.98	827.32	766.90	719.24	680.84	649.37
60000	988.34	902.53	836.62	784.62	742.73	708.41
65000	1070.70	977.74	906.34	850.01	804.62	767.44
70000	1153.06	1052.95	976.06	915.39	866.52	826.48
75000	1235.42	1128.17	1045.77	980.78	928.41	885.51
80000	1317.78	1203.38	1115.49	1046.16	990.31	944.54
85000	1400.15	1278.59	1185.21	1111.55	1052.20	1003.58
90000	1482.51	1353.80	1254.93	1176.93	1114.10	1062.61
95000	1564.87	1429.01	1324.65	1242.32	1175.99	1121.65
100000	1647.23	1504.22	1394.37	1307.70	1237.88	1180.68
200000	3294.46	3008.44	2788.73	2615.40	2475.77	2361.36
300000	4941.69	4512.66	4183.10	3923.11	3713.65	3542.04
400000	6588.92	6016.88	5577.47	5230.81	4951.54	4722.72
500000	8236.15	7521.10	6971.83	6538.51	6189.42	5903.40

9.75%

MONTHLY PAYMENT
Needed to repay a loan

TERM / AMOUNT	15 YEARS	20 YEARS	25 YEARS	30 YEARS	35 YEARS	40 YEARS
500	5.30	4.74	4.46	4.30	4.20	4.15
1000	10.59	9.49	8.91	8.59	8.41	8.30
2000	21.19	18.97	17.82	17.18	16.81	16.59
3000	31.78	28.46	26.73	25.77	25.22	24.89
4000	42.37	37.94	35.65	34.37	33.62	33.18
5000	52.97	47.43	44.56	42.96	42.03	41.48
6000	63.56	56.91	53.47	51.55	50.44	49.77
7000	74.16	66.40	62.38	60.14	58.84	58.07
8000	84.75	75.88	71.29	68.73	67.25	66.36
9000	95.34	85.37	80.20	77.32	75.65	74.66
10000	105.94	94.85	89.11	85.92	84.06	82.96
11000	116.53	104.34	98.03	94.51	92.46	91.25
12000	127.12	113.82	106.94	103.10	100.87	99.55
13000	137.72	123.31	115.85	111.69	109.28	107.84
14000	148.31	132.79	124.76	120.28	117.68	116.14
15000	158.90	142.28	133.67	128.87	126.09	124.43
16000	169.50	151.76	142.58	137.46	134.49	132.73
17000	180.09	161.25	151.49	146.06	142.90	141.02
18000	190.69	170.73	160.40	154.65	151.31	149.32
19000	201.28	180.22	169.32	163.24	159.71	157.62
20000	211.87	189.70	178.23	171.83	168.12	165.91
21000	222.47	199.19	187.14	180.42	176.52	174.21
22000	233.06	208.67	196.05	189.01	184.93	182.50
23000	243.65	218.16	204.96	197.61	193.34	190.80
24000	254.25	227.64	213.87	206.20	201.74	199.09
25000	264.84	237.13	222.78	214.79	210.15	207.39
30000	317.81	284.56	267.34	257.75	252.18	248.87
35000	370.78	331.98	311.90	300.70	294.21	290.35
40000	423.75	379.41	356.45	343.66	336.24	331.82
45000	476.71	426.83	401.01	386.62	378.27	373.30
50000	529.68	474.26	445.57	429.58	420.29	414.78
55000	582.65	521.68	490.13	472.53	462.32	456.26
60000	635.62	569.11	534.68	515.49	504.35	497.74
65000	688.59	616.54	579.24	558.45	546.38	539.21
70000	741.55	663.96	623.80	601.41	588.41	580.69
75000	794.52	711.39	668.35	644.37	630.44	622.17
80000	847.49	758.81	712.91	687.32	672.47	663.65
85000	900.46	806.24	757.47	730.28	714.50	705.12
90000	953.43	853.67	802.02	773.24	756.53	746.60
95000	1006.39	901.09	846.58	816.20	798.56	788.08
100000	1059.36	948.52	891.14	859.15	840.59	829.56
200000	2118.73	1897.03	1782.27	1718.31	1681.18	1659.12
300000	3178.09	2845.55	2673.41	2577.46	2521.77	2488.68
400000	4237.45	3794.07	3564.55	3436.62	3362.36	3318.23
500000	5296.81	4742.58	4455.69	4295.77	4202.95	4147.79

MONTHLY PAYMENT
Needed to repay a loan

10%

TERM / AMOUNT	1 YEAR	2 YEARS	3 YEARS	4 YEARS	5 YEARS	6 YEARS
500	43.96	23.07	16.13	12.68	10.62	9.26
1000	87.92	46.14	32.27	25.36	21.25	18.53
2000	175.83	92.29	64.53	50.73	42.49	37.05
3000	263.75	138.43	96.80	76.09	63.74	55.58
4000	351.66	184.58	129.07	101.45	84.99	74.10
5000	439.58	230.72	161.34	126.81	106.24	92.63
6000	527.50	276.87	193.60	152.18	127.48	111.16
7000	615.41	323.01	225.87	177.54	148.73	129.68
8000	703.33	369.16	258.14	202.90	169.98	148.21
9000	791.24	415.30	290.40	228.26	191.22	166.73
10000	879.16	461.45	322.67	253.63	212.47	185.26
11000	967.07	507.59	354.94	278.99	233.72	203.78
12000	1054.99	533.74	387.21	304.35	254.96	222.31
13000	1142.91	599.88	419.47	329.71	276.21	240.84
14000	1230.82	646.03	451.74	355.08	297.46	259.36
15000	1318.74	692.17	484.01	380.44	318.71	277.89
16000	1406.65	738.32	516.27	405.80	339.95	296.41
17000	1494.57	784.46	548.54	431.16	361.20	314.94
18000	1582.49	830.61	580.81	456.53	382.45	333.47
19000	1670.40	876.75	613.08	481.89	403.69	351.99
20000	1758.32	922.90	645.34	507.25	424.94	370.52
21000	1846.23	969.04	677.61	532.61	446.19	389.04
22000	1934.15	1015.19	709.88	557.98	467.43	407.57
23000	2022.07	1061.33	742.15	583.34	488.68	426.09
24000	2109.98	1107.48	774.41	608.70	509.93	444.62
25000	2197.90	1153.62	806.68	634.06	531.18	463.15
30000	2637.48	1384.35	968.02	760.88	637.41	555.78
35000	3077.06	1615.07	1129.35	887.69	743.65	648.40
40000	3516.64	1845.80	1290.69	1014.50	849.88	741.03
45000	3956.21	2076.52	1452.02	1141.32	956.12	833.66
50000	4395.79	2307.25	1613.36	1268.13	1062.35	926.29
55000	4835.37	2537.97	1774.70	1394.94	1168.59	1018.92
60000	5274.95	2768.70	1936.03	1521.76	1274.82	1111.55
65000	5714.53	2999.42	2097.37	1648.57	1381.06	1204.18
70000	6154.11	3230.14	2258.70	1775.38	1487.29	1296.81
75000	6593.69	3460.87	2420.04	1902.19	1593.53	1389.44
80000	7033.27	3691.59	2581.37	2029.01	1699.76	1482.07
85000	7472.85	3922.32	2742.71	2155.82	1806.00	1574.70
90000	7912.43	4153.04	2904.05	2282.63	1912.23	1667.33
95000	8352.01	4383.77	3065.38	2409.45	2018.47	1759.95
100000	8791.59	4614.49	3226.72	2536.26	2124.70	1852.58
200000	17583.18	9228.99	6453.44	5072.52	4249.41	3705.17
300000	26374.77	13843.48	9680.16	7608.78	6374.11	5557.75
400000	35166.35	18457.97	12906.87	10145.03	8498.82	7410.34
500000	43957.94	23072.46	16133.59	12681.29	10623.52	9262.92

10% MONTHLY PAYMENT
Needed to repay a loan

TERM AMOUNT	7 YEARS	8 YEARS	9 YEARS	10 YEARS	11 YEARS	12 YEARS
500	8.30	7.59	7.04	6.61	6.26	5.98
1000	16.60	15.17	14.08	13.22	12.52	11.95
2000	33.20	30.35	28.16	26.43	25.04	23.90
3000	49.80	45.52	42.24	39.65	37.56	35.85
4000	66.40	60.70	56.31	52.86	50.08	47.80
5000	83.01	75.87	70.39	66.08	62.60	59.75
6000	99.61	91.04	84.47	79.29	75.12	71.70
7000	116.21	106.22	98.55	92.51	87.64	83.66
8000	132.81	121.39	112.63	105.72	100.16	95.61
9000	149.41	136.57	126.71	118.94	112.68	107.56
10000	166.01	151.74	140.79	132.15	125.20	119.51
11000	182.61	166.92	154.87	145.37	137.72	131.46
12000	199.21	182.09	168.94	158.58	150.24	143.41
13000	215.82	197.26	183.02	171.80	162.76	155.36
14000	232.42	212.44	197.10	185.01	175.28	167.31
15000	249.02	227.61	211.18	198.23	187.80	179.26
16000	265.62	242.79	225.26	211.44	200.32	191.21
17000	282.22	257.96	239.34	224.66	212.84	203.16
18000	298.82	273.13	253.42	237.87	225.36	215.11
19000	315.42	288.31	267.50	251.09	237.88	227.06
20000	332.02	303.48	281.57	264.30	250.40	239.02
21000	348.62	318.66	295.65	277.52	262.92	250.97
22000	365.23	333.83	309.73	290.73	275.44	262.92
23000	381.83	349.01	323.81	303.95	287.96	274.87
24000	398.43	364.18	337.89	317.16	300.48	286.82
25000	415.03	379.35	351.97	330.38	313.00	298.77
30000	498.04	455.22	422.36	396.45	375.60	358.52
35000	581.04	531.10	492.75	462.53	438.20	418.28
40000	664.05	606.97	563.15	528.60	500.80	478.03
45000	747.05	682.84	633.54	594.68	563.39	537.79
50000	830.06	758.71	703.93	660.75	625.99	597.54
55000	913.07	834.58	774.33	726.83	688.59	657.29
60000	996.07	910.45	844.72	792.90	751.19	717.05
65000	1079.08	986.32	915.11	858.98	813.79	776.80
70000	1162.08	1062.19	985.51	925.06	876.39	836.55
75000	1245.09	1138.06	1055.90	991.13	938.99	896.31
80000	1328.09	1213.93	1126.29	1057.21	1001.59	956.06
85000	1411.10	1289.80	1196.69	1123.28	1064.19	1015.82
90000	1494.11	1365.67	1267.08	1189.36	1126.79	1075.57
95000	1577.11	1441.55	1337.48	1255.43	1189.39	1135.32
100000	1660.12	1517.42	1407.87	1321.51	1251.99	1195.08
200000	3320.24	3034.83	2815.74	2643.01	2503.98	2390.16
300000	4980.36	4552.25	4223.61	3964.52	3755.96	3585.23
400000	6640.47	6069.67	5631.47	5286.03	5007.95	4780.31
500000	8300.59	7587.08	7039.34	6607.54	6259.94	5975.39

MONTHLY PAYMENT 10%
Needed to repay a loan

TERM AMOUNT	15 YEARS	20 YEARS	25 YEARS	30 YEARS	35 YEARS	40 YEARS
500	5.37	4.83	4.54	4.39	4.30	4.25
1000	10.75	9.65	9.09	8.78	8.60	8.49
2000	21.49	19.30	18.17	17.55	17.19	16.98
3000	32.24	28.95	27.26	26.33	25.79	25.47
4000	42.98	38.60	36.35	35.10	34.39	33.97
5000	53.73	48.25	45.44	43.88	42.98	42.46
6000	64.48	57.90	54.52	52.65	51.58	50.95
7000	75.22	67.55	63.61	61.43	60.18	59.44
8000	85.97	77.20	72.70	70.21	68.77	67.93
9000	96.71	86.85	81.78	78.98	77.37	76.42
10000	107.46	96.50	90.87	87.76	85.97	84.91
11000	118.21	106.15	99.96	96.53	94.56	93.41
12000	128.95	115.80	109.04	105.31	103.16	101.90
13000	139.70	125.45	118.13	114.08	111.76	110.39
14000	150.44	135.10	127.22	122.86	120.35	118.88
15000	161.19	144.75	136.31	131.64	128.95	127.37
16000	171.94	154.40	145.39	140.41	137.55	135.86
17000	182.68	164.05	154.48	149.19	146.14	144.35
18000	193.43	173.70	163.57	157.96	154.74	152.85
19000	204.17	183.35	172.65	166.74	163.34	161.34
20000	214.92	193.00	181.74	175.51	171.93	169.83
21000	225.67	202.65	190.83	184.29	180.53	178.32
22000	236.41	212.30	199.91	193.07	189.13	186.81
23000	247.16	221.95	209.00	201.84	197.72	195.30
24000	257.91	231.61	218.09	210.62	206.32	203.80
25000	268.65	241.26	227.18	219.39	214.92	212.29
30000	322.38	289.51	272.61	263.27	257.90	254.74
35000	376.11	337.76	318.05	307.15	300.89	297.20
40000	429.84	386.01	363.48	351.03	343.87	339.66
45000	483.57	434.26	408.92	394.91	386.85	382.12
50000	537.30	482.51	454.35	438.79	429.84	424.57
55000	591.03	530.76	499.79	482.66	472.82	467.03
60000	644.76	579.01	545.22	526.54	515.80	509.49
65000	698.49	627.26	590.66	570.42	558.79	551.94
70000	752.22	675.52	636.09	614.30	601.77	594.40
75000	805.95	723.77	681.53	658.18	644.75	636.86
80000	859.68	772.02	726.96	702.06	687.74	679.32
85000	913.41	820.27	772.40	745.94	730.72	721.77
90000	967.14	868.52	817.83	789.81	773.71	764.23
95000	1020.87	916.77	863.27	833.69	816.69	806.69
100000	1074.61	965.02	908.70	877.57	859.67	849.15
200000	2149.21	1930.04	1817.40	1755.14	1719.34	1698.29
300000	3223.82	2895.06	2726.10	2632.71	2579.02	2547.44
400000	4298.42	3860.09	3634.80	3510.29	3438.69	3396.58
500000	5373.03	4825.11	4543.50	4387.86	4298.36	4245.73

10.25% MONTHLY PAYMENT

Needed to repay a loan

TERM AMOUNT	1 YEAR	2 YEARS	3 YEARS	4 YEARS	5 YEARS	6 YEARS
500	44.02	23.13	16.19	12.74	10.69	9.33
1000	88.03	46.26	32.38	25.48	21.37	18.65
2000	176.06	92.52	64.77	50.97	42.74	37.30
3000	264.10	138.78	97.15	76.45	64.11	55.96
4000	352.13	185.04	129.54	101.93	85.48	74.61
5000	440.16	231.30	161.92	127.41	106.85	93.26
6000	528.19	277.56	194.31	152.90	128.22	111.91
7000	616.23	323.82	226.69	178.38	149.59	130.57
8000	704.26	370.08	259.08	203.86	170.96	149.22
9000	792.29	416.34	291.46	229.35	192.33	167.87
10000	880.32	462.60	323.85	254.83	213.70	186.52
11000	968.35	508.86	356.23	280.31	235.07	205.17
12000	1056.39	555.12	388.62	305.79	256.44	223.83
13000	1144.42	601.39	421.00	331.28	277.81	242.48
14000	1232.45	647.65	453.39	356.76	299.18	261.13
15000	1320.48	693.91	485.77	382.24	320.55	279.78
16000	1408.52	740.17	518.16	407.73	341.92	298.43
17000	1496.55	786.43	550.54	433.21	363.29	317.09
18000	1584.58	832.69	582.92	458.69	384.66	335.74
19000	1672.61	878.95	615.31	484.17	406.04	354.39
20000	1760.64	925.21	647.69	509.66	427.41	373.04
21000	1848.68	971.47	680.08	535.14	448.78	391.70
22000	1936.71	1017.73	712.46	560.62	470.15	410.35
23000	2024.74	1063.99	744.85	586.10	491.52	429.00
24000	2112.77	1110.25	777.23	611.59	512.89	447.65
25000	2200.81	1156.51	809.62	637.07	534.26	466.30
30000	2640.97	1387.81	971.54	764.48	641.11	559.56
35000	3081.13	1619.11	1133.46	891.90	747.96	652.83
40000	3521.29	1850.42	1295.39	1019.31	854.81	746.09
45000	3961.45	2081.72	1457.31	1146.73	961.66	839.35
50000	4401.61	2313.02	1619.23	1274.14	1068.51	932.61
55000	4841.77	2544.32	1781.16	1401.55	1175.36	1025.87
60000	5281.93	2775.62	1943.08	1528.97	1282.22	1119.13
65000	5722.09	3006.93	2105.00	1656.38	1389.07	1212.39
70000	6162.25	3238.23	2266.93	1783.80	1495.92	1305.65
75000	6602.42	3469.53	2428.85	1911.21	1602.77	1398.91
80000	7042.58	3700.83	2590.78	2038.63	1709.62	1492.17
85000	7482.74	3932.13	2752.70	2166.04	1816.47	1585.43
90000	7922.90	4163.44	2914.62	2293.45	1923.32	1678.69
95000	8363.06	4394.74	3076.55	2420.87	2030.18	1771.95
100000	8803.22	4626.04	3238.47	2548.28	2137.03	1865.22
200000	17606.44	9252.08	6476.94	5096.56	4274.05	3730.43
300000	26409.66	13878.12	9715.41	7644.84	6411.08	5595.65
400000	35212.88	18504.16	12953.88	10193.13	8548.11	7460.86
500000	44016.10	23130.20	16192.34	12741.41	10685.13	9326.08

MONTHLY PAYMENT 10.25%

Needed to repay a loan

TERM AMOUNT	7 YEARS	8 YEARS	9 YEARS	10 YEARS	11 YEARS	12 YEARS
500	8.37	7.65	7.11	6.68	6.33	6.05
1000	16.73	15.31	14.21	13.35	12.66	12.10
2000	33.46	30.61	28.43	26.71	25.32	24.19
3000	50.19	45.92	42.64	40.06	37.99	36.29
4000	66.92	61.23	56.86	53.42	50.65	48.38
5000	83.65	76.53	71.07	66.77	63.31	60.48
6000	100.38	91.84	85.29	80.12	75.97	72.57
7000	117.11	107.15	99.50	93.48	88.63	84.67
8000	133.85	122.45	113.72	106.83	101.29	96.77
9000	150.58	137.76	127.93	120.19	113.96	108.86
10000	167.31	153.07	142.14	133.54	126.62	120.96
11000	184.04	168.37	156.36	146.89	139.28	133.05
12000	200.77	183.68	170.57	160.25	151.94	145.15
13000	217.50	198.99	184.79	173.60	164.60	157.24
14000	234.23	214.29	199.00	186.95	177.26	169.34
15000	250.96	229.60	213.22	200.31	189.93	181.43
16000	267.69	244.91	227.43	213.66	202.59	193.53
17000	284.42	260.22	241.65	227.02	215.25	205.63
18000	301.15	275.52	255.86	240.37	227.91	217.72
19000	317.88	290.83	270.07	253.72	240.57	229.82
20000	334.61	306.14	284.29	267.08	253.24	241.91
21000	351.34	321.44	298.50	280.43	265.90	254.01
22000	368.07	336.75	312.72	293.79	278.56	266.10
23000	384.80	352.06	326.93	307.14	291.22	278.20
24000	401.54	367.36	341.15	320.49	303.88	290.30
25000	418.27	382.67	355.36	333.85	316.54	302.39
30000	501.92	459.20	426.43	400.62	379.85	362.87
35000	585.57	535.74	497.50	467.39	443.16	423.35
40000	669.23	612.27	568.58	534.16	506.47	483.83
45000	752.88	688.80	639.65	600.93	569.78	544.30
50000	836.53	765.34	710.72	667.70	633.09	604.78
55000	920.19	841.87	781.79	734.46	696.40	665.26
60000	1003.84	918.41	852.87	801.23	759.71	725.74
65000	1087.49	994.94	923.94	868.00	823.01	786.22
70000	1171.15	1071.47	995.01	934.77	886.32	846.70
75000	1254.80	1148.01	1066.08	1001.54	949.63	907.17
80000	1338.45	1224.54	1137.15	1068.31	1012.94	967.65
85000	1422.10	1301.08	1208.23	1135.08	1076.25	1028.13
90000	1505.76	1377.61	1279.30	1201.85	1139.56	1088.61
95000	1589.41	1454.14	1350.37	1268.62	1202.87	1149.09
100000	1673.06	1530.68	1421.44	1335.39	1266.18	1209.57
200000	3346.13	3061.35	2842.88	2670.78	2532.35	2419.13
300000	5019.19	4592.03	4264.33	4006.17	3798.53	3628.70
400000	6692.26	6122.71	5685.77	5341.56	5064.70	4838.26
500000	8365.32	7653.38	7107.21	6676.95	6330.88	6047.83

10.25% MONTHLY PAYMENT
Needed to repay a loan

TERM AMOUNT	15 YEARS	20 YEARS	25 YEARS	30 YEARS	35 YEARS	40 YEARS
500	5.45	4.91	4.63	4.48	4.39	4.34
1000	10.90	9.82	9.26	8.96	8.79	8.69
2000	21.80	19.63	18.53	17.92	17.58	17.38
3000	32.70	29.45	27.79	26.88	26.37	26.06
4000	43.60	39.27	37.06	35.84	35.15	34.75
5000	54.50	49.08	46.32	44.81	43.94	43.44
6000	65.40	58.90	55.58	53.77	52.73	52.13
7000	76.30	68.72	64.85	62.73	61.52	60.82
8000	87.20	78.53	74.11	71.69	70.31	69.51
9000	98.10	88.35	83.37	80.65	79.10	78.19
10000	109.00	98.16	92.64	89.61	87.89	86.88
11000	119.89	107.98	101.90	98.57	96.67	95.57
12000	130.79	117.80	111.17	107.53	105.46	104.26
13000	141.69	127.61	120.43	116.49	114.25	112.95
14000	152.59	137.43	129.69	125.45	123.04	121.63
15000	163.49	147.25	138.96	134.42	131.83	130.32
16000	174.39	157.06	148.22	143.38	140.62	139.01
17000	185.29	166.88	157.49	152.34	149.41	147.70
18000	196.19	176.70	166.75	161.30	158.19	156.39
19000	207.09	186.51	176.01	170.26	166.98	165.08
20000	217.99	196.33	185.28	179.22	175.77	173.76
21000	228.89	206.15	194.54	188.18	184.56	182.45
22000	239.79	215.96	203.80	197.14	193.35	191.14
23000	250.69	225.78	213.07	206.10	202.14	199.83
24000	261.59	235.59	222.33	215.06	210.93	208.52
25000	272.49	245.41	231.60	224.03	219.71	217.20
30000	326.99	294.49	277.91	268.83	263.66	260.65
35000	381.48	343.58	324.23	313.64	307.60	304.09
40000	435.98	392.66	370.55	358.44	351.54	347.53
45000	490.48	441.74	416.87	403.25	395.49	390.97
50000	544.98	490.82	463.19	448.05	439.43	434.41
55000	599.47	539.90	509.51	492.86	483.37	477.85
60000	653.97	588.99	555.83	537.66	527.31	521.29
65000	708.47	638.07	602.15	582.47	571.26	564.73
70000	762.97	687.15	648.47	627.27	615.20	608.17
75000	817.46	736.23	694.79	672.08	659.14	651.61
80000	871.96	785.31	741.11	716.88	703.08	695.05
85000	926.46	834.40	787.43	761.69	747.03	738.50
90000	980.96	883.48	833.74	806.49	790.97	781.94
95000	1035.45	932.56	880.06	851.30	834.91	825.38
100000	1089.95	981.64	926.38	896.10	878.86	868.82
200000	2179.90	1963.29	1852.77	1792.20	1757.71	1737.64
300000	3269.85	2944.93	2779.15	2688.30	2636.57	2606.45
400000	4359.80	3926.57	3705.53	3584.41	3515.42	3475.27
500000	5449.75	4908.22	4631.92	4480.51	4394.28	4344.09

MONTHLY PAYMENT 10.5%
Needed to repay a loan

TERM AMOUNT	1 YEAR	2 YEARS	3 YEARS	4 YEARS	5 YEARS	6 YEARS
500	44.07	23.19	16.25	12.80	10.75	9.39
1000	88.15	46.38	32.50	25.60	21.49	18.78
2000	176.30	92.75	65.00	51.21	42.99	37.56
3000	264.45	139.13	97.51	76.81	64.48	56.34
4000	352.59	185.50	130.01	102.41	85.98	75.12
5000	440.74	231.88	162.51	128.02	107.47	93.89
6000	528.89	278.26	195.01	153.62	128.96	112.67
7000	617.04	324.63	227.52	179.22	150.46	131.45
8000	705.19	371.01	260.02	204.83	171.95	150.23
9000	793.34	417.38	292.52	230.43	193.45	169.01
10000	881.49	463.76	325.02	256.03	214.94	187.79
11000	969.63	510.14	357.53	281.64	236.43	206.57
12000	1057.78	556.51	390.03	307.24	257.93	225.35
13000	1145.93	602.89	422.53	332.84	279.42	244.13
14000	1234.08	649.26	455.03	358.45	300.91	262.91
15000	1322.23	695.64	487.54	384.05	322.41	281.68
16000	1410.38	742.02	520.04	409.65	343.90	300.46
17000	1498.53	788.39	552.54	435.26	365.40	319.24
18000	1586.67	834.77	585.04	460.86	386.89	338.02
19000	1674.82	881.14	617.55	486.46	408.38	356.80
20000	1762.97	927.52	650.05	512.07	429.88	375.58
21000	1851.12	973.90	682.55	537.67	451.37	394.36
22000	1939.27	1020.27	715.05	563.27	472.87	413.14
23000	2027.42	1066.65	747.56	588.88	494.36	431.92
24000	2115.57	1113.02	780.06	614.48	515.85	450.70
25000	2203.72	1159.40	812.56	640.08	537.35	469.47
30000	2644.46	1391.28	975.07	768.10	644.82	563.37
35000	3085.20	1623.16	1137.59	896.12	752.29	657.26
40000	3525.94	1855.04	1300.10	1024.14	859.76	751.16
45000	3966.69	2086.92	1462.61	1152.15	967.23	845.05
50000	4407.43	2318.80	1625.12	1280.17	1074.70	938.95
55000	4848.17	2550.68	1787.63	1408.19	1182.16	1032.84
60000	5288.92	2782.56	1950.15	1536.20	1289.63	1126.74
65000	5729.66	3014.44	2112.66	1664.22	1397.10	1220.63
70000	6170.40	3246.32	2275.17	1792.24	1504.57	1314.53
75000	6611.15	3478.20	2437.68	1920.25	1612.04	1408.42
80000	7051.89	3710.08	2600.20	2048.27	1719.51	1502.32
85000	7492.63	3941.96	2762.71	2176.29	1826.98	1596.21
90000	7933.37	4173.84	2925.22	2304.30	1934.45	1690.11
95000	8374.12	4405.72	3087.73	2432.32	2041.92	1784.00
100000	8814.86	4637.60	3250.24	2560.34	2149.39	1877.90
200000	17629.72	9275.21	6500.49	5120.68	4298.78	3755.79
300000	26444.58	13912.81	9750.73	7681.01	6448.17	5633.69
400000	35259.44	18550.42	13000.98	10241.35	8597.56	7511.59
500000	44074.30	23188.02	16251.22	12801.69	10746.95	9389.48

10.5% MONTHLY PAYMENT
Needed to repay a loan

TERM AMOUNT	7 YEARS	8 YEARS	9 YEARS	10 YEARS	11 YEARS	12 YEARS
500	8.43	7.72	7.18	6.75	6.40	6.12
1000	16.86	15.44	14.35	13.49	12.80	12.24
2000	33.72	30.88	28.70	26.99	25.61	24.48
3000	50.58	46.32	43.05	40.48	38.41	36.72
4000	67.44	61.76	57.40	53.97	51.22	48.97
5000	84.30	77.20	71.75	67.47	64.02	61.21
6000	101.16	92.64	86.11	80.96	76.83	73.45
7000	118.02	108.08	100.46	94.45	89.63	85.69
8000	134.89	123.52	114.81	107.95	102.44	97.93
9000	151.75	138.96	129.16	121.44	115.24	110.17
10000	168.61	154.40	143.51	134.93	128.04	122.41
11000	185.47	169.84	157.86	148.43	140.85	134.66
12000	202.33	185.28	172.21	161.92	153.65	146.90
13000	219.19	200.72	186.56	175.42	166.46	159.14
14000	236.05	216.16	200.91	188.91	179.26	171.38
15000	252.91	231.60	215.26	202.40	192.07	183.62
16000	269.77	247.04	229.61	215.90	204.87	195.86
17000	286.63	262.48	243.96	229.39	217.68	208.10
18000	303.49	277.92	258.32	242.88	230.48	220.35
19000	320.35	293.36	272.67	256.38	243.28	232.59
20000	337.21	308.80	287.02	269.87	256.09	244.83
21000	354.07	324.24	301.37	283.36	268.89	257.07
22000	370.93	339.68	315.72	296.86	281.70	269.31
23000	387.80	355.12	330.07	310.35	294.50	281.55
24000	404.66	370.56	344.42	323.84	307.31	293.79
25000	421.52	386.00	358.77	337.34	320.11	306.04
30000	505.82	463.20	430.53	404.80	384.13	367.24
35000	590.12	540.40	502.28	472.27	448.16	428.45
40000	674.43	617.60	574.03	539.74	512.18	489.66
45000	758.73	694.80	645.79	607.21	576.20	550.86
50000	843.03	772.00	717.54	674.67	640.22	612.07
55000	927.34	849.20	789.30	742.14	704.25	673.28
60000	1011.64	926.40	861.05	809.61	768.27	734.48
65000	1095.94	1003.60	932.81	877.08	832.29	795.69
70000	1180.25	1080.80	1004.56	944.54	896.31	856.90
75000	1264.55	1158.00	1076.31	1012.01	960.33	918.11
80000	1348.85	1235.20	1148.07	1079.48	1024.36	979.31
85000	1433.16	1312.40	1219.82	1146.95	1088.38	1040.52
90000	1517.46	1389.60	1291.58	1214.41	1152.40	1101.73
95000	1601.76	1466.80	1363.33	1281.88	1216.42	1162.93
100000	1686.07	1544.00	1435.09	1349.35	1280.45	1224.14
200000	3372.13	3088.00	2870.17	2698.70	2560.89	2448.28
300000	5058.20	4632.00	4305.26	4048.05	3841.34	3672.42
400000	6744.27	6176.01	5740.34	5397.40	5121.78	4896.56
500000	8430.34	7720.01	7175.43	6746.75	6402.23	6120.70

MONTHLY PAYMENT 10.5%
Needed to repay a loan

TERM AMOUNT	15 YEARS	20 YEARS	25 YEARS	30 YEARS	35 YEARS	40 YEARS
500	5.53	4.99	4.72	4.57	4.49	4.44
1000	11.05	9.98	9.44	9.15	8.98	8.89
2000	22.11	19.97	18.88	18.29	17.96	17.77
3000	33.16	29.95	28.33	27.44	26.94	26.66
4000	44.22	39.94	37.77	36.59	35.93	35.54
5000	55.27	49.92	47.21	45.74	44.91	44.43
6000	66.32	59.90	56.65	54.88	53.89	53.31
7000	77.38	69.89	66.09	64.03	62.87	62.20
8000	88.43	79.87	75.53	73.18	71.85	71.09
9000	99.49	89.85	84.98	82.33	80.83	79.97
10000	110.54	99.84	94.42	91.47	89.81	88.86
11000	121.59	109.82	103.86	100.62	98.79	97.74
12000	132.65	119.81	113.30	109.77	107.78	106.63
13000	143.70	129.79	122.74	118.92	116.76	115.51
14000	154.76	139.77	132.19	128.06	125.74	124.40
15000	165.81	149.76	141.63	137.21	134.72	133.29
16000	176.86	159.74	151.07	146.36	143.70	142.17
17000	187.92	169.72	160.51	155.51	152.68	151.06
18000	198.97	179.71	169.95	164.65	161.66	159.94
19000	210.03	189.69	179.39	173.80	170.65	168.83
20000	221.08	199.68	188.84	182.95	179.63	177.71
21000	232.13	209.66	198.28	192.10	188.61	186.60
22000	243.19	219.64	207.72	201.24	197.59	195.49
23000	254.24	229.63	217.16	210.39	206.57	204.37
24000	265.30	239.61	226.60	219.54	215.55	213.26
25000	276.35	249.59	236.05	228.68	224.53	222.14
30000	331.62	299.51	283.25	274.42	269.44	266.57
35000	386.89	349.43	330.46	320.16	314.35	311.00
40000	442.16	399.35	377.67	365.90	359.25	355.43
45000	497.43	449.27	424.88	411.63	404.16	399.86
50000	552.70	499.19	472.09	457.37	449.07	444.29
55000	607.97	549.11	519.30	503.11	493.97	488.71
60000	663.24	599.03	566.51	548.84	538.88	533.14
65000	718.51	648.95	613.72	594.58	583.79	577.57
70000	773.78	698.87	660.93	640.32	628.69	622.00
75000	829.05	748.78	708.14	686.05	673.60	666.43
80000	884.32	798.70	755.35	731.79	718.51	710.86
85000	939.59	848.62	802.55	777.53	763.41	755.28
90000	994.86	898.54	849.76	823.27	808.32	799.71
95000	1050.13	948.46	896.97	869.00	853.23	844.14
100000	1105.40	998.38	944.18	914.74	898.13	888.57
200000	2210.80	1996.76	1888.36	1829.48	1796.27	1777.14
300000	3316.20	2995.14	2832.55	2744.22	2694.40	2665.71
400000	4421.60	3993.52	3776.73	3658.96	3592.54	3554.28
500000	5526.99	4991.90	4720.91	4573.70	4490.67	4442.85

10.75%

MONTHLY PAYMENT
Needed to repay a loan

TERM AMOUNT	1 YEAR	2 YEARS	3 YEARS	4 YEARS	5 YEARS	6 YEARS
500	44.13	23.25	16.31	12.86	10.81	9.45
1000	88.27	46.49	32.62	25.72	21.62	18.91
2000	176.53	92.98	65.24	51.45	43.24	37.81
3000	264.80	139.48	97.86	77.17	64.85	56.72
4000	353.06	185.97	130.48	102.90	86.47	75.63
5000	441.33	232.46	163.10	128.62	108.09	94.53
6000	529.59	278.95	195.72	154.35	129.71	113.44
7000	617.86	325.44	228.34	180.07	151.33	132.34
8000	706.12	371.93	260.96	205.79	172.94	151.25
9000	794.39	418.43	293.58	231.52	194.56	170.16
10000	882.65	464.92	326.20	257.24	216.18	189.06
11000	970.92	511.41	358.82	282.97	237.80	207.97
12000	1059.18	557.90	391.45	308.69	259.42	226.88
13000	1147.45	604.39	424.07	334.42	281.03	245.78
14000	1235.71	650.89	456.69	360.14	302.65	264.69
15000	1323.98	697.38	489.31	385.86	324.27	283.59
16000	1412.24	743.87	521.93	411.59	345.89	302.50
17000	1500.51	790.36	554.55	437.31	367.51	321.41
18000	1588.77	836.85	587.17	463.04	389.12	340.31
19000	1677.04	883.35	619.79	488.76	410.74	359.22
20000	1765.30	929.84	652.41	514.49	432.36	378.13
21000	1853.57	976.33	685.03	540.21	453.98	397.03
22000	1941.83	1022.82	717.65	565.93	475.59	415.94
23000	2030.10	1069.31	750.27	591.66	497.21	434.84
24000	2118.36	1115.80	782.89	617.38	518.83	453.75
25000	2206.63	1162.30	815.51	643.11	540.45	472.66
30000	2647.95	1394.76	978.61	771.73	648.54	567.19
35000	3089.28	1627.21	1141.72	900.35	756.63	661.72
40000	3530.60	1859.67	1304.82	1028.97	864.72	756.25
45000	3971.93	2092.13	1467.92	1157.59	972.81	850.78
50000	4413.25	2324.59	1631.02	1286.21	1080.90	945.31
55000	4854.58	2557.05	1794.12	1414.84	1188.99	1039.85
60000	5295.91	2789.51	1957.23	1543.46	1297.08	1134.38
65000	5737.23	3021.97	2120.33	1672.08	1405.17	1228.91
70000	6178.56	3254.43	2283.43	1800.70	1513.26	1323.44
75000	6619.88	3486.89	2446.53	1929.32	1621.35	1417.97
80000	7061.21	3719.35	2609.64	2057.94	1729.44	1512.50
85000	7502.53	3951.81	2772.74	2186.56	1837.53	1607.03
90000	7943.86	4184.27	2935.84	2315.19	1945.62	1701.57
95000	8385.18	4416.73	3098.94	2443.81	2053.71	1796.10
100000	8826.51	4649.19	3262.05	2572.43	2161.80	1890.63
200000	17653.02	9298.37	6524.09	5144.86	4323.59	3781.26
300000	26479.53	13947.56	9786.14	7717.28	6485.39	5671.88
400000	35306.04	18596.74	13048.18	10289.71	8647.18	7562.51
500000	44132.54	23245.93	16310.23	12862.14	10808.98	9453.14

MONTHLY PAYMENT
Needed to repay a loan

10.75%

TERM AMOUNT	7 YEARS	8 YEARS	9 YEARS	10 YEARS	11 YEARS	12 YEARS
500	8.50	7.79	7.24	6.82	6.47	6.19
1000	16.99	15.57	14.49	13.63	12.95	12.39
2000	33.98	31.15	28.98	27.27	25.90	24.78
3000	50.97	46.72	43.46	40.90	38.84	37.16
4000	67.97	62.30	57.95	54.54	51.79	49.55
5000	84.96	77.87	72.44	68.17	64.74	61.94
6000	101.95	93.44	86.93	81.80	77.69	74.33
7000	118.94	109.02	101.42	95.44	90.64	86.72
8000	135.93	124.59	115.90	109.07	103.58	99.10
9000	152.92	140.17	130.39	122.70	116.53	111.49
10000	169.91	155.74	144.88	136.34	129.48	123.88
11000	186.90	171.31	159.37	149.97	142.43	136.27
12000	203.90	186.89	173.86	163.61	155.38	148.66
13000	220.89	202.46	188.34	177.24	168.32	161.04
14000	237.88	218.03	202.83	190.87	181.27	173.43
15000	254.87	233.61	217.32	204.51	194.22	185.82
16000	271.86	249.18	231.81	218.14	207.17	198.21
17000	288.85	264.76	246.30	231.78	220.12	210.60
18000	305.84	280.33	260.78	245.41	233.06	222.98
19000	322.83	295.90	275.27	259.04	246.01	235.37
20000	339.83	311.48	289.76	272.68	258.96	247.76
21000	356.82	327.05	304.25	286.31	271.91	260.15
22000	373.81	342.63	318.74	299.95	284.86	272.54
23000	390.80	358.20	333.22	313.58	297.80	284.92
24000	407.79	373.77	347.71	327.21	310.75	297.31
25000	424.78	389.35	362.20	340.85	323.70	309.70
30000	509.74	467.22	434.64	409.02	388.44	371.64
35000	594.69	545.09	507.08	477.19	453.18	433.58
40000	679.65	622.96	579.52	545.35	517.92	495.52
45000	764.61	700.83	651.96	613.52	582.66	557.46
50000	849.56	778.70	724.40	681.69	647.40	619.40
55000	934.52	856.56	796.84	749.86	712.14	681.34
60000	1019.48	934.43	869.28	818.03	776.88	743.28
65000	1104.43	1012.30	941.72	886.20	841.62	805.22
70000	1189.39	1090.17	1014.16	954.37	906.36	867.16
75000	1274.35	1168.04	1086.60	1022.54	971.10	929.10
80000	1359.30	1245.91	1159.04	1090.71	1035.84	991.04
85000	1444.26	1323.78	1231.48	1158.88	1100.58	1052.98
90000	1529.21	1401.65	1303.92	1227.05	1165.32	1114.92
95000	1614.17	1479.52	1376.36	1295.22	1230.06	1176.86
100000	1699.13	1557.39	1448.80	1363.39	1294.80	1238.80
200000	3398.25	3114.78	2897.60	2726.77	2589.60	2477.61
300000	5097.38	4672.17	4346.40	4090.16	3884.40	3716.41
400000	6796.51	6229.56	5795.20	5453.55	5179.20	4955.22
500000	8495.64	7786.95	7244.00	6816.93	6474.00	6194.02

10.75%

MONTHLY PAYMENT
Needed to repay a loan

TERM / AMOUNT	15 YEARS	20 YEARS	25 YEARS	30 YEARS	35 YEARS	40 YEARS
500	5.60	5.08	4.81	4.67	4.59	4.54
1000	11.21	10.15	9.62	9.33	9.18	9.08
2000	22.42	20.30	19.24	18.67	18.35	18.17
3000	33.63	30.46	28.86	28.00	27.53	27.25
4000	44.84	40.61	38.48	37.34	36.70	36.34
5000	56.05	50.76	48.10	46.67	45.88	45.42
6000	67.26	60.91	57.73	56.01	55.05	54.50
7000	78.47	71.07	67.35	65.34	64.23	63.59
8000	89.68	81.22	76.97	74.68	73.40	72.67
9000	100.89	91.37	86.59	84.01	82.58	81.76
10000	112.09	101.52	96.21	93.35	91.75	90.84
11000	123.30	111.68	105.83	102.68	100.93	99.92
12000	134.51	121.83	115.45	112.02	110.10	109.01
13000	145.72	131.98	125.07	121.35	119.28	118.09
14000	156.93	142.13	134.69	130.69	128.45	127.18
15000	168.14	152.28	144.31	140.02	137.63	136.26
16000	179.35	162.44	153.93	149.36	146.80	145.34
17000	190.56	172.59	163.56	158.69	155.98	154.43
18000	201.77	182.74	173.18	168.03	165.15	163.51
19000	212.98	192.89	182.80	177.36	174.33	172.60
20000	224.19	203.05	192.42	186.70	183.50	181.68
21000	235.40	213.20	202.04	196.03	192.68	190.76
22000	246.61	223.35	211.66	205.37	201.85	199.85
23000	257.82	233.50	221.28	214.70	211.03	208.93
24000	269.03	243.65	230.90	224.04	220.20	218.02
25000	280.24	253.81	240.52	233.37	229.38	227.10
30000	336.28	304.57	288.63	280.04	275.25	272.52
35000	392.33	355.33	336.73	326.72	321.13	317.94
40000	448.38	406.09	384.84	373.39	367.00	363.36
45000	504.43	456.85	432.94	420.07	412.88	408.78
50000	560.47	507.61	481.05	466.74	458.75	454.20
55000	616.52	558.38	529.15	513.41	504.63	499.62
60000	672.57	609.14	577.26	560.09	550.50	545.04
65000	728.62	659.90	625.36	606.76	596.38	590.46
70000	784.66	710.66	673.46	653.44	642.25	635.88
75000	840.71	761.42	721.57	700.11	688.13	681.30
80000	896.76	812.18	769.67	746.79	734.00	726.72
85000	952.81	862.94	817.78	793.46	779.88	772.14
90000	1008.85	913.71	865.88	840.13	825.75	817.56
95000	1064.90	964.47	913.99	886.81	871.63	862.98
100000	1120.95	1015.23	962.09	933.48	917.50	908.40
200000	2241.90	2030.46	1924.19	1866.96	1835.01	1816.79
300000	3362.84	3045.69	2886.28	2800.44	2752.51	2725.19
400000	4483.79	4060.92	3848.37	3733.93	3670.01	3633.59
500000	5604.74	5076.14	4810.46	4667.41	4587.51	4541.99

MONTHLY PAYMENT
Needed to repay a loan

11%

TERM / AMOUNT	1 YEAR	2 YEARS	3 YEARS	4 YEARS	5 YEARS	6 YEARS
500	44.19	23.30	16.37	12.92	10.87	9.52
1000	88.38	46.61	32.74	25.85	21.74	19.03
2000	176.76	93.22	65.48	51.69	43.48	38.07
3000	265.14	139.82	98.22	77.54	65.23	57.10
4000	353.53	186.43	130.95	103.38	86.97	76.14
5000	441.91	233.04	163.69	129.23	108.71	95.17
6000	530.29	279.65	196.43	155.07	130.45	114.20
7000	618.67	326.25	229.17	180.92	152.20	133.24
8000	707.05	372.86	261.91	206.76	173.94	152.27
9000	795.43	419.47	294.65	232.61	195.68	171.31
10000	883.82	466.08	327.39	258.46	217.42	190.34
11000	972.20	512.69	360.13	284.30	239.17	209.37
12000	1060.58	559.29	392.86	310.15	260.91	228.41
13000	1148.96	605.90	425.60	335.99	282.65	247.44
14000	1237.34	652.51	458.34	361.84	304.39	266.48
15000	1325.72	699.12	491.08	387.68	326.14	285.51
16000	1414.11	745.73	523.82	413.53	347.88	304.55
17000	1502.49	792.33	556.56	439.37	369.62	323.58
18000	1590.87	838.94	589.30	465.22	391.36	342.61
19000	1679.25	885.55	622.04	491.06	413.11	361.65
20000	1767.63	932.16	654.77	516.91	434.85	380.68
21000	1856.01	978.76	687.51	542.76	456.59	399.72
22000	1944.40	1025.37	720.25	568.60	478.33	418.75
23000	2032.78	1071.98	752.99	594.45	500.08	437.78
24000	2121.16	1118.59	785.73	620.29	521.82	456.82
25000	2209.54	1165.20	818.47	646.14	543.56	475.85
30000	2651.45	1398.24	982.16	775.37	652.27	571.02
35000	3093.36	1631.27	1145.86	904.59	760.98	666.19
40000	3535.27	1864.31	1309.55	1033.82	869.70	761.36
45000	3977.17	2097.35	1473.24	1163.05	978.41	856.53
50000	4419.08	2330.39	1636.94	1292.28	1087.12	951.70
55000	4860.99	2563.43	1800.63	1421.50	1195.83	1046.87
60000	5302.90	2796.47	1964.32	1550.73	1304.55	1142.04
65000	5744.81	3029.51	2128.02	1679.96	1413.26	1237.22
70000	6186.72	3262.55	2291.71	1809.19	1521.97	1332.39
75000	6628.62	3495.59	2455.40	1938.41	1630.68	1427.56
80000	7070.53	3728.63	2619.10	2067.64	1739.39	1522.73
85000	7512.44	3961.67	2782.79	2196.87	1848.11	1617.90
90000	7954.35	4194.71	2946.48	2326.10	1956.82	1713.07
95000	8396.26	4427.74	3110.18	2455.32	2065.53	1808.24
100000	8838.17	4660.78	3273.87	2584.55	2174.24	1903.41
200000	17676.33	9321.57	6547.74	5169.10	4348.48	3806.82
300000	26514.50	13982.35	9821.62	7753.66	6522.73	5710.22
400000	35352.66	18643.14	13095.49	10338.21	8696.97	7613.63
500000	44190.83	23303.92	16369.36	12922.76	10871.21	9517.04

11% MONTHLY PAYMENT

Needed to repay a loan

TERM AMOUNT	7 YEARS	8 YEARS	9 YEARS	10 YEARS	11 YEARS	12 YEARS
500	8.56	7.85	7.31	6.89	6.55	6.27
1000	17.12	15.71	14.63	13.78	13.09	12.54
2000	34.24	31.42	29.25	27.55	26.18	25.07
3000	51.37	47.13	43.88	41.33	39.28	37.61
4000	68.49	62.83	58.50	55.10	52.37	50.14
5000	85.61	78.54	73.13	68.88	65.46	62.68
6000	102.73	94.25	87.76	82.65	78.55	75.21
7000	119.86	109.96	102.38	96.43	91.65	87.75
8000	136.98	125.67	117.01	110.20	104.74	100.28
9000	154.10	141.38	131.63	123.98	117.83	112.82
10000	171.22	157.08	146.26	137.75	130.92	125.36
11000	188.35	172.79	160.88	151.53	144.02	137.89
12000	205.47	188.50	175.51	165.30	157.11	150.43
13000	222.59	204.21	190.14	179.08	170.20	162.96
14000	239.71	219.92	204.76	192.85	183.29	175.50
15000	256.84	235.63	219.39	206.63	196.39	188.03
16000	273.96	251.33	234.01	220.40	209.48	200.57
17000	291.08	267.04	248.64	234.18	222.57	213.10
18000	308.20	282.75	263.27	247.95	235.66	225.64
19000	325.33	298.46	277.89	261.73	248.75	238.18
20000	342.45	314.17	292.52	275.50	261.85	250.71
21000	359.57	329.88	307.14	289.28	274.94	263.25
22000	376.69	345.59	321.77	303.05	288.03	275.78
23000	393.82	361.29	366.39	316.83	301.12	288.32
24000	410.94	377.00	351.02	330.60	314.22	300.85
25000	428.06	392.71	365.65	344.38	327.31	313.39
30000	513.67	471.25	438.78	413.25	392.77	376.07
35000	599.29	549.79	511.91	482.13	458.23	438.74
40000	684.90	628.34	585.03	551.00	523.69	501.42
45000	770.51	706.88	658.16	619.88	589.16	564.10
50000	856.12	785.42	731.29	688.75	654.62	626.78
55000	941.73	863.96	804.42	757.63	720.08	689.46
60000	1027.35	942.51	877.55	826.50	785.54	752.13
65000	1112.96	1021.05	950.68	895.38	851.00	814.81
70000	1198.57	1099.59	1023.81	964.25	916.46	877.49
75000	1284.18	1178.13	1096.94	1033.13	981.93	940.17
80000	1369.79	1256.67	1170.07	1102.00	1047.39	1002.84
85000	1455.41	1335.22	1243.20	1170.88	1112.85	1065.52
90000	1541.02	1413.76	1316.33	1239.75	1178.31	1128.20
95000	1626.63	1492.30	1389.46	1308.63	1243.77	1190.88
100000	1712.24	1570.84	1462.59	1377.50	1309.23	1253.56
200000	3424.49	3141.69	2925.17	2755.00	2618.47	2507.11
300000	5136.73	4712.53	4387.76	4132.50	3927.70	3760.67
400000	6848.97	6283.37	5850.34	5510.00	5236.94	5014.22
500000	8561.22	7854.21	7312.93	6887.50	6546.17	6267.78

MONTHLY PAYMENT 11%

Needed to repay a loan

TERM AMOUNT	15 YEARS	20 YEARS	25 YEARS	30 YEARS	35 YEARS	40 YEARS
500	5.68	5.16	4.90	4.76	4.68	4.64
1000	11.37	10.32	9.80	9.52	9.37	9.28
2000	22.73	20.64	19.60	19.05	18.74	18.57
3000	34.10	30.97	29.40	28.57	28.11	27.85
4000	45.46	41.29	39.20	38.09	37.48	37.13
5000	56.83	51.61	49.01	47.62	46.85	46.41
6000	68.20	61.93	58.81	57.14	56.22	55.70
7000	79.56	72.25	68.61	66.66	65.59	64.98
8000	90.93	82.58	78.41	76.19	74.96	74.26
9000	102.29	92.90	88.21	85.71	84.33	83.55
10000	113.66	103.22	98.01	95.23	93.70	92.83
11000	125.03	113.54	107.81	104.76	103.07	102.11
12000	136.39	123.86	117.61	114.28	112.43	111.40
13000	147.76	134.18	127.41	123.80	121.80	120.68
14000	159.12	144.51	137.22	133.33	131.17	129.96
15000	170.49	154.83	147.02	142.85	140.54	139.24
16000	181.86	165.15	156.82	152.37	149.91	148.53
17000	193.22	175.47	166.62	161.89	159.28	157.81
18000	204.59	185.79	176.42	171.42	168.65	167.09
19000	215.95	196.12	186.22	180.94	178.02	176.38
20000	227.32	206.44	196.02	190.46	187.39	185.66
21000	238.69	216.76	205.82	199.99	196.76	194.94
22000	250.05	227.08	215.62	209.51	206.13	204.22
23000	261.42	237.40	225.43	219.03	215.50	213.51
24000	272.78	247.73	235.23	228.56	224.87	222.79
25000	284.15	258.05	245.03	238.08	234.24	232.07
30000	340.98	309.66	294.03	285.70	281.09	278.49
35000	397.81	361.27	343.04	333.31	327.94	324.90
40000	454.64	412.88	392.05	380.93	374.78	371.32
45000	511.47	464.48	441.05	428.55	421.63	417.73
50000	568.30	516.09	490.06	476.16	468.48	464.15
55000	625.13	567.70	539.06	523.78	515.33	510.56
60000	681.96	619.31	588.07	571.39	562.17	556.98
65000	738.79	670.92	637.07	619.01	609.02	603.39
70000	795.62	722.53	686.08	666.63	655.87	649.81
75000	852.45	774.14	735.08	714.24	702.72	696.22
80000	909.28	825.75	784.09	761.86	749.57	742.64
85000	966.11	877.36	833.10	809.47	796.41	789.05
90000	1022.94	928.97	882.10	857.09	843.26	835.46
95000	1079.77	980.58	931.11	904.71	890.11	881.88
100000	1136.60	1032.19	980.11	952.32	936.96	928.29
200000	2273.19	2064.38	1960.23	1904.65	1873.92	1856.59
300000	3409.79	3096.57	2940.34	2856.97	2810.87	2784.88
400000	4546.39	4128.75	3920.45	3809.29	3747.83	3713.18
500000	5682.98	5160.94	4900.57	4761.62	4684.79	4641.47

11.25%

MONTHLY PAYMENT
Needed to repay a loan

TERM AMOUNT	1 YEAR	2 YEARS	3 YEARS	4 YEARS	5 YEARS	6 YEARS
500	44.25	23.36	16.43	12.98	10.93	9.58
1000	88.50	46.72	32.86	25.97	21.87	19.16
2000	177.00	93.45	65.71	51.93	43.73	38.32
3000	265.49	140.17	98.57	77.90	65.60	57.49
4000	353.99	186.90	131.43	103.87	87.47	76.65
5000	442.49	233.62	164.29	129.84	109.34	95.81
6000	530.99	280.34	197.14	155.80	131.20	114.97
7000	619.49	327.07	230.00	181.77	153.07	134.14
8000	707.99	373.79	262.86	207.74	174.94	153.30
9000	796.48	420.52	295.72	233.70	196.81	172.46
10000	884.98	467.24	328.57	259.67	218.67	191.62
11000	973.48	513.96	361.43	285.64	240.54	210.79
12000	1061.98	560.69	394.29	311.61	262.41	229.95
13000	1150.48	607.41	427.14	337.57	284.28	249.11
14000	1238.98	654.14	460.00	363.54	306.14	268.27
15000	1327.47	700.86	492.86	389.51	328.01	287.44
16000	1415.97	747.58	525.72	415.47	349.88	306.60
17000	1504.47	794.31	558.57	441.44	371.74	325.76
18000	1592.97	841.03	591.43	467.41	393.61	344.92
19000	1681.47	887.76	624.29	493.37	415.48	364.09
20000	1769.97	934.48	657.14	519.34	437.35	383.25
21000	1858.46	981.20	690.00	545.31	459.21	402.41
22000	1946.96	1027.93	722.86	571.28	481.08	421.57
23000	2035.46	1074.65	755.72	597.24	502.95	440.73
24000	2123.96	1121.38	788.57	623.21	524.82	459.90
25000	2212.46	1168.10	821.43	649.18	546.68	479.06
30000	2654.95	1401.72	985.72	779.01	656.02	574.87
35000	3097.44	1635.34	1150.00	908.85	765.36	670.68
40000	3539.93	1868.96	1314.29	1038.68	874.69	766.49
45000	3982.42	2102.58	1478.58	1168.52	984.03	862.31
50000	4424.92	2336.20	1642.86	1298.35	1093.37	958.12
55000	4867.41	2569.82	1807.15	1428.19	1202.70	1053.93
60000	5309.90	2803.44	1971.43	1558.03	1312.04	1149.74
65000	5752.39	3037.06	2135.72	1687.86	1421.38	1245.55
70000	6194.88	3270.68	2300.01	1817.70	1530.71	1341.37
75000	6637.37	3504.30	2464.29	1947.53	1640.05	1437.18
80000	7079.87	3737.92	2628.58	2077.37	1749.38	1532.99
85000	7522.36	3971.54	2792.86	2207.20	1858.72	1628.80
90000	7964.85	4205.16	2957.15	2337.04	1968.06	1724.61
95000	8407.34	4438.78	3121.44	2466.87	2077.39	1820.43
100000	8849.83	4672.40	3285.72	2596.71	2186.73	1916.24
200000	17699.66	9344.80	6571.45	5193.42	4373.46	3832.47
300000	26549.49	14017.20	9857.17	7790.13	6560.19	5748.71
400000	35399.33	18689.60	13142.89	10386.84	8746.92	7664.95
500000	44249.16	23362.00	16428.62	12983.55	10933.65	9581.19

MONTHLY PAYMENT
Needed to repay a loan

11.25%

TERM AMOUNT	7 YEARS	8 YEARS	9 YEARS	10 YEARS	11 YEARS	12 YEARS
500	8.63	7.92	7.38	6.96	6.62	6.34
1000	17.25	15.84	14.76	13.92	13.24	12.68
2000	34.51	31.69	29.53	27.83	26.48	25.37
3000	51.76	47.53	44.29	41.75	39.71	38.05
4000	69.02	63.37	59.06	55.67	52.95	50.74
5000	86.27	79.22	73.82	69.58	66.19	63.42
6000	103.53	95.06	88.59	83.50	79.43	76.10
7000	120.78	110.91	103.35	97.42	92.66	88.79
8000	138.03	126.75	118.12	111.34	105.90	101.47
9000	155.29	142.59	132.88	125.25	119.14	114.16
10000	172.54	158.44	147.64	139.17	132.38	126.84
11000	189.80	174.28	162.41	153.09	145.61	139.52
12000	207.05	190.12	177.17	167.00	158.85	152.21
13000	224.30	205.97	191.94	180.92	172.09	164.89
14000	241.56	221.81	206.70	194.84	185.33	177.58
15000	258.81	237.65	221.47	208.75	198.56	190.26
16000	276.07	253.50	236.23	222.67	211.80	202.94
17000	293.32	269.34	251.00	236.59	225.04	215.63
18000	310.58	285.18	265.76	250.50	238.28	228.31
19000	327.83	301.03	280.52	264.42	251.51	240.99
20000	345.08	316.87	295.29	278.34	264.75	253.68
21000	362.34	332.72	310.05	292.25	277.99	266.36
22000	379.59	348.56	324.82	306.17	291.23	279.05
23000	396.85	364.40	339.58	320.09	304.46	291.73
24000	414.10	380.25	354.35	334.01	317.70	304.41
25000	431.35	396.09	369.11	347.92	330.94	317.10
30000	517.63	475.31	442.93	417.51	397.13	380.52
35000	603.90	554.53	516.75	487.09	463.31	443.94
40000	690.17	633.74	590.58	556.68	529.50	507.36
45000	776.44	712.96	664.40	626.26	595.69	570.78
50000	862.71	792.18	738.22	695.84	661.88	634.20
55000	948.98	871.40	812.04	765.43	728.06	697.62
60000	1035.25	950.62	885.86	835.01	794.25	761.04
65000	1121.52	1029.83	959.69	904.60	860.44	824.46
70000	1207.79	1109.05	1033.51	974.18	926.63	887.88
75000	1294.06	1188.27	1107.33	1043.77	992.81	951.29
80000	1380.33	1267.49	1181.15	1113.35	1059.00	1014.71
85000	1466.60	1346.70	1254.98	1182.94	1125.19	1078.13
90000	1552.88	1425.92	1328.80	1252.52	1191.38	1141.55
95000	1639.15	1505.14	1402.62	1322.10	1257.56	1204.97
100000	1725.42	1584.36	1476.44	1391.69	1323.75	1268.39
200000	3450.83	3168.72	2952.88	2783.38	2647.50	2536.79
300000	5176.25	4753.08	4429.32	4175.07	3971.26	3805.18
400000	6901.67	6337.43	5905.78	5566.76	5295.01	5073.57
500000	8627.08	7921.79	7382.21	6958.45	6618.76	6341.96

11.25%

MONTHLY PAYMENT
Needed to repay a loan

TERM / AMOUNT	15 YEARS	20 YEARS	25 YEARS	30 YEARS	35 YEARS	40 YEARS
500	5.76	5.25	4.99	4.86	4.78	4.74
1000	11.52	10.49	9.98	9.71	9.56	9.48
2000	23.05	20.99	19.96	19.43	19.13	18.97
3000	34.57	31.48	29.95	29.14	28.69	28.45
4000	46.09	41.97	39.93	38.85	38.26	37.93
5000	57.62	52.46	49.91	48.56	47.82	47.41
6000	69.14	62.96	59.89	58.28	57.39	56.90
7000	80.66	73.45	69.88	67.99	66.95	66.38
8000	92.19	83.94	79.86	77.70	76.52	75.86
9000	103.71	94.43	89.84	87.41	86.08	85.34
10000	115.23	104.93	99.82	97.13	95.65	94.83
11000	126.76	115.42	109.81	106.84	105.21	104.31
12000	138.28	125.91	119.79	116.55	114.78	113.79
13000	149.80	136.40	129.77	126.26	124.34	123.27
14000	161.33	146.90	139.75	135.98	133.91	132.76
15000	172.85	157.39	149.74	145.69	143.47	142.24
16000	184.38	167.88	159.72	155.40	153.04	151.72
17000	195.90	178.37	169.70	165.11	162.60	161.20
18000	207.42	188.87	179.68	174.83	172.17	170.69
19000	218.95	199.36	189.67	184.54	181.73	180.17
20000	230.47	209.85	199.65	194.25	191.30	189.65
21000	241.99	220.34	209.63	203.96	200.86	199.13
22000	253.52	230.84	219.61	213.68	210.43	208.62
23000	265.04	241.33	229.60	223.39	219.99	218.10
24000	276.56	251.82	239.58	233.10	229.56	227.58
25000	288.09	262.31	249.56	242.82	239.12	237.06
30000	345.70	314.78	299.47	291.38	286.95	284.48
35000	403.32	367.24	349.38	339.94	334.77	331.89
40000	460.94	419.70	399.30	388.50	382.60	379.30
45000	518.56	472.17	449.21	437.07	430.42	426.72
50000	576.17	524.63	499.12	485.63	478.25	474.13
55000	633.79	577.09	549.03	534.19	526.07	521.54
60000	691.41	629.55	598.94	582.76	573.90	568.95
65000	749.02	682.02	648.86	631.32	621.72	616.37
70000	806.64	734.48	698.77	679.88	669.55	663.78
75000	864.26	786.94	748.68	728.45	717.37	711.19
80000	921.88	839.40	798.59	777.01	765.20	758.61
85000	979.49	891.87	848.50	825.57	813.02	806.02
90000	1037.11	944.33	898.42	874.14	860.84	853.43
95000	1094.73	996.79	948.33	922.70	908.67	900.84
100000	1152.34	1049.26	998.24	971.26	956.49	948.26
200000	2304.69	2098.51	1996.48	1942.52	1912.99	1896.51
300000	3457.03	3147.77	2994.72	2913.78	2869.48	2844.77
400000	4609.38	4197.02	3992.96	3885.05	3825.98	3793.03
500000	5761.72	5246.28	4991.20	4856.31	4782.47	4741.29

MONTHLY PAYMENT
Needed to repay a loan

11.5%

TERM / AMOUNT	1 YEAR	2 YEARS	3 YEARS	4 YEARS	5 YEARS	6 YEARS
500	44.31	23.42	16.49	13.04	11.00	9.65
1000	88.62	46.84	32.98	26.09	21.99	19.29
2000	177.23	93.68	65.95	52.18	43.99	38.58
3000	265.85	140.52	98.93	78.27	65.98	57.87
4000	354.46	187.36	131.90	104.36	87.97	77.16
5000	443.08	234.20	164.88	130.45	109.96	96.46
6000	531.69	281.04	197.86	156.53	131.96	115.75
7000	620.31	327.88	230.83	182.62	153.95	135.04
8000	708.92	374.72	263.81	208.71	175.94	154.33
9000	797.54	421.56	296.78	234.80	197.93	173.62
10000	886.15	468.40	329.76	260.89	219.93	192.91
11000	974.77	515.24	362.74	286.98	241.92	212.20
12000	1063.38	562.08	395.71	313.07	263.91	231.49
13000	1152.00	608.92	428.69	339.16	285.90	250.79
14000	1240.61	655.76	461.66	365.25	307.90	270.08
15000	1329.23	702.60	494.64	391.34	329.89	289.37
16000	1417.84	749.45	527.62	417.42	351.88	308.66
17000	1506.46	796.29	560.59	443.51	373.87	327.95
18000	1595.07	843.13	593.57	469.60	395.87	347.24
19000	1683.69	889.97	626.54	495.69	417.86	366.53
20000	1772.30	936.81	659.52	521.78	439.85	385.82
21000	1860.92	983.65	692.50	547.87	461.84	405.11
22000	1949.53	1030.49	725.47	573.96	483.84	424.41
23000	2038.15	1077.33	758.45	600.05	505.83	443.70
24000	2126.76	1124.17	791.42	626.14	527.82	462.99
25000	2215.38	1171.01	824.40	652.23	549.82	482.28
30000	2658.45	1405.21	989.28	782.67	659.78	578.73
35000	3101.53	1639.41	1154.16	913.12	769.74	675.19
40000	3544.60	1873.61	1319.04	1043.56	879.70	771.65
45000	3987.68	2107.81	1483.92	1174.01	989.67	868.10
50000	4430.75	2342.02	1648.80	1304.45	1099.63	964.56
55000	4873.83	2576.22	1813.68	1434.90	1209.59	1061.01
60000	5316.90	2810.42	1978.56	1565.34	1319.56	1157.47
65000	5759.98	3044.62	2143.44	1695.79	1429.52	1253.93
70000	6203.05	3278.82	2308.32	1826.23	1539.48	1350.38
75000	6646.13	3513.02	2473.20	1956.68	1649.45	1446.84
80000	7089.20	3747.23	2638.08	2087.12	1759.41	1543.29
85000	7532.28	3981.43	2802.96	2217.57	1869.37	1639.75
90000	7975.35	4215.63	2967.84	2348.01	1979.33	1736.20
95000	8418.43	4449.83	3132.72	2478.46	2089.30	1832.66
100000	8861.51	4684.03	3297.60	2608.90	2199.26	1929.12
200000	17723.01	9368.06	6595.20	5217.80	4398.52	3858.23
300000	26584.52	14052.09	9892.80	7826.70	6597.78	5787.35
400000	35446.02	18736.13	13190.40	10435.60	8797.04	7716.46
500000	44307.53	23420.16	16488.00	13044.50	10996.30	9645.58

11.5% MONTHLY PAYMENT
Needed to repay a loan

TERM AMOUNT	7 YEARS	8 YEARS	9 YEARS	10 YEARS	11 YEARS	12 YEARS
500	8.69	7.99	7.45	7.03	6.69	6.42
1000	17.39	15.98	14.90	14.06	13.38	12.83
2000	34.77	31.96	29.81	28.12	26.77	25.67
3000	52.16	47.94	44.71	42.18	40.15	38.50
4000	69.55	63.92	59.61	56.24	53.53	51.33
5000	86.93	79.90	74.52	70.30	66.92	64.17
6000	104.32	95.88	89.42	84.36	80.30	77.00
7000	121.71	111.86	104.33	98.42	93.68	89.83
8000	139.09	127.83	119.23	112.48	107.07	102.67
9000	156.48	143.81	134.13	126.54	120.45	115.50
10000	173.86	159.79	149.04	140.60	133.84	128.33
11000	191.25	175.77	163.94	154.65	147.22	141.16
12000	208.64	191.75	178.84	168.71	160.60	154.00
13000	226.02	207.73	193.75	182.77	173.99	166.83
14000	243.41	223.71	208.65	196.83	187.37	179.66
15000	260.80	239.69	223.55	210.89	200.75	192.50
16000	278.18	255.67	238.46	224.95	214.14	205.33
17000	295.57	271.65	253.36	239.01	227.52	218.16
18000	312.96	287.63	268.27	253.07	240.90	231.00
19000	330.34	303.61	283.17	267.13	254.29	243.83
20000	347.73	319.59	298.07	281.19	267.67	256.66
21000	365.12	335.57	312.98	295.25	281.05	269.50
22000	382.50	351.55	327.88	309.31	294.44	282.33
23000	399.89	367.53	342.78	323.37	307.82	295.16
24000	417.28	383.50	357.69	337.43	321.20	308.00
25000	434.66	399.48	372.59	351.49	334.59	320.83
30000	521.59	479.38	447.11	421.79	401.51	384.99
35000	608.53	559.28	521.63	492.08	468.42	449.16
40000	695.46	639.17	596.15	562.38	535.34	513.33
45000	782.39	719.07	670.66	632.68	602.26	577.49
50000	869.32	798.97	745.18	702.98	669.18	641.66
55000	956.26	878.87	819.70	773.27	736.09	705.82
60000	1043.19	958.76	894.22	843.57	803.01	769.99
65000	1130.12	1038.66	968.74	913.87	869.93	834.16
70000	1217.05	1118.56	1043.26	984.17	936.85	898.32
75000	1303.98	1198.45	1117.77	1054.47	1003.76	962.49
80000	1390.92	1278.35	1192.29	1124.76	1070.68	1026.65
85000	1477.85	1358.25	1266.81	1195.06	1137.60	1090.82
90000	1564.78	1438.14	1341.33	1265.36	1204.52	1154.98
95000	1651.71	1518.04	1415.85	1335.66	1271.43	1219.15
100000	1738.65	1597.94	1490.37	1405.95	1338.35	1283.32
200000	3477.29	3195.87	2980.73	2811.91	2676.70	2566.63
300000	5215.94	4793.81	4471.10	4217.86	4015.05	3849.95
400000	6954.58	6391.75	5961.46	5623.82	5353.40	5133.27
500000	8693.23	7989.69	7451.83	7029.77	6691.75	6416.58

MONTHLY PAYMENT 11.5%
Needed to repay a loan

TERM AMOUNT	15 YEARS	20 YEARS	25 YEARS	30 YEARS	35 YEARS	40 YEARS
500	5.84	5.33	5.08	4.95	4.88	4.84
1000	11.68	10.66	10.16	9.90	9.76	9.68
2000	23.36	21.33	20.33	19.81	19.52	19.37
3000	35.05	31.99	30.49	29.71	29.28	29.05
4000	46.73	42.66	40.66	39.61	39.04	38.73
5000	58.41	53.32	50.82	49.51	48.81	48.41
6000	70.09	63.99	60.99	59.42	58.57	58.10
7000	81.77	74.65	71.15	69.32	68.33	67.78
8000	93.46	85.31	81.32	79.22	78.09	77.46
9000	105.14	95.98	91.48	89.13	87.85	87.15
10000	116.82	106.64	101.65	99.03	97.61	96.83
11000	128.50	117.31	111.81	108.93	107.37	106.51
12000	140.18	127.97	121.98	118.83	117.13	116.19
13000	151.86	138.64	132.14	128.74	126.89	125.88
14000	163.55	149.30	142.31	138.64	136.66	135.56
15000	175.23	159.96	152.47	148.54	146.42	145.24
16000	186.91	170.63	162.64	158.45	156.18	154.93
17000	198.59	181.29	172.80	168.35	165.94	164.61
18000	210.27	191.96	182.96	178.25	175.70	174.29
19000	221.96	202.62	193.13	188.16	185.46	183.97
20000	233.64	213.29	203.29	198.06	195.22	193.66
21000	245.32	223.95	213.46	207.96	204.98	203.34
22000	257.00	234.61	223.62	217.86	214.74	213.02
23000	268.68	245.28	233.79	227.77	224.50	222.70
24000	280.37	255.94	243.95	237.67	234.27	232.39
25000	292.05	266.61	254.12	247.57	244.03	242.07
30000	350.46	319.93	304.94	297.09	292.83	290.48
35000	408.87	373.25	355.76	346.60	341.64	338.90
40000	467.28	426.57	406.59	396.12	390.44	387.31
45000	525.69	479.89	457.41	445.63	439.25	435.73
50000	584.09	533.21	508.23	495.15	488.05	484.14
55000	642.50	586.54	559.06	544.66	536.86	532.56
60000	700.91	639.86	609.88	594.17	585.66	580.97
65000	759.32	693.18	660.70	643.69	634.47	629.38
70000	817.73	746.50	711.53	693.20	683.28	677.80
75000	876.14	799.82	762.35	742.72	732.08	726.21
80000	934.55	853.14	813.18	792.23	780.89	774.63
85000	992.96	906.47	864.00	841.75	829.69	823.04
90000	1051.37	959.79	914.82	891.26	878.50	871.45
95000	1109.78	1013.11	965.65	940.78	927.30	919.87
100000	1168.19	1066.43	1016.47	990.29	976.11	968.28
200000	2336.38	2132.86	2032.94	1980.58	1952.21	1936.56
300000	3504.57	3199.29	3049.41	2970.87	2928.32	2904.85
400000	4672.76	4265.72	4065.88	3961.17	3904.43	3873.13
500000	5840.95	5332.15	5082.34	4951.46	4880.54	4841.41

11.75% MONTHLY PAYMENT

Needed to repay a loan

TERM AMOUNT	1 YEAR	2 YEARS	3 YEARS	4 YEARS	5 YEARS	6 YEARS
500	44.37	23.48	16.55	13.11	11.06	9.71
1000	88.73	46.96	33.10	26.21	22.12	19.42
2000	177.46	93.91	66.19	52.42	44.24	38.84
3000	266.20	140.87	99.29	78.63	66.35	58.26
4000	354.93	187.83	132.38	104.85	88.47	77.68
5000	443.66	234.78	165.48	131.06	110.59	97.10
6000	532.39	281.74	198.57	157.27	132.71	116.52
7000	621.12	328.70	231.67	183.48	154.83	135.94
8000	709.86	375.65	264.76	209.69	176.95	155.36
9000	798.59	422.61	297.86	235.90	199.06	174.78
10000	887.32	469.57	330.95	262.11	221.18	194.20
11000	976.05	516.52	364.05	288.32	243.30	213.62
12000	1064.78	563.48	397.14	314.54	265.42	233.05
13000	1153.51	610.44	430.24	340.75	287.54	252.47
14000	1242.25	657.40	463.33	366.96	309.66	271.89
15000	1330.98	704.35	496.43	393.17	331.77	291.31
16000	1419.71	751.31	529.52	419.38	353.89	310.73
17000	1508.44	798.27	562.62	445.59	376.01	330.15
18000	1597.17	845.22	595.71	471.80	398.13	349.57
19000	1685.91	892.18	628.81	498.01	420.05	368.99
20000	1774.64	939.14	661.90	524.23	442.37	388.41
21000	1863.37	986.09	695.00	550.44	464.48	407.83
22000	1952.10	1033.05	728.09	576.65	486.60	427.25
23000	2040.83	1080.01	761.19	602.86	508.72	446.67
24000	2129.57	1126.96	794.28	629.07	530.84	466.09
25000	2218.30	1173.92	827.38	655.28	552.96	485.51
30000	2661.96	1408.70	992.85	786.34	663.55	582.61
35000	3105.62	1643.49	1158.33	917.39	774.14	679.72
40000	3549.28	1878.27	1323.80	1048.45	884.73	776.82
45000	3992.93	2113.06	1489.28	1179.51	995.32	873.92
50000	4436.59	2347.84	1654.75	1310.56	1105.92	971.02
55000	4880.25	2582.62	1820.23	1441.62	1216.51	1068.12
60000	5323.91	2817.41	1985.70	1572.68	1327.10	1165.23
65000	5767.57	3052.19	2151.18	1703.73	1437.69	1262.33
70000	6211.23	3286.98	2316.65	1834.79	1548.28	1359.43
75000	6654.89	3521.76	2482.13	1965.84	1658.87	1456.53
80000	7098.55	3756.54	2647.60	2096.90	1769.47	1553.63
85000	7542.21	3991.33	2813.08	2227.96	1880.06	1650.74
90000	7985.87	4226.11	2978.55	2359.01	1990.65	1747.84
95000	8429.53	4460.90	3144.03	2490.07	2101.24	1844.94
100000	8873.19	4695.68	3309.50	2621.13	2211.83	1942.04
200000	17746.38	9391.36	6619.01	5242.25	4423.66	3884.09
300000	26619.56	14087.04	9928.51	7863.38	6635.50	5826.13
400000	35492.75	18782.72	13238.01	10484.50	8847.33	7768.17
500000	44365.94	23478.40	16547.52	13105.63	11059.16	9710.22

MONTHLY PAYMENT 11.75%

Needed to repay a loan

TERM AMOUNT	7 YEARS	8 YEARS	9 YEARS	10 YEARS	11 YEARS	12 YEARS
500	8.76	8.06	7.52	7.10	6.77	6.49
1000	17.52	16.12	15.04	14.20	13.53	12.98
2000	35.04	32.23	30.09	28.41	27.06	25.97
3000	52.56	48.35	45.13	42.61	40.59	38.95
4000	70.08	64.46	60.17	56.81	54.12	51.93
5000	87.60	80.58	75.22	71.01	67.65	64.92
6000	105.12	96.69	90.26	85.22	81.18	77.90
7000	122.64	112.81	105.31	99.42	94.71	90.88
8000	140.15	128.93	120.35	113.62	108.24	103.87
9000	157.67	145.04	135.39	127.83	121.77	116.85
10000	175.19	161.16	150.44	142.03	135.30	129.83
11000	192.71	177.27	165.48	156.23	148.83	142.82
12000	210.23	193.39	180.52	170.44	162.36	155.80
13000	227.75	209.51	195.57	184.64	175.89	168.78
14000	245.27	225.62	210.61	198.84	189.42	181.77
15000	262.79	241.74	225.65	213.04	202.95	194.75
16000	280.31	257.85	240.70	227.25	216.48	207.73
17000	297.83	273.97	255.74	241.45	230.01	220.72
18000	315.35	290.08	270.78	255.65	243.55	233.70
19000	332.87	306.20	285.83	269.86	257.08	246.68
20000	350.39	322.32	300.87	284.06	270.61	259.67
21000	367.91	338.43	315.92	298.26	284.14	272.65
22000	385.42	354.55	330.96	312.46	297.67	285.63
23000	402.94	370.66	346.00	326.67	311.20	298.61
24000	420.46	386.78	361.05	340.87	324.73	311.60
25000	437.98	402.89	376.09	355.07	338.26	324.58
30000	525.58	483.47	451.31	426.09	405.91	389.50
35000	613.18	564.05	526.53	497.10	473.56	454.41
40000	700.77	644.63	601.74	568.12	541.21	519.33
45000	788.37	725.21	676.96	639.13	608.86	584.25
50000	875.97	805.79	752.18	710.15	676.51	649.16
55000	963.56	886.37	827.40	781.16	744.17	714.08
60000	1051.16	966.95	902.62	852.18	811.82	779.00
65000	1138.76	1047.53	977.83	923.19	879.47	843.91
70000	1226.35	1128.11	1053.05	994.21	947.12	908.83
75000	1313.95	1208.68	1128.27	1065.22	1014.77	973.74
80000	1401.55	1289.26	1203.49	1136.24	1082.42	1038.66
85000	1489.14	1369.84	1278.71	1207.25	1150.07	1103.58
90000	1576.74	1450.42	1353.92	1278.27	1217.73	1168.49
95000	1664.34	1531.00	1429.14	1349.28	1285.38	1233.41
100000	1751.93	1611.58	1504.36	1420.29	1353.03	1298.33
200000	3503.86	3223.16	3008.72	2840.59	2706.06	2596.65
300000	5255.80	4834.74	4513.08	4260.88	4059.09	3894.98
400000	7007.73	6446.32	6017.44	5681.18	5412.12	5193.30
500000	8759.66	8057.90	7521.80	7101.47	6765.15	6491.63

11.75% MONTHLY PAYMENT

Needed to repay a loan

TERM AMOUNT	15 YEARS	20 YEARS	25 YEARS	30 YEARS	35 YEARS	40 YEARS
500	5.92	5.42	5.17	5.05	4.98	4.94
1000	11.84	10.84	10.35	10.09	9.96	9.88
2000	23.68	21.67	20.70	20.19	19.92	19.77
3000	35.52	32.51	31.04	30.28	29.87	29.65
4000	47.37	43.35	41.39	40.38	39.83	39.53
5000	59.21	54.19	51.74	50.47	49.79	49.42
6000	71.05	65.02	62.09	60.56	59.75	59.30
7000	82.89	75.86	72.44	70.66	69.71	69.19
8000	94.73	86.70	82.78	80.75	79.66	79.07
9000	106.57	97.53	93.13	90.85	89.62	88.95
10000	118.41	108.37	103.48	100.94	99.58	98.84
11000	130.25	119.21	113.83	111.04	109.54	108.72
12000	142.10	130.04	124.18	121.13	119.50	118.60
13000	153.94	140.88	134.52	131.22	129.45	128.49
14000	165.78	151.72	144.87	141.32	139.41	138.37
15000	177.62	162.56	155.22	151.41	149.37	148.25
16000	189.46	173.39	165.57	161.51	159.33	158.14
17000	201.30	184.23	175.92	171.60	169.28	168.02
18000	213.14	195.07	186.26	181.69	179.24	177.91
19000	224.98	205.90	196.61	191.79	189.20	187.79
20000	236.83	216.74	206.96	201.88	199.16	197.67
21000	248.67	227.58	217.31	211.98	209.12	207.56
22000	260.51	238.42	227.66	222.07	219.07	217.44
23000	272.35	249.25	238.00	232.16	229.03	227.32
24000	284.19	260.09	248.35	242.26	238.99	237.21
25000	296.03	270.93	258.70	252.35	248.95	247.09
30000	355.24	325.11	310.44	302.82	298.74	296.51
35000	414.45	379.30	362.18	353.29	348.53	345.93
40000	473.65	433.48	413.92	403.76	398.32	395.35
45000	532.86	487.67	465.66	454.23	448.11	444.76
50000	592.07	541.85	517.40	504.70	497.90	494.18
55000	651.27	596.04	569.14	555.18	547.69	543.60
60000	710.48	650.22	620.88	605.65	597.48	593.02
65000	769.69	704.41	672.62	656.12	647.27	642.44
70000	828.89	758.59	724.36	706.59	697.06	691.85
75000	888.10	812.78	776.10	757.06	746.85	741.27
80000	947.31	866.97	827.84	807.53	796.64	790.69
85000	1006.51	921.15	879.58	858.00	846.42	840.11
90000	1065.72	975.34	931.32	908.47	896.21	889.53
95000	1124.92	1029.52	983.06	958.94	946.00	938.95
100000	1184.13	1083.71	1034.80	1009.41	995.79	988.36
200000	2368.26	2167.41	2069.60	2018.82	1991.59	1976.73
300000	3552.39	3251.12	3104.39	3028.23	2987.38	2965.09
400000	4736.53	4334.83	4139.19	4037.64	3983.18	3953.46
500000	5920.66	5418.54	5173.99	5047.05	4978.97	4941.82

MONTHLY PAYMENT 12%

Needed to repay a loan

TERM AMOUNT	1 YEAR	2 YEARS	3 YEARS	4 YEARS	5 YEARS	6 YEARS
500	44.42	23.54	16.61	13.17	11.12	9.78
1000	88.85	47.07	33.21	26.33	22.24	19.55
2000	177.70	94.15	66.43	52.67	44.49	39.10
3000	266.55	141.22	99.64	79.00	66.73	58.65
4000	355.40	188.29	132.86	105.34	88.98	78.20
5000	444.24	235.37	166.07	131.67	111.22	97.75
6000	533.09	282.44	199.29	158.00	133.47	117.30
7000	621.94	329.51	232.50	184.34	155.71	136.85
8000	710.79	376.59	265.71	210.67	177.96	156.40
9000	799.64	423.66	298.93	237.00	200.20	175.95
10000	888.49	470.73	332.14	263.34	222.44	195.50
11000	977.34	517.81	365.36	289.67	244.69	215.05
12000	1066.19	564.88	398.57	316.01	266.93	234.60
13000	1155.03	611.96	431.79	342.34	289.18	254.15
14000	1243.88	659.03	465.00	368.67	311.42	273.70
15000	1332.73	706.10	498.21	395.01	333.67	293.25
16000	1421.58	753.18	531.43	421.34	355.91	312.80
17000	1510.43	800.25	564.64	447.68	378.16	332.35
18000	1599.28	847.32	597.86	474.01	400.40	351.90
19000	1688.13	894.40	631.07	500.34	422.64	371.45
20000	1776.98	941.47	664.29	526.68	444.89	391.00
21000	1865.82	988.54	697.50	553.01	467.13	410.55
22000	1954.67	1035.62	730.71	579.34	489.38	430.10
23000	2043.52	1082.69	763.93	605.68	511.62	449.65
24000	2132.37	1129.76	797.14	632.01	533.87	469.20
25000	2221.22	1176.84	830.36	658.35	556.11	488.75
30000	2665.46	1412.20	996.43	790.02	667.33	586.51
35000	3109.71	1647.57	1162.50	921.68	778.56	684.26
40000	3553.95	1882.94	1328.57	1053.35	889.78	782.01
45000	3998.20	2118.31	1494.64	1185.02	1001.00	879.76
50000	4442.44	2353.67	1660.72	1316.69	1112.22	977.51
55000	4886.68	2589.04	1826.79	1448.36	1223.44	1075.26
60000	5330.93	2824.41	1992.86	1580.03	1334.67	1173.01
65000	5775.17	3059.78	2158.93	1711.70	1445.89	1270.76
70000	6219.42	3295.14	2325.00	1843.37	1557.11	1368.51
75000	6663.66	3530.51	2491.07	1975.04	1668.33	1466.26
80000	7107.90	3765.88	2657.14	2106.71	1779.56	1564.02
85000	7552.15	4001.25	2823.22	2238.38	1890.78	1661.77
90000	7996.39	4236.61	2989.29	2370.05	2002.00	1759.52
95000	8440.63	4471.98	3155.36	2501.71	2113.22	1857.27
100000	8884.88	4707.35	3321.43	2633.38	2224.44	1955.02
200000	17769.76	9414.69	6642.86	5266.77	4448.89	3910.04
300000	26654.64	14122.04	9964.29	7900.15	6673.33	5865.06
400000	35539.52	18829.39	13285.72	10533.53	8897.78	7820.08
500000	44424.39	23536.74	16607.15	13166.92	11122.22	9775.10

12%

MONTHLY PAYMENT
Needed to repay a loan

TERM AMOUNT	7 YEARS	8 YEARS	9 YEARS	10 YEARS	11 YEARS	12 YEARS
500	8.83	8.13	7.59	7.17	6.84	6.57
1000	17.65	16.25	15.18	14.35	13.68	13.13
2000	35.31	32.51	30.37	28.69	27.36	26.27
3000	52.96	48.76	45.55	43.04	41.03	39.40
4000	70.61	65.01	60.74	57.39	54.71	52.54
5000	88.26	81.26	75.92	71.74	68.39	65.67
6000	105.92	97.52	91.11	86.08	82.07	78.81
7000	123.57	113.77	106.29	100.43	95.75	91.94
8000	141.22	130.02	121.47	114.78	109.42	105.07
9000	158.87	146.28	136.66	129.12	123.10	118.21
10000	176.53	162.53	151.84	143.47	136.78	131.34
11000	194.18	178.78	167.03	157.82	150.46	144.48
12000	211.83	195.03	182.21	172.17	164.13	157.61
13000	229.49	211.29	197.40	186.51	177.81	170.74
14000	247.14	227.54	212.58	200.86	191.49	183.88
15000	264.79	243.79	227.76	215.21	205.17	197.01
16000	282.44	260.05	242.95	229.55	218.85	210.15
17000	300.10	276.30	258.13	243.90	232.52	223.28
18000	317.75	292.55	273.32	258.25	246.20	236.42
19000	335.40	308.80	288.50	272.59	259.88	249.55
20000	353.05	325.06	303.68	286.94	273.56	262.68
21000	370.71	341.31	318.87	301.29	287.24	275.82
22000	388.36	357.56	334.05	315.64	300.91	288.95
23000	406.01	373.82	349.24	329.98	314.59	302.09
24000	423.67	390.07	364.42	344.33	328.27	315.22
25000	441.32	406.32	379.61	358.68	341.95	328.35
30000	529.58	487.59	455.53	430.41	410.34	394.03
35000	617.85	568.85	531.45	502.15	478.73	459.70
40000	706.11	650.11	607.37	573.88	547.12	525.37
45000	794.37	731.38	683.29	645.62	615.50	591.04
50000	882.64	812.64	759.21	717.35	683.89	656.71
55000	970.90	893.91	835.13	789.09	752.28	722.38
60000	1059.16	975.17	911.05	860.83	820.67	788.05
65000	1147.43	1056.43	986.98	932.56	889.06	853.72
70000	1235.69	1137.70	1062.90	1004.30	957.45	919.39
75000	1323.95	1218.96	1138.82	1076.03	1025.84	985.06
80000	1412.22	1300.23	1214.74	1147.77	1094.23	1050.74
85000	1500.48	1381.49	1290.66	1219.50	1162.62	1116.41
90000	1588.75	1462.76	1366.58	1291.24	1231.01	1182.08
95000	1677.01	1544.02	1442.50	1362.97	1299.40	1247.75
100000	1765.27	1625.28	1518.42	1434.71	1367.79	1313.42
200000	3530.55	3250.57	3036.85	2869.42	2735.58	2626.84
300000	5295.82	4875.85	4555.27	4304.13	4103.36	3940.26
400000	7061.09	6501.14	6073.69	5738.84	5471.15	5253.68
500000	8826.37	8126.42	7592.12	7173.55	6838.94	6567.10

MONTHLY PAYMENT
Needed to repay a loan

12%

TERM AMOUNT	15 YEARS	20 YEARS	25 YEARS	30 YEARS	35 YEARS	40 YEARS
500	6.00	5.51	5.27	5.14	5.08	5.04
1000	12.00	11.01	10.53	10.29	10.16	10.08
2000	24.00	22.02	21.06	20.57	20.31	20.17
3000	36.01	33.03	31.60	30.86	30.47	30.25
4000	48.01	44.04	42.13	41.14	40.62	40.34
5000	60.01	55.05	52.66	51.43	50.78	50.42
6000	72.01	66.07	63.19	61.72	60.93	60.51
7000	84.01	77.08	73.73	72.00	71.09	70.59
8000	96.01	88.09	84.26	82.29	81.24	80.68
9000	108.02	99.10	94.79	92.58	91.40	90.76
10000	120.02	110.11	105.32	102.86	101.55	100.85
11000	132.02	121.12	115.85	113.15	111.71	110.93
12000	144.02	132.13	126.39	123.43	121.87	121.02
13000	156.02	143.14	136.92	133.72	132.02	131.10
14000	168.02	154.15	147.45	144.01	142.18	141.19
15000	180.03	165.16	157.98	154.29	152.33	151.27
16000	192.03	176.17	168.52	164.58	162.49	161.36
17000	204.03	187.18	179.05	174.86	172.64	171.44
18000	216.03	198.20	189.58	185.15	182.80	181.53
19000	228.03	209.21	200.11	195.44	192.95	191.61
20000	240.03	220.22	210.64	205.72	203.11	201.70
21000	252.04	231.23	221.18	216.01	213.27	211.78
22000	264.04	242.24	231.71	226.29	223.42	221.87
23000	276.04	253.25	242.24	236.58	233.58	231.95
24000	288.04	264.26	252.77	246.87	243.73	242.04
25000	300.04	275.27	263.31	257.15	253.89	252.12
30000	360.05	330.33	315.97	308.58	304.66	302.55
35000	420.06	385.38	368.63	360.01	355.44	352.97
40000	480.07	440.43	421.29	411.45	406.22	403.40
45000	540.08	495.49	473.95	462.88	457.00	453.82
50000	600.08	550.54	526.61	514.31	507.77	504.25
55000	660.09	605.60	579.27	565.74	558.55	554.67
60000	720.10	660.65	631.93	617.17	609.33	605.10
65000	780.11	715.71	684.60	668.60	660.11	655.52
70000	840.12	770.76	737.26	720.03	710.88	705.95
75000	900.13	825.81	789.92	771.46	761.66	756.37
80000	960.13	880.87	842.58	822.89	812.44	806.80
85000	1020.14	935.92	895.24	874.32	863.22	857.22
90000	1080.15	990.98	947.90	925.75	913.99	907.65
95000	1140.16	1046.03	1000.56	977.18	964.77	958.07
100000	1200.17	1101.09	1053.22	1028.61	1015.55	1008.50
200000	2400.34	2202.17	2106.45	2057.23	2031.10	2017.00
300000	3600.50	3303.26	3159.67	3085.84	3046.65	3025.50
400000	4800.67	4404.34	4212.90	4114.45	4062.20	4034.00
500000	6000.84	5505.43	5266.12	5143.06	5077.75	5042.50

12.25%

MONTHLY PAYMENT
Needed to repay a loan

TERM AMOUNT	1 YEAR	2 YEARS	3 YEARS	4 YEARS	5 YEARS	6 YEARS
500	44.48	23.60	16.67	13.23	11.19	9.84
1000	88.97	47.19	33.33	26.46	22.37	19.68
2000	177.93	94.38	66.67	52.91	44.74	39.36
3000	266.90	141.57	100.00	79.37	67.11	59.04
4000	355.86	188.76	133.34	105.83	89.48	78.72
5000	444.83	235.95	166.67	132.28	111.85	98.40
6000	533.79	283.14	200.00	158.74	134.23	118.08
7000	622.76	330.33	233.34	185.20	156.60	137.76
8000	711.73	377.52	266.67	211.65	178.97	157.44
9000	800.69	424.71	300.00	238.11	201.34	177.12
10000	889.66	471.90	333.34	264.57	223.71	196.80
11000	978.62	519.09	366.67	291.02	246.08	216.48
12000	1067.59	566.28	400.01	317.48	268.45	236.17
13000	1156.56	613.47	433.34	343.94	290.82	255.85
14000	1245.52	660.66	466.67	370.39	313.19	275.53
15000	1334.49	707.85	500.01	396.85	335.56	295.21
16000	1423.45	755.04	533.34	423.31	357.94	314.89
17000	1512.42	802.24	566.68	449.76	380.31	334.57
18000	1601.38	849.43	600.01	476.22	402.68	354.25
19000	1690.35	896.62	633.34	502.68	425.05	373.93
20000	1779.32	943.81	666.68	529.14	447.42	393.61
21000	1868.28	991.00	700.01	555.59	469.79	413.29
22000	1957.25	1038.19	733.34	582.05	492.16	432.97
23000	2046.21	1085.38	766.68	608.51	514.53	452.65
24000	2135.18	1132.57	800.01	634.96	536.90	472.33
25000	2224.14	1179.76	833.35	661.42	559.27	492.01
30000	2668.97	1415.71	1000.02	793.70	671.13	590.41
35000	3113.80	1651.66	1166.68	925.99	782.98	688.82
40000	3558.63	1887.61	1333.35	1058.27	894.84	787.22
45000	4003.46	2123.56	1500.02	1190.55	1006.69	885.62
50000	4448.29	2359.52	1666.69	1322.84	1118.55	984.02
55000	4893.12	2595.47	1833.36	1455.12	1230.40	1082.42
60000	5337.95	2831.42	2000.03	1587.41	1342.26	1180.83
65000	5782.78	3067.37	2166.70	1719.69	1454.11	1279.23
70000	6227.60	3303.32	2333.37	1851.97	1565.97	1377.63
75000	6672.43	3539.27	2500.04	1984.26	1677.82	1476.03
80000	7117.26	3775.22	2666.71	2116.54	1789.68	1574.44
85000	7562.09	4011.18	2833.38	2248.82	1901.53	1672.84
90000	8006.92	4247.13	3000.05	2381.11	2013.39	1771.24
95000	8451.75	4483.08	3166.71	2513.39	2125.24	1869.64
100000	8896.58	4719.03	3333.38	2645.68	2237.10	1968.04
200000	17793.16	9438.06	6666.77	5291.35	4474.20	3936.09
300000	26689.73	14157.09	10000.15	7937.03	6711.30	5904.13
400000	35586.31	18876.12	13333.54	10582.70	8948.39	7872.18
500000	44482.89	23595.15	16666.92	13228.38	11185.49	9840.22

MONTHLY PAYMENT
Needed to repay a loan

12.25%

TERM AMOUNT	7 YEARS	8 YEARS	9 YEARS	10 YEARS	11 YEARS	12 YEARS
500	8.89	8.20	7.66	7.25	6.91	6.64
1000	17.79	16.39	15.33	14.49	13.83	13.29
2000	35.57	32.78	30.65	28.98	27.65	26.57
3000	53.36	49.17	45.98	43.48	41.48	39.86
4000	71.15	65.56	61.30	57.97	55.31	53.14
5000	88.93	81.95	76.63	72.46	69.13	66.43
6000	106.72	98.34	91.95	86.95	82.96	79.72
7000	124.51	114.73	107.28	101.44	96.78	93.00
8000	142.29	131.12	122.60	115.94	110.61	106.29
9000	160.08	147.51	137.93	130.43	124.44	119.57
10000	177.87	163.91	153.26	144.92	138.26	132.86
11000	195.65	180.30	168.58	159.41	152.09	146.15
12000	213.44	196.69	183.91	173.90	165.92	159.43
13000	231.23	213.08	199.23	188.40	179.74	172.72
14000	249.01	229.47	214.56	202.89	193.57	186.00
15000	266.80	245.86	229.88	217.38	207.39	199.29
16000	284.59	262.25	245.21	231.87	221.22	212.58
17000	302.37	278.64	260.53	246.36	235.05	225.86
18000	320.16	295.03	275.86	260.86	248.87	239.15
19000	337.95	311.42	291.19	275.35	262.70	252.43
20000	355.73	327.81	306.51	289.84	276.53	265.72
21000	373.52	344.20	321.84	304.33	290.35	279.01
22000	391.31	360.59	337.16	318.82	304.18	292.29
23000	409.09	376.98	352.49	333.32	318.00	305.58
24000	426.88	393.37	367.81	347.81	331.83	318.86
25000	444.67	409.76	383.14	362.30	345.66	332.15
30000	533.60	491.72	459.77	434.76	414.79	398.58
35000	622.53	573.67	536.39	507.22	483.92	465.01
40000	711.47	655.62	613.02	579.68	553.05	531.44
45000	800.40	737.57	689.65	652.14	622.18	597.87
50000	889.34	819.53	766.28	724.60	691.31	664.30
55000	978.27	901.48	842.91	797.06	760.44	730.73
60000	1067.20	983.43	919.53	869.52	829.58	797.16
65000	1156.14	1065.38	996.16	941.98	898.71	863.59
70000	1245.07	1147.34	1072.79	1014.44	967.84	930.02
75000	1334.00	1229.29	1149.42	1086.90	1036.97	996.45
80000	1422.94	1311.24	1226.04	1159.36	1106.10	1062.88
85000	1511.87	1393.19	1302.67	1231.82	1175.23	1129.31
90000	1600.80	1475.15	1379.30	1304.28	1244.36	1195.74
95000	1689.74	1557.10	1455.93	1376.74	1313.49	1262.17
100000	1778.67	1639.05	1532.56	1449.20	1382.63	1328.60
200000	3557.34	3278.10	3065.11	2898.40	2765.25	2657.19
300000	5336.01	4917.15	4597.67	4347.60	4147.88	3985.79
400000	7114.68	6556.21	6130.22	5796.79	5530.50	5314.39
500000	8893.35	8195.26	7662.78	7245.99	6913.13	6642.98

12.25%

MONTHLY PAYMENT
Needed to repay a loan

TERM AMOUNT	15 YEARS	20 YEARS	25 YEARS	30 YEARS	35 YEARS	40 YEARS
500	6.08	5.59	5.36	5.24	5.18	5.14
1000	12.16	11.19	10.72	10.48	10.35	10.29
2000	24.33	22.37	21.43	20.96	20.71	20.57
3000	36.49	33.56	32.15	31.44	31.06	30.86
4000	48.65	44.74	42.87	41.92	41.41	41.15
5000	60.81	55.93	53.59	52.39	51.77	51.43
6000	72.98	67.11	64.30	62.87	62.12	61.72
7000	85.14	78.30	75.02	73.35	72.48	72.01
8000	97.30	89.49	85.74	83.83	82.83	82.29
9000	109.47	100.67	96.46	94.31	93.18	92.58
10000	121.63	111.86	107.17	104.79	103.54	102.87
11000	133.79	123.04	117.89	115.27	113.89	113.16
12000	145.96	134.23	128.61	125.75	124.24	123.44
13000	158.12	145.41	139.33	136.23	134.60	133.73
14000	170.28	156.60	150.04	146.71	144.95	144.02
15000	182.44	167.78	160.76	157.18	155.31	154.30
16000	194.61	178.97	171.48	167.66	165.66	164.59
17000	206.77	190.16	182.20	178.14	176.01	174.88
18000	218.93	201.34	192.91	188.62	186.37	185.16
19000	231.10	212.53	203.63	199.10	196.72	195.45
20000	243.26	223.71	214.35	209.58	207.07	205.74
21000	255.42	234.90	225.07	220.06	217.43	216.02
22000	267.59	246.08	235.78	230.54	227.78	226.31
23000	279.75	257.27	246.50	241.02	238.14	236.60
24000	291.91	268.46	257.22	251.50	248.49	246.88
25000	304.07	279.64	267.94	261.97	258.84	257.17
30000	364.89	335.57	321.52	314.37	310.61	308.61
35000	425.70	391.50	375.11	366.76	362.38	360.04
40000	486.52	447.43	428.70	419.16	414.15	411.47
45000	547.33	503.35	482.28	471.55	465.92	462.91
50000	608.15	559.28	535.87	523.95	517.69	514.34
55000	668.96	615.21	589.46	576.34	569.45	565.78
60000	729.78	671.14	643.05	628.74	621.22	617.21
65000	790.59	727.07	696.63	681.13	672.99	668.65
70000	851.41	783.00	750.22	733.53	724.76	720.08
75000	912.22	838.92	803.81	785.92	776.53	771.51
80000	973.04	894.85	857.40	838.32	828.30	822.95
85000	1033.85	950.78	910.98	890.71	880.07	874.38
90000	1094.67	1006.71	964.57	943.11	931.83	925.82
95000	1155.48	1062.64	1018.16	995.50	983.60	977.25
100000	1216.30	1118.56	1071.74	1047.90	1035.37	1028.69
200000	2432.60	2237.13	2143.49	2095.79	2070.74	2057.37
300000	3648.90	3355.69	3215.23	3143.69	3106.11	3086.06
400000	4865.19	4474.26	4286.98	4191.59	4141.48	4114.74
500000	6081.49	5592.82	5358.72	5239.48	5176.86	5143.43

12.5%

MONTHLY PAYMENT
Needed to repay a loan

TERM AMOUNT	1 YEAR	2 YEARS	3 YEARS	4 YEARS	5 YEARS	6 YEARS
500	44.54	23.65	16.73	13.29	11.25	9.91
1000	89.08	47.31	33.45	26.58	22.50	19.81
2000	178.17	94.61	66.91	53.16	45.00	39.62
3000	267.25	141.92	100.36	79.74	67.49	59.43
4000	356.33	189.23	133.81	106.32	89.99	79.24
5000	445.41	236.54	167.27	132.90	112.49	99.06
6000	534.50	283.84	200.72	159.48	134.99	118.87
7000	623.58	331.15	234.18	186.06	157.49	138.68
8000	712.66	378.46	267.63	212.64	179.98	158.49
9000	801.75	425.77	301.08	239.22	202.48	178.30
10000	890.83	473.07	334.54	265.80	224.98	198.11
11000	979.91	520.38	367.99	292.38	247.48	217.92
12000	1068.99	567.69	401.44	318.96	269.98	237.73
13000	1158.08	615.00	434.90	345.54	292.47	257.55
14000	1247.16	662.30	468.35	372.12	314.97	277.36
15000	1336.24	709.61	501.80	398.70	337.47	297.17
16000	1425.33	756.92	535.26	425.28	359.97	316.98
17000	1514.41	804.22	568.71	451.86	382.46	336.79
18000	1603.49	851.53	602.17	478.44	404.96	356.60
19000	1692.57	898.84	635.62	505.02	427.46	376.41
20000	1781.66	946.15	669.07	531.60	449.96	396.22
21000	1870.74	993.45	702.53	558.18	472.46	416.03
22000	1959.82	1040.76	735.98	584.76	494.95	435.85
23000	2048.91	1088.07	769.43	611.34	517.45	455.66
24000	2137.99	1135.38	802.89	637.92	539.95	475.47
25000	2227.07	1182.68	836.34	664.50	562.45	495.28
30000	2672.49	1419.22	1003.61	797.40	674.94	594.34
35000	3117.90	1655.76	1170.88	930.30	787.43	693.39
40000	3563.31	1892.29	1338.15	1063.20	899.92	792.45
45000	4008.73	2128.83	1505.41	1196.10	1012.41	891.50
50000	4454.14	2365.37	1672.68	1329.00	1124.90	990.56
55000	4899.56	2601.90	1839.95	1461.90	1237.39	1089.61
60000	5344.97	2838.44	2007.22	1594.80	1349.88	1188.67
65000	5790.39	3074.98	2174.49	1727.70	1462.37	1287.73
70000	6235.80	3311.51	2341.75	1860.60	1574.86	1386.78
75000	6681.21	3548.05	2509.02	1993.50	1687.35	1485.84
80000	7126.63	3784.58	2676.29	2126.40	1799.84	1584.89
85000	7572.04	4021.12	2843.56	2259.30	1912.32	1683.95
90000	8017.46	4257.66	3010.83	2392.20	2024.81	1783.01
95000	8462.87	4494.19	3178.09	2525.10	2137.30	1882.06
100000	8908.29	4730.73	3345.36	2658.00	2249.79	1981.12
200000	17816.57	9461.46	6690.73	5316.00	4499.59	3962.24
300000	26724.86	14192.19	10036.09	7974.00	6749.38	5943.35
400000	35633.15	18922.92	13381.45	10632.00	8999.18	7924.47
500000	44541.43	23653.65	16726.81	13290.00	11248.97	9905.59

12.5% — MONTHLY PAYMENT
Needed to repay a loan

TERM AMOUNT	7 YEARS	8 YEARS	9 YEARS	10 YEARS	11 YEARS	12 YEARS
500	8.96	8.26	7.73	7.32	6.99	6.72
1000	17.92	16.53	15.47	14.64	13.98	13.44
2000	35.84	33.06	30.94	29.28	27.95	26.88
3000	53.76	49.59	46.40	43.91	41.93	40.32
4000	71.68	66.12	61.87	58.55	55.90	53.75
5000	89.61	82.64	77.34	73.19	69.88	67.19
6000	107.53	99.17	92.81	87.83	83.85	80.63
7000	125.45	115.70	108.27	102.46	97.83	94.07
8000	143.37	132.23	123.74	117.10	111.80	107.51
9000	161.29	148.76	139.21	131.74	125.78	120.95
10000	179.21	165.29	154.68	146.38	139.75	134.39
11000	197.13	181.82	170.14	161.01	153.73	147.82
12000	215.05	198.35	185.61	175.65	167.71	161.26
13000	232.98	214.87	201.08	190.29	181.68	174.70
14000	250.90	231.40	216.55	204.93	195.66	188.14
15000	268.82	247.93	232.01	219.56	209.63	201.58
16000	286.74	264.46	247.48	234.20	223.61	215.02
17000	304.66	280.99	262.95	248.84	237.58	228.46
18000	322.58	297.52	278.42	263.48	251.56	241.89
19000	340.50	314.05	293.88	278.11	265.53	255.33
20000	358.42	330.58	309.35	292.75	279.51	268.77
21000	376.35	347.10	324.82	307.39	293.48	282.21
22000	394.27	363.63	340.29	322.03	307.46	295.65
23000	412.19	380.16	355.75	336.67	321.43	309.09
24000	430.11	396.69	371.22	351.30	335.41	322.53
25000	448.03	413.22	386.69	365.94	349.39	335.96
30000	537.64	495.86	464.03	439.13	419.26	403.16
35000	627.24	578.51	541.36	512.32	489.14	470.35
40000	716.85	661.15	618.70	585.50	559.02	537.54
45000	806.46	743.80	696.04	658.69	628.89	604.74
50000	896.06	826.44	773.38	731.88	698.77	671.93
55000	985.67	909.08	850.72	805.07	768.65	739.12
60000	1075.27	991.73	928.05	878.26	838.53	806.31
65000	1164.88	1074.37	1005.39	951.45	908.40	873.51
70000	1254.49	1157.02	1082.73	1024.63	978.28	940.70
75000	1344.09	1239.66	1160.07	1097.82	1048.16	1007.89
80000	1433.70	1322.30	1237.40	1171.01	1118.03	1075.09
85000	1523.31	1404.95	1314.74	1244.20	1187.91	1142.28
90000	1612.91	1487.59	1392.08	1317.39	1257.79	1209.47
95000	1702.52	1570.24	1469.42	1390.57	1327.67	1276.66
100000	1792.12	1652.88	1546.76	1463.76	1397.54	1343.86
200000	3584.25	3305.76	3093.51	2927.52	2795.09	2687.71
300000	5376.37	4958.64	4640.27	4391.29	4192.63	4031.57
400000	7168.50	6611.52	6187.02	5855.05	5590.17	5375.43
500000	8960.62	8264.40	7733.78	7318.81	6987.71	6719.29

MONTHLY PAYMENT — 12.5%
Needed to repay a loan

TERM AMOUNT	15 YEARS	20 YEARS	25 YEARS	30 YEARS	35 YEARS	40 YEARS
500	6.16	5.68	5.45	5.34	5.28	5.24
1000	12.33	11.36	10.90	10.67	10.55	10.49
2000	24.65	22.72	21.81	21.35	21.11	20.98
3000	36.98	34.08	32.71	32.02	31.66	31.47
4000	49.30	45.45	43.61	42.69	42.21	41.96
5000	61.63	56.81	54.52	53.36	52.76	52.45
6000	73.95	68.17	65.42	64.04	63.32	62.94
7000	86.28	79.53	76.32	74.71	73.87	73.42
8000	98.60	90.89	87.23	85.38	84.42	83.91
9000	110.93	102.25	98.13	96.05	94.97	94.40
10000	123.25	113.61	109.04	106.73	105.53	104.89
11000	135.58	124.98	119.94	117.40	116.08	115.38
12000	147.90	136.34	130.84	128.07	126.63	125.87
13000	160.23	147.70	141.75	138.74	137.18	136.36
14000	172.55	159.06	152.65	149.42	147.74	146.85
15000	184.88	170.42	163.55	160.09	158.29	157.34
16000	197.20	181.78	174.46	170.76	168.84	167.83
17000	209.53	193.14	185.36	181.43	179.39	178.32
18000	221.85	204.51	196.26	192.11	189.95	188.81
19000	234.18	215.87	207.17	202.78	200.50	199.29
20000	246.50	227.23	218.07	213.45	211.05	209.78
21000	258.83	238.59	228.97	224.12	221.60	220.27
22000	271.15	249.95	239.88	234.80	232.16	230.76
23000	283.48	261.31	250.78	245.47	242.71	241.25
24000	295.81	272.67	261.68	256.14	253.26	251.74
25000	308.13	284.04	272.59	266.81	263.81	262.23
30000	369.76	340.84	327.11	320.18	316.58	314.68
35000	431.38	397.65	381.62	373.54	369.34	367.12
40000	493.01	454.46	436.14	426.90	422.10	419.57
45000	554.63	511.26	490.66	480.27	474.86	472.01
50000	616.26	568.07	545.18	533.63	527.63	524.46
55000	677.89	624.88	599.69	586.99	580.39	576.91
60000	739.51	681.68	654.21	640.35	633.15	629.35
65000	801.14	738.49	708.73	693.72	685.92	681.80
70000	862.77	795.30	763.25	747.08	738.68	734.24
75000	924.39	852.11	817.77	800.44	791.44	786.69
80000	986.02	908.91	872.28	853.81	844.20	839.14
85000	1047.64	965.72	926.80	907.17	896.97	891.58
90000	1109.27	1022.53	981.32	960.53	949.73	944.03
95000	1170.90	1079.33	1035.84	1013.89	1002.49	996.47
100000	1232.52	1136.14	1090.35	1067.26	1055.25	1048.92
200000	2465.04	2272.28	2180.71	2134.52	2110.51	2097.84
300000	3697.57	3408.42	3271.06	3201.77	3165.76	3146.76
400000	4930.09	4544.56	4361.42	4269.03	4221.02	4195.68
500000	6162.61	5680.70	5451.77	5336.29	5276.27	5244.60

12.75% MONTHLY PAYMENT
Needed to repay a loan

TERM AMOUNT	1 YEAR	2 YEARS	3 YEARS	4 YEARS	5 YEARS	6 YEARS
500	44.60	23.71	16.79	13.35	11.31	9.97
1000	89.20	47.42	33.57	26.70	22.63	19.94
2000	178.40	94.85	67.15	53.41	45.25	39.88
3000	267.60	142.27	100.72	80.11	67.88	59.83
4000	356.80	189.70	134.29	106.81	90.50	79.77
5000	446.00	237.12	167.87	133.52	113.13	99.71
6000	535.20	284.55	201.44	160.22	135.75	119.65
7000	624.40	331.97	235.02	186.93	158.38	139.60
8000	713.60	379.40	268.59	213.63	181.00	159.54
9000	802.80	426.82	302.16	240.33	203.63	179.48
10000	892.00	474.24	335.74	267.04	226.25	199.42
11000	981.20	521.67	369.31	293.74	248.88	219.37
12000	1070.40	569.09	402.88	320.44	271.50	239.31
13000	1159.60	616.52	436.46	347.15	294.13	259.25
14000	1248.80	663.94	470.03	373.85	316.75	279.19
15000	1338.00	711.37	503.60	400.55	339.38	299.14
16000	1427.20	758.79	537.18	427.26	362.00	319.08
17000	1516.40	806.22	570.75	453.96	384.63	339.02
18000	1605.60	853.64	604.33	480.66	407.26	358.96
19000	1694.80	901.07	637.90	507.37	429.88	378.91
20000	1784.00	948.49	671.47	534.07	452.51	398.85
21000	1873.20	995.91	705.05	560.78	475.13	418.79
22000	1962.40	1043.34	738.62	587.48	497.76	438.73
23000	2051.60	1090.76	772.19	614.18	520.38	458.68
24000	2140.80	1138.19	805.77	640.89	543.01	478.62
25000	2230.00	1185.61	839.34	667.59	565.63	498.56
30000	2676.00	1422.73	1007.21	801.11	678.76	598.27
35000	3122.00	1659.86	1175.08	934.63	791.89	697.98
40000	3568.00	1896.98	1342.95	1068.14	905.01	797.70
45000	4014.00	2134.10	1510.81	1201.66	1018.14	897.41
50000	4460.00	2371.22	1678.68	1335.18	1131.27	997.12
55000	4906.00	2608.35	1846.55	1468.70	1244.39	1096.83
60000	5352.00	2845.47	2014.42	1602.21	1357.52	1196.54
65000	5798.00	3082.59	2182.29	1735.73	1470.64	1296.26
70000	6244.00	3319.71	2350.16	1869.25	1583.77	1395.97
75000	6690.00	3556.84	2518.02	2002.77	1696.90	1495.68
80000	7136.00	3793.96	2685.89	2136.29	1810.02	1595.39
85000	7582.00	4031.08	2853.76	2269.80	1923.15	1695.10
90000	8028.00	4268.20	3021.63	2403.32	2036.28	1794.82
95000	8474.00	4505.33	3189.50	2536.84	2149.40	1894.53
100000	8920.00	4742.45	3357.37	2670.36	2262.53	1994.24
200000	17840.01	9484.90	6714.73	5340.72	4525.06	3988.48
300000	26760.01	14227.34	10072.10	8011.07	6787.59	5982.72
400000	35680.01	18969.79	13429.47	10681.43	9050.12	7976.96
500000	44600.01	23712.24	16786.83	13351.79	11312.65	9971.20

MONTHLY PAYMENT 12.75%
Needed to repay a loan

TERM AMOUNT	7 YEARS	8 YEARS	9 YEARS	10 YEARS	11 YEARS	12 YEARS
500	9.03	8.33	7.81	7.39	7.06	6.80
1000	18.06	16.67	15.61	14.78	14.13	13.59
2000	36.11	33.34	31.22	29.57	28.25	27.18
3000	54.17	50.00	46.83	44.35	42.38	40.78
4000	72.23	66.67	62.44	59.14	56.50	54.37
5000	90.28	83.34	78.05	73.92	70.63	67.96
6000	108.34	100.01	93.66	88.70	84.75	81.55
7000	126.39	116.67	109.27	103.49	98.88	95.14
8000	144.45	133.34	124.88	118.27	113.00	108.74
9000	162.51	150.01	140.49	133.06	127.13	122.33
10000	180.56	166.68	156.10	147.84	141.25	135.92
11000	198.62	183.34	171.71	162.62	155.38	149.51
12000	216.68	200.01	187.32	177.41	169.50	163.10
13000	234.73	216.68	202.93	192.19	183.63	176.70
14000	252.79	233.35	218.54	206.98	197.76	190.29
15000	270.84	250.02	234.15	221.76	211.88	203.88
16000	288.90	266.68	249.76	236.54	226.01	217.47
17000	306.96	283.35	265.37	251.33	240.13	231.06
18000	325.01	300.02	280.98	266.11	254.26	244.66
19000	343.07	316.69	296.59	280.90	268.38	258.25
20000	361.13	333.35	312.20	295.68	282.51	271.84
21000	379.18	350.02	327.81	310.46	296.63	285.43
22000	397.24	366.69	343.43	325.25	310.76	299.02
23000	415.30	383.36	359.04	340.03	324.88	312.62
24000	433.35	400.03	374.65	354.82	339.01	326.21
25000	451.41	416.69	390.26	369.60	353.13	339.80
30000	541.69	500.03	468.31	433.52	423.76	407.76
35000	631.97	583.37	546.36	517.44	494.39	475.72
40000	722.25	666.71	624.41	591.36	565.02	543.68
45000	812.53	750.05	702.46	665.28	635.64	611.64
50000	902.82	833.39	780.51	739.20	706.27	679.60
55000	993.10	916.72	858.56	813.12	776.90	747.56
60000	1083.38	1000.06	936.61	887.04	847.52	815.52
65000	1173.66	1083.40	1014.67	960.96	918.15	883.48
70000	1263.94	1166.74	1092.72	1034.88	988.78	951.44
75000	1354.22	1250.08	1170.77	1108.80	1059.40	1019.40
80000	1444.51	1333.42	1248.82	1182.72	1130.03	1087.36
85000	1534.79	1416.76	1326.87	1256.64	1200.66	1155.32
90000	1625.07	1500.10	1404.92	1330.56	1271.28	1223.28
95000	1715.35	1583.43	1482.97	1404.48	1341.91	1291.24
100000	1805.63	1666.77	1561.02	1478.40	1412.54	1359.20
200000	3611.26	3333.54	3122.05	2956.80	2825.08	2718.40
300000	5416.90	5000.32	4683.07	4435.19	4237.61	4077.60
400000	7222.53	6667.09	6244.09	5913.59	5650.15	5436.80
500000	9028.16	8333.86	7805.12	7391.99	7062.69	6796.00

12.75%

MONTHLY PAYMENT
Needed to repay a loan

TERM AMOUNT	15 YEARS	20 YEARS	25 YEARS	30 YEARS	35 YEARS	40 YEARS
500	6.24	5.77	5.55	5.43	5.38	5.35
1000	12.49	11.54	11.09	10.87	10.75	10.69
2000	24.98	23.08	22.18	21.73	21.50	21.38
3000	37.47	34.61	33.27	32.60	32.26	32.08
4000	49.95	46.15	44.36	43.47	43.01	42.77
5000	62.44	57.69	55.45	54.33	53.76	53.46
6000	74.93	69.23	66.54	65.20	64.51	64.15
7000	87.42	80.77	77.63	76.07	75.26	74.84
8000	99.91	92.30	88.72	86.94	86.02	85.54
9000	112.40	103.84	99.81	97.80	96.77	96.23
10000	124.88	115.38	110.91	108.67	107.52	106.92
11000	137.37	126.92	122.00	119.54	118.27	117.61
12000	149.86	138.46	133.09	130.40	129.02	128.30
13000	162.35	150.00	144.18	141.27	139.78	139.00
14000	174.84	161.53	155.27	152.14	150.53	149.69
15000	187.33	173.07	166.36	163.00	161.28	160.38
16000	199.81	184.61	177.45	173.87	172.03	171.07
17000	212.30	196.15	188.54	184.74	182.78	181.76
18000	224.79	207.69	199.63	195.60	193.54	192.46
19000	237.28	219.22	210.72	206.47	204.29	203.15
20000	249.77	230.76	221.81	217.34	215.04	213.84
21000	262.26	242.30	232.90	228.21	225.79	224.53
22000	274.74	253.84	243.99	239.07	236.54	235.22
23000	287.23	265.38	255.08	249.94	247.30	245.92
24000	299.72	276.91	266.17	260.81	258.05	256.61
25000	312.21	288.45	277.26	271.67	268.80	267.30
30000	374.65	346.14	332.72	326.01	322.56	320.76
35000	437.09	403.83	388.17	380.34	376.32	374.22
40000	499.53	461.52	443.62	434.68	430.08	427.68
45000	561.98	519.22	499.07	489.01	483.84	481.14
50000	624.42	576.91	554.53	543.35	537.60	534.60
55000	686.86	634.60	609.98	597.68	591.36	588.06
60000	749.30	692.29	665.43	652.02	645.12	641.52
65000	811.74	749.98	720.88	706.35	698.88	694.98
70000	874.19	807.67	776.34	760.69	752.64	748.44
75000	936.63	865.36	831.79	815.02	806.40	801.90
80000	999.07	923.05	887.24	869.35	860.16	855.36
85000	1061.51	980.74	942.69	923.69	913.92	908.82
90000	1123.95	1038.43	998.15	978.02	967.68	962.28
95000	1186.40	1096.12	1053.60	1032.36	1021.44	1015.74
100000	1248.84	1153.81	1109.05	1086.69	1075.20	1069.20
200000	2497.67	2307.62	2218.10	2173.39	2150.39	2138.39
300000	3746.51	3461.43	3327.16	3260.08	3225.59	3207.59
400000	4995.35	4615.25	4436.21	4346.77	4300.78	4276.79
500000	6244.18	5769.06	5545.26	5433.47	5375.98	5345.98

MONTHLY PAYMENT
Needed to repay a loan

13%

TERM AMOUNT	1 YEAR	2 YEARS	3 YEARS	4 YEARS	5 YEARS	6 YEARS
500	44.66	23.77	16.85	13.41	11.38	10.04
1000	89.32	47.54	33.69	26.83	22.75	20.07
2000	178.63	95.08	67.39	53.65	45.51	40.15
3000	267.95	142.63	101.08	80.48	68.26	60.22
4000	357.27	190.17	134.78	107.31	91.01	80.30
5000	446.59	237.71	168.47	134.14	113.77	100.37
6000	535.90	285.25	202.16	160.96	136.52	120.44
7000	625.22	332.79	235.86	187.79	159.27	140.52
8000	714.54	380.33	269.55	214.62	182.02	160.59
9000	803.86	427.88	303.25	241.45	204.78	180.67
10000	893.17	475.42	336.94	268.27	227.53	200.74
11000	982.49	522.96	370.63	295.10	250.28	220.82
12000	1071.81	570.50	404.33	321.93	273.04	240.89
13000	1161.12	618.04	438.02	348.76	295.79	260.96
14000	1250.44	665.59	471.72	375.58	318.54	281.04
15000	1339.76	713.13	505.41	402.41	341.30	301.11
16000	1429.08	760.67	539.10	429.24	364.05	321.19
17000	1518.39	808.21	572.80	456.07	386.80	341.26
18000	1607.71	855.75	606.49	482.89	409.56	361.33
19000	1697.03	903.29	640.19	509.72	432.31	381.41
20000	1786.35	950.84	673.88	536.55	455.06	401.48
21000	1875.66	998.38	707.57	563.38	477.81	421.56
22000	1964.98	1045.92	741.27	590.20	500.57	441.63
23000	2054.30	1093.46	774.96	617.03	523.32	461.70
24000	2143.61	1141.00	808.65	643.86	546.07	481.78
25000	2232.93	1188.55	842.35	670.69	568.83	501.85
30000	2679.52	1426.25	1010.82	804.82	682.59	602.22
35000	3126.10	1663.96	1179.29	938.96	796.36	702.59
40000	3572.69	1901.67	1347.76	1073.10	910.12	802.96
45000	4019.28	2139.38	1516.23	1207.24	1023.89	903.33
50000	4465.86	2377.09	1684.70	1341.37	1137.65	1003.71
55000	4912.45	2614.80	1853.17	1475.51	1251.42	1104.08
60000	5359.04	2852.51	2021.64	1609.65	1365.18	1204.45
65000	5805.62	3090.22	2190.11	1743.79	1478.95	1304.82
70000	6252.21	3327.93	2358.58	1877.92	1592.72	1405.19
75000	6698.80	3565.64	2527.05	2012.06	1706.48	1505.56
80000	7145.38	3803.35	2695.52	2146.20	1820.25	1605.93
85000	7591.97	4041.05	2863.99	2280.34	1934.01	1706.30
90000	8038.55	4278.76	3032.46	2414.47	2047.78	1806.67
95000	8485.14	4516.47	3200.93	2548.61	2161.54	1907.04
100000	8931.73	4754.18	3369.40	2682.75	2275.31	2007.41
200000	17863.46	9508.36	6738.79	5365.50	4550.61	4014.82
300000	26795.18	14262.55	10108.19	8048.25	6825.92	6022.23
400000	35726.91	19016.73	13477.58	10731.00	9101.23	8029.64
500000	44658.64	23770.91	16846.98	13413.75	11376.54	10037.05

13%

MONTHLY PAYMENT
Needed to repay a loan

TERM AMOUNT	7 YEARS	8 YEARS	9 YEARS	10 YEARS	11 YEARS	12 YEARS
500	9.10	8.40	7.88	7.47	7.14	6.87
1000	18.19	16.81	15.75	14.93	14.28	13.75
2000	36.38	33.61	31.51	29.86	28.55	27.49
3000	54.58	50.42	47.26	44.79	42.83	41.24
4000	72.77	67.23	63.01	59.72	57.10	54.99
5000	90.96	84.04	78.77	74.66	71.38	68.73
6000	109.15	100.84	94.52	89.59	85.66	82.48
7000	127.34	117.65	110.28	104.52	99.93	96.22
8000	145.54	134.46	126.03	119.45	114.21	109.97
9000	163.73	151.27	141.78	134.38	128.48	123.72
10000	181.92	168.07	157.54	149.31	142.76	137.46
11000	200.11	184.88	173.29	164.24	157.04	151.21
12000	218.30	201.69	189.04	179.17	171.31	164.96
13000	236.50	218.49	204.80	194.10	185.59	178.70
14000	254.69	235.30	220.55	209.04	199.87	192.45
15000	272.88	252.11	236.30	223.97	214.14	206.19
16000	291.07	268.92	252.06	238.90	228.42	219.94
17000	309.26	285.72	267.81	253.83	242.69	233.69
18000	327.46	302.53	283.56	268.76	256.97	247.43
19000	345.65	319.34	299.32	283.69	271.25	261.18
20000	363.84	336.15	315.07	298.62	285.52	274.93
21000	382.03	352.95	330.83	313.55	299.80	288.67
22000	400.22	369.76	346.58	328.48	314.07	302.42
23000	418.42	386.57	362.33	343.41	328.35	316.16
24000	436.61	403.37	378.09	358.35	342.63	329.91
25000	454.80	420.18	393.84	373.28	356.90	343.66
30000	545.76	504.22	472.61	447.93	428.28	412.39
35000	636.72	588.25	551.38	522.59	499.66	481.12
40000	727.68	672.29	630.14	597.24	571.04	549.85
45000	818.64	756.33	708.91	671.90	642.42	618.58
50000	909.60	840.36	787.68	746.55	713.81	687.31
55000	1000.56	924.40	866.45	821.21	785.19	756.04
60000	1091.52	1008.44	945.22	895.86	856.57	824.78
65000	1182.48	1092.47	1023.98	970.52	927.95	893.51
70000	1273.44	1176.51	1102.75	1045.18	999.33	962.24
75000	1364.40	1260.54	1181.52	1119.83	1070.71	1030.97
80000	1455.36	1344.58	1260.29	1194.49	1142.09	1099.70
85000	1546.32	1428.62	1339.05	1269.14	1213.47	1168.43
90000	1637.28	1512.65	1417.82	1343.80	1284.85	1237.16
95000	1728.24	1596.69	1496.59	1418.45	1356.23	1305.89
100000	1819.20	1680.73	1575.36	1493.11	1427.61	1374.63
200000	3638.39	3361.45	3150.72	2986.21	2855.22	2749.25
300000	5457.59	5042.18	4726.08	4479.32	4282.83	4123.88
400000	7276.79	6722.90	6301.44	5972.43	5710.44	5498.50
500000	9095.98	8403.63	7876.79	7465.54	7138.05	6873.13

MONTHLY PAYMENT
Needed to repay a loan

13%

TERM AMOUNT	15 YEARS	20 YEARS	25 YEARS	30 YEARS	35 YEARS	40 YEARS
500	6.33	5.86	5.64	5.53	5.48	5.45
1000	12.65	11.72	11.28	11.06	10.95	10.90
2000	25.30	23.43	22.56	22.12	21.90	21.79
3000	37.96	35.15	33.84	33.19	32.86	32.69
4000	50.61	46.86	45.11	44.25	43.81	43.58
5000	63.26	58.58	56.39	55.31	54.76	54.48
6000	75.91	70.29	67.67	66.37	65.71	65.37
7000	88.57	82.01	78.95	77.43	76.66	76.27
8000	101.22	93.73	90.23	88.50	87.62	87.16
9000	113.87	105.44	101.51	99.56	98.57	98.06
10000	126.52	117.16	112.78	110.62	109.52	108.95
11000	139.18	128.87	124.06	121.68	120.47	119.85
12000	151.83	140.59	135.34	132.74	131.42	130.74
13000	164.48	152.30	146.62	143.81	142.38	141.64
14000	177.13	164.02	157.90	154.87	153.33	152.53
15000	189.79	175.74	169.18	165.93	164.28	163.43
16000	202.44	187.45	180.45	176.99	175.23	174.32
17000	215.09	199.17	191.73	188.05	186.18	185.22
18000	227.74	210.88	203.01	199.12	197.13	196.11
19000	240.40	222.60	214.29	210.18	208.09	207.01
20000	253.05	234.32	225.57	221.24	219.04	217.90
21000	265.70	246.03	236.85	232.30	229.99	228.80
22000	278.35	257.75	248.12	243.36	240.94	239.69
23000	291.01	269.46	259.40	254.43	251.89	250.59
24000	303.66	281.18	270.68	265.49	262.85	261.48
25000	316.31	292.89	281.96	276.55	273.80	272.38
30000	379.57	351.47	338.35	331.86	328.56	326.85
35000	442.83	410.05	394.74	387.17	383.32	381.33
40000	506.10	468.63	451.13	442.48	438.08	435.81
45000	569.36	527.21	507.53	497.79	492.84	490.28
50000	632.62	585.79	563.92	553.10	547.60	544.76
55000	695.88	644.37	620.31	608.41	602.36	599.23
60000	759.15	702.95	676.70	663.72	657.12	653.71
65000	822.41	761.52	733.09	719.03	711.88	708.18
70000	885.67	820.10	789.48	774.34	766.64	762.66
75000	948.93	878.68	845.88	829.65	821.39	817.14
80000	1012.19	937.26	902.27	884.96	876.15	871.61
85000	1075.46	995.84	958.66	940.27	930.91	926.09
90000	1138.72	1054.42	1015.05	995.58	985.67	980.56
95000	1201.98	1113.00	1071.44	1050.89	1040.43	1035.04
100000	1265.24	1171.58	1127.84	1106.20	1095.19	1089.51
200000	2530.48	2343.15	2255.67	2212.40	2190.39	2179.03
300000	3795.73	3514.73	3383.51	3318.60	3285.58	3268.54
400000	5060.97	4686.30	4511.34	4424.80	4380.77	4358.06
500000	6326.21	5857.88	5639.18	5531.00	5475.97	5447.57

13.5%

MONTHLY PAYMENT

Needed to repay a loan

TERM AMOUNT	1 YEARS	2 YEARS	3 YEARS	4 YEARS	5 YEARS	6 YEARS
500	44.78	23.89	16.97	13.54	11.50	10.17
1000	89.55	47.78	33.94	27.08	23.01	20.34
2000	179.10	95.55	67.87	54.15	46.02	40.68
3000	268.66	143.33	101.81	81.23	69.03	61.02
4000	358.21	191.11	135.74	108.31	92.04	81.36
5000	447.76	238.89	169.68	135.38	115.05	101.69
6000	537.31	286.66	203.61	162.46	138.06	122.03
7000	626.86	334.44	237.55	189.53	161.07	142.37
8000	716.42	382.22	271.48	216.61	184.08	162.71
9000	805.97	429.99	305.42	243.69	207.09	183.05
10000	895.52	477.77	339.35	270.76	230.10	203.39
11000	985.07	525.55	373.29	297.84	253.11	223.73
12000	1074.62	573.32	407.22	324.92	276.12	244.07
13000	1164.18	621.10	441.16	351.99	299.13	264.41
14000	1253.73	668.88	475.09	379.07	322.14	284.75
15000	1343.28	716.66	509.03	406.14	345.15	305.08
16000	1432.83	764.43	542.96	433.22	368.16	325.42
17000	1522.38	812.21	576.90	460.30	391.17	345.76
18000	1611.94	859.99	610.84	487.37	414.18	366.10
19000	1701.49	907.76	644.77	514.45	437.19	386.44
20000	1791.04	955.54	678.71	541.53	460.20	406.78
21000	1880.59	1003.32	712.64	568.60	483.21	427.12
22000	1970.14	1051.09	746.58	595.68	506.22	447.46
23000	2059.70	1098.87	780.51	622.76	529.23	467.80
24000	2149.25	1146.65	814.45	649.83	552.24	488.14
25000	2238.80	1194.43	848.38	676.91	575.25	508.47
30000	2686.56	1433.31	1018.06	812.29	690.30	610.17
35000	3134.32	1672.20	1187.74	947.67	805.34	711.86
40000	3582.08	1911.08	1357.41	1083.05	920.39	813.56
45000	4029.84	2149.97	1527.09	1218.43	1035.44	915.25
50000	4477.60	2388.85	1696.76	1353.82	1150.49	1016.95
55000	4925.36	2627.74	1866.44	1489.20	1265.54	1118.64
60000	5373.12	2866.62	2036.12	1624.58	1380.59	1220.34
65000	5820.88	3105.51	2205.79	1759.96	1495.64	1322.03
70000	6268.64	3344.39	2375.47	1895.34	1610.69	1423.73
75000	6716.40	3583.28	2545.15	2030.72	1725.74	1525.42
80000	7164.16	3822.16	2714.82	2166.11	1840.79	1627.12
85000	7611.92	4061.05	2884.50	2301.49	1955.84	1728.81
90000	8059.68	4299.93	3054.18	2436.87	2070.89	1830.51
95000	8507.44	4538.82	3223.85	2572.25	2185.94	1932.20
100000	8955.20	4777.70	3393.53	2707.63	2300.98	2033.90
200000	17910.41	9555.40	6787.06	5415.26	4601.97	4067.79
300000	26865.61	14333.10	10180.59	8122.90	6902.95	6101.69
400000	35820.81	19110.81	13574.11	10830.53	9203.94	8135.58
500000	44776.01	23888.51	16967.64	13538.16	11504.92	10169.48

MONTHLY PAYMENT

Needed to repay a loan

13.5%

TERM AMOUNT	7 YEARS	8 YEARS	9 YEARS	10 YEARS	11 YEARS	12 YEARS
500	9.23	8.54	8.02	7.61	7.29	7.03
1000	18.46	17.09	16.04	15.23	14.58	14.06
2000	36.93	34.18	32.08	30.45	29.16	28.11
3000	55.39	51.26	48.13	45.68	43.74	42.17
4000	73.86	68.35	64.17	60.91	58.32	56.23
5000	92.32	85.44	80.21	76.14	72.90	70.29
6000	110.79	102.53	96.25	91.36	87.48	84.34
7000	129.25	119.62	112.30	106.59	102.06	98.40
8000	147.72	136.71	128.34	121.82	116.64	112.46
9000	166.18	153.79	144.38	137.05	131.22	126.51
10000	184.65	170.88	160.42	152.27	145.80	140.57
11000	203.11	187.97	176.47	167.50	160.38	154.63
12000	221.58	205.06	192.51	182.73	174.96	168.69
13000	240.04	222.15	208.55	197.96	189.54	182.74
14000	258.51	239.23	224.59	213.18	204.12	196.80
15000	276.97	256.32	240.63	228.41	218.70	210.86
16000	295.44	273.41	256.68	243.64	233.28	224.91
17000	313.90	290.50	272.72	258.87	247.86	238.97
18000	332.37	307.59	288.76	274.09	262.44	253.03
19000	350.83	324.68	304.80	289.32	277.02	267.09
20000	369.30	341.76	320.85	304.55	291.60	281.14
21000	387.76	358.85	336.89	319.78	306.18	295.20
22000	406.23	375.94	352.93	335.00	320.76	309.26
23000	424.69	393.03	368.97	350.23	335.34	323.31
24000	443.16	410.12	385.02	365.46	349.92	337.37
25000	461.62	427.20	401.06	380.69	364.50	351.43
30000	553.95	512.64	481.27	456.82	437.40	421.72
35000	646.27	598.09	561.48	532.96	510.30	492.00
40000	758.60	683.53	641.69	609.10	583.19	562.29
45000	830.92	768.97	721.90	685.23	656.09	632.57
50000	923.24	854.41	802.12	761.37	728.99	702.86
55000	1015.57	939.85	882.33	837.51	801.89	773.14
60000	1107.89	1025.29	962.54	913.65	874.79	843.43
65000	1200.22	1110.73	1042.75	989.78	947.69	913.72
70000	1292.54	1196.17	1122.96	1065.92	1020.59	984.00
75000	1384.87	1281.61	1203.17	1142.06	1093.49	1054.29
80000	1477.19	1367.05	1283.39	1218.19	1166.39	1124.57
85000	1569.52	1452.49	1363.60	1294.33	1239.29	1194.86
90000	1661.84	1537.93	1443.81	1370.47	1312.19	1265.15
95000	1754.16	1623.38	1524.02	1446.61	1385.09	1335.43
100000	1846.49	1708.82	1604.23	1522.74	1457.99	1405.72
200000	3692.98	3417.63	3208.46	3045.49	2915.97	2811.43
300000	5539.47	5126.45	4812.69	4568.23	4373.96	4217.15
400000	7385.96	6835.26	6416.93	6090.97	5831.95	5622.87
500000	9232.45	8544.08	8021.16	7613.71	7289.93	7028.59

13.5%

MONTHLY PAYMENT
Needed to repay a loan

TERM AMOUNT	15 YEARS	20 YEARS	25 YEARS	30 YEARS	35 YEARS	40 YEARS
500	6.49	6.04	5.83	5.73	5.68	5.65
1000	12.98	12.07	11.66	11.45	11.35	11.30
2000	25.97	24.15	23.31	22.91	22.71	22.61
3000	38.95	36.22	34.97	34.36	34.06	33.91
4000	51.93	48.29	46.63	45.82	45.41	45.21
5000	64.92	60.37	58.28	57.27	56.77	56.51
6000	77.90	72.44	69.94	68.72	68.12	67.82
7000	90.88	84.52	81.60	80.18	79.47	79.12
8000	103.87	96.59	93.25	91.63	90.83	90.42
9000	116.85	108.66	104.91	103.09	102.18	101.72
10000	129.83	120.74	116.56	114.54	113.53	113.03
11000	142.82	132.81	128.22	126.00	124.89	124.33
12000	155.80	144.88	139.88	137.45	136.24	135.63
13000	168.78	156.96	151.53	148.90	147.59	146.93
14000	181.76	169.03	163.19	160.36	158.95	158.24
15000	194.75	181.11	174.85	171.81	170.30	169.54
16000	207.73	193.18	186.50	183.27	181.65	180.84
17000	220.71	205.25	198.16	194.72	193.01	192.14
18000	233.70	217.33	209.82	206.17	204.36	203.45
19000	246.68	229.40	221.47	217.63	215.71	214.75
20000	259.66	241.47	233.13	229.08	227.07	226.05
21000	272.65	253.55	244.79	240.54	238.42	237.35
22000	285.63	265.62	256.44	251.99	249.77	248.66
23000	298.61	277.70	268.10	263.44	261.13	259.96
24000	311.60	289.77	279.75	274.90	272.48	271.26
25000	324.58	301.84	291.41	286.35	283.84	282.57
30000	389.50	362.21	349.69	343.62	340.60	339.08
35000	454.41	422.58	407.98	400.89	397.37	395.59
40000	519.33	482.95	466.26	458.16	454.14	452.10
45000	584.24	543.32	524.54	515.44	510.90	508.62
50000	649.16	603.69	582.82	572.71	567.67	565.13
55000	714.08	664.06	641.10	629.98	624.44	621.64
60000	778.99	724.42	699.39	687.25	681.20	678.16
65000	843.91	784.79	757.67	744.52	737.97	734.67
70000	908.82	845.16	815.95	801.79	794.74	791.18
75000	973.74	905.53	874.23	859.06	851.51	847.70
80000	1038.65	965.90	932.52	916.33	908.27	904.21
85000	1103.57	1026.27	990.80	973.60	965.04	960.72
90000	1168.49	1086.64	1049.08	1030.87	1021.81	1017.24
95000	1233.40	1147.01	1107.36	1088.14	1078.57	1073.75
100000	1298.32	1207.37	1165.64	1145.41	1135.34	1130.26
200000	2596.64	2414.75	2331.29	2290.82	2270.68	2260.52
300000	3894.96	3622.12	3496.93	3436.24	3406.02	3390.78
400000	5193.27	4829.50	4662.58	4581.65	4541.36	4521.04
500000	6491.59	6036.87	5828.22	5727.06	5676.70	5651.31

MONTHLY PAYMENT
Needed to repay a loan

14%

TERM AMOUNT	1 YEAR	2 YEARS	3 YEARS	4 YEARS	5 YEARS	6 YEARS
500	44.89	24.01	17.09	13.66	11.63	10.30
1000	89.79	48.01	34.18	27.33	23.27	20.61
2000	179.57	96.03	68.36	54.65	46.54	41.21
3000	269.36	144.04	102.53	81.98	69.80	61.82
4000	359.15	192.05	136.71	109.31	93.07	82.42
5000	448.94	240.06	170.89	136.63	116.34	103.03
6000	538.72	288.08	205.07	163.96	139.61	123.63
7000	628.51	336.09	239.24	191.29	162.88	144.24
8000	718.30	384.10	273.42	218.61	186.15	164.85
9000	808.08	432.12	307.60	245.94	209.41	185.45
10000	897.87	480.13	341.78	273.26	232.68	206.06
11000	987.66	528.14	375.95	300.59	255.95	226.66
12000	1077.45	576.15	410.13	327.92	279.22	247.27
13000	1167.23	624.17	444.31	355.24	302.49	267.87
14000	1257.02	672.18	478.49	382.57	325.76	288.48
15000	1346.81	720.19	512.66	409.90	349.02	309.09
16000	1436.59	768.21	546.84	437.22	372.29	329.69
17000	1526.38	816.22	581.02	464.55	395.56	350.30
18000	1616.17	864.23	615.20	491.88	418.83	370.90
19000	1705.96	912.24	649.37	519.20	442.10	391.51
20000	1795.74	960.26	683.55	546.53	465.37	412.11
21000	1885.53	1008.27	717.73	573.86	488.63	432.72
22000	1975.32	1056.28	751.91	601.18	511.90	453.33
23000	2065.10	1104.30	786.09	628.51	535.17	473.93
24000	2154.89	1152.31	820.26	655.84	558.44	494.54
25000	2244.68	1200.32	854.44	683.16	581.71	515.14
30000	2693.61	1440.39	1025.33	819.79	698.05	618.17
35000	3142.55	1680.45	1196.22	956.43	814.39	721.20
40000	3591.48	1920.52	1367.11	1093.06	930.73	824.23
45000	4040.42	2160.58	1537.99	1229.69	1047.07	927.26
50000	4489.36	2400.64	1708.88	1366.32	1163.41	1030.29
55000	4938.29	2640.71	1879.77	1502.96	1279.75	1133.32
60000	5387.23	2880.77	2050.66	1639.59	1396.10	1236.34
65000	5836.16	3120.84	2221.55	1776.22	1512.44	1339.37
70000	6285.10	3360.90	2392.43	1912.85	1628.78	1442.40
75000	6734.03	3600.97	2563.32	2049.49	1745.12	1545.43
80000	7182.97	3841.03	2734.21	2186.12	1861.46	1648.46
85000	7631.90	4081.10	2905.10	2322.75	1977.80	1751.49
90000	8080.84	4321.16	3075.99	2459.38	2094.14	1854.52
95000	8529.78	4561.22	3246.87	2596.02	2210.48	1957.55
100000	8978.71	4801.29	3417.76	2732.65	2326.83	2060.57
200000	17957.42	9602.58	6835.53	5465.30	4653.65	4121.15
300000	26936.14	14403.86	10253.29	8197.94	6980.48	6181.72
400000	35914.85	19205.15	13671.05	10930.59	9307.30	8242.30
500000	44893.56	24006.44	17088.81	13663.24	11634.13	10302.87

14%

MONTHLY PAYMENT
Needed to repay a loan

TERM AMOUNT	7 YEARS	8 YEARS	9 YEARS	10 YEARS	11 YEARS	12 YEARS
500	9.37	8.69	8.17	7.76	7.44	7.19
1000	18.74	17.37	16.33	15.53	14.89	14.37
2000	37.48	34.74	32.67	31.05	29.77	28.74
3000	56.22	52.11	49.00	46.58	44.66	43.11
4000	74.96	69.49	65.33	62.11	59.55	57.49
5000	93.70	86.86	81.67	77.63	74.43	71.86
6000	112.44	104.23	98.00	93.16	89.32	86.23
7000	131.18	121.60	114.34	108.69	104.21	100.60
8000	149.92	138.97	130.67	124.21	119.09	114.97
9000	168.66	156.34	147.00	139.74	133.98	129.34
10000	187.40	173.72	163.34	155.27	148.87	143.71
11000	206.14	191.09	179.67	170.79	163.75	158.08
12000	224.88	208.46	196.00	186.32	178.64	172.46
13000	243.62	225.83	212.34	201.85	193.53	186.83
14000	262.36	243.20	228.67	217.37	208.41	201.20
15000	281.10	260.57	245.01	232.90	223.30	215.57
16000	299.84	277.94	261.34	248.43	238.19	229.94
17000	318.58	295.32	277.67	263.95	253.07	244.31
18000	337.32	312.69	294.01	279.48	267.96	258.68
19000	356.06	330.06	310.34	295.01	282.85	273.05
20000	374.80	347.43	326.67	310.53	297.73	287.43
21000	393.54	364.80	343.01	326.06	312.62	301.80
22000	412.28	382.17	359.34	341.59	327.51	316.17
23000	431.02	399.54	375.68	357.11	342.39	330.54
24000	449.76	416.92	392.01	372.64	357.28	344.91
25000	468.50	434.29	408.34	388.17	372.17	359.28
30000	562.20	521.15	490.01	465.80	446.60	431.14
35000	655.90	608.00	571.68	543.43	521.03	502.99
40000	749.60	694.86	653.35	621.07	595.47	574.85
45000	843.30	781.72	735.02	698.70	669.90	646.71
50000	937.00	868.58	816.69	776.33	744.33	718.56
55000	1030.70	955.43	898.35	853.97	818.77	790.42
60000	1124.40	1042.29	980.02	931.60	893.20	862.28
65000	1218.10	1129.15	1061.69	1009.23	967.63	934.13
70000	1311.80	1216.01	1143.36	1086.87	1042.07	1005.99
75000	1405.50	1302.86	1225.03	1164.50	1116.50	1077.85
80000	1499.20	1389.72	1306.70	1242.13	1190.93	1149.70
85000	1592.90	1476.58	1388.36	1319.76	1265.37	1221.56
90000	1686.60	1563.44	1470.03	1397.40	1339.80	1293.41
95000	1780.30	1650.29	1551.70	1475.03	1414.23	1365.27
100000	1874.00	1737.15	1633.37	1552.66	1488.67	1437.13
200000	3748.00	3474.30	3266.74	3105.33	2977.33	2874.25
300000	5622.00	5211.45	4900.11	4657.99	4466.00	4311.38
400000	7496.00	6948.60	6533.48	6210.66	5954.66	5748.51
500000	9370.01	8685.75	8166.85	7763.32	7443.33	7185.64

MONTHLY PAYMENT
Needed to repay a loan

14%

TERM AMOUNT	15 YEARS	20 YEARS	25 YEARS	30 YEARS	35 YEARS	40 YEARS
500	6.66	6.22	6.02	5.92	5.88	5.86
1000	13.32	12.44	12.04	11.85	11.76	11.71
2000	26.63	24.87	24.08	23.70	23.51	23.42
3000	39.95	37.31	36.11	35.55	35.27	35.13
4000	53.27	49.74	48.15	47.39	47.03	46.85
5000	66.59	62.18	60.19	59.24	58.78	58.56
6000	79.90	74.61	72.23	71.09	70.54	70.27
7000	93.22	87.05	84.26	82.94	82.30	81.98
8000	106.54	99.48	96.30	94.79	94.05	93.69
9000	119.86	111.92	108.34	106.64	105.81	105.40
10000	133.17	124.35	120.38	118.49	117.57	117.11
11000	146.49	136.79	132.41	130.34	129.32	128.83
12000	159.81	149.22	144.45	142.18	141.08	140.54
13000	173.13	161.66	156.49	154.03	152.84	152.25
14000	186.44	174.09	168.53	165.88	164.59	163.96
15000	199.76	186.53	180.56	177.73	176.35	175.67
16000	213.08	198.96	192.60	189.58	188.11	187.38
17000	226.40	211.40	204.64	201.43	199.86	199.09
18000	239.71	223.83	216.68	213.28	211.62	210.81
19000	253.03	236.27	228.71	225.13	223.38	222.52
20000	266.35	248.70	240.75	236.97	235.13	234.23
21000	279.67	261.14	252.79	248.82	246.89	245.94
22000	292.98	273.57	264.83	260.67	258.65	257.65
23000	306.30	286.01	276.87	272.52	270.40	269.36
24000	319.62	298.44	288.90	284.37	282.16	281.07
25000	332.94	310.88	300.94	296.22	293.92	292.79
30000	399.52	373.06	361.13	355.46	352.70	351.34
35000	466.11	435.23	421.32	414.71	411.49	409.90
40000	532.70	497.41	481.50	473.95	470.27	468.46
45000	599.28	559.58	541.69	533.19	529.05	527.01
50000	665.87	621.76	601.88	592.44	587.84	585.57
55000	732.46	683.94	662.07	651.68	646.62	644.13
60000	799.04	746.11	722.26	710.92	705.40	702.68
65000	865.63	808.29	782.44	770.17	764.19	761.24
70000	932.22	870.46	842.63	829.41	822.97	819.80
75000	998.81	932.64	902.82	888.65	881.75	878.36
80000	1065.39	994.82	963.01	947.90	940.54	936.91
85000	1131.98	1056.99	1023.20	1007.14	999.32	995.47
90000	1198.57	1119.17	1083.38	1066.38	1058.11	1054.03
95000	1265.15	1181.34	1143.57	1125.63	1116.89	1112.58
100000	1331.74	1243.52	1203.76	1184.87	1175.67	1171.14
200000	2663.48	2487.04	2407.52	2369.74	2351.35	2342.28
300000	3995.22	3730.56	3611.28	3554.62	3527.02	3513.42
400000	5326.97	4974.08	4815.04	4739.49	4702.69	4684.56
500000	6658.71	6217.60	6018.81	5924.36	5878.37	5855.70

14.5% MONTHLY PAYMENT

Needed to repay a loan

TERM AMOUNT	1 YEAR	2 YEARS	3 YEARS	4 YEARS	5 YEARS	6 YEARS
500	45.01	24.12	17.21	13.79	11.76	10.44
1000	90.02	48.25	34.42	27.58	23.53	20.87
2000	180.05	96.50	68.84	55.16	47.06	41.75
3000	270.07	144.75	103.26	82.73	70.58	62.62
4000	360.09	193.00	137.68	110.31	94.11	83.50
5000	450.11	241.25	172.10	137.89	117.64	104.37
6000	540.14	289.50	206.53	165.47	141.17	125.25
7000	630.16	337.75	240.95	193.05	164.70	146.12
8000	720.18	386.00	275.37	220.62	188.23	167.00
9000	810.20	434.24	309.79	248.20	211.75	187.87
10000	900.23	482.49	344.21	275.78	235.28	208.74
11000	990.25	530.74	378.63	303.36	258.81	229.62
12000	1080.27	578.99	413.05	330.94	282.34	250.49
13000	1170.29	627.24	447.47	358.51	305.87	271.37
14000	1260.32	675.49	481.89	386.09	329.40	292.24
15000	1350.34	723.74	516.31	413.67	352.92	313.12
16000	1440.36	771.99	550.74	441.25	376.45	333.99
17000	1530.38	820.24	585.16	468.83	399.98	354.87
18000	1620.41	868.49	619.58	496.40	423.51	375.74
19000	1710.43	916.74	654.00	523.98	447.04	396.61
20000	1800.45	964.99	688.42	551.56	470.57	417.49
21000	1890.47	1013.24	722.84	579.14	494.09	438.36
22000	1980.50	1061.49	757.26	606.71	517.62	459.24
23000	2070.52	1109.74	791.68	634.29	541.15	480.11
24000	2160.54	1157.99	826.10	661.87	564.68	500.99
25000	2250.56	1206.24	860.52	689.45	588.21	521.86
30000	2700.68	1447.48	1032.63	827.34	705.85	626.23
35000	3150.79	1688.73	1204.73	965.23	823.49	730.60
40000	3600.90	1929.98	1376.84	1103.12	941.13	834.98
45000	4051.01	2171.22	1548.94	1241.01	1058.77	939.35
50000	4501.13	2412.47	1721.05	1378.90	1176.41	1043.72
55000	4951.24	2653.72	1893.15	1516.79	1294.06	1148.09
60000	5401.35	2894.97	2065.26	1654.68	1411.70	1252.47
65000	5851.47	3136.21	2237.36	1792.57	1529.34	1356.84
70000	6301.58	3377.46	2409.47	1930.46	1646.98	1461.21
75000	6751.69	3618.71	2581.57	2068.35	1764.62	1565.58
80000	7201.80	3859.95	2753.68	2206.24	1882.26	1669.95
85000	7651.92	4101.20	2925.78	2344.13	1999.90	1774.33
90000	8102.03	4342.45	3097.89	2482.02	2117.55	1878.70
95000	8552.14	4583.70	3269.99	2619.91	2235.19	1983.07
100000	9002.25	4824.94	3442.10	2757.90	2352.83	2087.44
200000	18004.51	9649.89	6884.20	5515.59	4705.66	4174.89
300000	27006.76	14474.83	10326.29	8273.39	7058.48	6262.33
400000	36009.02	19299.77	13768.39	11031.18	9411.31	8349.77
500000	45011.27	24124.71	17210.49	13788.98	11764.14	10437.21

MONTHLY PAYMENT 14.5%

Needed to repay a loan

TERM AMOUNT	7 YEARS	8 YEARS	9 YEARS	10 YEARS	11 YEARS	12 YEARS
500	9.51	8.83	8.31	7.91	7.60	7.34
1000	19.02	17.66	16.63	15.83	15.20	14.69
2000	38.03	35.31	33.26	31.66	30.39	29.38
3000	57.05	52.97	49.88	47.49	45.59	44.07
4000	76.07	70.63	66.51	63.31	60.79	58.75
5000	95.09	88.29	83.14	79.14	75.98	73.44
6000	114.10	105.94	99.77	94.97	91.18	88.13
7000	133.12	123.60	116.39	110.80	106.38	102.82
8000	152.14	141.26	133.02	126.63	121.57	117.51
9000	171.16	158.92	149.65	142.46	136.77	132.20
10000	190.17	176.57	166.28	158.29	151.96	146.88
11000	209.19	194.23	182.90	174.12	167.16	161.57
12000	228.21	211.89	199.53	189.94	182.36	176.26
13000	247.22	229.54	216.16	205.77	197.55	190.95
14000	266.24	247.20	232.79	221.60	212.75	205.64
15000	285.26	264.86	249.42	237.43	227.95	220.33
16000	304.28	282.52	266.04	253.26	243.14	235.02
17000	323.29	300.17	282.67	269.09	258.34	249.70
18000	342.31	317.83	299.30	284.92	273.54	264.39
19000	361.33	335.49	315.93	300.74	288.73	279.08
20000	380.35	353.15	332.55	316.57	303.93	293.77
21000	399.36	370.80	349.18	332.40	319.13	308.46
22000	418.38	388.46	365.81	348.23	334.32	323.15
23000	437.40	406.12	382.44	364.06	349.52	337.84
24000	456.42	423.77	399.07	379.89	364.71	352.52
25000	475.43	441.43	415.69	395.72	379.91	367.21
30000	570.52	529.72	498.83	474.86	455.89	440.65
35000	665.61	618.00	581.97	554.00	531.88	514.10
40000	760.69	706.29	665.11	633.15	607.86	587.54
45000	855.78	794.58	748.25	712.29	683.84	660.98
50000	950.87	882.86	831.39	791.43	759.82	734.42
55000	1045.95	971.15	914.52	870.58	835.80	807.87
60000	1141.04	1059.44	997.66	949.72	911.79	881.31
65000	1236.12	1147.72	1080.80	1028.86	987.77	954.75
70000	1331.21	1236.01	1163.94	1108.01	1063.75	1028.19
75000	1426.30	1324.29	1247.08	1187.15	1139.73	1101.64
80000	1521.38	1412.58	1330.22	1266.29	1215.72	1175.08
85000	1616.47	1500.87	1413.36	1345.44	1291.70	1248.52
90000	1711.56	1589.15	1496.49	1424.58	1367.68	1321.96
95000	1806.64	1677.44	1579.63	1503.72	1443.66	1395.41
100000	1901.73	1765.73	1662.77	1582.87	1519.64	1468.85
200000	3803.46	3531.45	3325.54	3165.74	3039.29	2937.70
300000	5705.19	5297.18	4988.32	4748.60	4558.93	4406.55
400000	7606.92	7062.90	6651.09	6331.47	6078.58	5875.40
500000	9508.65	8828.63	8313.86	7914.34	7598.22	7344.24

14.5%

MONTHLY PAYMENT
Needed to repay a loan

TERM AMOUNT	15 YEARS	20 YEARS	25 YEARS	30 YEARS	35 YEARS	40 YEARS
500	6.83	6.40	6.21	6.12	6.08	6.06
1000	13.66	12.80	12.42	12.25	12.16	12.12
2000	27.31	25.60	24.84	24.49	24.32	24.24
3000	40.97	38.40	37.26	36.74	36.49	36.36
4000	54.62	51.20	49.69	48.98	48.65	48.49
5000	68.28	64.00	62.11	61.23	60.81	60.61
6000	81.93	76.80	74.53	73.47	72.97	72.73
7000	95.59	89.60	86.95	85.72	85.13	84.85
8000	109.24	102.40	99.37	97.96	97.29	96.97
9000	122.90	115.20	111.79	110.21	109.46	109.09
10000	136.55	128.00	124.22	122.46	121.62	121.21
11000	150.21	140.80	136.64	134.70	133.78	133.33
12000	163.86	153.60	149.06	146.95	145.94	145.46
13000	177.52	166.40	161.48	159.19	158.10	157.58
14000	191.17	179.20	173.90	171.44	170.26	169.70
15000	204.83	192.00	186.32	183.68	182.43	181.82
16000	218.48	204.80	198.75	195.93	194.59	193.94
17000	232.14	217.60	211.17	208.17	206.75	206.06
18000	245.79	230.40	223.59	220.42	218.91	218.18
19000	259.45	243.20	236.01	232.67	231.07	230.31
20000	273.10	256.00	248.43	244.91	243.23	242.43
21000	286.76	268.80	260.85	257.16	255.40	254.55
22000	300.41	281.60	273.28	269.40	267.56	266.67
23000	314.07	294.40	285.70	281.65	279.72	278.79
24000	327.72	307.20	298.12	293.89	291.88	290.91
25000	341.38	320.00	310.54	306.14	304.04	303.03
30000	409.65	384.00	372.65	367.37	364.85	363.64
35000	477.93	448.00	434.76	428.59	425.66	424.25
40000	546.20	512.00	496.87	489.82	486.47	484.85
45000	614.48	576.00	558.97	551.05	547.28	545.46
50000	682.75	640.00	621.08	612.28	608.09	606.07
55000	751.03	704.00	683.19	673.51	668.89	666.67
60000	819.30	768.00	745.30	734.73	729.70	727.28
65000	887.58	832.00	807.41	795.96	790.51	787.89
70000	955.85	896.00	869.51	857.19	851.32	848.49
75000	1024.13	960.00	931.62	918.42	912.13	909.10
80000	1092.40	1024.00	993.73	979.64	972.94	969.71
85000	1160.68	1088.00	1055.84	1040.87	1033.74	1030.31
90000	1228.95	1152.00	1117.95	1102.10	1094.55	1090.92
95000	1297.23	1216.00	1180.05	1163.33	1155.36	1151.53
100000	1365.50	1280.00	1242.16	1224.56	1216.17	1212.13
200000	2731.00	2560.00	2484.33	2449.11	2432.34	2424.27
300000	4096.50	3839.99	3726.49	3673.67	3648.51	3636.40
400000	5462.00	5119.99	4968.65	4898.22	4864.68	4848.53
500000	6827.50	6399.99	6210.81	6122.78	6080.85	6060.66

MONTHLY PAYMENT
Needed to repay a loan

15%

TERM AMOUNT	1 YEAR	2 YEARS	3 YEARS	4 YEARS	5 YEARS	6 YEARS
500	45.13	24.24	17.33	13.92	11.89	10.57
1000	90.26	48.49	34.67	27.83	23.79	21.15
2000	180.52	96.97	69.33	55.66	47.58	42.29
3000	270.77	145.46	104.00	83.49	71.37	63.44
4000	361.03	193.95	138.66	111.32	95.16	84.58
5000	451.29	242.43	173.33	139.15	118.95	105.73
6000	541.55	290.92	207.99	166.98	142.74	126.87
7000	631.81	339.41	242.66	194.82	166.53	148.02
8000	722.07	387.89	277.32	222.65	190.32	169.16
9000	812.32	436.38	311.99	250.48	214.11	190.31
10000	902.58	484.87	346.65	278.31	237.90	211.45
11000	992.84	533.35	381.32	306.14	261.69	232.60
12000	1083.10	581.84	415.98	333.97	285.48	253.74
13000	1173.36	630.33	450.65	361.80	309.27	274.89
14000	1263.62	678.81	485.31	389.63	333.06	296.03
15000	1353.87	727.30	519.98	417.46	356.85	317.18
16000	1444.13	775.79	554.65	445.29	380.64	338.32
17000	1534.39	824.27	589.31	473.12	404.43	359.47
18000	1624.65	872.76	623.98	500.95	428.22	380.61
19000	1714.91	921.25	658.64	528.78	452.01	401.76
20000	1805.17	969.73	693.31	556.61	475.80	422.90
21000	1895.42	1018.22	727.97	585.45	499.59	444.05
22000	1985.68	1066.71	762.64	612.28	523.38	465.19
23000	2075.94	1115.19	797.30	640.11	547.17	486.34
24000	2166.20	1163.68	831.97	667.94	570.96	507.48
25000	2256.46	1212.17	866.63	695.77	594.75	528.63
30000	2707.75	1454.60	1039.96	834.92	713.70	634.35
35000	3159.04	1697.03	1213.29	974.08	832.65	740.08
40000	3610.33	1939.47	1386.61	1113.23	951.60	845.80
45000	4061.62	2181.90	1559.94	1252.38	1070.55	951.53
50000	4512.92	2424.33	1733.27	1391.54	1189.50	1057.25
55000	4964.21	2666.77	1906.59	1530.69	1308.45	1162.98
60000	5415.50	2909.20	2079.92	1669.84	1427.40	1268.70
65000	5866.79	3151.63	2253.25	1809.00	1546.35	1374.43
70000	6318.08	3394.07	2426.57	1948.15	1665.30	1480.15
75000	6769.37	3636.50	2599.90	2087.31	1784.24	1585.88
80000	7220.66	3878.93	2773.23	2226.46	1903.19	1691.60
85000	7671.96	4121.37	2946.55	2365.61	2022.14	1797.33
90000	8123.25	4363.80	3119.88	2504.77	2141.09	1903.05
95000	8574.54	4606.23	3293.21	2643.92	2260.04	2008.78
100000	9025.83	4848.66	3466.53	2783.07	2378.99	2114.50
200000	18051.66	9697.33	6933.07	5566.15	4757.99	4229.00
300000	27077.49	14545.99	10399.60	8349.22	7136.98	6343.50
400000	36103.32	19394.66	13866.13	11132.30	9515.97	8458.01
500000	45129.16	24243.32	17332.66	13915.37	11894.97	10572.51

15%

MONTHLY PAYMENT
Needed to repay a loan

TERM AMOUNT	7 YEARS	8 YEARS	9 YEARS	10 YEARS	11 YEARS	12 YEARS
500	9.65	8.97	8.46	8.07	7.75	7.50
1000	19.30	17.95	16.92	16.13	15.51	15.01
2000	38.59	35.89	33.85	32.27	31.02	30.02
3000	57.89	53.84	50.77	48.40	46.53	45.03
4000	77.19	71.78	67.70	64.53	62.04	60.04
5000	96.48	89.73	84.62	80.67	77.55	75.04
6000	115.78	107.67	101.55	96.80	93.05	90.05
7000	135.08	125.62	118.47	112.93	108.56	105.06
8000	154.37	143.56	135.39	129.07	124.07	120.07
9000	173.67	161.51	152.32	145.20	139.58	135.08
10000	192.97	179.45	169.24	161.33	155.09	150.09
11000	212.26	197.40	186.17	177.47	170.60	165.10
12000	231.56	215.34	203.09	193.60	186.11	180.11
13000	250.86	233.29	220.02	209.74	201.62	195.11
14000	270.15	251.24	236.94	225.87	217.13	210.12
15000	289.45	269.18	253.87	242.00	232.64	225.13
16000	308.75	287.13	270.79	258.14	248.15	240.14
17000	328.04	305.07	287.71	274.27	263.66	255.15
18000	347.34	323.02	304.64	290.40	279.16	270.16
19000	366.64	340.96	321.56	306.54	294.67	285.17
20000	385.94	358.91	338.49	322.67	310.18	300.18
21000	405.23	376.85	355.41	338.80	325.69	315.18
22000	424.53	394.80	372.34	354.94	341.20	330.19
23000	443.83	412.74	389.26	371.07	356.71	345.20
24000	463.12	430.69	406.18	387.20	372.22	360.21
25000	482.42	448.64	423.11	403.34	387.73	375.22
30000	578.90	538.36	507.73	484.00	465.27	450.26
35000	675.39	628.09	592.35	564.67	542.82	525.31
40000	771.87	717.82	676.97	645.34	620.37	600.35
45000	868.35	807.54	761.60	726.01	697.91	675.39
50000	964.84	897.27	846.22	806.67	775.46	750.44
55000	1061.32	987.00	930.84	887.34	853.00	825.48
60000	1157.81	1076.72	1015.46	968.01	930.55	900.53
65000	1254.29	1166.45	1100.08	1048.68	1008.09	975.57
70000	1350.77	1256.18	1184.70	1129.34	1085.64	1050.61
75000	1447.26	1345.91	1269.33	1210.01	1163.19	1125.66
80000	1543.74	1435.63	1353.95	1290.68	1240.73	1200.70
85000	1640.22	1525.36	1438.57	1371.35	1318.28	1275.75
90000	1736.71	1615.09	1523.19	1452.01	1395.82	1350.79
95000	1833.19	1704.81	1607.81	1532.68	1473.37	1425.83
100000	1929.68	1794.54	1692.43	1613.35	1550.91	1500.88
200000	3859.35	3589.08	3384.87	3226.70	3101.83	3001.75
300000	5789.03	5383.62	5077.30	4840.05	4652.74	4502.63
400000	7718.70	7178.16	6769.73	6453.40	6203.66	6003.51
500000	9648.38	8972.70	8462.17	8066.75	7754.57	7504.38

MONTHLY PAYMENT
Needed to repay a loan

15%

TERM AMOUNT	15 YEARS	20 YEARS	25 YEARS	30 YEARS	35 YEARS	40 YEARS
500	7.00	6.58	6.40	6.32	6.28	6.27
1000	14.00	13.17	12.81	12.64	12.57	12.53
2000	27.99	26.34	25.62	25.29	25.14	25.06
3000	41.99	39.50	38.42	37.93	37.70	37.60
4000	55.98	52.67	51.23	50.58	50.27	50.13
5000	69.98	65.84	64.04	63.22	62.84	62.66
6000	83.98	79.01	76.85	75.87	75.41	75.19
7000	97.97	92.18	89.66	88.51	87.98	87.73
8000	111.97	105.34	102.47	101.16	100.55	100.26
9000	125.96	118.51	115.27	113.80	113.11	112.79
10000	139.96	131.68	128.08	126.44	125.68	125.32
11000	153.95	144.85	140.89	139.09	138.25	137.85
12000	167.95	158.01	153.70	151.73	150.82	150.39
13000	181.95	171.18	166.51	164.38	163.39	162.92
14000	195.94	184.35	179.32	177.02	175.95	175.45
15000	209.94	197.52	192.12	189.67	188.52	187.98
16000	223.93	210.69	204.93	202.31	201.09	200.52
17000	237.93	223.85	217.74	214.96	213.66	213.05
18000	251.93	237.02	230.55	227.60	226.23	225.58
19000	265.92	250.19	243.36	240.24	238.79	238.11
20000	279.92	263.36	256.17	252.89	251.36	250.64
21000	293.91	276.53	268.97	265.53	263.93	263.18
22000	307.91	289.69	281.78	278.18	276.50	275.71
23000	321.91	302.86	294.59	290.82	289.07	288.24
24000	335.90	316.03	307.40	303.47	301.64	300.77
25000	349.90	329.20	320.21	316.11	314.20	313.31
30000	419.88	395.04	384.25	379.33	377.04	375.97
35000	489.86	460.88	448.29	442.56	439.88	438.63
40000	559.83	526.72	512.33	505.78	502.73	501.29
45000	629.81	592.56	576.37	569.00	565.57	563.95
50000	699.79	658.39	640.42	632.22	628.41	626.61
55000	769.77	724.23	704.46	695.44	691.25	689.27
60000	839.75	790.07	768.50	758.67	754.09	751.93
65000	909.73	855.91	832.54	821.89	816.93	814.60
70000	979.71	921.75	896.58	885.11	879.77	877.26
75000	1049.69	987.59	960.62	948.33	942.61	939.92
80000	1119.67	1053.43	1024.66	1011.56	1005.45	1002.58
85000	1189.65	1119.27	1088.71	1074.78	1068.29	1065.24
90000	1259.63	1185.11	1152.75	1138.00	1131.13	1127.90
95000	1329.61	1250.95	1216.79	1201.22	1193.97	1190.56
100000	1399.59	1316.79	1280.83	1264.44	1256.81	1253.22
200000	2799.17	2633.58	2561.66	2528.89	2513.63	2506.45
300000	4198.76	3950.37	3842.49	3793.33	3770.44	3759.67
400000	5598.35	5267.16	5123.32	5057.78	5027.25	5012.90
500000	6997.94	6583.95	6404.15	6322.22	6284.07	6266.12

15.5%

MONTHLY PAYMENT
Needed to repay a loan

TERM AMOUNT	1 YEAR	2 YEARS	3 YEARS	4 YEARS	5 YEARS	6 YEARS
500	45.25	24.36	17.46	14.04	12.03	10.71
1000	90.49	48.72	34.91	28.08	24.05	21.42
2000	180.99	97.45	69.82	56.17	48.11	42.83
3000	271.48	146.17	104.73	84.25	72.16	64.25
4000	361.98	194.90	139.64	112.34	96.21	85.67
5000	452.47	243.62	174.55	140.42	120.27	107.09
6000	542.97	292.35	209.46	168.51	144.32	128.50
7000	633.46	341.07	244.37	196.59	168.37	149.92
8000	723.96	389.80	279.29	224.68	192.43	171.34
9000	814.45	438.52	314.20	252.76	216.48	192.76
10000	904.94	487.25	349.11	280.85	240.53	214.17
11000	995.44	535.97	384.02	308.93	264.59	235.59
12000	1085.93	584.69	418.93	337.02	288.64	257.01
13000	1176.43	633.42	453.84	365.10	312.69	278.43
14000	1266.92	682.14	488.75	393.19	336.74	299.84
15000	1357.42	730.87	523.66	421.27	360.80	321.26
16000	1447.91	779.59	558.57	449.36	384.85	342.68
17000	1538.41	828.32	593.48	477.44	408.90	364.10
18000	1628.90	877.04	628.39	505.53	432.96	385.51
19000	1719.39	925.77	663.30	533.61	457.01	406.93
20000	1809.89	974.49	698.21	561.70	481.06	428.35
21000	1900.38	1023.22	733.12	589.78	505.12	449.77
22000	1990.88	1071.94	768.03	617.87	529.17	471.18
23000	2081.37	1120.66	802.95	645.95	553.22	492.60
24000	2171.87	1169.39	837.86	674.04	577.28	514.02
25000	2262.36	1218.11	872.77	702.12	601.33	535.44
30000	2714.83	1461.74	1047.32	842.55	721.60	642.52
35000	3167.30	1705.36	1221.87	982.97	841.86	749.61
40000	3619.78	1948.98	1396.43	1123.39	962.13	856.70
45000	4072.25	2192.60	1570.98	1263.82	1082.39	963.79
50000	4524.72	2436.23	1745.53	1404.24	1202.66	1070.87
55000	4977.19	2679.85	1920.09	1544.67	1322.93	1177.96
60000	5429.66	2923.47	2094.64	1685.09	1443.19	1285.05
65000	5882.14	3167.10	2269.19	1825.52	1563.46	1392.14
70000	6334.61	3410.72	2443.75	1965.94	1683.72	1499.22
75000	6787.08	3654.34	2618.30	2106.36	1803.99	1606.31
80000	7239.55	3897.96	2792.85	2246.79	1924.26	1713.40
85000	7692.03	4141.59	2967.41	2387.21	2044.52	1820.49
90000	8144.50	4385.21	3141.96	2527.64	2164.79	1927.57
95000	8596.97	4628.83	3316.51	2668.06	2285.05	2034.66
100000	9049.44	4872.45	3491.07	2808.49	2405.32	2141.75
200000	18098.88	9744.91	6982.14	5616.97	4810.64	4283.50
300000	27148.32	14617.36	10473.20	8425.46	7215.96	6425.25
400000	36197.77	19489.82	13964.27	11233.94	9621.28	8567.00
500000	45247.21	24362.27	17455.34	14042.43	12026.60	10708.74

MONTHLY PAYMENT
Needed to repay a loan

15.5%

TERM AMOUNT	7 YEARS	8 YEARS	9 YEARS	10 YEARS	11 YEARS	12 YEARS
500	9.79	9.12	8.61	8.22	7.91	7.67
1000	19.58	18.24	17.22	16.44	15.82	15.33
2000	39.16	36.47	34.45	32.88	31.65	30.66
3000	58.74	54.71	51.67	49.32	47.47	46.00
4000	78.31	72.94	68.89	65.76	63.30	61.33
5000	97.89	91.18	86.12	82.21	79.12	76.66
6000	117.47	109.42	103.34	98.65	94.95	91.99
7000	137.05	127.65	120.56	115.09	110.77	107.32
8000	156.63	145.89	137.79	131.53	126.60	122.66
9000	176.21	164.12	155.01	147.97	142.42	137.99
10000	195.78	182.36	172.24	164.41	158.25	153.32
11000	215.36	200.60	189.46	180.85	174.07	168.65
12000	234.94	218.83	206.68	197.29	189.90	183.98
13000	254.52	237.07	223.91	213.73	205.72	199.32
14000	274.10	255.30	241.13	230.17	221.55	214.65
15000	293.68	273.54	258.35	246.62	237.37	229.98
16000	313.25	291.77	275.58	263.06	253.20	245.31
17000	332.83	310.01	292.80	279.50	269.02	260.64
18000	352.41	328.25	310.02	295.94	284.85	275.98
19000	371.99	346.48	327.25	312.38	300.67	291.31
20000	391.57	364.72	344.47	328.82	316.49	306.64
21000	411.15	382.95	361.69	345.26	332.32	321.97
22000	430.72	401.19	378.92	361.70	348.14	337.30
23000	450.30	419.43	396.14	378.14	363.97	352.64
24000	469.88	437.66	413.36	394.59	379.79	367.97
25000	489.46	455.90	430.59	411.03	395.62	383.30
30000	587.35	547.08	516.71	493.23	474.74	459.96
35000	685.24	638.26	602.82	575.44	553.87	536.62
40000	783.13	729.44	688.94	657.64	632.99	613.28
45000	881.03	820.62	775.06	739.85	712.11	689.94
50000	978.92	911.80	861.18	822.05	791.24	766.60
55000	1076.81	1002.98	947.29	904.26	870.36	843.26
60000	1174.70	1094.16	1033.41	986.46	949.48	919.92
65000	1272.59	1185.33	1119.53	1068.67	1028.61	996.58
70000	1370.48	1276.51	1205.65	1150.87	1107.73	1073.24
75000	1468.38	1367.69	1291.76	1233.08	1186.86	1149.90
80000	1566.27	1458.87	1377.88	1315.28	1265.98	1226.56
85000	1664.16	1550.05	1464.00	1397.49	1345.10	1303.22
90000	1762.05	1641.23	1550.12	1479.69	1424.34	1379.88
95000	1859.94	1732.41	1636.23	1561.90	1503.35	1456.54
100000	1957.83	1823.59	1722.35	1644.11	1582.47	1533.20
200000	3915.67	3647.18	3444.71	3288.21	3164.95	3066.41
300000	5873.50	5470.78	5167.06	4932.32	4747.42	4599.61
400000	7831.34	7294.37	6889.41	6576.42	6329.90	6132.82
500000	9789.17	9117.96	8611.76	8220.53	7912.37	7666.02

15.5% MONTHLY PAYMENT

Needed to repay a loan

TERM AMOUNT	15 YEARS	20 YEARS	25 YEARS	30 YEARS	35 YEARS	40 YEARS
500	7.17	6.77	6.60	6.52	6.49	6.47
1000	14.34	13.54	13.20	13.05	12.98	12.94
2000	28.68	27.08	26.39	26.09	25.95	25.89
3000	43.02	40.62	39.59	39.14	38.93	38.83
4000	57.36	54.16	52.79	52.18	51.90	51.78
5000	71.70	67.69	65.99	65.23	64.88	64.72
6000	86.04	81.23	79.18	78.27	77.86	77.66
7000	100.38	94.77	92.38	91.32	90.83	90.61
8000	114.72	108.31	105.58	104.36	103.81	103.55
9000	129.06	121.85	118.78	117.41	116.78	116.50
10000	143.40	135.39	131.97	130.45	129.76	129.44
11000	157.74	148.93	145.17	143.50	142.73	142.38
12000	172.08	162.47	158.37	156.54	155.71	155.33
13000	186.42	176.00	171.57	169.59	168.69	168.27
14000	200.76	189.54	184.76	182.63	181.66	181.22
15000	215.10	203.08	197.96	195.68	194.64	194.16
16000	229.44	216.62	211.16	208.72	207.61	207.10
17000	243.78	230.16	224.36	221.77	220.59	220.05
18000	258.12	243.70	237.55	234.81	233.57	232.99
19000	272.46	257.24	250.75	247.86	246.54	245.94
20000	286.80	270.78	263.95	260.90	259.52	258.88
21000	301.14	284.31	277.15	273.95	272.49	271.82
22000	315.48	297.85	290.34	286.99	285.47	284.77
23000	329.82	311.39	303.54	300.04	298.44	297.71
24000	344.16	324.93	316.74	313.08	311.42	310.66
25000	358.50	338.47	329.94	326.13	324.40	323.60
30000	430.20	406.16	395.92	391.36	389.28	388.32
35000	501.90	473.86	461.91	456.58	454.15	453.04
40000	573.60	541.55	527.90	521.81	519.03	517.76
45000	645.30	609.25	593.89	587.03	583.91	582.48
50000	717.00	676.94	659.87	652.26	648.79	647.20
55000	788.69	744.63	725.86	717.48	713.67	711.92
60000	860.39	812.33	791.85	782.71	778.55	776.64
65000	932.09	880.02	857.83	847.94	843.43	841.36
70000	1003.79	947.72	923.82	913.16	908.31	906.08
75000	1075.49	1015.41	989.81	978.39	973.19	970.80
80000	1147.19	1083.10	1055.80	1043.61	1038.07	1035.52
85000	1218.89	1150.80	1121.78	1108.84	1102.95	1100.24
90000	1290.59	1218.49	1187.77	1174.07	1167.83	1164.96
95000	1362.29	1286.19	1253.76	1239.29	1232.71	1229.68
100000	1433.99	1353.88	1319.75	1304.52	1297.58	1294.40
200000	2867.98	2707.76	2639.49	2609.03	2595.17	2588.80
300000	4301.97	4061.64	3959.24	3913.55	3892.75	3883.20
400000	5735.96	5415.52	5278.98	5218.07	5190.34	5177.60
500000	7169.95	6769.40	6598.73	6522.58	6487.92	6472.00

MONTHLY PAYMENT 16%

Needed to repay a loan

TERM AMOUNT	1 YEAR	2 YEARS	3 YEARS	4 YEARS	5 YEARS	6 YEARS
500	45.37	24.48	17.58	14.17	12.16	10.85
1000	90.73	48.96	35.16	28.34	24.32	21.69
2000	181.46	97.93	70.31	56.68	48.64	43.38
3000	272.19	146.89	105.47	85.02	72.95	65.08
4000	362.92	195.85	140.63	113.36	97.27	86.77
5000	453.65	244.82	175.79	141.70	121.59	108.46
6000	544.39	293.78	210.94	170.04	145.91	130.15
7000	635.12	342.74	246.10	198.38	170.23	151.84
8000	725.85	391.70	281.26	226.72	194.54	173.53
9000	816.58	440.67	316.41	255.06	218.86	195.23
10000	907.31	489.63	351.57	283.40	243.18	216.92
11000	998.04	538.59	386.73	311.74	267.50	238.61
12000	1088.77	587.56	421.88	340.08	291.82	260.30
13000	1179.50	636.52	457.04	368.42	316.13	281.99
14000	1270.23	685.48	492.20	396.76	340.45	303.69
15000	1360.96	734.45	527.36	425.10	364.77	325.38
16000	1451.69	783.41	562.51	453.44	389.09	347.07
17000	1542.42	832.37	597.67	481.78	413.41	368.76
18000	1633.16	881.34	632.83	510.13	437.73	390.45
19000	1723.89	930.30	667.98	538.47	462.04	412.14
20000	1814.62	979.26	703.14	566.81	486.36	433.84
21000	1905.35	1028.23	738.30	595.15	510.68	455.53
22000	1996.08	1077.19	773.45	623.49	535.00	477.22
23000	2086.81	1126.15	808.61	651.83	559.32	498.91
24000	2177.54	1175.11	843.77	680.17	583.63	520.60
25000	2268.27	1224.08	878.93	708.51	607.95	542.30
30000	2721.93	1468.89	1054.71	850.21	729.54	650.76
35000	3175.58	1713.71	1230.50	991.91	851.13	759.21
40000	3629.23	1958.52	1406.28	1133.61	972.72	867.67
45000	4082.89	2203.34	1582.07	1275.31	1094.31	976.13
50000	4536.54	2448.16	1757.85	1417.01	1215.90	1084.59
55000	4990.20	2692.97	1933.64	1558.72	1337.49	1193.05
60000	5443.85	2937.79	2109.42	1700.42	1459.08	1301.51
65000	5897.51	3182.60	2285.21	1842.12	1580.67	1409.97
70000	6351.16	3427.42	2460.99	1983.82	1702.26	1518.43
75000	6804.81	3672.23	2636.78	2125.52	1823.85	1626.89
80000	7258.47	3917.05	2812.56	2267.22	1945.44	1735.35
85000	7712.12	4161.86	2988.35	2408.92	2067.03	1843.81
90000	8165.78	4406.68	3164.13	2550.63	2188.63	1952.27
95000	8619.43	4651.50	3339.92	2692.33	2310.22	2060.72
100000	9073.09	4896.31	3515.70	2834.03	2431.81	2169.18
200000	18146.17	9792.62	7031.41	5668.06	4863.61	4338.37
300000	27219.26	14688.93	10547.11	8502.08	7295.42	6507.55
400000	36292.34	19585.24	14062.81	11336.11	9727.22	8676.74
500000	45365.43	24481.56	17578.52	14170.14	12159.03	10845.92

MONTHLY PAYMENT
Needed to repay a loan

TERM AMOUNT	7 YEARS	8 YEARS	9 YEARS	10 YEARS	11 YEARS	12 YEARS
500	9.93	9.26	8.76	8.38	8.07	7.83
1000	19.86	18.53	17.53	16.75	16.14	15.66
2000	39.72	37.06	35.05	33.50	32.29	31.32
3000	59.59	55.59	52.58	50.25	48.43	46.97
4000	79.45	74.12	70.10	67.01	64.57	62.63
5000	99.31	92.64	87.63	83.76	80.72	78.29
6000	119.17	111.17	105.15	100.51	96.86	93.95
7000	139.03	129.70	122.68	117.26	113.00	109.61
8000	158.90	148.23	140.20	134.01	129.15	125.27
9000	178.76	166.76	157.73	150.76	145.29	140.92
10000	198.62	185.29	175.25	167.51	161.43	156.58
11000	218.48	203.82	192.78	184.26	177.57	172.24
12000	238.34	222.35	210.30	201.02	193.72	187.90
13000	258.21	240.87	227.83	217.77	209.86	203.56
14000	278.07	259.40	245.35	234.52	226.00	219.22
15000	297.93	277.93	262.88	251.27	242.15	234.87
16000	317.79	296.46	280.40	268.02	258.29	250.53
17000	337.66	314.99	297.93	284.77	274.43	266.19
18000	357.52	333.52	315.45	301.52	290.58	281.85
19000	377.38	352.05	332.98	318.27	306.72	297.51
20000	397.24	370.58	350.51	335.03	322.86	313.17
21000	417.10	389.10	368.03	351.78	339.01	328.82
22000	436.97	407.63	385.56	368.53	355.15	344.48
23000	456.83	426.16	403.08	385.28	371.29	360.14
24000	476.69	444.69	420.61	402.03	387.44	375.80
25000	496.55	463.22	438.13	418.78	403.58	391.46
30000	595.86	555.86	525.76	502.54	484.30	469.75
35000	695.17	648.51	613.38	586.30	565.01	548.04
40000	794.48	741.15	701.01	670.05	645.73	626.33
45000	893.79	833.80	788.64	753.81	726.44	704.62
50000	993.10	926.44	876.26	837.57	807.16	782.91
55000	1092.41	1019.08	963.89	921.32	887.87	861.20
60000	1191.72	1111.73	1051.52	1005.08	968.59	939.50
65000	1291.03	1204.37	1139.14	1088.84	1049.31	1017.79
70000	1390.34	1297.02	1226.77	1172.59	1130.02	1096.08
75000	1489.65	1389.66	1314.39	1256.35	1210.74	1174.37
80000	1588.97	1482.30	1402.02	1340.10	1291.45	1252.66
85000	1688.28	1574.95	1489.65	1423.86	1372.17	1330.95
90000	1787.59	1667.59	1577.27	1507.62	1452.89	1409.24
95000	1886.90	1760.23	1664.90	1591.37	1533.60	1487.53
100000	1986.21	1852.88	1752.53	1675.13	1614.32	1565.83
200000	3972.41	3705.76	3505.05	3350.26	3228.63	3131.65
300000	5958.62	5558.64	5257.58	5025.39	4842.95	4697.48
400000	7944.83	7411.51	7010.10	6700.52	6457.27	6263.30
500000	9931.03	9264.39	8762.63	8375.66	8071.59	7829.13

MONTHLY PAYMENT
Needed to repay a loan

TERM AMOUNT	15 YEARS	20 YEARS	25 YEARS	30 YEARS	35 YEARS	40 YEARS
500	7.34	6.96	6.79	6.72	6.69	6.68
1000	14.69	13.91	13.59	13.45	13.38	13.36
2000	29.37	27.83	27.18	26.90	26.77	26.71
3000	44.06	41.74	40.77	40.34	40.15	40.07
4000	58.75	55.65	54.36	53.79	53.54	53.43
5000	73.44	69.56	67.94	67.24	66.92	66.78
6000	88.12	83.48	81.53	80.69	80.31	80.14
7000	102.81	97.39	95.12	94.13	93.69	93.50
8000	117.50	111.30	108.71	107.58	107.08	106.85
9000	132.18	125.21	122.30	121.03	120.46	120.21
10000	146.87	139.13	135.89	134.48	133.85	133.56
11000	161.56	153.04	149.48	147.92	147.23	146.92
12000	176.24	166.95	163.07	161.37	160.62	160.28
13000	190.93	180.86	176.66	174.82	174.00	173.63
14000	205.62	194.78	190.24	188.27	187.39	186.99
15000	220.31	208.69	203.83	201.71	200.77	200.35
16000	234.99	222.60	217.42	215.16	214.16	213.70
17000	249.68	236.51	231.01	228.61	227.54	227.06
18000	264.37	250.43	244.60	242.06	240.92	240.42
19000	279.05	264.34	258.19	255.50	254.31	253.77
20000	293.74	278.25	271.78	268.95	267.69	267.13
21000	308.43	292.16	285.37	282.40	281.08	280.49
22000	323.11	306.08	298.96	295.85	294.46	293.84
23000	337.80	319.99	312.54	309.29	307.85	307.20
24000	352.49	333.90	326.13	322.74	321.23	320.56
25000	367.18	347.81	339.72	336.19	334.62	333.91
30000	440.61	417.38	407.67	403.43	401.54	400.69
35000	514.05	486.94	475.61	470.66	468.46	467.48
40000	587.48	556.50	543.56	537.90	535.39	534.26
45000	660.92	626.07	611.50	605.14	602.31	601.04
50000	734.35	695.63	679.44	672.38	669.23	667.82
55000	807.79	765.19	747.39	739.62	736.16	734.61
60000	881.22	834.75	815.33	806.85	803.08	801.39
65000	954.66	904.32	883.28	874.09	870.01	868.17
70000	1028.09	973.88	951.22	941.33	936.93	934.95
75000	1101.53	1043.44	1019.17	1008.57	1003.85	1001.74
80000	1174.96	1113.00	1087.11	1075.81	1070.78	1068.52
85000	1248.40	1182.57	1155.06	1143.04	1137.70	1135.30
90000	1321.83	1252.13	1223.00	1210.28	1204.62	1202.08
95000	1395.27	1321.69	1290.94	1277.52	1271.55	1268.87
100000	1468.70	1391.26	1358.89	1344.76	1338.47	1335.65
200000	2937.40	2782.51	2717.78	2689.51	2676.94	2671.30
300000	4406.10	4173.77	4076.67	4034.27	4015.41	4006.95
400000	5874.80	5565.02	5435.56	5379.03	5353.88	5342.59
500000	7343.50	6956.28	6794.44	6723.78	6692.35	6678.24

16.5% MONTHLY PAYMENT
Needed to repay a loan

TERM AMOUNT	1 YEAR	2 YEARS	3 YEARS	4 YEARS	5 YEARS	6 YEARS
500	45.48	24.60	17.70	14.30	12.29	10.98
1000	90.97	49.20	35.40	28.60	24.58	21.97
2000	181.94	98.40	70.81	57.19	49.17	43.94
3000	272.90	147.61	106.21	85.79	73.75	65.90
4000	363.87	196.81	141.62	114.39	98.34	87.87
5000	454.84	246.01	177.02	142.99	122.92	109.84
6000	545.81	295.21	212.43	171.58	147.51	131.81
7000	636.77	344.42	247.83	200.18	172.09	153.78
8000	727.74	393.62	283.24	228.78	196.68	175.74
9000	818.71	442.82	318.64	257.37	221.26	197.71
10000	909.68	492.02	354.04	285.97	245.85	219.68
11000	1000.64	541.23	389.45	314.57	270.43	241.65
12000	1091.61	590.43	424.85	343.16	295.01	263.62
13000	1182.58	639.63	460.26	371.76	319.60	285.58
14000	1273.55	688.83	495.66	400.36	344.18	307.55
15000	1364.51	738.04	531.07	428.96	368.77	329.52
16000	1455.48	787.24	566.47	457.55	393.35	351.49
17000	1546.45	836.44	601.87	486.15	417.94	373.46
18000	1637.42	885.64	637.28	514.75	442.52	395.43
19000	1728.39	934.84	672.68	543.34	467.11	417.39
20000	1819.35	984.05	708.09	571.94	491.69	439.36
21000	1910.32	1033.25	743.49	600.54	516.27	461.33
22000	2001.29	1082.45	778.90	629.13	540.86	483.30
23000	2092.26	1131.65	814.30	657.73	565.44	505.27
24000	2183.22	1180.86	849.71	686.33	590.03	527.23
25000	2274.19	1230.06	885.11	714.93	614.61	549.20
30000	2729.03	1476.07	1062.13	857.91	737.54	659.04
35000	3183.87	1722.08	1239.15	1000.90	860.46	768.88
40000	3638.71	1968.09	1416.18	1143.88	983.38	878.72
45000	4093.54	2214.11	1593.20	1286.87	1106.30	988.56
50000	4548.38	2460.12	1770.22	1429.85	1229.23	1098.40
55000	5003.22	2706.13	1947.24	1572.84	1352.15	1208.24
60000	5458.06	2952.14	2124.26	1715.82	1475.07	1318.08
65000	5912.90	3198.15	2301.28	1858.81	1597.99	1427.92
70000	6367.73	3444.16	2478.31	2001.79	1720.92	1537.76
75000	6822.57	3690.18	2655.33	2144.78	1843.84	1647.60
80000	7277.41	3936.19	2832.35	2287.76	1966.76	1757.44
85000	7732.25	4182.20	3009.37	2430.75	2089.68	1867.28
90000	8187.09	4428.21	3186.39	2573.73	2212.61	1977.13
95000	8641.93	4674.22	3363.42	2716.72	2335.53	2086.97
100000	9096.76	4920.24	3540.44	2859.70	2458.45	2196.81
200000	18193.53	9840.47	7080.88	5719.40	4916.90	4393.61
300000	27290.29	14760.71	10621.31	8579.10	7375.36	6590.42
400000	36387.05	19680.94	14161.75	11438.80	9833.81	8787.22
500000	45483.82	24601.18	17702.19	14298.50	12292.26	10984.03

MONTHLY PAYMENT 16.5%
Needed to repay a loan

TERM AMOUNT	7 YEARS	8 YEARS	9 YEARS	10 YEARS	11 YEARS	12 YEARS
500	10.07	9.41	8.91	8.53	8.23	7.99
1000	20.15	18.82	17.83	17.06	16.46	15.99
2000	40.30	37.65	35.66	34.13	32.93	31.97
3000	60.44	56.47	53.49	51.19	49.39	47.96
4000	80.59	75.30	71.32	68.26	65.86	63.95
5000	100.74	94.12	89.15	85.32	82.32	79.94
6000	120.89	112.94	106.98	102.39	98.79	95.92
7000	141.04	131.77	124.81	119.45	115.25	111.91
8000	161.18	150.59	142.64	136.51	131.72	127.90
9000	181.33	169.42	160.47	153.58	148.18	143.89
10000	201.48	188.24	178.29	170.64	164.64	159.87
11000	221.63	207.06	196.12	187.71	181.11	175.86
12000	241.77	225.89	213.95	204.77	197.57	191.85
13000	261.92	244.71	231.78	221.83	214.04	207.84
14000	282.07	263.54	249.61	238.90	230.50	223.82
15000	302.22	282.36	267.44	255.96	246.97	239.81
16000	322.37	301.18	285.27	273.03	263.43	255.80
17000	342.51	320.01	303.10	290.09	279.89	271.78
18000	362.66	338.83	320.93	307.16	296.36	287.77
19000	382.81	357.66	338.76	324.22	312.82	303.76
20000	402.96	376.48	356.59	341.28	329.29	319.75
21000	423.11	395.30	374.42	358.35	345.75	335.73
22000	443.25	414.13	392.25	375.41	362.22	351.72
23000	463.40	432.95	410.08	392.48	378.68	367.71
24000	483.55	451.78	427.91	409.54	395.15	383.70
25000	503.70	470.60	445.74	426.61	411.61	399.68
30000	604.44	564.72	534.88	511.93	493.93	479.62
35000	705.18	658.84	624.03	597.25	576.25	559.56
40000	805.92	752.96	713.18	682.57	658.58	639.49
45000	906.66	847.08	802.33	767.89	740.90	719.43
50000	1007.39	941.20	891.47	853.21	823.22	799.37
55000	1108.13	1035.32	980.62	938.53	905.54	879.30
60000	1208.87	1129.44	1069.77	1023.85	987.86	959.24
65000	1309.61	1223.56	1158.92	1109.17	1070.18	1039.18
70000	1410.35	1317.68	1248.06	1194.50	1152.51	1119.11
75000	1511.09	1411.80	1337.21	1279.82	1234.83	1199.05
80000	1611.83	1505.92	1426.36	1365.14	1317.15	1278.99
85000	1712.57	1600.04	1515.51	1450.46	1399.47	1358.92
90000	1813.31	1694.16	1604.65	1535.78	1481.79	1438.86
95000	1914.05	1788.28	1693.80	1621.10	1564.12	1518.80
100000	2014.79	1882.40	1782.95	1706.42	1646.44	1598.73
200000	4029.58	3764.79	3565.90	3412.85	3292.88	3197.47
300000	6044.37	5647.19	5348.84	5119.27	4939.31	4796.20
400000	8059.16	7529.59	7131.79	6825.69	6585.75	6394.93
500000	10073.94	9411.99	8914.74	8532.11	8232.19	7993.67

16.5%

MONTHLY PAYMENT
Needed to repay a loan

TERM AMOUNT	15 YEARS	20 YEARS	25 YEARS	30 YEARS	35 YEARS	40 YEARS
500	7.52	7.14	6.99	6.93	6.90	6.88
1000	15.04	14.29	13.98	13.85	13.79	13.77
2000	30.07	28.58	27.96	27.70	27.59	27.54
3000	45.11	42.87	41.95	41.55	41.38	41.31
4000	60.15	57.16	55.93	55.41	55.18	55.08
5000	75.19	71.45	69.91	69.26	68.97	68.85
6000	90.22	85.73	83.89	83.11	82.77	82.62
7000	105.26	100.02	97.88	96.96	96.56	96.39
8000	120.30	114.31	111.86	110.81	110.36	110.16
9000	135.33	128.60	125.84	124.66	124.15	123.93
10000	150.37	142.89	139.82	138.51	137.95	137.70
11000	165.41	157.18	153.81	152.37	151.74	151.47
12000	180.45	171.47	167.79	166.22	165.53	165.24
13000	195.48	185.76	181.77	180.07	179.33	179.00
14000	210.52	200.05	195.75	193.92	193.12	192.77
15000	225.56	214.34	209.74	207.77	206.92	206.54
16000	240.59	228.62	223.72	221.62	220.71	220.31
17000	255.63	242.91	237.70	235.48	234.51	234.08
18000	270.67	257.20	251.68	249.33	248.30	247.85
19000	285.70	271.49	265.67	263.18	262.10	261.62
20000	300.74	285.78	279.65	277.03	275.89	275.39
21000	315.78	300.07	293.63	290.88	289.69	289.16
22000	330.82	314.36	307.61	304.73	303.48	302.93
23000	345.85	328.65	321.60	318.58	317.27	316.70
24000	360.89	342.94	335.58	332.44	331.07	330.47
25000	375.93	357.23	349.56	346.29	344.86	344.24
30000	451.11	428.67	419.47	415.54	413.84	413.09
35000	526.30	500.12	489.39	484.80	482.81	481.94
40000	601.48	571.56	559.30	554.06	551.78	550.78
45000	676.67	643.01	629.21	623.32	620.75	619.63
50000	751.85	714.45	699.12	692.57	689.73	688.48
55000	827.04	785.90	769.03	761.83	758.70	757.33
60000	902.23	857.34	838.95	831.09	827.67	826.18
65000	977.41	928.79	908.86	900.35	896.65	895.02
70000	1052.60	1000.23	978.77	969.60	965.62	963.87
75000	1127.78	1071.68	1048.68	1038.86	1034.59	1032.72
80000	1202.97	1143.12	1118.60	1108.12	1103.56	1101.57
85000	1278.15	1214.57	1188.51	1177.38	1172.54	1170.42
90000	1353.34	1286.01	1258.42	1246.63	1241.51	1239.26
95000	1428.52	1357.46	1328.33	1315.89	1310.48	1308.11
100000	1503.71	1428.90	1398.24	1385.15	1379.45	1376.96
200000	3007.42	2857.80	2796.49	2770.30	2758.91	2753.92
300000	4511.13	4286.70	4194.73	4155.44	4138.36	4130.88
400000	6014.83	5715.60	5592.98	5540.59	5517.82	5507.84
500000	7518.54	7144.50	6991.22	6925.74	6897.27	6884.80

17%

MONTHLY PAYMENT
Needed to repay a loan

TERM AMOUNT	1 YEAR	2 YEARS	3 YEARS	4 YEARS	5 YEARS	6 YEARS
500	45.60	24.72	17.83	14.43	12.43	11.12
1000	91.20	49.44	35.65	28.86	24.85	22.25
2000	182.41	98.88	71.31	57.71	49.71	44.49
3000	273.61	148.33	106.96	86.57	74.56	66.74
4000	364.82	197.77	142.61	115.42	99.41	88.98
5000	456.02	247.21	178.26	144.28	124.26	111.23
6000	547.23	296.65	213.92	173.13	149.12	133.48
7000	638.43	346.10	249.57	201.99	173.97	155.72
8000	729.64	395.54	285.22	230.84	198.82	177.97
9000	820.84	444.98	320.87	259.70	223.67	200.22
10000	912.05	494.42	356.53	288.55	248.53	222.46
11000	1003.25	543.86	392.18	317.41	273.38	244.71
12000	1094.46	593.31	427.83	346.26	298.23	266.95
13000	1185.66	642.75	463.49	375.12	323.08	289.20
14000	1276.87	692.19	499.14	403.97	347.94	311.45
15000	1368.07	741.63	534.79	432.83	372.79	333.69
16000	1459.28	791.08	570.44	461.68	397.64	355.94
17000	1550.48	840.52	606.10	490.54	422.49	378.18
18000	1641.69	889.96	641.75	519.39	447.35	400.43
19000	1732.89	939.40	677.40	548.25	472.20	422.68
20000	1824.10	988.85	713.05	577.10	497.05	444.92
21000	1915.30	1038.29	748.71	605.96	521.90	467.17
22000	2006.50	1087.73	784.36	634.81	546.76	489.41
23000	2097.71	1137.17	820.01	663.67	571.61	511.66
24000	2188.91	1186.61	855.67	692.52	596.46	533.91
25000	2280.12	1236.06	891.32	721.38	621.31	556.15
30000	2736.14	1483.27	1069.58	865.65	745.58	667.38
35000	3192.17	1730.48	1247.85	1009.93	869.84	778.61
40000	3648.19	1977.69	1426.11	1154.20	994.10	889.85
45000	4104.21	2224.90	1604.37	1298.48	1118.37	1001.08
50000	4560.24	2472.11	1782.64	1442.75	1242.63	1112.31
55000	5016.26	2719.32	1960.90	1587.03	1366.89	1223.54
60000	5472.29	2966.54	2139.16	1731.30	1491.15	1334.77
65000	5928.31	3213.75	2317.43	1875.58	1615.42	1446.00
70000	6384.33	3460.96	2495.69	2019.85	1739.68	1557.23
75000	6840.36	3708.17	2673.95	2164.13	1863.94	1668.46
80000	7296.38	3955.38	2852.22	2308.40	1988.21	1779.69
85000	7752.40	4202.59	3030.48	2452.68	2112.47	1890.92
90000	8208.43	4449.80	3208.75	2596.95	2236.73	2002.15
95000	8664.45	4697.02	3387.01	2741.23	2360.99	2113.38
100000	9120.48	4944.23	3565.27	2885.50	2485.26	2224.61
200000	18240.95	9888.45	7130.55	5771.01	4970.52	4449.23
300000	27361.43	14832.68	10695.82	8656.51	7455.77	6673.84
400000	36481.90	19776.91	14261.09	11542.02	9941.03	8898.45
500000	45602.38	24721.13	17826.36	14427.52	12426.29	11123.07

17% MONTHLY PAYMENT
Needed to repay a loan

TERM AMOUNT	7 YEARS	8 YEARS	9 YEARS	10 YEARS	11 YEARS	12 YEARS
500	10.22	9.56	9.07	8.69	8.39	8.16
1000	20.44	19.12	18.14	17.38	16.79	16.32
2000	40.87	38.24	36.27	34.76	33.58	32.64
3000	61.31	57.36	54.41	52.14	50.36	48.96
4000	81.74	76.49	72.54	69.52	67.15	65.28
5000	102.18	95.61	90.68	86.90	83.94	81.60
6000	122.61	114.73	108.82	104.28	100.73	97.92
7000	143.05	133.85	126.95	121.66	117.52	114.23
8000	163.49	152.97	145.09	139.04	134.31	130.55
9000	183.92	172.09	163.23	156.42	151.09	146.87
10000	204.36	191.21	181.36	173.80	167.88	163.19
11000	224.79	210.34	199.50	191.18	184.67	179.51
12000	245.23	229.46	217.63	208.56	201.46	195.83
13000	265.67	248.58	235.77	225.94	218.25	212.15
14000	286.10	267.70	253.91	243.32	235.04	228.47
15000	306.54	286.82	272.04	260.70	251.82	244.79
16000	326.97	305.94	290.18	278.08	268.61	261.11
17000	347.41	325.06	308.32	295.46	285.40	277.43
18000	367.84	344.19	326.45	312.84	302.19	293.75
19000	388.28	363.31	344.59	330.22	318.98	310.07
20000	408.72	382.43	362.72	347.60	335.77	326.38
21000	429.15	401.55	380.86	364.98	352.55	342.70
22000	449.59	420.67	399.00	382.35	369.34	359.02
23000	470.02	439.79	417.13	399.73	386.13	375.34
24000	490.46	458.91	435.27	417.11	402.92	391.66
25000	510.90	478.04	453.40	434.49	419.71	407.98
30000	613.07	573.64	544.09	521.39	503.65	489.58
35000	715.25	669.25	634.77	608.29	587.59	571.17
40000	817.43	764.86	725.45	695.19	671.53	652.77
45000	919.61	860.47	816.13	782.09	755.47	734.37
50000	1021.79	956.07	906.81	868.99	839.42	815.96
55000	1123.97	1051.68	997.49	955.89	923.36	897.56
60000	1226.15	1147.29	1088.17	1042.79	1007.30	979.15
65000	1328.33	1242.89	1178.85	1129.68	1091.24	1060.75
70000	1430.51	1338.50	1269.53	1216.58	1175.18	1142.35
75000	1532.69	1434.11	1360.21	1303.48	1259.12	1223.94
80000	1634.86	1529.72	1450.90	1390.38	1343.07	1305.54
85000	1737.04	1625.32	1541.58	1477.28	1427.01	1387.13
90000	1839.22	1720.93	1632.26	1564.18	1510.95	1468.73
95000	1941.40	1816.54	1722.94	1651.08	1594.89	1550.33
100000	2043.58	1912.15	1813.62	1737.98	1678.83	1631.92
200000	4087.16	3824.29	2627.24	3475.95	3357.66	3263.85
300000	6130.74	5736.44	5440.86	5213.93	5036.50	4895.77
400000	8174.32	7648.58	7254.48	6951.91	6715.33	6527.69
500000	10217.90	9560.73	9068.09	8689.88	8394.16	8159.61

MONTHLY PAYMENT 17%
Needed to repay a loan

TERM AMOUNT	15 YEARS	20 YEARS	25 YEARS	30 YEARS	35 YEARS	40 YEARS
500	7.70	7.33	7.19	7.13	7.10	7.09
1000	15.39	14.67	14.38	14.26	14.21	14.18
2000	30.78	29.34	28.76	28.51	28.41	28.37
3000	46.17	44.00	43.13	42.77	42.62	42.55
4000	61.56	58.67	57.51	57.03	56.82	56.73
5000	76.95	73.34	71.89	71.28	71.03	70.92
6000	92.34	88.01	86.27	85.54	85.23	85.10
7000	107.73	102.68	100.65	99.80	99.44	99.28
8000	123.12	117.34	115.02	114.05	113.64	113.47
9000	138.51	132.01	129.40	128.31	127.85	127.65
10000	153.90	146.68	143.78	142.57	142.05	141.83
11000	169.29	161.35	158.16	156.82	156.26	156.02
12000	184.68	176.02	172.54	171.08	170.46	170.20
13000	200.07	190.68	186.91	185.34	184.67	184.38
14000	215.46	205.35	201.29	199.59	198.87	198.57
15000	230.85	220.02	215.67	213.85	213.08	212.75
16000	246.24	234.69	230.05	228.11	227.28	226.93
17000	261.63	249.36	244.43	242.36	241.49	241.12
18000	277.02	264.02	258.80	256.62	255.69	255.30
19000	292.41	278.69	273.18	270.88	269.90	269.48
20000	307.80	293.36	287.56	285.14	284.11	283.66
21000	323.19	308.03	301.94	299.39	298.31	297.85
22000	338.58	322.70	316.32	313.65	312.52	312.03
23000	353.97	337.36	330.69	327.91	326.72	326.21
24000	369.36	352.03	345.07	342.16	340.93	340.40
25000	384.75	366.70	359.45	356.42	355.13	354.58
30000	461.70	440.04	431.34	427.70	426.16	425.50
35000	538.65	513.38	503.23	498.99	497.18	496.41
40000	615.60	586.72	575.12	570.27	568.21	567.33
45000	692.55	660.06	647.01	641.55	639.24	638.25
50000	769.50	733.40	718.90	712.84	710.26	709.16
55000	846.45	806.74	790.79	784.12	781.29	780.08
60000	923.40	880.08	862.68	855.41	852.32	850.99
65000	1000.35	953.42	934.57	926.69	923.34	921.91
70000	1077.30	1026.76	1006.46	997.97	994.37	992.83
75000	1154.25	1100.10	1078.35	1069.26	1065.39	1063.74
80000	1231.20	1173.44	1150.24	1140.54	1136.42	1134.66
85000	1308.15	1246.78	1222.13	1211.82	1207.45	1205.58
90000	1385.10	1320.12	1294.02	1283.11	1278.47	1276.49
95000	1462.05	1393.46	1365.91	1354.39	1349.50	1347.41
100000	1539.00	1466.80	1437.80	1425.68	1420.53	1418.32
200000	3078.01	2933.60	2875.59	2851.35	2841.05	2836.65
300000	4617.01	4400.40	4313.39	4277.03	4261.58	4254.97
400000	6156.02	5867.20	5751.19	5702.70	5682.10	5673.29
500000	7695.02	7334.00	7188.98	7128.38	7102.63	7091.62

17.5%

MONTHLY PAYMENT
Needed to repay a loan

TERM AMOUNT	1 YEAR	2 YEARS	3 YEARS	4 YEARS	5 YEARS	6 YEARS
500	45.72	24.84	17.95	14.56	12.56	11.26
1000	91.44	49.68	35.90	29.11	25.12	22.53
2000	182.88	99.37	71.80	58.23	50.24	45.05
3000	274.33	149.05	107.71	87.34	75.37	67.58
4000	365.77	198.73	143.61	116.46	100.49	90.10
5000	457.21	248.41	179.51	145.57	125.61	112.63
6000	548.65	298.10	215.41	174.69	150.73	135.16
7000	640.10	347.78	251.31	203.80	175.86	157.68
8000	731.54	397.46	287.22	232.91	200.98	180.21
9000	822.98	447.15	323.12	262.03	226.10	202.73
10000	914.42	496.83	359.02	291.14	251.22	225.26
11000	1005.86	546.51	394.92	320.26	276.34	247.79
12000	1097.31	596.19	430.82	349.37	301.47	270.31
13000	1188.75	645.88	466.73	378.49	326.59	292.84
14000	1280.19	695.56	502.63	407.60	351.71	315.36
15000	1371.63	745.24	538.53	436.72	376.83	337.89
16000	1463.08	794.93	574.43	465.83	401.96	360.42
17000	1554.52	844.61	610.34	494.94	427.08	382.94
18000	1645.96	894.29	646.24	524.06	452.20	405.47
19000	1737.40	943.97	682.14	553.17	477.32	427.99
20000	1828.84	993.66	718.04	582.29	502.44	450.52
21000	1920.29	1043.34	753.94	611.40	527.57	473.05
22000	2011.73	1093.02	789.85	640.52	552.69	495.57
23000	2103.17	1142.71	825.75	669.63	577.81	518.10
24000	2194.61	1192.39	861.65	698.74	602.93	540.63
25000	2286.06	1242.07	897.55	727.86	628.06	563.15
30000	2743.27	1490.49	1077.06	873.43	753.67	675.78
35000	3200.48	1738.90	1256.57	1019.00	879.28	788.41
40000	3657.69	1987.31	1436.08	1164.57	1004.89	901.04
45000	4114.90	2235.73	1615.59	1310.15	1130.50	1013.67
50000	4572.11	2484.14	1795.10	1455.72	1256.11	1126.30
55000	5029.32	2732.56	1974.61	1601.29	1381.72	1238.93
60000	5486.53	2980.97	2154.12	1746.86	1507.33	1351.56
65000	5943.74	3229.39	2333.63	1892.43	1632.94	1464.19
70000	6400.95	3477.80	2513.14	2038.01	1758.55	1576.82
75000	6858.17	3726.21	2692.65	2183.58	1884.17	1689.45
80000	7315.38	3974.63	2872.17	2329.15	2009.78	1802.08
85000	7772.59	4223.04	3051.68	2474.72	2135.39	1914.71
90000	8229.80	4471.46	3231.19	2620.29	2261.00	2027.34
95000	8687.01	4719.87	3410.70	2765.87	2386.61	2139.97
100000	9144.22	4968.28	3590.21	2911.44	2512.22	2252.60
200000	18288.44	9936.57	7180.41	5822.87	5024.44	4505.21
300000	27432.66	14904.85	10770.62	8734.31	7536.66	6757.81
400000	36576.88	19873.14	14360.83	11645.75	10048.89	9010.42
500000	45721.10	24841.42	17951.03	14557.19	12561.11	11263.02

MONTHLY PAYMENT
Needed to repay a loan

17.5%

TERM AMOUNT	7 YEARS	8 YEARS	9 YEARS	10 YEARS	11 YEARS	12 YEARS
500	10.36	9.71	9.22	8.85	8.56	8.33
1000	20.73	19.42	18.45	17.70	17.11	16.65
2000	41.45	38.84	36.89	35.40	34.23	33.31
3000	62.18	58.26	55.34	53.09	51.34	49.96
4000	82.90	77.68	73.78	70.79	68.46	66.62
5000	103.63	97.11	92.23	88.49	85.57	83.27
6000	124.35	116.53	110.67	106.19	102.69	99.92
7000	145.08	135.95	129.12	123.89	119.80	116.58
8000	165.81	155.37	147.56	141.58	136.92	133.23
9000	186.53	174.79	166.01	159.28	154.03	149.88
10000	207.26	194.21	184.45	176.98	171.15	166.54
11000	227.98	213.63	202.90	194.68	188.26	183.19
12000	248.71	233.05	221.34	212.37	205.38	199.85
13000	269.44	252.48	239.79	230.07	222.49	216.50
14000	290.16	271.90	258.23	247.77	239.61	233.15
15000	310.89	291.32	276.68	265.47	256.72	249.81
16000	331.61	310.74	295.13	283.17	273.84	266.46
17000	352.34	330.16	313.57	300.86	290.95	283.12
18000	373.06	349.58	332.02	318.56	308.07	299.77
19000	393.79	369.00	350.46	336.26	325.18	316.42
20000	414.52	388.42	368.91	353.96	342.30	333.08
21000	435.24	407.85	387.35	371.66	359.41	349.73
22000	455.97	427.27	405.80	389.35	376.53	366.39
23000	476.69	446.69	424.24	407.05	393.64	383.04
24000	497.42	466.11	442.69	424.75	410.76	399.69
25000	518.14	485.53	461.13	442.45	427.87	416.35
30000	621.77	582.64	553.36	530.94	513.45	499.62
35000	725.40	679.74	645.59	619.43	599.02	582.89
40000	829.03	776.85	737.81	707.92	684.60	666.15
45000	932.66	873.95	830.04	796.40	770.17	749.42
50000	1036.29	971.06	922.27	884.89	855.75	832.69
55000	1139.92	1068.17	1014.49	973.38	941.32	915.96
60000	1243.55	1165.27	1106.72	1061.87	1026.90	999.23
65000	1347.18	1262.38	1198.95	1150.36	1112.47	1082.50
70000	1450.81	1359.48	1291.17	1238.85	1198.05	1165.77
75000	1554.43	1456.59	1383.40	1327.34	1283.62	1249.04
80000	1658.06	1553.70	1475.63	1415.83	1369.19	1332.31
85000	1761.69	1650.80	1567.85	1504.32	1454.77	1415.58
90000	1865.32	1747.91	1660.08	1592.81	1540.34	1498.85
95000	1968.95	1845.01	1752.31	1681.30	1625.92	1582.12
100000	2072.58	1942.12	1844.53	1769.79	1711.49	1665.39
200000	4145.16	3884.24	3689.07	3539.58	3422.99	3330.77
300000	6217.74	5826.36	5533.60	5309.36	5134.48	4996.16
400000	8290.32	7768.48	7378.13	7079.15	6845.97	6661.55
500000	10362.90	9710.61	9222.67	8848.94	8557.47	8326.94

17.5%

MONTHLY PAYMENT
Needed to repay a loan

TERM AMOUNT	15 YEARS	20 YEARS	25 YEARS	30 YEARS	35 YEARS	40 YEARS
500	7.87	7.52	7.39	7.33	7.31	7.30
1000	15.75	15.05	14.78	14.66	14.62	14.60
2000	31.49	30.10	29.55	29.33	29.23	29.19
3000	47.24	45.15	44.33	43.99	43.85	43.79
4000	62.98	60.20	59.10	58.65	58.47	58.39
5000	78.73	75.25	73.88	73.32	73.08	72.99
6000	94.47	90.30	88.65	87.98	87.70	87.58
7000	110.22	105.35	103.43	102.64	102.32	102.18
8000	125.97	120.40	118.20	117.31	116.93	116.78
9000	141.71	135.44	132.98	131.97	131.55	131.38
10000	157.46	150.49	147.75	146.63	146.17	145.97
11000	173.20	165.54	162.53	161.30	160.78	160.57
12000	188.95	180.59	177.30	175.96	175.40	175.17
13000	204.70	195.64	192.08	190.62	190.02	189.77
14000	220.44	210.69	206.85	205.29	204.63	204.36
15000	236.19	225.74	221.63	219.95	219.25	218.96
16000	251.93	240.79	236.40	234.61	233.87	233.56
17000	267.68	255.84	251.18	249.28	248.48	248.15
18000	283.42	270.89	265.96	263.94	263.10	262.75
19000	299.17	285.94	280.73	278.60	277.72	277.35
20000	314.92	300.99	295.51	293.27	292.34	291.95
21000	330.66	316.04	310.28	307.93	306.95	306.54
22000	346.41	331.09	325.06	322.59	321.57	321.14
23000	362.15	346.14	339.83	337.25	336.19	335.74
24000	377.90	361.19	354.61	351.92	350.80	350.34
25000	393.64	376.24	369.38	366.58	365.42	364.93
30000	472.37	451.48	443.26	439.90	438.50	437.92
35000	551.10	526.73	517.14	513.21	511.59	510.91
40000	629.83	601.98	591.01	586.53	584.67	583.89
45000	708.56	677.22	664.89	659.85	657.75	656.88
50000	787.29	752.47	738.76	733.16	730.84	729.87
55000	866.02	827.72	812.64	806.48	803.92	802.85
60000	944.75	902.97	886.52	879.80	877.01	875.84
65000	1023.48	978.21	960.39	953.11	950.09	948.83
70000	1102.20	1053.46	1034.27	1026.43	1023.17	1021.81
75000	1180.93	1128.71	1108.15	1099.74	1096.26	1094.80
80000	1259.66	1203.95	1182.02	1173.06	1169.34	1167.79
85000	1338.39	1279.20	1255.90	1246.38	1242.42	1240.77
90000	1417.12	1354.45	1329.78	1319.69	1315.51	1313.76
95000	1495.85	1429.69	1403.65	1393.01	1388.59	1386.75
100000	1574.58	1504.94	1477.53	1466.33	1461.68	1459.73
200000	3149.16	3009.88	2955.06	2932.65	2923.35	2919.47
300000	4723.73	4514.83	4432.59	4398.98	4385.03	4379.20
400000	6298.31	6019.77	5910.12	5865.30	5846.70	5838.93
500000	7872.89	7524.71	7387.65	7331.63	7308.38	7298.67

18%

MONTHLY PAYMENT
Needed to repay a loan

TERM AMOUNT	1 YEAR	2 YEARS	3 YEARS	4 YEARS	5 YEARS	6 YEARS
500	45.84	24.96	18.08	14.69	12.70	11.40
1000	91.68	49.92	36.15	29.37	25.39	22.81
2000	183.36	99.85	72.30	58.75	50.79	45.62
3000	275.04	149.77	108.46	88.12	76.18	68.42
4000	366.72	199.70	144.61	117.50	101.57	91.23
5000	458.40	249.62	180.76	146.87	126.97	114.04
6000	550.08	299.54	216.91	176.25	152.36	136.85
7000	641.76	349.47	253.07	205.62	177.75	159.65
8000	733.44	399.39	289.22	235.00	203.15	182.46
9000	825.12	449.32	325.37	264.37	228.54	205.27
10000	916.80	499.24	361.52	293.75	253.93	228.08
11000	1008.48	549.17	397.68	323.12	279.33	250.89
12000	1100.16	599.09	433.83	352.50	304.72	273.69
13000	1191.84	649.01	469.98	381.87	330.11	296.50
14000	1283.52	698.94	506.13	411.25	355.51	319.31
15000	1375.20	748.86	542.29	440.62	380.90	342.12
16000	1466.88	798.79	578.44	470.00	406.29	364.92
17000	1558.56	848.71	614.59	499.37	431.69	387.73
18000	1650.24	898.63	650.74	528.75	457.08	410.54
19000	1741.92	948.56	686.90	558.12	482.48	433.35
20000	1833.60	998.48	723.05	587.50	507.87	456.16
21000	1925.28	1048.41	759.20	616.87	533.26	478.96
22000	2016.96	1098.33	795.35	646.25	558.66	501.77
23000	2108.64	1148.25	831.51	675.62	584.05	524.58
24000	2200.32	1198.18	867.66	705.00	609.44	547.39
25000	2292.00	1248.10	903.81	734.37	634.84	570.19
30000	2750.40	1497.72	1084.57	881.25	761.80	684.23
35000	3208.80	1747.34	1265.33	1028.12	888.77	798.27
40000	3667.20	1996.96	1446.10	1175.00	1015.74	912.31
45000	4125.60	2246.58	1626.86	1321.87	1142.70	1026.35
50000	4584.00	2496.21	1807.62	1468.75	1269.67	1140.39
55000	5042.40	2745.83	1988.38	1615.62	1396.64	1254.43
60000	5500.80	2995.45	2169.14	1762.50	1523.61	1368.47
65000	5959.20	3245.07	2349.91	1909.37	1650.57	1482.51
70000	6417.60	3494.69	2530.67	2056.25	1777.54	1596.55
75000	6876.00	3744.31	2711.43	2203.12	1904.51	1710.58
80000	7334.40	3993.93	2892.19	2350.00	2031.47	1824.62
85000	7792.80	4243.55	3072.95	2496.87	2158.44	1938.66
90000	8251.20	4493.17	3253.72	2643.75	2285.41	2052.70
95000	8709.60	4742.79	3434.48	2790.62	2412.38	2166.74
100000	9168.00	4992.41	3615.24	2937.50	2539.34	2280.78
200000	18336.00	9984.82	7230.48	5875.00	5078.69	4561.56
300000	27504.00	14977.23	10845.72	8812.50	7618.03	6842.34
400000	36672.00	19969.64	14460.96	11750.00	10157.37	9123.12
500000	45840.00	24962.05	18076.20	14687.50	12696.71	11403.90

18%

MONTHLY PAYMENT
Needed to repay a loan

TERM AMOUNT	7 YEARS	8 YEARS	9 YEARS	10 YEARS	11 YEARS	12 YEARS
500	10.51	9.86	9.38	9.01	8.72	8.50
1000	21.02	19.72	18.76	18.02	17.44	16.99
2000	42.04	39.45	37.51	36.04	34.89	33.98
3000	63.05	59.17	56.27	54.06	52.33	50.97
4000	84.07	78.89	75.03	72.07	69.78	67.96
5000	105.09	98.62	93.78	90.09	87.22	84.96
6000	126.11	118.34	112.54	108.11	104.67	101.95
7000	147.12	138.06	131.30	126.13	122.11	118.94
8000	168.14	157.79	150.06	144.15	139.55	135.93
9000	189.16	177.51	168.81	162.17	157.00	152.92
10000	210.18	197.23	187.57	180.19	174.44	169.91
11000	231.20	216.96	206.33	198.20	191.89	186.90
12000	252.21	236.68	225.08	216.22	209.33	203.89
13000	273.23	256.40	243.84	234.24	226.77	220.89
14000	294.25	276.12	262.60	252.26	244.22	237.88
15000	315.27	295.85	281.35	270.28	261.66	254.87
16000	336.29	315.57	300.11	288.30	279.11	271.86
17000	357.30	335.29	318.87	306.31	296.55	288.85
18000	378.32	355.02	337.62	324.33	314.00	305.84
19000	399.34	374.74	356.38	342.35	331.44	322.83
20000	420.36	394.46	375.14	360.37	348.88	339.82
21000	441.37	414.19	393.89	378.39	366.33	356.82
22000	462.39	433.91	412.65	396.41	383.77	373.81
23000	483.41	453.63	431.41	414.43	401.22	390.80
24000	504.43	473.36	450.17	432.44	418.66	407.79
25000	525.45	493.08	468.92	450.46	436.10	424.78
30000	630.54	591.70	562.71	540.56	523.33	509.74
35000	735.62	690.31	656.49	630.65	610.55	594.69
40000	840.71	788.93	750.28	720.74	697.77	679.65
45000	945.80	887.54	844.06	810.83	784.99	764.60
50000	1050.89	986.16	937.84	900.93	872.21	849.56
55000	1155.98	1084.78	1031.63	991.02	959.43	934.52
60000	1261.07	1183.39	1125.41	1081.11	1046.65	1019.47
65000	1366.16	1282.01	1219.20	1171.20	1133.87	1104.43
70000	1471.25	1380.62	1312.98	1261.30	1221.09	1189.38
75000	1576.34	1479.24	1406.77	1351.39	1308.31	1274.34
80000	1681.43	1577.86	1500.55	1441.48	1395.53	1359.30
85000	1786.52	1676.47	1594.34	1531.57	1482.76	1444.25
90000	1891.61	1775.09	1688.12	1621.67	1569.98	1529.21
95000	1996.69	1873.71	1781.90	1711.76	1657.20	1614.16
100000	2101.78	1972.32	1875.69	1801.85	1744.42	1699.12
200000	4203.57	3944.64	3751.38	3603.70	3488.84	3398.24
300000	6305.35	5916.96	5627.07	5405.56	5233.25	5097.36
400000	8407.14	7889.29	7502.76	7207.41	6977.67	6796.48
500000	10508.92	9861.61	9378.44	9009.26	8722.09	8495.60

MONTHLY PAYMENT
Needed to repay a loan

18%

TERM AMOUNT	15 YEARS	20 YEARS	25 YEARS	30 YEARS	35 YEARS	40 YEARS
500	8.05	7.72	7.59	7.54	7.51	7.51
1000	16.10	15.43	15.17	15.07	15.03	15.01
2000	32.21	30.87	30.35	30.14	30.06	30.02
3000	48.31	46.30	45.52	45.21	45.09	45.04
4000	64.42	61.73	60.70	60.28	60.12	60.05
5000	80.52	77.17	75.87	75.35	75.14	75.06
6000	96.63	92.60	91.05	90.43	90.17	90.07
7000	112.73	108.03	106.22	105.50	105.20	105.08
8000	128.83	123.46	121.39	120.57	120.23	120.09
9000	144.94	138.90	136.57	135.64	135.26	135.11
10000	161.04	154.33	151.74	150.71	150.29	150.12
11000	177.15	169.76	166.92	165.78	165.32	165.13
12000	193.25	185.20	182.09	180.85	180.35	180.14
13000	209.35	200.63	197.27	195.92	195.38	195.15
14000	225.46	216.06	212.44	210.99	210.40	210.17
15000	241.56	231.50	227.61	226.06	225.43	225.18
16000	257.67	246.93	242.79	241.13	240.46	240.19
17000	273.77	262.36	257.96	256.20	255.49	255.20
18000	289.88	277.80	273.14	271.28	270.52	270.21
19000	305.98	293.23	288.31	286.35	285.55	285.22
20000	322.08	308.66	303.49	301.42	300.58	300.24
21000	338.19	324.10	318.66	316.49	315.61	315.25
22000	354.29	339.53	333.83	331.56	330.64	330.26
23000	370.40	354.96	349.01	346.63	345.67	345.27
24000	386.50	370.39	364.18	361.70	360.69	360.28
25000	402.61	385.83	379.36	376.77	375.72	375.30
30000	483.13	462.99	455.23	452.13	450.87	450.35
35000	563.65	540.16	531.10	527.48	526.01	525.41
40000	644.17	617.32	606.97	602.83	601.16	600.47
45000	724.69	694.49	682.84	678.19	676.30	675.53
50000	805.21	771.66	758.71	753.54	751.45	750.59
55000	885.73	848.82	834.59	828.90	826.59	825.65
60000	966.25	925.99	910.46	904.25	901.74	900.71
65000	1046.77	1003.15	986.33	979.61	976.88	975.77
70000	1127.29	1080.32	1062.20	1054.96	1052.02	1050.83
75000	1207.82	1157.48	1138.07	1130.31	1127.17	1125.89
80000	1288.34	1234.65	1213.94	1205.67	1202.31	1200.95
85000	1368.86	1311.81	1289.82	1281.02	1277.46	1276.00
90000	1449.38	1388.98	1365.69	1356.38	1352.60	1351.06
95000	1529.90	1466.15	1441.56	1431.73	1427.75	1426.12
100000	1610.42	1543.31	1517.43	1507.09	1502.89	1501.18
200000	3220.84	3086.62	3034.86	3014.17	3005.78	3002.36
300000	4831.26	4629.93	4552.29	4521.26	4508.68	4503.55
400000	6441.68	6173.25	6069.72	6028.34	6011.57	6004.73
500000	8052.11	7716.56	7587.15	7535.43	7514.46	7505.91

18.5% MONTHLY PAYMENT
Needed to repay a loan

TERM AMOUNT	1 YEAR	2 YEARS	3 YEARS	4 YEARS	5 YEARS	6 YEARS
500	45.96	25.08	18.20	14.82	12.83	11.55
1000	91.92	50.17	36.40	29.64	25.67	23.09
2000	183.84	100.33	72.81	59.27	51.33	46.18
3000	275.75	150.50	109.21	88.91	77.00	69.27
4000	367.67	200.66	145.61	118.55	102.66	92.37
5000	459.59	250.83	182.02	148.18	128.33	115.46
6000	551.51	301.00	218.42	177.82	154.00	138.55
7000	643.43	351.16	254.83	207.46	179.66	161.64
8000	735.34	401.33	291.23	237.10	205.33	184.73
9000	827.26	451.49	327.63	266.73	231.00	207.82
10000	919.18	501.66	364.04	296.37	256.66	230.91
11000	1011.10	551.83	400.44	326.01	282.33	254.00
12000	1103.02	601.99	436.84	355.64	307.99	277.10
13000	1194.94	652.16	473.25	385.28	333.66	300.19
14000	1286.85	702.32	509.65	414.92	359.33	323.28
15000	1378.77	752.49	546.06	444.55	384.99	346.37
16000	1470.69	802.66	582.46	474.19	410.66	369.46
17000	1562.61	852.82	618.86	503.83	436.33	392.55
18000	1654.53	902.99	655.27	533.46	461.99	415.64
19000	1746.44	953.15	691.67	563.10	487.66	438.74
20000	1838.36	1003.32	728.07	592.74	513.32	461.83
21000	1930.28	1053.49	764.48	622.38	538.99	484.92
22000	2022.20	1103.65	800.88	652.01	564.66	508.01
23000	2114.12	1153.82	837.29	681.65	590.32	531.10
24000	2206.03	1203.98	873.69	711.29	615.99	554.19
25000	2297.95	1254.15	910.09	740.92	641.66	577.28
30000	2757.54	1504.98	1092.11	889.11	769.99	692.74
35000	3217.13	1755.81	1274.13	1037.29	898.32	808.20
40000	3676.72	2006.64	1456.15	1185.48	1026.65	923.65
45000	4136.32	2257.47	1638.17	1333.66	1154.98	1039.11
50000	4595.91	2508.30	1820.19	1481.85	1283.31	1154.57
55000	5055.50	2759.13	2002.20	1630.03	1411.64	1270.02
60000	5515.09	3009.96	2184.22	1778.21	1539.97	1385.48
65000	5974.68	3260.79	2366.24	1926.40	1668.30	1500.94
70000	6434.27	3511.62	2548.26	2074.58	1796.63	1616.39
75000	6893.86	3762.45	2730.28	2222.77	1924.97	1731.85
80000	7353.45	4013.28	2912.30	2370.95	2053.30	1847.31
85000	7813.04	4264.11	3094.32	2519.14	2181.63	1962.77
90000	8272.63	4514.94	3276.33	2667.32	2309.96	2078.22
95000	8732.22	4765.77	3458.35	2815.51	2438.29	2193.68
100000	9191.81	5016.60	3640.37	2963.69	2566.62	2309.14
200000	18383.62	10033.21	7280.74	5927.38	5133.24	4618.27
300000	27575.44	15049.81	10921.11	8891.07	7699.86	6927.41
400000	36767.25	20066.41	14561.49	11854.77	10266.48	9236.54
500000	45959.06	25083.01	18201.86	14818.46	12833.10	11545.68

MONTHLY PAYMENT 18.5%
Needed to repay a loan

TERM AMOUNT	7 YEARS	8 YEARS	9 YEARS	10 YEARS	11 YEARS	12 YEARS
500	10.66	10.01	9.54	9.17	8.89	8.67
1000	21.31	20.03	19.07	18.34	17.78	17.33
2000	42.62	40.05	38.14	36.68	35.55	34.66
3000	63.94	60.08	57.21	55.02	53.33	51.99
4000	85.25	80.11	76.28	73.37	71.10	69.32
5000	106.56	100.14	95.35	91.71	88.88	86.66
6000	127.87	120.16	114.42	110.05	106.66	103.99
7000	149.18	140.19	133.50	128.39	124.43	121.32
8000	170.50	160.22	152.57	146.73	142.21	138.65
9000	191.81	180.25	171.64	165.07	159.98	155.98
10000	213.12	200.27	190.71	183.42	177.76	173.31
11000	234.43	220.30	209.78	201.76	195.54	190.64
12000	255.74	240.33	228.85	220.10	213.31	207.97
13000	277.05	260.36	247.92	238.44	231.09	225.30
14000	298.37	280.38	266.99	256.78	248.86	242.64
15000	319.68	300.41	286.06	275.12	266.64	259.97
16000	340.99	320.44	305.13	293.47	284.42	277.30
17000	362.30	340.47	324.20	311.81	302.19	294.63
18000	383.61	360.49	343.27	330.15	319.97	311.96
19000	404.93	380.52	362.35	348.49	337.74	329.29
20000	426.24	400.55	381.42	366.83	355.52	346.62
21000	447.55	420.58	400.49	385.17	373.30	363.95
22000	468.86	440.60	419.56	403.52	391.07	381.29
23000	490.17	460.63	438.63	421.86	408.85	398.62
24000	511.49	480.66	457.70	440.20	426.62	415.95
25000	532.80	500.69	476.77	458.54	444.40	433.28
30000	639.36	600.82	572.12	550.25	533.28	519.93
35000	745.92	700.96	667.48	641.96	622.16	606.59
40000	852.48	801.10	762.83	733.67	711.04	693.25
45000	959.04	901.23	858.19	825.37	799.92	779.90
50000	1065.60	1001.37	953.54	917.08	888.80	866.56
55000	1172.16	1101.51	1048.89	1008.79	977.68	953.21
60000	1278.72	1201.65	1144.25	1100.50	1066.56	1039.87
65000	1385.27	1301.78	1239.60	1192.21	1155.44	1126.52
70000	1491.83	1401.92	1334.96	1283.92	1244.32	1213.18
75000	1598.39	1502.06	1430.31	1375.62	1333.20	1299.84
80000	1704.95	1602.20	1525.67	1467.33	1422.08	1386.49
85000	1811.51	1702.33	1621.02	1559.04	1510.96	1473.15
90000	1918.07	1802.47	1716.37	1650.75	1599.84	1559.80
95000	2024.63	1902.61	1811.73	1742.46	1688.72	1646.46
100000	2131.19	2002.74	1907.08	1834.17	1777.60	1733.11
200000	4262.38	4005.49	3814.16	3668.33	3555.20	3466.23
300000	6393.58	6008.23	5721.24	5502.50	5332.80	5199.34
400000	8524.77	8010.98	7628.33	7336.66	7110.40	6932.46
500000	10655.96	10013.72	9535.41	9170.83	8888.00	8665.57

18.5% — MONTHLY PAYMENT
Needed to repay a loan

TERM / AMOUNT	15 YEARS	20 YEARS	25 YEARS	30 YEARS	35 YEARS	40 YEARS
500	8.23	7.91	7.79	7.74	7.72	7.71
1000	16.47	15.82	15.57	15.48	15.44	15.43
2000	32.93	31.64	31.15	30.96	30.88	30.85
3000	49.40	47.46	46.72	46.44	46.33	46.28
4000	65.86	63.28	62.30	61.92	61.77	61.71
5000	82.33	79.09	77.87	77.40	77.21	77.13
6000	98.79	94.91	93.45	92.88	92.65	92.56
7000	115.26	110.73	109.02	108.36	108.09	107.99
8000	131.72	126.55	124.60	123.84	123.53	123.41
9000	148.19	142.37	140.17	139.32	138.98	138.84
10000	164.65	158.19	155.75	154.79	154.42	154.27
11000	181.12	174.01	171.32	170.27	169.86	169.69
12000	197.58	189.83	186.90	185.75	185.30	185.12
13000	214.05	205.65	202.47	201.23	200.74	200.55
14000	230.51	221.47	218.05	216.71	216.18	215.97
15000	246.98	237.28	233.62	232.19	231.63	231.40
16000	263.44	253.10	249.20	247.67	247.07	246.83
17000	279.91	268.92	264.77	263.15	262.51	262.25
18000	296.37	284.74	280.35	278.63	277.95	277.68
19000	312.84	300.56	295.92	294.11	293.39	293.11
20000	329.30	316.38	311.50	309.59	308.83	308.53
21000	345.77	332.20	327.07	325.07	324.28	323.96
22000	362.24	348.02	342.65	340.55	339.72	339.39
23000	378.70	363.84	358.22	356.03	355.16	354.81
24000	395.17	379.66	373.80	371.51	370.60	370.24
25000	411.63	395.47	389.37	386.99	386.04	385.67
30000	493.96	474.57	467.25	464.38	463.25	462.80
35000	576.28	553.66	545.12	541.78	540.46	539.93
40000	658.61	632.76	622.99	619.18	617.67	617.07
45000	740.94	711.85	700.87	696.58	694.88	694.20
50000	823.26	790.95	778.74	773.97	772.08	771.33
55000	905.59	870.04	856.62	851.37	849.29	848.47
60000	987.91	949.14	934.49	928.77	926.50	925.60
65000	1070.24	1028.23	1012.36	1006.16	1003.71	1002.73
70000	1152.57	1107.33	1090.24	1083.56	1080.92	1079.87
75000	1234.89	1186.42	1168.11	1160.96	1158.13	1157.00
80000	1317.22	1265.52	1245.99	1238.36	1235.33	1234.13
85000	1399.54	1344.61	1323.86	1315.75	1312.54	1311.26
90000	1481.87	1423.71	1401.74	1393.15	1389.75	1388.40
95000	1564.20	1502.80	1479.61	1470.55	1466.96	1465.53
100000	1646.52	1581.90	1557.48	1547.94	1544.17	1542.66
200000	3293.05	3163.79	3114.97	3095.89	3088.34	3085.33
300000	4939.57	4745.69	4672.45	4643.83	4632.50	4627.99
400000	6586.09	6327.59	6229.94	6191.78	6176.67	6170.66
500000	8232.62	7909.48	7787.42	7739.72	7720.84	7713.32

MONTHLY PAYMENT — 19%
Needed to repay a loan

TERM / AMOUNT	1 YEAR	2 YEARS	3 YEARS	4 YEARS	5 YEARS	6 YEARS
500	46.08	25.20	18.33	14.95	12.97	11.69
1000	92.16	50.41	36.66	29.90	25.94	23.38
2000	184.31	100.82	73.31	59.80	51.88	46.75
3000	276.47	151.23	109.97	89.70	77.82	70.13
4000	368.63	201.63	146.62	119.60	103.76	93.51
5000	460.78	252.04	183.28	149.50	129.70	116.88
6000	552.94	302.45	219.94	179.40	155.64	140.26
7000	645.10	352.86	256.59	209.30	181.58	163.64
8000	737.25	403.27	293.25	239.20	207.52	187.01
9000	829.41	453.68	329.90	269.10	233.46	210.39
10000	921.57	504.09	366.56	299.00	259.41	233.77
11000	1013.72	554.49	403.22	328.90	285.35	257.14
12000	1105.88	604.90	439.87	358.80	311.29	280.52
13000	1198.04	655.31	476.53	388.70	337.23	303.90
14000	1290.19	705.72	513.18	418.60	363.17	327.27
15000	1382.35	756.13	549.84	448.50	389.11	350.65
16000	1474.51	806.54	586.50	478.40	415.05	374.03
17000	1566.66	856.95	623.15	508.30	440.99	397.40
18000	1658.82	907.36	659.81	538.20	466.93	420.78
19000	1750.97	957.76	696.46	568.10	492.87	444.16
20000	1843.13	1008.17	733.12	598.00	518.81	467.53
21000	1935.29	1058.58	769.78	627.90	544.75	490.91
22000	2027.44	1108.99	806.43	657.80	570.69	514.29
23000	2119.60	1159.40	843.09	687.70	596.63	537.66
24000	2211.76	1209.81	879.74	717.60	622.57	561.04
25000	2303.91	1260.22	916.40	747.50	648.51	584.42
30000	2764.70	1512.26	1099.68	897.00	778.22	701.30
35000	3225.48	1764.30	1282.96	1046.50	907.92	818.19
40000	3686.26	2016.34	1466.24	1196.00	1037.62	935.07
45000	4147.05	2268.39	1649.52	1345.51	1167.32	1051.95
50000	4607.83	2520.43	1832.80	1495.01	1297.03	1168.84
55000	5068.61	2772.47	2016.08	1644.51	1426.73	1285.72
60000	5529.39	3024.52	2199.36	1794.01	1556.43	1402.60
65000	5990.18	3276.56	2382.64	1943.51	1686.14	1519.49
70000	6450.96	3528.60	2565.92	2093.01	1815.84	1636.37
75000	6911.74	3780.65	2749.20	2242.51	1945.54	1753.25
80000	7372.53	4032.69	2932.48	2392.01	2075.24	1870.14
85000	7833.31	4284.73	3115.76	2541.51	2204.95	1987.02
90000	8294.09	4536.78	3299.04	2691.01	2334.65	2103.91
95000	8754.87	4788.82	3482.32	2840.51	2464.35	2220.79
100000	9215.66	5040.86	3665.60	2990.01	2594.06	2337.67
200000	18431.32	10081.72	7331.20	5980.02	5188.11	4675.34
300000	27646.97	15122.59	10996.81	8970.04	7782.17	7013.02
400000	36862.63	20163.45	14662.41	11960.05	10376.22	9350.69
500000	46078.29	25204.31	18328.01	14950.06	12970.28	11688.36

19%

MONTHLY PAYMENT
Needed to repay a loan

TERM AMOUNT	7 YEARS	8 YEARS	9 YEARS	10 YEARS	11 YEARS	12 YEARS
500	10.80	10.17	9.69	9.33	9.06	8.84
1000	21.61	20.33	19.39	18.67	18.11	17.67
2000	43.22	40.67	38.77	37.33	36.22	35.35
3000	64.82	61.00	58.16	56.00	54.33	53.02
4000	86.43	81.34	77.55	74.67	72.44	70.69
5000	108.04	101.67	96.94	93.34	90.55	88.37
6000	129.65	122.00	116.32	112.00	108.66	106.04
7000	151.26	142.34	135.71	130.67	126.77	123.72
8000	172.86	162.67	155.10	149.34	144.88	141.39
9000	194.47	183.00	174.48	168.01	162.99	159.06
10000	216.08	203.34	193.87	186.67	181.10	176.74
11000	237.69	223.67	213.26	205.34	199.21	194.41
12000	259.30	244.01	232.64	224.01	217.32	212.08
13000	280.90	264.34	252.03	242.67	235.43	229.76
14000	302.51	284.67	271.42	261.34	253.54	247.43
15000	324.12	305.01	290.81	280.01	271.65	265.10
16000	345.73	325.34	310.19	298.68	289.77	282.78
17000	367.34	345.68	329.58	317.34	307.88	300.45
18000	388.94	366.01	348.97	336.01	325.99	318.13
19000	410.55	386.34	368.35	354.68	344.10	335.80
20000	432.16	406.68	387.74	373.34	361.21	353.47
21000	453.77	427.01	407.13	392.01	380.32	371.15
22000	475.38	447.35	426.52	410.68	398.43	388.82
23000	496.98	467.68	445.90	429.35	416.54	406.49
24000	518.59	488.01	465.29	448.01	434.65	424.17
25000	540.20	508.35	484.68	466.68	452.76	441.84
30000	648.24	610.02	581.61	560.02	543.31	530.21
35000	756.28	711.69	678.55	653.35	633.86	618.58
40000	864.32	813.35	775.48	746.69	724.41	706.95
45000	972.36	915.02	872.42	840.03	814.96	795.31
50000	1080.40	1016.69	969.35	933.36	905.52	883.68
55000	1188.44	1118.36	1066.29	1026.70	996.07	972.05
60000	1296.48	1220.03	1163.22	1120.03	1086.62	1060.42
65000	1404.52	1321.70	1260.16	1213.37	1177.17	1148.79
70000	1512.56	1423.37	1357.10	1306.71	1267.72	1237.16
75000	1620.60	1525.04	1454.03	1400.04	1358.27	1325.52
80000	1728.64	1626.71	1550.97	1493.38	1448.83	1413.89
85000	1836.68	1728.38	1647.90	1586.72	1539.38	1502.26
90000	1944.72	1830.05	1744.84	1680.05	1629.93	1590.63
95000	2052.76	1931.72	1841.77	1773.39	1720.48	1679.00
100000	2160.80	2033.39	1938.71	1866.72	1811.03	1767.36
200000	4321.60	4066.77	3877.42	3733.45	3622.07	3534.73
300000	6482.41	6100.16	5816.12	5600.17	5433.10	5302.09
400000	8643.21	8133.55	7754.83	7466.89	7244.13	7069.46
500000	10804.01	10166.93	9693.54	9333.62	9055.16	8836.82

MONTHLY PAYMENT
Needed to repay a loan

19%

TERM AMOUNT	15 YEARS	20 YEARS	25 YEARS	30 YEARS	35 YEARS	40 YEARS
500	8.41	8.10	7.99	7.94	7.93	7.92
1000	16.83	16.21	15.98	15.89	15.85	15.84
2000	33.66	32.41	31.95	31.78	31.71	31.68
3000	50.49	48.62	47.93	47.67	47.56	47.53
4000	67.32	64.83	63.91	63.56	63.42	63.37
5000	84.14	81.03	79.88	79.44	79.27	79.21
6000	100.97	97.24	95.86	95.33	95.13	95.05
7000	117.80	113.45	111.84	111.22	110.98	110.89
8000	134.63	129.65	127.81	127.11	126.84	126.73
9000	151.46	145.86	143.79	143.00	142.69	142.58
10000	168.29	162.07	159.77	158.89	158.55	158.42
11000	185.12	178.28	175.74	174.78	174.40	174.26
12000	201.95	194.48	191.72	190.67	190.26	190.10
13000	218.77	210.69	207.70	206.56	206.11	205.94
14000	235.60	226.90	223.68	222.44	221.97	221.78
15000	252.43	243.10	239.65	238.33	237.82	237.63
16000	269.26	259.31	255.63	254.22	253.68	253.47
17000	286.09	275.52	271.61	270.11	269.53	269.31
18000	302.92	291.72	287.58	286.00	285.39	285.15
19000	319.75	307.93	303.56	301.89	301.24	300.99
20000	336.58	324.14	319.54	317.78	317.10	316.83
21000	353.40	340.34	335.51	333.67	332.95	332.68
22000	370.23	356.55	351.49	349.56	348.81	348.52
23000	387.06	372.76	367.47	365.45	364.66	364.36
24000	403.89	388.96	383.44	381.33	380.52	380.20
25000	420.72	405.17	399.42	397.22	396.37	396.04
30000	504.86	486.21	479.30	476.67	475.65	475.25
35000	589.01	567.24	559.19	556.11	554.92	554.46
40000	673.15	648.27	639.07	635.56	634.20	633.67
45000	757.29	729.31	718.96	715.00	713.47	712.88
50000	841.44	810.34	798.84	794.45	792.75	792.09
55000	925.58	891.38	878.72	873.89	872.02	871.30
60000	1009.73	972.41	958.61	953.34	951.30	950.50
65000	1093.87	1053.45	1038.49	1032.78	1030.57	1029.71
70000	1178.01	1134.48	1118.38	1112.22	1109.85	1108.92
75000	1262.16	1215.51	1198.26	1191.67	1189.12	1188.13
80000	1346.30	1296.55	1278.14	1271.11	1268.40	1267.34
85000	1430.44	1377.58	1358.03	1350.56	1347.67	1346.55
90000	1514.59	1458.62	1437.91	1430.00	1426.95	1425.76
95000	1598.73	1539.65	1517.80	1509.45	1506.22	1504.97
100000	1682.88	1620.68	1597.68	1588.89	1585.49	1584.17
200000	3365.75	3241.37	3195.36	3177.78	3170.99	3168.35
300000	5048.63	4862.05	4793.04	4766.68	4756.48	4752.52
400000	6731.50	6482.74	6390.72	6355.57	6341.98	6336.70
500000	8414.38	8103.42	7988.40	7944.46	7927.47	7920.87

19.5% MONTHLY PAYMENT

Needed to repay a loan

TERM / AMOUNT	1 YEAR	2 YEARS	3 YEARS	4 YEARS	5 YEARS	6 YEARS
500	46.20	25.33	18.45	15.08	13.11	11.83
1000	92.40	50.65	36.91	30.16	26.22	23.66
2000	184.79	101.30	73.82	60.33	52.43	47.33
3000	277.19	151.96	110.73	90.49	78.65	70.99
4000	369.58	202.61	147.64	120.66	104.87	94.66
5000	461.98	253.26	184.55	150.82	131.08	118.32
6000	554.37	303.91	221.46	180.99	157.30	141.98
7000	646.77	354.56	258.37	211.15	183.52	165.65
8000	739.16	405.22	295.27	241.32	209.73	189.31
9000	831.56	455.87	332.18	271.48	235.95	212.97
10000	923.95	506.52	369.09	301.65	262.16	236.64
11000	1016.35	557.17	406.00	331.81	288.38	260.30
12000	1108.74	607.82	442.91	361.98	314.60	283.97
13000	1201.14	658.47	479.82	392.14	340.81	307.63
14000	1293.54	709.13	516.73	422.30	367.03	331.29
15000	1385.93	759.78	553.64	452.47	393.25	354.96
16000	1478.33	810.43	590.55	482.63	419.46	378.62
17000	1570.72	861.08	627.46	512.80	445.68	402.29
18000	1663.12	911.73	664.37	542.96	471.90	425.95
19000	1755.51	962.39	701.28	573.13	498.11	449.61
20000	1847.91	1013.04	738.19	603.29	524.33	473.28
21000	1940.30	1063.69	775.10	633.46	550.55	496.94
22000	2032.70	1114.34	812.00	663.62	576.76	520.61
23000	2125.09	1164.99	848.91	693.79	602.98	544.27
24000	2217.49	1215.65	885.82	723.95	629.19	567.93
25000	2309.88	1266.30	922.73	754.12	655.41	591.60
30000	2771.86	1519.56	1107.28	904.94	786.49	709.92
35000	3233.84	1772.82	1291.83	1055.76	917.58	828.24
40000	3695.81	2026.08	1476.37	1206.58	1048.66	946.56
45000	4157.79	2279.33	1660.92	1357.41	1179.74	1064.87
50000	4619.77	2532.59	1845.47	1508.23	1310.82	1183.19
55000	5081.75	2785.85	2030.01	1659.05	1441.90	1301.51
60000	5543.72	3039.11	2214.56	1809.88	1572.99	1419.83
65000	6005.70	3292.37	2399.11	1960.70	1704.07	1538.15
70000	6467.68	3545.63	2583.65	2111.52	1835.15	1656.47
75000	6929.65	3798.89	2768.20	2262.35	1966.23	1774.79
80000	7391.63	4052.15	2952.74	2413.17	2097.32	1893.11
85000	7853.61	4305.41	3137.29	2563.99	2228.40	2011.43
90000	8315.58	4558.67	3321.84	2714.81	2359.48	2129.75
95000	8777.56	4811.93	3506.38	2865.64	2490.56	2248.07
100000	9239.54	5065.19	3690.93	3016.46	2621.64	2366.39
200000	18479.07	10130.38	7381.86	6032.92	5243.29	4732.78
300000	27718.61	15195.56	11072.79	9049.38	7864.93	7099.17
400000	36958.15	20260.75	14763.72	12065.84	10486.58	9465.55
500000	46197.69	25325.94	18454.66	15082.30	13108.22	11831.94

MONTHLY PAYMENT 19.5%

Needed to repay a loan

TERM / AMOUNT	7 YEARS	8 YEARS	9 YEARS	10 YEARS	11 YEARS	12 YEARS
500	10.95	10.32	9.85	9.50	9.22	9.01
1000	21.91	20.64	19.71	19.00	18.45	18.02
2000	43.81	41.28	39.41	37.99	36.89	36.04
3000	65.72	61.93	59.12	56.99	55.34	54.06
4000	87.62	82.57	78.82	75.98	73.79	72.07
5000	109.53	103.21	98.53	94.98	92.24	90.09
6000	131.44	123.85	118.23	113.97	110.68	108.11
7000	153.34	144.50	137.94	132.97	129.13	126.13
8000	175.25	165.14	157.65	151.96	147.58	144.15
9000	197.16	185.78	177.35	170.96	166.02	162.17
10000	219.06	206.42	197.06	189.95	184.47	180.19
11000	240.97	227.07	216.76	208.95	202.92	198.21
12000	262.87	247.71	236.47	227.94	221.37	216.22
13000	284.78	268.35	256.17	246.94	239.81	234.24
14000	306.69	288.99	275.88	265.93	258.26	252.26
15000	328.59	309.64	295.58	284.93	276.71	270.28
16000	350.50	330.28	315.29	303.92	295.15	288.30
17000	372.40	350.92	335.00	322.92	313.60	306.32
18000	394.31	371.56	354.70	341.91	332.05	324.34
19000	416.22	392.21	374.41	360.91	350.50	342.35
20000	438.12	412.85	394.11	379.90	368.94	360.37
21000	460.03	433.49	413.82	398.90	387.39	378.39
22000	481.93	454.13	433.52	417.89	405.84	396.41
23000	503.84	474.78	453.23	436.89	424.28	414.43
24000	525.75	495.42	472.94	455.89	442.73	432.45
25000	547.65	516.06	492.64	474.88	461.18	450.47
30000	657.18	619.27	591.17	569.86	553.41	540.56
35000	766.71	722.49	689.70	664.83	645.65	630.65
40000	876.24	825.70	788.23	759.81	737.89	720.75
45000	985.78	928.91	886.75	854.78	830.12	810.84
50000	1095.31	1032.12	985.28	949.76	922.36	900.93
55000	1204.84	1135.34	1083.81	1044.74	1014.59	991.03
60000	1314.37	1238.55	1182.34	1139.71	1106.83	1081.12
65000	1423.90	1341.76	1280.87	1234.69	1199.06	1171.21
70000	1533.43	1444.97	1379.40	1329.67	1291.30	1261.31
75000	1642.96	1548.18	1477.92	1424.64	1383.53	1351.40
80000	1752.49	1651.40	1576.45	1519.62	1475.77	1441.49
85000	1862.02	1754.61	1674.98	1614.59	1568.01	1531.59
90000	1971.55	1857.82	1773.51	1709.57	1660.24	1621.68
95000	2081.08	1961.03	1872.04	1804.55	1752.48	1711.77
100000	2190.61	2064.25	1970.57	1899.52	1844.71	1801.86
200000	4381.22	4128.49	3941.13	3799.04	3689.43	3603.73
300000	6571.84	6192.74	5911.70	5698.57	5534.14	5405.59
400000	8762.45	8256.98	7882.26	7598.09	7378.85	7207.46
500000	10953.06	10321.23	9852.83	9497.61	9223.56	9009.32

19.5%

MONTHLY PAYMENT
Needed to repay a loan

TERM AMOUNT	15 YEARS	20 YEARS	25 YEARS	30 YEARS	35 YEARS	40 YEARS
500	8.60	8.30	8.19	8.15	8.13	8.13
1000	17.19	16.60	16.38	16.30	16.27	16.26
2000	34.39	33.19	32.76	32.60	32.54	32.51
3000	51.58	49.79	49.14	48.90	48.81	48.77
4000	68.78	66.39	65.52	65.20	65.07	65.03
5000	85.97	82.98	81.90	81.50	81.34	81.29
6000	103.17	99.58	98.28	97.80	97.61	97.54
7000	120.36	116.18	114.66	114.09	113.88	113.80
8000	137.56	132.77	131.04	130.39	130.15	130.06
9000	154.75	149.37	147.42	146.69	146.42	146.31
10000	171.95	165.97	163.80	162.99	162.69	162.57
11000	189.14	182.56	180.18	179.29	178.96	178.83
12000	206.34	199.16	196.56	195.59	195.22	195.09
13000	223.53	215.76	212.94	211.89	211.49	211.34
14000	240.73	232.35	229.32	228.19	227.76	227.60
15000	257.92	248.95	245.70	244.49	244.03	243.86
16000	275.12	265.55	262.08	260.79	260.30	260.11
17000	292.31	282.14	278.46	277.09	276.57	276.37
18000	309.50	298.74	294.84	293.39	292.84	292.63
19000	326.70	315.34	311.22	309.68	309.10	308.88
20000	343.89	331.93	327.60	325.98	325.37	325.14
21000	361.09	348.53	343.98	342.28	341.64	341.40
22000	378.28	365.13	360.36	358.58	357.91	357.66
23000	395.48	381.72	376.74	374.88	374.18	373.91
24000	412.67	398.32	393.12	391.18	390.45	390.17
25000	429.87	414.92	409.50	407.48	406.72	406.43
30000	515.84	497.90	491.40	488.98	488.06	487.71
35000	601.81	580.88	573.30	570.47	569.40	569.00
40000	687.79	663.87	655.20	651.97	650.75	650.28
45000	773.76	746.85	737.10	733.46	732.09	731.57
50000	859.74	829.83	819.00	814.96	813.43	812.85
55000	945.71	912.82	900.90	896.46	894.78	894.14
60000	1031.68	995.80	982.80	977.95	976.12	975.43
65000	1117.66	1078.78	1064.70	1059.45	1057.46	1056.71
70000	1203.63	1161.77	1146.60	1140.94	1138.81	1138.00
75000	1289.60	1244.75	1228.50	1222.44	1220.15	1219.28
80000	1375.58	1327.73	1310.40	1303.94	1301.49	1300.57
85000	1461.55	1410.71	1392.31	1385.43	1382.84	1381.85
90000	1547.52	1493.70	1474.21	1466.93	1464.18	1463.14
95000	1633.50	1576.68	1556.11	1548.42	1545.52	1544.42
100000	1719.47	1659.66	1638.01	1629.92	1626.87	1625.71
200000	3438.94	3319.33	3276.01	3259.84	3253.73	3251.42
300000	5158.41	4978.99	4914.02	4889.76	4880.60	4877.13
400000	6877.88	6638.66	6552.02	6519.68	6507.47	6502.84
500000	8597.35	8298.32	8190.03	8149.60	8134.33	8128.55

MONTHLY PAYMENT
Needed to repay a loan

20%

TERM AMOUNT	1 YEAR	2 YEARS	3 YEARS	4 YEARS	5 YEARS	6 YEARS
500	46.32	25.45	18.58	15.22	13.25	11.98
1000	92.63	50.90	37.16	30.43	26.49	23.95
2000	185.27	101.79	74.33	60.86	52.99	47.91
3000	277.90	152.69	111.49	91.29	79.48	71.86
4000	370.54	203.58	148.65	121.72	105.98	95.81
5000	463.17	254.48	185.82	152.15	132.47	119.76
6000	555.81	305.37	222.98	182.58	158.96	143.72
7000	648.44	356.27	260.15	213.01	185.46	167.67
8000	741.08	407.17	297.31	243.44	211.95	191.62
9000	833.71	458.06	334.47	273.87	238.44	215.58
10000	926.35	508.96	371.64	304.30	264.94	239.53
11000	1018.98	559.85	408.80	334.73	291.43	263.48
12000	1111.61	610.75	445.96	365.16	317.93	287.43
13000	1204.25	661.65	483.13	395.59	344.42	311.39
14000	1296.88	712.54	520.29	426.03	370.91	335.34
15000	1389.52	763.44	557.45	456.46	397.41	359.29
16000	1482.15	814.33	594.62	486.89	423.90	383.25
17000	1574.79	865.23	631.78	517.32	450.40	407.20
18000	1667.42	916.12	668.94	547.75	476.89	431.15
19000	1760.06	967.02	706.11	578.18	503.38	455.10
20000	1852.69	1017.92	743.27	608.61	529.88	479.06
21000	1945.32	1068.81	780.44	639.04	556.37	503.01
22000	2037.96	1119.71	817.60	669.47	582.87	526.96
23000	2130.59	1170.60	854.76	699.90	609.36	550.91
24000	2223.23	1221.50	891.93	730.33	635.85	574.87
25000	2315.86	1272.40	929.09	760.76	662.35	598.82
30000	2779.04	1526.87	1114.91	912.91	794.82	718.58
35000	3242.21	1781.35	1300.73	1065.06	927.29	838.35
40000	3705.38	2035.83	1486.54	1217.21	1059.76	958.11
45000	4168.55	2290.31	1672.36	1369.37	1192.22	1077.88
50000	4631.73	2544.79	1858.18	1521.52	1324.69	1197.64
55000	5094.90	2799.27	2044.00	1673.67	1457.16	1317.41
60000	5558.07	3053.75	2229.82	1825.82	1589.63	1437.17
65000	6021.24	3308.23	2415.63	1977.97	1722.10	1556.93
70000	6484.42	3562.71	2601.45	2130.13	1854.57	1676.70
75000	6947.59	3817.19	2787.27	2282.28	1987.04	1796.46
80000	7410.76	4071.66	2973.09	2434.43	2119.51	1916.23
85000	7873.93	4326.14	3158.90	2586.58	2251.98	2035.99
90000	8337.11	4580.62	3344.72	2738.73	2384.45	2155.75
95000	8800.28	4835.10	3530.54	2890.88	2516.92	2275.52
100000	9263.45	5089.58	3716.36	3043.04	2649.39	2395.28
200000	18526.90	10179.16	7432.72	6086.07	5298.78	4790.57
300000	27790.35	15268.74	11149.08	9129.11	7948.17	7185.85
400000	37053.80	20358.32	14865.43	12172.14	10597.55	9581.13
500000	46317.25	25447.90	18581.79	15215.18	13246.94	11976.41

MONTHLY PAYMENT
Needed to repay a loan

TERM AMOUNT	7 YEARS	8 YEARS	9 YEARS	10 YEARS	11 YEARS	12 YEARS
500	11.10	10.48	10.01	9.66	9.39	9.18
1000	22.21	20.95	20.03	19.33	18.79	18.37
2000	44.41	41.91	40.05	38.65	37.57	36.73
3000	66.62	62.86	60.08	57.98	56.36	55.10
4000	88.82	83.81	80.11	77.30	75.15	73.46
5000	111.03	104.77	100.13	96.63	93.93	91.83
6000	133.24	125.72	120.16	115.95	112.72	110.20
7000	155.44	146.67	140.19	135.28	131.50	128.56
8000	177.65	167.63	160.21	154.60	150.29	146.93
9000	199.86	188.58	180.24	173.93	169.08	165.29
10000	222.06	209.53	200.27	193.26	187.86	183.66
11000	244.27	230.49	220.29	212.58	206.65	202.03
12000	266.47	251.44	240.32	231.91	225.44	220.39
13000	288.68	272.39	260.34	251.23	244.22	238.76
14000	310.89	293.34	280.37	270.56	263.01	257.13
15000	333.09	314.30	300.40	289.88	281.80	275.49
16000	355.30	335.25	320.42	309.21	300.58	293.86
17000	377.51	356.20	340.45	328.53	319.37	312.22
18000	399.71	377.16	360.48	347.86	338.15	330.59
19000	421.92	398.11	380.50	367.19	356.94	348.96
20000	444.12	419.06	400.53	386.51	375.73	367.32
21000	466.33	440.02	420.56	405.84	394.51	385.69
22000	488.54	460.97	440.58	425.16	413.30	404.05
23000	510.74	481.92	460.61	444.49	432.09	422.42
24000	532.95	502.88	480.64	463.81	450.87	440.79
25000	555.15	523.83	500.66	483.14	469.66	459.15
30000	666.19	628.60	600.80	579.77	563.59	550.98
35000	777.22	733.36	700.93	676.39	657.52	642.81
40000	888.25	838.13	801.06	773.02	751.45	734.64
45000	999.28	942.89	901.19	869.65	845.39	826.47
50000	1110.31	1047.66	1001.33	966.28	939.32	918.30
55000	1221.34	1152.43	1101.46	1062.91	1033.25	1010.13
60000	1332.37	1257.19	1201.59	1159.53	1127.18	1101.97
65000	1443.40	1361.96	1301.72	1256.16	1221.11	1193.80
70000	1554.43	1466.72	1401.86	1352.79	1315.04	1285.63
75000	1665.46	1571.49	1501.99	1449.42	1408.98	1377.46
80000	1776.50	1676.26	1602.12	1546.05	1502.91	1469.29
85000	1887.53	1781.02	1702.25	1642.67	1596.84	1561.12
90000	1998.56	1885.79	1802.39	1739.30	1690.77	1652.95
95000	2109.59	1990.55	1902.52	1835.93	1784.70	1744.78
100000	2220.62	2095.32	2002.65	1932.56	1878.63	1836.61
200000	4441.24	4190.64	4005.30	3865.11	3757.27	3673.22
300000	6661.86	6285.96	6007.95	5797.67	5635.90	5509.83
400000	8882.48	8381.28	8010.60	7730.23	7514.54	7346.43
500000	11103.10	10476.60	10013.25	9662.78	9393.17	9183.04

MONTHLY PAYMENT
Needed to repay a loan

TERM AMOUNT	15 YEARS	20 YEARS	25 YEARS	30 YEARS	35 YEARS	40 YEARS
500	8.78	8.49	8.39	8.36	8.34	8.34
1000	17.56	16.99	16.78	16.71	16.68	16.67
2000	35.13	33.98	33.57	33.42	33.37	33.35
3000	52.69	50.96	50.35	50.13	50.05	50.02
4000	70.25	67.95	67.14	66.84	66.73	66.69
5000	87.81	84.94	83.92	83.55	83.41	83.36
6000	105.38	101.93	100.71	100.26	100.10	100.04
7000	122.94	118.92	117.49	116.97	116.78	116.71
8000	140.50	135.91	134.28	133.68	133.46	133.38
9000	158.07	152.89	151.06	150.39	150.15	150.05
10000	175.63	169.88	167.85	167.10	166.83	166.73
11000	193.19	186.87	184.63	183.81	183.51	183.40
12000	210.76	203.86	201.41	200.52	200.19	200.07
13000	228.32	220.85	218.20	217.23	216.88	216.74
14000	245.88	237.84	234.98	233.94	233.56	233.42
15000	263.44	254.82	251.77	250.65	250.24	250.09
16000	281.01	271.81	268.55	267.36	266.92	266.76
17000	298.57	288.80	285.34	284.07	283.61	283.43
18000	316.13	305.79	302.12	300.78	300.29	300.11
19000	333.70	322.78	318.91	317.49	316.97	316.78
20000	351.26	339.76	335.69	334.20	333.66	333.45
21000	368.82	356.75	352.47	350.91	350.34	350.13
22000	386.39	373.74	369.26	367.62	367.02	366.80
23000	403.95	390.73	386.04	384.33	383.70	383.47
24000	421.51	407.72	402.83	401.04	400.39	400.14
25000	439.07	424.71	419.61	417.75	417.07	416.82
30000	526.89	509.65	503.54	501.31	500.48	500.18
35000	614.70	594.59	587.46	584.86	583.90	583.54
40000	702.52	679.53	671.38	668.41	667.31	666.91
45000	790.33	764.47	755.30	751.96	750.73	750.27
50000	878.15	849.41	839.23	835.51	834.14	833.63
55000	965.96	934.35	923.15	919.06	917.55	917.00
60000	1053.78	1019.29	1007.07	1002.61	1000.97	1000.36
65000	1141.59	1104.24	1090.99	1086.16	1084.38	1083.72
70000	1229.41	1189.18	1174.92	1169.71	1167.79	1167.08
75000	1317.22	1274.12	1258.84	1253.26	1251.21	1250.45
80000	1405.04	1359.06	1342.76	1336.81	1334.62	1333.81
85000	1492.85	1444.00	1426.68	1420.37	1418.04	1417.17
90000	1580.67	1528.94	1510.61	1503.92	1501.45	1500.54
95000	1668.48	1613.88	1594.53	1587.47	1584.86	1583.90
100000	1756.30	1698.82	1678.45	1671.02	1668.28	1667.26
200000	3512.59	3397.65	3356.90	3342.04	3336.56	3334.53
300000	5268.89	5096.47	5035.36	5013.06	5004.83	5001.79
400000	7025.19	6795.30	6713.81	6684.07	6673.11	6669.06
500000	8781.48	8494.12	8392.26	8355.09	8341.39	8336.32

20.5% MONTHLY PAYMENT
Needed to repay a loan

TERM AMOUNT	1 YEAR	2 YEARS	3 YEARS	4 YEARS	5 YEARS	6 YEARS
500	46.44	25.57	18.71	15.35	13.39	12.12
1000	92.87	51.14	37.42	30.70	26.77	24.24
2000	185.75	102.28	74.84	61.39	53.55	48.49
3000	278.62	153.42	112.26	92.09	80.32	72.73
4000	371.50	204.56	149.68	122.79	107.09	96.97
5000	464.37	255.70	187.09	153.49	133.86	121.22
6000	557.24	306.84	224.51	184.18	160.64	145.46
7000	650.12	357.98	261.93	214.88	187.41	169.70
8000	742.99	409.12	299.35	245.58	214.18	193.95
9000	835.87	460.26	336.77	276.28	240.96	218.19
10000	928.74	511.40	374.19	306.97	267.73	242.44
11000	1021.61	562.54	411.61	337.67	294.50	266.68
12000	1114.49	613.68	449.03	368.37	321.27	290.92
13000	1207.36	664.83	486.44	399.07	348.05	315.17
14000	1300.24	715.97	523.86	429.76	374.82	339.41
15000	1393.11	767.11	561.28	460.46	401.59	363.65
16000	1485.98	818.25	598.70	491.16	428.37	387.90
17000	1578.86	869.39	636.12	521.86	455.14	412.14
18000	1671.73	920.53	673.54	552.55	481.91	436.38
19000	1764.61	971.67	710.96	583.25	508.68	460.63
20000	1857.48	1022.81	748.38	613.95	535.46	484.87
21000	1950.35	1073.95	785.80	644.65	562.23	509.11
22000	2043.23	1125.09	823.21	675.34	589.00	533.36
23000	2136.10	1176.23	860.63	706.04	615.78	557.60
24000	2228.98	1227.37	898.05	736.74	642.55	581.84
25000	2321.85	1278.51	935.47	767.43	669.32	606.09
30000	2786.22	1534.21	1122.57	920.92	803.19	727.31
35000	3250.59	1789.91	1309.66	1074.41	937.05	848.52
40000	3714.96	2045.62	1496.75	1227.90	1070.91	969.74
45000	4179.33	2301.32	1683.85	1381.38	1204.78	1090.96
50000	4643.70	2557.02	1870.94	1534.87	1338.64	1212.18
55000	5108.07	2812.72	2058.04	1688.36	1472.51	1333.39
60000	5572.44	3068.42	2245.13	1841.84	1606.37	1454.61
65000	6036.81	3324.13	2432.22	1995.33	1740.24	1575.83
70000	6501.18	3579.83	2619.32	2148.82	1874.10	1697.05
75000	6965.55	3835.53	2806.41	2302.30	2007.96	1818.27
80000	7429.92	4091.23	2993.51	2455.79	2141.83	1939.48
85000	7894.29	4346.93	3180.60	2609.28	2275.69	2060.70
90000	8358.66	4602.64	3367.70	2762.77	2409.56	2181.92
95000	8823.03	4858.34	3554.79	2916.25	2543.42	2303.14
100000	9287.40	5114.04	3741.88	3069.74	2677.29	2424.35
200000	18574.79	10228.08	7483.77	6139.48	5354.57	4848.71
300000	27862.19	15342.12	11225.65	9209.22	8031.86	7273.06
400000	37149.59	20456.16	14967.53	12278.96	10709.14	9697.41
500000	46436.99	25570.20	18709.42	15348.70	13386.43	12121.77

MONTHLY PAYMENT 20.5%
Needed to repay a loan

TERM AMOUNT	7 YEARS	8 YEARS	9 YEARS	10 YEARS	11 YEARS	12 YEARS
500	11.25	10.63	10.17	9.83	9.56	9.36
1000	22.51	21.27	20.35	19.66	19.13	18.72
2000	45.02	42.53	40.70	39.32	38.26	37.43
3000	67.52	63.80	61.05	58.97	57.38	56.15
4000	90.03	85.06	81.40	78.63	76.51	74.86
5000	112.54	106.33	101.75	98.29	95.64	93.58
6000	135.05	127.60	122.10	117.95	114.77	112.30
7000	157.56	148.86	142.45	137.61	133.90	131.01
8000	180.07	170.13	162.80	157.27	153.02	149.73
9000	202.57	191.39	183.15	176.92	172.15	168.44
10000	225.08	212.66	203.50	196.58	191.28	187.16
11000	247.59	233.93	223.85	216.24	210.41	205.87
12000	270.10	255.19	244.20	235.90	229.53	224.59
13000	292.61	276.46	264.54	255.56	248.66	243.31
14000	315.12	297.72	284.89	275.22	267.79	262.02
15000	337.62	318.99	305.24	294.87	286.92	280.74
16000	360.13	340.26	325.59	314.53	306.05	299.45
17000	382.64	361.52	345.94	334.19	325.17	318.17
18000	405.15	382.79	366.29	353.85	344.30	336.89
19000	427.66	404.06	386.64	373.51	363.43	355.60
20000	450.16	425.32	406.99	393.16	382.56	374.32
21000	472.67	446.59	427.34	412.82	401.69	393.03
22000	495.18	467.85	447.69	432.48	420.81	411.75
23000	517.69	489.12	468.04	452.14	439.94	430.47
24000	540.20	510.39	488.39	471.80	459.07	449.18
25000	562.71	531.65	508.74	491.46	478.20	467.90
30000	675.25	637.98	610.49	589.75	573.84	561.48
35000	787.79	744.31	712.24	688.04	669.48	655.06
40000	900.33	850.64	813.98	786.33	765.12	748.64
45000	1012.87	956.97	915.73	884.62	860.76	842.22
50000	1125.41	1063.30	1017.48	982.91	956.40	935.79
55000	1237.95	1169.63	1119.23	1081.20	1052.04	1029.37
60000	1350.49	1275.96	1220.98	1179.49	1147.67	1122.95
65000	1463.04	1382.29	1322.72	1277.78	1243.31	1216.53
70000	1575.58	1488.62	1424.47	1376.08	1338.95	1310.11
75000	1688.12	1594.95	1526.22	1474.37	1434.59	1403.69
80000	1800.66	1701.28	1627.97	1572.66	1530.23	1497.27
85000	1913.20	1807.62	1729.71	1670.95	1625.87	1590.85
90000	2025.74	1913.95	1831.46	1769.24	1721.51	1684.43
95000	2138.28	2020.28	1933.21	1867.53	1817.15	1778.01
100000	2250.82	2126.61	2034.96	1965.82	1912.79	1871.59
200000	4501.65	4253.21	4069.92	3931.65	3825.58	3743.18
300000	6752.47	6379.82	6104.88	5897.47	5738.37	5614.77
400000	9003.30	8506.42	8139.83	7863.29	7651.17	7486.36
500000	11254.12	10633.03	10174.79	9829.12	9563.96	9357.95

20.5%

MONTHLY PAYMENT
Needed to repay a loan

TERM AMOUNT	15 YEARS	20 YEARS	25 YEARS	30 YEARS	35 YEARS	40 YEARS
500	8.97	8.69	8.60	8.56	8.55	8.54
1000	17.93	17.38	17.19	17.12	17.10	17.09
2000	35.87	34.76	34.38	34.24	34.19	34.18
3000	53.80	52.14	51.57	51.37	51.29	51.27
4000	71.73	69.53	68.76	68.49	68.39	68.35
5000	89.67	86.91	85.95	85.61	85.49	85.44
6000	107.60	104.29	103.14	102.73	102.58	102.53
7000	125.53	121.67	120.33	119.85	119.68	119.62
8000	143.47	139.05	137.52	136.97	136.78	136.71
9000	161.40	156.43	154.71	154.10	153.88	153.80
10000	179.33	173.82	171.90	171.22	170.97	170.88
11000	197.27	191.20	189.09	188.34	188.07	187.97
12000	215.20	208.58	206.28	205.46	205.17	205.06
13000	233.14	225.96	223.47	222.58	222.26	222.15
14000	251.07	243.34	240.66	239.71	239.36	239.24
15000	269.00	260.72	257.85	256.83	256.46	256.33
16000	286.94	278.10	275.04	273.95	273.56	273.41
17000	304.87	295.49	292.23	291.07	290.65	290.50
18000	322.80	312.87	309.42	308.19	307.75	307.59
19000	340.74	330.25	326.61	325.31	324.85	324.68
20000	358.67	347.63	343.80	342.44	341.94	341.77
21000	376.60	365.01	360.99	359.56	359.04	358.86
22000	394.54	382.39	378.18	376.68	376.14	375.94
23000	412.47	399.78	395.37	393.80	393.24	393.03
24000	430.40	417.16	412.56	410.92	410.33	410.12
25000	448.34	434.54	429.75	428.05	427.43	427.21
30000	538.00	521.45	515.70	513.65	512.92	512.65
35000	627.67	608.35	601.65	599.26	598.40	598.09
40000	717.34	695.26	687.60	684.87	683.89	683.53
45000	807.01	782.17	773.55	770.48	769.38	768.98
50000	896.67	869.08	859.50	856.09	854.86	854.42
55000	986.34	955.98	945.45	941.70	940.35	939.86
60000	1076.01	1042.89	1031.40	1027.31	1025.83	1025.30
65000	1165.68	1129.80	1117.35	1112.92	1111.32	1110.74
70000	1255.34	1216.71	1203.30	1198.53	1196.81	1196.19
75000	1345.01	1303.62	1289.26	1284.14	1282.29	1281.63
80000	1434.68	1390.52	1375.21	1369.74	1367.78	1367.07
85000	1524.34	1477.43	1461.16	1455.35	1453.27	1452.51
90000	1614.01	1564.34	1547.11	1540.96	1538.75	1537.95
95000	1703.68	1651.25	1633.06	1626.57	1624.24	1623.39
100000	1793.35	1738.15	1719.01	1712.18	1709.72	1708.84
200000	3586.69	3476.31	3438.01	3424.36	3419.45	3417.67
300000	5380.04	5214.46	5157.02	5136.54	5129.17	5126.51
400000	7173.39	6952.62	6876.03	6848.72	6838.90	6835.35
500000	8966.73	8690.77	8595.04	8560.90	8548.62	8544.18

MONTHLY PAYMENT
Needed to repay a loan

21%

TERM AMOUNT	1 YEAR	2 YEARS	3 YEARS	4 YEARS	5 YEARS	6 YEARS
500	46.56	25.69	18.84	15.48	13.53	12.27
1000	93.11	51.39	37.68	30.97	27.05	24.54
2000	186.23	102.77	75.35	61.93	54.11	49.07
3000	279.34	154.16	113.03	92.90	81.16	73.61
4000	372.46	205.54	150.70	123.86	108.21	98.14
5000	465.57	256.93	188.38	154.83	135.27	122.68
6000	558.68	308.31	226.05	185.79	162.32	147.22
7000	651.80	359.70	263.73	216.76	189.37	171.75
8000	744.91	411.09	301.40	247.73	216.43	196.29
9000	838.02	462.47	339.08	278.69	243.48	220.82
10000	931.14	513.86	376.75	309.66	270.53	245.36
11000	1024.25	565.24	414.43	340.62	297.59	269.90
12000	1117.37	616.63	452.10	371.59	324.64	294.43
13000	1210.48	668.01	489.78	402.55	351.69	318.97
14000	1303.59	719.40	527.45	433.52	378.75	343.50
15000	1396.71	770.78	565.13	464.49	405.80	368.04
16000	1489.82	822.17	602.80	495.45	432.85	392.58
17000	1582.93	873.56	640.48	526.42	459.91	417.11
18000	1676.05	924.94	678.15	557.38	486.96	441.65
19000	1769.16	976.33	715.83	588.35	514.01	466.18
20000	1862.28	1027.71	753.50	619.31	541.07	490.72
21000	1955.39	1079.10	791.18	650.28	568.12	515.26
22000	2048.50	1130.48	828.85	681.25	595.17	539.79
23000	2141.62	1181.87	866.53	712.21	622.23	564.33
24000	2234.73	1233.26	904.20	743.18	649.28	588.86
25000	2327.84	1284.64	941.88	774.14	676.33	613.40
30000	2793.41	1541.57	1130.25	928.97	811.60	736.08
35000	3258.98	1798.50	1318.63	1083.80	946.87	858.76
40000	3724.55	2055.43	1507.00	1238.63	1082.13	981.44
45000	4190.12	2312.35	1695.38	1393.46	1217.40	1104.12
50000	4655.69	2569.28	1883.75	1548.28	1352.67	1226.80
55000	5121.26	2826.21	2072.13	1703.11	1487.93	1349.48
60000	5586.83	3083.14	2260.50	1857.94	1623.20	1472.16
65000	6052.40	3340.07	2448.88	2012.77	1758.47	1594.84
70000	6517.96	3597.00	2637.25	2167.60	1893.74	1717.52
75000	6983.53	3853.92	2825.63	2322.43	2029.00	1840.20
80000	7449.10	4110.85	3014.01	2477.26	2164.27	1962.88
85000	7914.67	4367.78	3202.38	2632.08	2299.54	2085.56
90000	8380.24	4624.71	3390.76	2786.91	2434.80	2208.24
95000	8845.81	4881.64	3579.13	2941.74	2570.07	2330.92
100000	9311.38	5138.57	3767.51	3096.57	2705.34	2453.60
200000	18622.75	10277.13	7535.01	6193.14	5410.67	4907.20
300000	27934.13	15415.70	11302.52	9289.71	8116.01	7360.80
400000	37245.51	20554.26	15070.03	12386.28	10821.34	9814.40
500000	46556.89	25692.83	18837.53	15482.85	13526.68	12268.00

21%

MONTHLY PAYMENT
Needed to repay a loan

TERM AMOUNT	7 YEARS	8 YEARS	9 YEARS	10 YEARS	11 YEARS	12 YEARS
500	11.41	10.79	10.34	10.00	9.74	9.53
1000	22.81	21.58	20.67	19.99	19.47	19.07
2000	45.62	43.16	41.35	39.99	38.94	38.14
3000	68.44	64.74	62.02	59.98	58.42	57.20
4000	91.25	86.32	82.70	79.97	77.89	76.27
5000	114.06	107.91	103.37	99.97	97.36	95.34
6000	136.87	129.49	124.05	119.96	116.83	114.41
7000	159.69	151.07	144.72	139.95	136.30	133.48
8000	182.50	172.65	165.40	159.95	155.77	152.54
9000	205.31	194.23	186.07	179.94	175.25	171.61
10000	228.12	215.81	206.75	199.93	194.72	190.68
11000	250.93	237.39	227.42	219.92	214.19	209.75
12000	273.75	258.97	248.10	239.92	233.66	228.82
13000	296.56	280.55	268.77	259.91	253.13	247.88
14000	319.37	302.13	289.45	279.90	272.61	266.95
15000	342.18	323.72	310.12	299.90	292.08	286.02
16000	365.00	345.30	330.80	319.89	311.55	305.09
17000	387.81	366.88	351.47	339.88	331.02	324.16
18000	410.62	388.46	372.15	359.88	350.49	343.22
19000	433.43	410.04	392.82	379.87	369.96	362.29
20000	456.24	431.62	413.50	399.86	389.44	381.36
21000	479.06	453.20	434.17	419.86	408.91	400.43
22000	501.87	474.78	454.85	439.85	428.38	419.50
23000	524.68	496.36	475.52	459.84	447.85	438.56
24000	547.49	517.94	496.20	479.84	467.32	457.63
25000	570.31	539.53	516.87	499.83	486.80	476.70
30000	684.37	647.43	620.25	599.80	584.15	572.04
35000	798.43	755.34	723.62	699.76	681.51	667.38
40000	912.49	863.24	826.99	799.73	778.87	762.72
45000	1026.55	971.15	930.37	899.69	876.23	858.06
50000	1140.61	1079.05	1033.74	999.66	973.59	953.40
55000	1254.67	1186.96	1137.12	1099.62	1070.95	1048.74
60000	1368.73	1294.86	1240.49	1199.59	1168.31	1144.08
65000	1482.79	1402.77	1343.87	1299.56	1265.67	1239.42
70000	1596.86	1510.67	1447.24	1399.52	1363.03	1334.76
75000	1710.92	1618.58	1550.62	1499.49	1460.39	1430.10
80000	1824.98	1726.48	1653.99	1599.45	1557.74	1525.44
85000	1939.04	1834.39	1757.36	1699.42	1655.10	1620.78
90000	2053.10	1942.29	1860.74	1799.39	1752.46	1716.12
95000	2167.16	2050.20	1964.11	1899.35	1849.82	1811.46
100000	2281.22	2158.10	2067.49	1999.32	1947.18	1906.80
200000	4562.45	4316.20	4134.97	3998.63	3894.36	3813.60
300000	6843.67	6474.30	6202.46	5997.95	5841.54	5720.40
400000	9124.89	8632.40	8269.95	7997.27	7788.72	7627.20
500000	11406.11	10790.50	10337.43	9996.58	9735.90	9534.01

MONTHLY PAYMENT
Needed to repay a loan

21%

TERM AMOUNT	15 YEARS	20 YEARS	25 YEARS	30 YEARS	35 YEARS	40 YEARS
500	9.15	8.89	8.80	8.77	8.76	8.75
1000	18.31	17.78	17.60	17.53	17.51	17.50
2000	36.61	35.55	35.19	35.07	35.02	35.01
3000	54.92	53.33	52.79	52.60	52.54	52.51
4000	73.22	71.11	70.39	70.14	70.05	70.02
5000	91.53	88.88	87.98	87.67	87.56	87.52
6000	109.84	106.66	105.58	105.20	105.07	105.03
7000	128.14	124.44	123.18	122.74	122.58	122.53
8000	146.45	142.21	140.77	140.27	140.10	140.03
9000	164.76	159.99	158.37	157.81	157.61	157.54
10000	183.06	177.76	175.97	175.34	175.12	175.04
11000	201.37	195.54	193.56	192.87	192.63	192.55
12000	219.67	213.32	211.16	210.41	210.14	210.05
13000	237.98	231.09	228.76	227.94	227.66	227.56
14000	256.29	248.87	246.35	245.48	245.17	245.06
15000	274.59	266.65	263.95	263.01	262.68	262.56
16000	292.90	284.42	281.55	280.54	280.19	280.07
17000	311.20	302.20	299.14	298.08	297.70	297.57
18000	329.51	319.98	316.74	315.61	315.22	315.08
19000	347.82	337.75	334.34	333.15	332.73	332.58
20000	366.12	355.53	351.93	350.68	350.24	350.08
21000	384.43	373.31	369.53	368.21	367.75	367.59
22000	402.73	391.08	387.13	385.75	385.26	385.09
23000	421.04	408.86	404.72	403.28	402.78	402.60
24000	439.35	426.63	422.32	420.82	420.29	420.10
25000	457.65	444.41	439.92	438.35	437.80	437.61
30000	549.18	533.29	527.90	526.02	525.36	525.13
35000	640.71	622.18	615.88	613.69	612.92	612.65
40000	732.24	711.06	703.87	701.36	700.48	700.17
45000	823.78	799.94	791.85	789.03	788.04	787.69
50000	915.31	888.82	879.83	876.70	875.60	875.21
55000	1006.84	977.70	967.81	964.37	963.16	962.73
60000	1098.37	1066.59	1055.80	1052.04	1050.72	1050.25
65000	1189.90	1155.47	1143.78	1139.71	1138.28	1137.78
70000	1281.43	1244.35	1231.76	1227.38	1225.84	1225.30
75000	1372.96	1333.23	1319.75	1315.05	1313.40	1312.82
80000	1464.49	1422.11	1407.73	1402.72	1400.96	1400.34
85000	1556.02	1511.00	1495.71	1490.39	1488.52	1487.86
90000	1647.55	1599.88	1583.70	1578.06	1576.08	1575.38
95000	1739.08	1688.76	1671.68	1665.73	1663.64	1662.90
100000	1830.61	1777.64	1759.66	1753.40	1751.20	1750.42
200000	3661.22	3555.29	3519.33	3506.80	3502.40	3500.85
300000	5491.84	5332.93	5278.99	5260.20	5253.60	5251.27
400000	7322.45	7110.57	7038.65	7013.60	7004.80	7001.69
500000	9153.06	8888.21	8798.31	8767.00	8756.00	8752.12

MONTHLY PAYMENT
Needed to repay a loan

TERM AMOUNT	1 YEAR	2 YEARS	3 YEARS	4 YEARS	5 YEARS	6 YEARS
500	46.68	25.82	18.97	15.62	13.67	12.42
1000	93.35	51.63	37.93	31.24	27.34	24.83
2000	186.71	103.26	75.86	62.47	54.67	49.66
3000	280.06	154.89	113.80	93.71	82.01	74.49
4000	373.42	206.53	151.73	124.94	109.34	99.32
5000	466.77	258.16	189.66	156.18	136.68	124.15
6000	560.12	309.79	227.59	187.41	164.01	148.98
7000	653.48	361.42	265.53	218.65	191.35	173.81
8000	746.83	413.05	303.46	249.88	218.68	198.64
9000	840.19	464.68	341.39	281.12	246.02	223.47
10000	933.54	516.32	379.32	312.35	273.35	248.30
11000	1026.89	567.95	417.26	343.59	300.69	273.13
12000	1120.25	619.58	455.19	374.82	328.02	297.96
13000	1213.60	671.21	493.12	406.06	355.36	322.79
14000	1306.95	722.84	531.05	437.29	382.70	347.62
15000	1400.31	774.47	568.98	468.53	410.03	372.45
16000	1493.66	826.11	606.92	499.76	437.37	397.28
17000	1587.02	877.74	644.85	531.00	464.70	422.11
18000	1680.37	929.37	682.78	562.23	492.04	446.94
19000	1773.72	981.00	720.71	593.47	519.37	471.77
20000	1867.08	1032.63	758.65	624.71	546.71	496.60
21000	1960.43	1084.26	796.58	655.94	574.04	521.43
22000	2053.79	1135.89	834.51	687.18	601.38	546.26
23000	2147.14	1187.53	872.44	718.41	628.71	571.09
24000	2240.49	1239.16	910.37	749.65	656.05	595.92
25000	2333.85	1290.79	948.31	780.88	683.38	620.75
30000	2800.62	1548.95	1137.97	937.06	820.06	744.91
35000	3267.39	1807.10	1327.63	1093.23	956.74	869.06
40000	3734.16	2065.26	1517.29	1249.41	1093.42	993.21
45000	4200.93	2323.42	1706.95	1405.59	1230.09	1117.36
50000	4667.70	2581.58	1896.61	1561.76	1366.77	1241.51
55000	5134.47	2839.74	2086.28	1717.94	1503.45	1365.66
60000	5601.23	3097.89	2275.94	1874.12	1640.12	1489.81
65000	6068.00	3356.05	2465.60	2030.29	1776.80	1613.96
70000	6534.77	3614.21	2655.26	2186.47	1913.48	1738.11
75000	7001.54	3872.37	2844.92	2342.64	2050.15	1862.26
80000	7468.31	4130.53	3034.58	2498.82	2186.83	1986.42
85000	7935.08	4388.68	3224.24	2655.00	2323.51	2110.57
90000	8401.85	4646.84	3413.90	2811.17	2460.18	2234.72
95000	8868.62	4905.00	3603.57	2967.35	2596.86	2358.87
100000	9335.39	5163.16	3793.23	3123.53	2733.54	2483.02
200000	18670.78	10326.31	7586.45	6247.05	5467.08	4966.04
300000	28006.17	15489.47	11379.68	9370.58	8200.61	7449.06
400000	37341.56	20652.63	15172.91	12494.10	10934.15	9932.08
500000	46676.95	25815.79	18966.14	15617.63	13667.69	12415.10

MONTHLY PAYMENT
Needed to repay a loan

TERM AMOUNT	7 YEARS	8 YEARS	9 YEARS	10 YEARS	11 YEARS	12 YEARS
500	11.56	10.95	10.50	10.17	9.91	9.71
1000	23.12	21.90	21.00	20.33	19.82	19.42
2000	46.24	43.80	42.00	40.66	39.64	38.84
3000	69.35	65.69	63.01	60.99	59.45	58.27
4000	92.47	87.59	84.01	81.32	79.27	77.69
5000	115.59	109.49	105.01	101.65	99.09	97.11
6000	138.71	131.39	126.01	121.98	118.91	116.53
7000	161.83	153.29	147.02	142.31	138.73	135.96
8000	184.95	175.18	168.02	162.64	158.54	155.38
9000	208.06	197.08	189.02	182.97	178.36	174.80
10000	231.18	218.98	210.02	203.30	198.18	194.22
11000	254.30	240.88	231.03	223.63	218.00	213.65
12000	277.42	262.78	252.03	243.96	237.82	233.07
13000	300.54	284.67	273.03	264.29	257.63	252.49
14000	323.65	306.57	294.03	284.62	277.45	271.91
15000	346.77	328.47	315.03	304.96	297.27	291.34
16000	369.89	350.37	336.04	325.29	317.09	310.76
17000	393.01	372.27	357.04	345.62	336.90	330.18
18000	416.13	394.16	378.04	365.95	356.72	349.60
19000	439.24	416.06	399.04	386.28	376.54	369.03
20000	462.36	437.96	420.05	406.61	396.36	388.45
21000	485.48	459.86	441.05	426.94	416.18	407.87
22000	508.60	481.76	462.05	447.27	435.99	427.29
23000	531.72	503.65	483.05	467.60	455.81	446.71
24000	554.84	525.55	504.06	487.93	475.63	466.14
25000	577.95	547.45	525.06	508.26	495.45	485.56
30000	693.54	656.94	630.07	609.91	594.54	582.67
35000	809.13	766.43	735.08	711.56	693.63	679.78
40000	924.73	875.92	840.09	813.21	792.72	776.90
45000	1040.32	985.41	945.10	914.87	891.81	874.01
50000	1155.91	1094.90	1050.12	1016.52	990.90	971.12
55000	1271.50	1204.39	1155.13	1118.17	1089.99	1068.23
60000	1387.09	1313.88	1260.14	1219.82	1189.08	1165.34
65000	1502.68	1423.37	1365.15	1321.47	1288.17	1262.45
70000	1618.27	1532.86	1470.16	1423.12	1387.26	1359.57
75000	1733.86	1642.35	1575.17	1524.78	1486.35	1456.68
80000	1849.45	1751.84	1680.19	1626.43	1585.44	1553.79
85000	1965.04	1861.33	1785.20	1728.08	1684.52	1650.90
90000	2080.63	1970.82	1890.21	1829.73	1783.61	1748.01
95000	2196.22	2080.31	1995.22	1931.38	1882.70	1845.13
100000	2311.81	2189.80	2100.23	2033.03	1981.79	1942.24
200000	4623.63	4379.61	4200.46	4066.07	3963.59	3884.48
300000	6935.44	6569.41	6300.70	6099.10	5945.38	5826.71
400000	9247.25	8759.21	8400.93	8132.13	7927.18	7768.95
500000	11559.07	10949.01	10501.16	10165.17	9908.97	9711.19

21.5%

MONTHLY PAYMENT
Needed to repay a loan

TERM AMOUNT	15 YEARS	20 YEARS	25 YEARS	30 YEARS	35 YEARS	40 YEARS
500	9.34	9.09	9.00	8.97	8.96	8.96
1000	18.68	18.17	18.00	17.95	17.93	17.92
2000	37.36	36.35	36.01	35.89	35.85	35.84
3000	56.04	54.52	54.01	53.84	53.78	53.76
4000	74.72	72.69	72.02	71.79	71.71	71.68
5000	93.40	90.86	90.02	89.73	89.64	89.60
6000	112.09	109.04	108.02	107.68	107.56	107.52
7000	130.77	127.21	126.03	125.63	125.49	125.44
8000	149.45	145.38	144.03	143.57	143.42	143.36
9000	168.13	163.56	162.04	161.52	161.34	161.28
10000	186.81	181.73	180.04	179.47	179.27	179.20
11000	205.49	199.90	198.05	197.41	197.20	197.12
12000	224.17	218.07	216.05	215.36	215.12	215.04
13000	242.85	236.25	234.05	233.31	233.05	232.96
14000	261.53	254.42	252.06	251.25	250.98	250.88
15000	280.21	272.59	270.06	269.20	268.91	268.80
16000	298.89	290.77	288.07	287.15	286.83	286.72
17000	317.57	308.94	306.07	305.09	304.76	304.64
18000	336.26	327.11	324.07	323.04	322.69	322.56
19000	354.94	345.28	342.08	340.99	340.61	340.48
20000	373.62	363.46	360.08	358.93	358.54	358.40
21000	392.30	381.63	378.09	376.88	376.47	376.32
22000	410.98	399.80	396.09	394.83	394.39	394.24
23000	429.66	417.97	414.09	412.77	412.32	412.17
24000	448.34	436.15	432.10	430.72	430.25	430.09
25000	467.02	454.32	450.10	448.67	448.18	448.01
30000	560.43	545.18	540.12	538.40	537.81	537.61
35000	653.83	636.05	630.14	628.13	627.45	627.21
40000	747.23	726.91	720.16	717.87	717.08	716.81
45000	840.64	817.78	810.18	807.60	806.72	806.41
50000	934.04	908.64	900.21	897.33	896.35	896.01
55000	1027.45	999.50	990.23	987.07	985.99	985.61
60000	1120.85	1090.37	1080.25	1076.80	1075.62	1075.21
65000	1214.26	1181.23	1170.27	1166.54	1165.26	1164.81
70000	1307.66	1272.10	1260.29	1256.27	1254.89	1254.42
75000	1401.06	1362.96	1350.31	1346.00	1344.53	1344.02
80000	1494.47	1453.83	1440.33	1435.74	1434.16	1433.62
85000	1587.87	1544.69	1530.35	1525.47	1523.80	1523.22
90000	1681.28	1635.55	1620.37	1615.20	1613.43	1612.82
95000	1774.68	1726.42	1710.39	1704.94	1703.07	1702.42
100000	1868.08	1817.28	1800.41	1794.67	1792.70	1792.02
200000	3736.17	3634.56	3600.82	3589.34	3585.40	3584.05
300000	5604.25	5451.84	5401.23	5384.01	5378.10	5376.07
400000	7472.34	7269.13	7201.64	7178.68	7170.80	7168.09
500000	9340.42	9086.41	9002.05	8973.35	8963.50	8960.11

MONTHLY PAYMENT
Needed to repay a loan

22%

TERM AMOUNT	1 YEAR	2 YEARS	3 YEARS	4 YEARS	5 YEARS	6 YEARS
500	46.80	25.94	19.10	15.75	13.81	12.56
1000	93.59	51.88	38.19	31.51	27.62	25.13
2000	187.19	103.76	76.38	63.01	55.24	50.25
3000	280.78	155.63	114.57	94.52	82.86	75.38
4000	374.38	207.51	152.76	126.02	110.48	100.50
5000	467.97	259.39	190.95	157.53	138.09	125.63
6000	561.57	311.27	229.14	189.04	165.71	150.76
7000	655.16	363.15	267.33	220.54	193.33	175.88
8000	748.76	415.03	305.52	252.05	220.95	201.01
9000	842.35	466.90	343.71	283.55	248.57	226.14
10000	935.94	518.78	381.90	315.06	276.19	251.26
11000	1029.54	570.66	420.09	346.57	303.81	276.39
12000	1123.13	622.54	458.29	378.07	331.43	301.51
13000	1216.73	674.42	496.48	409.58	359.05	326.64
14000	1310.32	726.29	534.67	441.09	386.66	351.77
15000	1403.92	778.17	572.86	472.59	414.28	376.89
16000	1497.51	830.05	611.05	504.10	441.90	402.02
17000	1591.10	881.93	649.24	535.60	469.52	427.14
18000	1684.70	933.81	687.43	567.11	497.14	452.27
19000	1778.29	985.68	725.62	598.62	524.76	477.40
20000	1871.89	1037.56	763.81	630.12	552.38	502.52
21000	1965.48	1089.44	802.00	661.63	580.00	527.65
22000	2059.08	1141.32	840.19	693.13	607.62	552.77
23000	2152.67	1193.20	878.38	724.64	635.23	577.90
24000	2246.27	1245.08	916.57	756.15	662.85	603.03
25000	2339.86	1296.95	954.76	787.65	690.47	628.15
30000	2807.83	1556.34	1145.71	945.18	828.57	753.78
35000	3275.80	1815.74	1336.67	1102.71	966.66	879.41
40000	3743.78	2075.13	1527.62	1260.24	1104.76	1005.05
45000	4211.75	2334.52	1718.57	1417.77	1242.85	1130.68
50000	4679.72	2593.91	1909.52	1575.30	1380.95	1256.31
55000	5147.69	2853.30	2100.47	1732.83	1519.04	1381.94
60000	5615.66	3112.69	2291.43	1890.36	1657.13	1507.57
65000	6083.63	3372.08	2482.38	2047.90	1795.23	1633.20
70000	6551.61	3631.47	2673.33	2205.43	1933.32	1758.83
75000	7019.58	3890.86	2864.28	2362.96	2071.42	1884.46
80000	7487.55	4150.25	3055.24	2520.49	2209.51	2010.09
85000	7955.52	4409.64	3246.19	2678.02	2347.61	2135.72
90000	8423.49	4669.03	3437.14	2835.55	2485.70	2261.35
95000	8891.47	4928.42	3628.09	2993.08	2623.80	2386.98
100000	9359.44	5187.82	3819.05	3150.61	2761.89	2512.61
200000	18718.88	10375.63	7638.09	6301.22	5523.78	5025.23
300000	28078.31	15563.45	11457.14	9451.82	8285.67	7537.84
400000	37437.75	20751.26	15276.18	12602.43	11047.56	10050.45
500000	46797.19	25939.08	19095.23	15753.04	13809.46	12563.06

22% MONTHLY PAYMENT
Needed to repay a loan

TERM AMOUNT	7 YEARS	8 YEARS	9 YEARS	10 YEARS	11 YEARS	12 YEARS
500	11.71	11.11	10.67	10.33	10.08	9.89
1000	23.43	22.22	21.33	20.67	20.17	19.78
2000	46.85	44.43	42.66	41.34	40.33	39.56
3000	70.28	66.65	64.00	62.01	60.50	59.34
4000	93.70	88.87	85.33	82.68	80.67	79.12
5000	117.13	111.09	106.66	103.35	100.83	98.89
6000	140.56	133.30	127.99	124.02	121.00	118.67
7000	163.98	155.52	149.32	144.69	141.16	138.45
8000	187.41	177.74	170.66	165.36	161.33	158.23
9000	210.83	199.95	191.99	186.03	181.50	178.01
10000	234.26	222.17	213.32	206.70	201.66	197.79
11000	257.69	244.39	234.65	227.37	221.83	217.57
12000	281.11	266.60	255.98	248.04	242.00	237.35
13000	304.54	288.82	277.31	268.71	262.16	257.13
14000	327.96	311.04	298.65	289.38	282.33	276.91
15000	351.39	333.26	319.98	310.05	302.49	296.68
16000	374.82	355.47	341.31	330.72	322.66	316.46
17000	398.24	377.69	362.64	351.38	342.83	336.24
18000	421.67	399.91	383.97	372.05	362.99	356.02
19000	445.09	422.12	405.31	392.72	383.16	375.80
20000	468.52	444.34	426.64	413.39	403.33	395.58
21000	491.94	466.56	447.97	434.06	423.49	415.36
22000	515.37	488.78	469.30	454.73	443.66	435.14
23000	538.80	510.99	490.63	475.40	463.82	454.92
24000	562.22	533.21	511.97	496.07	483.99	474.69
25000	585.65	555.43	533.30	516.74	504.16	494.47
30000	702.78	666.51	639.96	620.09	604.99	593.37
35000	819.91	777.60	746.62	723.44	705.82	692.26
40000	937.04	888.68	853.28	826.79	806.65	791.16
45000	1054.17	999.77	959.94	930.14	907.48	890.05
50000	1171.30	1110.85	1066.60	1033.48	1008.31	988.95
55000	1288.43	1221.94	1173.25	1136.83	1109.15	1087.84
60000	1405.56	1333.02	1279.91	1240.18	1209.98	1186.74
65000	1522.69	1444.11	1386.57	1343.53	1310.81	1285.63
70000	1639.82	1555.20	1493.23	1446.88	1411.64	1384.53
75000	1756.95	1666.28	1599.89	1550.23	1512.47	1483.42
80000	1874.08	1777.37	1706.55	1653.58	1613.30	1582.31
85000	1991.21	1888.45	1813.21	1756.92	1714.13	1681.21
90000	2108.33	1999.54	1919.87	1860.27	1814.97	1780.10
95000	2225.46	2110.62	2026.53	1963.62	1915.80	1879.00
100000	2342.59	2221.71	2133.19	2066.97	2016.63	1977.89
200000	4685.19	4443.42	4266.38	4133.94	4033.26	3955.79
300000	7027.78	6665.12	6399.57	6200.91	6049.89	5933.68
400000	9370.38	8886.83	8532.76	8267.88	8066.51	7911.57
500000	11712.97	11108.54	10665.95	10334.84	10083.14	9889.47

MONTHLY PAYMENT 22%
Needed to repay a loan

TERM AMOUNT	15 YEARS	20 YEARS	25 YEARS	30 YEARS	35 YEARS	40 YEARS
500	9.53	9.29	9.21	9.18	9.17	9.17
1000	19.06	18.57	18.41	18.36	18.34	18.34
2000	38.12	37.14	36.82	36.72	36.68	36.67
3000	57.17	55.71	55.24	55.08	55.03	55.01
4000	76.23	74.28	73.65	73.44	73.37	73.35
5000	95.29	92.85	92.06	91.80	91.71	91.68
6000	114.35	111.42	110.47	110.16	110.05	110.02
7000	133.40	129.99	128.89	128.52	128.40	128.35
8000	152.46	148.56	147.30	146.88	146.74	146.69
9000	171.52	167.14	165.71	165.24	165.08	165.03
10000	190.58	185.71	184.12	183.60	183.42	183.36
11000	209.63	204.28	202.54	201.96	201.76	201.70
12000	228.69	222.85	220.95	220.32	220.11	220.04
13000	247.75	241.42	239.36	238.68	238.45	238.37
14000	266.81	259.99	257.77	257.04	256.79	256.71
15000	285.86	278.56	276.19	275.40	275.13	275.04
16000	304.92	297.13	294.60	293.76	293.48	293.38
17000	323.98	315.70	313.01	312.12	311.82	311.72
18000	343.04	334.27	331.42	330.48	330.16	330.05
19000	362.09	352.84	349.84	348.84	348.50	348.39
20000	381.15	371.41	368.25	367.20	366.84	366.73
21000	400.21	389.98	386.66	385.56	385.19	385.06
22000	419.27	408.55	405.07	403.92	403.53	403.40
23000	438.32	427.12	423.49	422.28	421.87	421.74
24000	457.38	445.69	441.90	440.64	440.21	440.07
25000	476.44	464.26	460.31	459.00	458.56	458.41
30000	571.73	557.12	552.37	550.80	550.27	550.09
35000	667.01	649.97	644.43	642.59	641.98	641.77
40000	762.30	742.82	736.50	734.39	733.69	733.45
45000	857.59	835.68	828.56	826.19	825.40	825.13
50000	952.88	928.53	920.62	917.99	917.11	916.82
55000	1048.17	1021.38	1012.68	1009.79	1008.82	1008.50
60000	1143.45	1114.24	1104.75	1101.59	1100.53	1100.18
65000	1238.74	1207.09	1196.81	1193.39	1192.25	1191.86
70000	1334.03	1299.94	1288.87	1285.19	1283.96	1283.54
75000	1429.32	1392.79	1380.93	1376.99	1375.67	1375.22
80000	1524.60	1485.65	1472.99	1468.79	1467.38	1466.91
85000	1619.89	1578.50	1565.06	1560.59	1559.09	1558.59
90000	1715.18	1671.35	1657.12	1652.39	1650.80	1650.27
95000	1810.47	1764.21	1749.18	1744.19	1742.51	1741.95
100000	1905.76	1857.06	1841.24	1835.98	1834.22	1833.63
200000	3811.51	3714.12	3682.48	3671.97	3668.45	3667.27
300000	5717.27	5571.18	5523.73	5507.95	5502.67	5500.90
400000	7623.02	7428.24	7364.97	7343.94	7336.90	7334.53
500000	9528.78	9285.30	9206.21	9179.92	9171.12	9168.16

22.5%

MONTHLY PAYMENT
Needed to repay a loan

TERM AMOUNT	1 YEAR	2 YEARS	3 YEARS	4 YEARS	5 YEARS	6 YEARS
500	46.92	26.06	19.22	15.89	13.95	12.71
1000	93.84	52.13	38.45	31.78	27.90	25.42
2000	187.67	104.25	76.90	63.56	55.81	50.85
3000	281.51	156.38	115.35	95.33	83.71	76.27
4000	375.34	208.50	153.80	127.11	111.62	101.70
5000	469.18	260.63	192.25	158.89	139.52	127.12
6000	563.01	312.75	230.70	190.67	167.42	152.54
7000	656.85	364.88	269.15	222.45	195.33	177.97
8000	750.68	417.00	307.60	254.23	223.23	203.39
9000	844.52	469.13	346.05	286.00	251.14	228.81
10000	938.35	521.25	384.50	317.78	279.04	254.24
11000	1032.19	573.38	422.95	349.56	306.94	279.66
12000	1126.02	625.50	461.40	381.34	334.85	305.09
13000	1219.86	677.63	499.84	413.12	362.75	330.51
14000	1313.69	729.76	538.29	444.89	390.66	355.93
15000	1407.53	781.88	576.74	476.67	418.56	381.36
16000	1501.36	834.01	615.19	508.45	446.46	406.78
17000	1595.20	886.13	653.64	540.23	474.37	432.20
18000	1689.03	938.26	692.09	572.01	502.27	457.63
19000	1782.87	990.38	730.54	603.78	530.17	483.05
20000	1876.70	1042.51	768.99	635.56	558.08	508.48
21000	1970.54	1094.63	807.44	667.34	585.98	533.90
22000	2064.37	1146.76	845.89	699.12	613.89	559.32
23000	2158.21	1198.88	884.34	730.90	641.79	584.75
24000	2252.04	1251.01	922.79	762.68	669.69	610.17
25000	2345.88	1303.13	961.24	794.45	697.60	635.59
30000	2815.06	1563.76	1153.49	953.34	837.12	762.71
35000	3284.23	1824.39	1345.74	1112.24	976.64	889.83
40000	3753.41	2085.02	1537.98	1271.13	1116.16	1016.95
45000	4222.58	2345.64	1730.23	1430.02	1255.68	1144.07
50000	4691.76	2606.27	1922.48	1588.91	1395.20	1271.19
55000	5160.94	2866.90	2114.73	1747.80	1534.72	1398.31
60000	5630.11	3127.52	2306.98	1906.69	1674.24	1525.43
65000	6099.29	3388.15	2499.22	2065.58	1813.76	1652.54
70000	6568.46	3648.78	2691.47	2224.47	1953.28	1779.66
75000	7037.64	3909.40	2883.72	2383.36	2092.80	1906.78
80000	7506.81	4170.03	3075.97	2542.25	2232.32	2033.90
85000	7975.99	4430.66	3268.22	2701.14	2371.84	2161.02
90000	8445.17	4691.29	3460.46	2860.03	2511.36	2288.14
95000	8914.34	4951.91	3652.71	3018.92	2650.87	2415.26
100000	9383.52	5212.54	3844.96	3177.82	2790.39	2542.38
200000	18767.04	10425.08	7689.92	6355.63	5580.79	5084.75
300000	28150.56	15637.62	11534.88	9533.45	8371.18	7627.13
400000	37534.07	20850.16	15379.84	12711.26	11161.58	10169.51
500000	46917.59	26062.70	19224.80	15889.08	13951.97	12711.88

MONTHLY PAYMENT
Needed to repay a loan

22.5%

TERM AMOUNT	7 YEARS	8 YEARS	9 YEARS	10 YEARS	11 YEARS	12 YEARS
500	11.87	11.27	10.83	10.51	10.26	10.07
1000	23.74	22.54	21.66	21.01	20.52	20.14
2000	47.47	45.08	43.33	42.02	41.03	40.28
3000	71.21	67.61	64.99	63.03	61.55	60.41
4000	94.94	90.15	86.65	84.04	82.07	80.55
5000	118.68	112.69	108.32	105.06	102.58	100.69
6000	142.41	135.23	129.98	126.07	123.10	120.83
7000	166.15	157.77	151.65	147.08	143.62	140.96
8000	189.89	180.31	173.31	168.09	164.13	161.10
9000	213.62	202.84	194.97	189.10	184.65	181.24
10000	237.36	225.38	216.64	210.11	205.17	201.38
11000	261.09	247.92	238.30	231.12	225.68	221.51
12000	284.83	270.46	259.96	252.13	246.20	241.65
13000	308.56	293.00	281.63	273.15	266.72	261.79
14000	332.30	315.53	303.29	294.16	287.23	281.93
15000	356.03	338.07	324.95	315.17	307.75	302.06
16000	379.77	360.61	346.62	336.18	328.27	322.20
17000	403.51	383.15	368.28	357.19	348.79	342.34
18000	427.24	405.69	389.94	378.20	369.30	362.48
19000	450.98	428.22	411.61	399.21	389.82	382.61
20000	474.71	450.76	433.27	420.22	410.34	402.75
21000	498.45	473.30	454.94	441.23	430.85	422.89
22000	522.18	495.84	476.60	462.25	451.37	443.03
23000	545.92	518.38	498.26	483.26	471.89	463.17
24000	569.66	540.92	519.93	504.27	492.40	483.30
25000	593.39	563.45	541.59	525.28	512.92	503.44
30000	712.07	676.14	649.91	630.34	615.50	604.13
35000	830.75	788.84	758.23	735.39	718.09	704.82
40000	949.43	901.53	866.54	840.45	820.67	805.50
45000	1068.10	1014.22	974.86	945.50	923.26	906.19
50000	1186.78	1126.91	1083.18	1050.56	1025.84	1006.88
55000	1305.46	1239.60	1191.50	1155.62	1128.42	1107.57
60000	1424.14	1352.29	1299.81	1260.67	1231.01	1208.26
65000	1542.82	1464.98	1408.13	1365.73	1333.59	1308.95
70000	1661.49	1577.67	1516.45	1470.78	1436.17	1409.63
75000	1780.17	1690.36	1624.77	1575.84	1538.76	1510.32
80000	1898.85	1803.05	1733.09	1680.89	1641.34	1611.01
85000	2017.53	1915.74	1841.40	1785.95	1743.93	1711.70
90000	2136.21	2028.43	1949.72	1891.01	1846.51	1812.39
95000	2254.89	2141.12	2058.04	1996.06	1949.09	1913.07
100000	2373.56	2253.81	2166.36	2101.12	2051.68	2013.76
200000	4747.13	4507.63	4332.72	4202.24	4103.36	4027.52
300000	7120.69	6761.44	6499.07	6303.36	6155.03	6041.29
400000	9494.25	9015.26	8665.43	8404.47	8206.71	8055.05
500000	11867.82	11269.07	10831.79	10505.59	10258.39	10068.81

22.5%

MONTHLY PAYMENT
Needed to repay a loan

TERM AMOUNT	15 YEARS	20 YEARS	25 YEARS	30 YEARS	35 YEARS	40 YEARS
500	9.72	9.48	9.41	9.39	9.38	9.38
1000	19.44	18.97	18.82	18.77	18.76	18.75
2000	38.87	37.94	37.64	37.55	37.52	37.51
3000	58.31	56.91	56.46	56.32	56.27	56.26
4000	77.74	75.88	75.29	75.09	75.03	75.01
5000	97.18	94.85	94.11	93.87	93.79	93.76
6000	116.62	113.82	112.93	112.64	112.55	112.52
7000	136.05	132.79	131.75	131.41	131.30	131.27
8000	155.49	151.76	150.57	150.19	150.06	150.02
9000	174.93	170.73	169.39	168.96	168.82	168.77
10000	194.36	189.70	188.22	187.73	187.58	187.53
11000	213.80	208.67	207.04	206.51	206.33	206.28
12000	233.23	227.64	225.86	225.28	225.09	225.03
13000	252.67	246.61	244.68	244.05	243.85	243.78
14000	272.11	265.58	263.50	262.83	262.61	262.54
15000	291.54	284.55	282.32	281.60	281.37	281.29
16000	310.98	303.52	301.14	300.37	300.12	300.04
17000	330.42	322.48	319.97	319.15	318.88	318.79
18000	349.85	341.45	338.79	337.92	337.64	337.55
19000	369.29	360.42	357.61	356.69	356.40	356.30
20000	388.72	379.39	376.43	375.47	375.15	375.05
21000	408.16	398.36	395.25	394.24	393.91	393.80
22000	427.60	417.33	414.07	413.01	412.67	412.56
23000	447.03	436.30	432.89	431.79	431.43	431.31
24000	466.47	455.27	451.72	450.56	450.18	450.06
25000	485.90	474.24	470.54	469.33	468.94	468.81
30000	583.09	569.09	564.65	563.20	562.73	562.58
35000	680.27	663.94	658.75	657.07	656.52	656.34
40000	777.45	758.79	752.86	750.94	750.31	750.10
45000	874.63	853.64	846.97	844.80	844.10	843.86
50000	971.81	948.49	941.08	938.67	937.88	937.63
55000	1068.99	1043.33	1035.18	1032.54	1031.67	1031.39
60000	1166.17	1138.18	1129.29	1126.40	1125.46	1125.15
65000	1263.35	1233.03	1223.40	1220.27	1219.25	1218.91
70000	1360.53	1327.88	1317.51	1314.14	1313.04	1312.68
75000	1457.71	1422.73	1411.61	1408.00	1406.83	1406.44
80000	1554.89	1517.58	1505.72	1501.87	1500.61	1500.20
85000	1652.08	1612.42	1599.83	1595.74	1594.40	1593.96
90000	1749.26	1707.27	1693.94	1689.61	1688.19	1687.73
95000	1846.44	1802.12	1788.04	1783.47	1781.98	1781.49
100000	1943.62	1896.97	1882.15	1877.34	1875.77	1875.25
200000	3887.24	3793.94	3764.30	3754.68	3751.53	3750.50
300000	5830.85	5690.91	5646.45	5632.02	5627.30	5625.75
400000	7774.47	7587.88	7528.60	7509.36	7503.07	7501.01
500000	9718.09	9484.85	9410.76	9386.70	9378.83	9376.26

MONTHLY PAYMENT
Needed to repay a loan

23%

TERM AMOUNT	1 YEAR	2 YEARS	3 YEARS	4 YEARS	5 YEARS	6 YEARS
500	47.04	26.19	19.35	16.03	14.10	12.86
1000	94.08	52.37	38.71	32.05	28.19	25.72
2000	188.15	104.75	77.42	64.10	56.38	51.45
3000	282.23	157.12	116.13	96.15	84.57	77.17
4000	376.31	209.49	154.84	128.21	112.76	102.89
5000	470.38	261.87	193.55	160.26	140.95	128.62
6000	564.46	314.24	232.26	192.31	169.14	154.34
7000	658.53	366.61	270.97	224.36	197.33	180.06
8000	752.61	418.99	309.68	256.41	225.52	205.78
9000	846.69	471.36	348.39	288.46	253.71	231.51
10000	940.76	523.73	387.10	320.51	281.90	257.23
11000	1034.84	576.11	425.81	352.57	310.10	282.95
12000	1128.92	628.48	464.52	384.62	338.29	308.68
13000	1222.99	680.85	503.23	416.67	366.48	334.40
14000	1317.07	733.23	541.94	448.72	394.67	360.12
15000	1411.14	785.60	580.65	480.77	422.86	385.85
16000	1505.22	837.97	619.36	512.82	451.05	411.57
17000	1599.30	890.35	658.07	544.88	479.24	437.29
18000	1693.37	942.72	696.77	576.93	507.43	463.02
19000	1787.45	995.09	735.48	608.98	535.62	488.74
20000	1881.53	1047.47	774.19	641.03	563.81	514.46
21000	1975.60	1099.84	812.90	673.08	592.00	540.19
22000	2069.68	1152.21	851.61	705.13	620.19	565.91
23000	2163.76	1204.59	890.32	737.18	648.38	591.63
24000	2257.83	1256.96	929.03	769.24	676.57	617.35
25000	2351.91	1309.33	967.74	801.29	704.76	643.08
30000	2822.29	1571.20	1161.29	961.54	845.71	771.69
35000	3292.67	1833.07	1354.84	1121.80	986.67	900.31
40000	3763.05	2094.93	1548.39	1282.06	1127.62	1028.92
45000	4233.43	2356.80	1741.94	1442.32	1268.57	1157.54
50000	4703.82	2618.67	1935.49	1602.57	1409.52	1286.16
55000	5174.20	2880.53	2129.03	1762.83	1550.48	1414.77
60000	5644.58	3142.40	2322.58	1923.09	1691.43	1543.39
65000	6114.96	3404.26	2516.13	2083.35	1832.38	1672.00
70000	6585.34	3666.13	2709.68	2243.60	1973.33	1800.62
75000	7055.72	3928.00	2903.23	2403.86	2114.29	1929.23
80000	7526.11	4189.86	3096.78	2564.12	2255.24	2057.85
85000	7996.49	4451.73	3290.33	2724.38	2396.19	2186.46
90000	8466.87	4713.60	3483.87	2884.63	2537.14	2315.08
95000	8937.25	4975.46	3677.42	3044.89	2678.09	2443.70
100000	9407.63	5237.33	3870.97	3205.15	2819.05	2572.31
200000	18815.26	10474.66	7741.94	6410.29	5638.09	5144.62
300000	28222.90	15711.99	11612.92	9615.44	8457.14	7716.93
400000	37630.53	20949.32	15483.89	12820.59	11276.19	10289.24
500000	47038.16	26186.65	19354.86	16025.74	14095.24	12861.55

23% MONTHLY PAYMENT
Needed to repay a loan

TERM AMOUNT	7 YEARS	8 YEARS	9 YEARS	10 YEARS	11 YEARS	12 YEARS
500	12.02	11.43	11.00	10.68	10.43	10.25
1000	24.05	22.86	22.00	21.35	20.87	20.50
2000	48.09	45.72	43.99	42.71	41.74	41.00
3000	72.14	68.58	65.99	64.06	62.61	61.50
4000	96.19	91.44	87.99	85.42	83.48	81.99
5000	120.24	114.31	109.99	106.77	104.35	102.49
6000	144.28	137.17	131.98	128.13	125.22	122.99
7000	168.33	160.03	153.98	149.48	146.09	143.49
8000	192.38	182.89	175.98	170.84	166.96	163.99
9000	216.42	205.75	197.98	192.19	187.82	184.49
10000	240.47	228.61	219.97	213.55	208.69	204.98
11000	264.52	251.47	241.97	234.90	229.56	225.48
12000	288.57	274.33	263.97	256.26	250.43	245.98
13000	312.61	297.20	285.97	277.61	271.30	266.48
14000	336.66	320.06	307.96	298.97	292.17	286.98
15000	360.71	342.92	329.96	320.32	313.04	307.48
16000	384.76	365.78	351.96	341.68	333.91	327.97
17000	408.80	388.64	373.95	363.03	354.78	348.47
18000	432.85	411.50	395.95	384.39	375.65	368.97
19000	456.90	434.36	417.95	405.74	396.52	389.47
20000	480.94	457.22	439.95	427.10	417.39	409.97
21000	504.99	480.09	461.94	448.45	438.26	430.47
22000	529.04	502.95	483.94	469.81	459.13	450.96
23000	553.09	525.81	505.94	491.16	480.00	471.46
24000	577.13	548.67	527.94	512.51	500.87	491.96
25000	601.18	571.53	549.93	533.87	521.73	512.46
30000	721.42	685.84	659.92	640.64	626.08	614.95
35000	841.65	800.14	769.91	747.42	730.43	717.44
40000	961.89	914.45	879.89	854.19	834.78	819.93
45000	1082.12	1028.75	989.88	960.97	939.12	922.43
50000	1202.36	1143.06	1099.87	1067.74	1043.47	1024.92
55000	1322.60	1257.37	1209.85	1174.51	1147.82	1127.41
60000	1442.83	1371.67	1319.84	1281.29	1252.16	1229.90
65000	1563.07	1485.98	1429.83	1388.06	1356.51	1332.39
70000	1683.30	1600.28	1539.81	1494.83	1460.86	1434.89
75000	1803.54	1714.59	1649.80	1601.61	1565.20	1537.38
80000	1923.78	1828.90	1759.79	1708.38	1669.55	1639.87
85000	2044.01	1943.20	1869.77	1815.16	1773.90	1742.36
90000	2164.25	2057.51	1979.76	1921.93	1878.24	1844.85
95000	2284.48	2171.81	2089.75	2028.70	1982.59	1947.35
100000	2404.72	2286.12	2199.73	2135.48	2086.94	2049.84
200000	4809.44	4572.24	4399.46	4270.96	4173.88	4099.67
300000	7214.16	6858.36	6599.20	6406.43	6260.81	6149.51
400000	9618.88	9144.48	8798.93	8541.91	8347.75	8199.35
500000	12023.60	11430.60	10998.66	10677.39	10434.69	10249.19

MONTHLY PAYMENT 23%
Needed to repay a loan

TERM AMOUNT	15 YEARS	20 YEARS	25 YEARS	30 YEARS	35 YEARS	40 YEARS
500	9.91	9.69	9.62	9.59	9.59	9.58
1000	19.82	19.37	19.23	19.19	19.17	19.17
2000	39.63	38.74	38.46	38.37	38.35	38.34
3000	59.45	58.11	57.69	57.56	57.52	57.51
4000	79.27	77.48	76.93	76.75	76.69	76.68
5000	99.08	96.85	96.16	95.94	95.87	95.84
6000	118.90	116.22	115.39	115.12	115.04	115.01
7000	138.72	135.59	134.62	134.31	134.21	134.18
8000	158.53	154.96	153.85	153.50	153.39	153.35
9000	178.35	174.33	173.08	172.69	172.56	172.52
10000	198.17	193.70	192.31	191.87	191.73	191.69
11000	217.98	213.07	211.54	211.06	210.91	210.86
12000	237.80	232.44	230.78	230.25	230.08	230.03
13000	257.62	251.81	250.01	249.44	249.25	249.19
14000	277.43	271.18	269.24	268.62	268.43	268.36
15000	297.25	290.55	288.47	287.81	287.60	287.53
16000	317.07	309.92	307.70	307.00	306.77	306.70
17000	336.88	329.29	326.93	326.18	325.95	325.87
18000	356.70	348.66	346.16	345.37	345.12	345.04
19000	376.52	368.03	365.39	364.56	364.29	364.21
20000	396.33	387.40	384.63	383.75	383.47	383.38
21000	416.15	406.77	403.86	402.93	402.64	402.54
22000	435.97	426.14	423.09	422.12	421.81	421.71
23000	455.78	445.51	442.32	441.31	440.99	440.88
24000	475.60	464.88	461.55	460.50	460.16	460.05
25000	495.42	484.25	480.78	479.68	479.33	479.22
30000	594.50	581.10	576.94	575.62	575.20	575.06
35000	693.58	677.95	673.10	671.56	671.06	670.91
40000	792.67	774.80	769.25	767.49	766.93	766.75
45000	891.75	871.65	865.41	863.43	862.80	862.60
50000	990.83	968.50	961.56	959.37	958.66	958.44
55000	1089.91	1065.35	1057.72	1055.30	1054.53	1054.28
60000	1189.00	1162.20	1153.88	1151.24	1150.40	1150.13
65000	1288.08	1259.05	1250.03	1247.18	1246.26	1245.97
70000	1387.16	1355.90	1346.19	1343.11	1342.13	1341.81
75000	1486.25	1452.75	1442.35	1439.05	1438.00	1437.66
80000	1585.33	1549.60	1538.50	1534.98	1533.86	1533.50
85000	1684.41	1646.45	1634.66	1630.92	1629.73	1629.35
90000	1783.50	1743.30	1730.82	1726.86	1725.59	1725.19
95000	1882.58	1840.15	1826.97	1822.79	1821.46	1821.03
100000	1981.66	1937.00	1923.13	1918.73	1917.33	1916.88
200000	3963.33	3874.01	3846.26	3837.46	3834.65	3833.76
300000	5944.99	5811.01	5769.39	5756.19	5751.98	5750.63
400000	7926.65	7748.01	7692.52	7674.92	7669.31	7667.51
500000	9908.32	9685.02	9615.65	9593.65	9586.63	9584.39

23.5% MONTHLY PAYMENT

Needed to repay a loan

TERM AMOUNT	1 YEAR	2 YEARS	3 YEARS	4 YEARS	5 YEARS	6 YEARS
500	47.16	26.31	19.49	16.16	14.24	13.01
1000	94.32	52.62	38.97	32.33	28.48	26.02
2000	188.64	105.24	77.94	64.65	56.96	52.05
3000	282.95	157.87	116.91	96.98	85.44	78.07
4000	377.27	210.49	155.88	129.30	113.91	104.10
5000	471.59	263.11	194.85	161.63	142.39	130.12
6000	565.91	315.73	233.82	193.96	170.87	156.14
7000	660.22	368.35	272.80	226.28	199.35	182.17
8000	754.54	420.97	311.77	258.61	227.83	208.19
9000	848.86	473.60	350.74	290.93	256.31	234.22
10000	943.18	526.22	389.71	323.26	284.78	260.24
11000	1037.50	578.84	428.68	355.59	313.26	286.27
12000	1131.81	631.46	467.65	387.91	341.74	312.29
13000	1226.13	684.08	506.62	420.24	370.22	338.31
14000	1320.45	736.71	545.59	452.56	398.70	364.34
15000	1414.77	789.33	584.56	484.89	427.18	390.36
16000	1509.08	841.95	623.53	517.22	455.66	416.39
17000	1603.40	894.57	662.50	549.54	484.13	442.41
18000	1697.72	947.19	701.47	581.87	512.61	468.43
19000	1792.04	999.82	740.45	614.19	541.09	494.46
20000	1886.36	1052.44	779.42	646.52	569.57	520.48
21000	1980.67	1105.06	818.39	678.85	598.05	546.51
22000	2074.99	1157.68	857.36	711.17	626.53	572.53
23000	2169.31	1210.30	896.33	743.50	655.01	598.56
24000	2263.63	1262.92	935.30	775.82	683.48	624.58
25000	2357.94	1315.55	974.27	808.15	711.96	650.60
30000	2829.53	1578.66	1169.12	969.78	854.35	780.72
35000	3301.12	1841.77	1363.98	1131.41	996.75	910.84
40000	3772.71	2104.87	1558.83	1293.04	1139.14	1040.97
45000	4244.30	2367.98	1753.69	1454.67	1281.53	1171.09
50000	4715.89	2631.09	1948.54	1616.30	1423.92	1301.21
55000	5187.48	2894.20	2143.39	1777.93	1566.32	1431.33
60000	5659.07	3157.31	2338.25	1939.56	1708.71	1561.45
65000	6130.66	3420.42	2533.10	2101.19	1851.10	1691.57
70000	6602.25	3683.53	2727.96	2262.82	1993.49	1821.69
75000	7073.83	3946.64	2922.81	2424.45	2135.89	1951.81
80000	7545.42	4209.75	3117.66	2586.08	2278.28	2081.93
85000	8017.01	4472.86	3312.52	2747.71	2420.67	2212.05
90000	8488.60	4735.97	3507.37	2909.34	2563.06	2342.17
95000	8960.19	4999.08	3702.23	3070.97	2705.46	2472.29
100000	9431.78	5262.19	3897.08	3232.60	2847.85	2602.41
200000	18863.56	10524.37	7794.16	6465.21	5695.70	5204.83
300000	28295.34	15786.56	11691.24	9697.81	8543.54	7807.24
400000	37727.12	21048.75	15588.32	12930.41	11391.39	10409.65
500000	47158.90	26310.94	19485.40	16163.02	14239.24	13012.07

MONTHLY PAYMENT 23.5%

Needed to repay a loan

TERM AMOUNT	7 YEARS	8 YEARS	9 YEARS	10 YEARS	11 YEARS	12 YEARS
500	12.18	11.59	11.17	10.85	10.61	10.43
1000	24.36	23.19	22.33	21.70	21.22	20.86
2000	48.72	46.37	44.67	43.40	42.45	41.71
3000	73.08	69.56	67.00	65.10	63.67	62.58
4000	97.44	92.74	89.33	86.80	84.90	83.44
5000	121.80	115.93	111.67	108.50	106.12	104.31
6000	146.16	139.12	134.00	130.20	127.34	125.17
7000	170.52	162.30	156.33	151.90	148.57	146.03
8000	194.88	185.49	178.66	173.60	169.79	166.89
9000	219.25	208.68	201.00	195.30	191.02	187.75
10000	243.61	231.86	223.33	217.00	212.24	208.61
11000	267.97	255.05	245.66	238.70	233.46	229.47
12000	292.33	278.23	268.00	260.41	254.69	250.33
13000	316.69	301.42	290.33	282.11	275.91	271.19
14000	341.05	324.61	312.66	303.81	297.14	292.06
15000	365.41	347.79	335.00	325.51	318.36	312.92
16000	389.77	370.98	357.33	347.21	339.58	333.78
17000	414.13	394.17	379.66	368.91	360.81	354.64
18000	438.49	417.35	402.00	390.61	382.03	375.50
19000	462.85	440.54	424.33	412.31	403.26	396.36
20000	487.21	463.72	446.66	434.01	424.48	417.22
21000	511.57	486.91	468.99	455.71	445.70	438.08
22000	535.93	510.10	491.33	477.41	466.93	458.95
23000	560.29	533.28	513.66	499.11	488.15	479.81
24000	584.65	556.47	535.99	520.81	509.38	500.67
25000	609.01	579.65	558.33	542.51	530.60	521.53
30000	730.82	695.59	669.99	651.01	636.72	625.83
35000	852.62	811.52	781.66	759.52	742.84	730.14
40000	974.42	927.45	893.32	868.02	848.96	834.45
45000	1096.23	1043.38	1004.99	976.52	955.08	938.75
50000	1218.03	1159.31	1116.65	1085.02	1061.20	1043.06
55000	1339.83	1275.24	1228.32	1193.52	1167.32	1147.36
60000	1461.64	1391.17	1339.99	1302.03	1273.44	1251.67
65000	1583.44	1507.10	1451.65	1410.53	1379.56	1355.97
70000	1705.24	1623.03	1563.32	1519.03	1485.68	1460.28
75000	1827.04	1738.96	1674.98	1627.53	1591.80	1564.59
80000	1948.85	1854.90	1786.65	1736.03	1697.92	1668.89
85000	2070.65	1970.83	1898.31	1844.54	1804.04	1773.20
90000	2192.45	2086.76	2009.98	1953.04	1910.16	1877.50
95000	2314.26	2202.69	2121.64	2061.54	2016.28	1981.81
100000	2436.06	2318.62	2233.31	2170.04	2122.40	2086.11
200000	4872.12	4637.24	4466.62	4340.09	4244.81	4172.23
300000	7308.18	6955.86	6699.93	6510.13	6367.21	6258.34
400000	9744.24	9274.48	8933.24	8680.17	8489.61	8344.46
500000	12180.30	11593.10	11166.54	10850.22	10612.01	10430.57

23.5%

MONTHLY PAYMENT
Needed to repay a loan

TERM AMOUNT	15 YEARS	20 YEARS	25 YEARS	30 YEARS	35 YEARS	40 YEARS
500	10.10	9.89	9.82	9.80	9.79	9.79
1000	20.20	19.77	19.64	19.60	19.59	19.59
2000	40.40	39.54	39.28	39.20	39.18	39.17
3000	60.60	59.31	58.93	58.80	58.77	58.76
4000	80.80	79.09	78.57	78.41	78.36	78.34
5000	100.99	98.86	98.21	98.01	97.95	97.93
6000	121.19	118.63	117.85	117.61	117.53	117.51
7000	141.39	138.40	137.49	137.21	137.12	137.10
8000	161.59	158.17	157.13	156.81	156.71	156.68
9000	181.79	177.94	176.78	176.41	176.30	176.27
10000	201.99	197.72	196.42	196.02	195.89	195.85
11000	222.19	217.49	216.06	215.62	215.48	215.44
12000	242.39	237.26	235.70	235.22	235.07	235.02
13000	262.58	257.03	255.34	254.82	254.66	254.61
14000	282.78	276.80	274.98	274.42	274.25	274.19
15000	302.98	296.57	294.63	294.02	293.84	293.78
16000	323.18	316.34	314.27	313.62	313.42	313.36
17000	343.38	336.12	333.91	333.23	333.01	332.95
18000	363.58	355.89	353.55	352.83	352.60	352.53
19000	383.78	375.66	373.19	372.43	372.19	372.12
20000	403.98	395.43	392.83	392.03	391.78	391.70
21000	424.18	415.20	412.48	411.63	411.37	411.29
22000	444.37	434.97	432.12	431.23	430.96	430.87
23000	464.57	454.74	451.76	450.84	450.55	450.46
24000	484.77	474.52	471.40	470.44	470.14	470.04
25000	504.97	494.29	491.04	490.04	489.73	489.63
30000	605.97	593.15	589.25	588.05	587.67	587.55
35000	706.96	692.00	687.46	686.05	685.62	685.48
40000	807.95	790.86	785.67	784.06	783.56	783.40
45000	908.95	889.72	883.88	882.07	881.51	881.33
50000	1009.94	988.58	982.09	980.08	979.45	979.26
55000	1110.94	1087.43	1080.29	1078.08	1077.40	1077.18
60000	1211.93	1186.29	1178.50	1176.09	1175.34	1175.11
65000	1312.92	1285.15	1276.71	1274.10	1273.29	1273.03
70000	1413.92	1384.01	1374.92	1372.11	1371.23	1370.96
75000	1514.91	1482.86	1473.13	1470.12	1469.18	1468.88
80000	1615.91	1581.72	1571.34	1568.12	1567.12	1566.81
85000	1716.90	1680.58	1669.55	1666.13	1665.07	1664.73
90000	1817.90	1779.44	1767.76	1764.14	1763.01	1762.66
95000	1918.89	1878.29	1865.96	1862.15	1860.96	1860.59
100000	2019.88	1977.15	1964.17	1960.15	1958.90	1958.51
200000	4039.77	3954.30	3928.35	3920.31	3917.80	3917.02
300000	6059.65	5931.46	5892.52	5880.46	5876.70	5875.53
400000	8079.54	7908.61	7856.69	7840.61	7835.61	7834.04
500000	10099.42	9885.76	9820.86	9800.77	9794.51	9792.55

24%

MONTHLY PAYMENT
Needed to repay a loan

TERM AMOUNT	1 YEAR	2 YEARS	3 YEARS	4 YEARS	5 YEARS	6 YEARS
500	47.28	26.44	19.62	16.30	14.38	13.16
1000	94.56	52.87	39.23	32.60	28.77	26.33
2000	189.12	105.74	78.47	65.20	57.54	52.65
3000	283.68	158.61	117.70	97.81	86.30	78.98
4000	378.24	211.48	156.93	130.41	115.07	105.31
5000	472.80	264.36	196.16	163.01	143.84	131.63
6000	567.36	317.23	235.40	195.61	172.61	157.96
7000	661.92	370.10	274.63	228.21	201.38	184.29
8000	756.48	422.97	313.86	260.81	230.14	210.61
9000	851.04	475.84	353.10	293.42	258.91	236.94
10000	945.60	528.71	392.33	326.02	287.68	263.27
11000	1040.16	581.58	431.56	358.62	316.45	289.60
12000	1134.72	634.45	470.79	391.22	345.22	315.92
13000	1229.27	687.32	510.03	423.82	373.98	342.25
14000	1323.83	740.20	549.26	456.43	402.75	368.58
15000	1418.39	793.07	588.49	489.03	431.52	394.90
16000	1512.95	845.94	627.73	521.63	460.29	421.23
17000	1607.51	898.81	666.96	554.23	489.06	447.56
18000	1702.07	951.68	706.19	586.83	517.82	473.88
19000	1796.63	1004.55	745.42	619.43	546.59	500.21
20000	1891.19	1057.42	784.66	652.04	575.36	526.54
21000	1985.75	1110.29	823.89	684.64	604.13	552.86
22000	2080.31	1163.16	863.12	717.24	632.90	579.19
23000	2174.87	1216.04	902.36	749.84	661.66	605.52
24000	2269.43	1268.91	941.59	782.44	690.43	631.84
25000	2363.99	1321.78	980.82	815.05	719.20	658.17
30000	2836.79	1586.13	1176.99	978.06	863.04	789.80
35000	3309.59	1850.49	1373.15	1141.06	1006.88	921.44
40000	3782.38	2114.84	1569.31	1304.07	1150.72	1053.07
45000	4255.18	2379.20	1765.48	1467.08	1294.56	1184.71
50000	4727.98	2643.55	1961.64	1630.09	1438.40	1316.34
55000	5200.78	2907.91	2157.81	1793.10	1582.24	1447.98
60000	5673.58	3172.27	2353.97	1956.11	1726.08	1579.61
65000	6146.37	3436.62	2550.14	2119.12	1869.92	1711.24
70000	6619.17	3700.98	2746.30	2282.13	2013.76	1842.88
75000	7091.97	3965.33	2942.46	2445.14	2157.60	1974.51
80000	7564.77	4229.69	3138.63	2608.15	2301.44	2106.15
85000	8037.57	4494.04	3334.79	2771.16	2445.28	2237.78
90000	8510.36	4758.40	3530.96	2934.17	2589.12	2369.41
95000	8983.16	5022.75	3727.12	3097.17	2732.96	2501.05
100000	9455.96	5287.11	3923.29	3260.18	2876.80	2632.68
200000	18911.92	10574.22	7846.57	6520.37	5753.59	5265.37
300000	28367.88	15861.33	11769.86	9780.55	8630.39	7898.05
400000	37823.84	21148.44	15693.14	13040.73	11507.19	10530.73
500000	47279.80	26435.55	19616.43	16300.92	14383.98	13163.42

24%

MONTHLY PAYMENT
Needed to repay a loan

TERM AMOUNT	7 YEARS	8 YEARS	9 YEARS	10 YEARS	11 YEARS	12 YEARS
500	12.34	11.76	11.34	11.02	10.79	10.61
1000	24.68	23.51	22.67	22.05	21.58	21.23
2000	49.35	47.03	45.34	44.10	43.16	42.45
3000	74.03	70.54	68.01	66.14	64.74	63.68
4000	98.70	94.05	90.68	88.19	86.32	84.90
5000	123.38	117.57	113.35	110.24	107.90	106.13
6000	148.05	141.08	136.03	132.29	129.48	127.36
7000	172.73	164.59	158.70	154.34	151.06	148.58
8000	197.41	188.11	181.37	176.38	172.65	169.81
9000	222.08	211.62	204.04	198.43	194.23	191.03
10000	246.76	235.13	226.71	220.48	215.81	212.26
11000	271.43	258.64	249.38	242.53	237.39	233.48
12000	296.11	282.16	272.05	264.58	258.97	254.71
13000	320.79	305.67	294.72	286.63	280.55	275.94
14000	345.46	329.18	317.39	308.67	302.13	297.16
15000	370.14	352.70	340.06	330.72	323.71	318.39
16000	394.81	376.21	362.73	352.77	345.29	339.61
17000	419.49	399.72	385.40	374.82	366.87	360.84
18000	444.16	423.24	408.08	396.87	388.45	382.07
19000	468.84	446.75	430.75	418.91	410.03	403.29
20000	493.52	470.26	453.42	440.96	431.61	424.52
21000	518.19	493.78	476.09	463.01	453.19	445.74
22000	542.87	517.29	498.76	485.06	474.77	466.97
23000	567.54	540.80	521.43	507.11	496.36	488.19
24000	592.22	564.32	544.10	529.15	517.94	509.42
25000	616.90	587.83	566.77	551.20	539.52	530.65
30000	740.27	705.39	680.13	661.44	647.42	636.78
35000	863.65	822.96	793.48	771.68	755.32	742.91
40000	987.03	940.53	906.83	881.92	863.23	849.03
45000	1110.41	1058.09	1020.19	992.16	971.13	955.16
50000	1233.79	1175.66	1133.54	1102.40	1079.03	1061.29
55000	1357.17	1293.22	1246.90	1212.65	1186.94	1167.42
60000	1480.55	1410.79	1360.25	1322.89	1294.84	1273.55
65000	1603.93	1528.35	1473.61	1433.13	1402.74	1379.68
70000	1727.31	1645.92	1586.96	1543.37	1510.65	1485.81
75000	1850.69	1763.48	1700.31	1653.61	1618.55	1591.94
80000	1974.06	1881.05	1813.67	1763.85	1726.45	1698.07
85000	2097.44	1998.62	1927.02	1874.09	1834.36	1804.20
90000	2220.82	2116.18	2040.38	1984.33	1942.26	1910.33
95000	2344.20	2233.75	2153.73	2094.57	2050.16	2016.46
100000	2467.58	2351.31	2267.08	2204.81	2158.07	2122.59
200000	4935.16	4702.63	4534.17	4409.62	4316.13	4245.17
300000	7402.74	7053.94	6801.25	6614.43	6474.20	6367.76
400000	9870.32	9405.25	9068.34	8819.24	8632.27	8490.34
500000	12337.91	11756.56	11335.42	11024.05	10790.34	10612.93

MONTHLY PAYMENT
Needed to repay a loan

24%

TERM AMOUNT	15 YEARS	20 YEARS	25 YEARS	30 YEARS	35 YEARS	40 YEARS
500	10.29	10.09	10.03	10.01	10.00	10.00
1000	20.58	20.17	20.05	20.02	20.00	20.00
2000	41.17	40.35	40.11	40.03	40.01	40.00
3000	61.75	60.52	60.16	60.05	60.01	60.00
4000	82.33	80.70	80.21	80.06	80.02	80.01
5000	102.91	100.87	100.26	100.08	100.02	100.01
6000	123.50	121.04	120.32	120.10	120.03	120.01
7000	144.08	141.22	140.37	140.11	140.03	140.01
8000	164.66	161.39	160.42	160.13	160.04	160.01
9000	185.24	181.57	180.47	180.14	180.04	180.01
10000	205.83	201.74	200.53	200.16	200.05	200.01
11000	226.41	221.91	220.58	220.18	220.05	220.02
12000	246.99	242.09	240.63	240.19	240.06	240.02
13000	267.58	262.26	260.69	260.21	260.06	260.02
14000	288.16	282.44	280.74	280.22	280.07	280.02
15000	308.74	302.61	300.79	300.24	300.07	300.02
16000	329.32	322.79	320.84	320.26	320.08	320.02
17000	349.91	342.96	340.90	340.27	340.08	340.03
18000	370.49	363.13	360.95	360.29	360.09	360.03
19000	391.07	383.31	381.00	380.30	380.09	380.03
20000	411.65	403.48	401.05	400.32	400.10	400.03
21000	432.24	423.66	421.11	420.34	420.10	420.03
22000	452.82	443.83	441.16	440.35	440.11	440.03
23000	473.40	464.00	461.21	460.37	460.11	460.03
24000	493.99	484.18	481.27	480.39	480.12	480.04
25000	514.57	504.35	501.32	500.40	500.12	500.04
30000	617.48	605.22	601.58	600.48	600.15	600.04
35000	720.40	706.09	701.85	700.56	700.17	700.05
40000	823.31	806.96	802.11	800.64	800.20	800.06
45000	926.22	907.83	902.37	900.72	900.22	900.07
50000	1029.14	1008.70	1002.64	1000.80	1000.24	1000.07
55000	1132.05	1109.57	1102.90	1100.88	1100.27	1100.08
60000	1234.96	1210.44	1203.16	1200.96	1200.29	1200.09
65000	1337.88	1311.32	1303.43	1301.04	1300.32	1300.10
70000	1440.79	1412.19	1403.69	1401.12	1400.34	1400.10
75000	1543.71	1513.06	1503.96	1501.20	1500.37	1500.11
80000	1646.62	1613.93	1604.22	1601.28	1600.39	1600.12
85000	1749.53	1714.80	1704.48	1701.36	1700.42	1700.13
90000	1852.45	1815.67	1804.75	1801.44	1800.44	1800.13
95000	1955.36	1916.54	1905.01	1901.52	1900.46	1900.14
100000	2058.27	2017.41	2005.27	2001.60	2000.49	2000.15
200000	4116.55	4034.82	4010.55	4003.21	4000.98	4000.30
300000	6174.82	6052.22	6015.82	6004.81	6001.47	6000.45
400000	8233.09	8069.63	8021.10	8006.42	8001.95	8000.60
500000	10291.37	10087.04	10026.37	10008.02	10002.44	10000.74

24.5% MONTHLY PAYMENT

Needed to repay a loan

TERM AMOUNT	1 YEAR	2 YEARS	3 YEARS	4 YEARS	5 YEARS	6 YEARS
500	47.40	26.56	19.75	16.44	14.53	13.32
1000	94.80	53.12	39.50	32.88	29.06	26.63
2000	189.60	106.24	78.99	65.76	58.12	53.26
3000	284.41	159.36	118.49	98.64	87.18	79.89
4000	379.21	212.48	157.98	131.52	116.24	106.52
5000	474.01	265.60	197.48	164.39	145.29	133.16
6000	568.81	318.73	236.98	197.27	174.35	159.79
7000	663.61	371.85	276.47	230.15	203.41	186.42
8000	758.41	424.97	315.97	263.03	232.47	213.05
9000	853.22	478.09	355.46	295.91	261.53	239.68
10000	948.02	531.21	394.96	328.79	290.59	266.31
11000	1042.82	584.33	434.45	361.67	319.65	292.94
12000	1137.62	637.45	473.95	394.55	348.71	319.57
13000	1232.42	690.57	513.45	427.43	377.77	346.21
14000	1327.22	743.69	552.94	460.30	406.82	372.84
15000	1422.03	796.81	592.44	493.18	435.88	399.47
16000	1516.83	849.94	631.93	526.06	464.94	426.10
17000	1611.63	903.06	671.43	558.94	494.00	452.73
18000	1706.43	956.18	710.93	591.82	523.06	479.36
19000	1801.23	1009.30	750.42	624.70	552.12	505.99
20000	1896.03	1062.42	789.92	657.58	581.18	532.62
21000	1990.84	1115.54	829.41	690.46	610.24	559.25
22000	2085.64	1168.66	868.91	723.34	639.30	585.89
23000	2180.44	1221.78	908.40	756.21	668.36	612.52
24000	2275.24	1274.90	947.90	789.09	697.41	639.15
25000	2370.04	1328.02	987.40	821.97	726.47	665.78
30000	2844.05	1593.63	1184.88	986.37	871.77	798.94
35000	3318.06	1859.23	1382.36	1150.76	1017.06	932.09
40000	3792.07	2124.84	1579.83	1315.15	1162.36	1065.25
45000	4266.08	2390.44	1777.31	1479.55	1307.65	1198.40
50000	4740.09	2656.05	1974.79	1643.94	1452.95	1331.56
55000	5214.10	2921.65	2172.27	1808.34	1598.24	1464.72
60000	5688.10	3187.26	2369.75	1972.73	1743.53	1597.87
65000	6162.11	3452.86	2567.23	2137.13	1888.83	1731.03
70000	6636.12	3718.47	2764.71	2301.52	2034.12	1864.18
75000	7110.13	3984.07	2962.19	2465.92	2179.42	1997.34
80000	7584.14	4249.68	3159.67	2630.31	2324.71	2130.49
85000	8058.15	4515.28	3357.15	2794.70	2470.01	2263.65
90000	8532.16	4780.89	3554.63	2959.10	2615.30	2396.81
95000	9006.16	5046.49	3752.11	3123.49	2760.60	2529.96
100000	9480.17	5312.10	3949.59	3287.89	2905.89	2663.12
200000	18960.35	10624.20	7899.17	6575.77	5811.78	5326.24
300000	28440.52	15936.29	11848.76	9863.66	8717.67	7989.35
400000	37920.69	21248.39	15798.34	13151.55	11623.57	10652.47
500000	47400.87	26560.49	19747.93	16439.43	14529.46	13315.59

MONTHLY PAYMENT 24.5%

Needed to repay a loan

TERM AMOUNT	7 YEARS	8 YEARS	9 YEARS	10 YEARS	11 YEARS	12 YEARS
500	12.50	11.92	11.51	11.20	10.97	10.80
1000	24.99	23.84	23.01	22.40	21.94	21.59
2000	49.99	47.68	46.02	44.80	43.88	43.18
3000	74.98	71.53	69.03	67.19	65.82	64.78
4000	99.97	95.37	92.04	89.59	87.76	86.37
5000	124.96	119.21	115.05	111.99	109.70	107.96
6000	149.96	143.05	138.06	134.39	131.64	129.55
7000	174.95	166.89	161.07	156.78	153.57	151.15
8000	199.94	190.74	184.08	179.18	175.51	172.74
9000	224.94	214.58	207.10	201.58	197.45	194.33
10000	249.93	238.42	230.11	223.98	219.39	215.92
11000	274.92	262.26	253.12	246.38	241.33	237.52
12000	299.91	286.10	276.13	268.77	263.27	259.11
13000	324.91	309.95	299.14	291.17	285.21	280.70
14000	349.90	333.79	322.15	313.57	307.15	302.29
15000	374.89	357.63	345.16	335.97	329.09	323.89
16000	399.89	381.47	368.17	358.36	351.03	345.48
17000	424.88	405.31	391.18	380.76	372.97	367.07
18000	449.87	429.16	414.19	403.16	394.91	388.66
19000	474.86	453.00	437.20	425.56	416.85	410.26
20000	499.86	476.84	460.21	447.95	438.79	431.85
21000	524.85	500.68	483.22	470.35	460.72	453.44
22000	549.84	524.52	506.23	492.75	482.66	475.03
23000	574.84	548.37	529.24	515.15	504.60	496.63
24000	599.83	572.21	552.25	537.55	526.54	518.22
25000	624.82	596.05	575.26	559.94	548.48	539.81
30000	749.79	715.26	690.32	671.93	658.18	647.77
35000	874.75	834.47	805.37	783.92	767.87	755.74
40000	999.71	953.68	920.42	895.91	877.57	863.70
45000	1124.68	1072.89	1035.48	1007.90	987.27	971.66
50000	1249.64	1192.10	1150.53	1119.89	1096.96	1079.62
55000	1374.61	1311.31	1265.58	1231.88	1206.66	1187.59
60000	1499.57	1430.52	1380.63	1343.86	1316.36	1295.55
65000	1624.53	1549.73	1495.69	1455.85	1426.05	1403.51
70000	1749.50	1668.94	1610.74	1567.84	1535.75	1511.47
75000	1874.46	1788.15	1725.79	1679.83	1645.45	1619.44
80000	1999.43	1907.36	1840.85	1791.82	1755.14	1727.40
85000	2124.39	2026.57	1955.90	1903.81	1864.84	1835.36
90000	2249.36	2145.78	2070.95	2015.80	1974.53	1943.32
95000	2374.32	2264.99	2186.00	2127.78	2084.23	2051.29
100000	2499.28	2384.20	2301.06	2239.77	2193.93	2159.25
200000	4998.57	4768.39	4602.11	4479.55	4387.85	4318.49
300000	7497.85	7152.59	6903.17	6719.32	6581.78	6477.74
400000	9997.13	9536.78	9204.23	8959.09	8775.71	8636.99
500000	12496.42	11920.98	11505.28	11198.87	10969.63	10796.24

24.5%

MONTHLY PAYMENT
Needed to repay a loan

TERM AMOUNT	15 YEARS	20 YEARS	25 YEARS	30 YEARS	35 YEARS	40 YEARS
500	10.48	10.29	10.23	10.22	10.21	10.21
1000	20.97	20.58	20.46	20.43	20.42	20.42
2000	41.94	41.16	40.93	40.86	40.84	40.84
3000	62.90	61.73	61.39	61.29	61.26	61.25
4000	83.87	82.31	81.86	81.72	81.68	81.67
5000	104.84	102.89	102.32	102.15	102.10	102.09
6000	125.81	123.47	122.79	122.58	122.53	122.51
7000	146.78	144.04	143.25	143.02	142.95	142.93
8000	167.75	164.62	163.71	163.45	163.37	163.34
9000	188.71	185.20	184.18	183.88	183.79	183.76
10000	209.68	205.78	204.64	204.31	204.21	204.18
11000	230.65	226.35	225.11	224.74	224.63	224.60
12000	251.62	246.93	245.57	245.17	245.05	245.01
13000	272.59	267.51	266.04	265.60	265.47	265.43
14000	293.56	288.09	286.50	286.03	285.89	285.85
15000	314.52	308.66	306.96	306.46	306.31	306.27
16000	335.49	329.24	327.43	326.89	326.73	326.69
17000	356.46	349.82	347.89	347.32	347.15	347.10
18000	377.43	370.40	368.36	367.75	367.58	367.52
19000	398.40	390.98	388.82	388.19	388.00	387.94
20000	419.36	411.55	409.29	408.62	408.42	408.36
21000	440.33	432.13	429.75	429.05	428.84	428.78
22000	461.30	452.71	450.21	449.48	449.26	449.19
23000	482.27	473.29	470.68	469.91	469.68	469.61
24000	503.24	493.86	491.14	490.34	490.10	490.03
25000	524.21	514.44	511.61	510.77	510.52	510.45
30000	629.05	617.33	613.93	612.92	612.63	612.54
35000	733.89	720.22	716.25	715.08	714.73	714.63
40000	838.73	823.11	818.57	817.23	816.83	816.72
45000	943.57	925.99	920.89	919.39	918.94	918.81
50000	1048.41	1028.88	1023.21	1021.54	1021.04	1020.90
55000	1153.25	1131.77	1125.54	1123.69	1123.15	1122.99
60000	1258.09	1234.66	1227.86	1225.85	1225.25	1225.07
65000	1362.94	1337.55	1330.18	1328.00	1327.36	1327.16
70000	1467.78	1440.44	1432.50	1430.16	1429.46	1429.25
75000	1572.62	1543.32	1534.82	1532.31	1531.57	1531.34
80000	1677.46	1646.21	1637.14	1634.46	1633.67	1633.43
85000	1782.30	1749.10	1739.46	1736.62	1735.77	1735.52
90000	1887.14	1851.99	1841.79	1838.77	1837.88	1837.61
95000	1991.98	1954.88	1944.11	1940.93	1939.98	1939.70
100000	2096.82	2057.77	2046.43	2043.08	2042.09	2041.79
200000	4193.65	4115.53	4092.86	4086.16	4084.17	4083.58
300000	6290.47	6173.30	6139.28	6129.24	6126.26	6125.37
400000	8387.30	8231.06	8185.71	8172.32	8168.35	8167.17
500000	10484.12	10288.83	10232.14	10215.40	10210.43	10208.96

MONTHLY PAYMENT
Needed to repay a loan

25%

TERM AMOUNT	1 YEAR	2 YEARS	3 YEARS	4 YEARS	5 YEARS	6 YEARS
500	47.52	26.69	19.88	16.58	14.68	13.47
1000	95.04	53.37	39.76	33.16	29.35	26.94
2000	190.09	106.74	79.52	66.31	58.70	53.87
3000	285.13	160.11	119.28	99.47	88.05	80.81
4000	380.18	213.49	159.04	132.63	117.41	107.75
5000	475.22	266.86	198.80	165.79	146.76	134.69
6000	570.27	320.23	238.56	198.94	176.11	161.62
7000	665.31	373.60	278.32	232.10	205.46	188.56
8000	760.35	426.97	318.08	265.26	234.81	215.50
9000	855.40	480.34	357.84	298.41	264.16	242.43
10000	950.44	533.72	397.60	331.57	293.51	269.37
11000	1045.49	587.09	437.36	364.73	322.86	296.31
12000	1140.53	640.46	477.12	397.89	352.22	323.25
13000	1235.57	693.83	516.88	431.04	381.57	350.18
14000	1330.62	747.20	556.64	464.20	410.92	377.12
15000	1425.66	800.57	596.40	497.36	440.27	404.06
16000	1520.71	853.94	636.16	530.51	469.62	430.99
17000	1615.75	907.32	675.92	563.67	498.97	457.93
18000	1710.80	960.69	715.68	596.83	528.32	484.87
19000	1805.84	1014.06	755.44	629.99	557.68	511.81
20000	1900.88	1067.43	795.20	663.14	587.03	538.74
21000	1995.93	1120.80	834.96	696.30	616.38	565.68
22000	2090.97	1174.17	874.72	729.46	645.73	592.62
23000	2186.02	1227.54	914.48	762.61	675.08	619.56
24000	2281.06	1280.92	954.24	795.77	704.43	646.49
25000	2376.11	1334.29	994.00	828.93	733.78	673.43
30000	2851.33	1601.15	1192.79	994.71	880.54	808.12
35000	3326.55	1868.00	1391.59	1160.50	1027.30	942.80
40000	3801.77	2134.86	1590.39	1326.29	1174.05	1077.49
45000	4276.99	2401.72	1789.19	1492.07	1320.81	1212.17
50000	4752.21	2668.58	1987.99	1657.86	1467.57	1346.86
55000	5227.43	2935.43	2186.79	1823.64	1614.32	1481.54
60000	5702.65	3202.29	2385.59	1989.43	1761.08	1616.23
65000	6177.87	3469.15	2584.39	2155.21	1907.84	1750.92
70000	6653.09	3736.01	2783.19	2321.00	2054.59	1885.60
75000	7128.32	4002.86	2981.99	2486.78	2201.35	2020.29
80000	7603.54	4269.72	3180.79	2652.57	2348.11	2154.97
85000	8078.76	4536.58	3379.59	2818.36	2494.86	2289.66
90000	8553.98	4803.44	3578.38	2984.14	2641.62	2424.35
95000	9029.20	5070.29	3777.18	3149.93	2788.38	2559.03
100000	9504.42	5337.15	3975.98	3315.71	2935.13	2693.72
200000	19008.84	10674.30	7951.97	6631.43	5870.26	5387.44
300000	28513.26	16011.46	11927.95	9947.14	8805.40	8081.15
400000	38017.68	21348.61	15903.93	13262.85	11740.53	10774.87
500000	47522.10	26685.76	19879.91	16578.56	14675.66	13468.59

25%

MONTHLY PAYMENT
Needed to repay a loan

TERM AMOUNT	7 YEARS	8 YEARS	9 YEARS	10 YEARS	11 YEARS	12 YEARS
500	12.66	12.09	11.68	11.37	11.15	10.98
1000	25.31	24.17	23.35	22.75	22.30	21.96
2000	50.62	48.35	46.70	45.50	44.60	43.92
3000	75.93	72.52	70.06	68.25	66.90	65.88
4000	101.25	96.69	93.41	91.00	89.20	87.84
5000	126.56	120.86	116.76	113.75	111.50	109.80
6000	151.87	145.04	140.11	136.50	133.80	131.77
7000	177.18	169.21	163.47	159.25	156.10	153.73
8000	202.49	193.38	186.82	181.99	178.40	175.69
9000	227.80	217.55	210.17	204.74	200.70	197.65
10000	253.12	241.73	233.52	227.49	223.00	219.61
11000	278.43	265.90	256.87	250.24	245.30	241.57
12000	303.74	290.07	280.23	272.99	267.60	263.53
13000	329.05	314.24	303.58	295.74	289.90	285.49
14000	354.36	338.42	326.93	318.49	312.20	307.45
15000	379.67	362.59	350.28	341.24	334.50	329.41
16000	404.99	386.76	373.64	363.99	356.80	351.37
17000	430.30	410.94	396.99	386.74	379.10	373.34
18000	455.61	435.11	420.34	409.49	401.40	395.30
19000	480.92	459.28	443.69	432.24	423.70	417.26
20000	506.23	483.45	467.04	454.99	446.00	439.22
21000	531.54	507.63	490.40	477.74	468.30	461.18
22000	556.86	531.80	513.75	500.48	490.59	483.14
23000	582.17	555.97	537.10	523.23	512.89	505.10
24000	607.48	580.14	560.45	545.98	535.19	527.06
25000	632.79	604.32	583.80	568.73	557.49	549.02
30000	759.35	725.18	700.57	682.48	668.99	658.83
35000	885.91	846.04	817.33	796.23	780.49	768.63
40000	1012.47	966.91	934.09	909.97	891.99	878.44
45000	1139.02	1087.77	1050.85	1023.72	1003.49	988.24
50000	1265.58	1208.63	1167.61	1137.46	1114.99	1098.05
55000	1392.14	1329.50	1284.37	1251.21	1226.49	1207.85
60000	1518.70	1450.36	1401.13	1364.96	1337.99	1317.66
65000	1645.26	1571.22	1517.89	1478.70	1449.48	1427.46
70000	1771.81	1692.09	1634.65	1592.45	1560.98	1537.27
75000	1898.37	1812.95	1751.41	1706.20	1672.48	1647.07
80000	2024.93	1933.81	1868.18	1819.94	1783.98	1756.87
85000	2151.49	2054.68	1984.94	1933.69	1895.48	1866.68
90000	2278.05	2175.54	2101.70	2047.44	2006.98	1976.48
95000	2404.61	2296.40	2218.46	2161.18	2118.48	2086.29
100000	2531.16	2417.27	2335.22	2274.93	2229.98	2196.09
200000	5062.33	4834.53	4670.44	4549.86	4459.95	4392.19
300000	7593.49	7251.80	7005.66	6824.79	6689.93	6588.28
400000	10124.65	9669.07	9340.88	9099.72	8919.90	8784.37
500000	12655.82	12086.33	11676.10	11374.65	11149.88	10980.46

MONTHLY PAYMENT
Needed to repay a loan

25%

TERM AMOUNT	15 YEARS	20 YEARS	25 YEARS	30 YEARS	35 YEARS	40 YEARS
500	10.68	10.49	10.44	10.42	10.42	10.42
1000	21.36	20.98	20.88	20.85	20.84	20.83
2000	42.71	41.96	41.75	41.69	41.67	41.67
3000	64.07	62.95	62.63	62.54	62.51	62.50
4000	85.42	83.93	83.51	83.38	83.35	83.34
5000	106.78	104.91	104.38	104.23	104.18	104.17
6000	128.13	125.89	125.26	125.07	125.02	125.01
7000	149.49	146.88	146.13	145.92	145.86	145.84
8000	170.84	167.86	167.01	166.77	166.70	166.68
9000	192.20	188.84	187.89	187.61	187.53	187.51
10000	213.55	209.82	208.76	208.46	208.37	208.34
11000	234.91	230.80	229.64	229.30	229.21	229.18
12000	256.26	251.79	250.52	250.15	250.04	250.01
13000	277.62	272.77	271.39	271.00	270.88	270.85
14000	298.97	293.75	292.27	291.84	291.72	291.68
15000	320.33	314.73	313.14	312.69	312.55	312.52
16000	341.68	335.71	334.02	333.53	333.39	333.35
17000	363.04	356.70	354.90	354.38	354.23	354.18
18000	384.40	377.68	375.77	375.22	375.07	375.02
19000	405.75	398.66	396.65	396.07	395.90	395.85
20000	427.11	419.64	417.53	416.92	416.74	416.69
21000	448.46	440.63	438.40	437.76	437.58	437.52
22000	469.82	461.61	459.28	458.61	458.41	458.36
23000	491.17	482.59	480.16	479.45	479.25	479.19
24000	512.53	503.57	501.03	500.30	500.09	500.03
25000	533.88	524.55	521.91	521.14	520.92	520.86
30000	640.66	629.46	626.29	625.37	625.11	625.03
35000	747.44	734.38	730.67	729.60	729.29	729.20
40000	854.21	839.29	835.05	833.83	833.48	833.38
45000	960.99	944.20	939.43	938.06	937.66	937.55
50000	1067.76	1049.11	1043.82	1042.29	1041.85	1041.72
55000	1174.54	1154.02	1148.20	1146.52	1146.03	1145.89
60000	1281.32	1258.93	1252.58	1250.75	1250.22	1250.06
65000	1388.09	1363.84	1356.96	1354.98	1354.40	1354.23
70000	1494.87	1468.75	1461.34	1459.21	1458.59	1458.41
75000	1601.65	1573.66	1565.72	1563.43	1562.77	1562.58
80000	1708.42	1678.57	1670.10	1667.66	1666.96	1666.75
85000	1815.20	1783.48	1774.49	1771.89	1771.14	1770.92
90000	1921.98	1888.39	1878.87	1876.12	1875.33	1875.09
95000	2028.75	1993.31	1983.25	1980.35	1979.51	1979.27
100000	2135.53	2098.22	2087.63	2084.58	2083.69	2083.44
200000	4271.06	4196.43	4175.26	4169.16	4167.39	4166.88
300000	6406.59	6294.65	6262.89	6253.74	6251.08	6250.31
400000	8542.12	8392.86	8350.52	8338.31	8334.78	8333.75
500000	10677.64	10491.08	10438.15	10422.89	10418.47	10417.19

SECTION TWO

Annual Payment Schedules

Principle-to-Interest Ratio During a Thirty-Year Period

Based on a mortgage of $1,000, these tables follow amortization during a thirty year schedule of repayment at a fixed rate from 8% to 24%.

If you have an $85,000 loan at a fixed rate of 11% for thirty years, multiply the $9.52 by 85 to calculate your remaining balance at any given period.

ANNUAL PAYMENT SCHEDULE — 8%

Based on a loan of $1,000

30-YEAR TERM

Monthly Payment: $7.34 — Annual Payment: $88.06

YEAR	INTEREST PAID PER YEAR	PRINCIPAL PAID PER YEAR	BALANCE OWED AT YEAR END
1	$ 79.71	$ 8.35	$ 986.91
2	$ 79.01	$ 9.05	$ 977.86
3	$ 78.26	$ 9.80	$ 968.06
4	$ 77.45	$ 10.61	$ 957.45
5	$ 76.57	$ 11.49	$ 945.96
6	$ 75.61	$ 12.45	$ 933.51
7	$ 74.58	$ 13.48	$ 920.03
8	$ 73.46	$ 14.60	$ 905.43
9	$ 72.97	$ 15.09	$ 890.34
10	$ 70.94	$ 17.12	$ 873.22
11	$ 69.52	$ 18.54	$ 854.68
12	$ 67.97	$ 20.09	$ 834.59
13	$ 66.31	$ 21.75	$ 812.84
14	$ 64.51	$ 23.55	$ 789.29
15	$ 62.55	$ 25.51	$ 763.78
16	$ 60.43	$ 27.63	$ 736.15
17	$ 58.14	$ 29.92	$ 706.23
18	$ 55.66	$ 32.40	$ 673.83
19	$ 52.97	$ 35.09	$ 638.74
20	$ 50.06	$ 38.00	$ 600.74
21	$ 46.90	$ 41.16	$ 559.58
22	$ 43.49	$ 44.57	$ 515.01
23	$ 39.79	$ 48.27	$ 466.74
24	$ 35.76	$ 52.30	$ 414.44
25	$ 31.44	$ 56.62	$ 357.82
26	$ 26.74	$ 61.32	$ 296.50
27	$ 21.66	$ 66.40	$ 230.10
28	$ 16.14	$ 71.92	$ 158.18
29	$ 10.17	$ 77.89	$ 80.29
30	$ 7.77	$ 80.29	$ 0.00

9% ANNUAL PAYMENT SCHEDULE

Based on a loan of $1,000

30-YEAR TERM

Monthly Payment: $8.05 Annual Payment: $96.55

YEAR	INTEREST PAID PER YEAR	PRINCIPAL PAID PER YEAR	BALANCE OWED AT YEAR END
1	$ 89.73	$ 6.82	$ 993.17
2	$ 89.08	$ 7.47	$ 985.70
3	$ 88.37	$ 8.18	$ 977.52
4	$ 87.61	$ 8.94	$ 968.58
5	$ 86.77	$ 9.78	$ 958.80
6	$ 85.85	$ 10.70	$ 948.10
7	$ 84.85	$ 11.70	$ 936.40
8	$ 83.56	$ 12.99	$ 923.41
9	$ 82.55	$ 14.00	$ 909.41
10	$ 81.24	$ 15.31	$ 894.10
11	$ 79.80	$ 16.75	$ 877.35
12	$ 78.23	$ 18.32	$ 859.03
13	$ 76.51	$ 20.04	$ 838.99
14	$ 74.63	$ 21.92	$ 817.07
15	$ 72.58	$ 23.97	$ 793.10
16	$ 70.33	$ 26.22	$ 766.88
17	$ 67.87	$ 28.68	$ 738.20
18	$ 65.18	$ 31.37	$ 706.83
19	$ 62.24	$ 34.31	$ 672.52
20	$ 59.02	$ 37.53	$ 634.99
21	$ 55.50	$ 41.05	$ 593.94
22	$ 51.65	$ 44.90	$ 549.04
23	$ 47.44	$ 49.11	$ 499.93
24	$ 42.83	$ 53.72	$ 446.21
25	$ 37.78	$ 58.77	$ 387.44
26	$ 32.27	$ 64.28	$ 323.16
27	$ 26.24	$ 70.31	$ 252.85
28	$ 19.65	$ 76.90	$ 175.95
29	$ 12.44	$ 84.11	$ 91.84
30	$ 4.71	$ 91.84	$ .00

ANNUAL PAYMENT SCHEDULE 10%

Based on a loan of $1,000

30-YEAR TERM

Monthly Payment: $8.78 Annual Payment: $105.31

YEAR	INTEREST PAID PER YEAR	PRINCIPAL PAID PER YEAR	BALANCE OWED AT YEAR END
1	$ 99.71	$ 5.60	$ 994.40
2	$ 99.17	$ 6.14	$ 988.26
3	$ 98.53	$ 6.78	$ 981.48
4	$ 97.82	$ 7.49	$ 973.99
5	$ 97.03	$ 8.28	$ 965.71
6	$ 96.16	$ 9.15	$ 956.56
7	$ 95.21	$ 10.10	$ 946.46
8	$ 94.15	$ 11.16	$ 935.30
9	$ 92.98	$ 12.33	$ 922.97
10	$ 91.69	$ 13.62	$ 909.35
11	$ 90.26	$ 15.05	$ 894.30
12	$ 88.69	$ 16.62	$ 877.68
13	$ 86.95	$ 18.36	$ 859.32
14	$ 85.02	$ 20.29	$ 839.03
15	$ 82.90	$ 22.41	$ 816.62
16	$ 80.55	$ 24.76	$ 791.86
17	$ 77.96	$ 27.35	$ 764.51
18	$ 75.09	$ 30.22	$ 734.29
19	$ 71.93	$ 33.38	$ 700.91
20	$ 68.44	$ 36.87	$ 664.04
21	$ 64.57	$ 40.74	$ 623.30
22	$ 60.31	$ 45.00	$ 578.30
23	$ 55.60	$ 49.71	$ 528.59
24	$ 50.39	$ 54.92	$ 473.67
25	$ 44.64	$ 60.67	$ 413.00
26	$ 38.29	$ 67.02	$ 345.98
27	$ 31.27	$ 74.04	$ 271.94
28	$ 23.52	$ 81.79	$ 190.15
29	$ 14.95	$ 90.36	$ 99.79
30	$ 5.52	$ 99.79	$ 0.00

11% ANNUAL PAYMENT SCHEDULE

Based on a loan of $1,000

30-YEAR TERM

Monthly Payment: $9.52 Annual Payment: $114.27

YEAR	INTEREST PAID PER YEAR	PRINCIPAL PAID PER YEAR	BALANCE OWED AT YEAR END
1	$109.77	$ 4.50	$ 995.50
2	$109.25	$ 5.02	$ 990.48
3	$108.67	$ 5.60	$ 984.88
4	$108.02	$ 6.25	$ 978.63
5	$107.29	$ 6.98	$ 971.65
6	$106.49	$ 7.78	$ 963.87
7	$105.59	$ 8.68	$ 955.19
8	$104.58	$ 9.69	$ 945.50
9	$103.46	$ 10.81	$ 934.69
10	$102.21	$ 12.06	$ 922.63
11	$100.81	$ 13.46	$ 909.17
12	$ 99.26	$ 15.01	$ 894.16
13	$ 97.52	$ 16.75	$ 877.41
14	$ 95.58	$ 18.69	$ 858.72
15	$ 93.42	$ 20.85	$ 837.87
16	$ 91.05	$ 23.22	$ 814.65
17	$ 88.32	$ 25.95	$ 788.70
18	$ 85.31	$ 28.96	$ 759.74
19	$ 81.97	$ 32.30	$ 727.44
20	$ 78.22	$ 36.05	$ 691.39
21	$ 74.05	$ 40.22	$ 651.17
22	$ 69.40	$ 44.87	$ 606.30
23	$ 64.21	$ 50.06	$ 556.24
24	$ 58.41	$ 55.86	$ 500.38
25	$ 51.95	$ 62.32	$ 438.06
26	$ 44.71	$ 69.56	$ 368.50
27	$ 36.69	$ 77.58	$ 290.92
28	$ 27.71	$ 86.56	$ 204.36
29	$ 17.70	$ 96.57	$ 107.79
30	$ 6.48	$ 107.79	$ .00

ANNUAL PAYMENT SCHEDULE 12%

Based on a loan of $1,000

30-YEAR TERM

Monthly Payment: $10.29 Annual Payment: $123.43

YEAR	INTEREST PAID PER YEAR	PRINCIPAL PAID PER YEAR	BALANCE OWED AT YEAR END
1	$119.80	$ 3.63	$ 996.37
2	$119.34	$ 4.09	$ 992.28
3	$118.83	$ 4.60	$ 987.68
4	$118.24	$ 5.19	$ 982.49
5	$117.58	$ 5.85	$ 976.64
6	$116.84	$ 6.59	$ 970.05
7	$116.00	$ 7.43	$ 962.62
8	$114.70	$ 8.73	$ 953.89
9	$114.00	$ 9.43	$ 944.45
10	$112.80	$ 10.63	$ 933.83
11	$111.45	$ 11.98	$ 921.85
12	$109.94	$ 13.49	$ 908.36
13	$108.23	$ 15.20	$ 893.16
14	$106.29	$ 17.14	$ 876.02
15	$104.13	$ 19.30	$ 856.72
16	$101.67	$ 21.76	$ 834.95
17	$ 98.91	$ 24.52	$ 810.44
18	$ 95.80	$ 27.63	$ 782.81
19	$ 92.30	$ 31.13	$ 751.68
20	$ 88.35	$ 35.08	$ 716.60
21	$ 83.90	$ 39.53	$ 677.07
22	$ 78.89	$ 44.54	$ 632.53
23	$ 73.24	$ 50.19	$ 582.34
24	$ 66.88	$ 56.55	$ 525.79
25	$ 59.70	$ 63.73	$ 462.06
26	$ 51.63	$ 71.80	$ 390.26
27	$ 42.51	$ 80.92	$ 309.34
28	$ 32.25	$ 91.18	$ 218.16
29	$ 20.69	$ 102.74	$ 115.42
30	$ 8.01	$ 115.42	$ .00

13% ANNUAL PAYMENT SCHEDULE

Based on a loan of $1,000

30-YEAR TERM

Monthly Payment: $11.06 Annual Payment: $132.74

YEAR	INTEREST PAID PER YEAR	PRINCIPAL PAID PER YEAR	BALANCE OWED AT YEAR END
1	$129.83	$ 2.91	$ 997.09
2	$129.43	$ 3.31	$ 993.78
3	$128.97	$ 3.77	$ 990.01
4	$128.45	$ 4.29	$ 985.72
5	$127.86	$ 4.88	$ 980.84
6	$127.18	$ 5.56	$ 975.28
7	$126.41	$ 6.33	$ 968.95
8	$125.54	$ 7.20	$ 961.75
9	$124.54	$ 8.20	$ 953.55
10	$123.41	$ 9.33	$ 944.22
11	$122.57	$ 10.17	$ 934.05
12	$120.66	$ 12.08	$ 921.97
13	$118.99	$ 13.75	$ 908.22
14	$117.09	$ 15.65	$ 892.57
15	$114.94	$ 17.80	$ 874.77
16	$112.48	$ 20.26	$ 854.51
17	$109.68	$ 23.06	$ 831.45
18	$106.49	$ 26.25	$ 805.20
19	$102.87	$ 29.87	$ 775.33
20	$ 98.75	$ 33.99	$ 741.34
21	$ 94.06	$ 38.68	$ 702.66
22	$ 88.72	$ 44.02	$ 658.64
23	$ 82.65	$ 50.09	$ 608.55
24	$ 75.73	$ 57.01	$ 551.54
25	$ 67.86	$ 64.88	$ 486.66
26	$ 58.90	$ 73.84	$ 412.82
27	$ 48.71	$ 84.03	$ 328.79
28	$ 37.11	$ 95.63	$ 233.16
29	$ 23.91	$ 108.83	$ 124.33
30	$ 8.41	$ 124.33	$ .00

ANNUAL PAYMENT SCHEDULE 14%

Based on a loan of $1,000

30-YEAR TERM

Monthly Payment: $11.85 Annual Payment: $142.19

YEAR	INTEREST PAID PER YEAR	PRINCIPAL PAID PER YEAR	BALANCE OWED AT YEAR END
1	$139.86	$ 2.33	$ 997.67
2	$139.51	$ 2.68	$ 994.99
3	$139.11	$ 3.08	$ 991.91
4	$138.65	$ 3.54	$ 988.37
5	$138.12	$ 4.07	$ 984.30
6	$137.52	$ 4.67	$ 979.63
7	$136.87	$ 5.32	$ 974.31
8	$136.05	$ 6.14	$ 968.17
9	$135.11	$ 7.08	$ 961.09
10	$134.03	$ 8.16	$ 952.93
11	$132.82	$ 9.37	$ 943.56
12	$131.42	$ 10.77	$ 932.79
13	$129.81	$ 12.38	$ 920.41
14	$127.96	$ 14.23	$ 906.18
15	$125.83	$ 16.36	$ 889.82
16	$123.39	$ 18.80	$ 871.02
17	$120.58	$ 21.61	$ 849.41
18	$117.36	$ 24.83	$ 824.58
19	$113.65	$ 28.54	$ 796.04
20	$109.38	$ 32.81	$ 763.23
21	$104.48	$ 37.71	$ 725.52
22	$ 98.82	$ 43.37	$ 682.15
23	$ 92.38	$ 49.81	$ 632.34
24	$ 84.94	$ 57.25	$ 575.09
25	$ 76.39	$ 65.80	$ 509.29
26	$ 66.57	$ 75.62	$ 433.67
27	$ 55.27	$ 86.92	$ 346.75
28	$ 42.29	$ 99.90	$ 246.85
29	$ 27.37	$ 114.82	$ 132.03
30	$ 10.16	$ 132.03	$ 0.00

15% ANNUAL PAYMENT SCHEDULE

Based on a loan of $1,000

30-YEAR TERM

Monthly Payment: $12.64 Annual Payment: $151.73

YEAR	INTEREST PAID PER YEAR	PRINCIPAL PAID PER YEAR	BALANCE OWED AT YEAR END
1	$149.87	$ 1.86	$ 998.14
2	$149.57	$ 2.16	$ 995.98
3	$149.23	$ 2.50	$ 993.48
4	$148.82	$ 2.91	$ 990.57
5	$148.36	$ 3.37	$ 987.20
6	$147.82	$ 3.91	$ 983.29
7	$147.19	$ 4.54	$ 978.75
8	$146.46	$ 5.27	$ 973.48
9	$145.61	$ 6.12	$ 967.36
10	$144.62	$ 7.11	$ 960.25
11	$143.48	$ 8.25	$ 952.00
12	$142.16	$ 9.57	$ 942.43
13	$140.62	$ 11.11	$ 931.32
14	$138.83	$ 12.90	$ 918.42
15	$136.76	$ 14.97	$ 903.45
16	$134.35	$ 17.38	$ 886.07
17	$131.56	$ 20.17	$ 865.90
18	$128.31	$ 23.42	$ 842.48
19	$124.55	$ 27.18	$ 815.30
20	$120.18	$ 31.55	$ 783.75
21	$115.11	$ 36.62	$ 747.13
22	$109.22	$ 42.51	$ 704.62
23	$102.39	$ 49.34	$ 655.28
24	$ 94.45	$ 57.28	$ 598.00
25	$ 85.25	$ 66.48	$ 531.52
26	$ 74.56	$ 77.17	$ 454.35
27	$ 62.15	$ 89.58	$ 364.77
28	$ 47.75	$ 103.98	$ 260.79
29	$ 31.04	$ 120.69	$ 140.10
30	$ 11.63	$ 140.10	$ .00

ANNUAL PAYMENT SCHEDULE 16%

Based on a loan of $1,000

30-YEAR TERM

Monthly Payment: $13.45 Annual Payment: $161.38

YEAR	INTEREST PAID PER YEAR	PRINCIPAL PAID PER YEAR	BALANCE OWED AT YEAR END
1	$159.90	$ 1.48	$ 998.52
2	$159.65	$ 1.73	$ 996.79
3	$159.35	$ 2.03	$ 994.76
4	$159.00	$ 2.38	$ 992.38
5	$158.59	$ 2.79	$ 989.59
6	$158.11	$ 3.27	$ 986.32
7	$157.55	$ 3.83	$ 982.49
8	$156.89	$ 4.49	$ 978.00
9	$156.12	$ 5.26	$ 972.74
10	$155.21	$ 6.17	$ 966.57
11	$154.15	$ 7.23	$ 959.34
12	$152.90	$ 8.48	$ 950.86
13	$151.44	$ 9.94	$ 940.92
14	$149.73	$ 11.65	$ 929.27
15	$147.72	$ 13.66	$ 915.61
16	$145.37	$ 16.01	$ 899.60
17	$142.61	$ 18.77	$ 880.83
18	$139.38	$ 22.00	$ 858.83
19	$135.58	$ 25.80	$ 833.03
20	$131.14	$ 30.24	$ 802.79
21	$125.93	$ 35.45	$ 767.34
22	$119.82	$ 41.56	$ 725.78
23	$112.59	$ 48.79	$ 676.99
24	$104.27	$ 57.11	$ 619.88
25	$ 94.43	$ 66.95	$ 552.93
26	$ 82.90	$ 78.48	$ 474.45
27	$ 69.38	$ 92.00	$ 382.45
28	$ 53.53	$ 107.85	$ 274.60
29	$ 34.95	$ 126.43	$ 148.17
30	$ 13.21	$ 148.17	$ .00

17% ANNUAL PAYMENT SCHEDULE

Based on a loan of $1,000

30-YEAR TERM

Monthly Payment: $14.26 Annual Payment: $171.08

YEAR	INTEREST PAID PER YEAR	PRINCIPAL PAID PER YEAR	BALANCE OWED AT YEAR END
1	$169.91	$ 1.17	$ 998.83
2	$169.70	$ 1.38	$ 997.45
3	$169.44	$ 1.64	$ 995.81
4	$169.14	$ 1.94	$ 993.87
5	$168.78	$ 2.30	$ 991.57
6	$168.36	$ 2.72	$ 988.85
7	$167.86	$ 3.22	$ 985.63
8	$167.27	$ 3.81	$ 981.82
9	$166.57	$ 4.51	$ 977.31
10	$165.74	$ 5.34	$ 971.97
11	$164.75	$ 6.33	$ 965.64
12	$163.59	$ 7.49	$ 958.15
13	$162.22	$ 8.86	$ 949.29
14	$160.58	$ 10.50	$ 938.79
15	$158.65	$ 12.43	$ 926.36
16	$156.37	$ 14.71	$ 911.65
17	$153.66	$ 17.42	$ 894.23
18	$150.46	$ 20.62	S 873.61
19	$146.67	$ 24.41	S 849.20
20	$142.18	$ 28.90	$ 820.30
21	$136.87	$ 34.21	$ 786.09
22	$130.58	$ 40.50	$ 745.59
23	$123.13	$ 47.95	$ 697.64
24	$114.31	$ 56.77	$ 640.87
25	$103.87	$ 67.21	$ 573.66
26	$ 91.33	$ 79.75	$ 493.91
27	$ 76.88	$ 94.20	$ 399.71
28	$ 59.55	$ 111.53	$ 288.18
29	$ 39.04	$ 132.04	$ 156.14
30	$ 14.94	$ 156.14	$ .00

ANNUAL PAYMENT SCHEDULE 18%

Based on a loan of $1,000

30-YEAR TERM

Monthly Payment: $15.07 Annual Payment: $180.85

YEAR	INTEREST PAID PER YEAR	PRINCIPAL PAID PER YEAR	BALANCE OWED AT YEAR END
1	$179.93	$ 0.92	$ 999.08
2	$179.75	$ 1.10	$ 997.98
3	$179.53	$ 1.32	$ 996.66
4	$179.27	$ 1.58	$ 995.08
5	$178.96	$ 1.89	$ 993.19
6	$178.59	$ 2.26	$ 990.93
7	$178.15	$ 2.70	$ 988.23
8	$177.62	$ 3.23	$ 985.00
9	$176.99	$ 3.86	$ 981.14
10	$176.24	$ 4.61	$ 976.53
11	$175.33	$ 5.52	$ 971.01
12	$174.25	$ 6.60	$ 964.41
13	$172.97	$ 7.88	$ 956.53
14	$171.42	$ 9.43	$ 947.10
15	$169.58	$ 11.27	$ 935.83
16	$167.37	$ 13.48	$ 922.35
17	$164.74	$ 16.11	$ 906.24
18	$161.59	$ 19.26	$ 886.98
19	$157.82	$ 23.03	$ 863.95
20	$153.31	$ 27.54	$ 836.41
21	$147.92	$ 32.93	$ 803.48
22	$141.48	$ 39.37	$ 764.11
23	$133.77	$ 47.08	$ 717.03
24	$124.61	$ 56.24	$ 660.79
25	$113.57	$ 67.28	$ 593.51
26	$100.41	$ 80.44	$ 513.07
27	$ 84.67	$ 96.18	$ 416.89
28	$ 65.86	$ 114.99	$ 301.90
29	$ 43.36	$ 137.49	$ 164.41
30	$ 16.44	$ 164.41	$ .00

19% ANNUAL PAYMENT SCHEDULE
Based on a loan of $1,000

30-YEAR TERM

Monthly Payment: $15.89 **Annual Payment: $190.67**

YEAR	INTEREST PAID PER YEAR	PRINCIPAL PAID PER YEAR	BALANCE OWED AT YEAR END
1	$189.94	$ 0.73	$ 999.27
2	$189.79	$ 0.88	$ 998.39
3	$189.61	$ 1.06	$ 997.33
4	$189.39	$ 1.28	$ 996.05
5	$189.12	$ 1.55	$ 994.50
6	$188.80	$ 1.87	$ 992.63
7	$188.41	$ 2.26	$ 990.37
8	$187.95	$ 2.72	$ 987.65
9	$187.38	$ 3.29	$ 984.36
10	$186.70	$ 3.97	$ 980.39
11	$185.87	$ 4.80	$ 975.59
12	$184.88	$ 5.79	$ 969.80
13	$183.68	$ 6.99	$ 962.81
14	$182.22	$ 8.45	$ 954.36
15	$180.47	$ 10.20	$ 944.15
16	$178.36	$ 12.31	$ 931.85
17	$175.80	$ 14.87	$ 916.98
18	$172.72	$ 17.95	$ 899.03
19	$168.99	$ 21.68	$ 877.35
20	$164.50	$ 26.17	$ 851.18
21	$159.07	$ 31.60	$ 819.58
22	$152.51	$ 38.16	$ 781.42
23	$144.59	$ 46.08	$ 735.34
24	$135.01	$ 55.66	$ 679.68
25	$123.49	$ 67.18	$ 612.50
26	$109.56	$ 81.11	$ 531.39
27	$ 92.73	$ 97.94	$ 433.45
28	$ 72.41	$ 118.26	$ 315.19
29	$ 47.88	$ 142.79	$ 172.40
30	$ 18.27	$ 172.40	$ .00

ANNUAL PAYMENT SCHEDULE 20%
Based on a loan of $1,000

30-YEAR TERM

Monthly Payment: $16.71 **Annual Payment: $200.52**

YEAR	INTEREST PAID PER YEAR	PRINCIPAL PAID PER YEAR	BALANCE OWED AT YEAR END
1	$199.95	$ 0.57	$ 999.43
2	$199.82	$ 0.70	$ 998.73
3	$199.67	$ 0.85	$ 997.88
4	$199.48	$ 1.04	$ 996.84
5	$199.25	$ 1.27	$ 995.57
6	$198.98	$ 1.54	$ 994.03
7	$198.64	$ 1.80	$ 992.15
8	$198.22	$ 2.30	$ 989.85
9	$197.72	$ 2.80	$ 987.05
10	$197.11	$ 3.41	$ 983.64
11	$196.36	$ 4.16	$ 979.48
12	$195.45	$ 5.07	$ 974.41
13	$194.33	$ 6.19	$ 968.22
14	$192.97	$ 7.55	$ 960.67
15	$191.32	$ 9.20	$ 951.47
16	$189.29	$ 11.23	$ 940.24
17	$186.83	$ 13.69	$ 926.55
18	$183.83	$ 16.69	$ 909.86
19	$180.17	$ 20.35	$ 889.51
20	$175.70	$ 24.82	$ 864.69
21	$170.25	$ 30.27	$ 834.42
22	$163.62	$ 36.90	$ 797.52
23	$155.52	$ 45.00	$ 752.52
24	$145.65	$ 54.87	$ 697.65
25	$133.61	$ 66.91	$ 630.74
26	$118.93	$ 81.59	$ 549.15
27	$101.03	$ 99.49	$ 449.66
28	$ 79.20	$ 121.32	$ 328.34
29	$ 52.59	$ 147.93	$ 180.41
30	$ 20.11	$ 180.41	$ .00

SECTION THREE

Loan Progression Charts

As an example, turn to the 11% Loan Progression Chart: Find the original term in years going across the page; then go down the column, age of loan, to fifteen years. Multiply 838 by 85, an $85,000 loan. The balance remaining on an original $85,000 loan at a fixed rate of 11% for thirty years is $71,230.

LOAN PROGRESSION CHART — 5%

Showing dollar balance remaining on a $1000 loan

ORIGINAL TERM IN YEARS 5	8	10	12	15	16	17	18	19	20	21	AGE OF LOAN
819	896	921	938	954	959	962	965	967	970	973	1
630	786	838	872	906	914	922	928	933	939	944	2
430	671	751	803	855	868	880	889	897	906	913	3
220	550	659	731	802	820	835	848	860	871	881	4
	422	562	654	746	768	788	805	820	835	847	5
	289	461	574	687	715	739	760	779	796	812	6
	148	354	490	625	658	687	713	735	756	775	7
		242	402	560	599	633	663	689	714	735	8
		124	309	491	536	576	610	641	669	694	9
			211	419	471	516	555	590	622	651	10
			108	343	402	453	497	537	573	605	11
				264	329	386	437	481	521	557	12
				180	253	317	373	422	467	507	13
				92	173	243	305	360	410	454	14
					89	166	235	295	350	399	15
						85	160	227	287	340	16
							82	155	220	279	17
								79	150	214	18
									77	146	19
										75	20

ORIGINAL TERM IN YEARS 22	23	24	25	26	27	28	29	30	35	40	AGE OF LOAN
974	976	978	980	980	982	984	985	986	990	992	1
947	951	955	958	960	963	966	968	970	978	983	2
919	924	930	936	939	943	948	951	954	966	974	3
889	897	905	912	916	922	928	932	937	954	965	4
858	868	878	886	893	900	908	913	919	941	955	5
825	837	849	860	868	877	886	893	900	927	945	6
790	805	819	832	842	853	863	872	880	912	934	7
754	771	788	803	815	828	839	849	859	897	922	8
716	736	755	772	786	801	814	826	837	881	910	9
676	699	720	740	756	773	788	801	814	864	898	10
634	660	684	706	725	743	760	775	789	846	885	11
589	618	645	670	691	712	731	748	764	827	871	12
543	575	605	633	656	679	701	719	737	808	856	13
494	530	563	593	620	645	668	689	709	787	841	14
442	482	518	552	581	609	635	658	679	765	825	15
388	432	472	508	540	571	599	624	648	742	808	16
331	379	422	462	498	531	562	589	615	718	790	17
271	323	371	414	453	489	522	552	581	693	771	18
209	265	316	363	405	445	481	514	544	667	751	19
142	204	259	310	356	398	438	473	506	639	730	20
73	139	199	254	304	350	392	430	466	609	709	21
	71	136	195	249	298	344	386	424	578	686	22
		70	133	191	244	294	338	380	546	661	23
			68	131	188	241	289	333	512	636	24
				67	128	185	237	285	476	610	25
					66	126	182	233	438	582	26
						65	124	179	399	552	27
							64	122	357	521	28
								63	314	489	29
									268	454	30
									219	419	31
									168	381	32
									115	341	33
									59	299	34
										255	35

5.5% LOAN PROGRESSION CHART

Showing dollar balance remaining on a $1000 loan

AGE OF LOAN	5	8	10	12	15	16	17	18	19	20	21
	ORIGINAL TERM IN YEARS										
1	821	898	923	939	956	960	964	966	969	972	974
2	633	790	841	875	909	917	925	931	937	942	946
3	433	675	755	808	860	872	884	893	903	911	917
4	223	555	664	736	808	825	841	854	866	877	887
5		427	568	661	753	775	796	812	828	842	854
6		293	467	581	695	722	747	768	788	805	820
7		150	359	497	633	667	697	722	745	766	784
8			246	408	569	608	643	673	700	724	746
9			126	315	500	546	586	621	652	680	705
10				215	428	480	526	566	602	634	662
11				111	351	410	463	508	549	585	617
12					271	337	396	447	493	533	570
13					185	260	325	382	433	479	519
14					95	178	250	314	371	421	466
15						91	171	242	304	360	410
16							88	166	234	296	351
17								85	161	228	288
18									82	156	222
19										80	152
20											78

AGE OF LOAN	22	23	24	25	26	27	28	29	30	35	40
	ORIGINAL TERM IN YEARS										
1	976	977	979	981	982	983	985	986	987	990	993
2	951	954	957	960	963	966	968	971	973	980	986
3	924	929	934	939	943	947	951	955	958	969	978
4	896	903	910	916	922	928	933	938	942	958	970
5	866	875	884	893	900	907	914	920	925	946	961
6	834	846	857	867	877	885	893	901	907	933	952
7	800	815	828	841	852	862	872	881	888	920	942
8	765	782	798	813	826	838	849	860	869	905	931
9	728	748	766	783	798	812	825	837	848	890	920
10	688	711	732	751	769	785	800	814	826	874	909
11	647	673	697	718	738	756	773	789	802	858	897
12	603	632	659	683	705	726	745	762	778	840	884
13	556	589	619	646	671	694	715	734	752	821	870
14	507	543	577	607	635	660	683	705	724	802	856
15	455	495	532	566	596	624	650	674	695	781	840
16	400	445	485	522	556	586	615	641	664	759	824
17	342	391	436	476	513	546	577	606	632	735	807
18	281	335	383	427	467	504	538	570	598	711	789
19	217	275	328	376	420	460	497	531	562	685	770
20	148	212	269	321	369	413	453	490	523	657	750
21	76	145	207	264	316	363	406	447	483	628	729
22		74	142	203	259	310	357	401	440	598	707
23			73	139	200	255	306	353	395	565	683
24				72	137	196	251	302	348	531	658
25					70	134	193	248	297	495	632
26						69	132	191	244	457	604
27							68	131	188	416	574
28								67	129	374	543
29									66	329	510
30										281	475
31										231	439
32										178	400
33										122	359
34										63	316
35											270

LOAN PROGRESSION CHART 6%

Showing dollar balance remaining on a $1000 loan

5	8	10	12	15	16	17	18	19	20	21	AGE OF LOAN
ORIGINAL TERM IN YEARS											
823	899	925	941	958	961	965	968	971	973	976	1
635	793	845	879	913	920	928	934	940	944	950	2
436	680	760	813	865	877	889	898	907	914	922	3
225	560	670	743	814	831	847	860	872	882	893	4
	432	574	668	760	782	802	820	835	848	861	5
	296	473	589	703	730	755	777	796	812	828	6
	153	365	505	642	676	705	731	754	774	793	7
		250	416	578	617	652	683	710	734	756	8
		129	321	509	555	596	631	663	691	716	9
			220	437	489	536	577	613	645	674	10
			113	359	419	472	519	560	596	630	11
				277	345	405	457	504	545	582	12
				190	267	333	392	444	490	532	13
				98	183	257	323	381	432	478	14
					94	177	249	313	370	422	15
						91	171	242	305	362	16
							88	166	235	298	17
								86	162	230	18
									83	158	19
										81	20

22	23	24	25	26	27	28	29	30	35	40	AGE OF LOAN
ORIGINAL TERM IN YEARS											
977	979	981	982	984	985	986	987	988	991	993	1
953	957	960	963	966	968	971	973	975	982	987	2
928	934	939	943	948	951	955	958	962	972	980	3
901	909	916	922	928	933	938	942	947	962	972	4
872	882	891	899	907	914	919	925	931	951	965	5
842	854	865	875	885	893	900	908	915	939	956	6
809	824	838	849	861	871	880	889	897	927	947	7
775	793	808	822	836	848	858	869	878	913	938	8
739	759	777	794	810	823	836	847	859	900	928	9
700	723	744	763	781	797	811	825	837	885	917	10
659	686	709	731	751	769	785	801	815	869	906	11
615	645	672	696	719	739	758	775	791	852	894	12
569	603	633	660	686	708	729	748	766	834	881	13
520	557	591	621	650	675	698	719	739	816	868	14
468	509	546	580	612	639	665	689	711	796	854	15
412	458	499	536	571	602	630	656	681	774	838	16
353	404	449	490	528	562	593	622	649	752	822	17
291	346	396	441	482	520	554	586	615	728	805	18
225	285	339	389	434	475	512	547	579	702	787	19
154	220	279	333	383	427	468	506	540	675	768	20
79	151	216	274	328	377	421	462	500	647	747	21
	78	148	212	270	323	371	416	457	616	725	22
		76	145	208	266	318	366	411	584	702	23
			75	143	205	262	314	362	550	678	24
				74	141	202	258	310	513	652	25
					73	139	200	255	475	624	26
						71	137	197	434	595	27
							71	135	390	564	28
								70	344	531	29
									295	495	30
									243	458	31
									187	419	32
									129	376	33
									66	332	34
										284	35

6.5% LOAN PROGRESSION CHART

Showing dollar balance remaining on a $1000 loan

AGE OF LOAN	5	8	10	ORIGINAL TERM IN YEARS 12	15	16	17	18	19	20	21
1	825	902	926	943	959	963	967	970	973	975	976
2	639	797	848	882	916	924	931	938	943	948	952
3	439	684	764	818	869	882	893	903	912	920	926
4	227	565	675	749	820	837	853	867	878	889	898
5		437	580	675	767	790	809	827	842	856	868
6		301	479	596	711	739	763	785	804	821	836
7		155	370	512	651	685	714	741	764	784	802
8			255	423	587	627	662	693	720	745	765
9			132	327	518	565	606	642	674	702	727
10				225	445	499	546	588	624	657	685
11				116	367	429	482	530	571	609	641
12					284	354	414	468	515	557	594
13					196	274	342	402	455	502	544
14					101	188	265	332	391	444	490
15						97	182	257	323	381	433
16							94	177	250	315	372
17								91	172	243	307
18									89	167	238
19										86	163
20											84

AGE OF LOAN	22	23	24	ORIGINAL TERM IN YEARS 25	26	27	28	29	30	35	40
1	979	980	983	983	985	987	987	988	989	992	994
2	956	960	964	966	969	972	973	975	977	984	988
3	932	938	943	947	951	956	958	961	964	975	982
4	906	914	921	927	933	938	942	946	950	966	975
5	879	889	898	905	913	920	926	931	936	956	968
6	850	862	873	883	892	901	908	914	921	945	961
7	818	833	847	858	869	880	888	896	904	934	953
8	785	802	819	832	845	858	868	877	886	921	944
9	750	770	789	804	820	834	846	857	868	908	935
10	712	735	757	775	793	809	823	835	848	895	926
11	671	698	722	743	763	782	798	812	826	880	915
12	628	658	686	710	732	753	771	788	803	864	904
13	582	616	647	674	699	722	743	762	779	847	892
14	533	570	605	635	664	690	712	734	753	829	880
15	480	522	561	594	626	655	680	704	726	810	866
16	424	471	513	551	586	617	646	672	696	790	852
17	364	416	463	504	543	578	609	638	664	768	837
18	301	357	409	455	497	535	570	601	631	745	821
19	233	295	351	402	448	490	528	563	595	720	803
20	160	228	290	345	396	442	483	521	557	693	785
21	83	157	224	285	340	390	436	477	516	665	765
22		81	154	220	280	335	385	430	472	635	744
23			80	152	217	277	331	380	426	603	721
24				78	149	214	273	327	376	569	697
25					77	147	211	269	323	532	672
26						76	145	208	266	493	644
27							75	143	206	451	615
28								74	142	407	584
29									73	359	551
30										309	515
31										255	477
32										197	437
33										136	394
34										70	348
35											299

LOAN PROGRESSION CHART 7%

Showing dollar balance remaining on a $1000 loan

5	8	10	12	15	ORIGINAL TERM IN YEARS 16	17	18	19	20	21	AGE OF LOAN
827	903	928	944	961	965	969	972	974	976	978	1
641	799	852	885	919	927	935	941	946	950	954	2
442	688	769	822	874	886	898	908	916	923	929	3
229	569	681	754	826	843	859	872	883	894	903	4
	441	586	681	774	797	817	834	849	862	874	5
	304	485	603	719	747	772	793	812	829	843	6
	158	376	519	659	693	723	750	772	792	810	7
		259	429	596	636	672	703	730	754	775	8
		134	333	527	574	616	652	684	712	737	9
			230	454	509	557	599	635	667	696	10
			119	375	438	493	541	582	620	653	11
				291	362	424	479	526	568	606	12
				201	281	351	412	466	513	556	13
				104	194	272	341	401	455	502	14
					100	188	264	332	391	445	15
						97	182	257	324	383	16
							94	177	251	317	17
								92	173	245	18
									90	169	19
										88	20

22	23	24	25	26	ORIGINAL TERM IN YEARS 27	28	29	30	35	40	AGE OF LOAN
980	982	984	985	986	987	989	989	989	993	995	1
958	962	966	969	971	973	976	977	979	986	990	2
936	942	947	951	955	959	962	964	967	978	984	3
911	919	926	932	938	943	947	951	954	970	978	4
885	895	904	912	919	925	932	936	941	960	972	5
857	869	880	890	899	907	915	921	926	951	965	6
827	842	855	867	878	887	897	904	911	940	958	7
794	812	828	842	855	866	877	886	895	929	950	8
760	780	799	815	830	844	856	867	877	917	942	9
722	746	768	787	804	819	834	846	858	904	933	10
683	710	734	756	775	793	810	824	837	890	924	11
640	671	698	723	745	765	784	800	815	875	914	12
594	629	660	687	713	736	757	775	792	860	903	13
545	584	618	650	678	703	727	748	767	842	891	14
492	535	574	609	640	669	695	718	740	824	879	15
436	484	527	565	600	632	661	687	711	805	865	16
375	428	476	519	557	593	625	653	680	784	851	17
310	369	421	468	511	550	586	617	647	761	835	18
241	305	363	415	462	505	544	579	611	737	819	19
166	236	300	357	409	456	499	537	573	711	801	20
86	163	233	295	352	404	451	493	532	683	782	21
	84	160	229	291	347	399	445	488	653	761	22
		83	158	226	287	343	394	441	621	740	23
			82	156	223	284	339	390	587	716	24
				81	154	220	281	336	550	691	25
					80	152	218	278	511	664	26
						79	150	215	469	635	27
							78	149	423	604	28
								77	375	571	29
									323	535	30
									267	497	31
									207	455	32
									143	411	33
									74	364	34
										314	35

7.5% LOAN PROGRESSION CHART

Showing dollar balance remaining on a $1000 loan

AGE OF LOAN	ORIGINAL TERM IN YEARS 5	8	10	12	15	16	17	18	19	20	21
1	829	905	930	946	962	967	970	973	975	978	979
2	644	803	855	889	922	930	937	943	949	954	957
3	445	693	774	827	878	891	902	912	920	928	934
4	231	574	687	760	832	849	864	877	889	900	908
5		446	592	688	781	804	824	840	856	869	881
6		308	491	610	726	755	780	801	820	837	851
7		160	382	527	668	702	732	758	781	802	819
8			264	436	604	645	681	712	739	764	785
9			137	339	536	584	626	662	694	723	748
10				234	463	518	567	609	646	679	708
11				122	383	447	503	551	593	632	665
12					298	371	434	489	537	581	618
13					206	288	359	422	477	525	568
14					107	199	279	349	411	466	514
15						103	193	272	341	402	456
16							100	188	265	333	394
17								97	183	259	326
18									95	179	254
19										93	175
20											91

AGE OF LOAN	ORIGINAL TERM IN YEARS 22	23	24	25	26	27	28	29	30	35	40
1	982	983	985	986	986	988	989	990	990	994	996
2	962	964	968	971	973	976	978	980	981	987	991
3	940	945	950	954	957	962	965	968	970	980	987
4	917	923	931	936	941	947	951	955	958	972	981
5	892	901	910	917	924	931	936	942	946	964	976
6	865	876	888	897	905	914	921	927	932	955	970
7	836	849	863	875	885	895	903	912	918	945	964
8	805	821	837	851	863	875	885	895	903	935	957
9	771	790	809	825	839	853	865	876	886	924	949
10	734	757	779	797	814	830	844	857	868	912	941
11	695	721	746	767	786	805	821	836	848	899	932
12	653	683	711	735	757	778	796	813	827	885	923
13	607	641	673	700	725	749	769	788	805	870	913
14	558	596	632	663	691	717	740	762	780	854	902
15	505	548	588	623	654	683	709	733	754	837	890
16	448	496	540	579	614	647	676	702	726	818	878
17	387	440	489	532	571	607	640	669	695	798	864
18	321	380	434	482	525	565	601	633	662	776	850
19	249	315	374	427	475	519	559	595	627	752	834
20	172	245	310	369	422	470	514	553	589	727	817
21	89	169	241	306	364	417	465	509	548	700	798
22		88	167	238	302	360	412	460	503	670	779
23			86	164	234	298	356	408	456	639	757
24				85	162	232	295	352	404	605	735
25					84	160	229	292	349	568	710
26						83	158	227	289	528	683
27							82	157	225	485	654
28								81	155	439	624
29									81	390	590
30										336	554
31										279	516
32										217	474
33										150	429
34										78	381
35											328

LOAN PROGRESSION CHART 8%

Showing dollar balance remaining on a $1000 loan

ORIGINAL TERM IN YEARS 5	8	10	12	15	16	17	18	19	20	21	AGE OF LOAN
831	907	932	948	964	968	971	974	977	978	980	1
647	806	858	892	925	933	940	946	952	955	960	2
448	697	778	831	883	895	906	916	924	931	937	3
233	579	692	765	837	855	869	883	895	904	913	4
	451	598	694	788	810	830	847	862	875	887	5
	313	497	617	734	762	787	808	828	843	858	6
	163	387	534	676	711	740	767	790	809	827	7
		268	443	613	654	690	721	749	772	794	8
		139	345	545	593	635	672	705	732	758	9
			239	471	528	576	619	657	689	718	10
			124	392	456	512	561	605	642	676	11
				305	379	443	499	549	591	630	12
				211	295	368	432	488	536	580	13
				110	205	287	358	422	477	526	14
					106	199	279	350	412	468	15
						103	193	273	342	404	16
							101	189	267	336	17
								98	185	262	18
									96	181	19
										94	20

ORIGINAL TERM IN YEARS 22	23	24	25	26	27	28	29	30	35	40	AGE OF LOAN
982	984	986	987	989	989	990	991	992	994	996	1
964	967	970	973	976	977	980	981	983	988	992	2
943	948	953	958	962	964	968	970	973	982	988	3
921	928	935	941	946	950	955	959	962	975	983	4
897	906	915	923	930	935	941	946	951	968	979	5
871	883	894	903	912	919	927	933	939	960	973	6
843	857	871	882	893	901	911	918	925	951	967	7
813	830	845	859	872	882	893	902	910	941	961	8
780	800	818	835	849	862	874	885	895	931	954	9
745	768	789	808	825	839	854	866	878	920	947	10
706	733	757	779	798	815	832	846	859	908	939	11
664	695	722	747	770	789	808	824	839	895	931	12
619	654	685	713	739	761	782	800	817	881	921	13
570	609	645	676	705	730	754	774	794	865	911	14
517	561	601	636	668	697	723	746	768	849	900	15
460	509	553	593	629	661	690	716	740	831	889	16
398	452	502	546	586	621	654	684	711	811	876	17
330	391	446	495	540	579	616	648	678	790	862	18
257	325	386	440	490	533	574	610	643	768	847	19
178	253	320	381	435	484	528	568	605	743	831	20
93	175	250	316	376	430	479	523	564	716	813	21
	91	173	246	313	372	426	475	519	687	794	22
		90	171	243	309	368	422	471	656	774	23
			89	169	241	306	365	419	622	751	24
				88	167	238	303	362	585	727	25
					87	165	236	301	545	701	26
						86	164	234	502	673	27
							85	162	456	642	28
								84	405	609	29
									350	573	30
									291	534	31
									227	492	32
									157	446	33
									82	396	34
										343	35

8.5%

LOAN PROGRESSION CHART

Showing dollar balance remaining on a $1000 loan

AGE OF LOAN	ORIGINAL TERM IN YEARS 5	8	10	12	15	16	17	18	19	20	21
1	833	909	934	950	966	969	972	975	977	980	982
2	650	809	862	895	928	935	942	948	953	959	962
3	451	701	783	836	887	899	910	919	927	935	941
4	235	584	697	771	843	859	874	887	899	909	918
5		456	604	701	794	816	836	853	868	881	893
6		317	503	624	742	769	794	815	834	851	865
7		165	393	541	684	718	748	774	797	818	835
8			273	450	622	663	699	730	757	782	803
9			142	352	554	602	645	682	714	743	768
10				244	480	537	586	629	666	700	729
11				127	400	465	522	571	615	654	687
12					312	387	452	509	559	603	642
13					217	302	376	441	498	548	592
14					113	210	294	367	431	488	538
15						109	204	287	359	423	479
16							106	199	280	352	415
17								104	195	275	346
18									101	191	270
19										100	187
20											98

AGE OF LOAN	ORIGINAL TERM IN YEARS 22	23	24	25	26	27	28	29	30	35	40
1	983	985	987	988	989	989	991	992	993	995	997
2	966	969	972	974	977	979	981	983	984	990	993
3	946	952	956	960	964	967	970	973	975	984	990
4	925	933	939	945	949	954	958	962	966	978	986
5	903	912	920	928	934	940	945	951	955	972	981
6	878	890	900	909	917	925	932	938	943	964	977
7	851	865	878	889	899	908	916	924	931	956	972
8	822	839	854	867	879	890	900	909	917	947	966
9	790	810	828	843	857	870	882	893	902	938	960
10	755	778	799	817	834	849	863	875	886	928	953
11	717	744	768	789	808	826	841	856	868	916	946
12	676	707	734	759	780	800	818	835	849	904	938
13	631	666	697	725	750	773	793	812	828	891	930
14	582	622	657	689	717	743	766	787	806	877	920
15	529	574	614	649	681	710	736	760	781	861	910
16	471	522	566	606	642	674	704	730	754	844	899
17	408	465	515	559	599	636	668	698	725	825	887
18	340	403	458	508	553	593	630	663	693	805	874
19	265	335	397	453	503	548	588	625	658	783	860
20	184	262	331	392	448	498	543	584	620	759	845
21	96	182	258	327	388	443	493	538	579	732	828
22		95	179	255	323	384	439	489	534	704	810
23			93	177	252	320	381	436	486	673	790
24				92	175	250	317	378	433	639	768
25					91	173	247	314	375	602	744
26						90	172	246	312	563	719
27							90	170	244	519	691
28								89	169	472	660
29									88	420	627
30										364	591
31										303	552
32										237	509
33										164	463
34										86	412
35											357

LOAN PROGRESSION CHART

9%

Showing dollar balance remaining on a $1000 loan

ORIGINAL TERM IN YEARS 5	8	10	12	15	16	17	18	19	20	21	AGE OF LOAN
834	911	936	951	967	971	974	976	979	982	984	1
653	813	865	898	931	939	946	951	956	961	965	2
454	706	787	840	891	904	914	923	931	939	945	3
237	589	703	777	848	866	880	892	904	914	923	4
	461	610	707	800	824	843	859	874	887	899	5
	321	509	631	749	778	802	822	842	858	873	6
	168	398	548	692	727	757	783	806	826	844	7
		277	457	630	672	708	739	767	791	812	8
		145	358	563	612	655	691	724	752	778	9
			249	488	546	596	639	677	710	740	10
			130	407	475	532	582	626	665	699	11
				319	396	462	519	570	614	653	12
				222	310	385	451	509	559	604	13
				116	216	302	376	442	499	550	14
					113	210	294	368	434	491	15
						110	205	288	362	426	16
							107	201	283	356	17
								105	197	278	18
									103	194	19
										101	20

ORIGINAL TERM IN YEARS 22	23	24	25	26	27	28	29	30	35	40	AGE OF LOAN
985	986	988	989	990	991	991	992	994	996	997	1
968	971	975	976	979	981	982	984	986	991	994	2
950	955	960	963	967	970	972	975	978	986	991	3
930	937	944	948	954	958	962	965	969	980	987	4
908	917	926	933	939	945	950	954	959	974	983	5
885	896	907	915	924	930	937	943	949	968	979	6
859	873	885	896	906	915	922	930	937	960	975	7
830	847	862	875	887	898	907	916	924	952	970	8
799	819	837	852	867	879	890	900	910	944	964	9
765	788	809	827	844	858	871	883	895	934	958	10
728	755	779	800	819	836	851	865	878	924	952	11
688	718	746	770	792	811	829	845	860	912	945	12
643	678	710	737	763	785	805	823	840	900	937	13
595	634	670	701	730	755	778	799	818	886	928	14
541	586	627	662	695	723	749	772	794	871	919	15
483	534	580	620	656	688	717	743	767	855	908	16
420	477	528	573	614	650	682	712	739	837	897	17
350	414	471	521	567	608	644	677	707	818	885	18
274	345	409	465	516	562	603	639	673	796	872	19
191	270	341	404	461	512	557	598	635	773	857	20
100	188	267	337	400	457	507	553	594	747	841	21
	98	186	264	334	396	453	503	549	719	823	22
		97	184	261	331	393	449	500	689	804	23
			96	182	259	328	390	447	655	783	24
				95	180	257	325	388	619	760	25
					94	179	255	323	579	735	26
						93	177	253	535	708	27
							93	176	487	677	28
								92	435	645	29
									378	609	30
									315	569	31
									247	526	32
									172	479	33
									90	428	34
										371	35

9.5% LOAN PROGRESSION CHART

Showing dollar balance remaining on a $1000 loan

AGE OF LOAN	5	8	10	12	15	16	17	18	19	20	21
	ORIGINAL TERM IN YEARS										
1	836	912	937	953	968	972	975	978	980	982	984
2	656	816	868	901	933	941	948	954	959	963	966
3	457	710	792	844	895	907	918	927	935	942	947
4	239	593	708	782	853	870	885	898	909	918	926
5		465	616	713	807	829	849	865	880	893	903
6		325	515	638	756	784	809	830	848	864	878
7		170	404	555	700	735	765	791	814	833	850
8			282	464	639	681	717	748	775	799	820
9			148	364	571	621	664	701	733	762	786
10				254	497	555	606	649	687	720	749
11				133	416	483	542	592	636	675	709
12					326	404	471	530	581	625	664
13					227	317	394	461	519	570	615
14					119	221	309	385	452	510	561
15						116	216	302	378	444	502
16							113	211	296	371	437
17								110	207	291	365
18									108	203	286
19										106	200
20											105

AGE OF LOAN	22	23	24	25	26	27	28	29	30	35	40
	ORIGINAL TERM IN YEARS										
1	985	987	989	990	991	991	993	993	994	997	998
2	970	973	976	979	981	982	984	986	987	993	995
3	953	958	962	966	970	972	975	977	980	988	992
4	934	941	947	953	957	961	965	968	972	983	989
5	913	923	931	938	944	949	954	958	963	978	986
6	891	902	912	921	929	935	942	947	953	972	982
7	866	880	892	903	913	920	929	935	942	965	978
8	838	855	870	883	895	904	914	922	930	958	974
9	808	828	846	861	875	886	898	908	917	950	969
10	775	798	819	837	853	867	880	892	902	941	963
11	739	766	789	810	829	845	861	874	886	931	957
12	699	730	757	781	803	822	839	855	869	921	951
13	655	690	721	749	774	796	816	834	850	909	944
14	606	647	682	714	742	767	790	810	829	896	936
15	553	599	639	675	708	736	762	785	805	882	927
16	495	546	592	633	669	701	730	756	780	866	918
17	430	489	540	586	627	663	696	725	752	849	907
18	360	425	483	535	581	621	658	691	721	830	896
19	282	355	420	478	530	575	617	654	687	810	883
20	197	279	351	416	474	525	571	613	650	787	869
21	103	194	276	348	412	470	521	567	609	762	854
22		102	192	273	345	409	466	518	564	735	837
23			101	190	270	342	406	463	515	705	818
24				100	189	268	339	403	460	672	798
25					99	187	266	337	400	635	776
26						98	186	264	335	595	751
27							97	184	263	551	724
28								96	183	503	694
29									96	450	662
30										391	626
31										327	587
32										257	543
33										179	496
34										94	443
35											386

LOAN PROGRESSION CHART 10%

Showing dollar balance remaining on a $1000 loan

5	8	10	12	15	16	17	18	19	20	21	AGE OF LOAN
ORIGINAL TERM IN YEARS											
838	914	939	954	970	973	976	979	981	983	985	1
659	819	871	904	937	944	950	956	961	965	969	2
461	714	796	849	900	911	921	931	938	945	951	3
242	598	714	788	859	875	889	902	913	923	931	4
	470	622	720	813	835	854	871	885	898	909	5
	329	521	645	764	792	816	837	855	871	885	6
	173	410	562	708	743	773	799	821	841	858	7
		286	471	648	689	725	757	784	807	829	8
		150	370	580	630	673	710	742	771	796	9
			259	506	565	615	659	697	730	760	10
			136	424	492	551	602	646	685	720	11
				333	412	481	540	591	636	675	12
				233	324	403	471	530	581	627	13
				122	227	316	394	462	521	573	14
					119	221	310	387	454	513	15
						116	217	304	380	448	16
							114	213	299	375	17
								112	209	295	18
									110	206	19
										108	20

22	23	24	25	26	27	28	29	30	35	40	AGE OF LOAN
ORIGINAL TERM IN YEARS											
987	988	989	991	992	992	993	993	995	997	998	1
972	975	977	980	982	984	986	986	989	993	996	2
956	961	964	969	972	975	977	979	982	989	993	3
938	945	950	956	960	964	968	971	974	985	991	4
919	927	935	942	948	953	958	961	966	980	988	5
897	908	917	926	934	940	946	951	957	975	984	6
873	886	898	909	918	926	934	940	947	969	981	7
846	863	877	890	901	911	920	928	936	962	977	8
817	836	853	869	882	894	905	914	923	955	972	9
785	808	827	846	861	875	888	899	910	946	967	10
749	776	799	820	838	855	870	882	895	937	962	11
710	740	767	792	813	832	849	864	878	928	956	12
666	701	732	761	785	807	826	843	860	917	950	13
618	658	694	726	754	779	801	821	839	905	942	14
565	611	651	688	720	748	774	796	817	891	934	15
506	558	604	646	682	714	743	768	792	876	925	16
441	500	552	599	640	677	709	738	765	860	916	17
370	436	495	548	594	635	672	704	735	842	905	18
291	365	432	491	543	589	631	667	701	822	893	19
203	287	362	428	486	539	585	626	664	800	880	20
107	201	284	358	424	483	535	581	624	776	865	21
	105	199	282	355	421	479	531	579	749	849	22
		104	197	279	352	418	476	529	720	831	23
			103	195	277	350	415	474	687	812	24
				102	194	275	348	413	651	790	25
					102	192	273	346	611	766	26
						101	191	272	567	740	27
							100	190	518	710	28
								100	464	678	29
									405	642	30
									339	603	31
									267	560	32
									186	511	33
									98	458	34
										400	35

10.5% LOAN PROGRESSION CHART

Showing dollar balance remaining on a $1000 loan

AGE OF LOAN	ORIGINAL TERM IN YEARS 5	8	10	12	15	16	17	18	19	20	21
1	839	916	940	956	971	974	977	980	982	984	987
2	661	822	874	907	938	946	953	958	963	967	971
3	463	718	800	853	903	915	925	934	941	948	954
4	244	603	718	793	863	880	894	907	917	926	935
5		475	628	726	819	841	860	876	891	903	914
6		333	527	652	770	798	822	843	861	877	891
7		175	415	569	716	750	780	806	828	848	865
8			291	478	655	698	734	765	792	815	837
9			153	377	588	639	682	719	751	779	805
10				264	514	574	625	668	707	740	769
11				139	432	501	561	612	657	695	730
12					340	421	490	550	601	646	686
13					238	331	411	480	540	592	638
14					125	232	324	403	472	531	584
15						122	227	318	396	464	525
16							119	223	312	390	458
17								117	219	307	385
18									115	215	303
19										113	212
20											112

AGE OF LOAN	ORIGINAL TERM IN YEARS 22	23	24	25	26	27	28	29	30	35	40
1	988	989	990	991	992	993	994	994	995	997	999
2	975	977	979	981	984	985	987	988	990	994	997
3	959	964	967	971	974	976	980	981	984	990	995
4	943	949	954	959	963	967	971	973	977	986	992
5	924	932	939	946	952	956	962	965	969	982	990
6	903	914	922	931	939	945	951	955	961	977	987
7	880	893	904	915	924	932	939	945	951	971	984
8	855	870	884	896	908	917	927	933	941	965	980
9	826	845	861	876	890	901	912	920	929	959	976
10	795	817	836	854	870	883	896	906	916	951	972
11	760	786	808	829	848	863	878	890	902	943	967
12	721	751	778	802	823	841	859	873	886	934	962
13	678	713	743	771	796	817	837	853	869	923	956
14	630	670	706	737	765	790	813	831	849	912	949
15	577	623	663	700	732	760	786	807	828	899	942
16	518	571	617	658	694	726	756	780	804	885	933
17	453	512	565	611	653	689	722	751	777	870	924
18	380	448	507	560	607	648	686	718	747	853	914
19	299	376	443	503	556	602	645	681	715	834	903
20	210	296	372	439	499	552	599	640	678	812	890
21	110	207	293	369	436	495	549	595	633	789	877
22		109	205	290	366	433	493	545	593	763	861
23			108	204	288	363	430	489	543	734	844
24				107	202	286	361	428	487	701	825
25					106	201	285	359	426	666	804
26						106	199	283	357	626	781
27							105	198	282	582	755
28								104	197	533	726
29									104	478	694
30										418	659
31										351	619
32										276	576
33										194	527
34										102	473
35											414

LOAN PROGRESSION CHART 11%

Showing dollar balance remaining on a $1000 loan

ORIGINAL TERM IN YEARS 5	8	10	12	15	16	17	18	19	20	21	AGE OF LOAN
841	918	942	958	973	976	978	981	983	985	987	1
664	825	877	910	942	949	955	960	965	969	973	2
466	723	805	857	907	918	928	937	944	951	957	3
246	608	724	798	868	885	899	911	921	931	939	4
	480	634	732	825	847	866	882	896	908	919	5
	337	533	659	777	805	829	850	867	883	897	6
	178	421	577	724	758	788	813	835	855	872	7
		296	485	664	706	742	773	800	823	844	8
		156	383	597	648	691	728	760	788	813	9
			269	523	583	634	678	716	749	778	10
			142	440	510	570	622	667	706	740	11
				347	429	499	560	611	657	697	12
				244	339	420	490	550	603	649	13
				129	238	331	412	482	542	595	14
					125	233	325	405	475	535	15
						123	229	320	399	469	16
							121	225	315	394	17
								118	221	311	18
									117	219	19
										115	20

ORIGINAL TERM IN YEARS 22	23	24	25	26	27	28	29	30	35	40	AGE OF LOAN
988	990	991	992	993	994	994	995	995	997	998	1
976	979	981	983	985	987	988	990	990	995	997	2
961	966	970	973	976	979	980	983	985	991	995	3
945	952	957	962	966	970	973	976	978	988	993	4
928	936	943	949	955	960	964	969	971	984	990	5
908	919	928	936	943	949	954	960	964	979	988	6
886	899	910	920	929	937	943	950	955	975	985	7
861	877	891	903	914	923	931	939	945	969	982	8
834	853	869	884	896	908	917	927	934	963	978	9
803	826	845	862	877	891	902	914	922	956	974	10
769	795	818	838	856	872	885	899	909	948	970	11
731	762	788	812	832	851	867	882	894	940	965	12
689	724	755	782	806	827	846	863	877	930	960	13
641	682	717	749	776	801	822	842	858	920	954	14
588	635	676	711	743	771	796	819	838	908	947	15
529	582	629	670	706	739	767	793	814	895	939	16
463	524	577	624	665	702	734	763	788	880	931	17
390	459	519	572	619	661	698	731	759	863	921	18
308	386	454	515	568	616	657	695	727	845	911	19
216	305	382	451	511	565	612	654	691	824	899	20
114	214	302	379	448	508	561	609	651	802	886	21
	113	212	299	376	445	505	559	606	776	871	22
		112	210	297	374	442	503	556	747	855	23
			111	209	295	372	440	500	716	837	24
				110	207	294	370	438	680	816	25
					109	206	292	368	641	794	26
						109	205	291	596	769	27
							108	204	547	740	28
								108	492	709	29
									431	674	30
									363	634	31
									286	591	32
									201	542	33
									106	488	34
										427	35

11.5% LOAN PROGRESSION CHART

Showing dollar balance remaining on a $1000 loan

AGE OF LOAN	ORIGINAL TERM IN YEARS 5	8	10	12	15	16	17	18	19	20	21
1	843	919	943	959	973	977	980	982	984	986	988
2	667	828	880	913	944	951	957	962	967	971	975
3	469	727	809	861	910	922	932	940	947	953	960
4	248	613	729	803	873	889	903	915	925	934	943
5		485	639	738	831	853	871	887	901	913	924
6		341	539	665	784	812	835	856	873	888	902
7		180	426	583	731	766	795	820	842	861	878
8			300	492	672	714	750	781	808	831	851
9			159	389	605	656	700	737	769	797	821
10				274	531	591	643	687	725	758	788
11				145	448	519	580	632	676	715	750
12					354	437	508	569	622	667	707
13					249	346	429	499	560	613	660
14					132	244	339	421	492	553	606
15						129	239	333	414	485	546
16							126	234	328	409	479
17								124	231	323	404
18									122	228	320
19										120	225
20											119

AGE OF LOAN	ORIGINAL TERM IN YEARS 22	23	24	25	26	27	28	29	30	35	40
1	989	991	992	992	994	994	995	995	996	998	998
2	977	980	982	984	986	988	989	990	991	995	997
3	964	969	972	975	978	980	983	984	986	992	995
4	949	955	960	964	969	972	976	978	980	989	994
5	932	941	947	953	959	963	967	971	974	986	992
6	913	924	932	940	947	953	958	963	967	982	989
7	892	905	916	925	934	941	948	954	959	977	987
8	868	884	897	909	920	929	937	943	950	972	984
9	842	861	877	890	903	914	924	932	940	966	981
10	812	834	853	870	885	898	910	919	928	960	977
11	779	805	827	847	865	880	893	905	916	953	974
12	741	772	798	821	842	859	875	889	901	945	969
13	699	735	765	792	816	837	855	871	885	936	964
14	652	693	728	759	787	811	832	851	868	926	959
15	599	646	687	723	755	782	807	828	847	915	952
16	540	594	641	682	718	750	778	803	825	903	945
17	474	535	589	636	678	714	746	775	800	889	937
18	399	470	531	584	632	674	711	743	771	873	929
19	316	396	466	527	581	628	670	707	740	855	919
20	222	313	393	462	524	577	625	667	704	835	908
21	118	221	311	389	459	520	575	622	664	813	895
22		117	219	308	387	457	518	572	620	788	881
23			116	217	306	385	454	515	569	761	866
24				115	216	304	383	452	513	729	848
25					114	214	303	381	450	694	829
26						113	213	301	379	655	807
27							113	212	300	611	782
28								112	211	561	754
29									112	506	723
30										444	689
31										374	650
32										296	606
33										208	557
34										110	502
35											440

LOAN PROGRESSION CHART 12%

Showing dollar balance remaining on a $1000 loan

ORIGINAL TERM IN YEARS 5	8	10	12	15	16	17	18	19	20	21	AGE OF LOAN
845	921	945	960	974	978	981	983	985	987	989	1
670	831	883	915	946	953	959	964	969	973	976	2
472	731	813	865	914	925	935	943	950	956	962	3
250	617	734	808	877	894	907	919	929	938	946	4
	489	645	744	836	858	876	892	905	917	928	5
	345	545	672	790	818	842	862	879	894	907	6
	183	432	590	738	773	802	828	849	868	884	7
		305	499	680	722	758	789	815	838	858	8
		162	395	614	665	708	746	777	805	829	9
			279	539	601	652	696	734	767	796	10
			148	456	528	589	641	686	725	759	11
				361	446	517	579	632	677	717	12
				255	353	437	509	570	624	670	13
				135	249	347	430	501	563	617	14
					132	245	341	423	495	557	15
						130	240	336	418	490	16
							127	237	331	414	17
								125	234	328	18
									124	231	19
										123	20

ORIGINAL TERM IN YEARS 22	23	24	25	26	27	28	29	30	35	40	AGE OF LOAN
990	992	992	993	994	994	996	996	997	998	998	1
979	982	983	985	987	988	990	991	993	996	997	2
966	971	974	977	980	982	985	986	988	994	996	3
952	958	963	967	971	974	978	980	983	991	994	4
936	944	950	956	962	966	970	973	977	988	993	5
918	929	936	944	951	956	962	966	970	984	991	6
898	911	921	930	939	945	953	957	963	980	988	7
875	891	903	915	925	933	942	948	955	976	986	8
850	868	883	897	909	920	930	937	945	970	983	9
821	843	861	877	892	904	916	925	935	965	980	10
788	814	836	855	872	887	901	912	923	958	976	11
751	782	807	830	850	867	884	896	909	951	972	12
710	745	775	802	825	845	864	879	894	943	968	13
663	704	739	770	797	821	842	860	877	933	963	14
611	658	698	734	765	793	817	838	857	923	957	15
551	606	652	693	730	761	790	813	836	911	951	16
485	547	600	648	690	726	758	786	811	898	943	17
409	481	542	597	644	686	723	755	783	883	935	18
325	406	477	539	593	641	683	719	752	866	926	19
229	322	403	473	536	590	638	680	717	847	915	20
121	227	319	400	471	532	587	635	678	825	904	21
	120	225	317	398	468	530	585	633	801	890	22
		119	224	315	395	466	528	583	774	876	23
			119	222	313	394	464	526	743	859	24
				118	221	312	392	463	708	840	25
					117	220	311	391	669	819	26
						117	219	310	625	795	27
							116	219	576	767	28
								116	520	737	29
									457	703	30
									386	664	31
									306	620	32
									216	571	33
									114	516	34
										453	35

12.5% LOAN PROGRESSION CHART

Showing dollar balance remaining on a $1000 loan

AGE OF LOAN	ORIGINAL TERM IN YEARS 5	8	10	12	15	16	17	18	19	20	21
1	847	922	946	962	976	979	982	984	986	988	989
2	673	834	886	918	949	956	961	966	971	974	977
3	476	735	817	869	918	929	938	946	953	959	964
4	253	622	739	813	882	898	912	923	933	941	949
5		494	651	750	842	864	882	897	910	922	931
6		349	551	678	797	825	848	868	885	899	912
7		186	438	597	746	780	810	834	856	874	890
8			309	506	688	730	766	797	823	845	865
9			164	402	622	674	717	754	786	813	836
10				284	548	609	661	705	743	776	804
11				151	464	536	598	651	696	734	768
12					369	454	527	589	642	687	727
13					261	361	446	518	580	634	680
14					138	255	354	439	511	573	627
15						135	250	349	433	505	567
16							133	246	344	427	500
17								131	243	340	423
18									129	240	336
19										128	238
20											126

AGE OF LOAN	ORIGINAL TERM IN YEARS 22	23	24	25	26	27	28	29	30	35	40
1	991	992	993	993	994	995	996	997	997	998	999
2	981	983	985	986	988	990	991	992	993	996	998
3	969	973	976	979	981	983	986	988	989	994	997
4	955	961	966	970	973	977	980	982	984	991	996
5	940	948	954	959	964	969	973	976	979	989	994
6	923	933	941	948	954	960	965	969	973	985	992
7	904	916	926	935	943	950	956	961	966	982	990
8	882	897	909	920	930	938	946	953	958	978	988
9	857	875	890	903	915	925	935	943	949	973	986
10	829	850	868	884	898	911	922	931	939	968	983
11	797	822	844	863	879	894	907	919	928	962	980
12	761	791	816	839	858	875	891	904	915	955	976
13	720	755	785	811	834	854	872	888	901	947	972
14	674	714	749	780	807	830	851	869	884	938	967
15	622	669	709	745	776	803	827	848	866	929	962
16	562	617	664	705	741	772	800	824	845	917	956
17	495	558	612	659	701	737	769	797	821	905	949
18	419	491	554	608	656	698	734	766	794	891	942
19	333	416	488	550	605	653	695	732	763	874	933
20	235	330	413	484	547	602	650	692	729	856	923
21	125	234	328	410	482	545	600	648	690	835	912
22		124	232	326	408	480	543	598	646	812	900
23			123	230	324	406	478	541	595	785	885
24				122	229	323	404	476	539	755	869
25					122	228	321	403	474	721	851
26						121	227	320	401	682	830
27							121	226	319	638	807
28								120	226	589	781
29									120	533	751
30										469	717
31										397	678
32										315	635
33										223	585
34										118	529
35											466

LOAN PROGRESSION CHART 13%

Showing dollar balance remaining on a $1000 loan

ORIGINAL TERM IN YEARS 5	8	10	12	15	16	17	18	19	20	21	AGE OF LOAN
848	924	948	963	977	980	983	985	987	989	990	1
675	837	888	921	950	957	963	968	972	976	979	2
479	739	821	873	920	931	941	948	956	962	966	3
255	627	744	818	886	902	916	926	937	945	952	4
	499	656	756	847	869	887	901	915	926	935	5
	354	557	685	803	830	854	873	890	905	917	6
	188	443	604	753	787	816	841	862	880	896	7
		314	513	695	738	774	804	830	853	871	8
		167	408	630	682	725	762	794	821	844	9
			289	556	618	670	714	752	785	813	10
			154	472	545	607	660	705	744	777	11
				375	462	536	598	651	697	736	12
				266	368	454	527	590	644	690	13
				142	261	362	447	521	584	638	14
					139	256	356	442	515	578	15
						136	252	352	437	510	16
							134	249	348	432	17
								133	247	344	18
									131	244	19
										130	20

ORIGINAL TERM IN YEARS 22	23	24	25	26	27	28	29	30	35	40	AGE OF LOAN
991	993	993	994	995	995	996	996	997	998	1000	1
982	984	986	988	989	990	992	993	994	997	999	2
971	975	977	981	983	985	987	988	990	995	998	3
958	964	968	972	975	978	981	983	986	992	997	4
944	951	957	963	967	971	975	978	981	990	995	5
927	937	945	952	958	963	968	971	975	987	994	6
909	921	931	940	947	953	959	964	969	984	992	7
888	903	915	926	935	943	950	956	962	980	990	8
864	882	896	910	921	930	939	947	953	976	988	9
837	858	875	892	905	917	927	936	944	971	985	10
806	831	852	871	887	901	913	924	933	965	982	11
770	800	825	847	866	883	898	910	921	959	979	12
730	765	794	821	843	862	880	894	908	952	975	13
684	725	759	790	816	839	859	877	892	944	971	14
632	679	720	755	786	813	836	856	874	935	966	15
573	628	675	716	751	782	810	833	854	924	961	16
505	569	623	671	712	748	780	807	831	912	955	17
429	502	565	620	668	709	745	777	805	899	948	18
341	426	498	562	617	665	707	743	775	883	940	19
242	339	423	496	559	614	662	704	741	865	930	20
129	240	337	420	493	556	612	660	702	845	920	21
	128	239	335	418	491	554	610	658	823	908	22
		127	237	333	416	489	552	608	797	894	23
			126	236	332	415	487	551	767	879	24
				126	235	330	413	486	733	861	25
					125	234	329	412	695	842	26
						125	233	328	652	819	27
							124	233	602	793	28
								124	545	764	29
									481	730	30
									408	692	31
									325	649	32
									230	599	33
									123	543	34
										479	35

13.5% LOAN PROGRESSION CHART

Showing dollar balance remaining on a $1000 loan

AGE OF LOAN	ORIGINAL TERM IN YEARS 5	8	10	12	15	16	17	18	19	20	21
1	850	926	949	964	978	981	984	986	988	989	991
2	678	840	891	923	952	960	965	970	974	977	980
3	482	743	825	876	923	935	944	951	958	963	968
4	257	631	749	823	890	906	919	930	940	948	955
5		504	662	761	852	874	891	906	919	930	939
6		358	562	691	809	837	859	879	895	909	921
7		191	449	611	760	794	823	847	868	886	901
8			319	519	703	746	781	811	837	859	877
9			170	414	638	690	733	770	801	828	851
10				294	564	626	679	723	760	793	820
11				157	479	554	616	669	714	752	785
12					382	471	545	607	661	706	746
13					272	375	463	537	600	654	700
14					145	267	369	456	530	593	648
15						142	262	364	451	525	588
16							140	258	360	446	520
17								138	255	356	442
18									136	253	352
19										135	250
20											134

AGE OF LOAN	ORIGINAL TERM IN YEARS 22	23	24	25	26	27	28	29	30	35	40
1	992	993	994	995	995	996	997	997	997	998	999
2	983	985	987	989	990	992	993	993	994	997	998
3	973	976	980	982	984	987	988	989	991	995	997
4	961	966	971	975	977	981	983	985	987	993	996
5	947	954	960	966	970	974	977	980	982	991	995
6	932	941	949	956	961	966	971	974	977	988	994
7	914	926	935	944	951	957	963	967	971	985	992
8	894	908	920	931	939	947	954	960	965	982	991
9	871	888	903	915	926	936	944	951	957	978	989
10	844	865	883	898	911	923	933	941	948	974	987
11	814	839	860	878	893	908	919	929	938	969	984
12	780	809	834	855	874	890	904	916	927	963	981
13	740	774	804	829	851	871	887	901	914	956	978
14	695	735	770	800	825	848	868	884	899	949	974
15	643	690	731	766	796	822	845	865	882	940	969
16	584	639	686	727	762	793	820	842	862	930	964
17	516	580	635	682	723	759	790	817	840	919	959
18	438	512	576	631	679	721	757	787	815	906	952
19	350	435	509	573	628	676	718	754	785	891	945
20	248	347	433	507	570	626	674	716	752	874	936
21	133	247	345	431	504	568	624	672	714	855	926
22		132	245	344	428	502	566	622	670	833	915
23			131	244	342	427	501	564	620	807	902
24				130	243	341	425	499	563	778	887
25					130	242	339	424	498	745	870
26						129	241	338	423	708	851
27							129	240	337	664	829
28								128	240	615	804
29									128	558	775
30										493	742
31										419	704
32										334	661
33										238	612
34										127	556
35											491

LOAN PROGRESSION CHART 14%

Showing dollar balance remaining on a $1000 loan

ORIGINAL TERM IN YEARS 5	8	10	12	15	16	17	18	19	20	21	AGE OF LOAN
852	927	951	965	979	982	984	986	989	991	992	1
681	843	894	926	955	961	966	971	976	979	982	2
485	747	829	880	927	938	946	954	960	966	971	3
259	636	754	827	895	910	923	933	943	951	958	4
	508	667	767	858	879	896	910	923	934	943	5
	362	568	697	815	842	865	884	900	914	926	6
	193	454	618	767	801	829	853	874	892	906	7
		323	526	711	753	788	818	844	866	884	8
		173	420	646	698	741	778	809	836	858	9
			299	572	635	687	731	769	801	828	10
			160	487	562	625	678	723	762	794	11
				390	479	553	616	670	716	755	12
				277	383	471	546	610	664	710	13
				148	272	377	465	540	604	658	14
					146	268	372	460	535	598	15
						143	265	367	455	530	16
							141	262	364	451	17
								140	259	361	18
									139	257	19
										137	20

ORIGINAL TERM IN YEARS 22	23	24	25	26	27	28	29	30	35	40	AGE OF LOAN
993	994	995	995	996	997	997	998	998	999	999	1
984	986	989	990	991	993	993	995	995	998	999	2
975	978	981	984	986	988	989	991	992	996	998	3
963	968	973	977	980	983	985	987	988	995	997	4
951	957	963	968	972	976	979	982	984	993	996	5
936	944	952	959	964	969	973	977	980	990	995	6
919	930	940	948	955	961	966	971	974	988	994	7
900	913	925	935	944	952	958	964	968	984	992	8
877	894	909	921	931	941	948	955	961	981	990	9
852	872	889	904	917	928	938	946	953	977	988	10
822	846	867	885	900	914	925	935	944	972	986	11
788	817	842	863	881	897	911	923	933	967	983	12
749	783	813	838	859	878	894	908	920	961	980	13
705	744	779	809	834	857	875	892	906	954	977	14
653	700	741	775	805	832	854	873	890	946	973	15
594	649	697	737	772	803	829	852	871	936	968	16
526	590	646	693	734	770	800	827	849	926	963	17
448	523	587	642	690	732	767	798	825	913	957	18
358	445	520	584	640	688	729	765	796	899	950	19
255	356	443	517	582	638	686	727	763	883	942	20
136	253	354	441	515	580	636	684	725	864	932	21
	135	252	352	439	514	578	634	682	843	922	22
		135	251	351	437	512	577	632	818	910	23
			134	250	350	436	511	575	790	895	24
				134	249	348	435	509	757	879	25
					133	248	348	434	720	861	26
						133	247	347	677	839	27
							132	247	628	815	28
								132	571	787	29
									505	754	30
									430	717	31
									344	674	32
									245	625	33
									131	568	34
										503	35

14.5% LOAN PROGRESSION CHART

Showing dollar balance remaining on a $1000 loan

AGE OF LOAN	5	8	10	12	15	16	17	18	19	20	21
	ORIGINAL TERM IN YEARS										
1	853	929	952	967	980	983	985	988	989	991	992
2	684	846	897	928	957	963	968	973	977	980	983
3	488	751	832	883	930	940	949	956	963	968	973
4	261	640	758	832	899	914	926	937	946	954	960
5		513	673	772	863	883	900	915	927	937	946
6		366	574	704	822	848	870	889	905	918	930
7		196	460	624	774	807	835	859	880	897	911
8			328	533	718	760	795	825	850	871	890
9			176	427	654	706	749	785	816	842	865
10				304	581	643	695	740	777	809	836
11				163	495	570	633	687	732	770	802
12					397	487	562	626	679	725	764
13					283	390	479	555	619	673	719
14					152	278	384	474	549	613	668
15						149	274	379	468	544	608
16							147	271	375	464	540
17								145	268	372	461
18									144	265	369
19										142	263
20											141

AGE OF LOAN	22	23	24	25	26	27	28	29	30	35	40
	ORIGINAL TERM IN YEARS										
1	993	994	995	996	997	997	997	998	998	999	999
2	985	987	989	991	992	993	994	995	996	998	999
3	976	980	983	985	987	989	990	992	993	996	998
4	966	971	975	978	982	984	986	988	990	995	997
5	954	960	966	970	975	978	981	984	986	993	997
6	940	948	956	961	967	972	975	979	982	991	996
7	923	934	944	951	958	964	969	973	977	989	994
8	905	918	930	939	948	955	961	966	971	986	993
9	883	900	914	925	936	945	952	959	965	983	992
10	858	878	896	910	922	933	942	950	957	979	990
11	830	854	874	891	907	919	930	940	948	975	988
12	797	825	850	870	888	904	916	928	938	970	985
13	758	792	821	846	867	885	901	914	926	964	983
14	714	754	788	817	843	864	883	899	913	958	979
15	663	710	751	785	815	840	862	880	897	950	976
16	604	659	707	747	782	812	837	860	879	941	971
17	536	601	656	703	745	780	809	835	858	931	967
18	457	533	598	653	701	742	777	807	834	920	961
19	366	455	530	595	651	699	740	775	806	906	954
20	261	364	453	528	593	649	697	738	774	891	947
21	140	260	363	450	526	591	647	695	737	873	938
22		139	259	361	449	524	589	645	694	852	928
23			139	257	360	447	523	588	644	828	916
24				138	257	359	446	522	587	800	903
25					138	256	357	445	521	768	888
26						137	255	356	444	731	870
27							137	254	356	689	849
28								136	254	639	825
29									136	583	798
30										517	766
31										441	729
32										353	686
33										252	637
34										135	581
35											515

LOAN PROGRESSION CHART 15%

Showing dollar balance remaining on a $1000 loan

5	8	10	12	15	16	17	18	19	20	21	AGE OF LOAN
ORIGINAL TERM IN YEARS											
855	930	953	968	981	984	986	988	990	992	993	1
686	849	899	930	959	965	970	975	978	982	984	2
491	755	836	887	933	943	952	959	965	970	974	3
264	645	763	836	903	917	930	940	949	957	963	4
	518	678	778	868	888	905	919	931	941	949	5
	370	580	710	827	854	876	894	909	923	934	6
	199	465	631	780	814	842	865	885	902	916	7
		333	539	726	767	802	832	856	877	895	8
		179	433	662	714	757	793	823	849	871	9
			310	588	651	704	748	785	816	843	10
			166	503	579	642	695	740	778	810	11
				404	495	571	635	688	734	772	12
				289	397	488	564	628	682	728	13
				155	284	392	482	558	623	677	14
					153	280	387	477	554	618	15
						150	277	383	473	549	16
							149	274	380	470	17
								147	272	377	18
									146	270	19
										145	20

22	23	24	25	26	27	28	29	30	35	40	AGE OF LOAN
ORIGINAL TERM IN YEARS											
994	995	995	996	996	997	998	998	998	999	999	1
986	988	990	992	992	994	995	995	996	998	999	2
978	981	984	986	988	990	992	993	993	997	998	3
968	973	977	980	982	985	988	989	990	996	998	4
957	963	968	973	976	980	983	985	987	994	997	5
944	952	958	964	969	974	978	981	983	992	996	6
928	938	947	955	961	967	972	975	978	990	995	7
910	923	934	944	951	958	964	969	973	988	994	8
890	905	919	930	940	949	956	962	967	985	993	9
865	885	901	915	927	938	947	954	960	981	991	10
838	861	881	898	912	925	935	944	952	978	989	11
805	833	857	877	894	910	922	933	942	973	987	12
768	801	829	854	874	892	907	920	931	968	984	13
724	763	797	826	850	872	890	905	918	962	982	14
673	720	760	794	823	848	870	888	903	955	978	15
614	670	717	757	791	821	846	868	886	946	974	16
546	611	666	714	754	789	819	844	866	937	970	17
467	543	608	664	711	752	787	817	842	926	965	18
375	464	541	606	661	709	750	785	815	913	959	19
268	373	462	538	603	660	708	749	783	898	952	20
144	266	371	460	536	602	658	706	747	881	943	21
	143	265	370	458	535	601	657	704	861	934	22
		142	264	368	457	534	599	655	838	923	23
			142	263	367	456	533	598	810	910	24
				141	263	366	455	531	779	895	25
					141	262	365	454	743	878	26
						141	261	365	700	858	27
							140	261	651	835	28
								140	594	808	29
									528	777	30
									452	740	31
									363	698	32
									259	649	33
									139	593	34
										527	35

15.5% LOAN PROGRESSION CHART

Showing dollar balance remaining on a $1000 loan

AGE OF LOAN	5	8	10	12	15	16	17	18	19	20	21
				ORIGINAL TERM IN YEARS							
1	856	932	955	969	982	985	987	989	991	992	993
2	689	852	902	932	960	967	971	976	980	983	985
3	494	758	840	890	935	946	954	961	967	972	976
4	266	649	768	841	906	921	933	943	952	959	965
5		522	683	783	872	892	909	923	934	944	953
6		374	585	716	833	859	880	899	914	927	938
7		202	471	637	786	820	847	871	890	907	921
8			337	546	732	774	809	838	863	883	901
9			182	439	670	721	764	800	830	856	877
10				315	596	659	712	756	793	824	850
11				169	511	587	650	704	749	786	818
12					411	503	579	643	697	742	781
13					294	404	496	573	637	692	738
14					158	290	399	491	567	632	687
15						156	286	395	486	563	628
16							154	283	391	482	559
17								152	280	388	479
18									151	278	385
19										150	276
20											149

AGE OF LOAN	22	23	24	25	26	27	28	29	30	35	40
				ORIGINAL TERM IN YEARS							
1	994	995	996	997	997	997	998	998	999	1000	999
2	988	989	991	992	994	994	995	996	997	999	999
3	980	982	985	987	989	991	992	993	995	998	998
4	970	974	979	982	984	986	988	990	992	996	998
5	960	965	971	975	979	981	984	987	989	995	997
6	947	955	962	967	972	976	979	983	985	993	996
7	932	942	951	958	964	969	973	978	981	991	996
8	915	927	939	947	955	961	967	972	976	989	995
9	895	910	924	935	945	952	959	965	971	987	993
10	872	891	907	921	932	942	950	958	964	984	992
11	845	867	887	904	918	929	940	949	956	980	990
12	813	840	864	884	901	915	927	938	947	976	988
13	776	809	837	861	881	898	913	926	937	971	986
14	733	772	806	834	858	879	896	911	924	965	984
15	683	729	769	803	832	856	877	895	910	959	980
16	624	679	727	766	800	829	854	875	893	951	977
17	556	621	677	724	764	798	827	852	874	942	973
18	476	553	619	674	722	762	796	826	851	932	968
19	383	474	551	616	672	719	760	795	825	919	962
20	274	381	472	549	614	670	718	759	794	905	956
21	148	273	380	470	547	613	669	717	758	889	948
22		147	272	378	469	545	611	668	716	869	939
23			146	271	377	467	544	610	667	847	929
24				146	270	376	466	543	609	820	917
25					145	269	375	465	543	789	902
26						145	269	374	465	754	886
27							145	268	374	712	867
28								144	268	663	844
29									144	606	818
30										540	787
31										462	751
32										372	710
33										266	661
34										143	604
35											538

LOAN PROGRESSION CHART 16%

Showing dollar balance remaining on a $1000 loan

5	8	10	12	15	16	17	18	19	20	21	AGE OF LOAN
					ORIGINAL TERM IN YEARS						
858	933	956	970	983	985	987	989	991	992	993	1
692	854	904	935	962	968	973	977	981	984	986	2
497	762	843	894	938	948	956	963	969	973	977	3
268	654	772	845	910	924	936	946	955	961	967	4
	527	689	788	877	896	913	926	938	947	955	5
	378	591	722	838	864	885	903	918	931	941	6
	204	476	644	793	826	853	876	895	911	925	7
		342	553	740	781	815	844	868	888	905	8
		185	445	677	729	771	807	837	862	883	9
			320	604	667	719	763	800	830	856	10
			173	518	595	659	712	757	794	825	11
				418	511	588	652	706	751	789	12
				300	412	504	581	646	700	746	13
				162	296	406	499	577	641	696	14
					159	292	402	495	572	637	15
						157	289	399	491	568	16
							156	286	396	488	17
								155	284	393	18
									153	282	19
										152	20

22	23	24	25	26	27	28	29	30	35	40	AGE OF LOAN
					ORIGINAL TERM IN YEARS						
995	996	996	997	997	998	998	998	999	999	1000	1
988	990	991	993	994	995	996	996	997	998	1000	2
981	984	986	988	990	992	993	994	995	997	999	3
972	977	980	983	985	988	989	991	993	996	999	4
962	968	972	977	980	983	986	988	990	995	998	5
950	958	964	970	974	978	981	984	987	994	997	6
936	946	954	961	967	972	976	980	983	992	997	7
920	932	942	951	958	965	970	974	978	990	996	8
901	916	928	939	948	956	962	968	973	987	995	9
878	897	912	925	936	946	954	961	967	985	993	10
852	874	893	909	923	934	944	952	960	981	992	11
821	848	870	890	906	921	932	942	951	978	990	12
785	817	844	868	888	904	918	931	941	973	988	13
742	781	814	842	865	886	902	917	929	968	986	14
692	739	778	811	839	863	884	901	916	962	983	15
634	689	736	775	809	838	862	882	900	955	980	16
565	631	686	733	773	807	836	860	881	946	976	17
485	563	628	684	731	771	805	834	859	936	972	18
391	483	560	627	682	730	770	804	833	925	966	19
281	389	481	559	625	681	728	769	803	911	960	20
152	280	388	480	557	623	679	727	767	895	953	21
	151	278	387	478	556	622	678	726	876	945	22
		150	278	385	477	555	621	677	855	935	23
			150	277	385	476	554	620	829	923	24
				149	276	384	475	553	799	910	25
					149	276	383	475	763	894	26
						149	275	383	722	875	27
							148	275	674	853	28
								148	617	828	29
									550	798	30
									472	762	31
									381	721	32
									273	673	33
									147	616	34
										549	35

16.5% LOAN PROGRESSION CHART

Showing dollar balance remaining on a $1000 loan

AGE OF LOAN	5	8	10	12	15	16	17	18	19	20	21
	ORIGINAL TERM IN YEARS										
1	860	934	957	971	984	986	988	990	992	993	994
2	694	857	906	937	964	970	974	979	982	985	987
3	500	766	847	897	941	950	958	965	971	975	979
4	270	658	777	849	913	928	939	949	957	964	969
5		532	694	794	881	901	916	930	941	950	958
6		383	597	728	844	869	890	908	922	934	944
7		207	482	650	799	832	859	881	900	916	929
8			347	559	746	788	822	850	874	894	910
9			188	452	685	736	778	814	843	868	888
10				325	612	675	727	771	807	837	862
11				176	526	603	667	720	764	801	832
12					425	519	596	661	714	759	796
13					306	419	512	590	655	709	754
14					165	301	414	507	585	650	705
15						163	298	410	503	581	646
16							161	295	406	500	578
17								160	292	404	497
18									158	290	401
19										157	289
20											156

AGE OF LOAN	22	23	24	25	26	27	28	29	30	35	40
	ORIGINAL TERM IN YEARS										
1	995	995	996	997	998	998	998	998	999	999	1000
2	989	991	992	993	995	996	996	997	997	998	999
3	982	985	987	989	991	993	993	994	995	998	999
4	974	978	981	984	987	989	990	992	993	997	999
5	964	970	974	978	982	985	987	989	991	996	998
6	953	960	966	972	976	980	983	985	988	994	998
7	940	949	957	963	969	974	978	981	984	993	997
8	924	936	946	954	961	967	972	976	980	991	996
9	906	920	932	943	952	959	965	971	975	989	995
10	884	902	917	930	941	950	957	964	969	986	994
11	858	880	899	914	928	939	948	956	963	983	993
12	828	855	877	896	912	926	937	947	955	980	991
13	793	825	852	874	894	910	924	935	945	976	989
14	751	789	822	849	873	892	908	922	934	971	987
15	701	747	786	819	847	871	890	907	921	965	985
16	643	698	745	784	817	845	869	889	906	958	982
17	575	640	696	743	782	816	844	868	888	950	978
18	494	572	638	694	741	781	814	842	866	941	974
19	399	492	570	636	692	739	779	813	841	930	969
20	287	397	490	569	635	691	738	778	812	917	964
21	155	286	396	489	567	634	689	737	777	902	957
22		155	285	395	488	566	632	688	736	884	949
23			154	284	394	487	565	631	687	863	940
24				154	284	393	486	564	630	838	929
25					153	283	392	485	563	808	916
26						153	282	392	484	773	900
27							153	282	391	733	882
28								152	281	684	861
29									152	628	836
30										561	807
31										482	772
32										389	732
33										280	683
34										152	627
35											560

LOAN PROGRESSION CHART 17%

Showing dollar balance remaining on a $1000 loan

5	8	10	12	15	16	17	18	19	20	21	AGE OF LOAN
ORIGINAL TERM IN YEARS											
861	936	958	972	984	987	989	991	992	994	995	1
697	859	909	939	965	971	976	980	983	986	988	2
503	769	850	900	943	953	960	967	972	977	981	3
272	663	781	853	917	931	942	952	959	966	971	4
	536	699	799	886	905	920	933	944	953	961	5
	387	602	734	849	874	895	912	926	938	948	6
	210	487	657	805	838	864	886	904	920	933	7
		352	566	753	794	828	856	879	899	915	8
		191	458	692	743	786	820	849	874	894	9
			330	619	683	735	778	814	844	869	10
			179	533	611	675	728	772	809	839	11
				432	526	604	669	722	767	804	12
				311	426	521	599	663	718	763	13
				169	307	421	516	594	659	714	14
					167	304	417	512	590	656	15
						165	301	414	508	587	16
							163	299	411	506	17
								162	297	409	18
									161	295	19
										160	20

22	23	24	25	26	27	28	29	30	35	40	AGE OF LOAN
ORIGINAL TERM IN YEARS											
995	996	997	997	997	998	998	998	999	1000	1000	1
990	991	993	994	995	996	996	997	998	999	999	2
983	986	988	990	991	993	994	995	996	999	999	3
976	979	983	986	988	990	991	992	994	998	999	4
967	972	977	980	983	986	988	990	992	997	998	5
956	963	969	974	978	982	984	987	989	996	998	6
943	952	960	966	971	976	980	983	986	994	997	7
928	940	950	957	964	970	974	978	982	993	996	8
911	925	937	947	955	962	968	973	978	991	996	9
890	907	922	934	944	953	960	967	972	988	995	10
865	886	904	920	932	943	951	959	966	986	993	11
835	861	884	902	917	930	941	950	958	982	992	12
801	832	859	881	899	916	929	940	949	979	990	13
759	797	830	857	879	898	914	927	939	974	989	14
711	756	795	827	854	877	896	912	927	969	986	15
653	708	754	793	825	853	876	895	912	962	984	16
584	650	706	752	791	824	851	874	894	955	980	17
503	582	648	704	750	790	822	850	874	946	977	18
407	501	580	646	702	749	788	821	849	936	972	19
294	406	500	579	645	701	747	787	820	923	967	20
159	292	404	498	577	644	699	746	786	909	960	21
	159	292	403	497	576	642	698	746	891	953	22
		158	291	402	496	575	641	698	871	944	23
			158	290	402	495	574	641	846	934	24
				157	290	401	495	574	818	921	25
					157	289	400	494	784	907	26
						157	289	400	743	889	27
							156	288	695	869	28
								156	639	845	29
									572	816	30
									492	782	31
									399	742	32
									287	694	33
									156	637	34
										571	35

17.5% LOAN PROGRESSION CHART

Showing dollar balance remaining on a $1000 loan

AGE OF LOAN	5	8	10	12	15	16	17	18	19	20	21
				ORIGINAL TERM IN YEARS							
1	863	937	960	973	985	988	990	991	993	994	995
2	700	862	911	941	967	973	977	981	984	987	989
3	506	773	854	903	946	955	963	969	974	978	982
4	275	667	786	857	920	934	945	954	962	968	973
5		541	705	803	890	909	924	936	947	956	963
6		391	608	739	854	879	899	916	930	941	951
7		212	493	663	811	843	870	891	909	924	936
8			356	572	760	801	834	862	885	904	919
9			194	464	699	750	792	827	855	879	899
10				335	627	690	743	785	821	850	875
11				182	541	619	683	736	780	816	846
12					439	534	613	677	730	775	812
13					317	433	529	607	672	726	771
14					172	313	429	524	603	668	722
15						170	310	425	520	599	665
16							168	307	422	517	596
17								167	305	419	514
18									166	303	417
19										165	301
20											164

AGE OF LOAN	22	23	24	25	26	27	28	29	30	35	40
				ORIGINAL TERM IN YEARS							
1	996	997	997	998	998	998	999	999	999	1000	1000
2	991	992	993	995	995	996	997	997	998	999	1000
3	985	987	989	991	992	994	995	996	996	999	1000
4	978	981	984	987	989	991	992	994	994	998	999
5	969	974	978	982	984	987	989	991	992	997	999
6	959	966	971	976	979	983	986	988	990	996	998
7	947	956	963	969	974	978	982	985	987	995	998
8	933	944	953	961	966	972	977	980	983	993	997
9	916	929	941	951	958	965	971	975	979	992	997
10	895	912	926	939	948	957	964	970	974	989	996
11	871	892	909	924	936	947	955	962	968	987	995
12	842	868	889	908	922	935	945	954	961	984	993
13	808	840	865	887	905	921	934	944	953	981	992
14	768	806	837	864	885	904	919	932	943	976	990
15	719	765	803	835	861	884	903	918	931	971	988
16	662	717	763	801	833	860	883	901	917	966	986
17	593	660	715	761	799	832	859	881	900	959	983
18	512	592	657	713	759	798	831	858	880	950	979
19	415	510	590	656	711	758	797	829	857	940	975
20	300	414	509	588	654	710	757	796	828	929	970
21	163	299	413	508	587	653	709	756	795	914	964
22		163	298	412	506	586	653	708	755	898	957
23			162	297	411	506	585	652	707	878	949
24				162	297	410	505	584	651	854	939
25					161	296	409	504	584	826	927
26						161	296	409	504	793	913
27							161	295	408	753	897
28								161	295	705	877
29									160	649	853
30										582	825
31										502	792
32										407	752
33										294	704
34										160	648
35											581

LOAN PROGRESSION CHART 18%

Showing dollar balance remaining on a $1000 loan

5	8	10	12	15	16	17	18	19	20	21	AGE OF LOAN
					ORIGINAL TERM IN YEARS						
864	938	961	974	985	988	990	992	993	994	995	1
702	865	914	943	968	974	979	982	985	987	990	2
509	777	857	906	948	957	965	971	975	979	983	3
277	671	790	861	923	936	948	957	964	970	975	4
	545	710	808	894	912	928	940	950	958	965	5
	395	613	745	858	883	903	920	933	944	954	6
	215	498	669	816	848	875	896	913	928	940	7
		361	578	766	807	840	867	890	908	924	8
		197	470	706	757	799	833	861	885	904	9
			340	634	698	750	792	827	856	881	10
			185	548	627	691	744	787	823	852	11
				445	542	621	685	738	782	819	12
				322	440	537	616	680	734	779	13
				176	319	436	532	611	677	731	14
					174	316	432	528	608	673	15
						172	313	429	525	605	16
							170	311	427	523	17
								169	309	425	18
									168	308	19
										168	20

22	23	24	25	26	27	28	29	30	35	40	AGE OF LOAN
					ORIGINAL TERM IN YEARS						
996	997	997	997	998	998	999	999	999	1000	1000	1
991	993	994	995	996	996	997	997	998	999	1000	2
986	988	990	991	993	994	995	996	997	999	999	3
979	983	986	988	990	991	993	994	995	998	999	4
971	976	980	983	986	988	990	992	993	997	999	5
962	968	973	977	982	984	987	989	991	996	998	6
950	958	965	971	976	980	983	986	988	995	998	7
936	947	956	963	969	974	978	982	985	994	997	8
920	933	944	953	962	968	973	977	981	992	997	9
900	917	931	942	952	960	966	972	976	990	996	10
877	898	915	928	941	950	958	965	971	988	995	11
849	874	895	912	927	939	949	957	964	986	994	12
816	846	872	893	911	925	938	948	956	982	993	13
776	813	844	870	892	909	924	936	947	978	991	14
728	773	811	842	868	890	908	923	936	974	989	15
671	726	771	809	841	867	889	907	922	968	987	16
603	669	724	769	808	839	866	888	906	962	984	17
521	601	667	722	768	806	838	864	887	954	981	18
423	519	599	665	721	767	805	837	864	945	977	19
306	422	518	597	664	719	766	804	836	933	973	20
167	305	421	516	597	663	718	765	803	920	967	21
	166	305	420	516	595	662	717	764	904	961	22
		166	304	419	515	595	661	717	885	953	23
			165	303	418	514	594	661	862	943	24
				165	303	418	513	593	834	932	25
					165	302	417	513	801	919	26
						165	302	417	762	903	27
							164	302	715	883	28
								164	659	860	29
									592	833	30
									512	800	31
									416	761	32
									301	714	33
									164	658	34
										591	35

18.5% LOAN PROGRESSION CHART

Showing dollar balance remaining on a $1000 loan

AGE OF LOAN	ORIGINAL TERM IN YEARS 5	8	10	12	15	16	17	18	19	20	21
1	866	940	962	975	987	989	991	992	993	995	996
2	705	867	916	945	970	975	980	983	986	988	990
3	512	780	861	909	950	959	966	972	977	981	984
4	279	676	794	865	927	939	950	958	966	972	977
5		550	715	813	898	916	931	942	952	961	967
6		399	619	750	864	888	907	923	937	948	957
7		218	504	675	822	854	879	900	917	932	943
8			366	585	773	813	846	872	894	913	928
9			200	476	713	764	805	839	867	890	909
10				345	642	705	757	799	834	863	886
11				189	556	634	699	751	794	830	859
12					452	549	628	693	746	790	826
13					328	447	544	623	689	742	786
14					179	325	443	540	619	685	739
15						177	322	440	536	616	682
16							175	319	437	534	614
17								174	317	435	531
18									173	315	433
19										172	314
20											171

AGE OF LOAN	ORIGINAL TERM IN YEARS 22	23	24	25	26	27	28	29	30	35	40
1	996	997	998	998	998	999	999	999	999	1000	1000
2	992	994	995	995	996	997	998	998	998	999	1000
3	987	989	991	992	994	995	996	996	997	999	1000
4	980	984	987	989	991	993	994	995	996	998	1000
5	973	978	982	984	987	990	991	992	994	997	999
6	964	970	975	979	983	986	988	990	992	997	999
7	953	961	968	973	978	982	985	987	989	996	999
8	940	950	959	965	972	977	980	983	986	994	998
9	924	937	948	956	964	970	975	979	983	993	997
10	905	922	935	946	955	963	969	974	979	991	997
11	883	903	919	933	944	954	962	968	973	989	996
12	855	880	901	917	931	943	953	960	967	987	995
13	823	853	878	898	916	930	942	952	960	984	994
14	783	821	851	876	897	915	929	941	951	980	992
15	736	781	819	849	875	896	914	928	940	976	991
16	679	734	779	816	848	874	895	912	927	971	989
17	611	678	732	777	815	847	873	894	912	965	986
18	529	610	676	731	776	814	846	871	893	957	983
19	431	528	608	674	730	775	813	845	871	948	980
20	313	430	527	607	673	729	774	812	844	938	975
21	171	312	429	525	606	673	728	773	812	925	970
22		170	311	428	525	605	672	727	773	909	964
23			170	310	427	524	604	671	726	891	957
24				169	310	427	523	604	670	869	948
25					169	310	426	523	603	842	937
26						169	309	426	522	810	924
27							169	309	425	771	909
28								169	309	724	890
29									168	669	868
30										602	841
31										521	809
32										424	770
33										308	724
34										168	668
35											601

LOAN PROGRESSION CHART 19%

Showing dollar balance remaining on a $1000 loan

ORIGINAL TERM IN YEARS 5	8	10	12	15	16	17	18	19	20	21	AGE OF LOAN
868	941	963	976	987	989	991	993	994	995	996	1
708	870	918	947	971	976	980	984	987	989	991	2
515	784	864	911	952	961	968	973	978	982	985	3
281	680	799	869	929	942	952	961	968	974	978	4
	555	720	818	902	919	934	945	955	963	969	5
	403	624	756	868	892	911	927	940	951	959	6
	221	509	681	828	859	884	904	922	936	947	7
		370	591	779	819	851	877	899	917	931	8
		203	482	720	771	811	845	873	895	913	9
			351	649	712	764	806	840	868	891	10
			192	563	642	706	758	801	836	865	11
				459	557	636	701	754	797	833	12
				334	454	552	631	697	750	794	13
				183	330	450	548	628	693	747	14
					181	327	447	545	625	690	15
						179	325	444	542	622	16
							178	323	442	540	17
								177	322	440	18
									176	320	19
										175	20

ORIGINAL TERM IN YEARS 22	23	24	25	26	27	28	29	30	35	40	AGE OF LOAN
997	997	998	998	998	999	999	999	999	999	1000	1
993	994	995	996	996	997	997	998	998	999	1000	2
988	990	992	993	994	995	996	997	997	999	999	3
982	985	988	990	991	993	994	995	996	998	999	4
975	979	983	986	988	990	992	993	995	998	999	5
966	972	977	981	984	987	989	991	993	997	999	6
956	963	970	975	979	983	986	988	990	996	998	7
944	953	962	968	974	978	982	985	988	995	998	8
929	941	951	960	966	972	977	981	984	994	998	9
910	926	939	950	958	965	971	976	980	992	997	10
888	908	924	937	948	957	964	970	976	990	996	11
862	886	906	922	935	947	956	963	970	988	995	12
830	859	884	904	920	934	945	955	963	985	994	13
791	827	858	882	902	919	933	945	954	982	993	14
745	789	826	856	881	901	918	932	944	978	991	15
688	742	787	824	854	880	900	918	932	973	990	16
620	686	741	786	823	853	879	900	917	967	987	17
538	618	685	740	784	822	852	878	899	960	985	18
439	536	617	684	738	783	821	852	877	952	981	19
319	438	535	616	682	737	782	820	851	942	977	20
175	318	437	534	615	681	736	782	820	930	973	21
	174	318	436	533	614	681	736	781	915	967	22
		174	317	435	533	613	680	735	897	960	23
			173	316	435	532	613	680	875	951	24
				173	316	434	532	613	849	941	25
					173	316	434	531	818	929	26
						173	315	433	779	914	27
							173	315	734	896	28
								172	678	875	29
									611	849	30
									530	817	31
									432	779	32
									314	733	33
									172	678	34
										611	35

19.5% LOAN PROGRESSION CHART

Showing dollar balance remaining on a $1000 loan

AGE OF LOAN	5	8	10	12	15	16	17	18	19	20	21
				ORIGINAL TERM IN YEARS							
1	869	942	964	977	987	990	992	993	994	996	996
2	710	872	920	949	972	978	982	985	988	990	991
3	518	787	867	914	954	963	970	975	979	983	986
4	284	684	803	873	932	945	955	963	969	975	979
5		559	725	823	905	923	937	949	957	965	971
6		407	630	761	872	896	915	931	943	953	961
7		223	515	687	833	864	889	909	925	939	949
8			375	597	785	825	857	883	904	921	935
9			206	488	726	777	818	851	878	900	917
10				356	656	719	771	812	846	874	896
11				195	570	649	713	766	808	842	870
12					466	564	644	709	761	804	839
13					339	461	560	640	704	758	801
14					186	336	457	556	636	701	755
15						184	333	454	553	633	699
16							183	331	452	550	631
17								182	329	450	548
18									180	328	448
19										180	326
20											179

AGE OF LOAN	22	23	24	25	26	27	28	29	30	35	40
				ORIGINAL TERM IN YEARS							
1	997	997	998	998	999	999	999	999	999	1000	1000
2	993	994	996	996	997	998	998	998	999	1000	1000
3	988	991	992	994	995	996	996	997	998	999	1000
4	983	986	989	991	992	994	995	996	997	999	1000
5	976	981	984	987	989	991	993	994	995	998	999
6	968	974	979	982	986	988	990	992	993	998	999
7	958	966	972	977	981	985	987	989	991	997	999
8	947	956	964	970	976	980	983	986	989	996	999
9	932	944	954	962	969	975	979	983	986	995	998
10	915	930	943	953	961	968	973	978	982	993	998
11	893	912	928	941	951	960	967	973	978	992	997
12	868	891	911	926	940	950	959	966	972	990	996
13	836	865	890	909	925	939	949	958	966	987	995
14	798	834	864	888	908	924	937	949	958	984	994
15	752	796	833	862	887	907	923	937	948	980	993
16	696	750	795	831	861	886	906	923	936	976	991
17	629	695	749	794	830	860	885	905	922	970	989
18	546	627	693	748	793	829	859	884	905	964	986
19	446	545	626	692	747	792	828	859	884	956	983
20	325	445	544	625	691	746	791	828	858	946	980
21	178	325	445	543	624	691	745	790	827	934	975
22		178	324	444	542	623	690	745	790	920	970
23			178	323	443	542	623	689	744	903	963
24				177	323	443	541	622	689	882	955
25					177	323	442	541	622	857	946
26						177	322	442	540	826	934
27							177	322	442	788	920
28								177	322	743	902
29									176	688	881
30										621	856
31										539	825
32										441	788
33										321	742
34										176	687
35											620

LOAN PROGRESSION CHART 20%

Showing dollar balance remaining on a $1000 loan

5	8	10	12	15	16	17	18	19	20	21	AGE OF LOAN
					ORIGINAL TERM IN YEARS						
871	943	965	978	988	990	992	994	995	996	997	1
713	875	923	951	974	978	983	986	988	991	992	2
520	791	870	917	956	964	971	976	981	984	987	3
286	688	807	877	935	947	957	965	971	977	981	4
	564	730	827	909	926	940	951	960	967	973	5
	412	635	767	877	900	919	934	946	956	964	6
	226	520	693	838	868	893	913	929	942	953	7
		380	604	791	830	862	887	908	925	939	8
		209	494	733	783	824	856	883	904	922	9
			361	663	726	777	818	852	879	901	10
			198	577	656	721	772	814	848	876	11
				473	571	651	716	768	811	845	12
				345	468	567	647	712	765	808	13
				190	342	464	564	644	709	762	14
					188	339	461	561	641	707	15
						186	337	459	558	639	16
							185	335	457	556	17
								184	334	456	18
									183	333	19
										183	20

22	23	24	25	26	27	28	29	30	35	40	AGE OF LOAN
					ORIGINAL TERM IN YEARS						
997	998	998	998	999	999	999	999	999	1000	1000	1
994	995	996	996	997	998	998	998	999	999	1000	2
989	991	993	994	995	996	997	997	998	999	1000	3
984	987	990	991	993	995	995	996	997	999	999	4
978	982	985	988	990	992	993	995	996	998	999	5
970	976	980	984	987	989	991	993	994	998	999	6
961	968	974	978	982	986	988	990	992	997	999	7
950	959	966	972	977	982	985	988	990	996	998	8
936	948	957	965	971	977	981	984	987	995	998	9
919	934	946	955	964	971	976	980	984	994	998	10
899	917	932	944	954	963	969	975	979	992	997	11
873	896	915	930	943	954	962	969	974	990	996	12
843	871	895	914	929	942	953	961	968	988	995	13
806	841	870	893	913	929	941	952	961	985	994	14
760	804	839	868	892	912	928	941	951	982	993	15
705	758	802	838	867	892	911	927	940	978	992	16
637	703	757	801	837	867	891	910	927	973	990	17
555	636	702	756	800	836	866	890	910	966	987	18
454	553	634	701	755	799	835	865	889	959	985	19
332	453	552	633	700	754	798	835	865	950	981	20
182	331	452	551	633	699	753	798	834	939	977	21
	182	330	452	551	632	698	753	797	925	972	22
		181	330	451	550	631	698	752	908	966	23
			181	329	451	550	631	698	888	958	24
				181	329	450	549	631	863	949	25
					181	329	450	549	833	938	26
						181	329	450	796	924	27
							180	328	751	908	28
								180	696	887	29
									630	863	30
									548	832	31
									449	796	32
									328	751	33
									180	696	34
										629	35

SECTION FOUR

Points Discount Tables

Points are the fee charged by a lending institution for granting a loan. Each point is equal to 1% of the principal mortgage amount. For example, 2 points on a $100,000 loan will cost you 2 percent of $100,000 or $2,000.

POINTS DISCOUNT TABLES

TERM

INTEREST RATE	POINTS	5 YEARS	10 YEARS	15 YEARS	20 YEARS	25 YEARS	30 YEARS	35 YEARS	40 YEARS
	5	7.14	6.11	5.78	5.63	5.53	5.46	5.40	5.39
	4	6.70	5.88	5.64	5.49	5.40	5.36	5.32	5.30
5%	3	6.25	5.66	5.48	5.38	5.31	5.26	5.25	5.20
	2	5.85	5.43	5.31	5.22	5.19	5.17	5.15	5.14
	1	5.42	5.21	5.15	5.11	5.10	5.09	5.08	5.07
	5	8.16	7.16	6.80	6.66	6.54	6.50	6.44	6.41
	4	7.70	6.90	6.63	6.52	6.44	6.40	6.36	6.32
6%	3	7.26	6.65	6.48	6.38	6.32	6.27	6.25	6.24
	2	6.86	6.46	6.31	6.26	6.22	6.19	6.16	6.85
	1	6.44	6.23	6.15	6.13	6.12	6.09	6.09	6.08
	5	9.19	8.19	7.83	7.69	7.58	7.50	7.47	7.46
	4	8.74	7.92	7.65	7.52	7.47	7.42	7.36	7.34
7%	3	8.30	7.70	7.50	7.40	7.33	7.30	7.27	7.25
	2	7.86	7.47	7.32	7.25	7.23	7.20	7.19	7.18
	1	7.41	7.24	7.17	7.14	7.11	7.10	7.09	7.09
	5	10.19	9.18	8.87	8.70	8.60	8.56	8.52	8.47
	4	9.75	8.95	8.66	8.54	8.47	8.44	8.41	8.37
8%	3	9.29	8.71	8.50	8.40	8.37	8.33	8.31	8.28
	2	8.86	8.46	8.35	8.26	8.25	8.22	8.21	8.18
	1	8.42	8.22	8.16	8.14	8.12	8.11	8.10	8.09
	5	11.21	10.22	9.89	9.72	9.65	9.58	9.55	9.52
	4	10.75	9.98	9.71	9.59	9.50	9.47	9.44	9.41
9%	3	10.30	9.72	9.51	9.44	9.37	9.35	9.33	9.31
	2	9.88	9.47	9.34	9.27	9.25	9.22	9.21	9.20
	1	9.42	9.25	9.16	9.15	9.12	9.11	9.11	9.09
	5	12.25	11.25	10.90	10.77	10.66	10.61	10.58	10.57
	4	11.77	10.99	10.71	10.59	10.53	10.48	10.48	10.43
10%	3	11.33	10.72	10.55	10.45	10.41	10.38	10.36	10.34
	2	10.87	10.47	10.37	10.29	10.27	10.24	10.23	10.22
	1	10.42	10.25	10.17	10.15	10.12	10.12	10.11	10.11
	5	13.27	12.25	11.94	11.78	11.72	11.65	11.62	11.61
	4	12.80	12.00	11.75	11.63	11.58	11.53	11.50	11.47
11%	3	12.34	11.74	11.58	11.48	11.43	11.38	11.36	11.35
	2	11.88	11.50	11.36	11.31	11.28	11.27	11.25	11.23
	1	11.45	11.26	11.19	11.15	11.14	11.13	11.12	11.12
	5	14.29	13.28	12.98	12.81	12.75	12.69	12.67	12.65
	4	13.80	13.02	12.78	12.65	12.60	12.55	12.53	12.52
12%	3	13.35	12.77	12.58	12.48	12.45	12.40	12.40	12.38
	2	12.88	12.51	12.38	12.33	12.28	12.27	12.26	12.25
	1	12.45	12.24	12.20	12.17	12.15	12.14	12.13	12.13
	5	15.32	14.33	14.00	13.85	13.80	13.73	13.71	13.70
	4	14.82	14.04	13.80	13.67	13.63	13.58	13.57	13.56
13%	3	14.37	13.77	13.60	13.50	13.45	13.44	13.43	13.42
	2	13.91	13.51	13.40	13.33	13.30	13.29	13.28	13.27
	1	13.45	13.27	13.20	13.16	13.15	13.14	13.14	13.14

POINTS DISCOUNT TABLES

TERM

INTEREST RATE	POINTS	5 YEARS	10 YEARS	15 YEARS	20 YEARS	25 YEARS	30 YEARS	35 YEARS	40 YEARS
14%	5	16.32	15.35	15.02	14.88	14.81	14.78	14.76	14.75
	4	15.86	15.06	14.81	14.70	14.66	14.63	14.60	14.60
	3	15.37	14.78	14.60	14.52	14.47	14.45	14.45	14.44
	2	14.90	14.51	14.39	14.34	14.33	14.31	14.30	14.29
	1	14.46	14.27	14.19	14.16	14.16	14.15	14.14	14.14
15%	5	17.36	16.38	16.06	15.94	15.88	15.84	15.82	15.80
	4	16.88	16.10	15.84	15.75	15.67	15.66	15.65	15.64
	3	16.38	15.82	15.62	15.55	15.52	15.49	15.48	15.47
	2	15.93	15.55	15.44	15.36	15.35	15.33	15.32	15.31
	1	15.46	15.28	15.22	15.18	15.17	15.17	15.16	15.15
16%	5	18.39	17.41	17.11	16.98	16.90	16.88	16.86	16.85
	4	17.90	17.10	16.88	16.76	16.73	16.68	16.68	16.66
	3	17.40	16.84	16.65	16.58	16.54	16.52	16.51	16.50
	2	16.94	16.56	16.44	16.38	16.34	16.34	16.33	16.33
	1	16.47	16.28	16.22	16.20	16.18	16.17	16.17	16.16
17%	5	19.40	18.43	18.14	18.02	17.96	17.93	17.92	17.91
	4	18.89	18.12	17.91	17.81	17.76	17.74	17.72	17.71
	3	18.43	17.85	17.68	17.60	17.57	17.55	17.53	17.43
	2	17.95	17.57	17.44	17.40	17.37	17.36	17.35	17.35
	1	17.47	17.29	17.23	17.20	17.19	17.18	17.17	17.17
18%	5	20.43	19.47	19.17	19.06	19.00	18.98	18.97	18.96
	4	19.93	19.17	18.94	18.84	18.80	18.77	18.76	18.75
	3	19.44	18.88	18.69	18.63	18.59	18.58	18.57	18.56
	2	18.96	18.57	18.46	18.42	18.39	18.38	18.37	18.37
	1	18.48	18.29	18.23	18.21	18.19	18.19	18.18	18.18
19%	5	21.46	20.50	20.20	20.10	20.05	20.03	20.02	20.00
	4	20.95	20.19	19.97	19.86	19.83	19.82	19.81	19.80
	3	20.46	19.88	19.72	19.64	19.62	19.61	19.60	19.58
	2	19.97	19.60	19.48	19.43	19.41	19.40	19.39	19.39
	1	19.48	19.30	19.24	19.22	19.20	19.20	19.19	19.19
20%	5	22.47	21.58	21.25	21.14	21.09	21.08	21.07	21.06
	4	21.96	21.21	20.99	20.90	20.87	20.86	20.85	20.84
	3	21.47	20.90	20.74	20.68	20.65	20.64	20.63	20.62
	2	20.98	20.60	20.49	20.45	20.43	20.41	20.41	20.41
	1	20.49	20.30	20.25	20.23	20.22	20.21	20.20	20.20
21%	5	23.50	22.55	22.28	22.19	22.14	22.12	22.11	22.10
	4	22.99	22.25	22.02	21.94	21.91	21.88	21.88	21.88
	3	22.49	21.90	21.75	21.70	21.68	21.67	21.66	21.65
	2	21.99	21.59	21.51	21.47	21.45	21.44	21.43	21.43
	1	21.49	21.29	21.26	21.24	21.23	21.22	21.21	21.21
22%	5	24.53	23.59	23.33	23.23	23.19	23.17	23.16	23.15
	4	24.00	23.27	23.05	22.98	22.95	22.92	22.92	22.92
	3	23.50	22.93	22.78	22.71	22.70	22.69	22.68	22.68
	2	23.00	22.61	22.51	22.46	22.46	22.45	22.45	22.45
	1	22.50	22.31	22.26	22.23	22.23	22.22	22.22	22.22

POINTS DISCOUNT TABLES

TERM

INTEREST RATE	POINTS	5 YEARS	10 YEARS	15 YEARS	20 YEARS	25 YEARS	30 YEARS	35 YEARS	40 YEARS
23%	5	25.56	24.61	24.37	24.28	24.23	24.22	24.22	24.21
	4	25.02	24.29	24.09	24.00	23.99	23.96	23.96	23.96
	3	24.52	23.95	23.81	23.76	23.73	23.72	23.71	23.71
	2	24.00	23.64	23.54	23.48	23.48	23.47	23.47	23.47
	1	23.50	23.30	23.27	23.25	23.24	23.23	23.23	23.23
24%	5	26.59	25.66	25.41	25.32	25.29	25.27	25.27	25.25
	4	26.05	25.31	25.12	25.05	25.00	25.00	25.00	24.99
	3	25.52	24.97	24.82	24.76	24.75	24.75	24.74	24.73
	2	25.00	24.65	24.55	24.50	24.50	24.49	24.48	24.48
	1	24.50	24.33	24.26	24.24	24.24	24.24	24.24	24.24
25%	5	27.60	26.69	26.45	26.37	26.32	26.31	26.31	26.31
	4	27.08	26.35	26.15	26.09	26.06	26.06	26.05	26.04
	3	26.55	26.00	25.86	25.80	25.77	25.77	25.77	25.77
	2	26.01	25.65	25.55	25.53	25.53	25.52	25.51	25.51
	1	25.50	25.35	25.27	25.27	25.26	25.25	25.25	25.25